Columbia Pictures Movie Series, 1926–1955

Columbia Pictures Movie Series, 1926–1955

The Harry Cohn Years

Gene Blottner

McFarland & Company, Inc., Publishers
Jefferson, North Carolina, and London

LIBRARY OF CONGRESS CATALOGUING-IN-PUBLICATION DATA

Blottner, Gene, 1938–
Columbia Pictures movie series, 1926–1955 :
the Harry Cohn years / Gene Blottner.
p.   cm.
Includes bibliographical references and index.

ISBN 978-0-7864-3353-7
softcover : acid free paper ∞

1. Columbia Pictures Corporation — Catalogs.
2. Motion pictures — United States — Catalogs.
3 Motion pictures — History — 20th century — Catalogs.   I. Title.

PN1999.C57B56 2012   791.43097309'04 — dc23   2011042985

BRITISH LIBRARY CATALOGUING DATA ARE AVAILABLE

Front cover: *clockwise from top* Penny Singleton and Arthur Lake,
Blondie, 1938; Cornel Wilde, *The Bandit of Sherwood Forest*, 1946;
Charles Starret, *Prairie Roundup*, 1951; Amanda Blake and
Ron Randell, *Counterspy Meets Scotland Yard*, 1950.

Manufactured in the United States of America

*McFarland & Company, Inc., Publishers
Box 611, Jefferson, North Carolina 28640
www.mcfarlandpub.com*

To my son, Woody

Acknowledgments

Many people assisted me in obtaining information for this book. The following willingly shared their knowledge or helped me with my research: Charles Blottner; Larry Floyd; Martin Grams; Earl Hagen; Bill Sasser; Terry Salomonson; Graham Talbott.

A special thanks to the following: Elaine Brown, Assistant, Reference Services, National Library of Scotland; Susan Clementson and staff, Larchmont Public Library, Norfolk, Virginia; Laura Dodson and Mary-Ann Vandivort, Inter-Library Loan Department, Norfolk Public Library, Norfolk, Virginia.

Table of Contents

Preface

A series, as it applies to this book, consists of a group of films linked by a single fictional character(s). This book covers the years the studio was run by Harry Cohn, 1926–1955. (This means the Columbia films of Gene Autry, for example, are not included.) In doing the research for this book, I found three instances in which a film was produced with the intent to begin a series: *Tillie the Toiler*, *Mr. District Attorney* and *Night Editor*. Most of the series were short lived. Only about ten series can be called truly successful. Most of the entries were entertaining and pleased the general audiences of the time.

Here is an overview of the entry style of the films. The title of each film is followed by the production company and release date, as well as the advertising tagline.

Alternate Title: If a film used a title other than that given on initial release, this title is listed. Working titles will be found in the "Notes and Commentary" section of the entry.

Cast: All cast members listed before the designation "//" were identified in the credits. All cast members listed after that designation were identified by the author or by people considered knowledgeable about the film.

Credits: Major players beyond the cast.

Song(s): All identifiable songs have been named with composers and artists, if known.

Production Dates: When the film was made.

Source: If a film was derived from a published work, either a novel or story, this is stated along with the name(s) of the author. I was able to obtain copies of the original source and note similarities and differences. A few films were adapted from radio programs, most of which were not available.

Running Time: Running times came from various websites and reviews.

Story: This is an encapsulation of the film's scenario and not an attempt to describe every scene in detail. Only 26 of the 227 films were not available for viewing.

Notes and Commentary: These include facts obtained from various film historians and websites.

Reviews: To give the reader a flavor of how critics received the film at the time of release or in retrospective, selected reviews are printed.

Summation: My overall appraisal of the film, with which I can only hope the reader might agree.

HISTORICAL OVERVIEW

Columbia Pictures — The Harry Cohn Years

In 1919, Jack Cohn and his brother Harry, along with a close friend, Joe Brandt, formed a new motion picture company, C-B-C (Cohn-Brandt-Cohn) Film Sales. The company's focus was on short subjects, one based on the comic strip *The Hall-Room Boys*, and *Screen Snapshots*, which focused on movie stars at home. All three partners had experience in motion pictures with Carl Laemmle, president of Universal Pictures. Jack was the first to enter show business. In 1908, he joined Laemmle's Film Service, which became IMP (The Independent Motion Picture Company). In 1913, Jack founded the Universal Newsreel Department, which led to his responsibility of bringing in all of the one- and two-reel films on time and on budget. He became an editor when he worked on *Traffic in Souls* (Universal, 1913). In 1919, Jack left Universal to produce his own short subject, *Screen Snapshots*. At Jack's urging, Joe Brandt joined Universal around 1914 and became the general manager. In 1918, Harry became Carl Laemmle's secretary. Both Harry and Joe decided to take the gamble with Jack and they, also, left Universal. To make certain the short subjects that were being produced in Hollywood would stay within budget, Harry went west, leaving Jack and Joe in their New York offices.

Harry quickly became knowledgeable in maximizing expenses and his short films were considered economically but efficiently produced. Harry saw that the future in the company would be in feature films. *More to Be Pitied Than Scorned* (C-B-C Film Sales, 1922) was the initial production. The picture proved to be a financial success. The film was distributed through the "states-rights" system, wherein individual distributors in individual states would buy the film outright and keep the profits for themselves. Nine additional features were made through December 1923, and each one turned a profit. Others in the motion picture industry looked down on the fledgling company and referred to it as "Corned Beef and Cabbage," which irritated Harry. On January 10, 1924, the studio became known as Columbia Pictures. The main office was located at 727 7th Avenue in New York, with leased premises at 6070 Sunset Boulevard in Hollywood. Joe Brandt became president with Jack as the vice-president of sales, and Harry as the vice-president of production. In making decisions, Jack and Harry would argue violently with Joe acting as mediator. Over the years, each would need the others' expertise to run the company successfully.

Harry had a strong temper and was very crude and foul-mouthed, a trait that earned the hatred and fear of most of his associates. Harry had a special acumen, however, for guiding the company's progress in Hollywood. Instead of leasing offices as many of the "poverty row" companies did, Harry began to purchase space. He bought two sound stages and an office that he had been leasing. In 1926, the distribution process was changed to the exchange system in which the studio received a percentage of the profits. The films themselves catered to the taste of mass audiences. Budgets were kept low so exhibitors would not have to raise ticket prices. Columbia would have its own unique logo with a robed woman holding a torch. Later in 1936, the torch-bearing lady would be draped in a flag while standing on a pedestal. The company also made the decision not to purchase theaters (as did Paramount, Warner Bros. and Metro-Goldwyn-Mayer), but spent that money instead on making movies. This proved to be a wise decision. First, in 1929, the Depression caused a drop in movie theater attendance, almost sending Paramount and Radio Pictures into bankruptcy. Second, in 1948, the Justice Department finally put into effect the Consent Decree, which prohibited motion picture studios from making and exhibiting their own products. Studios were forced to sell at great losses. The theaters, also, had been subsidizing the parent studios.

Harry Cohn around 1950. He was president of Columbia Pictures from 1932 to 1958.

The year 1926 saw the first of Columbia's movie series with *The Lone Wolf Returns*, starring Bert Lytell. Lytell would star in three additional features. The following year, 1927, was a memorial year for the studio. They had their first big-time feature, *The Blood Ship*. Next, Harry hired Frank Capra to direct a film, a move that began a long-term association that lasted until 1939. Capra's first major hit was *Submarine* (1928) with Jack Holt and Ralph Graves. Capra followed this up with such features as *Flight* (1929), *Dirigible* (1931), *Platinum Blonde* (1931), *Lady for a Day* (1933) and, in 1934, he hit the jackpot with *It Happened One Night*. This film won Academy Awards for Best Actor (Clark Gable), Best Actress (Claudette Colbert), Best Director (Frank Capra), Best Screenplay adapted from another medium (Robert Riskin) and, of course, Best Picture.

In 1932, Harry bought out Joe Brandt and became president of Columbia Pictures. Harry had listening devices placed in offices so he could overhear what went on. He especially made the writers' offices his target to make certain they were working on his projects. He also could overhear conversations on the sound stages and would shout over loudspeakers if he heard anything that upset him. Actors who displeased him would feel the effect of his wrath. One of the great film icons, John Wayne, ran afoul of Harry. Harry learned that Wayne might have a romantic interest in Laura LaPlante, his co-star of *Arizona* (1931). At that time Harry was having an affair with LaPlante. Harry began a campaign to end Wayne's career by giving him bad roles and slandering his name. He spread the word that Wayne was a womanizer, a drunk and an overall troublemaker. Word of Cohn's actions finally reached Wayne. Enraged, he burst into Harry's office and grabbed him by the neck. Wayne told Cohn, "You son of a bitch, as long as I live I will never work one day for you or Columbia no matter how much you offer me." (Wayne was true to his word, turning down the starring role in *The Gunfighter* [1950]. The property went to 20th Century–Fox and the film was made with Gregory Peck in the lead.) Harry had the reputation for demanding or requesting sex from some of his starlets. Two notable stars that turned Harry down were Rita Hayworth and Joan Crawford. Crawford reportedly told Harry, "Keep it in your pants, Harry, I'm having lunch with Joan [Harry's wife] and the kids tomorrow."

To keep Columbia on the move to a higher status in the industry, Harry began to acquire additional property. Columbia now owned most of the area between Sunset Boulevard and Fountain Avenue, and between Gower Street and Beachwood Drive. Also, in 1935, Harry bought a 35-acre ranch near Burbank to be used in the making of his western features. By 1937, Cohn was producing two to three "A" pictures annually, plus programmers, B-westerns, series films, comedy shorts and serials. With the exception of the westerns, feature films ran at least 60 minutes, but rarely over 120 minutes. Later, Harry is reputed to have said, "Let me give you some facts of life. Every Friday, the front door of this studio opens and I spit a movie out onto Gower Street.... If that door opens and I spit and nothing comes out, it means a lot of people are out of work — drivers, distributors, exhibitors, projectionists, ushers, and a lot of other pricks.... I want one good picture a year, and I won't let an exhibitor have it unless he takes the bread-and-butter product, the *Boston Blackies*, the *Blondies*, the low-budget westerns and the rest of the junk we make." Harry once stated that when watching a film in the projection room, if his fanny squirmed, the picture was bad. Screenwriter Herman J. Mankiewicz then remarked, "Imagine, the whole world wired to Harry Cohn's ass." Mankiewicz was fired.

Another major decision Harry made was not to have a large number of high-priced actors and actresses under contract. He saw the problems Jack Warner was having at Warner Bros. and was content to borrow stars from other studios. He ultimately decided to develop his own stars, including Rosalind Russell, Glenn Ford, William Holden and Rita Hayworth. In 1935, Harry signed actresses Joan Perry and Rita Hayworth to contracts and stated, "Hayworth will be a star and you [Perry] will be my wife." Harry divorced Rose Barker Cohn in 1941 and married Joan Perry shortly thereafter. Thanks primarily to Frank Capra, Columbia had some popular films in the late '30s. *Mr. Deeds Goes to Town* (1936), *Lost Horizon* (1937), *You Can't Take It with You* (1938) and *Mr. Smith Goes to Washington* (1939) brought moviegoers into the theaters. But after *Mr. Smith*, Capra left Columbia. In the '40s, Cohn decided to increase the number of "A" films. Cohn finally released a film in Technicolor with *The Desperadoes* (1943). Other major color films that followed were *Cover Girl* (1944), *A Song to Remember* (1945) and *The Jolson Story* (1946). *The Jolson Story* would be Columbia's first blockbuster film.

Harry put Sam Briskin in charge of the "B" features, and Jules White and Hugh McCollum in charge of the comedy shorts. Some of the series films and Jack Holt's action films were made in conjunction with Larry Darmour Productions. Columbia's serials were, first, Weiss Productions (as Adventure Serials, Inc.) then turned over to Larry Darmour productions until the *Jungle Raiders* (1945), when Sam Katzman took the serial reins. Cohn entered into contracts with various production companies to provide films for Columbia release. Some of the producers were Sidney Buchman, Gene Autry and Walter Wanger.

By the early '50s, movie attendance was down. Most attributed this dip to the popularity of television. Harry endorsed moving into the television market with its subsidiary, Screen Gems. He began to cut back on his movie series. Old favorites like *Blondie, Boston*

Blackie and the *Crime Doctor* were discontinued. Although a few series, like *Gasoline Alley* and *Counterspy*, were introduced to movie audiences, only the *Jungle Jim* series was successful, continuing to thrill audiences until 1955. By 1953, the "B" westerns of Gene Autry and the *Durango Kid* were ended. Serials were produced until 1956. Harry found he could re-release the *Blondies*, the earlier westerns of Bill Elliott and Charles Starrett and the better-made serials of the '40s to new audiences. The '40s ended on a high note for Columbia. *All the King's Men* (1949) won Academy Awards for Best Picture, Best Actor (Broderick Crawford) and Best Supporting Actress (Mercedes McCambridge).

Columbia released some of the major films of the '50s: *From Here to Eternity* (1953), *On the Waterfront* (1954), and *The Bridge on the River Kwai* (1957) won Academy Awards for Best Picture. *Born Yesterday* (1950) and *The Caine Mutiny* (1954) were Best Picture nominees.

The dynasty began to unravel in 1956 with the death of Jack Cohn and, finally, with Harry's death on February 27, 1958. From the inception of Columbia Pictures and all through the reign of Harry Cohn, the studio never lost money. This was a record to be envied by all the other studios.

There was a large turnout for Harry Cohn's funeral. Comedian Red Skelton quipped, "It proves what Harry always said: Give the people what they want and they'll turn out for it," and "They came to make sure the S.O.B. was dead." Hedda Hopper added, "You had to stand in line to hate him." A rabbi was asked to say something nice about Harry, and he responded, "He's dead."

Director George Sherman, who directed nine films at Columbia between 1945 and 1948, had this to say about Harry: "Tough? Sure, Harry Cohn was tough, but he was also a helluva executive who kept track of everything that was going on at his studio, and knew how to cut a film. They don't have people in the industry like that today. No, he wasn't looking over my shoulder. On the other hand, if he had any complaints, he sure as hell let you know about them." Sherman added that he was probably much better off being associated with him.

What Is a Series?

In today's movie jargon, a group of films featuring the same fictional characters is known as a franchise. Harry Potter, Spider-man, Iron Man and Batman are some of the more popular franchises of the moment. Franchises are nothing new. In the beginning of movie history, they were known simply as series films. In the silent era, moviegoers flocked to their favorite theaters to see Sherlock Holmes, Boston Blackie, the Lone Wolf, Cheyenne Harry, Tarzan, Detective Tex and the Cohens and Kellys. When movies began to talk, almost every studio would release a number of series films each year. For the most part, the series films of the '30s, '40s and early '50s (the era of "B" films) had limited budgets and running times. Most running times would range between 60 to 70 minutes. The "B" series films would provide second-feature status in the larger markets and stand-alone status in the smaller markets and in the second-run neighborhood movie houses. If a series proved to be successful, one to three entries would be seen annually.

Most series would have limited favor. Some that proved to endear themselves during these years were Tarzan (Metro-Goldwyn-Mayer and RKO), The Thin Man (Metro-Goldwyn-Mayer), The Hardy Family/ Andy Hardy (Metro-Goldwyn-Mayer), Charlie Chan (20th Century–Fox, Monogram), Henry Aldrich (Paramount), Hopalong Cassidy (Paramount and United Artists), Frankenstein, Dracula, the Wolf Man (Universal), Sherlock Holmes (20th Century–Fox and Universal), The Saint (RKO), The Falcon (RKO and Film Classics), The Bowery Boys (Monogram and Allied Artists), The Three Mesquiteers (RKO and Republic) and Red Ryder (Republic).

This book features the series released by Columbia. Some of that studio's most successful series would include Blondie, The Lone Wolf, Boston Blackie, The Crime Doctor, Jungle Jim, The Durango Kid and The Whistler.

By the late '50s, the low-budget series from all studios would disappear. Series now would have increased budgets, running times, wide screen and color. Some of the popular series of the late '50s and early sixties were Tammy (Universal-International, 1957) in Technicolor and CinemaScope, Gidget (Columbia, 1959) in CinemaScope and Eastman Color and James Bond (United Artists, 1962) in Technicolor. Series over the years have covered all genres, from horror with Freddie Krueger in the Nightmare on Elm Street series and Michael Myers in the Halloween series to animation with *Shrek* and the Toy Story series. If you're in the mood for a contemporary series film as I write this, the choices would be *Harry Potter and the Deathly Hallows–Part 1, Saw 3D, Toy Story 3* and *Paranormal Activity 2*. It looks like series (or franchise) films will always be on the silver screen to entertain moviegoers.

Columbia Pictures Series
in Brief

For Columbia's first series, Harry Cohn chose The Lone Wolf and was able to obtain the services of Bert Lytell. Lytell was the screen's first Lone Wolf beginning with *The Lone Wolf* (Herbert Brenon Film Corporation/Selznick Distributing Company, 1917). Four films were produced between 1926–1930. Then the series was dropped. Through the '30s, Columbia tread tentatively in the series market. Thatcher Colt was the next series. Three features were announced but only two were produced. It is possible that Anthony Abbot did not like the adaptation of his books and ended the series. This fate befell two more of Columbia's series. The next series starred up-and-coming actor Ralph Bellamy as Inspector Trent. Four features were made, after which the series was discontinued. Columbia tested the waters with another Lone Wolf episode but additional films were put on hold. Author Rex Stout's famous detective Nero Wolfe was the next in line for a series, but only two were made. Stout was unhappy with the treatment of his detective and Wolfe did not appear onscreen until years after the author's death. Around 1937, the decision was made to produce more series features, and by 1938, three were produced. One centered around married sleuths Sally and Bill Reardon. Columbia hoped that the series would equal the charm and popularity of Metro-Goldwyn-Mayer's Thin Man Series. There were high hopes after the first entry, *There's Always a Woman* (1938), featuring sparkling performances from Joan Blondell and Melyvn Douglas. Blondell was not available for the second (*There's That Woman Again* [1939]). Blondell's replacement, Virginia Bruce, did not light up the screen as Blondell had and, coupled with a weak script, the series was discontinued.

Another Lone Wolf episode was released but the series that put Columbia on the series map came from the comic pages. Blondie and Dagwood came to the movie screen in 1938, much to moviegoers' delight. Columbia added the Lone Wolf series (with Warren William in the lead), a Wild Bill Saunders series (with rising western star Bill Elliott), and a series adapted from children's books by Margaret Sidney, *The Five Little Peppers*. After four features each, both the Wild Bill Saunders and Five Little Peppers series disappeared. The Five Little Peppers because, quite frankly, the screenplays were so saccharin that even the talented Edith Fellows couldn't save them. Elliott's Saunders series was rolled into the Wild Bill Hickok series, something that Columbia should have done from the beginning. In the 1940–41 season of eight films, Elliott would play Hickok in six. Why he was a different character name in the others is anybody's guess, since he played all eight in his own style. Warren William was given Eric Blore as his "gentleman's gentleman" in Williams' second Lone Wolf outing. This was inspired casting as the chemistry between them clicked and they elevated the entertainment level. The Ellery Queen series was added. The Durango Kid made his first appearance. Exhibitors wanted more, but the decision was not to star Charles Starrett in a series at that time. In 1941, Columbia signed Chester Morris to play another adventurer from the silent era, Boston Blackie.

Two other series were started and were short-lived. It has been mentioned that a series based on the comic strip *Tillie the Toiler* would be a replacement for the Blondie series. Critics and moviegoers gave a "thumbs down" and only one feature was made. Finally, Charles Starrett got his series, The Medico, based on novels by James L. Rubel. Some plot elements from Rubel's first book were used in the initial opus. Rubel's stories were much too involved for 60-minute programmers, and when the screenwriters chose not to use material from the other books, Rubel withdrew his support and the series was cancelled. Tex Ritter was added to Elliott's Hickok series. With the popularity of other studios' trio western series, the decision was to produce westerns with two action stars. In 1942, The Hickok series ended. Elliott, wanting to have his own series and not share the spotlight with Ritter, moved to Republic. The Ellery Queen series was also discontinued. Even though Columbia screenwriters played fast and loose with the Queen novels and injected some inane comedy, the authors were satisfied enough to demand four features annually. Harry Cohn retaliated by ending the series. William Gargan and Margaret Lindsay, who were under contract to play Ellery and Nikki Porter, were now without a series. In 1943, screenwriters came up with a Jess Arno–June Terry series, which was no great shakes and was discontinued after the initial feature. Margaret Lindsay then co-starred with Warner Baxter in *Crime Doctor* (Columbia, 1943). The feature was a hit, a series was in order and the decision was made not to give Baxter a permanent love interest. So Margaret Lindsay was written out of the series. In 1944, the Whistler came to the screen. This was an anthology series that starred Richard Dix. Dix would not play the same character in the series, but would alternate between good and evil. Another ploy Columbia used was not to use the series character in the title of the film. It was thought this would promote ticket sales. In 1945, three additional series came to the screen. The first was the I Love a Mystery series, based on the radio program of the same name. It was announced that there would be two films annually for five years, but only three were made. The second was the Durango Kid series, which effectively extended Charles Starrett's career. The intention was to just produce a few, but the reception was overwhelming. Starrett, in fact, would play Durango for the remainder of his screen career. The third was Rusty, a "boy-and-his-dog" series. Each feature included a moral lesson. The year 1946 saw Robin Hood's return to the screen. Actually, it was Robin's son in the forefront, in the person of Cornell Wilde. The other series was Night Editor, a proposed anthology series, which lasted for one production. The Lone Wolfe series was resurrected with Gerald Mohr in the lead, and Eric Blore as his valet. The chemistry wasn't there, and Mohr lacked the sophistication of the previous actors who played the role. Three features were made.

In 1947, two new series were attempted. Mr. District Attorney held great promise. It would be a premier series for Columbia, which wanted Edward G. Robinson in the lead but settled for Adolphe Menjou. After the first picture the decision was made not to continue the series. Bulldog Drummond was the other series. Two features were made before the series moved to 20th Century–Fox. Richard Dix played in his final Whistler feature, leaving the series for health reasons. The year 1948 saw the release of the last Whistler film, in which Michael Duane starred. Robin Hood was back for an encore. The last truly successful series, Jungle Jim, came to the screen. Johnny Weissmuller was Jim and played the part like Tarzan with clothes on. The year 1949 saw the last of Boston Blackie, the Crime Doctor and the Lone Wolf. Warner Baxter appeared as Jess Arno in one production, which was a decided improvement on the first entry. Even though the Durango Kid series was continued, a decision was made to no longer bill Charles Starrett as the Durango Kid. Starrett, as Durango, would be seen in scene cards but rarely on the title card. In 1950, the final Blondie film was released. That same year Phillips H. Lord's Counterspy came to the screen. Although two neat stories were produced, the series was discontinued. Rafael Sabatini's Captain Blood came to the screen, starring the swashbuckling Louis Hayward. The son of Robin Hood made his last appearance in *Rogues of Sherwood Forest* (Columbia, 1950). In 1951, three series were produced: Jungle Jim, the Durango Kid and Gasoline Alley. Columbia hoped to replace the Blondie series with Gasoline Alley, also from the comic strips, but ended the series after two films. In 1952, Durango hung up his spurs. Captain Blood made his final appearance, leaving Jungle Jim to carry on Columbia's series legacy. In 1954, Columbia sold the rights to the Jungle Jim character to their television subsidiary, Screen Gems. Screen Gems had plans for a television series, and then refused to let the parent company use the name "Jungle Jim" in the three remaining features with Weissmuller. So, in Weissmuller's final features, he plays — Johnny Weissmuller. The screenwriters even had to change Jungle Jim's chimpanzee's name from Tamba to Kimba. *Devil Goddess* (Columbia, 1955), also starring Weissmuller, was the last series film produced during Harry Cohn's tenure.

THE SERIES FILMS

Blondie

It was a struggle for cartoonist Chic Young to have his own successful comic strip. Earlier strips, *The Affairs of Jane* and *Beautiful Babs,* would quickly fall out of favor. A third strip, *Dumb Dora,* proved popular but Young gave up the strip in a dispute over ownership with King Features. King Features allowed Young to begin a new strip in which he would be the sole owner. Young came up with "Blondie," a strip that has endured for eight decades.

On September 8, 1930, Blondie first appeared in the newspapers. "Blondie Boopadoop" was a flapper who frequented jazz clubs. A flapper was a liberated woman of the '20s, sporting bobbed hair and wearing dresses designed to make her look young and boyish. Flappers would smoke cigarettes through long cigarette holders, sniff cocaine and engage in casual sex. Into Blondie's life would come playboy Dagwood Bumstead, scion of J. Bolling Bumstead of the Bumstead Locomotive Works. Dagwood was not the brightest of young men. In one incident, Dagwood became lost in his own mansion, only returning to familiar areas when he joined a tour of the mansion. Dagwood fell for Blondie and brought her home to meet his parents, at which time Blondie made a play for Dagwood's father. The couple split up, but Blondie finally realized that Dagwood was the man for her. His family forbade a marriage between the two. But after Dagwood went on a 28 day, seven hour, eight minute and 22 second hunger strike, his family relented.

On February 17, 1933, Blondie and Dagwood were married, and Dagwood was disinherited from the Bumstead fortune. He then obtained a job with the Dithers Construction Company, run with an iron fist by J.C. (Julius Caesar) Dithers. On April 15, 1934, the Bumsteads were blessed with the birth of a son, initially called Baby Dumpling. Later as he grew, his real name, Alexander, was used. The daily trials and tribulations of the Bumstead family were enjoyed by millions of readers. In 1941, the Bumsteads added a baby girl to their family. Their daughter was named in a readers' contest. Out of almost 500,000 suggestions, the winning selection was "Cookie." The winner received $100. To round out the family, the Bumsteads already had a dog, "Daisy." Daisy would later have pups; all would be well behaved, except the mischievous Elmer.

In 1937, Blondie first appeared in comic books with the first issue of *ACE Comics* (David McKay Publications). This issue also marked the first comic book appearances of Jungle Jim, Ripley's Believe It Or not and Krazy Kat. In the spring 1947 issue, *Blondie Comics* became a regular publication. The comic books lasted until the November 1976 issue. During those years *Blondie Comics* was published by David McKay, Harvey, King and Charlton. There were a number of spin-off publications: *Dagwood* (Harvey, 1950–1965), *Blondie & Dagwood Family* (Harvey, 1963–1965) and *Daisy & Her Pups* (Harvey, 1951–1955). Blondie, through Whitman Publishing, appeared in one Big Little Book (1937), 13 Better Little Books (1939–1949) and one New Better Little Book (1949).

In 1938, Columbia Pictures obtained the rights to the comic strip. Joan Blondell's sister, Gloria, was the first choice to play Blondie. Then, Una Merkel was announced for the part before assigning Shirley Deane. Deane fell ill, however, and Penny Singleton, after dying her hair, landed the role. This was a major turning point in her career; in the past she appeared primarily in support roles in Warner Bros. features. After starring in *Blondie* (Columbia, 1938), Singleton would only be seen in two non–Blondie features in her movie career: the lead in *Go West Young Lady* (Columbia, 1941), and a supporting role in *Young Widow* (United Artists, 1946).

Even though Stuart Erwin was the first choice to play Dagwood, the part eventually went to Arthur Lake. Lake had been top billed in features, notably *Harold Teen* (First National, 1928) and short subjects in the late twenties and the early '30s. By 1933, Lake's roles were relegated to supporting status. When Columbia suspended production of the series after *Footlight Glamour* (Columbia, 1942), Lake stayed busy with starring roles in *The Ghost That Walks Alone* (Columbia, 1944), *Sailor's Holiday* (Columbia, 1944), *The Big Show-off* (Republic, 1945) and a supporting role in *Three is a Family* (United Artists, 1944). When the Blondie series was resumed, Lake left the series for only one film, *16 Fathoms Deep* (Monogram, 1948). In 1950, King Features and Columbia could not agree on a new contract and the series was discontinued. With the series' demise, Lake's movie career ended. He made a failed attempt to revive the Blondie series with a television series in 1957.

Another major performer in the series was Larry Simms as Baby Dumpling/Alexander. Simms appeared in 36 feature films, 28 of which were in the Blondie series. Simms's other important role was as Pete Bailey in the Frank Capra classic, *It's a Wonderful Life* (Liberty Films, 1946). Cookie was the only role Marjorie Kent (a.k.a. Marjorie Ann Mutchie) played in her film career, appearing in 16 entries of the Blondie series.

The other important member of the Bumstead household was Daisy Bumstead, played by Spooks and his offspring. The "his" is correct, a male dog played Daisy. Daisy appeared in 27 entries in the series, missing only *Blondie's Holiday* (Columbia, 1947). Spooks would appear in 11 other films, most notably *The Valiant Hombre* (United Artists, 1948) with Duncan Renaldo as the Cisco Kid, and *Red Stallion* (Eagle-Lion, 1947).

Dagwood's boss, J.C. Dithers was played by Jonathan Hale. Hale had a long career in show business, usually playing people of prominence. Hale played Inspector Henry Fernack in five episodes of RKO's The Saint series (1938–1941). In the movie series, Dagwood would have another boss, George M. Radcliffe, played by Jerome Cowan. Cowan, also, had a long show business career. Probably Cowan's most notable performance was as Miles Archer, Sam Spade's murdered partner in the classic, *The Maltese Falcon* (Warner Bros., 1941).

Danny Mummert played Alvin Fuddle, Dagwood's nemesis in 24 entries. Like Larry Simms, Mummert would also have a role in *It's a Wonderful Life*.

Columbia screenwriters made some important changes in Blondie and Dagwood's background. First, Blondie's maiden name was now Miller. Second, they made Blondie and Dagwood high school sweethearts. Third, Dagwood's youthful nemesis in the comic strip was Elmo Tuttle, but in the movie series, he became Alvin Fuddle. When Jonathan Hale left the series, the decision was made to have the company sold to avoid trying to find an actor to play the role of Dithers. The Bumsteads' long-time neighbors, the Woodleys (from the comic strip) finally made an appearance in the final entry, *Beware of Blondie* (Columbia, 1950).

Due to the success of the movie series, Singleton and Lake were signed to reprise their roles on radio. They began on CBS on July 3, 1939, and appeared on the NBC Blue network. Singleton dropped out of the radio series in March 1949. During the program's final year on ABC, Alice White, Patricia Van Cleve and Ann Rutherford took on the role of Blondie. The final show aired July 6, 1950.

Columbia decided to replace the Blondie series with the comic strip *Gasoline Alley*. After two entries in that series, it was discontinued, only to be replaced with re-releases of the Blondie films.

There were five attempts to bring Blondie to television; two were failed attempts. The first, in 1952, was to star Jeff Donnell and John Harvey; the second in 1954 toplined Pamela Britton and Hal LeRoy. In 1957, Arthur Lake once again played Dagwood and Pamela Britton was Blondie for 15 episodes. In 1968, Patricia Hardy was Blondie and Will Hutchins, best known in his western role of Sugarfoot (Warner Bros.–ABC, 1957–1961), appeared as Dagwood. In 1987, an animated version of Blondie reached television audiences, with Loni Anderson as the voice of Blondie and Frank Welker, voicing Dagwood.

Blondie survives today. There have been many changes to update the strip. For example, no longer does Dagwood run for the bus; he carpools, and Blondie (with her next-door neighbor Tootsie Woodley) has a catering service.

We can only hope that Blondie and Dagwood can one day celebrate their 100th anniversary in the newspapers.

BLONDIE

Columbia (November 1938)

Out of the "Funnies" ... Straight into Your Heart!

Cast: Blondie, Penny Singleton; Dagwood, Arthur Lake; Baby Dumpling, Larry Simms; "Daisy"; C.P. Hazlip, Gene Lockhart; J.C. Dithers, Jonathan Hale; Chester Franey, Gordon Oliver; Alvin Fuddle, Danny Mummert; Mrs. Miller, Kathleen Lockhart; Elsie Hazlip, Ann Doran; Dot Miller, Dorothy Moore; Mrs. Fuddle, Fay Helm // Paperboy, Eugene Anderson, Jr.; Furniture salesman, Charles Lane; Mailman, Irving Bacon; Nelson, Richard Fiske; Mr. Hicks, Stanley Andrews; Mr. Morgan, Walter Soderling; Pie salesman, George Humbert; Mr. Phillips, Harold Minjir; S.W. Carey Salesman, Stanley Brown; Hotel porter, Willie Best; Optometrist patient, Josephine Whittell; Policeman at hotel, Edgar Dearing; *Daily Gazette* reporter, Dick Curtis; Mary, Mary Jane Carey; Man on bus, Hooper Atchley; Policeman in accident, James Flavin; Desk Sergeant, Emory Parnell; Judge, Ian Wolfe; Gardner, John Rand

Credits: Director, Frank R. Strayer; Associate Producer, Robert Sparks; Screenwriter, Richard Flournoy; Editor, Gene Havlick; Art Director, Lionel Banks; Interior Decorator, Babs Johnstone; Cinematographer, Henry Freulich; Gowns, Kalloch; Musical Director, M.W. Stoloff

Production Dates: September 12, 1938–October 7, 1938

Source: Based on the comic strip *Blondie*, created by Chic Young. Owned and copyrighted by King Features Syndicate, Inc.

Running Time: 70 min.

Story: For their fifth wedding anniversary, Penny Singleton plans to surprise Arthur Lake with all new furniture. The monthly payments are higher than Singleton anticipated, and she hopes Lake's raise comes through. Meanwhile Lake has troubles of his own. He co-signed a note for a former co-worker. The co-worker can't be found and Lake has to make good the loan or his furniture will be repossessed. His only way out is to land an important construction contract for Jonathan Hale's firm with Gene Lockhart. G. Lockhart is staying

at a local hotel but is no mood to deal with construction salesmen. By chance, Lake and
G. Lockhart meet, neither knowing the other's identity. A bond is formed when they spy
a hotel vacuum cleaner in need of repair. They take the vacuum to G. Lockhart's hotel
room. The next day they're still working on the vacuum. Singleton has found out that Lake
is in trouble. Singleton finds that he's gone to G. Lockhart's room. She calls the room and
G. Lockhart's daughter, Ann Doran, answers the phone. Immediately, Singleton is extremely
jealous, thinking the worse. Hale sees a newspaper story that G. Lockhart's project has been
cancelled. Lake tries to tell Hale that the story is not true, but Hale fires Lake before he
can explain. That night, Lake realizes how jealous Singleton has become and takes his
mother-in-law's (Kathleen Lockhart) car. K. Lockhart reports the car as stolen, not seeing
Lake behind the wheel. Lake is driving G. Lockhart, Doran and the hotel's vacuum to
explain to Singleton when he hits a police car. Lake is arrested for the accident, driving a
stolen car, and both Lake and G. Lockhart are accused of having the stolen vacuum in their
possession. In court the next morning, Singleton, having been told the circumstances by
Doran, tells Judge Ian Wolfe that she was responsible for the charges. Wolfe dismisses all
charges. Leaving the courtroom, G. Lockhart learns that Lake came to see him about the
construction project and awards the contract to him. Hale tells Lake and Singleton that all
is a misunderstanding and Lake was not fired. Singleton disagrees with Hale. For Lake's
return, Singleton negotiates a huge bonus and a nice raise for her husband.

Blondie (1938) movie still (left to right) Gene Lockhart, Penny Singleton and Arthur Lake.

Notes and Commentary: Penny Singleton was the fourth choice for the part of Blondie. Other actresses mentioned for the role were Gloria Blondell, Una Merkel, and Shirley Deane.

Stuart Erwin had previously been mentioned to play the part of Dagwood.

Gene and Kathleen Lockhart were husband and wife and appeared together in 18 feature films and one television program. They had one daughter, actress June Lockhart, and a granddaughter, actress Anne Lockhart. Gene, Kathleen and June had roles in *A Christmas Carol* (Metro-Goldwyn-Mayer, 1938).

Reviews: "Engaging start to the series." *The Columbia Story*, Hirshhorn

"Singleton and Lake bring charm and spontaneity to this film." *Motion Picture Guide*, Nash and Ross

"Clicko series for Columbia with pop cartoon characters. A particularly fine effort for the initial release." *Variety*, 11/02/38

Summation: This is a great start to the series! With a neat blend of comedy and sensitivity, this is a very entertaining entry. Penny Singleton and Arthur Lake are perfect as Blondie and Dagwood. Child actor Larry Simms and talented dog Daisy are legitimate scene-stealers. Gene Lockhart chips in with nice support. The rest of the cast is more than adequate. Richard Flournoy's script and Frank R. Strayer's direction are first-rate.

BLONDIE MEETS THE BOSS
Columbia (March 1939)

Movie audiences have taken the favorite family of the "funnies" right into their hearts!

Cast: Blondie, Penny Singleton; Dagwood, Arthur Lake; Baby Dumpling, Larry Simms; "Daisy"; J.C. Dithers, Jonathan Hale; Alvin Fuddle, Danny Mummert; Dot Miller, Dorothy Moore; Marvin Williams, Don Beddoe; Francine Rogers, Linda Winters; Ollie Shaw, Stanley Brown; Freddie Turner, Joel Dean; Nelson, Richard Fiske; Betty Lou Wood, Inez Courtney; Skinnay Ennis and his band // Paperboy, Eugene Anderson, Jr.; First mailman, Irving Bacon; Second mailman, Walter Sande; Mary, Mary Jane Carey; Mr. Morgan, Walter Soderling; Office worker/Nightclub patron with Dorothy Moore, Robert Sterling; Pots and pans peddler, Eddie Acuff; Marvin's wife, Sally Payne; Mr. Crane, Lew Kelly; Laundryman, George Chandler; Door-to-door saleswoman, Sarah Edwards; Officer in pool hall, Edgar Dearing; Elderly nightclub patron, William B. Davidson; Companion with elderly nightclub patron, Virginia Dabney; Harry Philpot, Wallis Clark

Credit: Director, Frank R. Strayer; Associate Producer, Robert Sparks; Story, Kay Van Riper and Richard Flournoy; Screenwriter, Richard Flournoy; Editor, Gene Havlick; Art Direction, Lionel Banks; Cinematographer, Henry Freulich; Gowns, Kalloch; Musical Director, M.W. Stoloff; Dance Director, Eddie Larkin

Song: "You Had It Coming to You" (Oakland and Lerner) — Sung and played by Skinnay Ennis and his band

Production Dates: December 27, 1938–January 24, 1939

Source: Based on the comic strip *Blondie*, created by Chic Young. Owned and copyrighted by King Features Syndicate, Inc.

Running Time: 75 min.

Story: When Jonathan Hale calls off Arthur Lake's vacation, Lake resigns. Penny Singleton goes to Hale's office to get Lake's job back, but Hale hires her. If a major deal goes through, then Lake will get his job back. Hale wants Singleton to purchase a piece of property before the news gets out. When Lake learns Singleton has his job, he goes on a fishing trip with neighbor Don Beddoe. Beddoe's fishing trips are an excuse to meet lovely ladies. One of the ladies, Linda Winters, a singer at the Golden Cafe, trips getting into the boat and Lake catches her. The picture of Winters in Lake's arms is caught on camera. Lake is uncomfortable being in the company of the women and goes home not knowing Winters's camera is in his fishing creel. Singleton finds the camera and has the film developed. Seeing the picture, Singleton thinks the worse and her jealousy goes into high gear. Singleton's sister, Dorothy Moore, and Dorothy's boyfriend, Joel Dean, are staying at Singleton's house. They're in town for a jitterbug contest. Lake leaves the house. Singleton has to stay at the office to wait for a telegram from Hale. She tells Moore and Dean to watch her son, Larry Simms. Moore and Dean take Simms and his dog, Daisy, to the Golden Cafe. When Lake comes home, he sees a note stating that Moore has taken Simms and Daisy. Lake goes to the club and sees Winters. Both want to keep the picture away from Singleton. Singleton gets the go-ahead to purchase the land. The owner, Willis Clark, runs the Golden Café. Singleton goes to the café and sees Lake coming out of Winters's dressing room, hits Lake over the head with her purse and leaves. The contents of the purse spill to the floor. Clark sees the telegram about the land deal and knows he can hold Hale up for more money. Singleton returns home and packs to leave Lake. Simms, who heard most of the conversation between Lake and Winters, tells Singleton how Winters ended up in Lake's arms. The jitterbug contest has started, but Moore and Dean have had an argument and Dean walked out. Moore is distraught until a woozy Lake slides out on the dance floor and Moore is able to manipulate Lake to the point that they are named the contest winners. Lake comes home and he and Singleton make up. Singleton now remembers she needs to see Clark, but Clark wants too much money and Singleton can't close the transaction. This turns out to be a great stroke of fortune, since the deal fell through and Hale had been unable to contact Singleton. Lake has his job back, and Hale tells him to take his vacation.

Notes and Commentary: The working title of this film was "Blondie Steps Out."

This was the first feature film for Robert Sterling. Sterling is probably best remembered for his role of George Kerby in the television series, *Topper* (CBS, 1953–55). Sterling has two roles in this film, so watch closely!

Reviews: "The series was predictable even this early." *Motion Picture Guide*, Nash and Ross

"It's amusing only in spots." *Variety*, 03/08/39

Summation: Not as much comedy in this one, but no matter, it's just as good as the first entry. Both Penny Singleton and Arthur Lake get a chance to stretch their acting skills, and acquit themselves well. The supporting cast does nicely, especially Larry Simms and Jonathan Hale. Frank R. Strayer directs with a sure hand.

BLONDIE TAKES A VACATION
Columbia (July 1939)

They're in the country now!

Cast: Blondie, Penny Singleton; Dagwood, Arthur Lake; Baby Dumpling, Larry Simms; "Daisy"; Alvin Fuddle, Danny Mummert; Jonathan Gillis, Donald Meek; Harvey

Morton, Donald MacBride; Matthew Dickerson, Thomas W. Ross; Emily Dickerson, Elizabeth Dunne; John Larkin, Robert Wilcox; Mr. Holden, Harlan Briggs; Mailman, Irving Bacon // Paperboy, Eugene Anderson, Jr.; Taxi driver, Lou Fulton; Train conductor, Emmett Vogan; Poker player, Harry Harvey; Drunk on train, Arthur Housman; Hotel desk clerk, Dave Willock; Plumbing creditor, Robert McKenzie; Bakery creditor, Gus Glassmire; Grocery creditor, Milton Kibbee; Resort singer, Christine McIntyre; Engineer, Wade Boteler; Sheriff Weaver. Arthur Aylesworth

Credits: Director, Frank R. Strayer; Producer, Robert Sparks; Story, Richard Flournoy, Karen DeWolf and Robert Chapin; Screenwriter, Robert Flournoy; Editor, Viola Lawrence; Art Director, Lionel Banks; Cinematography, Henry Freulich; Gowns, Kalloch; Musical Director, M.W. Stoloff

Filming Locations: Cedar Lake and Big Bear, California

Songs: "Love in Bloom" (Rainger and Robin) sung by Christine McIntyre; "For He's a Jolly Good Fellow" (traditional) sung by chorus

Production Dates: May 19, 1939–June 19, 1939

Source: Based on the comic strip *Blondie*, created by Chic Young. Owned and copyrighted by King Features Syndicate, Inc.

Running Time: 68 min.

Story: Finally, Penny Singleton, Arthur Lake, Larry Simms and Daisy go on vacation. On the train, they encounter Donald MacBride, who causes Daisy to be sent to the baggage car. They arrive at the hotel only to find MacBride is the owner. MacBride refuses to allow them to stay. Enraged, fellow traveler Donald Meek, who has a fascination for fire, cancels his reservation. They all find accommodations at the Westview Inn. Singleton and Lake find the inn too spooky and start to leave. They stay when they learn the owners, Thomas W. Ross and his wife Elizabeth Dunne, are in financial difficulty. MacBride talked Ross and Dunne into making improvements and then contrived to keep business away. Ross and Dunne are unable to pay off the note and MacBride is waiting to foreclose. Banker Harlan Briggs will not loan them money unless he can see their inn is a thriving business. Lake becomes acting manager and takes the inn's bus to see MacBride. MacBride and his employees intimidate Lake. In trying to leave, the bus catches fire. MacBride has Lake arrested and fined on various charges. Singleton is angry and wants to talk with MacBride. Meanwhile, Simms picks up a skunk thinking the animal is a cat. Daisy chases the skunk and its family into the mechanical room of MacBride's hotel. The skunks excrete a strong foul-smelling odor that goes through the air conditioning system, forcing all the guests to leave the premises. All the guests move to the Westview Inn. MacBride comes over and states that he'll take over the inn the next day. MacBride is told the skunk odor has permeated everything; it will take months to remove the odor and all the draperies, linens, etc. should be burned. Meek, who is a pyromaniac, decides to set fire to MacBride's hotel, not realizing Simms and Daisy have come to the hotel to look for the skunks. Simms and Daisy watch MacBride removing money and papers from his safe before starting the fire to destroy his property. Meek starts to leave when he hears Simms's voice. Meek rescues Simms and Daisy. MacBride tries to have Lake arrested for arson. Simms points out MacBride as the man who started the fire, and that he has money and papers in his coat pocket. MacBride is arrested. The inn is now a thriving business and Briggs will advance them the money needed to pay off the old loan. Singleton announces that the family is going on vacation — back to their home.

Notes and Commentary: Donald Meek was one of Hollywood's finest character actors, appearing in over 125 films. Usually playing milquetoast characters, Meek made an impression as Doc Boone's foil, Peacock in the classic western, *Stagecoach* (United Artists, 1939), Amos Budget in the Mae West–W.C. Fields western comedy, *My Little Chickadee* (Universal, 1940) and as Bartholomew in the short lived Nick Carter series at Metro-Goldwyn-Mayer (1939–1940).

Reviews: "Humorous piece of fluff." *Motion Picture Guide*, Nash and Ross
"Standard programmer for family trade." *Variety*, 07/19/39

Summation: The best in the series so far. There is a great mixture of comedy, drama and suspense. Director Frank R. Strayer's firm hand blends the ingredients nicely to everyone's satisfaction. Again, Penny Singleton and Arthur Lake turn in excellent performances, turning from comedy to drama with apparent ease. They have great support from the rest of the cast, especially Larry Simms, Daisy and Donald Meek.

BLONDIE BRINGS UP BABY

Columbia (November 1939)

Baby Goes to School ... and You Go Into Stitches

Cast: Blondie, Penny Singleton; Dagwood, Arthur Lake; Baby Dumpling, Larry Simms; "Daisy"; Alvin Fuddle, Danny Mummert; J.C. Dithers, Jonathan Hale; Abner Cartwright, Robert Middlemass; Encyclopedia Salesman, Olin Howland; Mrs. Fuddle, Fay Helm; Melinda Mason, Peggy Ann Garner; Mr. Mason, Roy Gordon; Miss White, Grace Stafford; Miss Ferguson, Helen Jerome Eddy; Mailman, Irving Bacon // Paperboy, Eugene Anderson, Jr.; Trashman, Milburn Morante; Mary, Mary Jane Carey; Dithers's employees, Stanley Brown, Richard Fiske and Robert Sterling; Tom Malcolm, Selmer Jackson; Dogcatchers, John Tyrell and Joe Palma; Mason's chauffeur, Bruce Bennett; Governess, Madelon Grey; Desk Sergeant, Ralph Dunn; Judge, Ian Wolfe; Bailiff, Harry Strang; Lars, Victol Potel: Captain James, Robert Homans, Policeman, Walter Sande

Credits: Director, Frank R. Strayer; Producer, Robert Sparks; Story, Robert Chapin, Karen DeWolf and Richard Flournoy; Screenwriters, Gladys Lehman and Richard Flournoy; Editor, Otto Meyer; Art Director, Lionel Banks; Cinematographer, Henry Freulich; Gowns, Kalloch; Musical Director, M.W. Stoloff

Song: "My Country 'Tis of Thee" (Carey) sung by children's chorus

Production Dates: August 31, 1939–October 10, 1939

Source: Based on the comic strip *Blondie*, created by Chic Young. Owned and copyrighted by King Features Syndicate, Inc.

Running Time: 67 min.

Story: Lake is in trouble again! Lake convinced developer Robert Middlemass to make changes in his proposed apartment complex to accommodate both children and dogs. Midddlemass never signed off on the changes, using them as an excuse to terminate his contract with Jonathan Hale and avoid bankruptcy. Consequently, Hale fires Lake. Meanwhile encyclopedia salesman Olin Howland convinces Penny Singleton that her son, Larry Simms, is brilliant and should start school early. Because of peer pressure, Simms won't allow Singleton to walk him to school, but will allow his dog Daisy to accompany him. Simms tells Daisy to stay outside of the school grounds until school is over. However, dogcatchers spy Daisy and take her to the pound. The next day, instead of going to school, Simms starts looking for Daisy. When school principal Helen Jerome Eddy calls Singleton to let her know that

Simms is absent, Singleton calls Hale's company looking for Lake. Hale, not wanting to tell Singleton that Lake was fired, decides to help Singleton find Simms. Daisy was taken from the pound to be a companion for Peggy Ann Garner. Garner had an illness leaving her unable to walk. Simms finds Daisy and reluctantly begins to play with Garner. Garner's father, Roy Gordon, is notified that Garner is missing. Singleton and Lake are present in the police station when Gordon reports Garner's disappearance. Daisy's name is mentioned, and Lake hurries to Gordon's estate. Through a series of mix-ups, Lake is thought to be a kidnapper. Since Simms is thought to be with Garner, they go to Lake's house. Simms and Garner are playing in the back yard. Additionally, Simms has encouraged Garner to walk. Gordon is so overjoyed that he wants to do something for other children in need. Lake suggests that Gordon take over the complex he had designed for Middlemass. Gordon thinks this is a great idea. Hale tells Lake he was never fired and will receive a substantial bonus.

Notes and Commentary: Peggy Ann Garner would become a major child star for 20th Century–Fox in the mid-'40s. Garner excelled in *A Tree Grows in Brooklyn* (Fox, 1945), *Nob Hill* (20th Century–Fox, 1945) and *Home Sweet Homicide* (20th Century–Fox, 1946). Primarily for her work in *Brooklyn*, Garner received an Academy Juvenile Award.

Reviews: "Only average, though Henry Freulich's camera work is particularly nice." *Motion Picture Guide*, Nash and Ross

"Further amusing adventures of Blondie and Dagwood." *Variety*, 11/08/39

Summation: The Blondie series rolls along nicely with this entry. Director Frank R. Strayer again mixes comedy, drama, and pathos and comes up with a tasty confection. Strayer coaxes winning performances from the cast, in particular Penny Singleton, Arthur Lake, Larry Simms, Jonathan Hale, Peggy Ann Garner and, of course, Daisy.

BLONDIE ON A BUDGET
Columbia (February 1940)

Balance your fun budget!

Cast: Blondie, Penny Singleton; Dagwood, Arthur Lake; Baby Dumpling, Larry Simms; "Daisy"; Joan Forrester, Rita Hayworth; Alvin Fuddle, Danny Mummert; Marvin Williams, Don Beddoe; Ed Fuddle, John Qualen; Mrs. Fuddle, Fay Helm; Mailman, Irving Bacon; Brice, Thurston Hall; Theater manager, William Brisbane // Paperboy, Willie Best; Tony, Dick Curtis; Bartender, Ralph Peters; Man outside theater, Gene Morgan; Anniversary cake usherette, Janet Shaw; Usherette, Claire James; Policeman Dempsey, Emory Parnell; Policeman, George Guhl; Bank teller, Hal K. Dawson; Saleslady, Mary Currier; Ticket agent, Chester Clute

Credits: Director, Frank R. Strayer; Producer, Robert Sparks; Story, Charles Molyneux Brown; Screenwriter, Richard Flournoy; Editor, Gene Havlick; Art Director, Lionel Banks; Cinematographer, Henry Freulich; Gowns, Kalloch; Musical Director, M.W. Stoloff

Production Dates: December 15, 1939–January 17, 1940

Source: Based on the comic strip *Blondie*, created by Chic Young. Owned and copyrighted by King Features Syndicate, Inc.

Running Time: 72 min.

Story: Arthur Lake wants two hundred dollars to join an exclusive fishing club. Penny Singleton wants two hundred dollars to purchase a fur coat. But the budget won't allow either. Lake and Singleton are arguing about this when an old flame of Lake's, Rita Hayworth, comes by. Hayworth is bringing papers needed for a deal with Lake's company. Singleton allows Lake to go fishing, and Hayworth offers to give Lake a ride. Hayworth takes Lake to a Lovers Lane spot where they used to spend time before Lake met Singleton. Lake becomes uncomfortable so they decide to leave, but Hayworth has car trouble. While waiting for the car to be repaired, Lake and Hayworth go to the movies. In the theater's anniversary contest, Lake gets a chance to win prize money. Lake, thinking he couldn't possibly win, tears up the chance. Lake confesses all to Singleton, who forgives him but tells him not to see Hayworth — except on business matters. Theater manager William Brisbane calls Lake to tell him he's won two hundred dollars. Hoping to surprise Singleton, Lake keeps the news to himself. When Lake calls to collect the money he finds out that he needs Hayworth since she filled out the chance. Lake plans to buy a fur coat for Singleton, and Hayworth agrees to help find the right size. Singleton withdraws two hundred dollars to give to Lake to join the fishing club. Singleton goes to the department store for one last look at the coat and finds the coat on Hayworth with Lake looking on. Singleton thinks divorce is the only alternative. Lawyer Thurston Hall, using reverse psychology, convinces Singleton to go home. Singleton finds the fur coat was really intended for her. She gives Lake money to join the fishing club then takes it back when she hears that fire has destroyed the club.

Notes and Commentary: A telling mistake: When Daisy, who had been drinking, leaps into a chair, you can see that Daisy is a male.

When Arthur Lake and Rita Hayworth go to the movies, the posters advertise *His Girl Friday* (Columbia, 1940) with Cary Grant and Rosalind Russell.

Reviews: "Notable for the presence of Hayworth." *Motion Picture Guide*, Nash and Ross

"Above average for series, entertaining programmer for the family trade." *Variety*, 02/28/40

Summation: Mild entry in the series. There is not a much true comedy with a too predictable story line. Rita Hayworth adds interest, but not enough to put the film in the preferred class.

BLONDIE HAS SERVANT TROUBLE
Columbia (July 1940)

A hot time ahead for the Bumsteads ... but a grand time ahead for you!

Alternate Title: *Blondie Has Trouble*

Cast: Blondie, Penny Singleton; Dagwood, Arthur Lake; Baby Dumpling, Larry Simms; "Daisy"; Alvin Fuddle, Danny Mummert; J.C. Dithers, Jonathan Hale; Eric Vaughn, Arthur Hohl; Anna Vaughn, Esther Dale; Mr. Crumb, Irving Bacon; Horatio Jones, Ray Turner; Mr. Morgan, Walter Soderling; Mrs. Fuddle, Fay Helm // Paperboy, Eugene Anderson, Jr.; Ollie, Frank Melton; Mary, Mary Jane Carey; Taxi driver, Murray Alper; Police commissioner, Ivan Miller

Credits: Director, Frank R. Strayer; Producer, Robert Sparks; Story, Albert Duffy; Screenwriter, Richard Flournoy; Editor, Gene Havlick; Art Director, Lionel Banks; Cinematographer, Henry Freulich; Gowns, Kalloch; Original Music, Leigh Harline; Musical Director, M.W. Stoloff

Production Dates: April 25, 1940–May 27, 1940

Source: Based on the comic strip *Blondie*, created by Chic Young. Owned and copyrighted by King Features Syndicate, Inc.

Running Time: 70 min.

Story: Jonathan Hale, executor of the Batterson estate, asks Arthur Lake and Penny Singleton to live in the house for a few weeks to prove it's not haunted. When Lake, Singleton, their son, Larry Simms, and their dog, Daisy, arrive; they find a visitor, Ray Turner. In order to join a lodge, Turner has to spend a night in the house .The doorbell rings. Arthur Hohl and Esther Dale are at the door. Singleton thinks they are the servants Hale is sending. Hohl is mentally unbalanced and thinks the house belongs to him. Simms notices that, while it's raining, Hohl and Dale are perfectly dry. Turner finds a newspaper article and calls out to Lake. Before Lake can respond, Turner is whisked into a secret passage. Dale decides to leave the house and is threatened by Hohl. Dale screams. Lake and Singleton find Dale unconscious, with a cut on her head. Lake calls Hale, but before he can finish the conversation, the line is cut. Then Dale disappears. Lake finds the newspaper article and realizes Hohl is crazy and is wanted by the police. Lake leaves Singleton, Simms and Turner in a locked room as he searches for Hohl. Hohl enters the room through a secret passage and walks toward Singleton, knife in hand. Lake comes through the passage in time to stop Hohl. Hale arrives with the police. Hohl is arrested. Lake, Singleton, Simms and Daisy are happy to return home.

Notes and Commentary: The working title for this film was "Blondie Beware."

Thank goodness, how times have changed! Penny Singleton threatens Larry Simms with being locked in a closet as punishment for misbehaving.

In one scene, Penny Singleton wears the fur coat she received in the previous film, *Blondie on a Budget* (1940).

Reviews: "Silly fluff." *Motion Picture Guide*, Nash and Ross

"Best of the Blondie's. Poor title hiding from the public a high laugh voltage. More like this and the Blondies will be in the major leagues." *Variety*, 08/07/40

Summation: This is an uneven but ultimately satisfying haunted house mystery. A lot of the comedy is forced and falls flat. The thrill quotient is first-rate in the last reel. Henry Freulich's camera work adds greatly to the suspense. Cast performances are fine, with Arthur Hohl excellent as the deranged "butler," and Arthur Lake registers strongly as the "scared" hero. Richard Flournoy's screenplay never tells what happened to Esther Dale and Walter Soderling.

BLONDIE PLAYS CUPID

Columbia (October 1940)

It's a Bumstead bombshell of fun when America's most
lovable family decides to come out for love!

Cast: Blondie, Penny Singleton; Dagwood, Arthur Lake; Dagwood "Baby Dumpling" Bumstead, Jr., Larry Simms; "Daisy"; J.C. Dithers, Jonathan Hale; Alvin Fuddle, Danny Mummert; Mr. Crumb, Irving Bacon; Charlie, Glenn Ford; Millie, Luana Walters; Mr. Tucker, Will Wright; Uncle Abner, Spencer Charters; Aunt Hannah, Leona Roberts // Ollie, Stanley Brown; Mary, Mary Jane Carey; Nelson, Richard Fiske; Train conductor, Charles Lane; Paperboy, Rex Moore; Newt Banks, Si Jenks; Reed, John Tyrell

Credits: Director, Frank R. Strayer; Producer, Robert Sparks; Story, Karen De Wolf and Charles M. Brown; Screenwriters, Richard Flournoy and Karen De Wolf; Editor, Gene Milford; Art Director, Lionel Banks; Cinematographer, Henry Freulich; Gowns, Kalloch; Musical Director, M.W. Stoloff

Filming Location: Union Station, 800 N. Alameda Street, Los Angeles, California

Production Dates: July 16, 1940–August 17, 1940

Source: Based on the comic strip *Blondie*, created by Chic Young. Owned and copyrighted by King Features Syndicate, Inc.

Running Time: 68 min.

Story: In order to have a safe Fourth of July, Penny Singleton decides the family should spend the holiday with her Aunt Leona Roberts. The family boards an express (instead of a local) and end up miles past their destination. The next day, Singleton, Arthur Lake, Larry Simms and Daisy are hiking their way to Roberts's farm. A young couple, Glenn Ford and Luana Walters, offer them a ride. Ford and Walters are heading for the justice of the peace, Si Jenks, to get married. As Jenks is performing the ceremony, Walters's father, Will Wright, armed with a shotgun, interrupts the ceremony. Jenks is unable to finish as Wright forces Walters into a car. Wright is angry with Ford because he constructed an oil well derrick on the wrong place on his farm. Ford believes that, if he had two more days, he could bring in the well. At Roberts's farm, Lake suggests to Ford that he and Walter elope. Ford thinks that's a great idea. Ford severely sprains his ankle and it's up to Lake to get Walters. Singleton and Simms go along for moral support. Lake ends up in Wright's bedroom and the chase is on. Lake finally stands his ground and KO's Wright with a roundhouse right. Simms finds a stick of dynamite that he thinks is a firecracker. The fuse is lit. Singleton panics and just tosses the dynamite away. The dynamite lands down the oil well shaft. The explosion causes a gusher. Wright is overjoyed and wants to give Ford and Walters a proper wedding. Singleton, Lake and Simms are covered with oil. Lake lights a match to see what's on their clothes. There is an explosion. A newspaper article notes that this was the safest Fourth of July on record with only three injuries: Singleton, Lake and Simms. Simms indicates there is a fourth injured family member, Daisy.

Notes and Commentary: The working title for this film was "Blondie Goes to the Country."

Reviews: "Delightful young lover pic." *Motion Picture Guide*, Nash and Ross

"Stereotyped slapstick issue for support in the family houses." *Variety*, 10/30/40

Summation: This is a mild episode in the Blondie series. Again, there is too much unfunny comedy in an otherwise engaging but somewhat predictable script. The performances are par for the series. It's nice to see Glenn Ford in an early role.

BLONDIE GOES LATIN

Columbia (February 1941)

They sing ... They dance ... They make music! ... The lovable
Bumsteads go on a rhythm-roaring tropical cruise!

Cast: Blondie, Penny Singleton; Dagwood, Arthur Lake; Baby Dumpling, Larry Simms; "Daisy"; Lovey Nelson, Ruth Terry; Alvin Fuddle, Danny Mummert; J.C. Dithers, Jonathan Hale; Little girl, Janet Burston; Hal Trent, Kirby Grant; Manuel Rodriguez, Tito Guizar/Mr.

Crumb, Irving Bacon; Cab Driver, Eddie Acuff; Ship captain, Joe King; Girl who picks up gloves, Cecilia Callejo; Steward who rings chimes and cries, William Newell; Messenger bringing drums, Marvin Stephens; Steward with Lake's sandwich, Paul Ellis, Sailor, Ralph Sanford

Credits: Director, Frank R. Strayer; Producer, Robert Sparks; Story, Quinn Martin; Screenwriters, Richard Flournoy and Karen De Wolf; Editor, Gene Havlick; Art Director, Lionel Banks; Cinematography, Henry Freulich; Gowns, Monica; Music Arranger, Leo Amaud; Musical Advisor, Paul Mertz; Musical Director, M.W. Stoloff

Songs: "You Don't Play a Drum, You Beat It" (Forrest and Wright) sung by Ruth Terry and played by Kirby Grant and Orchestra with Arthur Lake on drums; "I Hate Music Lessons" (Forrest and Wright) sung by Janet Burston and Larry Simms and played on piano by Janet Burston; "Solteiro a melhor" (Sores and Silva) sung by Tito Guizar and played by Kirby Grant and Orchestra with Tito Guizar on guitar; "Querida" (Forrest and Wright) sung by Tito Guizar and Penny Singleton and played by Kirby Grant and Orchestra with Tito Guizar on guitar; "Querida" (reprise) sung by Penny Singleton; "You Can Cry On My Shoulder" (Forrest and Wright) sung by Ruth Terry and orchestra quartet and played by Kirby Grant and Orchestra with Arthur Lake on drums; "Brazilian Cotillion" (Forrest and Wright) sung by Tito Guizar, Penny Singleton and orchestra quartet and danced by Penny Singleton; "You Don't Play a Drum, You Beat It" (reprise) sung by Ruth Terry and played by Kirby Grant and Orchestra; "Brazilian Cotillion" (reprise) danced by Penny Singleton and Arthur Lake, Larry Simms and Janet Burston and played by Kirby Grant and Orchestra

Production Dates: November 5, 1940–December 12, 1940

Source: Based on the comic strip *Blondie*, created by Chic Young. Owned and copyrighted by King Features Syndicate, Inc.

Running Time: 70 min.

Story: Jonathan Hale is taking a vacation to South America on a cruise ship. Accompanying him are Arthur Lake, Penny Singleton, Larry Simms and Daisy. Before the ship gets underway, Hale receives a telegram stating that a client will be coming to town to purchase some property that Hale had been trying to sell for a long time. Lake is selected to stay behind. Through a comedy of errors, Lake is unable to leave the ship before it sets sail. Now Lake has to avoid Hale and his family through the long voyage. Bandleader Kirby Grant needs Lake to plays drums in his orchestra. Singer Ruth Terry takes Lake under her wing. Passenger Tito Guizar receives a telegram requesting him to close a business deal with Hale. Singleton discovers Lake in Terry's stateroom and won't give Lake a chance to explain. When Lake shows up, dressed as a woman, to play in the orchestra, Singleton asks Guizar to play up to her. Lake is despondent. Finally, Terry is able to explain everything to Singleton. Singleton and Lake make up. Guizar makes a larger counter offer for the property, which makes Hale very happy. Now the vacation can proceed as planned.

Notes and Commentary: *The Hollywood Reporter* noted that, due to Frank R. Strayer's bout with the flu, producer Robert Sparks temporarily stepped in to direct.

Reviews: "Singleton gets a good chance to show off her Broadway origins by singing and dancing her way through several numbers that provide good reason to see another Blondie." *Motion Picture Guide*, Nash and Ross

"Set to music, latest Bumstead adventure gives series new life." *Variety*, 02/19/41

Summation: Great Blondie film! Fine comedy and music highlight this superior effort. The songs are tuneful and are given first-rate renditions by Penny Singleton, Tito Guizar and Ruth Terry. The comedy bits work, and Arthur Lake is a delight. The film leaves you with a smile on your face. Watch this one!

BLONDIE IN SOCIETY
Columbia (July 1941)

Blondie moves in the best circles.... No wonder the Bumsteads are dizzy!

Alternate Title: *Henpecked*

Cast: Blondie, Penny Singleton; Dagwood, Arthur Lake; Baby Dumpling, Larry Simms; "Daisy"; Choir, The Robert Mitchell's Boys Choir; J.C. Dithers, Jonathan Hale; Alvin Fuddle, Danny Mummert; Pincus, William Frawley; Doctor Glenn, Edgar Kennedy; Cliff Peters, Chick Chandler; Mr. Crumb, Irving Bacon; Dog show announcer, Bill Goodwin // Mr. Wilson, Arthur Stuart Hall; Mr. Jasper, Hal Cooke; Mr. Judson, Herbert Rawlinson; Chief of police, Cliff Clark; Andrews, William Forrest; Mary, Mary Jane Carey; Doghouse salesman, Grady Sutton; Neighbor with broom, Almira Sessons; Neighbor with pies, Georgia Backus; Neighbor with petunia beds, Harry C. Bradley; Neighbor with petition, Claire Du Brey; Neighbor with birthday cake, Edythe Elliott; Ollie Shaw, Stanley Brown; Nelson, Richard Fiske; Mr. Wade, Vince Barnett; Veterinarian's nurse, Patti McCarty; Washing Machine Salesman, Charles Lane; The Carpenter, Garry Owen; Blondie's lawyer, Edward Fielding; Dog collar saleslady, Bess Flowers; Little girl, Dorothy Ann Seese; Hot dog salesman, Ralph McCullough; Julie's owner, Charles Judels; Pincus's dog handler, Walter Sande; Boy show attendant, Warren McCollum; Mr. Griffin, Edward Earle; Dog show judge, Robert Strange

Credits: Director, Frank R. Strayer; Producer, Robert Sparks; Story, Eleanore Griffin; Screenplay, Karen De Wolf; Editor, Charles Nelson; Art Direction, Lionel Banks; Cinematography, Henry Freulich; Gowns, Monica; Musical Director, M.W. Stoloff

Songs: "In the Shade of the Old Apple Tree" (Van Alstyne and Williams) sung by Penny Singleton; "Where, Oh Where Has My Little Dog Gone" (music from the German folk song, "Der Deitcher's Dog," English lyrics by Winner) sung by the Robert Mitchell's Boys Choir; "Trees" (Kilmer and Rasbach) sung by Penny Singleton and the Robert Mitchell's Boys Choir

Production Dates: April 4, 1941–May 7, 1941

Source: Based on the comic strip *Blondie*, created by Chic Young. Owned and copyrighted by King Features Syndicate, Inc.

Running Time: 77 min.

Story: When Arthur Lake goes to collect $50 from an old school chum, he comes home with a pedigreed Great Dane. Penny Singleton tells Lake he can keep the dog temporarily. Lake tells his boss, Jonathan Hale, he's going to try to get William Frawley to sign a contract on a construction project. Lake meets Frawley and tells him that his Great Dane is better looking than Frawley's, and offers to sell the dog. Frawley wants to buy it and comes to Lake's office. Hale interferes, and Frawley thinks the dog was a ruse to get him to sign a contract. Lake thinks he's fired. Frawley tells Hale he'll sign a contract if Lake keeps his dog out of the competition in the upcoming dog show. Hale tells Lake he'll buy the dog as a present for Frawley, but Lake will have to keep the dog until the dog show. Meanwhile, Singleton reads about the dog show and the $500 prize money. When Singleton starts to work with the dog, the dog just lies around until she begins to sing. Singleton, without Lake's knowledge, enters the dog in the show. Frawley sees the dog at the show and thinks he's been double-crossed. Hale explains that the dog is a present, but Singleton brings the dog to the ring for the judging. The dog just lies there until Singleton sings with the Robert Mitchell's Boys Choir. Singleton's dog is the winner. Then chaos erupts over who owns the dog and, therefore, who gets the prize money. Finally, everything is sorted out: Frawley gets the dog, Singleton gets the prize money, Lake receives a thousand dollars for the dog from Hale, and Frawley signs the contract with Hale.

Notes and Commentary: William Frawley had a long career in show business, ranging from 1916 until 1965. He is best known for his role of Fred Mertz on the *I Love Lucy* television program (CBS, 1951–1957).

Reviews: "The canine burping display is a high point of this entry in the Blondie chronicles." *Motion Picture Guide*, Nash and Ross

"Blondie and her family provide good program entertainment. Best of the series." *Variety*, 07/02/41

Summation: Highly amusing entry in the Blondie series. Penny Singleton and Arthur Lake are perfect as the leads and are given a fine supporting cast. William Frawley and Edgar Kennedy are particular standouts. Again, Singleton is allowed to sing, which helps the film achieve its above-average status.

BLONDIE GOES TO COLLEGE

Columbia (January 1942)

The Bumsteads Are Going to College ...
So Folks Will Stop Calling Them the Dumbsteads!

Alternate Title: *The Boss Said "No"*

Cast: Blondie, Penny Singleton; Dagwood, Arthur Lake; Baby Dumpling, Larry Simms; "Daisy"; Laura Wadsworth, Janet Blair; J.C. Dithers, Jonathan Hale; Babs Connelly, Adele Mara; Alvin Fuddle, Danny Mummert; Rusty Bryant, Larry Parks; Ben Dixon, Lloyd Bridges; "Snookie" Wadsworth, Andrew Tombes // Fan with lost football charm, Boyd Davis; Captain Caswell, Byron Shores; Mrs. Dill's brother, Tom Fadden; Mrs. Dill, Esther Dale; Professor Mixwell, Cliff Nazarro; Gushing coed, Bertha Priestley; Mr. Howard, Emmett Vogan; Mr. Higby, Tim Ryan; Dean, Maurice Cass; Race announcer, Bill Goodwin; Motorcycle policemen, Eddy Chandler and Ralph Dunn; Police sergeant, Charles C. Wilson; Detective who grabs Dithers, Ken Christy; Coeds, Lois Collier, Marlo Dwyer, Eleanor Hansen and Jane Patten

Credits: Director, Frank R. Strayer; Producer, Robert Sparks; Story, Warren Wilson and Clyde Bruckman; Screenwriter, Lou Breslow; Editor, Otto Meyer; Art Director, Lionel Banks; Associate Art Director, Jerome Pycha, Jr.; Cinematography, Henry Freulich; Musical Director, M.W. Stoloff; Songwriters, Sammy Cahn and Saul Chaplin

Song: "Leighton School Song" sung by Penny Singleton and students

Production Dates: September 18, 1941–October 18, 1941

Source: Based on the comic strip *Blondie*, created by Chic Young. Owned and copyrighted by King Features Syndicate, Inc.

Running Time: 74 min.

Story: Arthur Lake has a desire to attend college, if only for one semester. His boss, Jonathan Hale, thinks it would be a good idea, adding that Penny Singleton should attend also. Singleton tells Hale she's going to have a baby but she hasn't informed Lake. Singleton and Lake attend school posing as unmarried students. Meanwhile, Larry Simms and Daisy go to a military school. Both Singleton and Lake are quickly involved in romantic entanglements. Larry Parks, the college's athletic star, makes a play for Singleton. Janet Blair, daughter of wealthy Andrew Tombes, likes Lake. Lake is disappointed because he's unable to make any of the sports teams. Singleton arranges to have Parks drop out of the rowing team and have Lake replace him. Prior to the big race, Lake meets Tombes. They talk about a major construction project Tombes is backing and Tombes likes Lake's ideas for the building. In the big race, Lake's team is comfortably in the lead until Lake develops a cramp and capsizes the boat. Hale wants Lake to leave college because he needs him to assist on negotiating a contract with Tombes. Hale enlists Simms's and Daisy's help. Through a series of mishaps, Lake and Hale are thought to be kidnapping Simms. Finally, Hale sends for Singleton to straighten everything out. Singleton and Lake return to the campus to tell the students that they're leaving. Hale is irate at Lake until he learns that Tombes will sign a contract only if Lake's ideas are incorporated. Lake gets a nice bonus and then finally learns that Singleton is going to have a baby.

Notes and Commentary: Songwriters Sammy Cahn and Saul Chaplin receive onscreen credit for the song "Do I Need You." The song was sung by Penny Singleton but ended up on the cutting-room floor.

To the author's eyes, it looks like Gary Grey as the student Larry Simms first meets at the military school.

Reviews: "The series was beginning to lose steam by this time, though it would struggle on for another nine years." *Motion Picture Guide*, Nash and Ross

"Switch in locale doesn't help series much." *Variety*, 02/11/42

Summation: Another good outing with the Bumsteads with many bright spots and touching moments. Penny Singleton, Arthur Lake, Larry Simms and Daisy do their usual good jobs, and the supporting cast is more than adequate. Director Frank R. Strayer guides the film nicely through the comedic and sentimental scenes.

BLONDIE'S BLESSED EVENT
Columbia (April 1942)

Blondie has a baby ... Dagwood has a fit ... You'll have hysterics!

Alternate Title: *A Bundle of Trouble*

Cast: Blondie, Penny Singleton; Dagwood, Arthur Lake; Baby Dumpling, Larry Simms; "Daisy"; J.C. Dithers, Jonathan Hale; Alvin Fuddle, Danny Mummert; George Wickley, Hans Conried; Ollie Shaw, Stanley Brown; Mr. Crumb, Irving Bacon; Sarah Miller, Mary Wickes // Paper boy, Eugene Anderson, Jr.; Little girl, Dorothy Ann Seese; Young mailman, Clarence Straight; Mary, Mary Jane Carey; Waiter, Don Barclay; Cab driver, Charles Jordan; Cookie, Norma Jean Wayne; William Lawrence, Paul Harvey

Credits: Director, Frank R. Strayer; Producer, Robert Sparks; Screenwriters, Connie Lee, Karen De Wolf and Richard Flournoy; Editor, Charles Nelson; Art Director, Lionel Banks; Associate Art Director, Jerome Pycha, Jr.; Cinematographer, Henry Freulich; Musical Director, M.W. Stoloff

Song: "Lullaby" (Cahn and Chaplin) sung by Penny Singleton

Production Dates: December 9, 1941–January 9, 1942

Source: Based on the comic strip *Blondie*, created by Chic Young. Owned and copy-righted by King
Features Syndicate, Inc.

Running Time: 69 min.

Story: Arthur Lake has a hard time keeping his mind on business since he's about to be a father again. Lake is overly attentive to Penny Singleton, which makes her extremely nervous. Jonathan Hale comes up with a solution. Lake will attend an architect's convention in Chicago and make a short speech. At the hotel, Lake meets impoverished playwright Hans Conried, who helps him write his speech. Lake's speech, based on people being their own architect and the use of new materials in construction, stuns the audience and closes the convention. Meanwhile Singleton goes to the hospital and gives birth to a baby girl. Returning home from the hospital, Lake and Singleton find Conried at their doorstep. Con-ried's stay proves to be lengthy and completely disrupts the household. Finally, Singleton tells Conried to leave the house. Just then, an angry Hale shows up and fires Lake. The speech promises to get Hale blacklisted and he's in danger of losing the architect's license. Paul Harvey arrives and offers Lake a job with the government. In retaliation, Hale makes Lake a junior partner. Harvey and Hale fight over where Lake will work. Conried tells Larry Simms, who had felt neglected since Wayne came home, how to stop the baby from crying. Simms becomes a hero in the family.

Blondie's Blessed Event (1942) scene card (left to right) Daisy, Arthur Lake and Larry Simms.

Notes and Commentary: The working title for the film was "Blondie Greets a Guest." In this one, Larry Simms wants to be called Alexander instead of Baby Dumpling. In an earlier episode, *Blondie Plays Cupid* (Columbia, 1940), Simms was called Dagwood Bumstead, Jr.

On the way home from the hospital, a motorcycle policeman calls the baby "Cookie," and the name sticks.

Review: "Typically frantic series entry." *1996 Movie & Video Guide*, Maltin

Summation: This is a neat Blondie episode. Penny Singleton really shines in this one and has great support from Arthur Lake and Larry Simms. In the supporting cast, Hans Conried is outstanding.

BLONDIE FOR VICTORY
Columbia (August 1942)

The Bumsteads Give First Aid For Laughter!

Alternate Title: *Troubles Through Billets*

Cast: Blondie, Penny Singleton; Dagwood, Arthur Lake; Baby Dumpling, Larry Simms; "Daisy"; "Cookie"; Private Herschel Smith, Stuart Erwin; J.C. Dithers, Jonathan Hale; Alvin Fuddle, Danny Mummert; Sergeant, Edward Gargan // Miss Clabber, Renie Riano; Mrs. Williams, Sylvia Field; Mrs. Webster, Mary Young; Mrs. Larkin, Almira Sessions; Mrs. Jones, Georgia Backus; Housewives of America, Volta Boyer, Ruth Cherrington, Helen Dickson, Minta Durfee, Edythe Elliott, Jean Inness, Bess Wade; Mrs. Holbrook, Nella Walker; Mr. Larkin, Don Beddoe; Gwendolyn's husband, Harry Harvey; Husband with socks problem, Eddie Acuff; Husband who threatens Dagwood, Dewey Robinson; Mysterious Man at dam, Charles Waggenheim; Mr. Crumb, Irving Bacon; Mr. Greene, Harrison Greene; Soldier who chases Dagwood, John Tyrell; Colonel, Russell Hicks

Credits: Director, Frank R. Strayer; Producer, Robert Sparks; Story, Fay Kanin; Screenwriters, Connie Lee and Karen De Wolf; Editor, Al Clark; Art Direction, Lionel Banks; Associate Art Director, Jerome Pycha, Jr.; Cinematographer, Henry Freulich; Music, John Leipold; Musical Director, M.W. Stoloff

Production Dates: April 14, 1942–May 5, 1942

Source: Based on the comic strip *Blondie*, created by Chic Young. Owned and copyrighted by King Features Syndicate, Inc.

Running Time: 72 min.

Story: Penny Singleton is determined to help the war effort by working with the Housewives of America. Her work plays havoc with Arthur Lake and his job. Singleton and the Housewives have the assignment of guarding the local dam. A mysterious prowler, Charles Waggenheim, scares all the Housewives away except Singleton. The club members' husbands have elected Lake to disband the Housewives of America. Lake borrows a soldier's uniform and goes to the dam to tell Singleton that he enlisted in the army and will be sent to Tokyo. Singleton decides to disband the organization. Singleton finds out the truth. Before Lake can get out of uniform, he is chased by military police. Waggenheim is seen carrying a suspicious package. Singleton and Lake think the package is a bomb and Lake gives chase. He eventually catches up with Waggenheim. The package turns out to contain sugar. Charges are dropped against Lake because he did nothing to disgrace the uniform. Singleton decides the Housewives of America can do more good at home.

Notes and Commentary: Majelle White was Cookie Bumstead this time out but did not receive onscreen billing.

It's fun to see Stuart Erwin dressed up in the Dagwood attire. Erwin was announced to play the role before Arthur Lake was finally signed for the part.

Reviews: "Good work by entire cast slightly redeems this programmer." *Motion Picture Guide*, Nash and Ross

"A crackerjack supporting film for the better duals." *Variety*, 10/14/42

Summation: Good entertainment with plenty of wartime propaganda. The performances are more than adequate. The story has several cute moments and some nice comedy.

IT'S A GREAT LIFE

Columbia (May 1943)

The Bumsteads are at it again ... with Hugh Herbert to add to
Blondie's woes! Watch Hughie help make this their funniest scream hit!

Alternate Title: *Blondie and Dagwood: It's a Great Life*

Cast: Blondie, Penny Singleton; Dagwood, Arthur Lake; Alexander, Larry Simms; "Daisy"; "Reggie"; Timothy Brewster, Hugh Herbert; J.C. Dithers, Jonathan Hale; Alvin Fuddle, Danny Mummert; Collender Martin, Alan Dinehart; Bromley, Douglas Leavitt; Mr. Crumb, Irving Bacon; Cookie Bumstead, Marjorie Ann Mutchie // Burly floor waxer, John Kelly; Alf, Alec Craig; Insurance agent, Andrew Tombes; Insurance physician, Douglas Wood; Policeman, Emory Parnell; Paper boy, Jack Low; Salesman, Ray Walker; Brewster attorneys, Edward Fielding and Stanley Andrews; Mary, Mary Jane Carey; Master of the hounds, Hal Taliaferro

Credits: Director and Producer, Frank R. Strayer; Screenwriters, Connie Lee and Karen De Wolf; Editor, Al Clark; Art Director, Lionel Banks; Associate Art Director, Walter Holscher; Set Decorator, Joseph Kish; Cinematographer, L.W. O'Connell; Musical Director, M.W. Stoloff

Production Dates: January 21, 1943–late February 1943

Source: Based on the comic strip *Blondie*, created by Chic Young. Owned and copyrighted by King Features Syndicate, Inc.

Running Time: 68 min.

Story: Misunderstanding his boss Jonathan Hale, Arthur Lake buys Reggie, a horse, instead of a house. Hale and competitor Alan Dinehart want to purchase property owned by Hugh Herbert. Hale is about to close the transaction when Lake shows up at the office with Reggie. Herbert wants the owner of Reggie to attend a fox hunt. Hale, unaware of this, tells Lake to sell the horse. Dinehart, aware of Herbert's request, purchases the horse from Penny Singleton. That night, Reggie returns to Lake. Dinehart arrives to take Reggie back, but Singleton tears up Dinehart's check. Dinehart shows up at the fox hunt with a bill of sale for Reggie and gives the horse to Herbert. Lake rides Reggie in the hunt and, thanks to his dog Daisy's interference, returns with the fox. Delighted with Lake and Reggie, Herbert signs the contract with Hale.

Notes and Commentary: The working title for this film was "Blondie Buys a Horse."

Penny Singleton calls Arthur Lake, Dagwood Aaron Bumstead. This is the first mention of Dagwood's middle name.

It is also mentioned that, prior to marriage, Blondie, was a stenographer.

It has been reported that this was Hugh Herbert's first role under his term contract at Columbia. Herbert stayed at Columbia until his death in 1952.

It was mentioned that the Woodleys were the Bumsteads' neighbors. The Woodleys, next door neighbors to the Bumsteads in the comic strips, would not make their screen appearance until the final Blondie film, *Beware of Blondie* (Columbia, 1950).

Reviews: "A typical Blondie film with comedy that is appealing to children and the childlike." *Motion Picture Guide*, Nash and Ross

"Typical slapstick trite that'll please the juves. But likely to be mildly trying to adults." *Variety*, 06/16/43

Summation: A delightful comedy in the Blondie series. The jokes are funny and the performances, especially those of Daisy and Reggie, are first rate. Frank R. Strayer's direction keeps the story continuously on the move.

FOOTLIGHT GLAMOUR
Columbia (September 1943)

Acting was easy as falling into trouble ... for Dagwood!

Cast: Blondie, Penny Singleton; Dagwood, Arthur Lake; Alexander, Larry Simms; "Daisy"; Vicki Wheeler, Ann Savage; J.C. Dithers, Jonathan Hale; Mr. Crumb, Irving Bacon; Cookie Bumstead, Marjorie Ann Mutchie; Alvin Fuddle, Danny Mummert // Carpool rider, Lew Kelly; Frances, Elspeth Dudgeon; Randolph Wheeler, Thurston Hall; Little girl at hotel, Janet Chapman; Mr. Phillips, James Flavin; Mr. Clark, Arthur Loft; First taxi driver, Syd Saylor; Cora Dithers, Grace Hayle; Jerry Grant, Rafael Storm; Baby sitter, Fern Emmett; Second taxi driver, William Newell; Third taxi driver, Gladys Blake

Credits: Director and Producer, Frank R. Strayer; Screenwriter, Karen De Wolf and Connie Lee; Editor, Richard Fantl; Art Director, Lionel Banks; Associate Art Director, Edward Jewell; Set Decorator, Robert Priestley; Cinematographer, Philip Tannura; Musical Director, M.W. Stoloff

Production Dates: June 24, 1943–July 17, 1943

Source: Based on the comic strip *Blondie*, created by Chic Young. Owned and copyrighted by King Features Syndicate, Inc.

Running Time: 68 min.

Story: Jonathan Hale constructed a housing development based upon plans to build a defense plant, which didn't materialize. Thurston Hall comes to visit Hale. Hale hopes that Hall will build a tool plant on the defense plant's site. Hall is in town to break up his daughter, Ann Savage's, desire for a show business career and to put an end to her romance with Rafael Storm. Hall believes that Storm is more interested in Savage's money than in Savage herself. Hale arranges for Savage to stay at Arthur Lake's house. Thinking Savage is a small child, Lake agrees. Penny Singleton, at first upset, calms down when Savage tells Singleton that she has potential to be an actress in a play Savage has written. With help from Hale's wife, Grace Hayle, Savage's play is to be performed at a local theater. Lake is pressured to play the male lead, and Storm arrives to direct the play. Meanwhile,

Hale has taken Hall to see the housing development. Hall is impressed and agrees to build a tool plant. Lake tells Hale about the play. Hale realizes if Hall finds out about the play, he'll cancel the agreement. Hale tries to close down the play until he finds that Hayle is firmly behind the project. The play goes on and becomes an unintentional comedy instead of a serious drama. Hall finds out about the play and cancels his contract with Hale. The play's disastrous turn upsets Savage to the point that she plans to elope with Storm. Thanks to Lake's interference, Savage finds out Storm's true intention; renounces both Storm and an acting career. Hall is so pleased that he decides to honor his contract with Hale.

Notes and Commentary: This would be Frank R. Strayer's last directorial effort in the Blondie series. His assistant director, Abby Berlin, would succeed him.

The *Hollywood Reporter* indicated the cinematographer for this outing was David Ragan.

Review: "A routine job but manages to net laughs in the last two reels via a slapstick play-within-a-play." *Variety*, 11/10/43

Summation: This is a mildly amusing episode in the Blondie series. Performances, direction and story are par for the series.

Footlight Glamour (1943) title card — Arthur Lake (upper left), Daisy (lower left), Penny Singleton (center); (left to right, right side) Penny Singleton, Arthur Lake, Rafael Storm, Ann Savage, Larry Simms (lower right).

Leave It to Blondie

Columbia (February 1945)

Dagwood wins prize in song contest! ... Naturally the *booby* prize!

Cast: Blondie, Penny Singleton; Dagwood, Arthur Lake; Alexander, Larry Simms; Cookie, Marjorie Ann Mutchie; "Daisy"; Rita Rogers, Marjorie Weaver; J.C. Dithers, Jonathan Hale; Eddie Baxter, Chick Chandler; Alvin Fuddle, Danny Mummert // Mr. Fuddle, Arthur Space; Emily Harding, Mary Newton; Ollie, Jack Rice; Mary, Ann Loos; Mrs. Laura Meredith, Eula Morgan; Henry, Fred Graff; Magda, Maude Eburne; Waitress at Gypsy Tea Room, Bess Flowers; Mailman, Eddie Acuff; Reporter, Robert Williams; Gilmore, Robert Emmett Keane; Audio engineer, Lester Dorr; Joe Potter, George Lloyd

Credits: Director, Abby Berlin; Producer, Burt Kelly; Screenwriter, Connie Lee; Editor, Al Clark; Art Director, Perry Smith; Set Decorator, Fay Babcock; Cinematographer, Franz F. Planer; Gowns, Jean Louis

Songs: "That Blue-Eyed Sweetheart of Mine" (Chaplin) sung by Danny Mummert; "That Blue-Eyed Sweetheart of Mine" (reprise) sung by Arthur Lake; "An Ounce of Bounce" (Chaplin and Samuels) sung by unknown singer; "Rumba Romance" sung by George Lloyd (dubbed by unknown singer); "That Blue-Eyed Sweetheart of Mine" (reprise) Sung by Chick Chandler

Production Dates: October 30, 1944–November 24, 1944

Source: Based on the comic strip *Blondie*, created by Chic Young. Owned and copyrighted by King Features Syndicate, Inc.

Running Time: 74 min.

Story: Both Penny Singleton and Arthur Lake write hundred-dollar checks for the underprivileged children's camp fund, but they only have one hundred dollars in the bank. Lake's boss, Jonathan Hale, has property he thinks would be perfect for the camp. Lake learns that there is a song-writing contest with a $250 grand prize. The contest sponsor, Eula Morgan, asks Hale to be a judge. Hale vehemently turns down the request. Larry Simms and his pal, Danny Mummert, find an old song written by Lake's uncle and enter the song as if it had been written by Lake. The song is one of the three finalists. Morgan sends singing coach Marjorie Weaver and accompanist Chick Chandler to prepare Lake for the finals. Singleton misunderstands the relationship between Lake and Weaver and locks Lake out of their house. Lake, forced to spend the night at a hotel, sleeps with two open windows, letting in a cool breeze. Lake catches a cold and is unable to sing. Chandler is persuaded to record the song and have Lake lip-synch the song at the finals. Hale learns that Morgan has the power to purchase land for the camp and wants Lake to influence Morgan to purchase the property Hale has for sale. Singleton has a change of heart and goes to the contest finals. Hale asks Singleton to get a note to Lake with the property's description. Disaster strikes and the record cannot be played. Lake ends up singing the property description. Lake, who entered the contest because he needed money to cover his check, admits he did not write the song. Morgan knew all along that Lake's uncle wrote the song because the song was written for her. Morgan decides to purchase Hale's property that results in a $500 bonus for Lake.

Notes and Commentary: *Leave It to Blondie* was Abby Berlin's first directorial effort. The Blondie series had been of the screen since September 1943.

Review: "'Leave it to Blondie' holds to the acceptable average of the series." *Variety*, 04/11/45

Summation: Amusing entry in the Blondie series. Plenty of chuckles throughout, especially when Arthur Lake catches a cold.

LIFE WITH BLONDIE
Columbia (December 1945)

Dagwood turns "cover boy" ... and is covered with confusion!

Cast: Blondie, Penny Singleton; Dagwood, Arthur Lake; Alexander, Larry Simms; Cookie, Marjorie Kent; "Daisy"; J.C. Dithers, Jonathan Hale; Theodore Glassby, Ernest Truex; Pete, Marc Lawrence; Hazel, Veda Ann Borg // "Elmer"; Dogcatcher, Edward Gargan; Tommy Cooper, Bobby Larson; Mary, Alyn Lockwood; Ollie, Jack Rice; Mrs. Brady, Josephine Whittell; Policeman, Eddie Dunn; Reporter, Hal K. Dawson; Mrs. Adams, Regina Wallace; Newspaper carrier, Bill Chaney; Buxom neighbor, Jody Gilbert; Mailman, Eddie Acuff; John, Lester Dorr; Anthony, Ray Walker; Models, Gloria Anderson and Doris Houck; Newspaper woman, Margie Liszt; Blackie Leonard, Douglas Fowley; Joe, Carl Deloro; Sailors, Mark Roberts and Robert Williams; Simon Rutledge, Francis Pierlot

Credits: Director, Abby Berlin; Screenwriter, Connie Lee; Editor, Jerome Thoms; Art Director, Perry Smith; Set Decorator, Joseph Kish; Cinematographer, L.W. O'Connell; Sound, Hugh McDowell; Musical Director, M.R. Bakaleinikoff

Production Dates: August 20, 1945–September 15, 1945

Source: Based on the comic strip *Blondie*, created by Chic Young. Owned and copyrighted by King Features Syndicate, Inc.

Running Time: 70 min.

Story: Daisy was voted the Navy's pin-up dog as a result of her picture on the cover of national magazines. Ernest Truex makes an arrangement with Penny Singleton and Arthur Lake to use Daisy in advertisements for Daisy Soap. Income from this agreement will allow them to pay off all their bills. Gangster Douglas Fowley sends henchman Marc Lawrence to buy Daisy for Fowley's girlfriend, Veda Ann Borg. Lawrence threatens Lake and his daughter, Marjorie Kent. Lake refuses the offer but Lawrence vows they will eventually get Daisy. Daisy's success disrupts the household. Lake and his children, Larry Simms and Kent, wish that Daisy were no longer a member of the family. Daisy overhears this and runs away from home. Minutes later, Lake, Simms and Kent regret their comments, but its too late. A citywide search is begun to find her. She winds up in the hands of Lawrence who gives the dog to Borg. Fowley learns that he and his gang are close to being arrested and decides to leave town. Knowing there is a major search for Daisy, Fowley contacts a disreputable doctor to alter her features. Lake guesses (correctly) that Fowley has Daisy. Fowley believes that Lake is the doctor and gives Daisy to him. As Lake starts to leave, Lawrence comes into the room and recognizes him. As the gangsters close in on Lake, sailors led by Mark Roberts and Robert Williams arrive with Singleton. The sailors had come to visit Daisy and learned of Fowley from Kent. A free-for-all breaks out between the sailors and gangsters. Police arrive to take Fowley and his gang into custody. Singleton takes Daisy from the clutches of Borg by knocking her out with a terrific right-hand punch. Fowley grabs Singleton to use as a shield, but Lake foils his escape. The family is now reunited.

Notes and Commentary: Marjorie Ann Mutchie's new screen name is Marjorie Kent. This was the first film in the series without the Alvin Fuddle character. Danny Mummert was filming *It's a Wonderful Life* at the time. Bobby Larson (as Tommy Cooper) replaces Mumert.

Reviews: "A better-than-average entry in the Columbia series. A standard programmer features some nice comic acting by Lake and Singleton, with good support from Truex and from Fowley as a gangster." *Motion Picture Guide*, Nash and Ross

"Another okay comedy in series based on the Chic Young cartoon strip." *Variety*, 01/23/46

Summation: Sparkling comedy proves there's still life in the series. The acting is on par, with a special nod to Daisy, with her many antics. Seeing Daisy walking upright in a naval uniform is worth the price of admission. Connie Lee's story is well paced by director Abby Berlin.

BLONDIE'S LUCKY DAY
Columbia (April 1946)

The Bumsteads go into business ... monkey business!

Cast: Blondie, Penny Singleton; Dagwood, Arthur Lake; Alexander, Larry Simms; Cookie, Marjorie Kent, "Daisy"; Johnny Butler, Jr., Robert Stanton; Betty Jane McDermott, Angelyn Orr; J.C. Dithers, Jonathan Hale; Mailman, Frank Jenks; Jonathan Butler, Sr., Paul Harvey; Mayor Richard Denby, Charles Arnt // Shaving kit salesman, Frank Orth; Ollie, Jack Rice; Mary, Margie Liszt; Mr. Emory, John Hamilton; Mr. Hankins, Dick Elliott; Corporal Atterbury, Jimmy Clark; Denby's secretary, Eric Wilton; Dan Carter, Edwin Mills; Miss Phelan, Lillian Bronson; Jensen, Sven Hugo Borg; Enrico, Alphonse Martell; Waiter at Continental Club, Marek Windheim; Policemen, Ralph Dunn, Pat O'Malley and Kernan Cripps

Credits: Director, Abby Berlin; Screenwriter, Connie Lee; Editor, Aaron Stell; Art Director, Perry Smith; Set Decorator, Herman Schoenbrun; Cinematographer, L.W. O'Connell; Sound, Jack Goodrich, Musical Director, Mischa Bakaleinikoff

Production Dates: September 24, 1945–October 16, 1945

Source: Based on the comic strip *Blondie*, created by Chic Young. Owned and copyrighted by King Features Syndicate, Inc.

Running Time: 69 min.

Story: Jonathan Hale has to leave town on business and puts Arthur Lake in charge of his company. Lake, through a campaign by Mayor Charles Arnt, hires a veteran, Angelyn Orr. At first Penny Singleton is upset at Lake hiring a woman but quickly warms to the idea. Singleton goes to the office to help Orr get settled in. Hale comes back unexpectedly and orders Lake to fire Orr. Singleton tells Lake not to fire Orr, which results in Lake being fired also. Singleton has Lake start his own company in competition with Hale's. Down to their last possible client, Lake decides to make a bid for an outdoor theater proposed by Paul Harvey's company. When Lake calls to set up an appointment with Harvey, he talks to Harvey's son, Robert Stanton. Stanton, who is no longer associated with Harvey due to his inattention to work and his high living, accepts, under false pretenses, a dinner invitation from Lake. Romance blossoms between Stanton and Orr. Finally, Lake brings up the subject of the theater and Stanton tells the truth, devastating Lake and Singleton. Orr makes Stanton realize what a cad he's been. Stanton decides to help Lake get the contract, not knowing that Harvey is close to signing with Hale. Through a ruse, Lake shows his plans for the theater, which are superior to Hale's. Hale lets Lake have the contract, but Lake can't raise the necessary financing. Lake comes back to work with Hale, with a bonus and a raise. Lake's plans will be used for the theater after all.

Notes and Commentary: Angelyn Orr is better known to fans of vintage radio programs as Joyce Ryan in the Captain Midnight series on the Mutual network in the late 1940s.

Reviews: "Predictable complications." *Motion Picture Guide*, Nash and Ross
"Good entertainment for any dual bill." *Variety*, 04/24/46

Summation: Amusing Blondie episode with Penny Singleton and Arthur Lake perfect in their roles. Some good comedy sequences move the film along to its happy, but predictable, conclusion.

BLONDIE KNOWS BEST
Columbia (October 1946)

At last it's happened! Dagwood fires the boss!!!

Cast: Blondie, Penny Singleton; Dagwood, Arthur Lake; Alexander, Larry Simms; Cookie, Marjorie Kent; "Daisy"; Dr. Schmidt, Steven Geray; J.C. Dithers, Jonathan Hale; Jim Gray, Shemp Howard; Charles Peabody, Jerome Cowan; Alvin Fuddle, Danny Mummert; Dr. Titus, Ludwig Donath; Mr. Conroy, Arthur Loft // Mary, Alyn Lockwood; Ollie, Jack Rice; Policeman, Ralph Sanford; Gloria Evans, Carol Hughes; Ruth Evans, Kay Mallory; David Armstrong, Edwin Cooper; Headwaiter, Gino Corrado; Hat check girl, Betty Alexander; Man on park bench, Fred Sears; Dr. Titus's nurse-receptionist, Jean Willes; Dr. Titus's intern, Coulter Irwin

Credits: Director, Abby Berlin; Story, Edward Bernds; Screenwriter, Edward Bernds and Al Martin; Editor, Aaron Stell; Art Director, Perry Smith; Set Decoration, James Crowe; Cinematographer, Philip Tannura; Musical Director, Mischa Bakaleinikoff

Song: "Put the Blame on Mame" (Roberts and Fisher) played by the nightclub orchestra

Production Dates: March 25, 1946–April 16, 1946

Source: Based on the comic strip *Blondie*, created by Chic Young. Owned and copyrighted by King Features Syndicate, Inc.

Running Time: 69 min.

Story: Jonathan Hale is in hot water when he realizes that the man with whom he'd had an angry confrontation was, in fact, a prospective client Jerome Cowan. Hale has Arthur Lake pretend to be the head of the construction company in order to obtain the contract. When Cowan sees Hale in the office, he insists that Lake fire Hale — if he wants his business. Next, Cowan wants to be wined and dined at an expensive nightclub in the company of beautiful single girls. Hale convinces Lake to comply, telling Lake he'll put things right with Penny Singleton. At the club, an acquaintance of Cowan's, Edwin Cooper, tells Lake he has a business proposition he'd like to discuss with him. Singleton makes Hale take her to the club. In the course of events, Cowan finds out the truth and backs out of the deal.

As always, Lake has money troubles, and he decides to be a guinea pig in an experiment for a truth serum. Cooper calls the office, looking for Lake. Hale needs Lake to close the deal. Singleton and Hale deduce where Lake has gone. Cooper, looking for Lake, follows Singleton and Hale. They locate Lake at the doctor's office and find that, for an hour, Lake can only tell the truth. Cooper is about to back out of any contractual agreement until Lake tells of the fine points of Hale and the company. Lake, in addition to receiving money from the doctor, is given a raise and a bonus from Hale.

Notes and Commentary: The song, *Put the Blame on Mame* was written for Rita Hayworth to perform in *Gilda* (Columbia, 1946).

Review: "Staple fare for family trade." *Variety*, 09/18/46

Summation: Arthur Lake is in money trouble again and this episode tells how he solves his dilemma. Both Lake and Penny Singleton acquit themselves well, but Shemp Howard (of The Three Stooges) is a hoot as a nearsighted process server.

BLONDIE'S BIG MOMENT
Columbia (January 1947)

Take a tip from Dagwood! Don't miss

Alternate Title: *Bundle of Trouble*

Cast: Blondie, Penny Singleton; Dagwood, Arthur Lake; Alexander, Larry Simms, Cookie, Marjorie Kent; "Daisy"; Harriet Gary, Anita Louise; George Radcliffe, Jerome Cowan; Alvin, Danny Mummert; Ollie, Jack Rice; Mr. Greenleaf, Jack Davis; Slugger, Johnny Granath // Mr. Little, Hal K. Dawson; Mailman, Eddie Acuff; Charlie, Dick Wessel; Mary, Alyn Lockwood; Joe, Robert Kellard; Office worker with pipe, Myron Healey; Pete, Robert De Haven; Theodore Payson, Douglas Wood

Credits: Director, Abby Berlin; Screenwriter, Connie Lee; Editor, Jerome Thoms; Art Director, Ben Hayne; Set Decorator, Louis Diage; Cinematographer, Allen Siegler; Musical Director, Mischa Bakaleinikoff

Production Dates: August 12, 1946–September 9, 1946

Source: Based on the comic strip *Blondie*, created by Chic Young. Owned and copyrighted by King Features Syndicate, Inc.

Running Time: 69 min.

Story: After returning from a two-week vacation, Arthur Lake finds he has a new boss, Jerome Cowan. Lake started on the wrong foot with Cowan when, on the bus ride to work, he spilled jelly on Cowan's coat. When Lake jeopardizes an important contract with Jack Davis, Cowan has Lake and his office rival, Jack Rice, switch responsibilities. Lake arrives home to find Larry Simms's teacher, Anita Louise, waiting for him. With Penny Singleton's blessings, Louise wants her class to make a field trip to Lake's office. In addition to Simms, the class includes Danny Mummert and Johnny Granath. Granath has a problem relating to other people and will not speak, but he enjoys being a guest in Singleton and Lake's home. Davis decides to give Cowan's firm the business if a suitable lot can be located, but the lot Davis selected is not for sale. Neighbor boys are playing softball, and a ball hit by Granath lands on Cowan's head. Cowan is infuriated. That night, Cowan is Singleton and Lake's dinner guest. This is a ploy to help get Lake's old job back. The dinner proves to be a disaster, especially when Cowan sees that Granath is a guest. In trying to obtain the property, the only contact is with lawyer Douglas Wood, who tells Cowan the owner does not wish to sell. Through a ruse, Lake has Cowan and Rice go to the lot in anticipation of meeting Wood. This gives Lake a chance to have Louise bring her class to the office. Unfortunately, Cowan returns before the class can leave. Lake is fired. When Cowan finally talks with Wood, Wood tells him that the owner will sell to Lake. Cowan rushes to Lake's house to try to obtain the lot. The young Granath is the owner. Granath, a millionaire, will give the lot to Lake. Granath will allow Lake to give the lot to Cowan if Lake gets his job and office back plus a sizeable bonus. The deal with Davis will now go through.

Notes and Commentary: Dagwood's rival, Ollie, was always Ollie Shaw as played by Stanley Brown. Now, with Jack Rice in the part, Ollie's last name is Merton.

This is Jerome Cowan's first outing as Arthur Lake's boss. Cowan replaced Jonathan Hale.

Review: "Nothing new." *1996 Movie & Video Guide*, Maltin

Summation: This is an amusing comedy in the Blondie series. Again, Penny Singleton and Arthur Lake are on target. Jerome Cowan scores highly as Lake's new boss. There are more than a few chuckles in this episode.

BLONDIE'S HOLIDAY
Columbia (April 1947)

Dagwood's got a hot tip on a horse ... but he forgot to tell the horse!

Cast: Blondie, Penny Singleton; Dagwood, Arthur Lake; Alexander, Larry Simms, Cookie, Marjorie Kent; George Radcliffe, Jerome Cowan; Samuel Breckenbridge, Grant Mitchell; Pete Brody, Sid Tomack; Mrs. Breckenbridge, Mary Young; Paul Madison, Jeff York; Bea Mason, Ann Nagel; Cynthia Thompson, Jody Gilbert; Ollie, Jack Rice // "Elmer"; Mailman, Eddie Acuff; Tommy Cooper, Bobby Lawson; Mary, Alyn Lockwood; Bank secretary, Elmer Jerome; Tom Henley, Rodney Bell; Charlie, Charles Jordan; Bouncer, Allen Mathews; Mike, Tim Ryan; J.L., Fred Sears; Pierre, Leonardo Scavino

Credits: Director, Abby Berlin; Screenwriter, Constance Lee; Editor, Jerome Thoms; Art Director, Ben Hayne; Set Decorators, Wilbur Menafee and Frank Kramer; Cinematographer, Vincent Farrar; Musical Director, Mischa Bakaleinikoff

Production Dates: November 5, 1946–November 27, 1946

Source: Based on the comic strip *Blondie*, created by Chic Young. Owned and copyrighted by King Features Syndicate, Inc.

Running Time: 67 min.

Story: Jerome Cowan hears that influential banker Grant Mitchell is interested in having a new bank constructed. With Arthur Lake's assistance, Cowan is set to sign a contract with Mitchell and gives Lake a $2.50-a-week raise. Meanwhile Penny Singleton is working on a high school reunion banquet with Jody Gilbert and Jeff York. Lake calls Singleton with the good news and Gilbert and York hear Singleton say, "two fifty." Gilbert and York assume that Lake is now making $250 a week and can pay all banquet expenses. Singleton is too proud to tell the truth. To help raise money, Singleton creates women's hats, which she can sell for $200. Lake, in trying to raise money, has bookie Sid Tomack come to the office to give him tips on betting on horses. Cowan and Mitchell break into Lake's office while Tomack is listening to a radio broadcast of a horse race. Mitchell is horrified and refuses to deal with Cowan. Cowan then fires Lake. On the day of the banquet, Lake picks up the money for the hats. Lake meets Tomack on the street, and he steers Lake to a bookie joint. Lake is undecided on which horse to bet. An older lady, Mary Young, gives Lake a tip on one of the races. Lake's horse wins and, as he's about to collect his proceeds, the police stage a raid. Lake is about to get away when he sees that Young needs help in getting away. Lake helps Young escape and, in turn, is arrested. Singleton, not knowing Lake is in jail, finally has to attend the banquet without him. Lake calls Cowan to bail him out. While Cowan is deciding whether or not to help Lake, Mitchell and Young arrive. Young is Mitchell's wife, and Lake's action prevented a horrible scandal. Mitchell is so grateful that, providing Lake is still Cowan's employee, the deal is back on. As a bonus, Cowan gives Lake enough money to cover the class reunion banquet expense. Singleton is about to confess that she doesn't have the money to pay for the banquet when Lake shows up to save her pride.

Notes and Commentary: Both Daisy and Danny Mummert are missing in this episode, as they were working in other motion pictures. Elmer carries on Daisy's responsibilities, and Bobby Lawson does the same for Mummert. Daisy was playing Curley in *Red Stallion* (Eagle-Lion, 1947); Mummert had the role of Benny in *Magic Town* (RKO, 1947)

Review: "A solid hour of laughs." *Variety*, 03/05/47

Summation: Engaging addition to the Blondie series. Director Abby Berlin keeps the story moving swiftly with enough amusing moments to satisfy audiences.

BLONDIE IN THE DOUGH
Columbia (October 1947)

"Woo! Woo!" It's Hugh ... adding to the Bumstead hullabaloo!

Cast: Blondie, Penny Singleton; Dagwood, Arthur Lake; Alexander, Larry Simms; Cookie, Marjorie Kent; "Daisy"; Llewellyn Simmons, Hugh Herbert; George Radcliffe, Jerome Cowan; J.T. Thorpe, Clarence Kolb; Alvin Fuddle, Danny Mummert; Robert Dixon, William Forrest; Mailman, Eddie Acuff // Milkmen, Michael Forrest and Ralph Volkie; Premier Biscuit board members, James Conaty, Boyd Davis, Franklyn Farnum, John Hamilton, and Victor Travers; Caterer, Gino Corrado; Mrs. Thorpe, Mary Emery; Miss Marsh, Jean Willes; Mr. Taylor, Hal K. Dawson; Mrs. Dixon, Bess Flowers; Ollie, Norman Phillips, Jr.; Mary, Alyn Lockwood; Woman buying cookies, Cecil Weston; Quinn, Fred Sears; Baxter, Kernan Cripps

Credits: Director, Abby Berlin; Story, Arthur Marx; Screenwriters, Arthur Marx and Jack Henley; Editor, Henry Batista; Art Director, George Brooks; Set Decorator, James Crowe; Cinematographer, Vincent Farrar; Musical Director, Mischa Bakaleinikoff

Song: "Bringing in the Sheaves" (Minor and Shaw) played by a string assembly

Production Dates: April 2, 1947–April 24, 1947

Source: Based on the comic strip *Blondie*, created by Chic Young. Owned and copyrighted by King Features Syndicate, Inc.

Running Time: 69 min.

Story: Radio station owner Clarence Kolb needs to have a new station built to accommodate the request of their largest sponsor, the Premier Biscuit Company, to provide coast-to-coast broadcasts. Jerome Cowan and Arthur Lake are set to play a round of golf with Kolb and then discuss a contract. Lake has to caddy with disastrous results. Disgusted, Kolb tells Cowan he'll look for another contractor. Cowan rescinds Lake's raise. Needing money,

Lake decides to learn how to repair radios, and Penny Singleton plans to bake and sell her special cookies. Lake had placed one his clubs, along with his plans for the radio station, in Kolb's golf bag. Kolb loves the plans and wants to do business with Cowan. Cowan and Lake come to Kolb's station. Lake needs to make one slight modification while Kolb and Cowan tour the studio. Seeing that the speaker in Kolb's radio is defective, Lake begins to repair it, with disastrous results. To keep Kolb's contract, Cowan is forced to fire Lake. In gathering supplies for her baking, Singleton meets Hugh Herbert, president of the Premier Biscuit Company. Herbert, who loves to bake, much to the irritation of his company's board members, offers to help Singleton. Kolb invites Cowan and other selected guests to hear the Premier Biscuit radio program. Meanwhile, Herbert wants to see the powerful radio Lake put together. Herbert asks Singleton to read her flyer. As Singleton reads, Herbert's arm hits the "on" switch, and her voice is broadcast over Kolb's station. Kolb and William Forrest, chairman of the Premier Biscuit Company, want to find the parties responsible to the rival commercial and prosecute them to the limit of the law. Detectives Fred Sears and Kernan Cripps locate the radio and Singleton. Singleton is arrested and taken to the radio station. Cowan, believing correctly that Lake was involved, asks Lake to come to his office. Cowan gets a call from Singleton, and Cowan and Lake hurry to the station. But Lake first calls home and talks with Herbert. Herbert heads for the radio station, also. Kolb is ready to prosecute Singleton, Lake and Herbert. Forrest, wisely, prevents this. Herbert has brought some of Singleton's cookies and passes them around. All agree the cookies are excellent and Forrest wants the recipe. Singleton sorts everything out. Kolb keeps the contract with the Premier Biscuit Company and will have Cowan build his new radio station. Lake gets his job back with a raise and a bonus. Herbert gets his own kitchen in which to invent and bake new cookies. As a result, Singleton will give her cookie recipe to Forrest. As Singleton and Lake leave Kolb's office, Kolb turns on his radio. The sound is awful. Lake takes a step toward the radio, but is guided out of the office by Singleton, averting another disaster.

Review: "Nine years into the series Lake and Singleton are beginning to show their age. So is the series in this programmer." *Motion Picture Guide*, Nash and Ross

Summation: This edition is slow starting and too predictable. The story seems like a few two-reel comedies strung together. Thanks to the deft performance by Hugh Herbert, however, the film is watchable.

BLONDIE'S ANNIVERSARY
Columbia (December 1947)

With squirrels who know their nuts the best ... It's Dagwood 10 to 1!

Cast: Blondie, Penny Singleton; Dagwood, Arthur Lake; Alexander, Larry Simms; Cookie, Marjorie Kent; "Daisy"; Gloria Stanford, Adele Jergens; George Radcliffe, Jerome Cowan; Samuel Breckenridge, Grant Mitchell; Sharkey, William Frawley // Parker, Larry Steers; Ollie, Jack Rice; Mailman, Eddie Acuff; Man with book, Cosmo Sardo; Acme Loan Company employee, Al Thompson; Carter, Frank Wilcox; Mary, Alyn Lockwood; Man in park, Paul E. Burns; Bob Burley, Edmund MacDonald; Bert Dalton, Fred F. Sears

Credits: Director, Abby Berlin; Screenwriter, Jack Henley; Editor, Al Clark; Art Director, George Brooks; Set Decorator, William Kiernan; Cinematography, Vincent Farrar; Musical Director, Mischa Bakaleinikoff

Song: "Anniversary Song" (Chaplin and Jolson) — hummed by Penny Singleton
Production Dates: August 8, 1947–August 29, 1947
Source: Based on the comic strip *Blondie*, created by Chic Young. Owned and copyrighted by King Features Syndicate, Inc.
Running Time: 67 min
Story: While visiting Grant Mitchell's bank to bid on a contract to build a new hospital, Jerome Cowan finds himself attracted to Mitchell's secretary, Adele Jergens. Cowan decides to give Jergens a new and expensive watch and instructs Arthur Lake to deliver it the following morning. Lake has forgotten his wedding anniversary. Penny Singleton finds the watch and thinks this is her anniversary present from Lake. Lake is too embarrassed to tell the truth. Next morning, Lake borrows $30 from a loan shark, William Frawley, to buy a cheap imitation. The watch immediately falls apart and Jergens calls the jeweler, Frank Wilcox. Lake tells Cowan that Singleton is wearing the watch, whereupon Cowan fires Lake. It takes Lake a week to tell Singleton the truth. Singleton returns the watch to Cowan. At the same time unscrupulous contractors, Edmund MacDonald and Fred F. Sears, give Jergens an expensive broach to help influence their chances of winning the contract. Jergens gives MacDonald information on Cowan's contract and bid. MacDonald plans to use sub-par materials to undercut Cowan's bid. MacDonald hires Lake to draw up plans for the hospital. By accident, Lake discovers MacDonald and Sears are crooks. Lake obtains the needed proof to take to Mitchell, but is captured by MacDonald. Frawley, trying to get money from Lake, frees him. Singleton, unaware of Lake's plight, tells Mitchell that MacDonald is a crook. Lake arrives in time to provide proof. Mitchell tells MacDonald and Sears to leave town. Jergens decides to leave town, also. Mitchell thinks Lake's plans are the best. Lake gets his job back (with a nice raise) and Cowan gives Singleton the expensive watch.
Notes and Commentary: In this episode, the audience learns that Dagwood's title at the Radcliffe Construction Company is Head Draftsman and that he and Blondie have been married 15 years.
Review: "Slender gist." *The Columbia Story*, Hirschhorn
Summation: This is only an okay entry. To its credit, it does hold the audience's interest, but the laughs are sparse.

BLONDIE'S REWARD
Columbia (June 1948)

Dagwood bites man for job and Blondie! Your favorite fun family's newest howl hit!

Cast: Blondie, Penny Singleton; Dagwood, Arthur Lake; Alexander, Larry Simms; Cookie, Marjorie Kent; George M. Radcliffe, Jerome Cowan; Alice Dickson, Gay Nelson; Ted Scott, Ross Ford; Alvin Fuddle, Danny Mummert; John D. Dickson, Paul Harvey; Ed Vance, Frank Jenks; Bill Cooper, Chick Chandler; "Daisy" // Officer Carney, Frank Sully; Mr. Johnson (mailman), Eddie Acuff; Mary, Alyn Lockwood; Ollie Merton, Jack Rice; Leroy J. Blodgett, Chester Clute; Gardner, Nacho Galindo; Butler, Vesey O'Davoren; Cluett Day, Myron Healey; Marie, Virginia Hunter
Credits: Director, Abby Berlin; Screenwriter, Edward Bernds; Editor, Al Clark; Art Director, George Brooks; Set Decorator, Sidney Clifford; Cinematographer, Vincent Farrar; Musical Director, Mischa Bakaleinikoff

Production Dates: September 15, 1947–October 6, 1947

Source: Based on the comic strip *Blondie*, created by Chic Young. Owned and copyrighted by King Features Syndicate, Inc.

Running Time: 66 min.

Story: Jerome Cowan sends Arthur Lake to buy a particular tract of land. Lake meets two con men, Chick Chandler and Frank Jenks, who sell him the wrong property. When Lake forgets to pick up a set of plans from Paul Harvey, Penny Singleton asks a neighbor, Ross Ford, to pick up the plans. At Harvey's estate, Ford sees Myron Healey manhandling Harvey's daughter, Gay Nelson. Ford steps in. A fight ensues with Ford knocking Healey into the swimming pool. Harvey asks to see Lake, believing him to be the man who hit Healey. Harvey wants to see the punch he used to hit Healey, and Lake knocks out Harvey. Harvey is impressed and decides to award the contract to Cowan, as soon as he obtains the property he needs. Harvey and Nelson confront Lake and Ford in Cowan's office and void the contract. Ford and Nelson clear the matter up and begin a romance. It turns out that the property Lake purchased by mistake is the very property Harvey needs. Chandler and Jenks also find out how valuable the property is and decide to trick Lake into selling it to them. Danny Mummert overhears the two men plotting. Mummert, with some help from Lake's children, Larry Simms and Marjorie Kent (and their dog, Daisy) prevent Lake from relinquishing the property. Chandler and Jenks take the deed and try to escape. Before they can leave, Cowan and Harvey arrive. Singleton arranges for Lake to make a small profit on selling the property to Harvey and get a week off with pay. Lake expects to have a carefree vacation at home, but Singleton tells Lake that he will be varnishing all of the floors.

Notes and Commentary: The working title for the film was "Blondie's Night Out."

This was last series entry to be directed by Abby Berlin. Screenwriter Edward Bernds would take the helm for the remained of the series.

Reviews: "Predictable comedy with ten-year old gags. Mercifully brief." *Motion Picture Guide*, Nash and Ross

"One of the better offerings in the series." *Variety*, 08/18/48

Summation: Engaging Bumstead entry. Some laughs in this episode.

BLONDIE'S SECRET
Columbia (December 1948)

O-o-o-h-h-h!!! What you'll see! How you'll roar ... learning

Cast: Blondie, Penny Singleton; Dagwood, Arthur Lake; Alexander, Larry Simms; Cookie, Marjorie Kent; "Daisy"; Radcliffe, Jerome Cowan; Mr. Whiteside, Thurston Hall; Ollie, Jack Rice; Alvin Fuddle, Danny Mummert; Philpotts, Frank Orth; Mary, Alyn Lockwood; Mailman, Eddie Acuff // Larry, Murray Alper; Police sergeant, Joseph Crehan; Mack, Kernan Cripps; Bathing girls in dream, Carole Gallagher, Joi Lansing and Kathleen O'Malley; The butcher, Edward Gargan; Mona, Greta Granstedt; Jim, Robert Malcolm; Big man, Allen Matthews; Mr. Ford, William Newell; Chips, William "Bill" Phipps; Dr. Mason's nurse, Paula Raymond; Ken Marcy, Grandon Rhodes; Cab driver, Ralph Sanford; Grocery store clerk, Emil Sitka

Credits: Director, Edward Bernds; Screenwriter, Jack Henley; Editor, Richard Fantl; Art Director, George Brooks; Set Decorator, Louis Diage; Cinematographer, Vincent Farrar; Musical Director, Mischa Bakaleinikoff

Songs: "Oh! Susanna" (Foster) sung by Arthur Lake (modified lyrics)

Production Dates: May 18, 1948–June 5, 1948

Source: Based on the comic strip *Blondie*, created by Chic Young. Owned and copyrighted by King Features Syndicate, Inc.

Running Time: 68 min.

Story: After four postponements, Penny Singleton and Arthur Lake finally plan to take a vacation. Unfortunately, Lake is needed to correct Jack Rice's mistakes in an architectural drawing for a building commissioned by Thurston Hall. To keep Lake at home, Rice steals the luggage. As Rice is getting away, Daisy takes the seat out of his pants. To find the identity of the thief, Singleton has the radio station announce that Daisy has rabies. This is done to force the thief to seek medical attention. Lake inadvertently tips off Rice, who cancels his doctor's appointment. Meanwhile, Greta Granstedt, who is an accomplice in a counterfeit scheme, switches Singleton's purse. Because of the possibility of rabies, Daisy is taken to the dog pound. A release from Rice is needed before Lake can bring Daisy home. At the same time, crooks try to retrieve Granstedt's purse and Rice tries to return the luggage. A wild melee ensues: the crooks are arrested and Singleton discovers that Rice stole the luggage. Rice signs Daisy's release. Lake and Singleton receive an additional week's vacation.

Notes and Commentary: Dream girl bathing beauty Joi Lansing would be featured on the cover of *Life* magazine (March 28, 1949). Lansing had an undistinguished career, with highlights as the female lead in the Bowery Boys' comedy, *Hot Shots* (Allied Artists, 1956) and the recurring role of Gladys Flatt in the classic TV comedy series, *The Beverly Hillbillies* (CBS) from 1963–68.

Nurse Paula Raymond had a durable career in both films and television. Raymond had the female lead in director Anthony Mann's *Devil's Doorway* (Metro-Goldwyn-Mayer, 1950) and *The Tall Target* (Metro-Goldwyn-Mayer, 1951). Raymond was probably best known for appearing in the sci-fi classic *The Beast from 20,000 Fathoms* (Warner Bros., 1953). Raymond then appeared in many television series into 1964.

Reviews: "Not one of the better entries in this series." *Motion Picture Guide*, Nash and Ross

"Trivial fluff, with the tired series coming into the home stretch." *Movie and Video Guide*, Maltin

"Very good entry in the Columbia series based on the comic strip." *Variety*, 01/26/49

Summation: This is a very amusing entry in the series. Even the old jokes are still funny.

BLONDIE'S BIG DEAL
Columbia (March 1949)

Anybody gotta match for Dagwood! As if anyone could match the Bumsteads for laughs!

Alternate Title: *The Big Deal*

Cast: Blondie, Penny Singleton; Dagwood, Arthur Lake; Alexander, Larry Simms; Cookie, Marjorie Kent; "Daisy"; George M. Radcliffe, Jerome Cowan; Norma Addison, Colette Lyons; Joe Dillon, Wilton Graff; Harry Slack, Ray Walker; Mr. Forsythe, Stanley Andrews; Rollo, Alan Dinehart III; Mr. Beasley (mailman), Eddie Acuff // Alvin Fuddle, Danny Mummert; Girard, Ronnie Ralph; Marvin, David Sandell; "Elmer"; Ollie, Jack Rice;

Mary, Alyn Lockwood; Mayor A.K. Ramsey, Chester Clute; Fire chief, George Lloyd; Woman at demonstration, Sue Casey; Photographer, Allen Matthews

Credits: Director, Edward Bernds; Producer, Ted Richmond; Story and Screenwriter, Lucile Watson Henley; Editor, Henry Batista; Art Director, Perry Smith; Set Decorator, George Montgomery; Cinematographer, Vincent Farrar; Musical Director, Mischa Bakaleinikoff

Production Dates: September 8, 1948–September 25, 1948

Source: Based on the comic strip *Blondie*, created by Chic Young. Owned and copyrighted by King Features Syndicate, Inc.

Running Time: 66 min.

Story: Arthur Lake invents a fire-repellant paint that Jerome Cowan plans to use if he wins the contract to build a new school. With this invention, rival contractors Wilton Graff and Ray Walker realize they will lose the bid. Prior to a demonstration using Cowan's fishing cabin, Walker is able to substitute regular paint. In the demonstration, Cowan's cabin is destroyed by fire. Lake's dog, Daisy, and neighborhood boy, Alan Dinehart III, find the empty paint cans. Dinehart believes Graff and Walker may be behind the substitution and suggests that Penny Singleton take a job as their secretary and investigate. Graff and Walker plan to use Lake's paint and claim the original formula belongs to them. As Graff and Walker are about to be awarded the contract, Singleton arrives with proof of their duplicity. Cowan is awarded the contract. Graff and Walker are arrested.

Notes and Commentary: In *Blondie's Reward*, Eddie Acuff's character's name was Johnson. Now, two films later, Acuff is Mr. Beasley, which was the mailman's name in the comic strip.

Reviews: "*Blondie's Big Deal* is a shade better than most Blondie movies." *Motion Picture Guide*, Nash and Ross

"Good light programmer, cut above the average Blondie." *Variety*, 03/16/49

Summation: This is a sparkling Bumstead episode. Penny Singleton has more screen time than in most of the later films. Director Edward Bernds successfully meshes good comedy with a dash of suspense.

BLONDIE HITS THE JACKPOT
Columbia (September 1949)

Blondie hits the crackpot jackpot of laughs!

Alternate Title: *Hitting the Jackpot*

Cast: Blondie, Penny Singleton; Dagwood, Arthur Lake; Alexander, Larry Simms; Cookie, Marjorie Kent; "Daisy"; George Radcliffe; Jerome Cowan; J.B. Hutchins, Lloyd Corrigan; Louise Hutchins, Ann Carter; Alvin Fuddle, Danny Mummert; Brophy, James Flavin // Mailman, Dick Wessel; Mary, Alyn Lockwood; Chauffeur, Eric Wilton; Sally, Sherlee Collier; Senate president, Sam Harris; Floorwalker with toupee, George Meador; Angelo, George Humbert; Diner, Heinie Conklin; Pierre Dubois, Maurice Cass; Delivery man, Al Thompson; Luke, David Sharpe; Truck driver, Rodney Bell; Swedish plaster mixer, Emil Sitka; Policeman, Kernan Cripps

Credits: Director, Edward Bernds; Producer, Ted Richmond; Screenwriter, Jack Henley; Editor, Henry Batista; Art Director, Perry Smith; Set Decorator, George Montgomery; Cinematographer, Vincent Farrar; Musical Director, Mischa Bakaleinikoff

Song: "Romance in ¾ Time" played by an orchestra

Production Dates: December 6, 1938–December 17, 1948

Source: Based on the comic strip *Blondie*, created by Chic Young. Owned and copyrighted by King Features Syndicate, Inc.

Running Time: 66 min.

Story: In order to further goodwill with client Lloyd Corrigan, Jerome Cowan arranges for Arthur Lake's son, Larry Simms, to be Corrigan's daughter Amy Carter's date at her birthday party. Since she is a spoiled brat, Simms ends up spending most of his time with Sherlee Collier, much to Carter's displeasure. Corrigan advises Simms to be stern with Carter, and demonstrates this in a way that looks like the two are fighting. Lake, who has come to the party to take Simms home, misunderstands and knocks Corrigan into the swimming pool. At Carter's demand, Corrigan has Cowan fire Lake in order to keep the construction contract. With Lake out of a job, Simms takes a newspaper route and has Daisy deliver the paper to Corrigan's estate. Carter spies Daisy and wants the dog for herself. When she learns that the dog belongs to Simms, she plans further revenge on Lake. Carter arranges for Lake to obtain a job with Corrigan's company and has the foreman, James Flavin, assign him to the hardest, dirtiest jobs. Lake overhears Flavin talk with worker Ray Teal about using defective steel girders. Lake investigates and finds the defective materials. Lake telephones Penny Singleton and asks her to tell Corrigan. Meanwhile, Flavin and Teal chase Lake in attempt to shut him up. As Flavin and Teal finally get their hands on Lake, Singleton and Corrigan arrive. Singleton steps in and levels both crooks with a two-by-four to the head. Lake thinks he knocked out both men. Now Corrigan wants Lake to be in full charge of the construction of his new building. Carter realizes she's been a spoiled brat and now sees Singleton as a role model. Singleton negotiates a new salary for Lake with Cowan.

Notes and Commentary: This was Jerome Cowan's last appearance in the series. In *Beware of Blondie*, Edward Earle (as J.C. Dithers) regains control of the construction company.

Ace stuntman David Sharpe plays construction worker Luke. Sharpe, known for his fondness for cigars, is allowed to perform two stunts with a cigar in his mouth. At Republic, Sharpe was famous for doing the practice stunts with a cigar in his mouth to prevent those stunts from being used in the film. In *Blondie Hits the Jackpot*, Sharpe also doubles Arthur Lake.

Child actress Ann Carter is best known for her role as the troubled little girl, Amy Reed, in *The Curse of the Cat People* (RKO, 1944).

Reviews: "Not a very good example of the series." *Motion Picture Guide*, Nash and Ross

"Trite comedy in the "Blondie" series. One of the most belabored in the series." *Variety*, 09/14/49

Summation: An only moderately funny but nevertheless pleasing Bumstead feature. The cast performs up to standard with a special nod to Lloyd Corrigan and Amy Carter. Director Edward Bernds's judicious handling of the close-ups adds to the film's enjoyment.

BLONDIE'S HERO

Columbia (March 1950)

What a hero! ... What a family! ... What fun!...

Cast: Blondie, Penny Singleton; Dagwood, Arthur Lake; Alexander, Larry Simms; Cookie, Marjorie Kent; "Daisy"; Marty Greer, William Frawley; Alvin Fuddle, Danny

Mummert; Sergeant Gateson, Joe Sawyer; Danny Gateson, Teddy Infuhr; Mary Reynolds, Alyn Lockwood; Mae, Iris Adrian; Tim Saunders, Frank Jenks // "Elmer"; Fruit vendor, Ted Mapes; Recruiting sergeant, Pat Flaherty; Mr. Collins, Robert Emmett Keane; Mailman, Dick Wessel; Mike McClusky, Frank Sully; Captain Masters, Robert Wilcox; Corporal Biff Touhey, Jimmy Lloyd; Richard Rogers, Edward Earle; Agnes Rogers, Mary Newton; Army waiter, Allen Mathews; Police officer, Cliff Clark

Credits: Director, Edward Bernds; Producer, Ted Richmond; Screenwriter, Jack Henley; Editor, Aaron Stell; Art Director, Perry Smith; Set Decorator, George Montgomery; Cinematographer, Vincent Farrar; Military Advisor, Captain Alfred Landau; Musical Director, Mischa Bakaleinikoff

Location: ORC Training Center, Fort MacArthur, California

Song: "Reveille" (traditional)

Production Dates: April 26, 1949–May 10, 1949

Source: Based on the comic strip *Blondie*, created by Chic Young. Owned and copyrighted by King Features Syndicate, Inc.

Running Time: 60 min.

Story: After an altercation with fruit vendor Ted Mapes, during which Arthur Lake is punched in the nose, Recruiting sergeant Pat Flaherty convinces Lake to join the army reserves. Lake then goes to the bank to make the final payment on the mortgage. Con man William Frawley overhears Lake say that he is in the reserves. Frawley approaches Lake and, learning the house would be empty on Sunday, tells him he has a buyer willing to pay four times the amount Lake paid on the house. With no one home, Frawley has Iris Adrian and Frank Jenks impersonate Penny Singleton and Lake. Frawley sells the house to Edward Earle and Mary Newton. Lake and Singleton return home to find their house occupied. The matter is resolved and Singleton hatches a plan to have the crooks arrested and get Earle and Newton's money back. The plan works, and Lake punches out Frawley and Jenks while Singleton takes care of Adrian. Before the police take charge, Lake is able to retrieve all but $16. Lake also settles matters with Mapes, who tries to hit Lake again but is instead punched out by him.

Notes and Commentary: The *Hollywood Reporter* stated that *Blondie's Hero* was "made with the cooperation of the 13th Armored Division O.R.C. and the officers and men of the Training Center at Fort MacArthur in California."

In the next Bumstead episode, Edward Earle would play the part of J.C. Dithers.

Review: "Stock service farce." *1996 Video & Movie Guide*, Maltin

Summation: Moderately entertaining Blondie and Dagwood comedy. The change of locale helps a little, but the jokes are still too old.

BEWARE OF BLONDIE

Columbia (April 1950)

Dagwood's sticking his neck out again ... leading Blondie on the funniest spree ever!

Cast: Blondie, Penny Singleton; Dagwood, Arthur Lake; Alexander, Larry Simms; Cookie, Marjorie Kent; "Daisy"; Toby Clifton, Adele Jergens; Mailman, Dick Wessel; Ollie, Jack Rice; Mary, Alyn Lockwood // Trash collectors, Ralph Peters and Emil Sitka; Herb Woodley, Emory Parnell; Harriett Woodley, Isabel Withers; Gossips, Symona Boniface,

Jessie Arnold and Gail Bonney; Alvin Fuddle, Danny Mummert; Maitre'd, Steven Geray; Adolph, Douglas Fowley; Samuel P. Dutton, William E. Green; Convict, Harry Wilson; Guard, George Lloyd; Sheriff, Vernon Dent; Policeman, Fred Sears; J.C. Dithers, Edward Earle

Credits: Director, Edward Bernds; Producer, Milton Feldman; Screenwriter, Jack Henley; Editor, Richard Fantl; Art Director, Perry Smith; Set Decorator, Faye Babcock; Cinematographers, Henry Freulich and Vincent Farrar; Musical Director, Mischa Bakaleinikoff

Production Dates: August 18, 1949–September 1, 1949

Source: Based on the comic strip *Blondie*, created by Chic Young. Owned and copyrighted by King Features Syndicate, Inc.

Running Time: 66 min.

Story: Arthur Lake is left in charge when Edward Earle goes on vacation. Lake is instructed to close an important deal and Lake, mistakenly, believes Adele Jergens is the client. Jergens learns that Lake has three signed checks from Earle in his possession. Jergens tells Lake she will sign the contract in her hotel room. Once there, Jergens changes into something "comfortable" and falls into Lake's arms just as Douglas Fowley come into the room. Fowley demands $5,000 not to make a scene. Jergens convinces Lake to lend her the money using one of Earle's checks, with a promise to repay Lake the following day. Jergens and Fowley and skip town immediately with the intention of getting the check cashed in Cleveland. The next day, Lake meets the actual client, William E. Green, and learns Jergens has checked out of her hotel room. Lake thinks he will be sent to prison unless he can replace the money. Earle gives Lake a call to tell him the checks are worthless because that account was closed.

Notes and Commentary: This was the last feature film for Arthur Lake and Marjorie Kent.

The "Spider Lady" set from the serial *Superman* (Columbia, 1948), was used as the courtroom in Dagwood's dream sequence.

Edward Earle's scenes are shot to suggest that Jonathan Hale had returned to the series. To add to the illusion, Hale's voice was used.

Reviews: "It's all good fun and innocent as a new born babe." *Motion Picture Guide*, Nash and Ross

"'Beware of Blondie' never lets the long series down, nor does it stand out as anything more unusual than its celluloid predecessors." *Variety*, 04/05/50

Summation: The series ends on a positive note. The script sparkles at times with fine performances from the cast, with a special nod to Adele Jergens and Jack Rice. One caveat: there should have a smoother transition from the Radcliffe Construction Company back to the Dithers Construction Company. No clue is given as to why Radcliffe sold out. Was it because of Dagwood?

Boston Blackie

"Enemy to those who make him an enemy.... Friend to those who have no friend."

Jack Boyle's Boston Blackie began as an opium-using safecracker in stories that appeared in the *American Magazine* in 1914. Blackie's piercing black eyes and his New England birthplace are said to be the origin for his name. Within a few years Boyle reworked the Boston Blackie character. He was now a university graduate, a renowned safecracker and an international crook. Blackie's earlier opium habit was a thing of the past. He had acquired a lovely wife, Mary, who assisted him in some of his illegal ventures.

Boyle's story, "The Baby and the Burglar" (*American Magazine*, June 1918) was the basis for the first Boston Blackie picture, *Boston Blackie's Little Pal* (Metro, 1918). Bert Lytell took the lead in this and the subsequent entry, *Blackie's Redemption* (Metro, 1919). Through the silent era, nine films depicted Blackie's exploits. Most told of Blackie's redemption accomplished with the understanding and assistance of Mary, who had various last names. Other actors who played Blackie were Sam De Grasse, David Powell, Lionel Barrymore, William Russell, Thomas Carrigan, Forrest Stanley and Raymond Glenn (a.k.a. western star Bob Custer). *The Return of Boston Blackie* (Chadwick Pictures Corporation, 1927) featured Strongheart, the dog.

Blackie was absent from the screen until 1941 when Columbia released *Meet Boston Blackie*, with veteran actor Chester Morris. Blackie had undergone some significant changes. He was now completely reformed and worked as an amateur sleuth to solve mysteries. Like his series counterpart the Lone Wolf, Blackie would have a law officer would could not believe he had changed and was prepared to blame Blackie for any major crime. Morris's screen careen began in silent films with *An Amateur Orphan* (Thanhouser/Pathé, 1917). He easily made the transition to sound, receiving an Academy Award nomination as best actor for his role as Chick Williams in *Alibi* (United Artists, 1929). By the mid–'30s, Morris was headlining "B" features. Morris played other roles in the 1940s, primarily in Pine-Thomas action films for Paramount, while also starring as Blackie. After the Blackie series was discontinued, Morris guest starred on many television shows and, in 1965, appeared on Broadway as Jack Albertson's replacement in *The Subject Was Roses*.

Blackie's sidekick, The Runt, appeared in all entries of the Boston Blackie series. George E. Stone, the Runyonesque character actor, played the part to perfection. Other actors who appeared in the role were Charles Wagenheim and Sid Tomack. Also aiding Blackie in many episodes was the flighty, eccentric millionaire Arthur Manleder, primarily played by Lloyd Corrigan. (Other actors in that role were Harrison Greene and Harry Hayden.) Jumbo Madigan, an underworld character, would help Blackie from time to time as well. The role was played by two actors, Cy Kendall (who fit the role like a glove) and Joseph Crehan. Inspector Farraday, who never quite believed that Blackie had reformed, was played by veteran actor Richard Lane. (Lane later became a noted announcer for Hot Rod Derby, roller derby and professional wrestling. His signature trademark was to shout, "Whoooooah Nellie!" to accentuate exciting moments. In the early days of televised wrestling, Lane would make up names for the various holds, some of which are still used today.) Farraday's assistant was the beleaguered, completely out-of-his-depth Sergeant Mathews. The role was alternately played by Walter Sande, Lyle Latell and Frank Sully. The popular series produced 14 entries between 1941 and 1949. On June 23, 1944, the *Boston Blackie* radio program was broadcast on NBC, and was sponsored by Rinso Soap. This was a summer replacement for *The Amos 'n' Andy Show*. Morris and Lane reprised their roles of Blackie and Farraday. In the interest of being politically correct, The Runt's name was changed to Shorty. Some websites indicate that the radio Blackie had a girlfriend, Mary Wesley, played by Lesley Woods. In the seven broadcasts that survive, Mary does not appear.

Blackie returned to the airwaves on April 25, 1945, as a syndicated show. Richard Kollmer played Blackie, Maurice Tarplin was Farraday, and Jan Minor took the part of Mary Wesley. In the first episode, "The Wentworth Diamonds" (April 25, 1945), Blackie introduces Mary to his friend, Shorty. This leads the author to believe that perhaps Mary was not in the Morris episodes. The program was popular, running for 220 episodes; it ended on June 29, 1949.

By 1951, Blackie had made the conversion to television with Kent Taylor as Blackie, Lois Collier as Mary, Frank Orth as Inspector Faraday, and Whitey the dog. Interestingly, sometimes the Inspector's last name would be spelled with 2 "r's" in most of the Columbia entries, and with only one on the television series. For the television series, a change was made in the relationship between Blackie and Faraday. They now were close friends. In all, 58 30-minute episodes would be produced, the last 32 in color. New episodes were filmed until 1953. It would take until November 2002 for Blackie to reappear, this time in a graphic comic book from Moonstone. Writer Stefan Petrucha and artist Kirk Van Wormer take Blackie back to his roots. Blackie is married to Mary and is an opium-using safecracker with a moral sense. Blackie finds the murderer of a child killed during a robbery committed by Blackie. It may have taken 88 years, but Blackie has come full circle.

MEET BOSTON BLACKIE

Columbia (February 1941)

That beloved rogue is back ... up to his neck in fantastic adventure!

Alternate Title: The Return of Boston Blackie
Cast: Boston Blackie, Chester Morris; Cecelia Bradley, Rochelle Hudson; Inspector Farraday, Richard Lane; The Runt, Charles Wagenheim; Marilyn Howard, Constance Worth; Monk, Jack O'Malley; Georgie, George Magrill; Mechanical Man, Michael Rand// Martin Vestrick, Nestor Paiva; First cab driver, Charles Sullivan; Second cab driver, Ralph Peters; Immigration officer, Lee Shumway; Freak show doorman, John Tyrell; Tunnel of Horror barker, Jack Gardner; Tunnel of Horror attendant, Philo McCullough; Brakeman, Ethan Laidlaw; Max, Stanley Brown; Telescope man, Sam Bernard; Blind man, Byron Foulger; Weight guesser, John Harmon; Amusement park officer, Walter Sande; McCarthy, William Lally; Second freak show barker, Eddie Fetherston; Princess Betty, Schlitze

Credits: Director, Robert Florey; Story and Screenplay, Jay Dratler; Editor, James Sweeney; Cinematographer, Franz Planer

Production Dates: December 6, 1940–December 27, 1940

Running Time: 61 min.

Source: Based upon the character created by Jack Boyle

Story: Returning to the New York after a few years' absence, Chester Morris finds himself embroiled in murder and international intrigue. His only clues are the so-called "Mechanical Man" and a blinking sign at Coney Island. The Mechanical Man is an act performed by Michael Rand. Rand attempts to murder Morris. Morris escapes with the aid of the beautiful Rochelle Hudson. Morris discovers that Rand plans to smuggle a Navy bombsite to a foreign country. A neon sign is used to transmit information to an offshore vessel. With help from Police Inspector Richard Lane, the plot is thwarted and Rand is cut down by a policeman's bullet. Morris is exonerated of all criminal charges.

Notes and Commentary: In a continuity goof, the chair Morris uses to secure Hudson in her Murphy bed is not the one Lane removes to free her. The original chair has a round back while the second chair is square backed.

This is the only appearance by Charles Waggenheim as the Runt. Beginning with the next episode, *Confessions of Boston Blackie* (Columbia, 1942), George E. Stone takes over for 12 episodes. Waggenheim returns to the series for an unbilled role as Mr. Sobel in *Boston Blackie Booked on Suspicion* (Columbia, 1945).

Beat patrolman Walter Sande becomes a series regular in *Confessions of Boston Blackie* (Columbia, 1942). He has the recurring role of Detective Mathews, Richard Lane's somewhat inept assistant. Sande would play the role in five entries.

In print advertising, it would be stated, "Boston Blackie of 'Get-Rich-Quick Wallingford' Fame." Unfortunately, that Blackie was no relation to Jack Boyle's character.

Reviews: "Mystery yarn that fails to jell. Principal defect in a slim yarn that rings as true as a tin cup." *Variety*, 3/4/41

"Franz Planer's stylish cinematography enhances this solid programmer." *Movie and Video Guide*, Maltin

Summation: Chester Morris's winning personality saves this picture. The story moves briskly, but is too swift in the handling of the villainy and the capture of the espionage ring.

CONFESSIONS OF BOSTON BLACKIE

Columbia (January 1942)

Blackie's Blackmailed By a Female ... and Nearly Blacked-out By Killers!

Cast: Boston Blackie, Chester Morris; Diane Parrish, Harriet Hilliard; Inspector Faraday, Richard Lane; The Runt, George E. Stone; Arthur Manleder, Lloyd Corrigan; Mona, Joan Woodbury; Detective Mathews, Walter Sande; Buchanan, Ralph Theodore; Caulder, Kenneth MacDonald; Eric Allison, Walter Soderling; Ice cream man, Billy Benedict// Auctioneer, Eddie Kane; Dr. Crane, Julius Tannen; First taxi driver, Jack O'Malley; Nurse-Receptionist, Lorna Dunn; Jimmy Parrish, Martin Spellman; Second nurse, Gwen Kenyon; Intern, John Tyrell; Third nurse, Jessie Arnold; Albert, Herbert Clifton; Plainclothesman, Harry Hollingworth; Mr. Bigsby, Harry Depp; Second taxi driver, Eddie Fetherston; Express men, Eddie Laughton and Budd Fine; Desk sergeant, Al Hill; Officer McCarthy, Ralph Dunn

Credits: Director, Edward Dmytryk; Producer, William Berke; Story, Paul Yawitz and Jay Dratler; Screenwriter, Paul Yawitz; Editor, Gene Milford; Art Directors, Lionel Banks and Robert Peterson; Cinematographer, Philip Tannura; Musical Director, M.W. Stoloff

Production Dates: September 10, 1941–September 24, 1941

Running Time: 65 min.

Source: Based upon the character created by Jack Boyle

Story: Harriet Hilliard, needing money for medical expenses for her brother, Martin Spellman, enlists art dealers Ralph Theodore, Kenneth MacDonald and Walter Soderling to auction a valuable statue. Unknown to Hilliard, the art dealers are crooks. They plan to make a copy of the statue, auction the copy and then sell the original. On the day of the auction, Hilliard notices that the statue is a fake. Wealthy Lloyd Corrigan and his friend, former jewel thief Chester Morris, attend the auction. Theodore tries to stop Hilliard's outburst by shooting her. Morris springs into action and fires a shot at Theodore. Theodore's shot ricochets off the statue, slightly wounding Hilliard and killing Soderling. Morris gives chase, but Theodore is able to elude capture. Theodore, not wanting the police to compare the bullet in Soderling's body to Morris's gun, hides Soderling in the fake statue. Inspector Richard Lane, Morris's old nemesis, arrests Morris for Soderling's death. Meanwhile, MacDonald sells the fake statue to Corrigan. Morris is able to escape from police custody. MacDonald offers to buy the statue from Corrigan. Morris tells Corrigan to sell the statue and plans to see where it will be taken. Morris meets Hilliard and plans to help her find the real statue while clearing his name. Morris sends Hilliard to his apartment, not knowing that Theodore is waiting there for him. Morris and Corrigan follow the statue to Theodore's warehouse. Morris gains entry to the warehouse and the secret underground workshop where he captures MacDonald. Theodore arrives with Hilliard and a standoff results until Corrigan shows up with Lane and his assistant, Walter Sande. Lane battles Theodore who falls to the workshop floor. One shot from Sande kills Theodore, and another shot disables the electrical system, leaving the group to suffocate. Morris starts a fire that travels up a ventilator shaft. The fire department arrives and all are saved.

Notes and Commentary: The working title of this film was "The Secret of Boston Blackie."

George W. Stone took over the role of Chester Morris' sidekick, The Runt. Stone would play the role until he was replaced by Sid Tomack for the series finale, *Boston Blackie's Chinese Venture.*

Review: "Compact, deftly paced murder meller, embroiled with light comedy touches. Chester Morris is excellent in the lead." *Variety*

"Action-packed and well acted. This may not be art but its pace and sense of its own ridiculousness could give today's filmmakers a lesson." *Motion Picture Guide*, Nash and Ross

Summation: Good entry in the Boston Blackie series. This is a well-acted film with Chester Morris perfect in the title role. Director Edward Dmytryk balances the action and comedy for full audience enjoyment.

ALIAS BOSTON BLACKIE
Columbia (April 1942)

Blackie's got an eye-full of alibi ... but cops don't believe in looks!

Cast: Boston Blackie, Chester Morris; Eve Sanders, Adele Mara; Inspector Farraday,

Richard Lane; The Runt, George E. Stone; Arthur Manleder, Lloyd Corrigan, Detective Mathews, Walter Sande; Joe Trilby, Larry Parks; Roggi McKay, George McKay; Jumbo Madigan, Cy Kendall; Steve Caveroni, Paul Fix; Warden, Ben Taggart// Meggs, Cyril Thornton; Pop, Ernie Adams; Bus driver, Lloyd Bridges; Mack, Frank Richards; Frank (prison guard), Lee Prather; Bill, James T. Mack; Laundry proprietor, Francis Sayles; Herman, Sidney Miller; Henry, Lester Dorr; Taxi driver, Kit Guard; Dr. Crane, Walter Soderling; Ambulance driver, Eddie Laughton; Ambulance attendant, John Tyrell; Lead singing telegram boy, Teddy Mangean; Police dispatcher, Edmund Cobb; Squad car 29 policemen, Dick Jensen and Duke York; Elevator boy, George Hickman; Angry desk clerk, Harry Depp; Hotel maid, Eileen O'Hearn

Credits: Director, Lew Landers; Producer, Wallace MacDonald; Screenwriter, Paul Yawitz; Editor, Richard Fantl; Art Directors, Lionel Banks and Robert Peterson; Cinematographer, Philip Tannura; Musical Director, M.W. Stoloff

Production Dates: January 6, 1942–January 22, 1942

Running Time: 67 min.

Source: Based upon the character created by Jack Boyle

Story: On Christmas Eve, Chester Morris takes a show troupe to perform for the State Prison inmates. One of the troupe's members, Adele Mara's brother, Larry Parks, is serving a sentence for bank robbery. Parks was framed and wants to escape to exact his revenge. Parks gets his chance when he's able to change places with one of the performers. Morris gets to one of the men who framed Parks, but finds him murdered. When Parks shows up afterwards, Morris knows Parks is innocent. Morris hides Parks while he runs down a clue to the other bank robber, Paul Fix, who is now driving cabs. Working with Mara, Morris is able to get Fix to the scene of the murder. Inspector Lane has a reason to return to the crime scene and is able to hear Fix admit to the murder and exonerate Parks. Fix makes an escape attempt but is gunned down by police bullets.

Notes and Commentary: In a reference to the previous entry, *Confessions of Boston Blackie* (Columbia, 1941), in which Chester Morris saved Richard Lane's life, Lane remarks, "Saved my life once." At the end of this one, Lane returns the favor.

In real life, Chester Morris loved magic tricks and was an amateur magician.

Review: "Enjoyable entry." *Blockbuster Video Guide to Movies and Videos 1995*, Castell

Summation: Neat, fast-moving Boston Blackie, thanks to Lew Landers's strong direction and Paul Yamitz's nifty screenplay. Chester Morris is engaging, as always, with the rest of the cast chipping in with fine performances.

BOSTON BLACKIE GOES HOLLYWOOD

Columbia (November 1942)

What a moving picture ... when Blackie moves in on this blonde picture!
Hollywood gets a new kind of thrill!

Alternate Title: Blackie Goes Hollywood

Cast: Boston Blackie, Chester Morris; Slick Barton, William Wright; Gloria Lane, Constance Worth; Arthur Manleder, Lloyd Corrigan; Inspector Farraday, Richard Lane; The Runt, George E. Stone; Whipper, Forrest Tucker// Detective Mathews, Walter Sande; Desk clerk, Stanley Brown; Al, James C. Morton; Pharmacist, Eddie Laughton; Jumbo

Madigan, Cy Kendall; First taxi driver, Jack Gardner; Ticket clerk, Robert Kellard; Gift counter clerk, Virginia Sale; Stewardess, Shirley Patterson; Steve, John Tyrell; Police sergeant, Ralph Dunn; Jailer, Al Hill; Elderly couple at radio, Dorothy Phillips and Victor Travers; Last cab driver, Charles Sullivan

Credits: Director, Michael Gordon; Producer, Wallace MacDonald; Screenwriter, Paul Yawitz; Editor, Arthur Seid; Art Directors, Lionel Banks and Arthur Royce; Interior Decorator, Robert Priestley; Cinematographer, Henry Freulich; Musical Director, M.W. Stoloff

Production Dates: June 18, 1942–July 3, 1942

Running Time: 68 min.

Source: Based upon the character created by Jack Boyle

Story: The Monterey Diamond is stolen in California. On the East Coast, Inspector Richard Lane believes that somehow Chester Morris is involved. Morris gets a distress call from Lloyd Corrigan, who is in Los Angeles. Corrigan desperately needs Morris to open his wall safe and bring him $60,000. Gangsters Forrest Tucker and John Tyrell make Corrigan believe that he's responsible for the disappearance of the Monterey Diamond, which could be ransomed for that amount. The money is needed to have the diamond cut up. Morris believes that an old nemesis, William Wright, is behind the robbery. Tyrell and Tucker are able to get control of the money. Through a ruse, Morris gets all the principals together. Wright decides to double-cross his confederates and tries to get away with the diamond and the money. Morris gives chase, recovers the diamond and money and brings Wright to justice.

Notes and Commentary: Forrest Tucker had a long and distinguished career, playing both lead and support roles. Tucker is probably best remember as Sergeant Morgan O'Rourke on *F Troop* (ABC, 1965–67).

Review: "Good whodunit." *Motion Picture Guide*, Nash and Ross

"One of the best Blackie's is helped along by nice ensemble playing and terrific atmosphere." *Blockbuster Video Guide to Movies and Videos 1995*, Castell

Summation: Neat Boston Blackie caper with Chester Morris as charming as ever. The supporting cast performs admirably, with the exception of Morris's nemesis William Wright. Wright is unable to be fully convincing as a tough guy. Director Michael Gordon is on top of Paul Yawitz's screenplay and keeps the proceedings briskly paced.

AFTER MIDNIGHT WITH BOSTON BLACKIE

Columbia (March 1943)

Blackie keeps the action boiling!

Cast: Boston Blackie, Chester Morris; Inspector Farraday, Richard Lane; Betty Barnaby, Ann Savage; The Runt, George E. Stone; Arthur Manleder, Lloyd Corrigan// Joe Herschel, Cy Kendall; Sammy Walsh, Al Hill; Marty Beck, George McKay; Diamond Ed Barnaby, Walter Baldwin; Warden, Robert F. Hill; Detective Mathews, Walter Sande; Porter, Sam McDaniel; Waiter in dining car, Jesse Graves; Florist, Harry Semels; Taxi driver, Ray Johnson; Dixie Rose Blossom, Jan Buckingham; Mr. Potts, Dick Elliott; Cigar clerk, Don Barclay; Key man, Victor Travers; Workman, Heinie Conklin; The Fence, John Harmon; Air raid warden, Eddie Kane; Police lieutenant, Robert Homans; Bullfiddle player, Dudley Dickerson; Songstress, Marguerite Whitten; Police captain, Eddy Chandler

Credits: Director, Lew Landers; Producer, Sam White; Story, Aubrey Wisberg; Screenwriter, Howard J. Green; Editor, Richard Fantl; Art Directors, Lionel Banks and Walter Holscher; Interior Decorator, William Kiernan; Cinematographer, L.W. O'Connell; Musical Director, M.W. Stoloff

Production Dates: November 13, 1942–December 12, 1942

Running Time: 64 min.

Source: Based upon the character created by Jack Boyle

Story: Released from prison, Walter Baldwin plans to give diamonds to his daughter, Ann Savage, and then leave town. When Baldwin disappears, Savage turns to Chester Morris for help. Gangster nightclub owner, Cy Kendall, and his confederates, Al Hill and George McKay, who covet the diamonds, have kidnapped Baldwin. Baldwin finally succumbs and tells that the diamonds are hidden in a safe deposit box. Left alone, Baldwin tries to call for help but a shot rings out, killing him. Morris figures out the location of the diamonds and opens the safe deposit box, only to find it empty. Hill and McKay believe that Morris has the diamonds and kidnapped Savage in exchange for the diamonds. But it was Kendall who shot Baldwin and stole the diamonds, planning to double-cross Hill and McKay. Morris goes to Kendall's nightclub and, through a keyhole, sees Kendall place the diamonds in his safe. Morris easily opens the safe and retrieves the diamonds. Before Morris can leave the room, Hill and McKay confront him. Morris is able to hide the diamonds in a pitcher of water on Kendall's desk. Morris has some fake diamonds and exchanges them for Savage's freedom. Freedom is short-lived when Kendall interferes and declares that the diamonds Morris gave his confederates were fakes. Morris and Savage are able to escape. Morris returns to Kendall's office to retrieve the diamonds when he sees Hill gun down Kendall. Morris enters the room and gets the diamonds without Hill's knowledge. Hill wants the diamonds, and Morris agrees to take him to them. Morris steals a police car and turns the police radio to the "send" mode. Morris gets Hill to confess to Kendall's murder and reveal that Kendall had murdered Baldwin. Hill realizes the police are closing in. Morris deliberately crashes the police car. Morris and Hill climb out of the wreckage and begin a short fight, one that Morris wins. Morris returns the diamonds to Savage.

Notes and Commentary: In this film we learn Boston Blackie's given name: Horatio Black.

Cy Kendall, who played Jumbo Madigan in two previous series entries, is one of the main gangsters in this film. In the next Boston Blackie episode, Kendall was back as Madigan.

Ann Savage will forever be remembered in film noir history as Vera in *Detour* (PRC, 1945). In 2007, *Time* listed Savage as one of the 25 top villains, along with Barbara Stanwyck for *Double Indemnity* (Paramount, 1944) and Angela Lansbury in *The Manchurian Candidate* (United Artists, 1962). In 2005, the Academy of Motion Picture Arts and Sciences cited Savage as an icon and legend.

Review: "Amiable whodunit, with cult star Savage good as the prisoner's daughter." *Blockbuster Video Guide to Movies and Videos 1995,* Castell

Summation: A fun Boston Blackie episode. As always, Chester Morris is glib and charming in the title role. Supporting performances are above average with the villainy in the capable hands of Cy Kendall and Al Hill.

The Chance of a Lifetime
Columbia (October 1943)

Arrested for a murder he didn't commit! Yet he confessed!

Cast: Boston Blackie, Chester Morris; Dooley Watson, Erik Rolf; Mary Watson, Jeanne Bates; Inspector Farraday, Richard Lane; The Runt, George E. Stone; Arthur Manleder, Lloyd Corrigan// Governor Rutledge, Pierre Watkin; Parole board chairman, Forbes Murray; Warden Edwards, George Anderson; Detective Mathews, Walter Sande; Manny Vogel, Trevor Bardette; George Phillips, Jerry Frank; Joe Painter, Joel Friedkin; Wilfred Thompson, Kit Guard; Tex Stewart, Arthur Hunnicutt; Benny Hines, Sid Melton; William Jones, Al Murphy; Parker Gray, Brian O'Hara; Jerome Wagner, Harry Semels; Nails Blanton, Douglas Fowley; Red Taggart, John Harmon; Johnny Watson, Larry Olsen; Women in hallway, Jessie Arnold and Minta Durfee; Joe, Ray Teal; Frank, Eddy Chandler; Carpet men, Richard Alexander and Jack Carr; Richie, Sally Cairns; Desk sergeant, Heine Conklin; Miss Bailey, Marie De Becker; Miss Counihan, Maude Eburne; Driver, John Tyrell; Reporter, Eddie Bruce; Jumbo Madigan, Cy Kendall; Warden Root, Ben Erway

Credits: Director, William Castle; Producer, Wallace MacDonald; Screenwriter, Paul Yawitz; Editor, Jerome Thoms; Art Directors, Lionel Banks and Paul Murphy; Set Decorator, Robert Priestley; Cinematographer, Ernie Miller; Makeup, S. Clay Campbell; Musical Director, M.W. Stoloff

Production Dates: July 26, 1943–August 9, 1943

Running Time: 65 min.

Source: Based upon the character created by Jack Boyle

Story: Chester Morris's plan to allow model prisoners to help in the war effort by working in Lloyd Corrigan's factory is approved on a trial basis. There is an early problem when convict Erik Rolf fails to show up for work. Rolf had been involved in $60,000 payroll robbery with two confederates, Douglas Fowley and John Harmon. Rolf had been given permission to spend the first night with his wife, Jeanne Bates, and their son, Larry Olson. During the night Rolf retrieves the money and wants Bates to skip town with him. Bates persuades Rolf to go straight and return the money. Fowley and Harmon confront Rolf and demand their share of the money. When Harmon threatens to harm Olson, Rolf and Harmon begin fighting. In the struggle the gun goes off, killing Harmon. Morris arrives to take Rolf to work, giving Fowley the opportunity to escape. In order not to jeopardize the Model Prisoner Program, Morris makes Rolf report to Corrigan's factory. Inspector Richard Lane catches Morris with Harmon's body and the payroll money. Morris confesses to the crime but escapes to prove his innocence by making Fowley tell the truth about the incident. Fowley believes that Morris now has the money. Morris is able to make Fowley come to him and allows Fowley to get the upper hand. Fowley forces Morris to go to his apartment to produce the money. In the apartment, Fowley is jumped by Rolf and the other convicts. Fowley is tied, blindfolded and dangled outside a window on the 14th floor. Believing he will be dropped to his death, Fowley confesses to how the incident really happened. Inspector Lane arrives at Morris' apartment in time to hear the confession. The trial program is a success and will be offered to other prisons.

Notes and Commentary: The working title for this film was "The Gamble of Boston Blackie." Columbia thought that by eliminating Boston Blackie's name from the title, non-Blackie fans might take a chance on the film.

In the onscreen credits, makeup artist S. Clay Campbell should have been correctly billed as H. Clay Campbell.

The Chance of a Lifetime marked the first screen appearance of Jeanne Bates and the directorial debut of William Castle. It has been stated that Castle rearranged the order of the reels to make the picture work. That statement is probably a work of fiction since the flow of the storyline seems to be in an orderly fashion.

Review: "Action moves swiftly." *Motion Picture Guide*, Nash and Ross

"Chester Morris in a fast-moving 'Boston Blackie' cops-and-robbers. Good dual." *Variety*, 12/22/43

Summation: Moderately entertaining but definitely not up to the standards of the previous Boston Blackie entries. For his part, Chester Morris is given a chance to expand his acting range and succeeds admirably. William Castle's direction is a little shaky and Paul Yawitz's screenplay is a bit slack. A firm hand on the directorial reins and tighter screenplay would have resulted in a better film.

One Mysterious Night
Columbia (October 1944)

Blackie, wipe that smile off your face! You have an appointment with <u>death</u>!

Alternate Title: Behind Closed Doors

Cast: Boston Blackie, Chester Morris; Dorothy Anderson, Janis Carter; Paul Martens, William Wright; Inspector Farraday, Richard Lane; The Runt, George E. Stone; Matt Healy, Robert Williams; George Daley, Robert E. Scott// Eileen Daley, Dorothy Maloney; Switchboard operator, Early Cantrell; Woman in Daley's office, Constance Purdy; Mothers, Edythe Elliott and Cecil Weston; Boys, Kenneth Brown and Billy Lenhart; Commissioner Howard, Edward Keane; Detective Mathews, Lyle Latell; Reporter, Jack Gardner; Arthur Manleder, Harrison Greene; Newsstand clerk, Ann Loos; Sergeant McNulty, George McKay; Jumbo Madigan, Joseph Crehan; Miss Wilkinson, Minerva Urecal

Credits: Director, Oscar Boetticher Jr.; Producer, Ted Richmond; Screenwriter, Paul Yawitz; Editor, Al Clark; Art Directors, Lionel Banks and George Brooks; Set Decorator, Robert Priestley; Cinematographer, L.W. O'Connell; Musical Director, Mischa Bakaleinikoff

Production Dates: May 31, 1944–June 13, 1944

Running Time: 61 min.

Source: Based upon the character created by Jack Boyle

Story: Blinded with the promise of easy money from William Wright and Robert Williams, Robert E. Scott steals the Blue Star Diamond from an exhibit at the Carlton-Plaza Hotel. Completely stymied, Inspector Richard Lane enlists Chester Morris's help in retrieving the diamond. Morris figures out how Scott stole the diamond and convinces him to return it. Before Morris can take the diamond to headquarters, Wright and Williams appear. A fight breaks out, Scott is shot and killed, the diamond falls in Wright's hands, and Morris is captured. Morris tells Wright that the diamond he has is a fake and that he was planning to switch it with the real diamond. Wright goes to underworld fence Joseph Crehan to confirm Morris's story. Crehan, tipped off by Morris, confirms Morris's story. Wright gives the Blue Star Diamond to Morris but holds his pal George E. Stone as hostage. Morris returns the diamond to Lane. Morris and Lane rescue Stone and capture Wright and Williams.

"Blackie, wipe that smile off your face. You have an appointment with death!"

One Mysterious Night (1944) scene card — Janis Carter and Chester Morris.

Notes and Commentary: The working title for this film was "Boston Blackie's Appointment with Death."

One Mysterious Night marked Oscar Boetticher's first directorial assignment. Later in his career, Boetticher was billed as Budd. Boetticher will be remembered for his collaboration with Randolph Scott to bring seven first rate westerns to the screen.

There was a casting shake-up in this entry: Harrison Greene, not Lloyd Corrigan, played Arthur Manleder; Lyle Latell, instead of Walter Sande, played Detective Mathews; and Joseph Crehan, not Cy Kendall, played Jumbo Madigan.

Dorothy Maloney would achieve stardom as Dorothy Malone.

Reviews: "Solid cast makes up for the rather slow-moving story." *Motion Picture Guide*, Nash and Ross

"Another in the Boston Blackie series, one that adds up lightly as film entertainment in the detective fiction groove." *Variety*, 10/25/44

Summation: Breezy Boston Blackie episode. Chester Morris is a delight and the supporting cast performances are up to par. Paul Yawitz's loopy screenplay is well handled by novice director Oscar (later Budd) Boetticher. Boetticher adroitly paces the film so that the comedy sequences seem almost believable.

BOSTON BLACKIE BOOKED ON SUSPICION
Columbia (May 1945)

A Beautiful Girl Turns Killer and Blackie Is Taking the Rap!

Alternate Title: Booked on Suspicion

Cast: Boston Blackie, Chester Morris; Gloria Mannard, Lynn Merrick; Inspector Farraday, Richard Lane; Sergeant Mathews, Frank Sully; Jack Higgins, Steve Cochran; The Runt, George E. Stone; Arthur Manleder, Lloyd Corrigan// Wilfred Kittredge, George M. Carleton; Dr. Barclay, Edward Keane; Frank, Nolan Leary; Steven Culbacker, George Meader; Alexander Harmon, Douglas Wood; Leslie Paisley, Dan Stowell; Landlady, Isabel Withers; Police photographer, Eddie Bruce; Mr. Sobel, Charles Wagenheim; Officer Lee, Robert Williams; Newsboy, Bob Alden; Reporter, Philip Van Zandt; Mr. Obie, Jack Rice; Bookstore customer, Cecil Weston; Housekeeper, Jessie Arnold; Telegraph clerk, Dick Jensen; Diz, George Lloyd

Credits: Director, Arthur Dreifuss; Producer, Michel Krauke; Story, Malcolm Stuart Boylan; Screenwriter, Paul Yawitz; Editor, Richard Fantl; Art Director, Perry Smith; Set Decorator, Fay Babcock; Cinematographer, George B. Meehan; Sound, William Randall and Philip Faulkner

Production Dates: January 23, 1945–February 8, 1945

Running Time: 66 min.

Source: Based upon the character created by Jack Boyle

Story: Chester Morris, in disguise, decides to impersonate a noted rare book expert at an auction at Lloyd Corrigan's bookstore. Unbeknownst to Morris, The rare Dickens first edition is a fake. Counterfeit book expert George Meader and bookstore assistant Lynn Merrick are working together in the scam. After the sale, the book is discovered to be a fake, and Morris gets a line on where Meader might be hiding. Merrick beats Morris to Meader. Merrick accuses Meader of planning a double-cross and shoots him. As the shots ring out, Morris enters the building. Merrick is able to escape but loses the envelope containing the money. Inspector Lane believes that Morris is guilty of the scam and the murder. Merrick wants the money so that she and her escaped convict husband, Steve Cochran, can leave town. Morris thwarts Merrick and Cochran's attempts to steal the money. Cochran, in disguise, arranges to meet Morris in a restaurant. Morris sees through Cochran's disguise and asks about his marriage. Morris is able to verify that Merrick is Cochran's wife. Morris captures Cochran in Merrick's apartment. When Merrick arrives, Morris is able to convince him that he murdered Cochran. Merrick writes and signs a confession. He later is able to destroy the confession when Cochran revives and engages Morris in a rugged fight. As Morris finishes off Cochran, Lane, with his fellow police officers, break into the apartment and take Cochran into custody. As Lane is about to arrest Morris, Morris is able to trick Merrick into admitting that she is a thief and murderess.

Notes and Commentary: Steve Cochran was signed to a shared contract between Columbia and Samuel Goldwyn Productions. *Boston Blackie Booked on Suspicion* was his first picture for Columbia.

Review: "Merrick adds interest to this caper." *Motion Picture Guide*, Nash and Ross

Summation: Another good Boston Blackie caper with a delightful cat-and-mouse game between Chester Morris and Lynn Merrick. Merrick is a cool customer as a femme fatale and gives Morris a run for the money in the acting honors department. The film is well directed by Arthur Driefuss, who adroitly balances drama and comedy.

Boston Blackie's Rendezvous
Columbia (July 1945)

Strangler on the loose! Copper on the trail! Shocker on the screen!

Alternate Title: Blackie's Rendezvous

Cast: Boston Blackie, Chester Morris; Sally Brown, Nina Foch; James Cook, Steve Cochran; Inspector Farraday, Richard Lane; The Runt, George E. Stone; Detective Mathews, Frank Sully; Martha, Iris Adrian// Arthur Manleder, Harry Hayden; Hotel desk clerk, Dan Stowell; Doorman, Tom Kennedy; Patricia Powers, Adele Roberts; Steve Caveroni, Joe Devlin; Reporters, Frank Stevens, Perc Landers and Charles Jordan; Dr. Volkman, Philip Van Zandt; Chambermaid, Marilyn Johnson; Hotel Porter, Clarence Muse; Policemen, John Tyrell, Robert Williams and Joe Palma; Martha's cousins, Richard Alexander, Bing Conley and Charles Sullivan

Credits: Director, Arthur Dreifuss; Producer, Alexis Thurn-Taxis; Story, Fred Schiller; Screenwriter, Edward Dein; Editor, Aaron Stell; Art Director, Perry Smith; Set Decorator, Fay Babcock; Cinematographer, George B. Meehan, Jr.; Sound, Philip Faulkner; Musical Director, M.R. Bakaleinikoff

Production Dates: February 15, 1945–March 2, 1945

Running Time: 64 min.

Source: Based upon the character created by Jack Boyle

Story: Harry Hayden's nephew Steve Cochran has been diagnosed with an incurable mental condition. Cochran violently escapes from the sanitarium and breaks into Chester Morris' hotel suite. Morris offers to help Cochran if he returns to the sanitarium. Cochran chokes Morris into unconsciousness and takes some of his clothes. Cochran is looking for a taxi dancer, Nina Foch, whose picture he saw in a newspaper. Morris tries to stop Cochran but, complications ensue when Inspector Lane believes Morris is the strangler, and Foch believes that Cochran is Morris. Cochran takes Foch to Morris' apartment, where she realizes Cochran is the strangler. In trying to call for help, hotel desk clerk Dan Stovall tells Lane and Morris that someone is in Morris' suite. Lane and Morris break into the suite and are able to subdue Cochran.

Notes and Commentary: The working title for this film was "Surprise in the Night."

On one web site, it was stated that Steve Cochran's character name was Jimmy Casey. This is an erroneous statement. Cochran's character name was James Cook.

One major goof: after rendering Chester Morris unconscious, Steve Cochran puts on Morris' clothes which fit him perfectly. The problem being that Cochran is a much bigger man than Morris.

The music being played in the dance hall scene, at one point, is the theme music for the Blondie series.

This film marked the final appearance of the continuing character, Arthur Manleder. Manleder appeared in eight Boston Blackie episodes with Lloyd Corrigan, essaying the role six times. In *Rendezvous*, Boston Blackie explains his relationship with Manleder as the parole board member who helped him when he needed a friend.

Reviews: "Pretty good, especially Cochran." *Motion Picture Guide*, Nash and Ross
"Well-paced, well-acted killer-thriller." *Variety*, 08/22/45

Summation: A chilling Boston Blackie story with some good performances by Steve Cochran as the psychotic killer and Nina Foch as Cochran's intended victim. There is some politically incorrect comedy, by today's standards, from Chester Morris and George E. Stone as they attempt to stop Cochran's murder spree. Director Arthur Dreifuss does a fine job of balancing the suspense and humor.

A CLOSE CALL FOR BOSTON BLACKIE
Columbia (January 1946)

Blackie answers the call to arms ... and lands in the arms of the law!

Alternate Title: Lady of Mystery

Cast: Boston Blackie, Chester Morris; Gerry Peyton, Lynn Merrick; Inspector Farraday, Richard Lane; Detective Mathews, Frank Sully; The Runt, George E. Stone// John Peyton, Mark Roberts; Coroner, Emmett Vogan; Smiley Slade, Erik Rolf; Hack Hagan, Charles Lane; Mamie Kirwin, Claire Carleton; Milk woman, Ruth Warren; Blackie's cab driver, Brian O'Hara; Cab driver, Jack Gordon; Landlady, Kathryn Card; Harcourt, Russell Hicks; Janitor, George Lloyd; Policeman, John Tyrell; Josie, Doris Houck

Credits: Director, Lew Landers; Producer, John Stone; Story, Paul Yawitz; Screenwriter, Ben Markson; additional dialogue, Malcolm Stuart Boylan; Editor, Jerome Thoms; Art Directors, Carl Anderson and Jerome Pycha, Jr.; Set Decorator, Albert Rickerd; Cinematographer, Burnett Guffey; Sound, Philip Faulkner; Musical Director, Mischa Bakaleinikoff

Production Dates: October 1, 1945–October 13, 1945

Running Time: 60 min.

Source: Based upon the character created by Jack Boyle

Story: Chester Morris sees Lynn Merrick, a former girlfriend, being manhandled by two men and comes to her rescue. Merrick tells Morris that she left her baby in his apartment. Merrick wants to keep the baby away from her ex-convict husband, Mark Roberts. Roberts shows up at Morris apartment and demands the baby. Erik Rolf opens the apartment door and guns down Roberts. Rolf and Merrick are working a scam to pass off Charles Lane's baby as the grandson of Merrick's wealthy father-in-law. Morris discovers that the baby is a ringer because there's no birth certificate registered to Merrick and Roberts. From Merrick's father-in-law's lawyer, Russell Hicks, Morris learns that a note was received about the baby. Morris decides to impersonate Merrick's father-in-law. When Lane changes his mind about giving up his baby, Rolf shoots him. Morris shows up, in disguise, and tells Merrick that the baby isn't hers. When Morris sees Lane's dead body, Rolf pulls a gun. Morris and Rolf fight with Morris finally getting the upper hand. Rolf and Merrick are arrested.

Review: "An entertaining Boston Blackie vehicle made appealing by Morris' charm." *Motion Picture Guide*, Nash and Ross

"Good 'B' detective comedy." *Variety*, 02/20/46

Summation: This Boston Blackie entry is played primarily for comedy, and director Lew Landers keeps a light touch throughout. Chester Morris' performance is again on target as the glib ex-jewel thief. The rest of the cast chips in with good support. Lynn Merrick does not register as strong a femme fatale as she did in *Boston Blackie Booked on Suspicion* (Columbia, 1945). Erik Rolf makes a sinister and very effective villain.

THE PHANTOM THIEF
Columbia (May 1946)

All Blackie's got is a ghost of a chance ... 'cause a phantom's his only alibi!

Cast: Boston Blackie, Chester Morris; Anne Duncan, Jeff Donnell; Inspector Farraday, Richard Lane; Sandra, Dusty Anderson; The Runt, George E. Stone; Detective Mathews, Frank Sully; Dr. Nejino, Marvin Miller; Rex Duncan, Wilton Graff// Eddie Anderson, Murray Alper; Officer Kowalski, George Magrill; Police sergeant, Eddie Dunn; Dr. Nash, Forbes Murray; Dinny McGonagle, Tom Dillon; Waitress, Doris Houck; Elderly police officer, Pat O'Malley; Patrolman, John Tyrell; Second police sergeant, Eddie Fetherston; Jumbo Madigan, Joseph Crehan; Nurse, Adele Roberts; Policemen at Hospital, Charles Jordan and George Eldredge

Credits: Director, D. Ross Lederman, Producer, John Stone; Story, G.A. Snow; Screenwriters, Richard Wormser and Richard Weil; Additional Dialogue, Malcolm Stuart Boylan; Editor, Al Clark; Art Director, Robert Peterson; Set Decorator, George Montgomery; Cinematography, George B. Meehan, Jr.; Sound, George Cooper; Musical Director, Mischa Bakaleinikoff

Production Dates: January 7, 1946–January 21, 1946
Running Time: 65 min.
Source: Based upon the character created by Jack Boyle

Story: Jeff Donnell sends her chauffeur, Murray Alper, to retrieve some papers in a leather case from her doctor, Marvin Miller. Miller had been blackmailing Donnell, threatening to reveal that he never got their marriage annulled. Donnell, thinking that she was again single, had married Wilton Graff. When Alper sees the case containing a valuable necklace, he calls on his pal George E. Stone for help. Both men have to rely on Chester Morris to set things right. Miller tells Morris that Donnell is neurotic and is using séances to help cure her. Morris decides not to return the necklace until he sees an actual séance. Miller arranges one for Donnell with Graff, Morris, Stone and Alper present. During the séance, Alper is murdered. When Morris meets with Donnell, she tells him about being blackmailed by Miller. From pawnbroker Joseph Crehan, also an underworld figure, Morris learns that Graff was penniless when he married Donnell. Morris telephones Donnell and asks her to meet him at the pawnshop. Unbeknownst to Morris and Donnell, Graff was listening in on an extension. Morris tells Donnell the truth about Graff, and that he was a party to the blackmail scheme. Graff is at the window, listening, and fires a shot at Donnell. Donnell is rushed to a hospital. Graff is told that Donnell did not survive her wounds. Graff goes to Miller's office. Inspector Lane arrives and requests that he conduct a séance to ask Donnell to name her murderer. Morris confronts Miller and the two men fight, with Miller apparently knocking Morris out. During the séance, Donnell appears and names Graff as her murderer. Enraged, Graff pulls a gun and fires at Donnell, only hitting her reflection in the mirror. Donnell was unharmed, as the bullet fired by Graff in Miller's office missed. Graff blurts out that Miller is responsible for Alper's death. Graff tries to escape but is grabbed by Detective Frank Sully. Morris and Lane, working together, had already taken Miller into custody to allow Morris to conduct the séance.

Notes and Commentary: The working title for this film was "Boston Blackie's Private Ghost."

A January 1946 edition of the *Hollywood Reporter* stated that Jim Bannon would play a romantic lead in the film.

This marked the last appearance of Jumbo Madigan, who had appeared in five entries. Cy Kendall played the role three times, with Joseph Crehan handling the part twice.

Review: "Neat series entry with plenty of haunted-house comic relief from Stone." *1996 Movie & Video Guide*, Maltin

Summation: For once a Boston Blackie entry is a pure murder mystery, and it turns out to be a good one thanks to Richard Wormser's and Richard Weil's taut screenplay. Laughs are present, but only mildly intrusive. Acting is above par with Chester Morris a standout in the title role. Director D. Ross Lederman, known for his stint with western films, is at the helm and guides it through in an entertaining fashion.

BOSTON BLACKIE AND THE LAW
Columbia (December 1946)

Blackie waves a magic wand ... and a woman vanishes ... a murderer appears!

Alternate Title: Blackie and the Law

Cast: Boston Blackie, Chester Morris; Irene, Trudy Marshall; Dinah Moran, Constance Dowling; Inspector Farrady, Richard Lane; Detective Mathews, Frank Sully; John Lampau, Warren Ashe// Prisoner, Jessie Arnold; Warden Lund, Selmer Jackson; Prison guard operating siren, Chuck Hamilton; Peterson, Eddie Dunn; Jackson, Eddie Fetherston; Callahan, Kernan Cripps; Miss Burton, Maudie Prickett; Mephistopheles the Great, Eugene Borden; Cab driver, Frank O'Connor; Locksmith, Eddy Waller; Bank guard, Ralph Dunn; Andrews, Edward Keane; Harry Burton, Ted Hecht; Tom, Tom Kingston; Mr. Jones, William Newell; Syd, Syd Saylor; Coroner, Pat O'Malley; Runt, George E. Stone

Credits: Director, D. Ross Lederman; Producer, Ted Richmond; Screenplay, Harry J. Essex; Additional Dialogue, Malcolm Stuart Boylan; Editor, James Sweeney; Art Director, Charles Clague; Set Decorator, Bill Calvert; Cinematographer, George B. Meehan, Jr.; Musical Director, Mischa Bakaleinikoff

Production Dates: August 8, 1946–August 21, 1946

Running Time: 70 min.

Source: Based upon the character created by Jack Boyle

Story: Chester Morris goes to the women's prison for the Thanksgiving holiday to perform magic tricks. In is final trick, he asks for a volunteer to assist him. The volunteer will step into the booth and disappear and then Morris will make her reappear. Constance Dowling volunteers. Morris is unaware that she is a former magician's assistant and is familiar with the trick. Dowling is able to make a successful escape from prison. A note is found in Dowling's cell stating her ex-husband, Warren Ashe, is planning to marry his new assistant, Trudy Marshall. Dowling and Ashe were suspected of being responsible for a robbery-murder, but only Dowling was convicted. Meanwhile, Ashe has changed his stage name and is still performing. Morris confronts Ashe in his dressing room. While there Dowling arrives, gun in hand, and demands her share of the robbery money. During the altercation, the gun goes off, wounding Ashe in the hand. Dowling leaves the theater. Morris decides to impersonate

Ashe so that Dowling will come looking for him. Morris takes a key from Ashe and determines it is for a safe deposit box. In the box, Morris finds the robbery money. Dowling makes an unsuccessful attempt to take the money from Morris. He tells Marshall that Ashe and Dowling stole the money. Morris had been hiding Ashe in a friend's apartment, with George E. Stone to watch him. Stone is decoyed and knocked out and Ashe is murdered. Inspector Lane arrests Morris for the murder. In jail, Morris tells Marshall that the money is hidden in a magic box at the theater. Morris escapes from jail and goes there. Entering the theater, Morris hears a shot and finds Marshall, gun in hand, standing over Dowling's dead body. Morris determines that it was Marshall who also murdered Ashe. Marshall admits that she never loved Ashe and only wanted the money. Marshall holds the gun on Morris and calls Lane, planning to blame the murders on Morris. Lane arrives, planning to arrest Morris. Morris is able to trick a confession out of Marshall.

Notes and Commentary: The working title for this film was "Quicker Than the Eye."

Since Chester Morris was an amateur magician, he was able to gain permission from the Magician's Association to show how the "sawing the woman in half" magic trick worked. In the release print, the sequence does not appear. Morris does attempt to saw George E. Stone in half, but Stone topples the box to end the trick.

George E. Stone sports a mustache in this Boston Blackie entry.

Reviews: "Fairly entertaining." *Motion Picture Guide*, Nash and Ross

"Mediocre entry utilizing a distaff version of the ALIAS BOSTON BLACKIE plot." *1996 Movie & Video Guide*, Maltin

Summation: Entertaining Boston Blackie saga. The story moves nicely after we get past some prolonged, forced "comedy" with Frank Sully and a magician's box. Acting is par with Chester Morris still on target.

TRAPPED BY BOSTON BLACKIE
Columbia (May 1948)

Blackie crashes society ... to see how the other half kills!

Cast: Boston Blackie, Chester Morris; Doris Bradley, June Vincent; Inspector Farraday, Richard Lane; Joan Howell, Patricia White; Igor Bono, Edward Norris; Detective Mathews, Frank Sully; Sandra Doray, Fay Baker// Mrs. Helen Kenyon, Mary Currier; Claire Carter, Sarah Selby; Mason Carter, William Forrest; Mrs. Worthington, Helen Dickson; Mrs. Treadwell, Laura Treadwell; Party guest, Franklyn Farnum; Henry, Charles Jordan; Police Matron, Bryn Davis; Receptionist, Abigail Adams; Janitor, Frank O'Connor; Dunn, Pierre Watkin; Louis Gehrig, Ben Weldon

Credits: Director, Seymour Friedman; Producer, Rudolph C. Flothow; Story, Charles Marion and Edward Bock; Screenwriter, Maurice Tombragel; Editor, Dwight Caldwell; Art Director, George Brooks; Set Decorator, Louis Diage; Cinematographer, Philip Tannura; Musical Director, Mischa Bakaleinikoff

Production Dates: December 8, 1947–December 18, 1947

Running Time: 67 min.

Source: Based upon the character created by Jack Boyle

Story: Mary Currier's private detective husband, who was working on an important case, dies in a car crash. Her friends, Chester Morris and George E. Stone, convince Currier to run the agency. Needing detectives to act as guards at Sarah Selby's party, Morris and

Stone volunteer. Currier has Selby's niece take Morris and Stone to the party. Morris's main concern is to watch Selby's necklace. The necklace is used in a dance performed by ballet artist Edward Norris and his troupe. When the necklace is returned to Selby, she notices that it is an imitation. Inspector Richard Lane is called in to investigate. A search of the guests is initiated. Morris finds the necklace in a pocket of his coat and hides the necklace in a vase. Lane recognizes Morris and Stone. Before they can be arrested, Morris and Stone escape. The lights go out and a hand reaches into the vase and takes the necklace. Currier is questioned by Lane and is told that he believes her husband was murdered. In disguise, Morris and Stone go to Vincent's apartment. Vincent's friend Patricia White enters and Morris finds the missing necklace in White's wrap. Morris wants to keep the necklace to draw the guilty parties to him. The necklace is hidden in a file cabinet in Currier's office. Morris believes that either Norris or his assistant, Fay Baker, could be involved in the theft, as both seem to be indifferent to retrieving the necklace. Stone searches Baker's apartment and finds evidence that she and a notorious fence, Ben Welden, were suspected for a major jewel robbery but released for lack of evidence. Morris visits Welden and finds Baker, gun in hand, waiting for him. Morris makes a deal to sell the necklace to Baker that night in a cemetery. Baker shows up with Selby's husband, William Forrest, who demands the necklace. Morris tells Forrest and Baker the necklace is now in a safe in Currier's office. Later that night, Morris and Stone go to Currier's office and find Forrest and Baker trying to break into the safe. There is a scuffle, but Forrest gets the upper hand and calls Lane. Forrest tries to blame Morris for the theft. Morris responds that he would not need to use a blowtorch to open the safe when he has the combination. Forrest bolts. Lane orders Forrest to stop and shoots him when he ignores the command. Forrest was working in a robbery ring with Baker and Welden. Forrest's position in society would enable Baker to get into the richest homes to steal jewels for Welden to fence. Baker also states that Forrest tampered with Currier's husband's car when he was starting to get too close to them.

Notes and Commentary: This was Seymour Friedman's first solo directorial effort.

We finally find out that William is Inspector Farraday's first name.

This was the last appearance of George E. Stone in the role of The Runt. Stone played the part in 12 features. Stone' s mustache was shaved off for this final effort.

Reviews: "The film follows formula. Morris and Stone put on disguises, once as an older couple, and that is so old hat in the series that the story sags a bit." *Motion Picture Guide*, Nash and Ross

"Standard melodrama in the 'Blackie' series." *Variety*, 04/28/48

Summation: A good Boston Blackie mystery with the villain's identity well hidden. The performances are up to par, with Chester Morris still glib and breezy as ever. Seymour Friedman's first directorial stint is very much on target, guiding this intriguing convoluted plot to its satisfying conclusion.

BOSTON BLACKIE'S CHINESE VENTURE
Columbia (March 1949)

Blackie catches a red-head red-handed!

Alternate Title: Chinese Venture

Cast: Boston Blackie, Chester Morris; Mei Ling, Maylia; Inspector Farraday, Richard

Boston Blackie's Chinese Venture (1949) scene card (left to right) Louis Van Rooten, Joan Woodbury, Chester Morris, George Lloyd.

Lane; Les, Don McGuire; Red, Joan Woodbury; The Runt, Sid Tomack; Detective Mathews, Frank Sully; Pop Gerard, Charles Arnt; Craddock, Louis Van Rooten; Wong Chung Shee, Philip Ahn// Henry, George Lloyd; Fantan players, Eddie Lee, George Lee and William Yip; Chinese hatchet man, James B. Leong; Ah Hing, Benson Fong; Rolfe, Peter Brocco; McAllister, Henry Strang; Reiber, Edgar Dearing; Police chemist, Fred Sears; Cynical tourist, Robert Williams; Officer Jim, Pat O'Malley; Theater ticket taker, Victor Sen Yung

   Credits: Director, Seymour Friedman; Producer, Rudolph C. Flothow; Screenwriter, Maurice Tombragel; Editor, Richard Fantl; Art Director, Paul Palmentola; Set Decorator, James Crowe; Cinematographer, Vincent Farrar; Musical Director, Mischa Bakaleinikoff

   Production Dates: May 18, 1948–June 5, 1948

   Running Time: 59 min.

   Source: Based upon the character created by Jack Boyle

   Story: Chester Morris and his pal, Sid Tomack, are seen by Maylia leaving a Chinese laundry. When Maylia enters she finds the owner has been murdered. Maylia, believing Morris to be innocent, asks him to investigate the murder. Morris learns that the owner had called nightclub owner Louis Van Rooten and told him that a valuable package had been left in the laundry and was picked up from his club. In the club, Morris sees Van Rooten give a valuable broach to Joan Woodbury. Morris follows Woodbury to the local movie theater. Morris learns that Woodbury acts as a shill for Don McGuire's Chinatown tour. During the tour Woodbury disappears. Woodbury delivers jewelry to an imprisoned diamond cutter, Peter Brocco. At the conclusion of the tour, McGuire buys a special blend of tea from shop clerk Benson Fong. Morris is able to switch boxes of tea with McGuire and finds diamonds in the package. Morris confronts Van Rooten, only to have Van Rooten murdered right before his eyes. The second murder brings Inspector Richard Lane back to Chinatown. Morris and Tomack hide in the movie theater where they spot Woodbury leaving. Morris and Tomack investigate and discover Brocco. Theater owner Charles Arnt gets the drop on Morris and Tomack and leaves them to be guarded by Brocco. Brocco tells Morris that Arnt is the murderer. Morris then bests Brocco in a fistfight. Arnt returns and a gunfight ensues. A bullet from Arnt's gun hits Brocco. The sound of the gunshots bring Lane, who arrests Arnt. Woodbury is unsuccessful in leaving Chinatown with another box of tea with stolen recut jewels.

Notes and Commentary: The working titles for the film were "Boston Blackie's Honor" and "Boston Blackie's Chinese Adventure."

Columbia used the movie theater in this episode to advertise two of their films, *The Prince of Thieves* (January 1948) with Jon Hall, and *The Mating of Millie* (April 1948) with Glenn Ford and Evelyn Keyes.

Two of Charlie Chan's screen offspring appeared in the film: Benson Fong played Tommy Chan, "number three son," with Sidney Toler at Monogram; Victor Sen Yung was "number two son," Jimmy, with Sidney Toler at both 20th Century–Fox and Monogram; Sen Yung was also Tommy in five features with Roland Winters at Monogram.

Review: "A surprise ending. Plenty of action." *Motion Picture Guide*, Nash and Ross "Last *Blackie* film is one of the weakest." *Blockbuster Video Guide to Movies and Videos 1995*, Castell

Summation: Neat Boston Blackie mystery. Chester Morris still sparkles, but Sid Tomack is a disappointment as The Runt. Tomack had neither the sensitivity nor the vulnerability for the part. All Tomack had going for him was his short stature. Seymour Friedman scores again in his second Boston Blackie directorial effort, as he keeps the story continually on the move.

Bulldog Drummond

"Out of the fog ... out of the night ... comes another Bulldog Drummond story"

This was the introduction the famed soldier of fortune and adventurer to radio audiences on April 6, 1941. We need to go back 21 years to H.C. McNeile's novel, *Bulldog Drummond*. McNeile used the pseudonym "Sapper." (During World War I, a sapper was a term used in the British army for a soldier who performs combat engineering duties that may include demolitions and the laying or clearing of minefields.) The character of Bulldog Drummond was once a captain in His Majesty's Royal Loamshires, but was now bored with life. Placing an ad, Drummond advertised his willingness to participate in some exciting project. A damsel in distress, Phyllis Benton, plunged him into an adventure, pitting him against one of the great villains of fiction, Carl Peterson. Phyllis, by the second novel, became Drummond's wife. Peterson is assisted in his schemes by his wife/mistress Irma Peterson. (Peterson and Irma's relationship is never made clear.) It took four novels before Drummond finally killed Peterson. In the novel, *Female of the Species* (1928), Irma is unsuccessful in exacting her revenge.

This popular adventurer was brought to the screen in *Bulldog Drummond* (Astra-National, 1922) with Carlyle Blackwell in the lead. In the film, Drummond is portrayed as a suave, handsome individual. In McNeile's novels, Drummond was considered homely, perhaps ugly, but with a charming smile and beautiful eyes. To this author's thinking, the perfect Drummond might have been Victor McLaglen. Drummond hit his stride with *Bulldog Drummond* (United Artists, 1929) with Ronald Colman as the suave adventurer. Colman would repeat the role five years later in *Bulldog Drummond Strikes Back* (20th Century, 1935). McNeile wrote Drummond novels until his death in 1937. In 1938, author Gerald Fairle took over and wrote seven additional novels, the last being published in 1954. In 1937, Paramount thought the time was right for a "B"-movie series. Ray Milland received the nod for the first entry, *Bulldog Drummond Escapes* (Paramount, 1937). John Howard took over for six subsequent entries. Throughout the series, Drummond and Phyllis were trying to wed and finally pulled it off in *Bulldog Drummond's Bride* (Paramount, 1939).

Drummond would next be heard on radio, with a series aired over the Mutual network and starring George Coulouris. The initial 13 episodes were based in England, but the 14th moved the adventurer to America. The introduction was changed to "Out of the night ... out of the fog comes Bulldog Drummond in another American adventure." Santos Ortega took over the role from May 25, 1942, until March 8, 1943, when he was replaced by Ned Weaver. Weaver played Drummond until the series ended, on March 28, 1954.

After an eight-year absence, Drummond would return to the screen with *Bulldog Drummond at Bay* (Columbia, 1947), with Australian actor Ron Randell in the lead. This would be his American screen debut. Only the first few chapters were taken from the novel;

the rest was Columbia screenwriter imagination. A second entry was released four months later, *Bulldog Drummond Strikes Back* (Columbia, 1947). This time only a few pages from the novel were used. This was not a remake of the Ronald Colman film. Although Randell made an acceptable Drummond, he was relocated to the Lone Wolf series. The series moved to 20th Century–Fox where Tom Conway took over the lead for two adventures in 1948. Back in November 1946, United Artists had purchased the rights to various Bulldog Drummond titles. UA then gave the rights to Edward Small Productions, which then assigned the rights to Bernard Small, Edward's son, and Ben Pivar. Small co-produced the two Columbia entries before Small and Pivar teamed up for the two Fox releases. Drummond stayed off the screen until Walter Pidgeon essayed the role in *Calling Bulldog Drummond* (Metro-Goldwyn-Mayer, 1951). An attempt was made to revive Drummond on the Douglas Fairbanks, Jr., anthology television program, *The Reingold Theater*. Robert Beatty took over the role in the half-hour drama, "The Ludlow Affair" (January 1957). At the end, Fairbanks promised more adventures, but none were forthcoming.

Ten years would pass before Drummond would again return to the screen. This time he was a British Agent who has to thwart the plans of master villain Carl Petersen (note the change in spelling). The film was *Deadlier Than the Male* (Universal, 1967) with Richard Johnson as Drummond. This was an unsuccessful attempt to jump on the James Bond craze even though a second adventure, *Some Girls Do* (United Artists, 1969) followed.

The Drummond character remained dormant until Moonstone Comics brought him back in 2004. Moonstone went back to the charter's roots. Again, disenchanted with life and desiring adventure, Drummond places an ad and Phyllis leads him into direct conflict with Carl Peterson. Outmaneuvered through most of the story, Drummond, nevertheless, defeats Peterson and causes his death. The major surprise of the narrative is that Phyllis and Irma are one and the same. Drummond, who had a sexual liaison with Phyllis, doesn't care and wants to be with Irma/Phyllis.

BULLDOG DRUMMOND AT BAY
Columbia (May 1947)

The new Bulldog Drummond comes out shooting....

Cast: Doris Hamilton, Anita Louise; Algy Longworth, Pat O'Moore; Seymour, Terry Kilburn; Inspector McIvar, Holmes Herbert; Shannon, Lester Matthews; Meredith, Leonard Mudie; and introducing Ron Randell as Bulldog Drummond// Richard Hamilton, Oliver Thorndike; Nannie, Aminta Dyne; Peter, Jimmy Aubrey; Barmaid, Eleanor Counts; Hatcheck girl, Olive Larkin; Hotel clerk, Clyde Cook

Credits: Director, Sidney Salkow; Producers, Louis B. Appleton, Jr., and Bernard Small; Screenwriter, Frank Gruber; Editor, Aaron Stell; Art Director, Charles Clague; Set Decorators, Wilbur Menefee and Sidney Clifford; Cinematography, Philip Tannura; Musical Director, Mischa Bakaleinikoff

Production Dates: December 9, 1946–December 21, 1946

Source: Based upon the novel by SAPPER

Running Time: 70 min.

Story: Ron Randell is vacationing in a cottage in Medwick when a stone comes crashing through a front window. A wounded man, Oliver Thorndike, threw the stone. Randell races outside to find the culprit when Lester Matthews and a confederate come on the scene wielding guns. Randell acts like an itinerant farmer. Matthews searches the house and, finding nothing, he leaves. At the edge of the woods he finds the wounded man who tells him that he'll never find the jewels. Meanwhile, Randell finds part of a claim check in the broken window's debris. The next day, Matthews and jeweler Leonard Mudie realize who Randell is. He sends his secretary, Anita Louise, to find a clue to the whereabouts of the jewels. Randell gains an ally in cub reporter Terry Kilburn, who comes to the cottage to cover the story of Randell's broken window. Louise tries to send Randell on a false trail but Randell instead meets an old comrade, Pat O'Moore, who is more than willing to help. Randell calls Inspector Holmes Herbert and relays a notation he found on the claim check: A-5. From Herbert's reaction, Randell surmises that A-5 is a Scotland Yard operative. Matthews takes Louise and some men to search Randell's cottage. In the process, one of Randell's dogs is killed and his housekeeper, Aminta Dyne, is drugged. Randell secretly goes to see Louise and she tells him that Thorndike is her brother. Matthews overhears most of the conversation between Randell and Louise. He then plans to have Randell find the jewels, after which Louise will lead them to the location. Randell finally gives the claim check to Herbert and, by snooping on his desk, learns the code is for a Sambo doll. Randell arranges to pick up a decoy Sambo doll, which is taken by force by Matthews. Matthews also takes Louise to meet with Thorndike, hoping to learn the location of the jewels. Randell has Kilburn follow on his motorcycle, with Randell and O'Moore in pursuit. Thorndike inadvertently reveals where the Sambo doll with the jewels is hidden. Wanting the jewels for himself, Matthews kills Mudie. Matthews speeds away, chased by Randell, O'Moore, Kilburn, Louise and Thorndike. After Matthews obtains the jewels, he is confronted by Randell, who punches Matthews in the jaw. Herbert arrives on the scene to take Matthews into custody. Herbert tells Randell that Scotland Yard is grateful that Thorndike is saved, and, he believes, so is Louise.

Notes and Commentary: Sapper was a pseudonym for H.C. McNeille.

The film is based on H.C. McNeille's novel, *Bulldog Drummond at Bay* (Hodder & Stroughton, 1935). The opening scene to the one involving the drugging of Nannie and the murder of Drummond's dog is taken directly from the book. The rest is pure Columbia screenwriter's invention. The novel had Drummond's adversaries attempting to gain control of plans for a deadly gas, and an advanced airplane instead of jewels.

Review: "Quickie entry." *1996 Movie & Video Guide*, Maltin

Summation: This is a neat mystery-drama, heralding the return of Bulldog Drummond to the screen after an eight-year absence. Ron Randell is very acceptable in the title role. Pat O'Moore is fine as Drummond's pal, Algy Longworth. Terry Kilburn, thankfully, is not a liability as Seymour, a cub reporter. Anita Louise is as lovely as always. She makes a fetching heroine and acts the part capably. Lester Matthews is properly villainous. Director Sidney Salkow does what he's supposed to do: keep the story moving at a brisk pace.

Bulldog Drummond Strikes Back

Columbia (September 1947)

Beauty against beauty with Drummond in the middle ... of murder!

Cast: Bulldog Drummond, Ron Randell; Ellen Curtiss, Gloria Henry; Algy Longworth,

Pat O'Moore; Ellen Curtiss #2, Anabel Shaw; Seymour, Terry Kilburn; Inspector McIver, Holmes Herbert; Cedric Mason, Wilton Graff; William Cosgrove, Matthew Boulton// Inspector Sanderson, Carl Harbord; Hat check girl, Lee Anderson; Bartender, Eric Wilton; Vincent Cummings, Barry Bernard; Sergeant Schubeck, Leslie Denison; Williams, Frank Marlowe; Nanny, Elspeth Dudgeon

Credits: Director, Frank McDonald; Producers, Louis B. Appleton, Jr., and Bernard Small; Screenwriters, Edna and Edward Anhalt; Adaptation, Lawrence Edward Taylor; Editor, Richard Fantl; Art Director, Robert Peterson; Set Decorator, George Montgomery; Cinematographer, Henry Freulich; Musical Director, Mischa Bakaleinikoff

Production Dates: May 6, 1947–May 15, 1947

Source: Based upon the novel by SAPPER

Running Time: 65 min.

Story: Scotland Yard Inspector Carl Harbord is investigating a new racket in which false heirs lay claim to unclaimed estates. Harbord calls on lawyer Wilton Graff for information. Harbord finds two women, Anabel Shaw and Gloria Henry, both claiming to be heirs to an estate worth £75,000. Harbord runs into his good friend Ron Randell, and tells him he's on an important case. He then asks Randell to come to his house that night. Randall arrives with his good friends Pat O'Moore and Terry Kilburn. When Harbord doesn't answer the doorbell, Randell looks through the study window to find Harbord dead

Bulldog Drummond Strikes Back (1947) scene card — Gloria Henry and Ron Randell.

and the door to a closet closing. Randell enters the room, rummages through Harbord's briefcase and finds an envelope with birth certificates for the two claimants. Randell also finds Henry in the closet. Henry swears she didn't shoot Harbord, but merely hid in the closet after the shot. Randell decides to help Henry and has O'Moore and Kilburn take her to his apartment. Randell arranges to have Henry and Shaw meet. Shaw denounces Henry as an impostor and leaves. Henry still insists that she is the rightful heir. Henry has an appointment to meet with Graff, but Randell goes instead. At Graff's office, Randell meets the uncle of the heir, Matthew Boulton, who insists that Shaw is the rightful heir. Randell spreads the rumor that he is in possession of important papers concerning the case. That night, two men, Barry Bernard and Frank Marlowe, break into Randell's apartment. Randell and O'Moore are there waiting. A fistfight ensues but ends when Bernard pulls a gun and the intruders quickly leave. Henry, who is a guest in Randell's apartment, is missing. O'Moore sees a hotel key that had been dropped during the scuffle. Randell and O'Moore go to the hotel and rescue Henry. Henry tells Randell that her old nanny, Elspeth Dudgeon, would confirm her identity. Randell arranges to have Inspector Holmes Herbert meet them at Dudgeon's cottage. Boulton overhears the conversation and Shaw, Graff and he decide to attend the confrontation. When all parties have assembled, Dudgeon identifies Henry as the true heir. Randell then proves that Dudgeon is lying. Dudgeon confesses that she was bribed to name Henry and Shaw is the true heir to the estate. Herbert is interested in arresting the murderer of Harbord. Henry then breaks down and implicates Graff in the scheme. Randell proves Graff is the murderer. Graff tries to escape but is victim to a knockout punch from Randell. Randell and Shaw plan to have breakfast together.

Notes and Commentary: The only plot thread used by screenwriters Edna and Edward Anhalt from H.C. McNeille's *Bulldog Drummond Strikes Back* (Doubleday, Doran & Company, 1933) was the murder of Sanderson that launched Hugh Drummond on his latest adventure. In the book, he thwarted a monstrous plot to undermine England's financial standing.

After this entry, the Bulldog Drummond saga now moved to 20th Century–Fox for two episodes, *13 Lead Soldiers* (1948) and *The Challenge* (1948). Tom Conway took over the role of Drummond. Of course, Algy Longworth was on hand. Also, Terry Kilburn was signed to reprise his role of Seymour. Rather than revert back to Neilsen as had been in the films of the '30s, the Scotland Yard inspector was still McIvar.

Reviews: "Uninspired occasion." *The Columbia Story*, Hirshhorn

"Pedestrian entry." *1996 Movie & Video Guide*, Maltin

"Teems with good times and snappy action." *Blockbuster Video Movies and Videos, 1995*, Castell

Summation: This time out we have a real murder-mystery with the culprits finally identified in the closing minutes of the film. Ron Randell handles both the action and the acting in fine style. His two leading ladies, Gloria Henry and Anabel Shaw, are beautiful and fulfill their acting requirements adequately. Screenwriters Edna and Edward Anhalt provide director Frank McDonald with an engaging story which unspools nicely. A good show.

Captain Blood

Prolific author Rafael Sabatini followed his extremely popular work *Scaramouche* (1921) with another rousing classic, *Captain Blood* (1922). Physician Peter Blood, former adventurer, has the misfortune to treat a patient who happened to be an enemy of the English government. Sentenced to be hanged, Blood's punishment is commuted; he is to be sent to the Caribbean to work as a slave. While Spanish forces attack the town, Blood and a number of convict-slaves take possession of the Spanish ship. Blood quickly becomes the most feared pirate in the Caribbean. With a change of command in England, Blood saves an important British colony from the French, is pardoned and becomes the colony's governor.

Captain Blood came to the screen in *Captain Blood* (Vitagraph, 1924) with J. Warren Kerrigan in the title role. Sabatini came up with two additional novels, *Captain Blood Returns* (a.k.a. *The Chronicles of Captain Blood*) (1931) and *The Fortunes of Captain Blood* (1936). Warner Bros. produced the definitive version of Sabatini's novel, *Captain Blood* (1935) which made a star of the then-unknown Errol Flynn.

Captain Blood was off the screen until Louis Hayward essayed the role in *The Fortunes of Captain Blood* (Columbia, 1950). Hayward was no stranger to swashbuckling epics with *The Man in the Iron Mask* (United Artists, 1939), *The Son of Monte Cristo* (United Artists, 1940), *The Return of Monte Cristo* (Columbia, 1946), *The Black Arrow* (Columbia, 1948) and *Captain Sirocco* (Film Classics, 1949) under his belt. Patricia Medina would co-star as the object of Blood's affections, Isabelita (or Dona Isabella), in the series. Between *Fortunes* and *Captain Pirate* (Columbia, 1952), Hayward and Medina would appear together in *The Lady and the Bandit* (Columbia, 1951) and *The Lady in the Iron Mask* (20th Century–Fox, 1952). After *Captain Pirate*, Hayward would concentrate primarily on television, appearing in one additional swashbuckler, *The Highwayman* (NBC, 1958).

In 2009, SLG Comics began publishing an adaptation of Sabatini's novel. Two issues are now available. The goal is to complete the saga in five issues. It has been announced that, in 2011, Warner Bros. will release a remake of their classic adventure, with a difference. It seems that Captain Blood will somehow be launched into outer space.

FORTUNES OF CAPTAIN BLOOD

Columbia (May 1950)

Greatest of Sabatini thrillers — on the screen for the first time!

Cast: Captain Peter Blood, Louis Hayward; Isabelita, Patricia Medina; Marquis de Riconete, George Macready; Carmilio, Alfonso Bedoya; Pepita Maria Rosados, Dona Drake; George Fairfax, Lowell Gilmore; Captain Alvarado, Wilson Graff; King Charles II, Curt

Bois; Tom Mannering, Lumsden Hare; Billy Bragg, William Bevan; Will Ward, Harry Cording; Andrew Hardy, Duke York; Swede, Sven Hugo Borg; Antonio Viamonte, Martin Garralaga; Nat Russell, James Fairfax; Smitty, Charles Irwin; Kenny Jensen, Terry Kilburn; Miguel Gonzales, Alberto Morin; Papa Rosados, Nick Volpe// Quinn, Charles Stevens; Seaman, Ethan Laidlaw; Prison guard, Trevor Bardette; Spanish officer, Nestor Paiva; Lieutenant, Paul Marion; Salto, Julian Rivero; Valdez, Donald Murphy

Credits: Director, Gordon Douglas; Assistant Director, Mel Dellar; Producer, Harry Joe Brown; Screenwriters, Michael Hogan, Robert Libott and Frank Burt; Editor, Gene Havlick; Art Director, George Brooks; Set Decorator, Frank Tuttle; Cinematographer, George E. Diskant; Gowns, Jean Louis; Makeup, Clay Campbell; Hair Stylist, Helen Hunt; Sound, Jack Goodrich; Musical Score, Paul Sawtell; Musical Director, Morris Stoloff

Production Dates: November 8, 1949–December 10, 1949

Source: Based on the novel by Rafael Sabatini

Running Time: 91 min.

Story: Dr. Louis Hayward was falsely imprisoned by the English and was sent to the Caribbean as a slave. After managing not only his own escape but others as well, Hayward became the most feared pirate in the Caribbean. King Curt Bois of Spain instructs Marquis George Macready to capture Hayward. In an attempt to obtain provisions, Hayward sends men ashore, not knowing that his men are walking into a trap set by slave trader Lowell Gilmore. All the men except Charles Irvin are captured and imprisoned as slaves, forced to dive in shark-infested waters for pearls. Hayward assumes the role of a fruit peddler to find a way to free his men. Arousing suspicion, Gilmore has Hayward captured and is about to kill him when Macready's niece, Patricia Medina, arrives. Medina wants to return to Spain, and she wants Gilmore to take her. Macready had previously warned Gilmore to stay away from Medina, and he has had his men follow her. Thanks to Hayward's expertise with a sword, the trio escapes to hide in William Bevan's inn. Bevan recognizes Hayward, and tells Gilmore. Gilmore wants Bevan to tell Macready when he can capture Hayward. Bevan refuses to be an informer. Through a ruse and a fierce battle, Hayward sets his men free. Macready captures Gilmore and Bevan. Gilmore tells Macready that Hayward is on the island. Bevan, though tortured, refuses to tell Macready where Hayward is. Medina, who wanted Hayward to take her away, tells Macready how to capture Hayward. Afterwards, Medina realizes she has made a mistake and hurries to warn Hayward. Macready sails in his 40-gun vessel to attack Hayward's ship. Warned by Medina, Hayward has his men go ashore. When Macready boards Hayward's ship, Hayward and his men swim to Macready's vessel and capture it. Macready, in command of the ship, decides to ram the vessel, but Hayward's men send a barrage of cannonballs into the ship, sinking it, with Macready on board. Hayward plans to continue his fight to promote freedom. Medina plans to stay on the island to make it a free country. Hayward tells Medina that he will return some day.

Notes and Commentary: Little is found in this screenplay from the novel, *The Fortunes of Captain Blood* (Grosset & Dunlap, 1936). There is the Marquis de Riconete, an enemy of Captain Blood's, who appeared in the story *The Dragon's Jaw*. Blood only outwits the marquis. George Fairfax and Isabelita appear in the final story, *The Eloping Hidalga*, as eloping lovers. When Fairfax's true colors are shown, Blood is able to return the very young Isabelita to her family. Fairfax's plan to turn Blood over to the Marquis de Riconte is upset. Fairfax sails from Isabelita's hometown before her family can exact vengeance. The chronicles of Blood being sold into slavery in the Caribbean and his decision to become a pirate are revisited in each Sabatini novel.

In the credits, Charles Irwin's character name is listed as Smitty, but is called "Scotty" throughout the film.

Reviews: "Misfortunes might have been a more appropriate label to pin onto Michael Hogan, Robert Libott and Frank Burt's enervating adaptation of Rafael Sabatini's stirring adventure." *The Columbia Story*, Hirshhorn

"Yet another rehash of familiar material." *Motion Picture Guide*, Nash and Ross

"An okay programmer for the general action market." *Variety*, 05/17/50

Summation: This is a rousing swashbuckler, albeit on a small budget and certainly not in the same league with Errol Flynn's *Captain Blood* (Warner Bros., 1935), but entertaining nevertheless. Louis Hayward is in fine form as the hero, with George Macready properly villainous and Patricia Medina very attractive. Gordon Douglas's direction is on target with the battle scenes a highlight of the picture.

CAPTAIN PIRATE
Columbia (August 1952)

Passions run hot and blood runs cold

Alternate Title: Captain Blood, Fugitive

Cast: Dr. Peter Blood, Louis Hayward; Dona Isabella, Patricia Medina; Hilary Evans, John Sutton; Angus McVickers, Charles Irwin; Easterling, Ted de Corsia; Governor Henry Carlyle, Rex Evans; Amanda, Malú Gatica; Tomas Velasquez, George Givot; Manuelito, Robert McNeeley; Madame Duval, Nina Koshetz; Col. Ramsey, Lester Matthews; Swede, Sven Hugo Borg; Don Ramon, Sandro Giglio; Viceroy, Ian Wolfe; Egyptian, Jay Novello; Coulevain, Maurice Marsac; Celeste, Geneviève Aumont; General Chavez, Mario Siletti; Lieutenant, Robert Bice// Ramsey's Overseer, Harry Cording; Brag, Reed Howes; Turk, Martin Garralaga; Cabin Boy, Davis Hammond; Waitress, Charlita; Martinique policeman, Ben Welden; Dr. Le Grand, Franklyn Farnum

Credits: Director, Ralph Murphy; Assistant Director, Milton Feldman; Producer, Harry Joe Brown; Assistant to producer, Herbert Stewart; Screenwriters, Robert Libott, John Meredyth Lucas and Frank Burt; Editor, Gene Havlick; Art Director, George Brooks; Set Decorator, Frank Tuttle; Cinematographer, Charles Lawton, Jr.; Gowns, Jean Louis; Makeup, Clay Campbell; Hair Stylist, Helen Hunt; Technicolor Color Consultant, Francis Cugat; Sound, Jack Goodrich; Musical Score, George Duning; Musical Director, Morris Stoloff

Song: "Largo al factotum" (Rossini), sung by Malú Gatica

Production Dates: mid August 1951–early September 1951

Source: Based upon the novel *Captain Blood Returns* by Rafael Sabatini

COLOR by TECHNICOLOR

Running Time: 85 min.

Story: Having been pardoned by the English government for his career as a pirate, Louis Hayward resumes his career as a physician, practicing in the West Indies. Hayward is set to marry Patricia Medina. John Sutton, a rival suitor for Medina's hand, brings word that Hayward has returned to his pirating ways. Hayward is arrested and Sutton is responsible for transporting Hayward to England for trial. Medina, realizing Hayward would not receive a fair trial, arranges for his old pirate crew to take over Sutton's vessel and free Hayward.

Captain Pirate (1952) scene card — (left) Louis Hayward and Patricia Medina (center) — Louis Hayward and John Sutton), (lower right) Louis Hayward and John Sutton.

Hayward is determined to find out who's using his name and finally learns that it's a French pirate, Maurice Marsac. Medina has been arrested for aiding Hayward and has been imprisoned in Puerto Bello. Hayward also discovers that Marsac plans to raid Puerto Bello and that Sutton is in league with Marsac. Hayward, in disguise, reaches Puerto Bello first and persuades Viceroy Ian Wolfe to allow him to set up cannons to defend the city. Sutton arrives and tells Wolfe that Hayward is a notorious pirate. Wolfe is shot by Sutton when he allows Hayward to carry out his battle plan. Hayward's strategy works. Marsac and his ship are destroyed. Sutton tries to escape but is chased by Hayward. The two men fight and Hayward emerges victorious. Hayward and Medina finally marry.

Notes and Commentary: The working title for this film was "Captain Blood Returns." Reportedly based on the Sabatini novel, *Captain Blood Returns* (Grosset & Dunlap, 1930), only a few incidents were used. Captain Blood does defend a town from invasion by sinking his own ship to block the entrance to the harbor, and then firing a cannon from the shore, sinking the vessel. Captain Blood, using his wits to set two captors against each other, is used, but modified, in the film. Only two supporting characters find their way to the screen: Easterling, a cruel rival pirate, and Coulevain, originally a corrupt French governor but reworked to become a pirate. Wearing a disguise, Captain Blood uses the alias Peter Vandermeer in the film as he did in the novel. The framework of having another pirate assume the identity was lifted from "The Pretender," one of the stories from *The Fortunes of Captain Blood* (Grosset & Dunlap, 1936). In the original story, the perpetrator was never named.

In the flashback sequence, footage from *Fortunes of Captain Blood* was used. The flashback was in black and white, as was *Fortunes*.

Although the story takes place in 1690, Malú Gatica sings "Largo al factotum" from *The Barber of Seville*. The problem: Rossini wrote the opera in 1816.

Reviews: "As period adventures went, this was par-for-the-course." *The Columbia Story*, Hirshhorn

"Average adventure yarn. Good action scenes and likable performances by the principals." *Motion Picture Guide*, Nash and Ross

"A conventionally contrived swashbuckler. It measures an acceptable feature material for the general action situation." *Variety*, 07/23/52

Summation: This is a rousing sequel to *Fortunes of Captain Blood*. Plenty of action helps keep the story on the move. Louis Hayward makes a striking figure as the stalwart hero. Patricia Medina shines as Hayward's lady faire. John Sutton is hissable as the jealous suitor for Medina's hand. The use of Technicolor enhances the story.

Counterspy

Washington calling Counterspy.... Washington calling Counterspy

Harding, counterspy, calling Washington ... Harding, counterspy, calling Washington

[There would then be an explanation of a "counterspy":]

[On ABC] A counterspy is a United States undercover agent whose duty it is to smash the professional enemy spies operating in our midst. Imagine the ace counterspy of them all as David Harding.

[On NBC] United States Counterspies, especially appointed to investigate and combat the enemies of our country, both home and abroad

[On the Mutual Network] Program especially transcribed to help investigate and combat the enemies home and abroad

Counterspy was the brain child of Phillips H. Lord, who had been successful with two previous real-life crime dramas, *Gang Busters* and *Mr. District Attorney*. In the beginning, David Harding (with his assistant, Harry Peters) thwarted threats from the Axis powers. After World War II, they had to deal with Cold War activities. Finally, they addressed all manner of illegal activities, e.g., illegal alcohol, diamond theft, postal theft, arson and narcotics. Lord kept his subject matter topical with stories of rackets that targeted the families of dead heroes and a female spy. *Counterspy* aired these stories just prior to having them break in the headlines. A favorite story of this author is "Case of the Fight against Narcotics," in which the then recently enacted Boggs Act (1951) played a major part in the successful conclusion of the story. The show ran for better than 15 years, beginning on May 18, 1942 on ABC, moving to NBC in 1950 and finally to the Mutual network in 1953. The final show was broadcast on November 29, 1957. Don MacLaughlin played Harding and Mandel Kramer was Peters.

In 1950, Columbia decided to launch a series based on the radio program and chose Howard St. John to play Harding and actor-director Fred Sears to take the role of Peters. St. John had been a stage actor from 1925 until his screen debut in *Shockproof* (Columbia, 1949), followed by *The Undercover Man* (Columbia, 1949), *Customs Agent* (Columbia, 1950) and *711 Ocean Drive* (Columbia, 1950). This belied St. John's billing in *Counterspy* as listed in the opening credits as "introducing Howard St. John as David Harding." St. John's film career lasted until 1969. His most memorable role was that of General Bullmoose in *Li'l Abner* (Paramount, 1959), a role he originated on the Broadway stage. Fred Sears was a prolific director (54 films) and actor (72 appearances). *The Return of Rusty* (Columbia, 1946) was his first acting role; his last was as an offscreen narrator in *Crash Landing* (Columbia, 1958). Sears's first directorial assignment was *Desert Vigilante* (Columbia, 1949); his last was *Ghost of China Sea* (Columbia, 1958).

DAVID HARDING, COUNTERSPY
Columbia (July 1950)

Behind the headlines of today's spy round-ups with radio's sensational spy-smasher!

Cast: Commander Jerry Baldwin, Willard Parker; Betty Iverson, Audrey Long; Dr. George Vickers, Raymond Greenleaf; Hopkins, Harlan Warde; Charles Kingston, Alex Gerry; and introducing Howard St. John as David Harding// Peters, Fred F. Sears; Frank Reynolds, John Dehner; Barrington, Anthony Jochim; Nurse, Jean Willes; Bartender, Peter Virgo; Newspaper Vendor, Earle Hodgins; Frank Edwards, Steve Darrell; Brown, Jock Mahoney; Burton, Jimmy Lloyd; Baker, Allen Mathews; Man in theater, Joey Ray; Grady, Charles Quigley; McCullough, John Pickard; Lt. Van Dyke, Grant Calhoun; Sentry, William Henry; Radio operator, William Tannen

Credits: Director, Ray Nazarro; Producer, Milton Feldman; Story and Screenwriters, Clint Johnson and Tom Reed; Editor, Henry Batista; Art Director, Harold MacArthur; Set Decorator, Frank Tuttle; Cinematographer, George E. Diskant; Musical Director, Mischa Bakaleinikoff

Song: "Let's Fall In Love" (Arlen/Koehler), hummed by Willard Parker

Source: Based on the radio program, *Counterspy* created by Phillip H. Lord

Production Dates: January 17, 1950–January 27, 1950

Running Time: 71 min.

Story: With the death of Audrey Long's husband, counterspy Howard St. John suspects espionage agents are at work at the Molino torpedo plant. St. John has Commander Willard Parker assigned to take Long's husband's place at the plant. Long was also her husband's secretary. Parker, who is love with Long, takes the job when he learns that her husband was murdered. In the ensuing investigation, St. John discovers Harlan Warde is taking pictures of classified information. Parker sees Warde pass something to Long, but Long insists Warde was returning a pack of cigarettes. Realizing Parker is suspicious, Long, who is a member of the espionage ring, reports to the ringleader, Dr. Raymond Greenleaf. Greenleaf decides that Parker must be killed. Long, who has fallen in love with Parker, alerts authorities who prevent his own demise. St. John makes his move and arrests Warde. St. John then spreads rumors that important plans are coming to the facility. The plans are stolen, but St. John has Greenleaf and his men trailed to an out-of-the-way airfield. St. John informs Parker that Long is an enemy agent and the daughter of Greenleaf. St. John allows one agent to escape with the plans, which are phony. In the roundup of the espionage ring, both Long and Greenleaf are killed.

Notes and Commentary: When Willard Parker and Audrey Long go to a movie theater, posters of *Sahara* (Columbia, 1943) with Humphrey Bogart can be seen.

Fred F. Sears appeared in 64 films; he directed 50 others.

David Harding, Counterspy was a remake of *Walk a Crooked Mile* (Columbia, 1948)

Reviews: "Modestly successful effort." *The Columbia Story*, Hirschhorn

"A fast-paced programmer." *Motion Picture Guide*, Nash and Ross

"New series based on the radio program. Good secondary feature." *Variety*, 05/24/50

Summation: This is a good espionage drama and a good start to the series. The treatment remains faithful to the popular radio program. The acting is good, especially by Willard Parker, Audrey Long, Howard St. John and Raymond Greenleaf. Ray Nazarro paces the film adroitly and has excellent assistance from cinematographer George E. Diskant, who gives the proceedings a film noir effect.

COUNTERSPY MEETS SCOTLAND YARD
Columbia (November 1950)

Guided-missile spy plot smashed!

Cast: David Harding, Howard St. John; Karen Michelle, Amanda Blake; Simon Langton, Ron Randell; Barbara Taylor, June Vincent; Peters, Fred Sears; Bob Reynolds, John Dehner; Hugo Borne (Dr. Victor Gilbert), Lewis Martin// Martin, Harry Lauter; Burton, Jimmy Lloyd; McCullough, Rick Vallin; Hugo Borin (a.k.a. Doc Ritter), Everett Glass; Martha, Gloria Henry; Professor Schuman, Gregory Gay; Col. Kilgore, Douglas Evans; Fields, Robert Bice; Paul Heisl, Paul Marion; Larry, John Doucette; Jimmy, Don Brodie; Brown, Ted Jordan; Power company clerk, Jack Rice; Assistant lab technician, George Eldredge; Danning, Taylor Reid; Laundry man, Al Hill

Counterspy Meets Scotland Yard (1950) title card—(upper left) Amanda Blake and Ron Randell, (center left) Howard St. John, (lower left) Amanda Blake, unknown actor, Lewis Martin (center)-John Dehner and Ron Randell.

Credits: Director, Seymour Friedman; Producer, Wallace MacDonald; Screenwriter, Harold Greene; Editor, Aaron Stell; Art Director, Victor Greene; Set Decorator, George Montgomery; Musical Director, Mischa Bakaleinikoff

Source: Based on the radio program, *Counterspy* created by Phillip H. Lord

Production Dates: June 12, 1950–June 24, 1950

Running Time: 67 min.

Story: Harry Lauter discovers how top-secret information is getting into the hands of an espionage ring. He is murdered before he can tell his boss, Howard St. John. Scotland Yard is interested in the problem and assigns their top agent, Ron Randell, to help. St. John arranges to have Randell take Lauter's place. Randell's secretary, Amanda Blake, has psychological problems and is a patient of Dr. Lewis Martin. Martin is drugging Blake to learn the secret missile data. The information is then taken to the leader, Charles Meredith, in the stopper of an empty water jug. The spies learn Randell is a federal agent and make an attempt to murder him. Randell believes Martin is using a hypnotic drug to obtain information from Blake. St. John places Martin's office under surveillance. Blake goes for her weekly appointment and gives the last of the information. In disguise, Randell goes to Martin's office as a patient. Martin's nurse, June Vincent, had met Randell previously and sees through the disguise. Martin attempts to drug Randell but is only partially successful. Randell is able to alert St. John, who then rounds up the espionage ring. Meanwhile, Randell and Blake have fallen in love and marry.

Notes and Commentary: Ron Randell appears to have had bad luck in Columbia's series efforts. He appeared in the short-lived Bulldog Drummond series, the final Lone Wolf effort and this final Counterspy film.

Reviews: "Childish was the word." *The Columbia Story*, Hirshhorn

"Cast seems to be having fun, and audiences should too." *Motion Picture Guide*, Nash and Ross

"The modest programmer packs enough excitement to please mystery fans and juvenile audiences." *Variety*, 11/15/50

Summation: This effort was not as good as the initial entry in the Counterspy series, but is still quite entertaining. Director Seymour Friedman paces the story in documentary fashion and with the more-than-capable cast, everything works.

Crime Doctor

With this statement, *The Philip Morris Crime Doctor* radio program was on the air. The show, created by playwright and screenwriter Max Marcin, aired on CBS from 1940 to 1947. Unfortunately, only two April 1945 radio shows survive. Ray Collins was the original Crime Doctor, Dr. Benjamin Ordway. Other actors who essayed the role were House Jameson, Everett Sloan and John McIntire. From the two surviving shows, a definite format can be found. Basically, each story built up into a murder. From the outset, the audience knows the killer's identity. Ordway, upon investigation, deduces the murderer's mistake and can prove guilt. At this point the announcer would state, "Dr. Ordway will be back in exactly 59 seconds with the solution to tonight's case."

Columbia Pictures decided to bring the popular radio show to the screen in 1943. Warner Baxter was chosen to play the Crime Doctor, who underwent a slight name change to Robert Ordway. Baxter had been a star in silent films. He received an Academy Award in 1929 for *In Old Arizona*, in which he was the sound era's first Cisco Kid. By the late 1930s, Baxter's health deteriorated; he suffered a nervous breakdown. Once under contract to Columbia, Baxter would only star in the Crime Doctor films, which he did until the series ended in 1949. Baxter would appear in three more programmers (one as Jess Arno) for the studio before his death in 1951. In viewing Baxter's filmography, you will see *Lady in the Dark* (Paramount, 1944) interspersed with his Crime Doctor mysteries. (*Lady* was filmed prior to *The Crime Doctor* but postponed by Paramount for release due to a backlog of other features.) The initial entry of the series had Baxter as a criminal, Phil Moran, who was double-crossed by his gang and thrown from a speeding car to die. Teenagers discover Moran and take him quickly to a nearby hospital, where he recovers from his physical injuries. Moran, who is suffering from amnesia, is given the name Robert Ordway and becomes a noted physician. His past comes back to haunt him but, because of his numerous good deeds, he is sentenced to ten years' probation and allowed to continue his career as a physician.

Margaret Lindsay played Baxter's girlfriend and, at the picture's end, they walk out of the courtroom together. With the decision to launch a series, Lindsay's part was dropped. The actress would be cast in the Rusty series as Ted Donaldson's stepmother. An unusual touch in the series was to have Ordway work with various police officials, not one particular individual like most other series of the time. In all, Baxter starred in ten Crime Doctor entries, most of which have stood the test of time.

CRIME DOCTOR
Columbia (June 1943)

His greatest mystery was his own amazing life story!

Cast: Dr. Robert Ordway, Warner Baxter; Grace Fielding, Margaret Lindsay; Emilio Caspari, John Litel; Dr. John Carey, Ray Collins; Joe Dylan, Harold Huber; Nick Ferris, Don Costello; William Wheeler, Leon Ames// Betty, Constance Worth; Detectives, Ray Teal and Elliott Sullivan; Murphy, George McKay; Mrs. Harrington, Bess Flowers; Myrtle Perrin, Vi Athens; Headwaiter, Chester Clute; Dave, Harry Strang; Jim, Craig Woods; Slipsy, Dewey Robinson; Warden, Addison Richards; Turnkey, Kernan Cripps; Governor, Edward Fielding; Pearl Adams, Dorothy Tree; Mac, Kit Guard; Martin, Housley Stevenson; Man evicted from booth in bar, Milton Kibbee; Judge, Wallis Clark; Court reporters, Anthony Warde, Donald Kerr, Charles Jordan, Anne Jeffreys and Phil Arnold

Credits: Director, Michael Gordon; Producer, Ralph Cohn; Screenwriters, Graham Baker and Louis Lantz; Adaptation, Jerome Odlum; Editor, Dwight Caldwell; Cinematographer, James S. Brown, Jr.; Music, Lee Zahler

Production Dates: March 25, 1943–April 13, 1943

Running Time: 66 min.

Source: From the radio program *Crime Doctor* by Max Marcin

Story: Warner Baxter, presumed dead, is throw from a speeding car to the side of a highway. Teenagers discover Baxter and take him to a hospital. When Baxter finally regains consciousness, he finds he has total amnesia. A visitor to the hospital, John Litel, believes Baxter was a gang leader and that Baxter knows where he stashed $200,000 in robbery money. His physician, Ray Collins, champions Baxter and encourages him to become a psychologist. Baxter champions people who no longer want a criminal career. Through his work he meets social worker Margaret Lindsay. The two soon fall in love. While dining at a noted nightclub, Baxter is spotted by two underworld figures, Don Costello and Harold Huber, who believe he is their former gang leader. Litel joins Costello and Huber in the quest to retrieve the money. Litel goes to Baxter's office posing as a patient, but is just trying to see if Baxter's amnesia is genuine. When Litel leaves the office, Lindsay follows him to a seedy bar. Since Baxter is now chairman of the parole board, Litel gets Baxter's former girlfriend and now convict, Dorothy Tree, to request a parole. Litel figures that, if Baxter grants Tree a parole, Baxter's amnesia is phony. Baxter denies the parole but a conversation with Tree leads Baxter to believe that he was once a criminal. Lindsay tells Baxter about following Litel, and Baxter goes to the bar. While there, Baxter meets Litel, Costello and Huber, and convinces them to reenact the events that led up to his being thrown from a car. The situation grows violent. Litel brandishes a gun. A struggle ensues, and the lights go out. When the lights are turned back on, Baxter has possession of the gun. During the fight, Baxter received a blow to his head that completely restored his memory. He immediately calls the police to arrest the trio. The money is recovered. Baxter is arrested and put on trial. He tells the jury they have a tough decision: their conviction of a guilty man will also mean the conviction of an innocent one. The jury returns a verdict of guilty, with a provision for clemency. Judge Clark sentences Baxter to ten years' probation. Baxter and Lindsay walk out of the court together.

Notes and Commentary: In the original radio program, Ordway's given name was Benjamin, not Robert.

Ray Collins, who plays Dr. John Carey, was the original Dr. Ordway for the popular radio program.

Review: "Much-better-than-average melodrama holds the interest all the way." *Variety*, 07/07/43

Summation: This is good beginning to the Crime Doctor series. Warner Baxter plays his role convincingly. Margaret Lindsay is perfect as the woman who loves Baxter no matter what happened in his past life. John Litel, Don Costello and Harold Huber are properly tough as gangsters; never overacting so the toughness is realistic. Ray Collins chips in a nice performance as the physician who tries to help Baxter find himself. Michael Gordon directs the fine screenplay of Graham Baker and Louis Lantz, getting just what he needs out of every scene.

CRIME DOCTOR'S STRANGEST CASE
Columbia (December 1943)

Radio's greatest crime expert solves his most spectacular case!

Cast: Dr. Robert Ordway, Warner Baxter; Ellen Trotter, Lynn Merrick; Evelyn Cartwright, Gloria Dickson; Detective Rief, Barton MacLane; Mallory Cartwright, Jerome Cowan; Paul Ashley, Reginald Denny; Mrs. Diana Burns, Rose Hobart; Patricia Cornwall, Virginia Brissac; Jimmy Trotter, Lloyd Bridges; Ann Watson, Constance Worth// Addison Burns, Sam Flint; Dr. Carter, Creighton Hale; Detective Yarnell, Thomas E. Jackson; Walter Burns, George Lynn; George Fenton, Ray Walker

Credits: Director, Eugene J. Forde; Producer, Rudolph C. Flothow; Story and Screenwriter, Eric Taylor; Editor, Dwight Caldwell; Art Director, George Van Marter; Set Decorator, Emile Kuri; Cinematographer, James S. Brown; Musical Director, Lee Zahler

Production Dates: September 15, 1943–October 5, 1943

Running Time: 68 min.

Source: From the radio program *Crime Doctor* by Max Marcin

Story: Warner Baxter goes to see George Lynn, employer of Lloyd Bridges. Baxter wants to learn why he hired Bridges, a man accused of poisoning his former employer, even though a second trial resulted in an acquittal. Upon arriving, the housekeeper, Virginia Brissac, informs Baxter that Lynn had been murdered by poisoned coffee. Suspicion falls on Bridges, who had been the last person to see Lynn alive. Detectives Barton MacLane and Thomas E. Jackson place Bridges under arrest, but he escapes. Brissac believes Bridges is innocent and that Lynn's young wife, Rose Hobart, is the guilty party. Brissac makes an appointment to meet Baxter in his office the next day. During the confusion, the cook, Gloria Dickson, removes her disguise and leaves the premises. Bridges goes to his apartment to see his new bride, Merrick. She believes Bridges is innocent but has her doubts when he finds a box marked "poison" in his coat. Merrick takes the box to Baxter, who believes someone is trying to frame Bridges. Brissac comes to Baxter's office. Under hypnosis, Brissac tells of her long-standing love for Lynn; a riff between Lynn and his partner, Ray Walker, in the Golden Nights nightclub; Lynn's accusation that Walker stole $50,000; Walker's subsequent disappearance; and reveals that Dickson is Walker's daughter and that she is now married to Jerome Cowan. Baxter believes that the clue to Lynn's murder lies in the empty, worthless nightclub that Lynn continued to pay taxes on over the past 30 years. At the club, Baxter finds the dead body of Lynn's brother, Sam Flint. Baxter decides to investigate the basement, where he's knocked unconscious by an unknown individual and left to die in a fire. Baxter is able to escape and goes to Cowan's apartment. There, Baxter finds that Cowan is extremely careless with matches. Baxter then talks with Dickson and finds she took the position with Lynn to find what happened to Walker. Dickson believes Lynn murdered Walker and framed him as an embezzler. MacLane and Jackson show up and arrest both Dickson and Cowan. Bridges and Merrick have also been taken into custody. Baxter returns to Lynn's estate and investigates the shrubbery outside Lynn's window. Baxter finds a straw with a residue of poison and a hole in the screen big enough to accommodate the straw. Baxter believes someone blew poison into Lynn's coffee cup. Hobart sees someone outside and calls Lynn's nephew, Reginald Denny. Denny accuses Hobart of killing Lynn, but is still willing to marry her, since she is probably the principal heir. Baxter convinces MacLane and Jackson to release all the suspects. In exchange, Baxter shows the detectives exactly why Lynn was murdered. Baxter has Hobart and Denny meet him at the abandoned nightclub. Searching through the basement, they discover Walker's body. Cowan and Dickson show up and explain to Hobart that money is owed them from Walker's estate. Hobart says that if Dickson's claim can be upheld in court, she will personally give her the money. Hobart, Dickson and Cowan leave to explain their arrangement to the police. Baxter finds an old safe, which he believes is a clue to the murders. Denny says that Flint killed Lynn and that he later killed Flint in self-defense and tried to make it look like suicide. Denny, who has possession of Baxter's gun, pulls the trigger three times on empty chambers. MacLane and Jackson step in to arrest Denny. Baxter tells Denny that the police have already removed Lynn's money from the safe. Denny tries to make the case that he's not really a murderer, but Baxter reminds him that he tried to murder him twice.

Notes and Commentary: Most cast listings list Constance Worth's character name as Betty Watson. In the film, Warner Baxter calls her Ann.

Gloria Dickson prophetically utters one line of dialogue that she's practically cremated, in reference to Jerome Cowan's propensity for loosely handling lighted matches. About two years later, Dickson was killed in a house fire, which was reportedly started by a discarded cigarette.

Reviews: "Nothing really strange about this film in the Crime Doctor series." *Motion Picture Guide*, Nash and Ross

"Though plotted well, sustaining suspense *Crime Doctor's Strangest Case* has a tendency to drag due to detail involved in running down clues and questioning of suspects in the murder that has been committed." *Variety*, 12/15/43

Summation: This is a good murder mystery with a lot of red herrings. Of course, the person with the weakest motive turns out to be the guilty party, but that's okay. Warner Baxter makes the Crime Doctor role his own and does a good job. Baxter is given a good supporting cast. The young Lloyd Bridges shows the promise that made him a star. Eugene J. Forde directs the proceedings briskly, and is benefitted by Eric Taylor's screenplay.

SHADOWS IN THE NIGHT

Columbia (July 1944)

Only radio's famous crime doctor could solve this baffling
mystery that almost drove a beautiful girl mad!

A Crime Doctor picture

Cast: Dr. Robert Ordway, Warner Baxter; Lois Garland, Nina Foch; Frank Swift, George Zucco; Jess Hilton, Edward Norris; Stanley Carter, Lester Matthews; Nick Kallus, Ben Welden; Adele Carter, Jeanne Bates// Frederick Gordon, Minor Watson; Sheriff, Charles C. Wilson; Doc Stacey, Charles Halton; Riggs, Arthur Hohl

Credit: Director, Eugene J. Forde; Producer, Rudolph C. Flothow; Story and Screenplay, Eric Tayor; Editor, Dwight Caldwell; Art Director, John Datu, Set Decorator, Sidney Clifford; Cinematographer, James S. Brown, Jr.

Production Dates: April 2, 1944–May 5, 1944

Running Time: 67 min.

Source: From the radio program *Crime Doctor* by Max Marcin

Story: On a dark, rainy night Nina Foch shows up at Warner Baxter's front door, and tells him that she's afraid she will not live until morning. Foch relates a recurring dream in which a woman appears out of a mist in her bedroom, walks to the bedroom door and beckons to her. Foch believes she followed this woman and ended up on a rocky beach. Foch asks Baxter to come to her estate. He at first refuses, until he sees evidence that Foch had been followed to his house. At Foch's house, she asks Baxter to stay in her room. Mist covers the room, a woman appears and Baxter follows her to the beach where he slips on a rock and falls to the ground. Foch's uncle George Zucco sees Baxter and helps him back to the house. There, Baxter finds a murdered man in the upstairs hall. Baxter goes to get Foch, but when they return, the body is missing. The following morning Baxter finds the body, which has washed up on the beach. The dead man is Foch's employer. Other visitors in the house are Jeanne Bates, Foch's sister; Foch's brother-in-law, Lester Matthews, a would-be actor; the dead man's partner, Edward Norris; and Matthews's lawyer, Minor Watson. While others want to dismiss the man's death as accidental, Baxter believes that it was murder and begins his investigation. Baxter finds a laundry chute in which the dead man could have been moved quickly to the cellar. Then Baxter finds a pathway from the cellar to the beach. In addition, Baxter finds a candlestick that he believes to be the murder weapon. In Foch's room, Baxter and Foch discuss the candlestick and Baxter's plans to turn it over to Sheriff Charles C. Wilson. That night, the mist incapacitates Baxter and an unknown figure enters the room to search for the candlestick. The figure finally discovers where Baxter has hidden it. Before the mysterious figure can leave the room, handyman Arthur Hohl enters and is struck on the head with the candlestick. Hohl is killed instantly. Baxter tells Wilson that Foch's employer was killed because he saw how Foch's dreams were managed, and that Hohl was killed because he had incriminating information for Baxter. Baxter believes that someone was in the attic and overheard the conversation he had with Foch. In the attic, Baxter finds the chemicals that cause the mist, and an envelope addressed to Watson. Baxter and Foch confront Watson, who tells them that he gave the envelope to Matthews. Foch demands to know if Watson is working to help Matthews gain custody of his son. Foch tells Watson that if this is so, she will testify that Matthews is morally unfit. Matthews, it seems, has embezzled some funds and Foch covered for him. Meanwhile, Watson is searching the basement when a mask, gown and the candlestick come down the laundry chute. Everyone is quickly accounted for — except Matthews. He is found tied up in a locked closet. Baxter then shows how Matthews could have tied himself up. Baxter also shows proof that Matthews was trying to drive Foch insane so that she could not testify against him in the quest to gain custody of his son.

Notes and Commentary: The working title for this film was "Crime Doctor's Rendezvous."

Reviews: "A fairly eerie and suspenseful thriller." *Motion Picture Guide*, Nash and Ross "Better-than-average meller in the Crime Doctor series." *Variety*, 08/02/44

Summation: Another good Crime Doctor mystery. This time out, the story has supernatural overtones and is successful. Warner Baxter is great in the leading role. He has a fine supporting cast, especially Nina Foch in the difficult role of a woman being driven to madness. Eugene J. Forde's direction is steady and on target.

THE CRIME DOCTOR'S COURAGE
Columbia (February 1945)

Radio's crime doctor returns in his greatest thriller!

Cast: Dr. Robert Ordway, Warner Baxter; Kathleen Carson, Hillary Brooke; Jeff Jerome, Jerome Cowan; Bob Rencoret, Robert Scott; John Massey, Lloyd Corrigan; Captain Birch, Emory Parnell; Butler, Charles Arnt; Miguel Braggs, Anthony Caruso; Dolores Braggs, Lupita Tovar//David Lee, Dennis Moore; Sheriff, Edgar Dearing; Caterer, William H. O'Brien; Detective Fanning, Jack Carrington; Headwaiter, John Maxwell; Master of Ceremonies, Ken Carpenter; Luga, "King Kong" Kashey

Credits: Director, George Sherman; Producer, Rudolph C. Flothow; Story and Screenplay, Eric Taylor; Editor, Dwight Caldwell; Art Director, John Datu; Set Decorator, Sidney Clifford; Cinematographer, L.W. O'Connell; Choreographer, Tito Valdez

Production Dates: November 3, 1944–November 21, 1944

Running Time: 70 min.

Source: From the radio program *Crime Doctor* by Max Marcin

Story: Warner Baxter is vacationing in Southern California when Hillary Brooke comes to see him. Brooke had received a letter containing newspaper clippings. These articles reveal that two previous wives of her new husband, Stephen Crane, had died in mysterious accidents only a few days after they were wed. Brooke wants Baxter to come to a dinner party at their home to observe Crane to see if he is insane. At the party Baxter meets an old friend, novelist Jerome Cowan; Brooke's eccentric father, Lloyd Corrigan; a family friend, Robert Scott; and a mysterious dance team, Anthony Caruso and Lupita Tovar. As the guests are seated for dinner, one of the waiters, Dennis Moore, a brother of Crane's first wife, declares that Crane is a murderer. The party quickly breaks up, and Crane retires to his study. A shot is heard. Baxter and Cowan break open the door and find the lifeless Crane on the floor. It looks like suicide: the study door was locked and the only windows had iron bars to prevent entry. When Captain Emory Parnell arrives to investigate, Baxter tells him that Crane was likely murdered: the supposed murder weapon was cold, and would have been warm had it been fired. Brooke tells Scott that she married Crane only because he was wealthy and would help finance projects for Corrigan. Scott reveals that he is in love with Brooke and wants to take her to Reno to get married. Brooke informs Scott that she's really in love with Caruso. Caruso and Tovar's act includes the disappearance and reappearance of Tovar. Caruso states that Tovar actually becomes invisible. Added to the dance couple's mystique is the fact that they are never seen in the daylight, they allow no mirrors in their dressing rooms and coffins are found in the basement of their home. Parnell postures that perhaps an invisible Caruso murdered Crane. Baxter discovers there is a trick mechanism to collapse two of the bars in the window, allowing passage in or out of the room. In his investigation, Baxter and Brooke go to Cowan's room and find writings of Cowan which indicate that he believes the dancers are vampires, and that he plans to destroy them by driving stakes into their hearts. They hurry to the dancers' house and find Cowan mortally wounded. Baxter retrieves a pistol Cowan had in his coat pocket. He then quickly goes to the coffin and finds Caruso and Tovar still alive. Baxter sees a mysterious figure in the basement and a gunfight ensues, with Baxter wounding the man. It is revealed that the mysterious aura surrounding Caruso and Tovar was a publicity gimmick devised by Cowan. The murderer turns out to be Scott, who killed Crane and Cowan and was planning to murder Caruso and Tovar to clear the way to convince Brooke to marry him.

Notes and Commentary: Hillary Brooke had a long career in movies and television, from 1937 until 1960. High spots include the role of Lorelei Kilbourne in Paramount's *Big Town* series (1947–48) and was Roberta, the girlfriend of Charles Farrell on *My Little Margie* (Roland Reed TV Productions/Rovan Films, 1952–55), and the girlfriend of Lou Costello on *The Abbott and Costello Show* (Television Corporation of America, 1952–53).

Reviews: "A poorer entry in the Crime Doctor series." *Motion Picture Guide*, Nash and Ross

"One of the poorer entries in the series, this 'Crime Doctor' pic lacks suspense or mystery." *Variety*, 03/07/45

Summation: The story unspools nicely, but the script is somewhat deficient this time out. For example, it is hard to believe that the murderer knew about the trick bars in the study window. Warner Baxter is comfortable in the title role, and a fine supporting cast has been assembled. Director George Sherman does his usual fine job and, as a result, delivers some entertainment value. But in this entry, the script is the main culprit.

THE CRIME DOCTOR'S WARNING

Columbia (September 1945)

Murder in the Latin Quarter! It's radio's Crime Doctor's <u>weirdest</u> case!

Alternate Title: The Doctor's Warning

Cast: Dr. Robert Ordway, Warner Baxter; Inspector Dawes, John Litel; Connie Mace, Dusty Anderson; Clive Lake, Coulter Irwin; Frederick Malone, Miles Mander; Jimmy Gordon, John Abbott// Nick Petroni, Edward Ciannelli; Joseph Duval, Franco Corsaro; Mrs. Wellington Lake, Alma Kruger; Mrs. Lake's attorneys, George Meeker and Arthur Aylesworth; Turnkey, Jack Cheatham; Dr. Forday Booth, Boyd Davis; Bridge players, Bess Flowers and Sam Harris; Robert MacPherson, J.M. Kerrigan

Credits: Director, William Castle; Producer, Rudolph C. Flothow; Story and Screenplay, Eric Taylor; Editor, Dwight Caldwell; Cinematographer, L.W. O'Connell; Sound, Hugh McDowell; Musical Director, Paul Sawtell

Production Dates: June 14, 1945–June 30, 1945

Running Time: 70 min.

Source: From the radio program *Crime Doctor* by Max Marcin

Story: An artist's model is murdered in Greenwich Village. Inspector John Litel asks Warner Baxter to assist in the case. Coulter Irwin, a struggling artist who has a studio in the same building, becomes a patient of Baxter's. Irwin has frequent blackouts and, when he recovers, he cannot remember what he did. Baxter tells Irwin to call him when he feels a blackout coming on. Also, to help Irwin, Baxter arranges for him to take a painting to Miles Mander's exclusive art gallery to be sold. Baxter plans to buy the painting. That night, when Irwin is working with Dusty Anderson, he feels another spell coming on and calls Baxter. Irwin, in a trance, goes up to the roof. At this time, a mysterious figure comes down from the roof and murders Anderson. As the intruder leaves, he drops a key. When Baxter shows up at the studio, there is a party going on, a celebration of Irwin selling a painting. Before Baxter leaves, Anderson's body is discovered. Irwin is the prime suspect. Baxter returns to the studio not knowing that someone else is in the studio. Baxter finds the key and is followed home. The intruder enters Baxter's bedroom. Baxter feigns sleep. The intruder finds the key and leaves the room. Baxter follows but is knocked out as he leaves his bedroom. Under hypnosis by Baxter, Irwin says he saw other persons on the roof. Baxter wants Irwin placed in his care, but Litel places him under arrest. Baxter returns to Mander's gallery to pick up Irwin's painting, but Mander explains that he sold it to another buyer. Baxter thinks the purchaser might be interested in the model in the picture. He then learns that Anderson knew the other murdered model. Those two, along with a third model, posed for a painting titled "The Ring." Baxter finds out the name of the third model and that she married someone in the city. Baxter asks Irwin to check marriage records to identify the third model's husband. Baxter returns to Mander's gallery to see if he knew anything about the third model. Mander says he'll ask around. That night Baxter breaks in Mander's gallery. First Baxter finds the frame for Irwin's painting. Then Baxter finds the painting which shows the three models. Finally, Baxter finds a wax figure of the third model. At that point, Mander enters the room and holds Baxter at gunpoint. Mander tells him that his wife was planning to leave him. He wanted the make a wax figure of her but the mould suffocated his wife. To prevent the other two models from asking about his dead wife, he had to murder them. As Mander is about to kill Baxter, Litel and Irwin enter the room and prevent the murder. Litel puts Mander under arrest. Irwin had uncovered Mander's name in the marriage records and had called Litel.

Notes and Commentary: The working title for the film was "The Paper Doll Murders."

Edward Ciannelli receives seventh billing in the print ads but is left out of the screen credits. Before World War II, Ciannelli was usually billed as Eduardo instead of Edward.

Reviews: "Another good film in the Crime Doctor series." *Motion Picture Guide*, Nash and Ross

"Warner Baxter in good whodunit." *Variety*, 12/19/45

Summation: The Crime Doctor series is back on target with this episode, thanks to a tauter, well-constructed script by Eric Taylor. Again, Warner Baxter is perfect in the title role.

Just Before Dawn

Columbia (March 1946)

The Crime Doctor murders ... and then traps the real murderer!

A Crime Doctor Picture

Cast: Dr. Robert Ordway, Warner Baxter; Claire Foster, Adelle Roberts; Karl Ganss, Martin Kosleck; Harriet Travers, Mona Barrie; Casper, Marvin Miller; Inspector Burns,

Charles D. Brown; Clyde Travers, Robert H. Barrat// Walter Foster, George Meeker; Alec Girard, Wilton Graff; Jack Swayne, Craig Reynolds; Dr. Steiner, Charles Lane; Allen Tobin, Charles Arnt; Tobin's servant, Walter Soderling; Armand, Ted Hecht; Connie Day, Peggy Converse; Florence White, Irene Tedrow; Louie, Skelton Knaggs; Dr. Evans, Egon Brecher; Walter Cummings, Thomas E. Jackson; Harris, Byron Foulger

Credits: Director, William Castle; Producer, Rudolph C. Flothow; Screenwriters, Eric Taylor and Aubrey Wisberg; Editor, Dwight Caldwell; Art Director, Hans Radon; Set Decorator, William Kiernan; Cinematographer, Henry Freulich; Sound, Howard Fogetti; Musical Director, Mischa Bakaleinikoff

Production Dates: November 5, 1945–November 20, 1945

Running Time: 66 min.

Source: From the radio program *Crime Doctor* by Max Marcin

Story: Marvin Miller goes to Martin Kosleck's mortuary to receive a vial marked insulin, but in reality contains a deadly poison. Later that night, Mona Barrie summons Warner Baxter to treat George Meeker, her brother-in-law. Finding that Meeker is diabetic, Baxter asked that Meeker's medicine be brought to him. Baxter injects Meeker with the substance from the vial marked insulin. Within minutes, Meeker collapses to the floor; before he dies he says, "I've given you one face." Since Baxter was the instrument of Meeker's death, Inspector Charles D. Brown asks him to assist on the case. Baxter finds he has many suspects. Meeker was sponging off his sister, Adelle Roberts. Meeker was blocking the marriage between Roberts and Craig Reynolds. Lawyer Charles Arnt was upset because Meeker took all his inheritance in a lump sum instead of allowing him to invest and manage it. Barrie had been involved with Meeker and had given him substantial sums of money. Barrie was then thrown over for another woman, Peggy Converse, who works for Kosleck. Barrie's husband, Robert H. Barrat, was angry over her actions. Roberts discovers the exact quote Meeker was trying to make, "God has given you one face and you make yourselves another." Roberts asks Baxter to come to her house so she can explain more fully. Before Baxter can arrive, Miller kidnaps Roberts and takes her to Kosleck's mortuary. When Baxter sees Barrie and Barrat are selling their house, he learns from realtor Wilton Graff that the couple is separating. Baxter locates Converse and arranges to meet her at her apartment after she gets off work at Kosleck's mortuary. Kosleck had listened in on the phone call and prevents her from meeting Baxter. Later, Miller tells Converse that she told Meeker to blackmail the doctor as he leads her to be murdered. Miller brings Skelton Knaggs to Baxter's office and prompts Knaggs to shoot Baxter. Baxter falls to the floor. Miller throws Knaggs out of Baxter's office window, to his death. The glancing shot injures Baxter's optic nerve, and Baxter is blind. Through treatment Baxter regains his sight. With Brown's urging, Baxter pretends to be blind when he's in the presence of any of the suspects. Because Baxter's nurse can recognize Miller, Baxter engages private detective Thomas E. Jackson to protect her and see if Miller is following her. Baxter discovers Miller's true identity and concludes that he has undergone plastic surgery. With this information, Baxter disguises himself as a notorious bank robber. He convinces Miller to send him to Kosleck so he can have his facial features changed. As Baxter is making arrangements with Kosleck, Miller hears a news bulletin that the real bank robber has been shot and killed by police. Miller calls Kosleck with this information, adding that he's on the way to the mortuary. Kosleck tells Baxter that he has to inject him with medication prior to the surgery. As he is about to inject the drug, Baxter suddenly hits Kosleck with a terrific right to the jaw, knocking him out. Baxter calls the police, and when Miller arrives, the police arrest him. Baxter and Brown want to catch the murderer. Baxter, again pretending to be blind, invites all the suspects to his house and tells them that they are no longer suspects. But privately, Baxter tells each individual that the murderer is in the house. Graff returns after the party to retrieve a forgotten item. Baxter suggests Graff pour them a nightcap. Graff slips poison in Baxter's drink. After he has consumed it, Graff tells Baxter that he's been poisoned and that he murdered Meeker and is responsible for the deaths of Roberts and Converse. The police have been listening to Graff's confession and arrest him. Baxter had lined his stomach with chalk and then has the contents of his stomach pumped out before the poison can harm him.

Notes and Commentary: The working title for this film was "Exposed by the Crime Doctor."

According to the *Hollywood Reporter*, the role of Karl Ganns was originally assigned to Ludwig Donath.

Review: "One of the best of the Crime Doctor series. Dark and brooding B-mystery." *Blockbuster Video Guide to Movies and Videos 1995*, Castell

Summation: This is an excellent entry in the Crime Doctor series. Warner Baxter again essays the title role in fine style. Kudos to the makeup job of Baxter as a wanted criminal. You would have to look extremely close to tell it's Baxter.

CRIME DOCTOR'S MAN HUNT
Columbia (October 1946)

Radio's Crime Doctor reads murder in a lover's mind ... in a woman's heart!

Cast: Dr. Robert Ordway, Warner Baxter; Irene Cotter, Ellen Drew; Inspector Harry B. Manning, William Frawley; Bigger, Frank Sully; Ruby Farrell, Claire Carleton; Waldo, Bernard Nedell; Sergeant Bradley, Jack Lee; Gerald Cotter, Francis Pierlot// Philip Armstrong, Myron Healey; Miss White, Wanda Perry; Landlady, Minerva Urecal; Officer Reynolds, Ralph Linn; Marcus Le Blaine, Olin Howland; Joe, Cy Malis; Sailors, Frank Cody and Robert De Haven; Tom, Paul E. Burns; Martha, Mary Newton; Waiter, John Manning; Alfredi, Ivan Triesault; Mr. Herrera, Leon Lenoir

Credit: Director, William Castle; Producer, Rudolph C. Flothow; Story, Eric Taylor; Screenwriter, Leigh Brackett; Editor, Dwight Caldwell; Art Director, Hans Radon; Set Decorator, George Montgomery; Cinematographer, Philip Tannura; Musical Director, Mischa Bakaleinikoff

Production Dates: May 6, 1946–May 21, 1946

Running Time: 61 min.

Source: From the radio program *Crime Doctor* by Max Marcin

Story: Myron Healey becomes a patient of Warner Baxter. Healey finds himself in strange places, without knowing how or why he came to be there. He always ends at the same destination, looking for the fortune-teller who predicted his imminent death. After Healey leaves Baxter's office, Healey's fiancée, Ellen Drew, comes to Baxter's office to inquire about Healey. Baxter wanders down to the area Healey described. He sees Healey being placed in a car by two men, Frank Sully and Bernard Nedell. Baxter approaches, pretending to be drunk, and sees that Healey is dead. Baxter calls Inspector William Frawley and they investigate the rooming house from which Healey had been removed. Sully and Nedell report to a mysterious woman, demanding more money for the disposal of Healey's body.

The Crime Doctor finds a gun talks louder than words!

Crime Doctor's Man Hunt (1946) scene card — Ellen Drew and Warner Baxter.

Since no shot was heard, Baxter notices a nearby shooting gallery that uses air pistols. The owner, Claire Carleton, tells Baxter that it was possible one of guns had been stolen. Baxter is also advised to investigate the abandoned house behind the rooming house because she noticed the lights were on the night Healey was murdered. Baxter enters the house and is struck on the head by Sully. The police find Healey's body at a crematorium. The house is owned by Francis Pierlot. Baxter and Frawley go to Pierlot's estate and tell him that Healey is dead. Drew overhears the conversation. Sully and Nedell come to the estate, looking for the mysterious woman thought to be Pierlot's daughter, and are told she hasn't lived there for the past three years. Drew still hasn't forgiven Pierlot for sending her sister away. Sully and Nedell finally see the mysterious woman in her apartment and, using a gas heater, she asphyxiates the two men. In one of the dead men's pockets there is an address book with the information on the fortune-teller, Ivan Triesault. Triesault is arrested and tells Baxter and Frawley that Drew's sister hired him to tell Healey that he would soon die; he also hired Sully and Nedell to rough up Healey. Drew's sister tried to break up the romance between Healey and Drew and, when that failed, left for New Orleans. A newspaper article (stating that the police were searching for Drew's sister in connection with three murders) brings Leon Lenoir to the police station. Lenoir states that Drew's sister was his wife and that she died six months earlier. Baxter has Drew meet him at the abandoned house. There, Baxter finds a glove and asks Drew to go next door and phone the police. Minutes later, the mysterious woman enters the room, gun in hand, planning to kill Baxter. Frawley and Sergeant

Jack Lee are waiting as she goes into the hall and arrest her. Baxter then shows Frawley that Drew was masquerading as her sister. Drew was so dependent on her, at times he assumed her identity. Drew killed Healey because he learned of her dual personality. He refused treatment for fear of being institutionalized.

Notes and Commentary: The working title for this film was "The Crime Doctor's Horror."

As Warner Baxter passes a movie theater, you can see posters advertising *The Bandit of Sherwood Forest* (Columbia, 1946).

Reviews: "A jumbled plot with a lot of unexplained twists." *Motion Picture Guide*, Nash and Ross

"Minor murder meller with Warner Baxter." *Variety*, 09/18/46

Summation: This is a very good Crime Doctor entry, possibly the best in the series. Warner Baxter is steady in the role, as usual. William Frawley adds much to the picture with his droll personality. His repartee with Baxter at the film's conclusion provides the perfect ending. But Ellen Drew takes the acting honors, enveloping herself with two distinct personalities, exhibiting two different voices and mannerisms. Expert help from wardrobe and makeup departments adds to the deception. Leigh Brackett's screenplay is first-rate.

THE MILLERSON CASE
Columbia (May 1947)

Jealousy Brews murder for radio's amazing Crime Doctor!

Cast: Dr. Robert Ordway, Warner Baxter; Belle Englehart, Nancy Saunders; Sheriff Luke Akers, Clem Bevens; Doc Sam Millerson, Griff Barnett; Jud Rookstool, Paul Gilfoyle; Ezra Minnich, James Bell; Dr. Wickersham, Addison Richards; Bije Minnich, Mark Dennis// Receptionist, Virginia Hunter; Miss White, Barbara Woodell; Dr. Shaw; Walden Boyle; Jeremiah Dobbs, Eddy Waller; Ward Beechy, Trevor Bardette; Squire Tuttle, Russell Simpson; Eadie Rookstool, Barbara Pepper; Emma Millerson, Sarah Padden; Eben Tuttle, Elvin Field; Jonas Beechy, Vincent Graeff; Mathilda Beechy, Joyce Arling; Link Hazen, Walter Baldwin; Lt. Callahan, Eddie Parker; Dr. Prescott, Robert Kellard; Zeke, Ernie Adams; Mort Crowell, Jack Davis; Harley Rumford, Paul Bryar; Hank Nixon, Victor Potel; Littleton, Robert Emmett Keane; Clem Ogle, Dick Wessel; Myra Minnich, Eilene Janssen; Ella Minnich, Frances Morris; Fiddling contest judge, Dorothy Vernon

Credits: Director, George Archainbaud; Producer, Rudolph C. Flothow; Story, Gordon Rigby and Carlton Sand; Screenwriter, Raymond L. Schrock; Editor, Dwight Caldwell; Art Director, Harold MacArthur; Set Decorators, Sidney Clifford and Wilbur Minefee; Cinematographer, Philip Tannura; Sound, Jack Goodrich; Musical Director, Mischa Bakaleinikoff

Location Filming: Iverson, California
Production Dates: January 3, 1947–January 18, 1947
Running Time: 72 min.
Source: From the radio program *Crime Doctor* by Max Marcin
Story: Warner Baxter takes a much-deserved vacation in the rustic community of Brook Falls. The community has been beset with a mysterious illness, labeled by the old country doctor, Griff Barnett, as "summer complaints." The latest victim is barber Trevor

Bardette, who will trade his skill for corn liquor from horticulturist James Bell. The illness turns out to be typhoid fever, and Baxter is recruited in the vaccination program. Baxter reviews blood samples from the deceased; all show evidence of typhoid except Bardette. Baxter thinks Bardette was murdered, and there are many suspects. Bardette had affairs with Bell's wife, guide Paul Gilfoyle's wife and Dick Wessell's girlfriend. Barnett is suspected because of his displeasure of Bardette seeking medical care at a nearby clinic. Bardette was killed by a poison which had been sold to Barnett and Bell. Barnett receives a note to meet someone at the town's swimming hole with proof of his innocence. Instead, Barnett receives a bullet, ending his life. Investigating further, Baxter finds that Bell was responsible for the note. Bell offers Baxter some cider laced with poison. When Baxter doesn't drink the cider, a fight begins between the two men. Bell is finally getting the better of Baxter, when local officers step in and arrest Bell. Bell had murdered Bardette because he was trying to break up his home. Barnett was killed because Bell was afraid that the doctor would remember that he asked how much plant spray it would take to kill a person. In custody, Bell feigns insanity, but Baxter proves Bell to be sane.

Notes and Commentary: The working title for *The Millerson Case* was "The Crime Doctor's Vacation."

Eddie Parker doubled Warner Baxter in the fight sequence.

When Baxter says he's going on vacation, Barbara Woodell tells Baxter he needs to help Inspector Manning. Manning was William Frawley's character name in *The Crime Doctor's Man Hunt* (1946).

Robert Emmett Keane talks about Baxter's work in solving the Paper Doll Murders. This was a reference to *The Crime Doctor's Warning* (1945).

Review: "Par for the series." *1996 Movie & Video Guide*, Maltin

Summation: This is a neat, well-constructed murder-mystery. Warner Baxter, with another fine performance, is given a good supporting cast made up of some of Hollywood's best character actors, including James Bell, Clem Bevens, Griff Barnett and Trevor Bardette. Watching these veteran actors work adds to the viewer's enjoyment.

THE CRIME DOCTOR'S GAMBLE
Columbia (November 1947)

A spree in gay paree ends up in murder!

Alternate Title: Doctor's Gamble

Cast: Dr. Robert Ordway, Warner Baxter; Mignon Duval Jardin, Micheline Cheirel; Henri Jardin, Roger Dann; Jules Daudet, Steven Geray; Inspector Morrell, Marcel Journet; Maurice Duval, Eduardo Ciannelli// Institute superintendent, Alphonse Martel; Apache dancers, Don Graham and Dolores Graham; Jacques, Jack Chefe; Anton Geroux, Maurice Marsac; Theodore, Jean Del Val; Louis Chabonet, Henri Letondal; Coroner, Bernard DeRoux; Auctioneer, Leon Lenoir; Brown, Wheaton Chambers; O'Reilly, Emory Parnell; Wagon driver, Peter Camlin

Credits: Director, William Castle; Producer, Rudolph C. Flothow; Story, Raymond L. Schrock and Jerry Warner; Screenwriter, Edward Bock; Editor, Dwight Caldwell; Art Director, George Brooks; Set Decorator, Louis Diage; Cinematography, Philip Tannura; Musical Director, Mischa Bakaleinikoff

Production Dates: July 14, 1947–July 26, 1947
Running Time: 66 min.
Source: from the radio program *Crime Doctor* by Max Marcin

Story: Warner Baxter, in Paris to deliver a series of lectures, is persuaded by Inspector Marcel Journel to assist on a murder case: an enraged Roger Dann has murdered his father after he had been disinherited. Lawyer Steven Geray, a friend of the family, offers to take the case. He believes Dann should plead guilty while insane because of Dann's prior mental problems. Baxter is not satisfied that Dann is the murderer and finds others with a motive. Prior to World War II, Eduardo Ciannellt, Dann's father-in-law, entered into an arrangement with Dann's father in which valuable properties were put up a security for a significant loan. When Ciannelli tried to repay the loan after the end of the war, Dann's father refused the payment and kept the properties. Artist Maurice Marsac is in love with Dann's wife, Micheline Cheirel, and would like to see Dann out of the way. Marsac makes a living copying great paintings that will be used in advertising campaigns. Baxter is impressed with how one of Marsac's painting looks like an original master. Marsac asks Baxter to meet him at Henri Letondal's gallery in anticipation of selling him one. Before Baxter arrives, a mysterious intruder attacks Marsac and kills him. Letondal comes to the gallery and discovers that all copies have been stolen. Baxter arranges for Dann to be released and awarded his father's fortune. Baxter convinces Dann to auction all the valuable objects d'art. Baxter is the highest bidder on all items. Finally, a valuable painting is put up for auction. Two American art dealers are present to bid. Wheaton Chambers enters a bid of $50,000. Emory Parnell insists that the painting is a fake, and he proves it. To help Dann, Geray offers to buy the copy for $500. The painting is delivered to his residence. Baxter enters the basement and discovers the stolen copies. Geray brings the copy he had purchased to the basement and finds Baxter with the paintings. A fight ensues, with Geray the victor. Geray plans to place the copies and Baxter's body in the furnace. Suddenly, Baxter turns and lands a hard right to Geray's jaw, knocking him out. Baxter signals for the police and Geray is arrested. Geray had murdered Dann's father when he was caught substituting the fake painting for the original. He also killed Marsac. Geray went to Letondal's gallery, in which he was part owner, to retrieve Dann's father's valuable painting that he had hidden in the gallery. When Geray discovered Marsac in the gallery, he felt that he had to kill him.

Notes and Commentary: The *Hollywood Reporter* noted that Charles Vidor was originally assigned to direct this film.

Review: "Okay supporter for twin bill situations." *Variety*, 11/26/47

Summation: Entertaining little murder-mystery. The script plays fair, so attentive audiences should deduce the motive and, consequently, the murderer. The acting is up to par, with Warner Baxter tuning his usual fine performance as the Crime Doctor. Director William Castle forgoes his usual suspense and chills, but provides a straightforward story that holds the interest.

THE CRIME DOCTOR'S DIARY

Columbia (June 1949)

Bullet-hot murder brewed by love turned cold!

Cast: Dr. Robert Ordway, Warner Baxter; Steve Carter, Stephen Dunne; Jane Darrin,

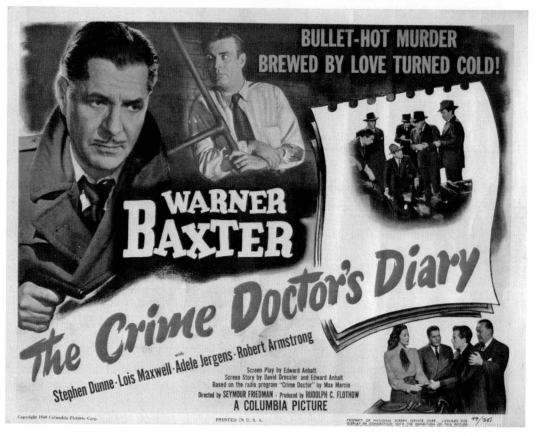

The Crime Doctor's Diary (1949) title card—(upper left) Warner Barter, (center) Stephen Dunne, (upper right, left to right) Whit Bissell, Crane Whitley, Warner Baxter, unknown actor, Cliff Clark, Fred Sears, George Meeker (on floor), (lower right, left to right)—Lois Maxwell, Warner Baxter, Whit Bissell, Don Beddoe.

Lois Maxwell; Inez Gray, Adele Jergens; Goldie Harrigan, Robert Armstrong; Phillip Bellem, Don Beddoe; Pete Bellem, Whit Bissell// Warden, Selmer Jackson; Carter's cellmate, Ray Bennett; Turnkey, Pat O'Malley; Carl Anson, George Meeker; Roma, Lois Fields; Bartender, Billy Nelson; Blaney the Dip, Sid Tomack; Louise, Claire Carleton; Inspector John D. Manning, Cliff Clark; Ballistics detective, Fred F. Sears; Detective MacDonald, Crane Whitley; Eddie, Syd Saylor; Eddie's wife, Phyllis Kennedy; Police pathologist, Robert Emmett Keane

Credits: Director, Seymour Friedman; Producer, Rudolph C. Flothow; Story, David Dressler and Edward Anhalt; Screenwriter, Edward Anhalt; Editor, Jerome Thoms; Art Direction, Harold MacArthur; Set Decorator, George Montgomery; Musical Director, Mischa Bakaleinikoff

Production Dates: August 19, 1948–September 1, 1948

Running Time: 61 min.

Source: from the radio program *Crime Doctor* by Max Marcin

Story: Under Warner Baxter's recommendation, Stephan Dunne is paroled from prison. Dunne was convicted of arson at his employer Don Beddoe's music company. Beddoe was convinced to rehire Dunne by his secretary, Lois Maxwell. Maxwell is in love with Dunne, even though she knows he loves Adele Jergens. Dunne thinks that either George Meeker, sales manager of Beddoe's company, or Robert Armstrong, owner of a rival company, committed the crime. Dunne goes to Armstrong's office where he finds Jergens, now Armstong's secretary and girlfriend. The spark of romance still exists between the two. Beddoe's slow-witted brother, Whit Bissell, believes himself to be a talented songwriter. Bissell begins recording his song when Meeker interrupts him and makes him leave the building. Bissell then sees Dunne enter the building. Later, Bissell returns to the office and finds that Meeker had been murdered. Police Inspector Cliff Clark asks Baxter to help in the case. Baxter believes Dunne to be innocent and begins his own investigation. Baxter asks Beddoe if he can talk with Bissell. Beddoe sends Maxwell to bring Bissell to his office. Maxwell finds Bissell listening to the record of the song he had begun when Meeker stopped him. Bissell leaves the room. Maxwell then hears the confrontation between Bissell and Meeker. Bissell is unable to help Baxter, but asks if he would like a record of his song. Bissell, Baxter and Beddoe enter the room, as Maxwell is about to smash the record. Bissell retrieves it and gives it to Baxter. Baxter takes the record home and starts to play it when Maxwell arrives. Together, Baxter and Maxwell listen to the record. On the record is the confrontation between Meeker and Maxwell. Meeker tells Maxwell that he'll tell Dunne that she started the fire and framed him. Maxwell then fires two bullets into Meeker, killing him instantly. Maxwell is about to shoot Baxter when the police arrive. In an exchange of gunfire, Maxwell is killed. Maxwell framed Dunne for arson to separate him from Jergens. But now, Dunne and Jergens realize they love each other.

Notes and Commentary: Lois Maxwell would go on to cinema fame as Miss Moneypenny in the James Bond series.

In this film, Warner Baxter is back as head of the parole board.

Inspector Manning is back as the police official in the case. Interesting, when William Frawley played the part in *Crime Doctor's Man Hunt* (1946), he was Henry B. Manning. Cliff Clark is John D. Manning in this entry.

Review: "A standard mystery but one of the better films in the series." *Motion Picture Guide*, Nash and Ross

"Standard mystery-actioner in Columbia's celluloid series based upon the 'Crime Doctor' radio show. Helped by a fair amount of suspense and a plausible story, this latest entry will provide adequate supporting fare for the duals." *Variety*, 03/23/49

Summation: The Crime Doctor series ends on a positive note with a well-written little crime story. Warner Baxter has less to do in this entry. A veteran cast takes up the slack and performs admirably. The acting honors, though, go to Lois Maxwell as a psychotic woman scorned.

The Durango Kid

For western star Charles Starrett's 1944–45 release schedule, production head Harry Decker devised a group of westerns featuring the Durango Kid, "A mysterious masked rider whose name became a by-word in Texas 1875." Now, for those readers with good memories, there was a stand-alone feature, *The Durango Kid* (Columbia, 1941), with Starrett. In this early saga, Durango wore a white hat rather than the black one in the official series. No additional Durango movies were forthcoming at that time.

Starrett took on a short-lived series, The Medico. But Durango emerged again in *Sagebrush Heroes* (Columbia, 1944), in which Starrett played the Durango Kid on his radio program. In the first group of eight Durango adventures, Starrett's character went by the name Steve in 4, and a variety of other first names in the others. Starrett had the habit of revealing his identity to the ones he helped before riding on to new adventures. (This might have been a reason for Starrett's name changes.) Tex Harding was the secondary hero in the initial Durango, playing Tex Harding in all but the first. Curiously, Harding did not seem to know Starrett's secret in all of the films. In fact, Harding would occasionally don the Durango outfit to shift suspicion from Starrett. Harding, not a handsome individual, would raise his voice in song sometime throughout the proceedings. It came as a shock to western historians to discover that supporting actor James T. "Bud" Nelson did the actual vocalizing. Harding left after the initial eight. He would be seen in two more Durangos, *Last Days of Boot Hill* (Columbia, 1947) utilizing archive footage, and *Desert Vigilante* (Columbia, 1949). In neither case did he receive onscreen billing.

The other recurring character was Cannonball, played in the final seven of the first season by Dub Taylor. Taylor had been on the scene in western movies since *Taming of the West* (Columbia, 1939) with Bill Elliott. Taylor appeared with Elliott in 13 features before riding with Russell Hayden in eight, and with Starrett in eight non–Durangos before signing on for the Durango series. After *Frontier Gun Law* (Columbia, 1946), both Harding and Taylor left the series. Columbia decided to stay with Starrett as the Durango Kid. A few changes would be made; hereafter Starrett's first name would always be Steve, although he had a myriad of last names. Of the few times the last name was repeated, it usually would be as a sequel. The series took on a surreal quality, with lightning changes to the masked hero. Also, no matter how Starrett came into an area, his white horse, Raider, and his black garb would be uncannily at hand.

Taylor's departure from the series was predicated by the availability of Smiley Burnette. Burnette entered big time show business when he was hired by Gene Autry to appear in his music group in 1933. The two became fast friends and when Autry was beckoned to Hollywood, Burnette came along. Burnette became Autry's comic sidekick at Republic, playing the part of Frog Millhouse in all but Autry's first starring western, *Tumbling Tumbleweeds*

(Republic, 1935) in which Burnette was just Smiley. When Autry enlisted in the Air Force, Burnette became a sidekick for Roy Rogers (nine films), Eddie Dew (two films), Bob Livingston (three films) and Sunset Carson (four films). Sunset had the unenviable distinction of being the only action star to receive billing secondary to a sidekick. After the Carson sagas, Burnette's contact with Republic was up. He was proving to be difficult to work with, so his contract was not renewed. Columbia took the opportunity to sign him for the Durango series, giving the exhibitors and moviegoing public two Top Ten western stars.

Starrett appeared in the *Motion Picture Herald* popularity poll 15 times, with his highest position of fourth place in 1941 and 1951. Burnette was almost as popular, placing in the poll 13 times, coming in at third place in 1943 and 1944. It has been said that Starrett and Burnette never became fast friends but learned to work with each other. Burnette always played Smiley Burnette in the Durangos, never Smiley Butterbeam as has been stated by some historians. Oddly, in the series, Smiley's relationship with Starrett could change from picture to picture: at times as fast friends, even with Burnette knowing Starrett's secret identity; sometimes knowing Starrett but not his secret identity; and sometime just meeting Starrett for the first time. When the screenwriters didn't let Burnette's "funnies" get out of control, he could be an asset, but beware if he was allowed to run wild. Possibly the best Durango epic was *Prairie Roundup* (Columbia, 1951) in which everything was right. It had a strong story, rugged action, excellent camera work and a fine performance by Burnette. Burnette handily whips brawny bad man John Cason in a fist fight and sings a show-stopping musical number, "Deep Froggie Blues."

Starrett had two top stuntmen who thrilled audiences with spectacular stunt work. The first was Ted Mapes, who was frequently seen as a villain. When Jacques O'Mahoney took over, he first played various support roles until, billed sometimes as Jock Mahoney, sometimes as Jack Mahoney, he became a series regular in the final seven entries. Mahoney, like Burnette, had various relationships with Starrett, but was always on the side of the law.

The Durango Kid series had its good stories and those that should have been forgotten. Columbia found they could make some episodes in each season on the cheap by utilizing stock footage from the earlier Durangos. In some of these sequels, time would be taken for long flashbacks from an earlier film. In fact, some features had too little new footage.

In 1949, ME comics began a bi-monthly series, "Charles Starrett as the Durango Kid." The series ran for 41 issues, ending with the October/November 1955 issue. In the comic book, Durango's alter-ego was Steve Brand and his sidekick was Muley Pike. ME could not use Smiley Burnette as Burnette had his own comic book with Fawcett Publications. With *The Kid from Broken Gun* (Columbia, 1952), the series was discontinued. This was the first film that at the story's end, Starrett did not ride off to new adventures. The actor retired from the screen. Burnette would make personal appearances, even appearing at shopping center openings. He would be seen on television as a regular on *Ranch Party* (Screen Gems, 1958) and would assume the role of Charley Pratt on *Petticoat Junction* (CBS, 1963–67) and *Green Acres* (CBS, 1965–66). It was mentioned that Durango would resurface with Mahoney in the role, but nothing came of it. Before the end of the Durango series, Mahoney had been signed on as the title character in the television show, *The Range Rider* (Flying A Productions, 1951–53). This led to his starring in six western features for Universal-International, and a second television series, *Yancey Derringer* (CBS, 1958). Mahoney would become the screen's 13th Tarzan in *Tarzan Goes to India* (Metro-Goldwyn-Mayer, 1962). His film and television career would last until 1985.

THE DURANGO KID
Columbia (August 1940)

Masked terror stalks the rhythm-ringin' bad lands!

Alternate Title: The Masked Stranger

Cast: Bill Lowery, Charles Starrett; Nancy Winslow, Luana Walters; Mace Ballard, Kenneth MacDonald; Steve, Francis Walker; Ben Winslow, Forrest Taylor; Marshal Trayboe, Melvin Lang; Bob, Bob Nolan; Pat, Pat Brady; Sam Lowry, Frank LaRue; the Sons of the Pioneers (Hugh Farr, Karl Farr, Lloyd Perryman and Tim Spencer)// Bixby, Steve Clark; Evans, Jack Rockwell; Mrs. Evans, Marin Sais; Taylor, Ralph Peters; Banning, John Tyrrell

Credits: Director, Lambert Hillyer; Screenwriter, Paul Franklin; Editor, Richard Fantl; Cinematographer, John Stumar

Songs: "Tumbling Tumbleweeds" (Nolan) sung and played by the Sons of the Pioneers; "There's a Rainbow Over the Range" (Nolan and Spencer) sung and played by the Sons of the Pioneers; "The Prairie Sings a Lullaby" (Nolan and Spencer) sung and played by the Sons of the Pioneers; "Yippi-Yi Your Troubles Away" (Nolan and Spencer) sung and played by the Sons of the Pioneers

Location Filming: Agoura and Lone Pine, California

Production Dates: May 9, 1940–May 17, 1940

Running Time: 61 min.

Story: Pretending friendship to other ranchers, Kenneth actually wants to drive all homesteaders off the range. Frank LaRue discovers MacDonald's duplicity and is subsequently murdered. MacDonald claims to have seen the murder and tells LaRue's son, Charles Starrett, that homesteaders were responsible. Starrett believes MacDonald is behind all the trouble. In his guise as the Durango Kid, Starrett begins robbing MacDonald and giving money to the homesteaders. MacDonald sets a trap for Starrett. Starrett turns the tables and gets MacDonald to confess that he murdered LaRue. About to be arrested, MacDonald makes a break for freedom and Starrett follows in pursuit. In a gun duel, Starrett shoots MacDonald.

Notes and Commentary: Although the actual Durango Kid series would not begin until the release of *The Return of the Durango Kid* (Columbia, 1945), most "B" western fans consider this film to be a part of the series.

Ben Taggart was originally cast to play Marshal Trayboe. The part would eventually go to Melvin Lang.

Review: "Familiarly-tailored but meritorious six-shooter drama." *Variety*, 08/28/40

Summation: This is a good beginning to the Durango Kid character: a well-paced western by veteran director Lambert Hillyer, with good acting by the principals, especially Charles Starrett and Kenneth MacDonald.

THE RETURN OF THE DURANGO KID
Columbia (April 1945)

Meet a great new western thrill star!

Alternate Title: Stolen Time

Cast: Bill Blayden, Charles Starrett; Jim Gill, Tex Harding; Paradise Flo, Jean Stevens;

The Return of the Durango Kid (1945) scene card — (left to right) George Chesbro, Britt Wood, Tex Harding, Charles Starrett, Ted Mapes (over Starrett's head), Jean Stevens, unknown actor, Ray Bennett.

Lee Kirby, John Calvert; The Jesters (Guy Bonham, Walter Carlson and Dwight Latham)// "Raider"; Buckskin Liz, Betty Roadman; Tom, Hal Price; Sheriff, Dick Botiller; Curly, Britt Wood; Cherokee, Ray Bennett; Ringo, Paul Conrad; Murdered card player, Steve Clark; Tom, Carl Sepulveda; Luke, Elmo Lincoln; Henchmen, Ted Mapes, Dan White, William Desmond, Carl Mathews and Herman Hack; Townsman, James T. "Bud" Nelson; Saloon patron, Jack O'Shea

    Credits: Director, Derwin Abrahams; Producer, Colbert Clark; Screenwriter, J. Benton Cheney; Editor, Aaron Stell; Art Directors, Lionel Banks and Charles Clague; Set Decorator, John W. Pascoe; Cinematographer, Glen Gano.

    Songs: "Old Pinto (and His Cowboy Pal)" sung by Tex Harding; "When They Fiddle Out the Polka" (Seiler, Neiburg and Marcus) sung by Jean Stevens and the Jesters; "He Holds the Lantern (While His Mother Cuts the Wood)" (Gray, Terker and Jacobs), sung by the Jesters; "We'll Hang Old Leland Kirby" sung by Tex Harding and the Jesters; "Old Pinto (and His Cowboy Pal)" (reprise) sung by Tex Harding and the Jesters

    Location Filming: Corriganville, California

    Production Dates: June 5, 1944–June 15, 1944

    Running Time: 58 min.

    Story: Charles Starrett comes to Silver City to clear his father's name as outlaw and killer. The town is under the control of saloon owner John Calvert. Calvert wants control of Betty Roadman's stage line. Starrett helps Roadman and begins to thwart Calvert's attacks on the line. Starrett is able to get the gang members arguing with each other. Starrett confronts gang member Hal Price and has him give the information he needs to clear his father's name. Calvert enters Price's office and gets the drop on Starrett and Price. Using Starrett's gun, Calvert murders Price and frames Starrett. Starrett convinces Sheriff Dick Botiller of his innocence. Starrett asks for 24 hours to prove Calvert is the killer. Using the mysterious persona of the Durango Kid, Starrett puts fear into the hearts of Calvert's henchmen. Finally, only Calvert and his lead henchman, Paul Conrad, are left. Starrett is able to turn Conrad against Calvert. When Calvert almost kills Conrad, he blurts out that Calvert killed Price. Botiller overhears this outburst. Calvert bolts out of the door only to be greeted by Starrett. He is taking Calvert to jail when Calvert turns, brandishing a hidden derringer in his hand. Starrett is faster than Calvert and a well-placed bullet ends his outlaw career. Starrett rides to new adventures.

Notes and Commentary: Tex Harding's singing was dubbed by James T. "Bud" Nelson.

Charles Starrett paves the way for the next entry, telling folks he has to track down train robber Dan Cass. Dan Cass is one of the outlaws in *Both Barrels Blazing* (Columbia, 1945).

John Calvert liked his role as the villainous Lee Kirby. He enjoyed manipulating the spring that released the derringer that was hidden in his right sleeve into his hand.

Henchman Luke was played by Elmo Lincoln, the screen's first Tarzan. Lincoln was seen in *Tarzan of the Apes* (National Film Corp. of America, 1918), *The Romance of Tarzan* (National Film Corp. of America, 1918) in which Tarzan battles western outlaws in California, and the serial *The Adventures of Tarzan* (Numa Pictures Corporation, 1921).

Review: "Mediocre film." *Western Movies*, Pitts

Summation: This is not a bad effort in the first official Durango Kid series entry. Charles Starrett is fine as the masked hero, and he's pretty well matched by John Calvert with his smooth villainy. Derwin Abrams's direction keeps the story moving nicely to the climactic shootout.

BOTH BARRELS BLAZING
Columbia (May 1945)

The Durango Kid Thunders Into Action!

Alternate Title: The Yellow Streak

Cast: Kip Allen, Charles Starrett; Tex Harding, Tex Harding; Cannonball, Dub Taylor; Gail Radford, Pat Parrish; The Jesters (Guy Bonham, Walter Carlson and Dwight Latham)// "Raider"; Captain Rogers, Jack Rockwell; Lucky Thorpe, Al Bridge; Dan Cass, Robert Barron; Nevada, Charles King; Shad, John Cason; Lefty Dean, Bert Dillard; Spike, Edward Howard; Grubstake, Emmett Lynn; Henchmen, Dan White and James T. "Bud" Nelson

Credits: Director, Derwin Abrahams; Producer, Colbert Clark; Screenwriter, William Lively; Editor, Henry Batista; Art Director, Charles Clague; Set Decorator, John W. Pascoe; Cinematographer, George Meehan

Songs: "Sidekick Joe" sung by The Jesters; "Through the Night" sung by Tex Harding

Shooting it out with desperate rustlers!

Both Barrels Blazing (1945) scene card — Charles Starrett, Emmett Lynn (on ground).

and the Jesters; "Look Before Your Leap" sung by the Jesters; "Cowboys and Indians" sung by the Jesters; "Look Before Your Leap" (reprise) sung by Tex Harding and the Jesters; "Through the Night" (reprise) sung by Tex Harding and the Jesters

Location Filming: Corriganville, California

Production Dates: June 22, 1944–June 30, 1944

Running Time: 58 min.

Story: Robert Barron steals gold belonging to needy Texas families. Texas Ranger Charles Starrett, in the guise of the Durango Kid, trails after Barron. Town boss Al Bridge has Barron murdered. Bridge takes the stolen money and places the blame on the Durango Kid. Bridge arranges to have prospector Emmett Lynn appear as a rich mine owner when his granddaughter comes to visit. Through Lynn's mine, Barron can move the stolen gold. Starrett's pal, Tex Harding, discovers the ore from Lynn's mine is minted gold. Starrett allows Lynn to set a trap for Bridge. Bridge is aware and sets a trap for Starrett and Harding. Lynn warns Starrett at the cost of his own life. Bridge returns to his saloon to get the gold. Starrett follows, after which he and Bridge exchange shots. Starrett's bullet ends Bridge's outlaw career. Starrett takes the stolen gold back to Texas. Harding marries Parrish.

Notes and Commentary: The working title was "Texas Rifles."

This time out, James T. "Bud" Nelson performed double duty. He sang for Tex Harding and played one of the henchmen.

Scenes from this film would later be used in *Last Days of Boot Hill* (Columbia, 1947)

Review: "Fair entry in the 'Durango Kid' series." *Western Movies*, Pitts

Summation: This is a good Durango Kid episode. There is sufficient action and the story moves well until a musical interlude about halfway through brings the film to a temporary halt. Charles Starrett makes a good hero, but acting honors go to Alan Bridge and Emmett Lynn. Pat Parrish is one of the loveliest leading ladies in the Durango Kid series.

RUSTLERS OF THE BADLANDS
Columbia (August 1945)

The Durango Kid roars to new glory!

Alternate Title: By Whose Hand?

Cast: Steve Lindsay, Charles Starrett; Tex Harding, Tex Harding; Cannonball, Dub Taylor; Sally Boylston, Sally Bliss; Jim Norton, George Eldredge; Regan, Edward M. Howard; Blake, Ray Bennett; Packard, Ted Mapes; Sheriff Mallory, Karl Hackett; Al Trace and His Silly Symphonists// "Raider"; Boylston, Steve Clark; Emerson, Frank LaRue; Stage driver, Bud Osborne; Tom, Edmund Cobb; Outlaw cook, Ted French; Dr. Burton, Nolan Leary; Major Ostrand, Jack Ingram; Cowhand, Frank Ellis; Henchmen, James T. "Bud" Nelson, Frank McCarroll and Carl Sepulvada

Credits: Director, Derwin Abrahams; Producer, Colbert Clark; Story, Richard Hill Wilkinson; Screenwriter, J. Benton Cheney; Editor, Aaron Stell; Art Director, Charles Clague; Set Decorator, John W. Pascoe; Cinematographer, George Meehan

Songs: "Dusty Saddle on the Ole Barn Wall" (Stoner and Rice); "Yodelin' Kate" (B. Trace and A. Trace); "Hay! Louella" (Davis, Levy, Cody, Braverman and Brookhouse)

Location Filming: Iverson, California

Production Dates: July 12, 1944–July 21, 1944

Running Time: 55 min.

Story: Charles Starrett and Tex Harding are assigned to investigate cattle rustling and the murder of an army lieutenant in New Mexico. Taking separate trails to Antelope Valley, Starrett is accused of being a rustler by George Eldredge, foreman of Steve Clark's ranch. Harding and Dub Taylor break Starrett out of jail. In his guise as the Durango Kid, Starrett goes to Clark's ranch to talk with his daughter, Sally Bliss. Bliss is worried because Clark is missing. Bliss tells Starrett that Eldredge is ignoring the threat of rustlers and plans a cattle drive. Starrett, Harding and Taylor prevent the cattle from being rustled. In trailing the rustlers, they rescue Clark, who had been wounded. Bliss and Harding take Clark to town for medical assistance. Starrett and Taylor engage the rustlers in a gunfight. Sheriff Karl Hackett and a posse arrive. Starrett and Taylor are accused of being rustlers. Starrett and Taylor break free. Again as the Durango Kid, Starrett finds evidence that Eldredge is in league with the rustlers. Confronting Eldredge, Starrett gets him to confess and lead him to the rustlers' hideout. A gunfight breaks out at the hideout. Just as things are looking grim, Taylor and Hackett arrive to place Eldredge and his gang in custody.

Notes and Commentary: The working title was "Renegade Roundup."

Again, James T. "Bud" Nelson performed double duty. He sang for Tex Harding and played one of the henchmen.

This was the last role Sally Bliss had as Sally Bliss for five years. Bliss was back in the films as Carla Balenda for six years before reverting back to being billed as Bliss. Bliss ended her career as Miss Hazlett in fifteen episodes of the Lassie (CBS) from 1958–63.

Review: "Standard "Durango Kid" offering." *Western Movies*, Pitts

Summation: This film was unavailable for viewing by the author.

Outlaws of the Rockies
Columbia (September 1945)

Hard-riding action! Pulse-tingling rhythms!

Alternate Title: A Roving Rogue

Cast: Steve Williams, Charles Starrett; Tex Harding, Tex Harding, Cannonball, Dub Taylor; Jane Stuart, Carole Mathews; Singer, Carolina Cotton; Spade, Spade Cooley, the King of Western Swing// "Raider"; Honest Dan Chantry, Philip Van Zandt; Pete, James T. "Bud" Nelson; Bill, Horace B. Carpenter; Tom, the banker, Frank LaRue; Ace Lanning, I. Stanford Jolley; Jason, George Chesebro; Sheriff Potter, Steve Clark; Deputies, Kermit Maynard and John Tyrell; Frank, Frank O'Connor, Sheriff Hall, Jack Rockwell; Red, Nolan Leary; Musicians, Smokey Rogers (Singer, guitar), Deuce Spriggins (singer, bass) and Tex Williams (singer)

Credits: Director, Ray Nazarro; Producer, Colbert Clark, Screenwriter, J. Benton Cheney; Editor, Aaron Stell; Art Director, Charles Clague; Cinematographer, George Kelley

Songs: "Hilda Was a Darn Good Cook" sung by Smokey Rogers, Deuce Spriggins and Carolina Cotton with Spade Cooley and his band; "You'll Know What It Means to be Blue" sung by Tex Williams with Spade Cooley and his band; "The Tear in Your Eyes" sung by Tex Harding with Spade Cooley and his band; "Do Ya or Don't Cha" (Cooley and Rogers) sung by Carolina Cotton and Smokey Rogers with Spade Cooley and his band; "The Tear in Your Eyes" (reprise) sung by Tex Harding with Spade Cooley and his band

Location Filming: Iverson and Corriganville, California

Production Dates: April 11, 1945–April 21, 1945

Running Time: 55 min.

Story: Peddler Philip Van Zandt is the real leader of I. Stanford Jolley's outlaw gang. Sheriff Charles Starrett is lured out of town so the bank can be robbed without interference. In the getaway, Tex Harding tries to stop the holdup. Harding wounds one outlaw who drops some of the bank money. Stopping to pick up the money, Harding is accused by banker Frank LaRue as being a member of the gang. Although Harding is a friend of Starrett's, Starrett has to jail Harding until he can find evidence to clear him. Harding is impatient and breaks out of jail. Starrett is accused of allowing Harding to escape. Starrett has to get away at gunpoint so he, too, can prove his innocence. Starrett and Harding finally work together and capture Jolley and his gang. Van Zandt is able to free them and also alert Sheriff Jack Rockwell that Starrett and Harding are hiding out at Carole Mathews's mine. Starrett and Harding are arrested. Van Zandt has Jolley rob the bank where Mathews' has stored $50,000 in gold. Starrett and Harding escape, but too late to prevent the robbery.

In searching for the robbers, Starrett comes upon Van Zandt on the trail. Starrett notices the deep ruts that Van Zandt's wagon wheels are making. Starrett and Harding follow him. Van Zandt goes to the outlaw hide-out. A gun battle ensues. Van Zandt tricks Starrett and Harding into the hide-out shack where the only way out is the front door. Van Zandt sets fire to a wagon loaded with explosives and sends it toward the shack. Starrett is able to set off the explosives with a well-placed shot. The shock of the explosion stuns the outlaws long enough for Starrett to capture them. Starrett rides to new adventures.

Notes and Commentary: Again, James T. "Bud" Nelson performs double duty. He sings for Tex Harding and plays Pete, the outlaw shot in the first bank robbery.

Both Spade Cooley and Tex Williams had their chance at western stardom. Cooley had the lead in a quartet of films for various small companies in 1950. The best was probably a western musical, *Everybody's Dancing* (Lippert, 1950). Tex Williams starred in 18 featurettes for Universal-International from 1948 to 1950). Some of Williams's entries featured footage from earlier Universal westerns, headlined by either Bob Baker or Johnny Mack Brown.

Reviews: "Fast moving but somewhat hard to follow 'Durango Kid' segment." *Western Movies*, Pitts

"A weak western. A low-budgeted film, lack of originality and poor attempts at humor groove it for the grade school kids." *Variety*, 11/14/45

Summation: This is a good, fast moving entry in the Durango Kid series. The performances are up to par and Carole Mathews makes a fetching heroine.

BLAZING THE WESTERN TRAIL
Columbia (October 1945)

The Durango Kid blazes a new thrill trail!
Roaring guns ... strumming guitars ... swingy tunes ... sizzling action!

Alternate Title: Who Killed Waring?

Cast: Jeff Waring, Charles Starrett; Tex Harding, Tex Harding; Cannonball, Dub Taylor; Mary Halliday, Carole Mathews; Bob, Bob Wills; The Texas Playboys (Noel Boggs [steel guitar], Alex Brashear [trumpet], Tommy Duncan [singer], Cameron Hill [guitar], Joe Holley [fiddle], Monte Montjoy [drums] and Jimmy Wyble [guitar])// "Raider"; Brent, Al Bridge; Perkins, John Tyrell; Halliday, Nolan Leary; Dan Waring, Steve Clark; Nellie, Virginia Sale; McMasters, Mauritz Hugo; Santry, Ethan Laidlaw; Sheriff Turner, Edmund Cobb; Henchmen, Edward M. Howard and Ted Mapes; Deputy, James T. "Bud" Nelson; Stagecoach passenger, Budd Buster; Postal Inspector Spencer, Frank LaRue

Credits: Director, Vernon Keays; Producer, Colbert Clark; Screenwriter, J. Benton Cheney; Editor, Henry Batista; Art Director, Charles Clague; Set Decorator, John W. Pascoe; Cinematographer, George Meehan

Songs: "Ida Red" (White) sung by Tommy Duncan with Bob Wills and the Texas Playboys; "Goodbye, Liza Jane" (traditional) sung by Tommy Duncan with Bob Wills and the Texas Playboys; "Time Changes Everything" (Duncan) sung by Tommy Duncan with Bob Wills and the Texas Playboys; "I Wonder if You Feel the Way I Do" (Wills) sung by Tex Harding with Bob Wills and the Texas Playboys; "Time Changes Everything" (reprise) sung by Tommy Duncan with Bob Wills and the Texas Playboys

Location Filming: Corriganville and Providencia Ranch, California

Production Dates: August 21, 1944–September 1, 1944

Running Time: 57 min.

Story: Ruthless Al Bridge needs to control the stage line in Quanto Basin in order to obtain a lucrative mail contract. Unable to purchase Nolan Leary's line, Bridge proceeds to destroy it. Bridge sets up a rival stage line managed by Steve Clark who has a reputation for honesty. When Clark learns of Bridge's duplicity, he hurries to Leary's office. Before he can explain the situation to Leary, Bridge's henchman, Mauritz Hugo, kills Clark and Leary is arrested for the crime. Clark's nephew, Charles Starrett, is determined to uncover his uncle's murderer. Bridge hires Starrett to run his line. Starrett arranges for his friend Tex Harding to help Leary's daughter, Carole Mathews, to run her line. In his guise of the Durango Kid, Starrett blunts the attacks on Mathews' line and begins robbing Bridge's stagecoaches. In one attack of Starrett's attacks against Bridge, Sheriff Edmund Cobb finds evidence that Starrett is the Durango Kid. Because everything stolen from Bridge's line had been delivered to him to be returned to the rightful owners, Cobb lets Starrett continue with his plan. To determine which line will receive the mail contract, a race between the rival stage lines will be held. Bridge's men try to prevent Mathews' line from finishing the race, even to the point of wounding Harding so he can't finish the race. Starrett comes to the rescue and guides the stage to victory. Starrett is able to trick Hugo into admitting that Bridge hired him to kill Clark. Starrett brings Bridge to justice before riding to new adventures.

Notes and Commentary: The working title was "Raiders of Quanto Basin."

This time James T. "Bud" Nelson plays Sheriff Edmund Cobb's deputy as well as providing the singing voice of Tex Harding.

It has been printed that Paul Borofsky is the film's editor, but it is Henry Batista who receives onscreen credit.

In Charles R. Townsend's book, *San Antonio Rose* (University of Illinois Press, 1986), Millard Kelso is listed as one of the Texas Playboys in the film. There is an unidentified bass player in the film.

In the montage at the beginning of the picture, a stagecoach drops from a dynamited bridge into a river. This scene had been used in the serial *The Great Adventures of Wild Bill Hickok* (Columbia, 1938), as well as another Durango Kid adventure, *Pecos River* (Columbia, 1951).

Review: "Pretty good 'Durango Kid' episode." *Western Movies*, Pitts

Summation: This is a superior "B" western. Director Vernon Keays paces this one fast, fast, fast. Starrett is in top form. Al Bridge is a formidable adversary. The western swing music by Bob Wills and His Texas Playboys is excellent. Dub Taylor and Virginia Sale provide some pretty funny comic relief. See This One!

LAWLESS EMPIRE
Columbia (November 1945)

The Durango Kid blazes into action!

Alternate Title: Power of Possession

Cast: Steve Ranson, Charles Starrett; Reverend Tex Harding, Tex Harding; Cannonball, Dub Taylor; Vicky Harding, Mildred Law; Bob Wills and His Texas Playboys (Noel Boggs [steel guitar], Tommy Duncan [singer], Cameron Hill [guitar], Chuck MacKay [trumpet], Joe Holley [fiddle], Millard Kelso [accordion], Teddy Adams [bass] and Jimmy Wyble [guitar])// "Raider"; Mr. Murphy, Lloyd Ingraham; Mrs. Murphy, Jessie Arnold; Duke, Ethan Laidlaw; Lenny, George Chesebro; Skids, Boyd Stockman; Blaze Howard, John Calvert; Marty Foster, Johnny Walsh; Doc Weston, Forrest Taylor; Jeff Stevens, Jack Rockwell; Homesteaders, Edward M. Howard and James T. "Bud" Nelson; Editor Sam Enders, Tom Chatterton; Cattle Buyer, Jack Kirk.

Credits: Director, Vernon Keays; Producer, Colbert Clark; Story, Elizabeth Beecher; Screenwriter, Bennett Cohen; Editor, Paul Borofsky; Art Director, Charles Clague; Set Decorations, John W. Pascoe; Cinematographer, George Meehan

Songs: "(Stay All Night) Stay a Little Longer" (Duncan and Wills) sung by Tommy Duncan with Bob Wills and His Texas Playboys; "Home in San Antone" (Jenkins) sung by Tommy Duncan with Bob Wills and His Texas Playboys; "Farther Along" (Stevens) sung by Tex Harding, Mildred Law, Tommy Duncan with Bob Wills and His Texas Playboys; "Dev'lish Mary" sung by Tommy Duncan with Bob Wills and His Texas Playboys; "Farther Along" (reprise) sung by Bob Wills and His Texas Playboys

Location Filming: Iverson and Walker Ranch, California

Production Dates: October 5, 1944–October 16, 1944

Running Time: 58 min.

Story: Outlaws are driving homesteaders off their lands. Saloon owner John Calvert is thought to be behind the outlawry. Charles Starrett as the Durango Kid and Reverend Tex Harding pledge to aid the homesteaders. Calvert convinces Starrett to become marshal and track down the Durango Kid. Starrett has an ulterior motive: to find who murdered Starrett's brother, the previous marshal. Starrett as the Durango Kid is able to stop Calvert's efforts to harm the homesteaders, thanks to information provided by Dub Taylor. D. Taylor is working as a swamper in Calvert's saloon. The homesteaders plan to sell their cattle. Forrest Taylor, masquerading as a kindly doctor, is the actual leader of the gang. F. Taylor orders Calvert to stop the roundup. Again, thanks to D. Taylor's information, Starrett is able to thwart the outlaw raids. F. Taylor now plans to murder Harding and place the blame on Starrett. Starrett walks into their trap, then springs a trap of his own. F. Taylor and Calvert try to get away but Starrett brings them to justice.

Notes and Commentary: When Charles Starrett rounds up John Calvert and Forrest Taylor at the end of the picture, Starrett shoots a gun out of Taylor's hand. When the camera cuts back to Taylor, he is now holding his shoulder.

The working title was "The Taming of Helldorado."

In this entry, James T. "Bud" Nelson plays a homesteader as well as providing the singing voice of Tex Harding.

Reviews: "Choppy, but fast moving 'Durango Kid' episode." *Western Movies*, Pitts

"There's nothing novel or startling in this horse-opera, but the combination of hard-riding, shooting, sheriff-vs.-outlaws story, suspense, insertions of music, makes a pleasant enough confection for western fans." *Variety*, 02/13/46

Summation: This is an above average "B" western with plenty of action and some excellent music from Bob Wills and His Texas Playboys. We get to see some long fistic encounters, something somewhat lacking in previous Durango Kid entries. Charles Starrett is fine as the masked hero. Dub Taylor's comedy is silly and predictable this time out. Elizabeth Beecher's story and Bennett Cohen's screenplay is serviceable, but the mystery villain is too easy to spot.

Texas Panhandle

Columbia (December 1945)

Blazing a glory trail through the west!

Cast: Steve Buckner, Charles Starrett; Tex Harding, Tex Harding; Cannonball, Dub Taylor; Ann Williams, Nanette Parks; Carolina, Carolina Cotton; Spade, Spade Cooley, The King of Western Swing// "Raider"; Spade Cooley's Band, "Muddy" Berry (harmonica); "Spike" Featherstone (zither); Gibby Gibson (fiddle); Joaquin Murphy (steel guitar); Smokey Rogers (singer, guitar); Johnny Weis (guitar); Tex Williams (singer); Chief Harrington, William Gould; Harrington's secretary, Budd Buster; Dinero, Edward M. Howard; Slash, George Chesebro; Ace Galatan, Forrest Taylor; Bistro, Jack Kirk; Millicent, Jody Gilbert; Trig, Ted Mapes; Shorty, Hugh Hooker; Bartender, Robert Walker

Credits: Director, Ray Nazarro; Producer, Colbert Clark; Screenwriter, Ed Earl Repp; Editor, Paul Borofsky; Art Director, Charles Clague; Cinematographer, George Kelly

Songs: "I Love to Yodel" (Hagstrom) sung by Carolina Cotton and Smokey Rogers with Spade Cooley and his band; "Heavenly Range" (Cooley and Rogers) sung by Tex Williams with Spade Cooley and his band; "Take Me Back to Tulsa" (Wills and Duncan) sung by Tex Williams, Smokey Rogers, Spade Cooley and Carolina Cotton with Cooley's band; "At Sunset" (Silva and Walter) sung by Tex Harding with Spade Cooley and his band; "I Love to Yodel" (reprise) sung by Carolina Cotton with Spade Cooley and his band

Location Filming: Iverson, California

Production Dates: April 30, 1945–May 9, 1945

Running Time: 58 min.

Story: Secret Service Agent Charles Starrett reports to William Gould for his next assignment, hoping to be assigned to track down the outlaw gang responsible for attacks on the Texas trails. Instead Starrett finds he's been suspended, on the suspicion that he's the Durango Kid. Starrett, posing as a lawyer, goes west with a wagon train led by Tex Harding. The outlaw gang captures the wagon train and takes it to Crow Springs. Most of the men are forced to prove up a section of land and then give a quick claim deed to outlaw boss Forrest Taylor. Taylor claims to own the land that actually belongs to Nanette Parks. Starrett goes to work for Taylor. A letter taken from Harding contains a will giving Parks the rights to the land claimed by Taylor. Starrett, as the Durango Kid, takes the will from Taylor. Starrett then takes the land registry and tells Taylor that the Durango Kid stole it. Starrett, as Durango, almost retrieves stolen gold from Taylor's safe. Taylor decides to melt the gold into bullion and hide it in the blacksmith shop. There, Taylor finds Starrett's horse, Raider, Durango's outfit and all the missing papers. Taylor confronts Starrett and orders his henchman, Edward M. Howard, to gun him down. Harding causes a distraction, enabling Starrett to escape. Starrett is then able to arm the homesteaders. Taylor calls all his gunmen to town to prepare for battle. Starrett has the homesteaders round up the wild horses in the area and stampede them into town. During the ensuing confusion, Starrett and his men rout out the outlaws, and Taylor is brought to justice. Starrett is reinstated in the Secret Service.

Notes and Commentary: Helen Hagstrom wrote, "I Love to Yodel." Hagstrom was Carolina Cotton's real name.

In this entry James T. "Bud" Nelson only provides the singing voice of Tex Harding.

Review: "Okay 'Durango Kid' series entry." *Western Movies*, Pitts

Summation: This is a routine western, with Charles Starrett again in charge as the Durango Kid. Ed Earl Repp's screenplay is only adequate. A mild windup with Starrett bringing villain Forrest Taylor to justice mars this effort.

FRONTIER GUNLAW

Columbia (January 1946)

Outlaws meet their master ... the Durango Kid!

Alternate Titles: Frontier Gun Law and Menacing Shadows

Cast: Jim Stewart, Charles Starrett; Tex Harding, Tex Harding; Cannonball, Dub Taylor; Kitty, Jean Stevens; Al Trace and His Silly Symphonists// "Raider." Matt Edwards, Weldon Heyburn; Hank Watson, Jack Rockwell; Sheriff Kincaid, Frank LaRue; Pop Evans, John Elliott; Mace, Robert Kortman; Sam, Stanley Price; Musician, Jack Guthrie

Credits: Director, Derwin Abrahams; Producer, Colbert Clark; Story, Victor McLeod; Screenwriter, Bennett Cohen; Editor, Aaron Stell; Art Director, Charles Clague; Set Decorator, John W. Pascoe; Cinematographer, Glen Gano

Songs: "Oh! Please Tell Me, Darling" (Hoffman, Trace and Livingston); "The Antelope and the Lion" (Wexler); "Out in the Cow Country"

Production Dates: August 2, 1944–August 11, 1944

Running Time: 60 min.

Story: Charles Starrett arrives in Mesa City to buy a cattle ranch from Weldon Heyburn, the crippled editor of the *Mesa City News*. Tex Harding's ranch is the only one the Phantom Raiders have never attacked. Consequently, Harding is suspected of being the leader of the outlaw gang. Starrett's ranch is raided. One of his men is killed and he decides to settle the score in his Durango Kid guise. Starrett learns the outlaws use columns in the Mesa City newspaper to contact one another. Meanwhile, Harding is arrested as the leader of the outlaw gang. Starrett believes that Harding is innocent and breaks him out of jail. They ride to Harding's ranch followed by the Phantom Raiders. Sheriff Frank LaRue and a posse enter into the fray. All of the gang is rounded up except the leader. Starrett, as the Durango Kid, rides to Heyburn's office and proves that Heyburn is not crippled. Heyburn and Starrett fight. Harding arrives in time to help subdue Heyburn. Starrett rides to new adventures.

Notes and Commentary: At the conclusion, Tex Harding, Dub Taylor and the singing voice of James T. "Bud" Nelson would be replaced by Smiley Burnette. Harding would be seen in future Durango Kid features, those for which flashback footage is used.

The working titles were "Phantom Outlaws" and "Prairie Raiders."

Review: "Pretty fair entry in the popular 'Durango Kid' series." *Western Movies*, Pitts

Summation: This film was unavailable for viewing by the author.

ROARING RANGERS

Columbia (February 1946)

The wild west's most exciting action team

Alternate Title: False Hero

Cast: Steve Randall, Charles Starrett; Doris Connor, Adele Roberts; Merle Travis and his Bronco Busters (Slim Duncan [Fiddle and Piccolo], Red Murrell [guitar] and Alan Reinhart [bass]); Smiley Burnette, Smiley Burnette// "Raider"; "Ring Eye"; Outlaw Leader, Bob Wilke; Sheriff Jeff Connor, Jack Rockwell; Taggart, Edmund Cobb; Larry Connor, Mickey Kuhn; Bill Connor, Ed Cassidy; Slade, Ted Mapes; Rancher, Kermit Maynard; Boy with money, Teddy Infuhr; Scrud, Gerald Mackey; Henchmen, Ethan Laidlaw, Herman Hack, Chick Hannon, Tex Harper and Carol Henry

Credits: Director, Ray Nazarro; Producer, Barry Shipman; Screenwriter, Barry Shipman; Editor, Jerome Thoms; Art Director, Charles Clague; Cinematographer, George Kelley

Songs: "Listen to the Mocking Bird" (Hawthorne) played by Smiley Burnette; "The New Ten-Gallon Hat" (Penny, Wills and Burnette) sung by Smiley Burnette with Merle Travis and His Bronco Busters; "The Old Chisholm Trail" (traditional) sung by Merle Travis with His Bronco Busters; "Lazy Daily Dozen" (Burnette) sung by Smiley Burnette with Merle Travis and His Bronco Busters; "The New Ten-Gallon Hat (reprise) sung by Smiley Burnette

Location Filming: Iverson and Providencia Ranch, California

Production Dates: May 17, 1945–May 26, 1945

Running Time: 56 min.

Story: Many of the ranchers in the Powder River area are delinquent in their taxes. Edmund Cobb is most vocal in having these ranches put up for auction. There is a good chance the railroad will be coming though, and whoever owns these ranches will stand to make a huge profit. Sheriff Jack Rockwell supports the ranchers opposed to the auction. Rockwell's brother, Ed Cassidy, wants the auction to take place at any cost. Rockwell's son, Mickey Kuhn, sends a letter to the Durango Kid, asking him for help. Fearing that the Durango Kid will show up, Cassidy has henchman Ted Mapes impersonate Durango. Kuhn, who hero-worships Durango, follows Mapes. Mapes shoots Kuhn, possibly crippling him for life. Charles Starrett and his sidekick, Smiley Burnette, arrive in Powder River. Starrett convinces Rockwell to go to the capital and get the railroad project pushed through. Both Starrett and Cassidy know when Rockwell is returning to Powder River with good news for the ranchers. Cassidy tells Mapes he must impersonate Durango one last time. The plan is for both Rockwell and Mapes to be killed. Starrett, as Durango, foils the plan. Starrett has captured Mapes and shows Rockwell the Durango Kid never shot Kuhn. The word is spread that Rockwell is dead. Cobb proclaims himself sheriff and schedules the auction. Cassidy believes Rockwell to be alive and goes to Rockwell's hiding place. As Cassidy is about to murder Rockwell, Starrett, as Durango, arrives in time to shoot Cassidy. Burnette delays the auction with comedic and musical antics. Cobb instructs his henchmen to put a stop to Burnette's foolishness. Burnette and the townspeople overcome the outlaws. Rockwell arrives to arrest Cobb. Since Kuhn learns the Durango Kid was a hero, he now wants to get well, and does. Starrett and Burnette ride to new adventures.

Notes and Commentary: The working title was "Powder River."

With this picture, Charles Starrett was forever "Steve," although his last name usually changed.

Some sources list Smiley Burnette's character name as Smiley Butterbeam, but Charles Starrett introduces him as Smiley Burnette.

Review: "Pretty good 'Durango Kid' segment." *Western Movies*, Pitts

Summation: This is an above-average "B" western and a pretty good start for the

Charles Starrett-Smiley Burnette team. Director Ray Nazarro keeps the story moving at a brisk place, with plenty of action. Barry Shipman's story is well done until the final minutes when Smiley and the townsmen each connect simultaneously with a punch to the outlaw's jaws. This is pretty thin comedy at this juncture.

GUNNING FOR VENGEANCE
Columbia (March 1946)

Hitting a double high in outdoor action ... fun ... music!

Alternate Title: Jail Break
Cast: Steve Landry, Charles Starrett; Elaine Jenkins, Marjean Neville; The Trailsmen (Curt Barrett [guitar], Slim Duncan [fiddle], Stanley Ellison [accordion], Bud Dooley [bass]); Smiley Burnette, Smiley Burnette// "Raider"; "Ring Eye"; Mike, George Chesebro; Curly, Bob Kortman; Banker, Dick Rush; Jenkins, Nolan Leary; Dr. Hawkins, Frank Fanning; Mayor, Frank LaRue; Belle Madden, Phyllis Adair; Jim Clayburn, Lane Chandler; Shorty, Robert Williams; Raid leader, Jack Kirk; Henchmen, Blackie Whiteford, Tommy Coats, Matty Roubert and Chick Hannon; Smiley's deputy, John Tyrell
Credits: Director, Ray Nazarro; Producer, Colbert Clark; Story, Louise Rousseau; Screenwriters, Louise Rousseau and Ed. Earl Repp; Editor, Paul Borofsky; Art Director, Charles Clague; Cinematographer, George Kelley
Songs: "A Blacksmith of the Village" (Burnette) sung by Smiley Burnette with the Trailsmen; "Twenty Long Years" (Burnette) sung by Smiley Burnette with the Trailsmen; "The Belle of Sonora is Mine" (Barrett and Wilkin) sung by the Trailsmen; "Hominy Grits" (Burnette) sung by Smiley Burnette with the Trailsmen; "A Blacksmith of the Village" (reprise) sung by the Trailsmen
Location Filming: Iverson, California
Production Dates: June 4, 1945–June 13, 1945
Running Time: 54 min.
Story: Around Split Rock, Kansas, outlaws are running wild. Charles Starrett comes to take the job of town marshal. Starrett is reunited with his old pal Smiley Burnette, who becomes his deputy. When Starrett finds his authority ends at the nearby state line, he dons the garb of his alter ego, The Durango Kid. He then begins to protect the homesteaders, foil robberies and bring lawbreakers to justice. Outlaw leader Lane Chandler tells the saloon owners that he wants relaxed law enforcement to encourage trail-herding cowboys to visit Split Rock. Saloon owner Phyllis Adair believes Starrett is the Durango Kid. A plot is hatched to trap him. Adair tells Starrett that a little girl, Marjean Neville, is being held at the outlaw camp. Starrett, as the Durango Kid, rides to rescue Neville, not knowing the girl is safe in the back room of Adair's saloon. Burnette finds out the truth and rides to warn Starrett that he's riding into trouble. Burnette reaches Starrett in time, then rides to town while Starrett leads the outlaws on a long chase. The outlaws decide to ride back to town to Adair's saloon. Chandler sees Burnette ride back to town and the outlaws try unsuccessfully to shoot him. Finally, Chandler decides to set a trap to kill both Starrett and Burnette. Neville, in the saloon, hears the plot and runs out the door. A shot from Chandler, meant for Neville, kills Adair. Adair's devoted employee, Robert Williams, decides to help Burnette. Both walk into the trap, and a gunfight ensues. The tide is turned when Starrett,

as the Durango Kid, enters the fray. Starrett defeats Chandler in a rugged fistfight and the outlaws are brought to justice. Starrett rides to new adventures.

Notes and Commentary: The working title was "Burning the Trail."

The *Hollywood Reporter* stated the editor would be Al Clark. Paul Borofsky received onscreen credit.

Review: "Fairly good 'Durango Kid' series entry." *Western Movies*, Pitts

Summation: This is a good "B" western and a worthy entry in the Durango Kid series. Both Charles Starrett and Smiley Burnette are in top form. Director Ray Nazarro keeps the story moving at a brisk pace. The film is highlighted by two very good fistfights. Starrett takes on Bob Kortman and then Lane Chandler in the film's windup.

GALLOPING THUNDER
Columbia (April 1946)

See rustlers run! Wild stampedes! Smiley and Durango in action!
Your favorite Western stars in a roaring adventure film!

Cast: Steve Reynolds, Charles Starrett; Jud Temple, Adelle Roberts; Merle Travis and His Bronco Busters (Slim Duncan [fiddle, fife] and Alan Reinhart [bass]); Smiley Burnette, Smiley Burnette// "Raider"; "Ring Eye"; Lawson, Nolan Leary; Regan, John Merton; Colonel Collins, Forrest Taylor; Grat Hanlon, Richard Bailey; Barstow, Edmund Cobb; Krag, Kermit Maynard; Wyatt, Ray Bennett; the barber, Budd Buster

Credits: Director, Ray Nazarro; Producer, Colbert Clark; Screenwriter, Ed. Earl Repp; Editor, Richard Fantl; Art Director, Charles Clague; Cinematographer, George Kelley

Songs: "I Want to Play the Fife" (Burnette) sung by Smiley Burnette with Merle Travis and His Bronco Busters; "He'll Be Getting Some Sleep" (Burnette) sung by Smiley Burnette with Merle Travis and His Bronco Busters; "Texas Home Here I Come" (Travis and Atchinson) sung by Merle Travis with His Bronco Busters; "The Wind Sings A Cowboy Song" (Burnette) sung by Smiley Burnette with Merle Travis; "Texas Home Here I Come" (reprise) sung by Merle Travis with His Bronco Busters

Production Dates: June 21, 1945–June 29, 1945

Running Time: 54 min.

Story: Outlaws have been preventing the ranchers around Splitrock from delivering horses to the Army. Charles Starrett is assigned to investigate the situation. He believes banker Richard Bailey is behind the outlaw activity. Starrett, as the Durango Kid, captures henchman John Merton. Before Merton can talk, Bailey shoots him. Bailey convinces his fiancée, Adelle Roberts, to drive a herd of horses through Oro Canyon. Starrett realizes Bailey's men are planning to stampede the horses. Starrett sends word to drive the horses through Wagon Wheel Pass. Roberts disregards Starrett's advice. As the Durango Kid, Starrett organizes the ranchers to fight the outlaws. Bailey, seeing that all is lost, tries to escape but is no match for Starrett. The horses are delivered, and Starrett rides to new adventures.

Notes and Commentary: The working title was "Bronco Busters."

Review: "Only a passable effort in the 'Durango Kid' series." *Western Movies*, Pitts

Summation: This is an okay but undistinguished "B" western. Charles Starrett and Smiley Burnette perform capably. The supporting cast is adequate, with the exception of Richard Bailey. Bailey's acting is not up to the standard of previous boss villains in the Durango Kid series, seeming at times to have difficulty delivering his lines.

Two-Fisted Stranger

Columbia (May 1946)

Dynamite in their fists! Desperadoes on their trail!

Alternate Title: High Stakes

Cast: Steve Gordon, Charles Starrett; Jennifer Martin, Doris Houck; Zeke Clements (of the Grand Ole Opry); Smiley Burnette, Smiley Burnette// "Raider"; "Ring Eye"; Benson, Ted Mapes; Sourdough, Nolan Leary; Sheriff Condon, Jack Rockwell; J.P. Martin, Davison Clark; Brady, Lane Chandler; Doyle, George Chesebro; Ted Randolph, Charles Murray, Jr.; Widow Simpson, Maudie Prickett; Mr. O'Connor, Frank O'Connor; Deputy, Robert Walker

Credits: Director, Ray Nazarro; Producer, Colbert Clark; Story, Robert Lee Johnson; Screenwriters, Peter Whitehead and Robert Lee Johnson; Editor, Paul Borofsky; Art Director, Charles Clague; Set Decorator, Richard Mansfield; Cinematographer, Vincent Farrar

Songs: "The Old Chisholm Trail" (traditional) played by Zeke Clements and trio; "Trombone Song" (Burnette) sung by Smiley Burnette with Zeke Clements and trio; "You're Free Again" (Clements) sung by Zeke Clements and trio; "Will You Meet Me Little Darlin'" (Clements) sung by Zeke Clements and trio; "Someone Swell" (Burnette and Penny) sung by Smiley Burnette; "Trombone Song" (reprise) sung by Smiley Burnette with Zeke Clements and trio

Location Filming: Corriganville, California

Production Dates: July 30, 1945–August 8, 1945

Running Time: 50 min.

Story: Lane Chandler tells banker Davison Clark that some mud samples may contain diamonds. Afraid of a possible bank robbery, Clark needs to move some money to another facility. Clark enlists the help of Sheriff Jack Rockwell. Outlaws attack the stagecoach and Rockwell is killed. The outlaw leader discovers the cash boxes are empty. Rockwell had summoned Charles Starrett as his deputy. Starrett assumes the office of sheriff. Starrett discovers the bank's money in Rockwell's safe. The money is returned to Clark, only to be robbed by Mapes and his gang. Chandler, the actual leader of the gang, needs the money to purchase cheap industrial diamonds to salt Clark's land. Chandler encourages Clark to sell shares in a potential diamond mine. Clark discovers the scam and confronts Chandler. Chandler knocks out Clark, steals the money and kidnaps Clark's daughter, Doris Houck. Starrett, as the Durango Kid, gives chase. A posse rounds up Mapes and his gang. Starrett overtakes Chandler and defeats him in a brief fistfight. Starrett rides to new adventures.

Notes and Commentary: *"When Durango Rode"* was the title of Peter Whitehead's original screen story.

Review: "Short, but not much of an effort in the 'Durango Kid' series." *Western Movies*, Pitts

Summation: Entertaining and fast-moving Durango Kid entry. Charles Starrett is first-rate as the masked hero, and Smiley Burnette provides some nice comedic moments.

The Desert Horseman

Columbia (July 1946)

The west's top action, fun and tune team!

Alternate Title: Checkmate

Cast: Steve Godfrey, Charles Starrett; Mary Ann Jarvis, Adelle Roberts; Walt Shrum and his Colorado Hillbillies; Smiley Burnette, Smiley Burnette// "Raider"; "Ring Eye"; Tom Jarvis, Bud Osborne; Eddie, Riley Hill; Treadway, Richard Bailey; Rex Young, John Merton; Pete, George Morgan; Baldy, Tommy Coats; Sheriff, Jack Kirk

Credits: Director, Ray Nazarro; Producer, Colbert Clark; Story and Screenwriter, Sherman Lowe; Editor, Paul Borofsky; Art Director, Charles Clague; Set Decorator, Richard Mansfield; Cinematographer, L.W. O'Connell

Songs: "He Was An Amateur Once" (Burnette) sung by Smiley Burnette with Walt Shrum and his Colorado Hillbillies; "Ring the Bell" (Burnette) sung by Smiley Burnette; "There's a Tear in Your Eye" (Shrum and Hoag) sung by Walt Shrum with his Colorado Hillbillies; "I Wish I Could Be a Singing Cowboy" (Cahn and Chaplin) sung by Smiley Burnette with Walt Shrum and his Colorado Hillbillies; "Ring the Bell" (reprise) sung by Smiley Burnette with Walt Shrum and his Colorado Hillbillies

Location Filming: Iverson and Agoura, California

Production Dates: August 23, 1945–August 31, 1945

Story: A mysterious desert rat has murdered both Adelle Roberts's father and uncle. Charles Starrett arrives, hopefully, to find who instigated an army payroll robbery and clear both his and Roberts's uncle's names. Family lawyer Richard Bailey is behind a conspiracy to get Roberts to sell her ranch. Bailey has discovered gold on the ranch. Starrett, as the Durango Kid, advises Roberts to hold on to her ranch. After Starrett foils an attempt to make Roberts sign a quick claim deed to henchman John Merton, Bailey sets a trap for Starrett, as Durango. Starrett's old Army buddy, ranch cook Smiley Burnette, upsets the outlaw's plans. An attempt by the mysterious desert rat to murder Starrett fails. Bailey convinces Roberts to meet him on the ranch so that he can show her the gold strike. Burnette alerts Starrett. Burnette and the ranch hands corral Merton and his gang. The mysterious desert rat is set to ambush Roberts, but Starrett, as Durango, shows up in time to shoot the rifle out of his hands. Starrett unmasks the desert rat as Bailey. Bailey's confession clears both Starrett and Roberts's uncle's names. Starrett leaves for Army headquarters.

Notes and Commentary: "Phantom of the Desert" was the working title.

The song, "I Wish I Could Be a Singing Cowboy," was performed by Allen Jenkins and Ann Miller in *Go West, Young Lady* (Columbia, 1941)

Review: "Enjoyable, if undistinguished, programmer." *Motion Picture Guide*, Nash and Ross

Summation: This is another enjoyable Durango Kid episode. Acting is up to par in this entry; even Richard Bailey acquits himself favorably this time out. Ray Nazarro's directing keeps the story constantly on the move.

HEADING WEST

Columbia (August 1946)

Heading for action!

Alternate Title: The Cheat's Last Throw

Cast: Steve Randall, Charles Starrett; Anne Parker, Doris Houck; Hank Penny and His Plantation Boys; Smiley Burnette, Smiley Burnette// "Raider"; "Ring Eye"; Indian, Charles Soldani; Rance Hudson, Norman Willis; Kelso, John Merton; Jim Mallory, Hal Taliaferro; Sam Parker, Nolan Leary; Blaze Curlew, Bud Geary; Red Curlew, Frank McCarroll;

Drag, Matty Roubert; Stage driver, Post Park; Wounded henchman, Stanley Price; Doctor Wyatt, Tom Chatterton; Henchman, Tommy Coats

Credits: Director, Ray Nazarro; Producer, Colbert Clark; Story and Screenwriter, Ed. Earl Repp; Editor, Henry Batista; Art Director, Charles Clague; Set Decorator, Richard Mansfield; Cinematographer, George B. Meehan

Songs: "Sally Goodin" (Foree and Rose) sung by Hank Penny with his Plantation Boys; "That Old Ice Cream Freezer" (Burnette) sung by Smiley Burnette with Hank Penny and his Plantation Boys; "Scaredy Cat Blues" (Burnette) sung by Smiley Burnette; "Bless Your Heart" (Penny and Hensley) sung by Smiley Burnette with Hank Penny and His Plantation Boys; "Sally Goodin" (reprise) sung by Hank Penny with His Plantation Boys

Location Filming: Iverson, California

Production Dates: September 24, 1945–October 2, 1945

Running Time: 54 min.

Story: Charles Starrett reads in the Bonanza City newspaper that the Durango Kid is raiding miners. Starrett and his sidekick, Smiley Burnette, ride to investigate. In Bonanza City, Norman Willis, owner of a mining business, is behind the outrages. He has hired notorious outlaw Bud Geary and his gang to pull off the robberies. Willis is trying to break all the miners so he can control all the mines in the Bonanza area. Also, Willis and Geary plan to doublecross each other. Willis's next target is miner Norman Leary. One attempt to steal Leary's gold ore is thwarted by Starrett, as the Durango Kid. In a second attempt, Starrett arrives too late. Burnette trails the outlaws and is captured. Burnette make his escape and is chased by the outlaws. Starrett, as Durango, rescues Burnett and captures one of the henchmen, Stanley Price. Price tells Starrett the location of Geary's hideout. Starrett tells Willis where he can find Geary. Willis orders his henchman, John Merton, to gun down Geary's gang and bring back all the gold his gang has stolen. The two gangs meet and a gunfight ensues. During the altercation, Starrett loads the gold in a wagon and returns it to Leary. Leary tells Willis that he's making a shipment to pay off his debt. Merton and his men attack, only to be rebuffed by Starrett, as Durango. Knowing all is lost, Willis and Merton try to get away but are no match for the quick-shooting Starrett.

Notes and Commentary: "Massacre Mesa" was the working title.

Review: "Fair 'Durango Kid' series entry." *Western Movies*, Pitts

Summation: Good, fast and exciting Durango Kid western that finds both Charles Starrett and Smiley Burnette in top form. The villainy is in the capable hands of Norman Willis, Bud Geary and John Merton.

Songs and comedy are just fine.

LANDRUSH

Columbia (October 1946)

Topping their best!

Alternate Titles: Land Rush and The Claw Strikes

Cast: Steve Harmon, Charles Starrett; Mary Parker, Doris Houck; Ozie Waters and His Colorado Rangers (Edward "Tookie" Cronenbold [fiddle], Eddie Kirk [guitar] and Scotty Harrel [bass]); Smiley Burnette, Smiley Burnette// "Raider"; "Ring Eye"; "Claw" Hawkins, Bud Geary; Bill, George Chesebro; Sheriff Collins, Bud Osborne; Editor Jake

Parker, Emmett Lynn; Kirby Garvey, Steve Barcley; Sackett, Bob Kortman; Sweeper, George Hoey; The minister, Curt Barrett; Stage driver, John Hawks

Credits: Director, Vernon Keays; Producer, Colbert Clark; Story and Screenwriter, Michael Simmons; Editor, James Sweeney; Art Director, Charles Clague; Set Decorator, George Montgomery; Cinematography, George B. Meehan, Jr.

Songs: "Darling Nellie Gray" (Hanby) sung by Ozie Waters and His Colorado Rangers; "Dentist's Song" (Burnette) sung by Smiley Burnette with Ozie Waters and His Colorado Rangers; "De Camptown Races" (Foster) sung by Ozie Waters and His Colorado Rangers; "Oh! Susanna" (Foster) sung by Ozie Waters and His Colorado Rangers; "Darling Nellie Gray" (Hanby) sung by Smiley Burnette with Ozie Waters and His Colorado Rangers

Location Filming: Iverson, California

Production Dates: November 5, 1945–November 13, 1945

Story: Spur Valley, a haven for outlaws, is being opened by the federal government for homesteading. Outlaws, led by Bud Geary, are turning back homesteaders to prevent a land rush. Into this tense situation rides Charles Starrett as the Durango Kid. The real leader of the outlaw activities is businessman Steve Barclay. Even though the outlaws continue the attempt to stop the land rush, Starrett, as Durango, is able to spread the word. Realizing the land rush will be held, Barclay schemes to block the homesteaders so his hirelings can stake out the best sites in Spur Valley. As Durango, Starrett stops Barclay's men from staking any claim. Geary, realizing Barclay's plan will fail, tries to warn Barclay. Barclay shoots Geary and then tries to get away. Starrett reaches Barclay before he can mount his horse. In a rugged fight, Barclay collapses under the pounding of Starrett's fists. Starrett now rides to new adventures.

Notes and Commentary: This film was made after *Terror Trail* (Columbia, 1946), but was released about a month before.

The song "Darling Nellie Gray" tells the story of a young maiden taken into slavery.

Footage from this film would find its way into a later Durango Kid entry, *Streets of Ghost Town* (Columbia, 1950).

There was an interesting dialogue exchange:

DORIS HOUCK: Want to know something, Smiley?
SMILEY BURNETTE: What?
DORIS HOUCK: Maybe someday you will.

Reviews: "Generic western format. Performances are stiff and direction is uneven — at best." *Motion Picture Guide*, Nash and Ross

"More than passable 'Durango Kid' segment." *Western Movies*, Pitts

"'Landrush' will probably excite the weekend moppets. Kids who will enjoy almost anything will take this." *Variety*, 09/18/46

Summation: This is a well-paced Durango Kid episode by director Ray Nazarro. Charles Starrett performs well and Smiley Burnette keeps most of his slapstick comedy under control. Nazarro is able to generate some suspense in the scene in which Starrett approaches the outlaw's cabin.

TERROR TRAIL

Columbia (November 1946)

Hail Durango and Smiley ... in a hail of hot lead and top tunes!

Cast: Steve Haverly, Charles Starrett; Karen Kemp, Barbara Pepper; Ozie Waters and His Colorado Rangers (Edward "Tookie" Cronenbold [fiddle], Eddie Kirk [guitar, accordion] and Scotty Harrel [guitar, bass]); Smiley Burnette, Smiley Burnette// "Raider"; "Ring Eye"; Duke Catlett, Lane Chandler; Waco, Ted Mapes; Drag, George Chesebro; Bart Matson, Zon Murray, Ed, Edward M. Howard; Rocky Kemp, Elvin Field; Relief stage driver, Budd Buster

Credits: Director, Ray Nazarro; Producer, Colbert Clark; Story and Screenplay, Ed. Earl Repp; Editor, Aaron Stell; Art Director, Charles Clague; Set Decorator, Richard Mansfield; Cinematographer, George B. Meehan

Songs: "The Road That Leads to Nowhere" sung by Ozie Waters with His Colorado Rangers; "Way Down Low" (Burnette) sung by Smiley Burnette with Ozie Waters and His Colorado Rangers; "Louisville Lady" sung by Ozie Waters with His Colorado Rangers; "Peg-Leg" (Burnette) sung by Smiley Burnette with Ozie Waters and His Colorado Rangers; "Peg-Leg" (reprise) sung by Smiley Burnette with Ozie Waters and His Colorado Rangers

Location Filming: Iverson, California

Production Dates: October 17, 1945–October 25, 1945

Running Time: 55 min.

Story: Charles Starrett returns to Red Buette, Wyoming, to sell his ranch, not realizing a range war between cattlemen and sheepmen is brewing. Saloon owner Lane Chandler is behind all the unrest, while pretending to be a friend of the cattlemen. Barbara Pepper is coming west to buy a half-interest in the sheep venture. Accompanying her is her trouble-prone younger brother, Elvin Field. First, Chandler sends his henchmen to rob Pepper, but Starrett, as the Durango Kid, recovers the money. Then Chandler allows Pepper to be his partner figuring the cattlemen won't fight a woman. Starrett finally convinces Pepper to move her sheep to another range, under protection of the cattlemen. Chandler sees this as an opportunity to rustle cattle and plans to start with Starrett's. Pepper refuses to join in and is locked in a closet in Chandler's saloon. Entertainer Smiley Burnette rescues Pepper and together they race to warn Starrett. Meanwhile, Field, thinking Chandler is a big shot, decides to ride with him. Starrett guesses correctly when Chandler plans to strike. A gunfight ensues and the cattle stampede. Field's horse throws him in the path of the stampede. Chandler leaves Field to die. Starrett rescues Field and Burnette rounds up Chandler and his gang. Pepper buys Starrett's ranch and Field becomes Burnette's assistant.

Notes and Commentary: "Renegade Range" was the working title.

Plenty of stock footage from previous Durango Kid films can be seen in this outing: the stagecoach holdup and chase of Durango by the outlaws; Durango on Raider, rearing and turning (usually used in the introduction of the Durango Kid); Durango leaping out of the saloon window onto Raider, then riding around to the back of a building where Durango seeks refuge; and Durango being chased on horseback by Ted Mapes and George Chesebro, only to be unseated by a rope stretched across the road.

When Ozie Waters and His Colorado Rangers back up Smiley Burnette on "Way Down Low," an accordion is definitely heard, even though none of the band members is playing one.

Review: "Pretty fair 'Durango Kid' episode with good supporting work by Lane Chandler and Barbara Pepper." *Western Movies*, Pitts

Summation: This is just a standard Durango Kid entry, but benefits from the energy infused by Barbara Pepper. Otherwise, this is strictly routine fare.

THE FIGHTING FRONTIERSMAN
Columbia (December 1946)

The west's action-rhythm-and-fun champs!

Alternate Title: Golden Lady

Cast: Steve Reynolds, Charles Starrett; Dixie King, Helen Mowery; Hank Newman and The Georgia Crackers (Bob Newman, Slim Newman and Johnny Spies); Smiley Burnette, Smiley Burnette// "Raider"; "Ring Eye"; "Cimarron" Dobbs, Emmett Lynn: John Munro, Robert Filmer; Rankin, George Chesebro; Waco, Jock O'Mahoney; Slade, Zon Murray; Blaze, Jim Diehl; Kate, Maudie Prickett; The Printer, Ernie Adams; Banker Roberts, Frank LaRue

Credits: Director, Derwin Abrahams; Producer, Colbert Clark; Screenwriter, Ed. Earl Repp; Editor, Jerome Thoms; Art Director, Charles Clague; Set Decorator, Robert Bradfield; Cinematographer, Philip Tannura

Songs: "Old Folks at Home" (Foster) sung by Emmett Lynn; "Little Brown Jug"(Winner) played by Hank Newman and The Georgia Crackers; "Swamp Woman Blues" (Burnette) sung by Smiley Burnette; "Don't Be Mad at Me" (Burnette) sung by Smiley Burnette with Hank Newman and The Georgia Crackers; "Following the Trail" (B. Newman) sung and played by Hank Newman and The Georgia Crackers; "Blue Tail Fly" (traditional) played by Hank Newman and The Georgia Crackers; "Coyote Chorus" (Burnette) sung by Smiley Burnette with Hank Penny and The Georgia Crackers; "Don't Be Mad at Me" (reprise) sung by Smiley Burnette with Hank Newman and The Georgia Crackers

Location Filming: Iverson, California

Production Dates: June 11, 1946–June 19, 1946

Running Time: 61 min.

Story: Prospector Emmett Lynn discovers Santa Ana's lost treasure. Lynn confides in saloon girl Helen Mowery and tells her he's going to contact Texas Ranger Charles Starrett. Saloon owner Robert Filmer and his gang see one of the Mexican coins and kidnap Lynn. Mowery sends a letter to Starrett about Lynn's disappearance. Starrett and his pal, Smiley Burnette, ride to investigate. Lynn is being held captive without food or water, but refuses to disclose the location of the treasure. Starrett, as the Durango Kid, offers a $5,000 reward for information of Lynn's whereabouts. Starrett begins to organize a massive search. Filmer gets Mowery to talk to Lynn and tell her where to find the treasure. Filmer plans to kill Mowery after she gets the information. Lynn tells Mowery he'll tell her if she gets a certain badge from Durango. Mowery obtains the badge, but tells Filmer she failed to get it. Mowery realizes she's going to be killed. Showing Lynn the badge, Mowery has Lynn draw a map. Starrett locates the cabin and has Burnette and Hank Newman's musicians create a diversion. Starrett, as Durango, reaches the cabin in time to prevent Lynn and Mowery's deaths. Starrett rescues Lynn, and Mowery throws in with Filmer. He goes after Starrett and Lynn and is captured by Starrett. Filmer turns the tables, knocks out Starrett and removes his mask. Filmer goes back to the cabin to set off some explosives. As he is leaving the cabin, he and Starrett exchange shots, and Filmer is wounded. Filmer is trying to crawl to safety when the charge goes off, ending his outlaw career. Burnette rounds up Mowery and the rest of the gang. Starrett, Burnette and Lynn give up their shares in the treasure, donating the money to impoverished ranchers in the area.

Notes and Commentary: "Big Bend Badmen" was the working title.

The Fighting Frontiersman was the first directorial effort for Derwin Abrahams in the Durango Kid series. Abrahams would direct seven additional entries.

The scene in which the Durango Kid distributes flyers offering a reward for finding "Cimarron" Dobbs was first used in *Landrush* (Columbia, 1946), released just two months ahead of *The Fighting Frontiersman*.

Steve Reynolds (Charles Starrett) and Dixie King (Helen Mowery) will show up in the final Durango Kid episode, *The Kid from Broken Gun* (Columbia, 1952).

Summation: This one of the better Durango Kid entries. Both Charles Starrett and Smiley Burnette are in top form. Burnette performs "Swamp Woman Blues," which is a show stopper. Acting honors go to Emmett Lynn, who delivers probably his best performance of his long career. Director Derwin Abrahams comes through with a winner is his first time out with the series.

SOUTH OF THE CHISHOLM TRAIL

Columbia (January 1947)

There's hot lead flyin' and music in the air ...

Cast: Steve Haley/The Durango Kid, Charles Starrett; Nora Grant, Nancy Saunders; Hank Newman and The Georgia Crackers (Bob Newman, Slim Newman and Johnny Spies); Smiley Burnette, Smiley Burnette// "Raider"; "Ring Eye"; Big Jim Grady, Frank Sully; Milt, Milton Kibbee; Bonecrusher, Victor Holbrook; Doc Walker, George Chesebro; Thorpe, Jock O'Mahoney; Sheriff Palmer, Eddie Parker; Deputy, Kermit Maynard; Pop Grant, Frank LaRue; Chet Tobin, Jack Ingram; Rancher, Ethan Laidlaw; Townsman, Steve Clark; Johnson, Fred Sears; Abilene Deputy Marshal, Robert Barron

Credits: Director, Derwin Abrahams; Producer, Colbert Clark; Story and Screenwriter, Michael Simmons; Editor, Paul Borofsky; Art Director, Charles Clague; Set Decorator, Robert Bradfield; Cinematographer, George F. Kelley

Songs: "Froggy Went A-Courtin'" (traditional) sung by Smiley Burnette and Hank Newman and The Georgia Crackers; "Dr. Burnette, King of Pain" (Burnette) sung by Smiley Burnette and Hank Newman and The Georgia Crackers; "I Get the Sillies" (Burnette) sung by Smiley Burnette and Hank Newman and The Georgia Crackers; "Hi-Nellie, Lo-Nellie" sung by Hank Newman with The Georgia Crackers; "I'd Learn to Yodel" (Newman) sung by Smiley Burnette; "Down in Abilene" sung by Hank Newman and The Georgia Crackers; "Down in Abilene" (reprise) sung by Hank Newman and The Georgia Crackers with Smiley Burnette

Location Filming: Providencia Ranch, California

Production Dates: June 24, 1946–July 2, 1946

Running Time: 58 min.

Story: Rustlers are terrorizing the cattle trails in Kansas. Investor Frank Sully is responsible for bringing the railroad to Abilene. On the trail, Smiley Burnette and his pals see a holdup and take the money from the outlaws. Sheriff Eddie Parker catches Burnette with the money and places him under arrest. Charles Starrett, as the Durango Kid, steps in, frees Burnette and takes the money. In Bearcat, Parker tries to arrest Burnette again, but Starrett gives the money to Parker. Rancher Frank LaRue offers Starrett a job fighting the rustlers, but Starrett turns him down. Burnette takes a job with veterinarian George Chesebro, who is one of the men behind the outlaw gang. Both Starrett and Burnette learn of Chesebro's villainy. Starrett finds that Sully is Chesebro's partner and takes a job with Chesebro. Sully is suspicious of Starrett and the two men shoot it out, with Starrett killing Sully. Chesebro and his men try to rob the Cattleman's Association exchange and are met by Starrett (as the Durango Kid) and Burnette. Chesebro is captured and his men are killed. Starrett rides to new adventures.

Notes and Commentary: "The Outlaw Tamer" was the working title.

Review: "Complicated and hard to follow 'Durango Kid' entry." *Western Movies*, Pitts

Summation: This is a good, fast moving Durango Kid western. Everything is pretty much standard in the acting department, but it was a relief not to see Smiley as a buffoon in this outing.

THE LONE HAND TEXAN

Columbia (March 1947)

Burstin' with bullets and ballads!

Alternate Title: The Cheat

Cast: Steve Driscoll/The Durango Kid, Charles Starrett; Mustard, Frank Rice; Gravy, Ernest Stokes; Smiley, Smiley Burnette// "Raider"; "Ring Eye"; Sam Jason, Fred F. Sears; Henchmen, John Cason and George Russell; Clarabelle Adams, Mary Newton; Williams, Jasper Weldon; Hattie Hatfield, Maudie Prickett; J.E. Clark, Art Dillard; Boomer Kildea, Robert Stevens; Scanlon, George Chesebro; Stagecoach Driver, Post Park; Well workers, Blackie Whiteford and Herman Hack

Credits: Director, Ray Nazarro; Producer, Colbert Clark; Screenwriter, Ed. Earl Repp; Editor, Paul Borofsky; Art Director, Charles Clague; Set Decorator, Frank Kramer; Cinematographer, George F. Kelley

Songs: "Crow Song" (Burnette) sung by Smiley Burnette with Mustard and Gravy; "They Never Say 'Love You' On a Postcard" (Burnette) sung by Smiley Burnette with Mustard and Gravy; "The Birthday Song" (Burnette) sung by Smiley Burnette with Mustard and Gravy; "What Makes You So Sweet" (Burnette) sung by Smiley Burnette with Mustard and Gravy; "We Had a Big Time" sung by Mustard and Gravy; "We Had a Big Time" (reprise) sung by Mustard and Gravy

Location Filming: Corriganville, California

Production Dates: September 27, 1946–October 5, 1946

Running Time: 54 min.

Story: Outlaws blow up Fred F. Sears's oil well and are chased by Charles Starrett, in his guise of the Durango Kid. Starrett gets the drop on the outlaws and warns them to stay away from the oil well. Sears's men, afraid of outlaw retaliation, quit. Sears has sent for Starrett to help him. With Starrett's help, Sears starts over and gets wildcat oilman Robert Stevens to sign on. Starrett discovers that ranch owner Mary Newton has been receiving correspondence from an unscrupulous oil company. Newton is behind Sears's troubles and wants the oil leases. Sears raises additional money to finance his well. Newton's foreman George Chesebro, dressed as the Durango Kid, steals the money. Starrett, as the Durango Kid, goes to Newton's ranch, where his suspicions about her are confirmed, and he brings her and her men to justice. Stevens brings in a gusher for Sears.

Notes and Commentary: The working title was "Blue Prairie."

Reviews: "Okay 'Durango Kid' western." *Western Movies*, Pitts

"A routine entry from Starrett as the Durango Kid." *The Western*, Hardy

Summation: A fast-moving Durango Kid entry with an incoherent storyline. At the end, Charles Starrett has the bag of stolen money before he brings robber George Chesebro to justice. Starrett is fine as the hero, and rest of the cast deliver satisfactory performances. Smiley Burnette's "funnies" are not as obtrusive in this entry. The songs with Burnette and Mustard and Gravy are below par. Overall, the film is only average.

WEST OF DODGE CITY

Columbia (March 1947)

The west's top thrill-tune-and-fun team!

Alternate Title: The Sea Wall

Cast: Steve Ramsey/The Durango Kid, Charles Starrett; Anne Avery, Nancy Saunders; Mustard, Frank Rice; Gravy, Ernest Stokes; Smiley, Smiley Burnette// "Raider"; "Ring Eye"; Henry Hardison, Fred F. Sears; John Avery, Nolan Leary; Dirk, Zon Murray; Stage driver, Bud Osborne; Flint, Marshall Reed; Hod Barker, George Chesebro; Danny Avery, Glenn Stuart; Borger, I. Stanford Jolley; Adams, Bob Wilke; Office manager, Tom Chatterton; Sheriff, Steve Clark; Mrs. Throckbottom, Almira Sessions

Credits: Director, Ray Nazarro; Producer, Colbert Clark; Screenwriter, Bert Horswell; Editor, Edwin Bryant; Art Director, Charles Clague; Set Decorator, Robert Bradfield; Cinematographer, George F. Kelley

Songs: "The Circus Parade" (Rice and Stokes) sung by Mustard and Gravy; "Satchel Up and Go" (Rice and Stokes) sung by Smiley Burnette with Mustard and Gravy; "Cricket Song" (Burnette) sung by Smiley Burnette with Mustard and Gravy; "Can't Cry for Laughin'" (Burnette) sung by Smiley Burnette with Mustard and Gravy

Location Filming: Iverson, California

Production Dates: September 11, 1946–September 19, 1946

Running Time: 57 min.

Story: Fred F. Sears wants to purchase Nolan Leary's ranch for a power project scam. Leary has hired engineer/surveyor Charles Starrett to publicly discredit Sears. In the guise of a stagecoach holdup, Sears shoots Leary. Sears wants to stop Starrett from making a survey and revealing that the ranch is not a basin for a natural reservoir. Starrett convinces Leary's daughter Nancy Saunders from selling the ranch to Sears. Saunders's brother, Glenn Stuart, wants to sell the ranch. Hothead Stuart is goaded into shooting up the town while henchmen Marshall Reed and Zon Murray rob the bank. Sheriff Steve Clark believes Stuart is one of the bandits and arrests him. As the Durango Kid, Starrett tells Sears to leave town. Sears pretends to leave but plans to blow up the dam, flooding Saunders's ranch. Starrett is unable to prevent the explosion. The flood waters catch up with Sears, but Starrett pulls Sears to safety. Sears makes a confession which clears Stuart. Starrett rides to new adventures.

Notes and Commentary: The working title was "Trigger Law."

Review: "Fair 'Durango Kid' entry." *Western Movies*, Pitts

Summation: Speedy, but less plausible than usual. Bert Horswell should "satchel up and go" after delivering this screenplay. Charles Starrett plays a surveyor without surveying equipment and probably should have been a geologist. His quick changes are even more unbelievable, from eluding the outlaws as Durango to minutes later riding with George Chesebro as if he had been with him for hours. The resolution is just too pat, but the younger audience probably won't notice or care. Fred F. Sears plays the villain as if he is Oil Can Harry from the Mighty Mouse cartoons. On a positive side, the musical interludes with Smiley Burnette and Mustard and Gravy are simply delightful.

LAW OF THE CANYON
Columbia (April 1947)

Sizzlin' gunplay! Tuneful horseplay!

Alternate Title: The Price of Crime

Cast: Steve Langtry/The Durango Kid, Charles Starrett; Mary Coleman, Nancy Saunders; Spike Coleman, Buzz Henry; Texas Jim Lewis and His Lone Star Cowboys (Spud Goodall [guitar], Buddy Hayes [bass], Harold Hensley [fiddle] and Billy Liebert [accordion]); Smiley, Smiley Burnette// "Raider"; "Ring-Eye"; Ben, Jack Kirk; Fletcher, Zon Murray; Henchman, Bob Wilke; Henchman lying in road, Stanley Price; Dr. Middleton, Fred F. Sears; Sheriff Coleman, George Chesebro; T.D. Wilson, Edmund Cobb; Wagon driver, Art Dillard; Hotel clerk, Douglas D. Coppin; Dr. D. Kay, Frank LaRue; Blackie, Frank Merlo

Credits: Director, Ray Nazarro; Producer, Colbert Clark; Screenwriter, Eileen Gary; Editor, Burton Kramer; Art Director, Harold MacArthur; Set Decorator, Dave Montrose; Cinematographer, George F. Kelley

Songs: "My Luck" (Burnette) sung by Smiley Burnette; "Riding the Trail Back Home" (Lewis) sung by Texas Jim Lewis with His Lone Star Cowboys; "Trouble Always Finds Me" (Burnette) sung by Smiley Burnette with Texas Jim Lewis and His Lone Star Cowboys; "Way Back in Grandpa's Day" (Lewis and Cargill) sung by Texas Jim Lewis with His Lone Star Cowboys; "My Luck" (reprise) sung by Smiley Burnette with Texas Jim Lewis and His Lone Star Cowboys

Location Filming: Iverson, California

Production Dates: October 14, 1946–October 22, 1946

Running Time: 56 min.

Story: Special government agent Charles Starrett, posing as an eastern businessman, is bringing a wagon train with goods to Jackson City. The wagon train is attacked by the Hood gang, with Starrett sustaining a bullet wound to his right hand. While obtaining treatment by Dr. Fred F. Sears, Starrett is told that his wagon train will be put up for ransom. Sears is called on to deliver the ransom money, and the wagon trains are returned the next morning. Starrett, as the Durango Kid, begins to interfere with the Hood gang. Sears, who is the gang leader and only masquerading as a physician, orders henchman Zon Murray to get him. Sears, while "treating" Sheriff George Chesebro, has actually been sedating him. At Chesebro's ranch, Smiley Burnette is asked to put Sears's medical bag on his horse. Burnette, instead, plays with the medications and replaces them with water. Starrett attempts to get another wagon train through. Starrett, as Durango, routs the gang and the wagon train gets through safely. Since Starrett disappeared before the fight started, he is jailed. Burnette, who knows that Starrett is a government agent, helps him break jail. Meanwhile, Murray tells Sears that since Durango's hand is bandaged, Starrett must be the Durango Kid. Starrett comes to Sears's office, where Sears gives him an injection. Starrett is rendered unconscious and taken to the outlaw's hideout. But Starrett had only pretended to be knocked out, and soon overcomes his captors. Returning as Durango, he confronts Sears and captures his gang. Sears makes a getaway, followed by Starrett, as Durango. Starrett tries to capture Sears but Sears falls from a high cliff to his death. Starrett rides to new adventures.

Notes and Commentary: Shades of Dick Tracy! The dentist's name in this picture is Dr. D. Kay.

Review: "Less than mediocre 'Durango Kid' feature." *Western Movies*, Pitts

Summation: Fast-moving; one of the best Durango Kid entries. Kudos to screenwriter Eileen Gary for keeping the narrative flowing and on track. Also, the ending explains the title as Fred F. Sears falls to his death in a canyon. The performances are satisfactory and Smiley Burnette's comedy routines are easy to take.

PRAIRIE RAIDERS
Columbia (May 1947)

A two-man whirlwind of action and song!

Alternate Title: The Forger

Cast: Steve Bolton/The Durango Kid, Charles Starrett; Ann Bradford, Nancy Saunders; Bronc Masters, Robert Scott; Ozie Waters and His Colorado Rangers (Edward "Tookie" Cronenbold [fiddle], Scotty Harrel [bass] and Eddie Kirk [guitar]); Smiley, Smiley Burnette// "Raider"; "Ring-Eye"; Briggs, Douglas D. Coppin; Stark, Lane Bradford; Cinco, John Cason; Shorty, Tommy Coats; Flagg, Ray Bennett; Sheriff, Steve Clark; Bart Henley, Hugh Prosser; Bradford, Frank LaRue; Secretary of the Interior Meeker, Sam Flint

Credits: Director, Derwin Abrahams; Producer, Colbert Clark; Screenwriter, Ed. Earl Repp; Editor, Paul Borofsky; Art Director, Charles Clague; Set Decorator, Dave Montrose; Cinematographer, George F. Kelley

Songs: "Raisin' Rabbits" (Burnette) sung by Smiley Burnette with Ozie Waters and His Colorado Rangers; "My Country and You Dear" sung by Ozie Waters with His Colorado Rangers; "The Thieving Burro" (Burnette) sung by Smiley Burnette with Ozie Waters and His Colorado Rangers; "Roll On" (traditional) sung by Ozie Waters with His Colorado Rangers; "My Country and You Dear" (reprise) sung by Smiley Burnette with Ozie Water and His Colorado Rangers

Location Filming: Corriganville, California

Production Dates: October 31, 1946–November 8, 1946

Running Time: 54 min.

Story: To ensure a steady supply of horses for the Army, Charles Starrett, agent for the Department of the Interior, leases 50,000 acres of range land to Robert Stevens. Trouble brews when Hugh Prosser produces a lease for the same area signed by Secretary of the Interior Sam Flint. Prosser's lease is a forgery. Starrett gives Stevens the okay to round up horses. Prosser's men stampede the horses into town and to the railhead. Starrett, as the Durango Kid, and Stevens prevent Prosser from sending the horses to market. Still as Durango, Starrett gets proof that Prosser's lease is a forgery and brings him to justice. Starrett then rides to new adventures.

Notes and Commentary: The working title was "Whispering Range."
The *Hollywood Reporter* stated that, prior to principal photography, Derwin Abrahams replaced Ray Nazarro.

Review: "Another lookalike entry in the 'Durango Kid' series." *Western Movies*, Pitts

Summation: Only an average Durango Kid entry. Ed. Earl Repp's screenplay and Derwin Abraham's direction fail to bring the necessary energy to the story. In a plot flaw, Charles Starrett identifies Douglas D. Coppin as the forger, with no evidence to support his accusation.

THE STRANGER FROM PONCA CITY
Columbia (July 1947)

Sharpshootin' thrills!

Cast: Steve Larkin/The Durango Kid, Charles Starrett; Terry Saunders, Virginia Hunter; Texas Jim Lewis and His Lone Star Cowboys (Buddy Hayes [jug], Billy Liebert [concertina] and Charlie Linville [fiddle]); Smiley, Smiley Burnette// "Raider"; "Ring Eye"; Fargo, Ted Mapes; Tensleep, Jock O'Mahoney; Billy, "Harmonica Bill" Russell; Grat Carmody, Forrest Taylor; Tug Carter, Paul Campbell; Duke, Johnny Carpenter; Bill, Tom McDonough; Flip Dugan, Jim Diehl

Credits: Director, Derwin Abrahams; Producer, Colbert Clark; Screenwriter, Ed. Earl Rapp; Editor, Burton Kramer; Art Director, Charles Clague; Set Decorator, Dave Montrose; Cinematography, George F. Kelley

Songs: "Top It" sung by "Harmonica Bill" Russell, Smiley Burnette and Texas Jim Lewis and His Lone Star Cowboys; "Catfish, Take a Look at That Worm" (Burnette) sung by Smiley Burnette and Texas Jim Lewis and His Lone Star Cowboys; "Hillbilly Lil" sung by Texas Jim Lewis and His Lone Star Cowboys; "Hoot'n Nannie Annie" sung by Texas Jim Lewis and His Lone Star Cowboys; "Rubbing Out the Deadline" sung by Smiley Burnette and Texas Jim Lewis and His Lone Star Cowboys

Location Filming: Iverson Ranch, Walker Ranch and Providencia Ranch, California
Production Dates: November 15, 1946–November 23, 1946
Running Time: 56 min.

Story: After cleaning up the outlaw problem in Ponca City, Charles Starrett moves on to Red Mound, a town with a white line painted down the middle. There's a feud between the businessmen and the rough citizens. Starrett wants to purchase the Atkins ranch. To date, all prospective buyers have been frightened off. As the Durango Kid, Starrett is able to have the sale recorded by storekeeper Forrest Taylor. Starrett, Sheriff Paul Campbell and restaurant owner Smiley Burnette search the ranch to find out why people have been run off. Starrett finds that Jim Diehl is mixed up in the scheme. Starrett believes that outlaws are using the ranch to hide stolen cattle. He then tricks Taylor into revealing himself as the outlaw leader. In the ensuing showdown, Campbell guns down Diehl. Starrett rounds up Taylor and the rest of the gang. With all of the rustlers rounded up, the white line is rubbed out. Campbell becomes the city marshal, and Starrett rides to new adventures.

Notes and Commentary: Texas Jim Lewis had a 55-year career that began in 1929. Although proficient with both the guitar and doghouse bass, Lewis is known for his "Hootin'nanny" that consisted of automobile horns, hand-cranked sirens, percussive clackers, two washboards and a blank firing gun. Lewis was seen in 42 films, mainly short subjects like *Swingin' in the Barn* (Universal, 1940). Lewis had some best-selling records, such as "Who Broke the Lock on the Henhouse Door" (Vocalion, 1936), "Seven Beers with the Wrong Woman" (Decca, 1940) and "Too Late to Worry, Too Blue to Cry" (Decca, 1944). After leaving Hollywood, Lewis concentrated on local TV with his *Sheriff Tex's Safety Junction* on KING-TV in Seattle.

Review: "Fair 'Durango Kid' series segment." *Western Movies*, Pitts

Summation: This Durango Kid entry is fast moving and above average. Acting is par for the series, with Charles Starrett, Virginia Hunter and Paul Campbell rising above the rest of the cast. Only sour note: it's too easy to spot Forrest Taylor as the mystery villain.

Riders of the Lone Star
Columbia (August 1947)

Bullets sing! As melodies ring!

Cast: Steve Mason/The Durango Kid, Charles Starrett; Doris McCormick, Virginia Hunter; Curly Williams and His Georgia Peach Pickers; Smiley, Smiley Burnette// "Raider"; "Ring Eye"; Murdock, Steve Darrell; Rank, Lane Bradford: Sheriff Banning, Eddie Parker; Mike Morton, Mark Dennis; Blake, Edmund Cobb; Faro, George Chesebro; Slade, Ted Mapes; Brock, Peter Perkins; Doctor, Nolan Leary; Man in wagon, Bud Osborne

Credits: Director, Derwin Abrahams; Producer, Colbert Clark; Screenwriter, Barry Shipman; Editor, Paul Borofsky; Art Director, Harvey Gillett; Set Decorator, David Montrose; Cinematographer, George F. Kelly

Songs: "Granddaddy Bullfrog" (Burnette) sung by Smiley Burnette and Curly Williams and His Georgia Peach Pickers; "A Happy Birthday" sung by Smiley Burnette and Curly Williams and His Georgia Peach Pickers; "Oh, Mona" (Weems and Washburn) sung by Curly Williams and His Georgia Peach Pickers; "Prairie Dog's Lament" (Burnette) sung by Smiley Burnette and Curly Williams and His Georgia Peach Pickers; "Let Me By" sung by Curly Williams and His Georgia Peach Pickers and Smiley Burnette; "Oh, Mona" (reprise) sung by Curly Williams and His Georgia Peach Pickers

Location Filming: Corriganville and Providencia Ranch, California

Production Dates: December 9, 1946–December 17, 1946

Running Time: 55 min.

Story: Ranger Charles Starrett and his sidekick, Smiley Burnette, are sent to investigate the gold robberies of Virginia Hunter's mine. In town, Starrett meets young Mark Dennis, a stagecoach bandit's son, although Dennis believes his father is innocent. George Chesebro, the town drunk, has been taking care of Dennis. Outlaws kidnap the boy to try to find the location of $50,000 from a stagecoach robbery. As the Durango Kid, Starrett rescues Dennis. Starrett suspects Steve Darrell is really Dennis's father, but Darrell is just trying to find the missing money. At Dennis's birthday party, Chesebro gives him a note from his father telling the location of the money. Darrell's men capture Dennis and force him to tell where the money is hidden. As Durango, Starrett gets Chesebro to tell where Dennis has been taken. Chesebro is Dennis's father. Starrett and Chesebro ride to rescue the boy. A gunfight ensues. Darrell fires a shot at Dennis, but Chesebro takes the fatal bullet instead. Starrett shoots Darrell.

Notes and Commentary: *Riders of the Lone Star* was noted in the October 1946 *Hollywood Reporter* to be the last of the Durango Kid series. There was obviously a change of heart. On May 20, 1947, production began on the next Durango entry, *Buckaroo from Powder River* (Columbia, 1947).

Review: "Pretty good 'Durango Kid' film." *Western Movies*, Pitts

Summation: Although familiar, this Durango Kid episode is better than average. The performances are up to par, with a nod to George Chesebro. Smiley Burnette keeps his comedy in check and is a decided asset in this one.

BUCKAROO FROM POWDER RIVER
Columbia (October 1947)

Roarin' range warfare!

Cast: Steve Lacey/The Durango Kid, Charles Starrett; Molly Parnell, Eve Miller; Pop Ryland, Forrest Taylor; Tommy Ryland, Paul Campbell; The Cass County Boys (Jerry Scoggins [guitar], Fred Martin [accordion] and Bert Dodson [bass]), Smiley, Smiley Burnette// "Raider"; "Ring-Eye"; Clint Ryland, Douglas D. Coppin; Dave Ryland, Casey MacGregor; Ben Trask, Ethan Laidlaw; McCall, Frank McCarroll; Sheriff Parnell, Philip Morris; Stagecoach driver, Tex Palmer; Stagecoach guard, Kermit Maynard; Lon Driscoll, Ted Adams; Half-shaved customer, Roy Butler; Half-haircut customer, Phil Arnold; Baldheaded customer, Buster Brodie

Credits: Director, Ray Nazarro; Producer, Colbert Clark; Screenwriter, Norman Hall; Editor, Paul Borofsky; Art Director, Charles Clague; Set Decorator, David Montrose; Cinematographer, George F. Kelly

Songs: "It Sure Sounds Good to Me" (Burnette) sung by Smiley Burnette with The Cass County Boys; "Carry Me Back to Old Virginny" (Bland) sung by Smiley Burnette with The Cass County Boys; "Cecil Could See What He Wanted to See" (Burnette) sung by Smiley Burnette with The Cass County Boys; "When I Saw Sweet Nellie Home" (Kyle and Fletcher) sung by The Cass County Boys

Location Filming: Walker Ranch and Providencia Ranch, California

Production Dates: May 20, 1947–May 28, 1947

Running Time: 55 min.

Story: Forrest Taylor's outlaw gang consists of his two sons, Douglas D. Coppin and Casey MacGregor, and his step-son, Paul Campbell. After a bank robbery, Campbell wants to quit the gang, but he is stopped by Taylor. In addition to money, some Territorial Bonds are stolen. Taylor plans to flood the area with counterfeit bonds. Taylor then sends for gunman Frank McCarroll to kill Campbell. Charles Starrett, as the Durango Kid, intercepts McCarroll and takes the letter identifying him to Taylor. Starrett agrees to kill Campbell, but is able to fake Campbell's death. Starrett searches Taylor's ranch house and finds printing equipment and counterfeit bonds. Coppin confronts Starrett while he's gathering evidence. In an exchange of shots, Coppin is killed. McCarroll finally gets to Taylor's ranch and Taylor hires him to kill Starrett. In a gunfight, Starrett shoots McCarroll. Starrett, as Durango, rides to Taylor's ranch. In a gunfight, Starrett dispatches Taylor and MacGregor. Starrett, still as Durango, rides away.

Notes and Commentary: The working title was "Blazing Through Cimarron."

The *Hollywood Reporter* stated that Virginia Hunter would appear in the film. Eve Miller subsequently took the part.

Reviews: "Passable entertainment." *Motion Picture Guide*, Nash and Ross

"Entertaining 'Durango Kid' series segment." *Western Movies*, Pitts

"A standard oatuner in Columbia's Durango Kid series. George F. Kelley's lensing incorporated some nice outdoor shots." *Variety*, 04/07/48

Summation: This is a decidedly uneven Durango Kid episode. Screenwriter Norman Hall's script is pretty well on target during the first half, then falls apart in the second. There is a silly subplot with Smiley Burnette and a cash register. And where did the usually single-gun carrying Charles Starrett have the second gun in the barber chair? Performances are standard, except for Forrest Taylor's exceptional on-the-mark portrayal of the outlaw gang's patriarch.

LAST DAYS OF BOOT HILL
Columbia (November 1947)

Rhythm-roaring action!

Alternate Title: On Boot Hill

Cast: Steve Waring/The Durango Kid, Charles Starrett; Paula Thorpe, Virginia Hunter; Frank Rayburn, Paul Campbell; Clara Brent, Mary Newton; The Cass County Boys (Jerry Scoggins [guitar], Fred Martin [accordion] and Bert Dodson [bass]); Smiley, Smiley Burnette// "Raider"; Reed Brokaw, Bill Free; Dan McCoy, J.C. Lytton; Bronc Peters, Bob Wilke; Man coming out saloon, Heine Conklin; Hank, Syd Saylor; Lucky Thorpe/Forrest Brent, Al Bridge; Dan Cass, Robert Barron; Nevada, Charles King; Grubstake, Emmett Lynn; Henchman, John Cason; Dan Waring, Steve Clark; Steve's friend, Tex Harding; Masters, Mauritz Hugo; Bill Halliday, Nolan Leary; Mary Halliday, Carole Mathews; Perkins, John Tyrell; Sheriff, Victor Cox, Henchman, Ethan Laidlaw

Credits: Director, Ray Nazarro; Producer, Colbert Clark; Screenwriter, Norman S. Hall; Editor, Paul Borofsky; Art Director, Charles Clague; Set Decorator, David Montrose; Cinematographer, George F. Kelley

Songs: "Texas Belle" (Zimmer, Parker and Neerson) sung by Smiley Burnette with The Cass County Boys; "Inside Looking Out" (Drake) sung by Smiley Burnette with The Cass County Boys; "On My Way Back Home" (Burnette) sung by The Cass County Boys; "Giddy Up. Jerico" (Burnette) sung by Smiley Burnette

Location Filming: Corriganville and Providencia Ranch, California

Production Dates: June 9, 1947–June 14, 1947

Running Time: 55 min.

Story: Mary Newton is looking for the $100,000 hidden by her deceased husband, Al Bridge. Newton takes possession of Bridge's ranch since she believes that's where the money is hidden. Complications arise when Bridge's daughter with his first wife, Virginia Hunter, shows up to claim the ranch. Secret Service Agent Charles Starrett shows up believing Newton will eventually find the money. Newton sends confederate Bill Free to steal the documents supporting Hunter's claim. Free gets away with Starrett, as the Durango Kid, in pursuit. In the chase, one of Starrett's shots kills Free and he recovers the documents. Newton suspects Starrett is the Durango Kid and henchman Bob Wilke is ordered to kill him. Before

Wilke can pull the trigger, Starrett grabs Wilke and the two men fight. Meanwhile, Hunter comes to the ranch with a letter supporting her claim. In the letter there is a clue as to the money's hiding place. Finding the money, Newton prepares to shoot Hunter. Starrett, who has defeated Wilke in the fight, arrives in time to save Hunter's life, arrest Newton and confiscate the money.

Notes and Commentary: For the flashbacks, stock footage from two earlier Durango Kid films, *Both Barrels Blazing* (Columbia, 1945) and *Blazing the Western Trail* (Columbia, 1945), was used.

Although Charles Starrett's character name was Steve Waring in this film, he was Kip Hardy in *Both Barrels Blazing* and Jeff Waring in *Blazing the Western Trail*.

Up to this film, nine days was the usual filming time but, with the use of so much stock footage, filming was completed in only six days.

"Inside Looking Out" was originally sung by Dub Taylor in *Wildcat of Tucson* (Columbia, 1940). The author identified the song as "Looking Out and Looking In" in his book, *Wild Bill Elliott* (McFarland, 2007).

Reviews: "The direction is evenly paced, the performances standard. The story suffers from too many gunfights and chases." *Motion Picture Guide*, Nash and Ross

"Tacky 'Durango Kid' series entry mostly made up of footage from the earlier series film *Both Barrels Blazing*." *Western Movies*, Pitts

"Okay oater for the Saturday matinee trade." *Variety*, 03/31/48

Summation: Okay Durango Kid entry even though most of the action sequences came from earlier Durango Kid entries. Even so, Charles Starrett, in his Steve persona, is a little more rugged in this one.

Six-Gun Law

Columbia (January 1948)

Goin' great guns with action and song!

Cast: Steve Norris/The Durango Kid, Charles Starrett; June Wallace, Nancy Saunders; Jim Wallace, Paul Campbell; Boss Decker, Hugh Prosser; Curly Clements and His Rodeo Rangers; Smiley, Smiley Burnette// "Raider"; "Ring-Eye"; Larson, Bob Wilke; Ben, John Cason; Crowl, Billy Dix; Sheriff Brackett, Ethan Laidlaw; Bret Wallace, George Chesebro; Duffy, Budd Buster; Stage driver, Bud Osborne; Marshal Jack Reed, Pierce Lyden; Drunk cowboy, Louis "Slim" Gaut

Credits: Director, Ray Nazarro; Producer, Colbert Clark; Screenwriter, Barry Shipman; Editor, Henry DeMond; Art Director, Charles Clague; Set Decorator, David Montrose; Cinematographer, George F. Kelley

Songs: "If I Were the Boss" (Burnette) sung by Smiley Burnette with Curly Clements and His Rodeo Rangers; "Around the Clock" (Burnette) sung by Smiley Burnette with Curly Clements and His Rodeo Rangers; "Darling Nellie Gray"(Hanby) played by Curly Clements and His Rodeo Rangers; "Cowboy Shindig" (Clements) sung by Curly Clements with His Rodeo Rangers

Location Filming: Iverson, California
Production Dates: June 24, 1947–July 2, 1947
Running Time: 54 min.

Six-Gun Law (1947) title card —(lower left) Smiley Burnett, (right) Charles Starrett.

Story: Rancher Charles Starrett is accused of cattle rustling by Sheriff Ethan Laidlaw. An argument ensues. Laidlaw goes for his gun while Starrett grabs a gun on Laidlaw's desk. The gun goes off and Laidlaw falls to the floor. The gun was loaded with blanks and set to go off when pointed. Town boss Hugh Prosser forces Starrett to sign a confession and then take over the office of sheriff. Prosser then has Laidlaw killed. Starrett, as the Durango Kid, foils a bank robbery by taking the money before Prosser's gang shows up. Fellow rancher George Chesebro is given the money to hide until Federal Marshal Pierce Lyden can come to town. Prosser's henchmen spot Chesebro and give chase. One of the outlaws' bullets hits Chesebro and he barely makes it to Smiley Burnette's cabin with the money. By a ruse, Burnette gets rid of the outlaws. He then finds that Chesebro has died of his wound. Prosser orders Starrett to arrest Chesebro's son, Paul Campbell. As Durango, Starrett rescues Campbell and has Burnette hide him. Burnette and Campbell also hide the bank money. Prosser learns that Starrett has been working against him and makes an unsuccessful attempt to kill him. Starrett confronts Prosser, looking for the signed confession, but instead finds the trick gun. Prosser's men attack the stagecoach bringing Lyden to town but Lyden escapes, thanks to the quick action of Starrett, as Durango. Starrett tells Campbell to bring the bank money to his ranch. Starrett makes a deal with Prosser to produce the bank money in exchange for the signed confession. Prosser and his men accompany him to Campbell's ranch. Campbell brings the money that Starrett gives to Prosser. Enraged, Campbell grabs the gun from Starrett's holster which fires. Starrett falls to the floor. Prosser is about to shoot down Campbell and his sister, Nancy Saunders, when Starrett gets the drop on the outlaws. The weapon used by Campbell was Prosser's trick gun. Lyden, who had been listening in the next room, arrests Prosser and his men.

Reviews: "Okay Durango Kid series entry. The film is at its best when there's action and gunplay. The script shows some wit and the direction isn't bad, though the plot development scenes aren't quite up to par." *Motion Picture Guide*, Nash and Ross

"Fair 'Durango Kid' film." *Western Movies*, Pitts

"This is a modest Starrett entry in his Durango Kid series." *The Western*, Hardy

"There's ample shootin' and hard ridin' in 'Six-Gun Law' which will make this oater an audience satisfier in the action situations." *Variety*, 02/25/48

Summation: Not as fast moving as most Durango Kid stories, but a solid script by Barry Shipman more than compensates, elevating the film to one of the preferred films in the series. Charles Starrett delivers one of his best performances. Smiley Burnette adds to the film's enjoyment with some clever comedy sequences.

PHANTOM VALLEY
Columbia (February 1948)

Song-studded thrills!

Cast: Steve Collins/The Durango Kid, Charles Starrett; Jancy Littlejohn, Virginia Hunter; Ozie Waters and His Colorado Rangers (Slim Duncan [piccolo, fiddle]); Smiley, Smiley Burnette// "Raider"; "Ring-Eye"; Sam Littlejohn, Joel Friedkin; Craig, Mikel Conrad; Reynolds, Robert Filmer; Jim Durant, Sam Flint; Ben Theibold, Fred F. Sears; Frazer, Zon Murray; Chips, Teddy Infuhr; Henchman, Matty Roubert: Bart, Jerry Jerome

Credits: Director, Ray Nazarro; Producer, Colbert Clark; Screenwriter, J. Benton Cheney; Editor, Paul Borofsky; Art Director, Charles Clague; Set Decorator, David Montrose; Cinematographer, George F. Kelley

Songs: "I'll Be Glad to See You" (Burnette), sung by Smiley Burnette; "The Big Corral" (traditional) sung by Ozie Waters with His Colorado Rangers; "Streets of Laredo (The Cowboy's Lament)" (traditional) sung by Ozie Waters with His Colorado Rangers

Location Filming: Iverson, Providencia Ranch, California

Production Dates: July 16, 1947–July 24, 1947

Running Time: 53 min.

Story: Bank president/rancher Robert Filmer accuses homesteader Sam Flint of rustling. Incensed, Flint withdraws all the homesteaders' money from Filmer's bank. To help Flint get the money to a bank in a neighboring town, Joel Friedkin suggests his daughter, Virginia Hunter, drive him. Outlaws attack them, force Hunter to walk back to town and take Flint and the money. Hunter tells Marshal Charles Starrett that someone is trying to start a range war between the cattlemen and the homesteaders. With the homesteaders' backs to the wall, Starrett arranges for a loan. Meanwhile, homesteader Fred F. Sears learns that land he owns in Pennsylvania is oil rich. Before he can spread the news, he is shot during an ambush, and Sears is badly wounded. Starrett captures outlaw Zon Murray. Before he can name the gang's leader, a shot ends Murray's outlaw career. Hunter accuses Filmer of being behind all the troubles. At the crime scene, a cane tip with the smell of gunpowder is found. Starrett confronts Friedkin and asks to see his cane. Hunter brings the cane and

Starrett discovers it is a cane gun. Friedkin is arrested. Filmer's top hand, Mikel Conrad, plants evidence linking him to Flint's disappearance. Starrett arrests Filmer. A key and a note are thrown into the jail cell. A wagon is waiting and, as Friedkin and Filmer make their escape, outlaws attack. Starrett, as the Durango Kid, routs out the outlaws. Starrett tells the men to hide out, and Starrett tells Hunter that Friedkin was killed. Hunter goes to a cabin to congratulate Conrad on his success of getting Friedkin and Filmer out of the way. Starrett enters the cabin and places Hunter and her men under arrest. Starrett had known that Hunter was behind the troubles because of the handwriting on the note and only she could have substituted Friedkin's cane for a cane gun. Hunter admits that her real father had owned Phantom Valley and she was trying to get it back at any cost. Enraged, she races to the door but is shot by Conrad.

Notes and Commentary: The working title was "Call of the Prairie."

Reviews: "A fairly routine Starrett B western — until the end when our hero guns down the female villain, Hunter, by shooting her in the back. It takes so long for Starrett to uncover this that nobody cares anymore." *Motion Picture Guide*, Nash and Ross

"Better than average 'Durango Kid' film." *Western Movies*, Pitts

"Film is an assembly-line oatuner cranked out for the juve trade." *Variety*, 08/11/48

Summation: This is a well-written mystery-western story, with a surprise villain. One of the best Durango Kid entries.

WEST OF SONORA
Columbia (March 1948)

Blazing Guns and Rhythms!

Cast: Steve Rollins/The Durango Kid, Charles Starrett; "Black" Murphy, Steve Darrell; Sheriff Jeff Clinton, George Chesebro; Penelope Clinton, Anita Castle; The Sunshine Boys (Fred Daniel, Ace Richman, J.D. Sumner and Eddie Wallace); Smiley, Smiley Burnette// "Raider"; Jack Bascom, Emmett Lynn; Sandy Clinton, Hal Taliaferro; Brock, Bob Wilke; Dickson, Lynn Farr; Three Strike O'Toole, Blackie Whiteford

Credits: Director, Ray Nazarro; Producer, Colbert Clark; Screenwriter, Barry Shipman; Editor, Jerome Thoms; Art Director, Charles Clague; Set Decorator, George Montgomery; Cinematographer, Ira H. Morgan

Songs: "Dese Bones Gonna Rise Again" (traditional) sung by The Sunshine Boys; "The Glory Train" (traditional) sung by The Sunshine Boys; "I Ain't Gonna Do Tomorrow" (Burnette) sung by Smiley Burnette with the Sunshine Boys; "Li'l Indian" (Burnette) sung by Smiley Burnette; "I Ain't Gonna Do Tomorrow" (reprise) sung by The Sunshine Boys

Location Filming: Iverson, California

Production Dates: September 19, 1947–September 26, 1947

Running Time: 55 min.

Story: Little Anita Castle is taken off the stagecoach to Seco City by outlaw Steve Darrell, one of her grandfathers. Darrell has a hook in place of his left hand. Her other grandfather is George Chesebro, sheriff of Seco City. Chesebro asks Texas Ranger Charles Starrett to help him capture Darrell and return Castle to him. Darrell is being blamed for the lawlessness around Seco City when, in actuality, the leader is Chesebro's brother, Hal Taliaferro. Starrett has his doubts regarding Darrell's guilt when he saves the life of miner Emmett

Lynn. Starrett wants Chesebro and Darrell to meet and resolve their differences, but Taliaferro plots to have Darrell killed. Darrell and his men are about to ambush Chesebro and the posse when Starrett, as the Durango Kid, rides between them and places Castle in Chesebro's arms. At Darrell's camp, Taliaferro reports that Lynn has been murdered by a hook. Darrell comes to the jail for revenge on Starrett and Chesebro, but Starrett is too fast on the draw and captures Darrell. Taliaferro has his henchmen, Bob Wilke and Lynn Farr, break Darrell out of jail so he can be lynched. Starrett, as Durango, interferes and Darrell gets away. Taliaferro's plans are upset when he learns that Lynn has left his gold mine to Castle. Taliaferro plans to murder Chesebro and place the blame on Darrell and then murder Castle. Starrett, as Durango, prevents the deaths of Darrell and Chesebro and captures Wilke. Wilke confesses that Taliaferro murdered Lynn. Meanwhile, Taliaferro is alone with Castle and advances menacingly, brandishing a hook. As he draws close, Starrett, as Durango, crashes through a window and subdues Taliaferro. As Starrett rides away, Castle now has two grandfathers to look after her.

Notes and Commentary: *Junction City* (Columbia, 1952) was the sequel to this film.

Reviews: "Pretty good 'Durango Kid' segment enhanced by a well written, mystery-laden script." *Western Movies*, Pitts

"An unpretentious oatuner. The film is average action fare for the duals and Saturday matinee trade." *Variety*, 11/10/48

Summation: This is another well-written screenplay by Barry Shipman; well performed, especially by Steve Darrell and Hal Taliaferro. Director Ray Nazarro even generates suspense as Hal Taliaferro attempts to murder Anita Castle with a vicious-looking hook.

WHIRLWIND RAIDERS
Columbia (May 1948)

Bullet-and-rhythm tornado!

Alternate Title: State Police

Cast: Steve Lanning/The Durango Kid, Charles Starrett; Tracy Beaumont, Fred Sears; Claire Ross, Nancy Saunders; Tommy Ross, "Little Brown Jug"; Doye O'Dell and The Radio Rangers; Smiley, Smiley Burnette// "Raider"; "Ring-Eye"; Captain Buff Tyson, Jack Ingram; Slim, Lynn Farr; Red Jordan, Eddie Parker; Homer Ross, Philip Morris; Bill Webster, Patrick Hurst; Mrs. Wallace, Maudie Prickett; Wilson, Frank LaRue

Credits: Director, Vernon Keays; Producer, Colbert Clark; Screenwriter, Norman Hall; Editor, Paul Borofsky; Art Director, Charles Clague; Set Decorator, David Montrose; Cinematographer, M.A. Andersen

Songs: "Lookin' Poor But Feelin' Rich" (Burnette) sung by Smiley Burnette; "Fiddlin' Fool" (Burnette) sung by Smiley Burnette with Doye O'Dell and The Radio Rangers; "Give Me Texas" (Rice) sung by Doye O'Dell with The Radio Rangers; "Jimmy Crack Corn (The Blue Tail Fly)" (traditional) sung by Doye O'Dell with The Radio Rangers; "Lookin' Poor But Feelin' Rich" (reprise) sung by Smiley Burnette with Doye O'Dell and The Radio Rangers

Location Filming: Corriganville, California

Production Dates: September 3, 1947–September 11, 1947

Running Time: 54 min.

Story: The Texas Rangers have been disbanded. The corrupt state police becomes the new law in Texas. Ex-Ranger Charles Starrett, masquerading as a bank robber, comes to Indian Springs to break the stranglehold Fred Sears has on the West Texas area. In debt to Sears, rancher Philip Morris is being forced to become police commissioner and help Sears gain control of the ranches in the area. Morris is going to defy Sears, but Starrett, as Durango, tells him to play along. Upon leaving Morris's ranch, Starrett is followed by Morris' son, Little Brown Jug. Brown Jug learns Durango's identity and is sworn to secrecy by Starrett. As Durango, Starrett is disrupting Sears's plans. Sears tells his chief henchman, Jack Ingram, to dress as Durango and rob the bank. While trying to make a getaway, Brown Jug recognizes Ingram as Durango. Brown Jug is stopped by Sears and lets it slip that Starrett is actually Durango. Brown Jug is kidnapped and taken to Sears's ranch. Starrett rescues Brown Jug, who tells him about Sears and Ingram. Starrett, as Durango, and Morris confront Ingram and Sears. In a gunfight, Ingram and Sears are killed. Word reaches Indian Springs that the Texas Rangers have replaced the state police.

Notes and Commentary: The song "Lookin' Poor But Feelin' Rich" was a hit on the Exclusive Label for Doye O'Dell.

"Little Brown Jug" was the nickname for Don Reynolds.

Reviews: "'Durango Kid' fans will like this actionful series entry." *Western Movies*, Pitts

"Shapes up tepidly compared to some of its predecessors. Standard hoss opera has a fair amount of shootin' and ridin'." *Variety*, 05/12/48

Summation: Exciting Durango Kid feature with a nice blend of action, songs and comedy. Performances are standard, with a special nod to Little Brown Jug.

Blazing Across the Pecos

Columbia (July 1948)

On the thrill-'n-rhythm warpath

Alternate Title: Under Arrest

Cast: Steve Blake/The Durango Kid, Charles Starrett; Lola Carter, Patricia White; Jim Traynor, Paul Campbell; Ace Brockway, Charles Wilson; Matt Carter, Thomas Jackson; Red Arnall and The Western Aces; Smiley, Smiley Burnette// "Raider"; Buckshot Thomas, Jack Ingram; Mike Doyle, Pat O'Malley; Chief Bear Claw, Chief Thundercloud; Bill, Jock O'Mahoney; Townsman, Blackie Whiteford; Gunsmoke Ballard, Frank McCarroll; Jason, Pierce Lyden; Sleepy Larsen, Paul Conrad

Credits: Director, Ray Nazarro; Producer, Colbert Clark; Screenwriter, Norman S. Hall; Editor, Richard Fantl; Art Director, Charles Clague; Set Decorator, Sidney Clifford; Cinematographer, Ira H. Morgan

Songs: "That's All Brother, That's All" (Burnette) sung by Smiley Burnette with Red Arnall and The Western Aces; "Goin' Back to Texas" (Brockman and Cornell) sung by Red Arnall with The Western Aces; "It Ain't Much Help" (Burnette) sung by Smiley Burnette; "Crawdad Song" (traditional) sung by Red Arnall with The Western Aces

Location Filming: Iverson, California

Production Dates: November 18, 1947–November 25, 1947

Running Time: 55 min.

Story: Charles Starrett, as the Durango Kid, is following up on raids on Thomas Jackson's trading posts. Charles Wilson, mayor and saloon owner, and henchman Jack Ingram are behind the raids. Wilson has been supplying an Indian tribe with rifles and, in return, the Indians conduct the raids. To obtain money to keep his remaining posts open, Jackson sells a large herd of cattle to the Army. Wilson gets the Indians to steal the cattle. Starrett, as Durango, convinces Chief Thundercloud to return the cattle to the Army. Additionally, Thundercloud implicates Wilson. Wilson and Ingram, knowing their scheme to take over providing supplies to settlers is finished plan to make a getaway. Before they leave, they plan to steal the money the Army gave Jackson. Starrett foils their plans and arrests Wilson and Ingram.

Notes and Commentary: Stock footage from *Arizona* (Columbia, 1940) was used in the Indian attacks on the supply train and cattle drive.

Review: "Actionful and well written 'Durango Kid' saga." *Western Movies*, Pitts

Summation: Entertaining and slightly above average Durango Kid with enough action to satisfy western fans. One note: Charles Starrett only has to deal with two badmen. Signs of budget cutting somewhat saved by Norman S. Hall's script and Richard Fantl's astute editing. Smiley Burnette's comedy is pretty well under control.

Trail to Laredo
Columbia (August 1948)

Hot with a gun! Tops with a tune!

Alternate Title: Sign of the Dagger

Cast: Steve Ellison/The Durango Kid, Charles Starrett; Dan Parks, Jim Bannon; Classy, Virginia Maxey; Ronnie Parks, Tommy Ivo; Fenton, Hugh Prosser; The Cass County Boys (Jerry Scoggins [guitar], Fred S. Martin [accordion] and Bert Dodson [bass]); Smiley, Smiley Burnette// "Raider"; Duke, Bob Wilke; Walt Morgan, George Chesebro; Sheriff Kennedy, John Merton; Deputy, Jock O'Mahoney; Blaze, John Cason; Card Player, Ethan Laidlaw; Chuck, Ted Mapes

Credits: Director, Ray Nazarro; Producer, Colbert Clark; Screenwriter, Barry Shipman; Editor, Paul Borofsky; Art Director, Charles Clague; Set Decorator, David Montrose; Cinematographer, Henry Freulich

Songs: "Go West Young Lady" (Cahn and Chaplin) sung by Virginia Maxey and The Cass County Boys; "Listen to the Mockingbird" (Winner) played by Smiley Burnette; "It's My Turn" (Burnette) sung by Smiley Burnette; "Flo from St. Joe Mo." (Roseland and McDermott) sung by Virginia Maxey and The Cass County Boys; "The Yodeler" (Burnette) sung by Smiley Burnette and The Cass County Boys

Location Filming: Iverson and Providencia Ranch, California

Production Dates: December 6, 1947–December 16, 1947

Running Time: 54 min.

Story: Freighter Jim Bannon finds that he's been shipping stolen government gold in boxes marked "ring bolts." He confides in his partner, George Chesebro, not knowing that he's working with outlaw boss Hugh Prosser. Prosser and Chesebro frame Bannon and he's arrested by Sheriff John Merton. Bannon's friend, Treasury Agent Charles Starrett, as the Durango Kid, throws a scare into Chesebro. Prosser decides to break Bannon out of jail in order to kill Chesebro and frame Bannon. Bannon is then held captive. Starrett, as Durango, locates the outlaw hideout and, while Merton and his posse are shooting it out with the outlaw gang, makes off with the gold. Starrett, as Durango, rescues Bannon and gets the drop on Merton. Starrett, still as Durango, gets Prosser to admit that he had Chesebro killed. Merton and Bannon are in an adjoining room and hear Prosser's confession. With Starrett's help, Merton arrests Prosser.

Notes and Commentary: Look closely and you can see Jock O'Mahoney double Charles Starrett in the saloon fight sequence. What a leap O'Mahoney makes during the fight!

Singer Virginia Maxey had a short screen career at Columbia, appearing in *Trail to Laredo* and three musical shorts. Maxey sang with the orchestras of Charlie Barnet, Tony Pastor and Ziggy Elman, and with the Modernaires. Maxey was married to singer/pianist/bandleader Matt Dennis. Together they wrote "We've Reached the Point of No Return," "Snuggle Up, Baby" and "You Can Believe in Me."

The song, "Go West, Young Lady" was first sung by Ann Miller in *Go West, Young Lady* (Columbia, 1941).

Review: "Actionful 'Durango Kid' film." *Western Movies*, Pitts

Summation: This could have been a good Durango Kid outing but it barely comes in as average due to a very mild windup (as Hugh Prosser and Bob Wilke are brought to justice too easily) and some unfunny antics by Smiley Burnette. This is the one where Burnette attempts to paint the saloon while four men oblivious to the antics play poker. This is too silly and very much out of place.

EL DORADO PASS
Columbia (October 1948)

Six-gun action ... double-barreled fun!

Alternate Title: Desperate Men

Cast: Steve Clayton/The Durango Kid, Charles Starrett; Dolores Martinez, Elena Verdugo; Page, Steve Darrell; Shorty Thompson and his Saddle Rockin' Rhythm; Smiley, Smiley Burnette// "Raider"; Sheriff Tom Wright, Rory Mallinson; Dodd, Ted Mapes; Barlow, Stanley Blystone; Don Martinez, Harry Vejar; Snowflower, Gertrude Chorre; Henchman, Blackie Whiteford

Credits: Director, Ray Nazarro; Producer, Colbert Clark; Screenwriter, Earle Snell; Editor, Burton Kramer; Art Director, Carl Anderson; Set Decorator, Frank Kramer; Cinematographer, Rex Wimpy

Songs: "Black, Black Jack of All Trades" (Burnette) sung by Smiley Burnette; "On the Banks of the Sunny San Juan" (Dean and Strange); "The Yellow Rose of Texas" (traditional)

Production Dates: May 18, 1948–May 26, 1948

Running Time: 55 min.

Story: In a stagecoach robbery, $20,000 in gold is stolen from Mexican rancher Harry Vejar. Cowboy Charles Starrett is framed for the crime and is arrested. Starrett's friend, Smiley Burnette, helps him break out of jail. Starrett trails the gold to rancher Steve Darrell. As the Durango Kid, Starrett arranges to exchange the gold for cash. Starrett attempts to turn Darrell over to Sheriff Rory Mallinson. Darrell's gang intervenes and, thinking Darrell was planning to double-cross them, kill him. The gang then captures Starrett and takes him to the outlaw hideout. The gang plans to kill Starrett and collect the reward. Burnette comes through again and helps Starrett escape. As the Durango Kid, Starrett gets Mallinson and a posse to follow him to the hideout. The gang is captured and the gold recovered.

Notes and Commentary: The working title was "Crossroads of the West."

Elena Verdugo is best remembered for her roles in two television series, as Millie Bronson on *Meet Millie* (CBS, 1952–56) and as Consuelo Lopez on *Marcus Welby, M.D.* (ABC, 1969–1976).

Reviews: "Nothing noteworthy in this entry in the Durango Kid series." *Motion Picture Guide*, Nash and Ross

"Passable 'Durango Kid' series segment." *Western Movies*, Pitts

"Familiar action fare. There's little in this entry that makes it stand out from its many predecessors. Routine." *Variety*, 05-04-49

Summation: This film was not available for viewing by the author.

QUICK ON THE TRIGGER
Columbia (December 1948)

Hot lead singin'! Hot tunes ringin'!

Alternate Title: Condemned in Error

Cast: Steve Warren/The Durango Kid, Charles Starrett; Garvey Yager, Lyle Talbot; Nora Reed, Helen Parrish, The Sunshine Boys (Ace Richman, Freddie Daniel, Eddie Wallace and J.D. Sumner); Smiley, Smiley Burnette// "Raider"; Alfred Murdock, George Eldredge; Sheriff Martin Oaks, Ted Adams; Judge Kormac, Alan Bridge; Fred Reed, Russell Arms; Telegrapher, Budd Buster; Stage Driver, Bud Osborne; Jury Foreman, Russell Meeker; Henchmen, Blackie Whiteford and Sandy Sanders; Juror, Tex Cooper

Credits: Director, Ray Nazarro; Producer, Colbert Clark; Screenwriter, Elmer Clifton; Editor, Paul Borofsky; Art Director, Charles Clague; Set Decorator, Frank Kramer; Cinematography, Rex Wimpy

Songs: "Ring Eye Rhythm" (Burnette); "Bugle Boy" (Burnette); "Better Get Down and Pray" (The Sunshine Boys); "Midnight Flyer" (Rose and Heath)

Production Dates: June 9, 1948–June 16, 1948

Running Time: 54 min.

Story: Sheriff Charles Starrett is after the outlaws plaguing Helen Parrish's stagecoach line. He catches up with one of the gang members, Parrish's brother Russell Arms. Starrett brings Arms to the jail and begins questioning him. Before Arms can reveal the leaders of the gang, he is shot. Starrett returns fire but his shots miss the assailant. Parrish finds Starrett standing over Arms's body with a recently fired gun in his hand. Parrish accuses Starrett of murder. Prosecuting Attorney Lyle Talbot fired the fatal shot. Starrett's father had sent Talbot to jail, and now Talbot wants revenge. George Eldredge, Talbot's partner in crime, is assisting Talbot to convict Starrett. Starrett breaks jail, and as the Durango Kid, begins investigating Talbot and Eldredge. Starrett's pal, Smiley Burnette, unwittingly helps in Starrett's capture. Starrett is convicted of Arms's murder, but again breaks jail. Starrett obtains proof that Talbot is not a lawyer. As Durango, Starrett finds proof of Talbot and Eldredge's guilt. Starrett is cleared and takes over as sheriff.

Notes and Commentary: The working title was "Gun Brand."

This was the last film that billed "Charles Starrett as the Durango Kid" above the title.

Reviews: "Typical Starrett outing." *Motion Picture Guide*, Nash and Ross

"Well written 'Durango Kid' series entry." *Western Movies*, Pitts

"Another in the Durango Kid series, 'Quick on the Trigger' unwinds as an okay dualer for the wild and wooly aficionados." *Variety*, 05-25-49

Summation: This film was not available for viewing by the author.

CHALLENGE OF THE RANGE
Columbia (February 1949)

Action-'n-rhythm rampage!

Alternate Title: Moonlight Raid

Cast: Steve Roper/The Durango Kid, Charles Starrett; Judy Barton, Paula Raymond; Reb Matson, William Halop; Cal Matson, Steve Darrell; Jim Barton, Henry Hall; Grat Largo, Robert Filmer, The Sunshine Boys (Fred Daniel, Ace Richmond, J.D. Sumner and Eddie Wallace); Smiley, Smiley Burnette// "Raider"; "Ring-Eye"; Henley, John Cason; Dugan, Frank McCarroll; Lon Collins, George Chesebro; Ezra, Milton Kibbee; Cliff, John McKee; Saunders, Frank O'Connor; Henchmen, Edmund Cobb, Ray Bennett and Kermit Maynard; Henchman, Cactus Mack; Sheriff, Pat O'Malley

Credits: Director, Ray Nazarro; Producer, Colbert Clark; Screenwriter, Ed. Earl Repp; Editor, Paul Borofsky; Art Director, Charles Clague; Set Decorator, David Montrose; Cinematography, Rex Wimpy

Songs: "I Kin Dance" (Burnette) sung by Smiley Burnette with the Sunshine Boys; "My Home Town" (Burnette) sung by the Sunshine Boys; "The More We Get Together" (Roberts and Fisher) sung by Smiley Burnette with the Sunshine Boys; "The Old Scrubbin' Bucket" sung by Smiley Burnette; "My Home Town" (reprise) sung by the Sunshine Boys

Location Filming: Iverson, California

Production Dates: June 24, 1948–July 2, 1948

Running Time: 56 min.

Story: Outlaws are running settlers out of Rincon Valley. John Cason and his men attack Henry Hall's farm. Charles Starrett as the Durango Kid breaks up the raid. Hall believes cattleman Steve Darrell is behind the raids. Robert Filmer and George Chesebro, of the Farmer's Association, hire Charles Starrett as gun guard. Hall's daughter, Paula Raymond, doesn't believe that either Darrell or his son, William Halop, is responsible. After another raid on Hall's farm, Hall and Darrell meet to settle issues with guns. Shots ring out and Hall is hit in the shoulder. Starrett saw the shot come from behind Hall and not from Darrell's gun. Starrett, as Durango, gets Halop to work with him until Starrett finds evidence that would prove Darrell guilty. Halop believes that Chesebro is guilty. Darrell is arrested. Halop is baited into coming into town not knowing that outlaws are waiting to gun him down. Chesebro discovers that Filmer is behind the outlawry. Filmer wants to possess the farmer's land, which would then allow him to control the water rights. Starrett, as Durango, and Halop team up to kill or capture the outlaw gang. Filmer attempts to ambush Darrell in his jail cell but is shot by Chesebro before he can pull the trigger. Range war in Rincon Valley is over.

Notes and Commentary: With this film and for the remainder of the series, it would only have Charles Starrett's name above the title. Most title lobby cards from this time on would not indicate that Starrett was playing the Durango Kid. The character, however, would appear in scene lobby cards.

Smiley Burnette sings "The Old Scrubbin' Bucket" to the tune of "The Old Oaken Bucket." The original tune came from "Jesse, the Flower of Dunbane" by George Krallmark.

The scene in which Smiley Burnette is attacked by Edmund Cobb, Ray Bennett and Kermit Maynard, and the one showing Durango's entry to rescue Burnette, were lifted from *Galloping Thunder* (Columbia, 1946).

Reviews: "High class entry in the popular 'The Durango Kid' series." *Western Movies*, Pitts

"One of the better Charles Starrett Durango Kid westerns, 'Challenger of the Range' is a breezy entry for the action market. *Variety*, 06-22-49

Summation: Above average Durango Kid entry with Smiley Burnette's comedy held in check. The plot unfolds nicely, with plenty of hard-riding, hard-shooting action. William Halop, an original member of the Dead End Kids, is surprisingly effective.

LARAMIE

Columbia (May 1949)

War chants echo! Range songs ring!

Cast: Steve Holden/The Durango Kid, Charles Starrett; Colonel Ron Dennison, Fred Sears; Denny Dennison, Tommy Ivo; The singing sergeant, Elton Britt; Smiley, Smiley Burnette// " Raider"; "Ring-Eye"; Sergeant Duff, George Lloyd; Stage driver, Kermit Maynard; Lt. Reed, Myron Healey; Cronin, Bob Wilke; Chief Eagle, Shooting Star; Running Wolf, Jay Silverheels; L.D. Brecker, Jim Diehl; Henchmen, John Cason and Ethan Laidlaw; Peace Commisioner, Nolan Leary

Credits: Director, Ray Nazarro; Producer, Colbert Clark; Screenwriter, Barry Shipman; Editor, Paul Borofsky; Art Director, Charles Clague; Set Decorator, James Crowe; Cinematographer, Rex Wimpy

Songs: "The Happy Cobbler" (Burnette) sung by Smiley Burnette; "Chime Bells" (Britt and Miller) sung by Elton Britt; "Who Don't" (Burnette) sung by Smiley Burnette; "Millie Darling" (Hays) sung by Elton Britt

Location Filming: Iverson and Corriganville, California

Production Dates: October 11, 1949–October 19, 1949

Running Time: 55 min.

Story: Charles Starrett comes to Fort Sanders to initiate a peace treaty with Shooting Star's Indian tribe. Scout Bob Wilke wants to start an Indian uprising, knowing he can get rich selling guns to the Indians. To further his cause, Wilke murders Shooting Star and arranges a massacre of Army soldiers. To delay the hostilities, Starrett, as Durango, tells new chief Jay Silverheels that he'll bring Shooting Star's murderer to him. Shoemaker Smiley Burnette discovers that Wilke is the murderer. Colonel Fred Sears decides to avenge the deaths of the Army soldiers and attack the Indians. Thanks to Wilke, Silverheels knows of the Army's plans and is set to ambush them. Starrett finds Wilke's confederate, Jim Diehl, in Laramie, and the rifles destined for the Indians. As he gets the drop on Diehl and two henchmen, Wilke captures Starrett. Burnette, looking for him, starts a diversion that allows Starrett to gun down the underlings but Wilke gets away. Burnette tells Starrett that Wilke kidnapped Sears' son, Tommy Ivo. Starrett rescues Ivo, who tells him that Wilke and his men, disguised as Indians, are planning an attack on a stagecoach with Peace Commissioner Nolan Leary. Starrett reaches the stagecoach and helps hold the outlaws at bay until the cavalry arrives. Silverheels sees Wilke has been apprehended, and peace is assured.

Notes and Commentary: The scene in which the Indians attack the stagecoach with the cavalry coming to the rescue was lifted from the John Ford classic western, *Stagecoach* (United Artists, 1939). In the long shots, it's either John Wayne or Yakima Canutt on top of the stagecoach. In this sequence, the stagecoach passed through Beale's Cut and Luzerne Dry Lake, California, and Monument Valley, Utah.

Reviews: "Written and directed without conviction. Performances are adequate, with a few welcome moments of comic relief." *Motion Picture Guide*, Nash and Ross

"Mediocre 'Durango Kid' film." *Western Movies*, Pitts

"As the latest in the 'Durango Kid' westerns, 'Laramie' doesn't quite measure up to some of its predecessors. Film's only saving grace is a well-staged chase in the final reel." *Variety*, 10-19-49

Summation: Okay Durango Kid effort marred by the decision to use footage of the famous Indian attack on the stagecoach from *Stagecoach*. To match the footage, Charles Starrett is dressed like John Wayne, which is completely out of character.

THE BLAZING TRAIL
Columbia (July 1949)

Rapid-fire thrills and songs!

Alternate Title: The Forged Will

Cast: Steve Allen/The Durango Kid, Charles Starrett; Janet Masters, Marjorie Stapp; Luke Masters, Fred Sears; Sam Brady, Steve Darrell; "Full-House" Patterson, Jock O'Mahoney; Jess Williams, Trevor Bardette; Musical cowboys, Hank Penny and Slim Duncan; Smiley, Smiley Burnette// "Raider"; "Ring-Eye"; Mike Brady, Robert Malcolm; Kirk Brady, Steve Pendleton; Colton, John Cason; Brady house guard, John Merton; Newspaper customer, Blackie Whiteford; Donald Thorp, Frank O'Connor

Credits: Director, Ray Nazarro; Producer, Colbert Clark; Screenwriter, Barry Shipman; Editor, Paul Borofsky; Art Director, Charles Clague; Set Decorator, Frank Tuttle; Cinematographer, Ira H. Morgan

Songs: "You Put Me on My Feet" (Burnette) sung by Smiley Burnette with Slim Duncan and Hank Penny; "Want a Gal From Texas" (LaVerne and Bartlett) Sung by Slim Duncan and Hank Penny; "Extra, Extra" (Burnette) sung by Smiley Burnette; "Cheer Up" (Duncan and Penny) sung by Slim Duncan and Hank Penny

Location Filming: Iverson, California

Production Dates: January 18, 1949–January 25, 1949

Running Time: 59 min.

Story: Robert Malcolm is murdered. Suspects include Malcolm's sons, Steve Darrell and Steve Pendleton, lawyer Fred Sears, Sears' daughter Marjorie Stapp, saloon owner Jock O'Mahoney and Malcolm's foreman, Trevor Bardette. Marshal Charles Starrett investigates and no one wants to cooperate. Malcolm's will is read. Steve Pendleton inherits the ranch and Steve Darrell receives a worthless gold mine. Starrett believes the will is a forgery. Starrett finds the shells from the bullets that killed Malcolm. As the Durango Kid, Starrett discovers bullets from the guns of Darrell and O'Mahoney don't match. Starrett takes Sears' gun — that Sears says was stolen and mysteriously returned. Sears' gun is the murder weapon. Before Starrett can question him, Sears is found murdered. Stapp goes to Pendleton's ranch where she finds the owner and Bardette looking for something in the walls of the house. Starrett and Stapp go to the ranch and find a secret hiding place containing a more recent will. Starrett arrests Pendleton for murder and deputizes Bardette to take him to jail. Starrett gets newspaperman Smiley Burnette to print one copy of the newspaper with the terms of the new will and take it to the jail. Starrett, as Durango, has spread the news that gold has been discovered in Darrell's mine. Bardette rides to warn Darrell that Pendleton and O'Mahoney are coming to kill him. Bardette has pretended to be unable to read or write. Malcolm, it seems, was unable to read or write and had Bardette write for him. All the wills were written by Bardette who wrote a new will when he believed the mine contained a rich vein of gold. Bardette read the newspaper in the sheriff's office and now claims the gold mine. Starrett accuses Bardette of having murdered Malcolm and Sears. Actually, the mine is worthless. Pendleton wants Darrell to run the ranch with him. It also looks like Pendleton and Stapp will marry.

Notes and Commentary: Hank Penny was the "King of Hillbilly Bebop," fusing jazz with country music. Penny had a few hit records including "Steel Guitar Stomp" (King, 1946) with Noel Boggs on steel guitar and Merle Travis on guitar, "Get Yourself a Red Head" (King, 1946) and "Bloodshot Eyes" (King, 1950).

Reviews: "*The Blazing Trail* packs lots of action in one hour, plus has some time for a few funnies by Burnette, as well as a couple of tunes by Hank Penny and Slim Duncan. What more could a person want?" *Motion Picture Guide*, Nash and Ross

"A fair 'Durango Kid' series film." *Western Movies*, Pitts

"One of the better entries in Columbia's Durango Kid series. Low-budgeter is aided by a good script with a suspenseful whodunit atmosphere." *Variety*, 11-16-49

Summation: A very good Durango Kid film, thanks to Barry Shipman's deft screenplay. Shipman keeps the mystery villain well hidden until the last few minutes of the film. Smiley Burnette's comedy is on target and he is an asset in this one.

SOUTH OF DEATH VALLEY
Columbia (August 1949)

Starrett's a two-gun terror! Smiley's a hit tune riot!

Alternate Title: River of Poison

Cast: Steve Downey/The Durango Kid, Charles Starrett; Molly Tavish, Gail Davis; Sam Ashton, Fred Sears; Scotty Tavish, Lee Roberts; Tommy Tavish, Richard Emory; Bead, Clayton Moore; Tommy Duncan and his Western All Stars; Smiley, Smiley Burnette// "Raider"; "Ring-Eye"; Major Mullen, Jason Robards, Sr.

Credits: Director, Ray Nazarro; Producer, Colbert Clark; Story, James Gruen; Screenwriter, Earle Snell; Editor, Paul Borofsky; Art Director, Charles Clague; Set Decorator, George Montgomery; Cinematographer, Fayte Browne

Songs: "The Ever-Loving Marshal" (Burnette) sung by Smiley Burnette and Tommy Duncan and his Western All Stars; "Saturday Night in San Antone" (Drake) sung by Tommy Duncan and his Western All Stars; "Rock-A-Bye Baby" (Canning, with additional lyrics by Marie Duncan) sung by Tommy Duncan and his Western All Stars; "When You Go" (Burnette) sung by Smiley Burnette

Location Filming: Iverson, California

Production Dates: April 6, 1949–April 13, 1949

Running Time: 54 min.

Story: A range war seems imminent between cattlemen and miners. Cattlemen complain that runoff water from the miners' claims is poisoning their cattle. Charles Starrett comes to Nugget City to investigate his brother-in-law's death. Lee Roberts, Gail Davis and Richard Emory warn him to leave. Miner and influential citizen Fred Sears is afraid that Starrett will want to reopen his brother-in-law's mine and orders his chief henchman, Clayton Moore, to kill Starrett and place the blame on Roberts. When that fails, Moore murders Emory and frames Starrett. Sheriff Smiley Burnette is forced to arrest Starrett, who is able to break jail. To cover himself, Burnette arranges pillows on the jail cot to look as if Starrett is sleeping. Moore fires two shots into the bed, thinking he's killed him. Starrett convinces Burnette to allow him to play dead. Starrett suspects Sears since he brought a sample of ore from his brother-in-law's mine to be assayed. Starrett then switched his ore sample for Sears's valuable ore sample. Sears tells Starrett that the ore sample is worthless. Starrett frightens Sears' assayer into admitting he made up poison to be placed in water where cattle drank. Through a secret tunnel, Sears has been stealing valuable ore from Starrett's brother-in-law's mine. Sears decides it time to leave the area with all the gold. Starrett, as the Durango Kid, and Burnette find the outlaw hideout. A gunfight breaks out and Starrett is trapped in Sears' mine shaft. Burnette is able to escape, and he goes to Roberts and Davis for help. Starrett has taken the fight to the outlaws. While successful at first, the odds begin to overwhelm him. Roberts, Burnette and Davis show up in time to turn the tables.

Notes and Commentary: A picture of Smiley Burnette demonstrating his rope tricks was used on the title card for *Last Days of Boot Hill* (Columbia, 1947)

Reviews: "Another assembly line 'Durango Kid' segment." *Western Movies*, Pitts

"Story is no gem of originality, but it's an adequate prop on which to hang a bunch of action. Film will satisfy oater fans," *Variety*, 07-12-50

Summation: Another strong Durango Kid western. The story moves well with good action sequences. Smiley Burnette is an asset in this one. Even with the great Tommy Duncan, the songs are undistinguished, but the lyrics of "When You Go" will bring a few chuckles.

BANDITS OF EL DORADO

Columbia (October 1949)

South of the border action-'n'-rhythm thrills!

Alternate Titles: Bandits of Eldorado and Tricked

Cast: Steve Carson/The Durango Kid, Charles Starrett; Colonel Jose Vargas, George J. Lewis; Captain Richard Henley, Fred Sears; Charles Bruton, John Dehner; Morgan, Clayton Moore; Mustard (Frank Rice) and Gravy (Ernest Stokes); Smiley, Smiley Burnette//

"Raider"; "Bullet"; "Ring-Eye"; Stage guard, Kermit Maynard; Tucker, John Doucette; Tim Starling, Jock O'Mahoney; Paul, Max Wagner; Rider knocked from horse, Ted Mapes; El Raton patron, Blackie Whiteford; Spade, Henry Kulky

Credits: Director, Ray Nazarro; Producer, Colbert Clark; Screenwriter, Barry Shipman; Editor, Paul Borofsky; Art Director, Charles Clague; Set Decorator, George Montgomery; Cinematographer, Fayte Browne

Songs: "The Rich Get Richer" (Burnette) sung by Smiley Burnette with Mustard and Gravy; "Tricky Senor" (Burnette) sung by Smiley Burnette; "The Last Great Day" (Rice and Stokes) sung by Mustard and Gravy

Location Filming: Iverson, California

Production Dates: May 17, 1949–May 26, 1949

Running Time: 56 min.

Story: To find out what has happened to some missing outlaws, Charles Starrett goes undercover. His only lead is a Copper City storekeeper, Clayton Moore. Moore is set to do business with him until the outlaw leader, John Dehner, suspects that Starrett might be a Texas Ranger. As the Durango Kid, Starrett intimidates henchman John Doucette into revealing that the key can be found at the El Raton cantina in El Dorado, Mexico. The answer can be found in Dehner's hacienda, which is attached to the cantina. Dehner has a trapdoor in his living room that opens to a raging river. Ranger Captain Fred Sears, disguised as a Mexican peasant, gains entry to the cantina office and begins to search it. Sears is caught by Moore and Cantina manager Henry Kulky. As Sears is being beaten, Starrett, as Durango, comes to his aid. In the fight, Kulky is killed. Starrett gains entry into Dehner's hacienda. A fight starts between Starrett and Moore and Dehner's butler, Max Wagner. In the scuffle, Moore and Wagner fall into the river. Dehner is about to end Starrett's life when the gun is shot out of his hand. Sears, Texas Ranger Jock O'Mahoney and Colonel Jose Vargas, George J. Lewis, arrive in time. Through Sears' intervention, Starrett is allowed to escape.

Notes and Commentary: Charles Starrett, as Steve, finally calls his horse by name, which is "Bullet."

There is a wanted poster at the sheriff's office for Black Murphy. Murphy was a character name in an earlier series entry, *West of Sonora* (Columbia, 1948).

Reviews: "A short film, it manages to pack lots of story into the time frame, but no real emotional involvement." *Motion Picture Guide*, Nash and Ross

"Fairly good 'Durango Kid' series outing." *Western Movies*, Pitts

"Run-of-the-mill yarn interspersed with enough fisticuffs and gunplay to please the hoss-loving clientele." *Variety*, 06-27-51

Summation: A good Durango Kid entry, well written by screenwriter Barry Shipman and well paced by director Ray Nazarro. Smiley Burnette and Mustard and Gravy chip in with a few good songs.

DESERT VIGILANTE

Columbia (November 1949)

Rhythm-riddled thrill round-up!

Cast: Steve Woods/The Durango Kid, Charles Starrett; Betty Long, Peggy Stewart; Thomas Hadley, Tristram Coffin; Angel, Mary Newton; Bill Martin, George Chesebro; The

Georgia Crackers (Hank Newman [vocals, guitar], Slim Newman [vocals], Bob Newman [vocals, bass], unknown musician [accordion]); Smiley, Smiley Burnette// "Raider," "Bullet," "Ring-Eye"; Ace, I. Stanford Jolley; Border patrol sergeant, Jack Ingram; Bob Gill, Paul Campbell; Little Arrow, Jerry Hunter; Jim Gill, Tex Harding

Credits: Director, Fred F. Sears; Producer, Colbert Clark; Screenwriter, Earle Snell; Editor, Paul Borofsky; Art Director, Charles Clague; Set Decorator, David Montrose; Cinematographer, Rex Wimpy

Songs: "It Can't Be As Bad As That" (Burnette) sung by Smiley Burnette with The Georgia Crackers; "He Don't Like Work" (Burnette) sung by Smiley Burnette with The Georgia Crackers; "I'll Never Let You Go, Little Darlin'" (Wakely) sung by The Georgia Crackers; "The Sky Over California" sung by The Georgia Crackers

Location Filming: Iverson and Bronson, California

Production Dates: September 14, 1948–September 22, 1948

Running Time: 56 min.

Story: Paul Campbell, mortally wounded by outlaws, asks Charles Starrett to deliver a hat to his mother, Mary Newton, who is staying at the Lazy Z ranch. In the lining of the hatbox are valuable silver certificates. Starrett finds that silver smuggling is running rampant along the U.S. Mexico border. Starrett is assigned to run down the smugglers and reports to Assistant U.S. Attorney Tristram Coffin, not knowing that he is the gang leader. Coffin is working with Newton, who is pretending to be bedridden. Coffin and Newton find the silver certificates that they don't intend to share with his henchmen. There is a tunnel that runs from Mexico to the basement room under the Lazy Z's kitchen. Tex Harding shows up looking for Campbell. Coffin has his gang led, by George Chesebro, attack Harding. Starrett, as the Durango Kid, foils the attack. There is another shipment coming through to the Lazy Z. Chesebro and his men plan to double-cross Coffin and Newton and hijack the ore. Starrett, as Durango, and Harding capture the gang, but Chesebro and his confederate, I. Stanford Jolley, escape and ride to the Lazy Z. At the ranch house, Chesbro guns down Coffin and Newton. Chesebro and Jolley try to escape through the tunnel into Mexico. Starrett, as Durango, follows and shoots Jolley before he can gain access to the tunnel. In Mexico, there is a gunfight between Starrett and the gang. Chesebro tries to sneak up on Starrett, but Starrett, aware of this, knocks out Chesebro. Starrett, with the help of the Mexican Rurales, rounds up the gang.

Notes and Commentary: The Georgia Crackers also performed as the Newman Brothers.

The scene in which the Durango Kid is knocked from his horse by a low-hanging branch was first seen in *Outlaws of the Rockies* (Columbia, 1945).

This was Tex Harding's first film with Charles Starrett since *Frontier Gunlaw* (Columbia, 1946).

Reviews: "Mediocre 'Durango Kid' series film." *Western Movies,* Pitts

"Slower paced than recent Starretts." *The Western,* Hardy

"While not as action-packed as some of its predecessors, Columbia's 'Desert Vigilante' is a fair entry in the Charles Starrett-Smiley Burnette mesa series." *Variety,* 08-24-49

Summation: A good Durango Kid entry. Screenwriter Earle Snell pulls a surprise when he has George Chesebro cold-bloodedly murder Tristram Coffin and Mary Newton. Fred F. Sears' direction is fast paced and on target. The music is good in this one.

HORSEMAN OF THE SIERRAS

Columbia (September 1949)

Song-swept western thriller!

Alternate Title: Remember Me

Cast: Steve Saunders/The Durango Kid, Charles Starrett; T. Texas Tyler; Patty McGregor, Lois Hall; Robin Grant, Tommy Ivo; Smiley, Smiley Burnette// "Raider"; Duke Webster, John Dehner; Phineas Grant, Jason Robards, Sr.; Morgan Webster, Daniel M. Sheridan; Bill Grant, Jock O'Mahoney; Ellory Webster, George Chesebro; Henchmen, Emile Avery, Ethan Laidlaw, Charles Soldani and Al Wyatt

Credits: Director, Fred F. Sears; Producer, Colbert Clark; Screenwriter, Barry Shipman; Editor, Paul Borofsky; Art Director, Charles Clague; Set Decorator, George Montgomery; Cinematography, Fayte Browne

Songs: "My Night to Howl" (Burnette) sung by Smiley Burnette; "No Kid" (Burnette) sung by Smiley Burnette; "Remember Me" (Wiseman) sung by T. Texas Tyler; "Fair Weather Baby" (Tyler and Hensley) sung by T. Texas Tyler

Location Filming: Iverson and Columbia/Warner Bros. Ranch, California

Production Dates: March 9, 1949–March 17, 1949

Running Time: 56 min.

Story: With the death of his parents, Tommy Ivo inherits the Rocky Moon Ranch. U.S. Marshal Charles Starrett is assigned to uncover the murderer of a government surveyor working on the ranch. Two of Ivo's relatives, Jason Robards, Sr. and John Dehner, plan to start a feud to eliminate all potential heirs to the ranch. As Starrett begins his investigation, an attempt is made on his life. Dehner is arrested. Robards kidnaps Ivo and breaks Dehner out of jail. Starrett, as the Durango Kid, rescues Ivo. Starrett then confronts Robards and Dehner and forces them to admit they are working together. Dehner is named the murderer of the surveyor because he was going to spread the news that oil deposits are on the ranch. Ivo becomes the ranch owner.

Notes and Commentary: T. Texas Tyler obtained his stage name by combining the names of western stars Tex Ritter and Tom Tyler. Tyler's biggest hit record was "The Deck of Cards" (4-Star, 1948).

Reviews: "Standard 'Durango Kid' drama." *Western Movies*, Pitts

"A marked improvement on his [Sears] first film, it sees him bringing fresh camera angles to the Durango Kid series. Nonetheless the plot is routine." *The Western*, Hardy

"A fair entry for the action market." *Variety*, 03-08-50

Summation: The film was unavailable for viewing by the author

RENEGADES OF THE SAGE

Columbia (November 1949)

Crashing to new action-and-rhythm highs!

Alternate Title: The Fort

Cast: Steve Duncan/The Durango Kid, Charles Starrett; Ellen Miller, Leslie Banning; Lt. Hunter, Jock O'Mahoney; Lt. Jones, Fred Sears; Smiley, Smiley Burnette// "Raider";

Miller, Trevor Bardette; Sloper, Douglas Fowley; Johnny, Jerry Hunter; Worker, George Chesebro; Drew, Frank McCarroll, Brown, Selmer Jackson

Credits: Director, Ray Nazarro; Producer, Colbert Clark; Screenwriter, Earle Snell; Editor, Paul Borofsky; Art Director, Charles Clague; Set Decorator, David Montrose; Cinematographer, Fayte M. Browne

Songs: "Pussy Foot" (Burnette) sung by Smiley Burnette; "Let Me Sleep" (Burnette) sung by Smiley Burnette; "I'm Thankful for Small Favors" (Raye and de Paul) sung by Smiley Burnette; "America" (Smith and Carey)

Location Filming: Iverson and Corriganville, California

Production Dates: August 17, 1949–August 25, 1949

Running Time: 56 min.

Story: An outlaw gang is sabotaging telegraph lines in western territories. The Secret Service sends top agent Charles Starrett to bring the gang to justice. The primary suspect is a former medical student, Trevor Bardette, who operated in the same manner for the Confederates during the Civil War. The real leader, however, is Douglas Fowley, who has Starrett ambushed and left for dead. Smiley Burnette finds the wounded Starrett and takes him to Bardette's trading post. Bardette is operating the post under a different name. Bardette tends to Starrett's wounds in a professional manner. Starrett thinks Bardette might be the man for whom he was searching. After Bardette performs a delicate operation to save an orphan, Jerry Hunter, he reveals his true identity to Starrett. In his Durango Kid guise, Starrett finds Fowley involved with the outlaw gang and proves Bardette's innocence. Fowley leads his men on another attack, this time on a telegraph supply train. Starrett, as Durango, and Bardette lead the fight against the outlaws. In the fight, Fowley is killed.

Reviews: "Better-than-average series western. The action is almost nonstop, with Burnette around for some comic relief." *Motion Picture Guide*, Nash and Ross

"Fair 'Durango Kid' series segment." *Western Movies*, Pitts

"This 56 minute entry, heavy in the action department and sporting a better-than-average story for a low-budget western rates with choicer Charles Starrett starrer." *Variety*, 09-20-50

Summation: The film was unavailable for viewing by the author

---

FRONTIER OUTPOST
Columbia (December 1949)

A rampage of action and rhythm!

Cast: Steve Lawton/The Durango Kid, Charles Starrett; Alice Tanner, Lois Hall; Forsythe, Steve Darrell; Copeland, Fred Sears; Krag Benson, Bob Wilke; Musicians, Hank Penny and Slim Duncan; Smiley, Smiley Burnette// "Raider"; "Bullet"; "Ring Eye"; Stage driver, Bud Osborne; Gopher, Chuck Roberson; Captain Tanner, Paul Campbell; Lt. Peck, Jock O'Mahoney; Col. Warrick, Pierre Watkin; Sgt. Murphy, Dick Wessel; Chalmers, Everett Glass; Stage employee, Blackie Whiteford

Credits: Director, Ray Nazarro; Producer, Colbert Clark; Screenwriter, Barry Shipman; Editor, Paul Borofsky; Art Director, Charles Clague; Set Decorator, George Montgomery; Cinematographer, Fayte Browne

Songs: "Twister" (Burnette) sung by Smiley Burnette with Hank Penny and Slim Duncan;

"I Love to Eat" (Burnette) sung by Smiley Burnette; "The Warning Song" (Burnette) sung by Smiley Burnette

Location Filming: Corriganville, California

Production Dates: September 8, 1949–September 16, 1949

Running Time: 55 min.

Story: Outlaws are intercepting gold shipments to Santa Fe. A stagecoach carrying three passengers — Fred Sears, Lois Hall and Steve Darrell — is held up by Charles Starrett, as the Durango Kid, who takes the gold. Later outlaws led by Bob Wilke hold up the coach, but are driven off by Starrett and Smiley Burnette. The stagecoach travels on to Fort Navajo, which is deserted. Lois Hall had come to Fort Navajo to be with her husband, Paul Campbell, who is in command of the fort. Sears is really an Army officer and takes command of the deserted fort. Starrett and Burnette, on assignment to bring the gold robbers, have the gold taken by Durango. Sears orders Starrett and Burnette to take the gold to Santa Fe. After they leave, Steve Darrell shows his true colors by murdering Sears and takes Hall prisoner. Campbell has already been taken captive. Darrell, by threatening to harm Hall, forces Campbell to do his bidding. Upon arrival in Santa Fe, Starrett is placed under arrest as Darrell brands him a murderer. Starrett is able to make his escape and learns more gold is to be shipped. Darrell forces Campbell to help him steal the gold shipment. Starrett, as the Durango Kid, gains control of the stagecoach and races to Fort Navajo, followed by Darrell and his men. Campbell, in gaining access to the fort so the stage can enter, receives a gunshot wound. Starrett, as Durango, is able to get behind the outlaws and force them to surrender.

Notes and Commentary: This film sat on the shelf for about 15 1/2 months before it was released.

Reviews: "A better than average Starrett oater." *Motion Picture Guide*, Nash and Ross

"Rather jumbled episode." *Western Movies*, Pitts

"Story line in this Charles Starrett entry wavers a bit, but film nevertheless rates as satisfactory for oater followers." *Variety*, 12-30-50

Summation: Okay Durango Kid outing. Performances are standard, with Smiley Burnette in fine form as Charles Starrett's official sidekick. Entertaining, but nothing special.

TRAIL OF THE RUSTLERS

Columbia (February 1950)

Sizzling Starrett action! Sparkling Smiley rhythms!

Alternate Title: Lost River

Cast: Steve Armitage/The Durango Kid, Charles Starrett; Mary Ellen Hyland, Gail Davis; Todd Hyland, Tommy Ivo; Mrs. J.G. Mahoney, Mira McKinney; Chick Mahoney, Don Harvey; Eddie Cletro and His Roundup Boys; Smiley, Smiley Burnette// "Raider"; "Ring-Eye"; "Bullet"; Ben Mahoney, Myron Healey; Jake, Boyd "Red" Morgan; Bob, Chuck Roberson; Sheriff Dave Wilcox, Gene Roth; Stage driver, Post Park; Rancher, Herman Hack

Credit: Director, Ray Nazarro; Producer, Colbert Clark; Screenwriter, Victor Arthur; Editor, Paul Borofsky; Art Director, Charles Clague; Set Decorator, George Montgomery; Cinematographer, Fayte Browne

Songs: "I Wish I'd Said That" (Burnette) sung by Smiley Burnette with Eddie Cletro and His Roundup Boys; "I Should Say" (Burnette) sung by Smiley Burnette; "Shoot Me

Dead for That One" (Burnette) sung by Smiley Burnette with Eddie Cletro and His Roundup Boys

Location Filming: Iverson, California
Production Dates: September 29, 1949–October 6, 1949
Running Time: 55 min.

Story: Mira McKinney believes Charles Starrett, as the Durango Kid, is responsible for her eldest son's death. Working with her other two sons, Don Harvey and Myron Healey, McKinney plans revenge on Starrett. Harvey plans to dress as the Durango Kid in cattle raids, and McKinney plots to buy up all the ranches in the area. An underground spring has been discovered that will increase the value of the properties. Hearing about the Durango Kid's supposed atrocities, Starrett come to Rio Perdito to investigate. Tommy Ivo and his sister, Gail Davis, see Harvey, as Durango, murder their father. Starrett's friend Smiley Burnette has a letter from a St. Louis company authorizing him to buy all the ranches in the area. Burnette is unaware the letter actually came from McKinney. Burnette is placed in an uncomfortable situation with both Starrett and the outlaws who are threatening to murder him if he doesn't follow their wishes. Working with Starrett as Durango, Ivo discovers the underground river. Unfortunately, he first tells McKinney. She has two henchmen hold Ivo captive until all the ranches have been sold to Burnette. Starrett learns that Ivo left town with two men. Starrett, as Durango, finds Ivo, learns about the water and races to town. Disgusted with Burnette's stalling tactics, Harvey dresses in his Durango outfit in order to force Burnette to purchase the ranches. Starrett arrives in time to expose Harvey as the false Durango. McKinney brandishes a derringer and points it at Starrett. Ivo arrives in time to snatch the gun from her hand. McKinney and her sons are arrested.

Notes and Commentary: Some sources mistakenly list "Blame it on Granpappy" for the song "Shoot Me Dead for That One"

On a theatrical poster, Smiley Burnette's last name is misspelled as Burnett.

Review: "Fair 'Durango Kid' actioner." *Western Movies*, Pitts

Summation: This is another good Durango Kid story. Charles Starrett and Smiley Burnette work well together, as usual. Ray Nazarro directs confidently and the end result shows it.

OUTCASTS OF BLACK MESA
Columbia (April 1950)

Pistols bark as melodies ring!

Alternate Title: The Clue

Cast: Steve Norman/The Durango Kid, Charles Starrett; Ruth Dorn, Martha Hyer; Andrew Vaning, Richard Bailey; Ozie, Ozie Waters; Smiley, Smiley Burnette// "Raider"; Sheriff Grasset, Stanley Andrews; Dayton, William Haade; Ted Thorp, Lane Chandler; Walt Dorn, William Gould; Curt, Bob Wilke; Kramer, Chuck Roberson; Nixon, George Chesebro

Credits: Director, Ray Nazarro; Producer, Colbert Clark; Story, Elmer Clifton; Screenwriter, Barry Shipman; Editor, Paul Borofsky; Art Director, Charles Clague; Set Decorator, Sidney Clifford; Cinematography, Fayte Browne

Songs: "Nobody Fires the Boss" (Burnette) sung by Smiley Burnette; "Donkey Engine" (Burnette) sung by Smiley Burnette; "Just Sittin' Around in Jail" (Clark) sung by Ozie Waters

Location Filming: Iverson, California

Production Dates: July 6, 1949–July 16, 1949

Running Time: 54 min.

Story: Charles Starrett, Lane Chandler and William Gould are partners in a gold mine. Gould is murdered. An attempt is made on Chandler's life. Chandler's daughter, Martha Hyer, claims Starrett fired the bullet. Starrett escapes custody. As the Durango Kid, Starrett believes William Haade made the murder attempt on Chandler. Still as Durango, Starrett has photographer Smiley Burnette send a picture of Haade to a U.S. marshal. Haade is wanted for murder. As Durango, Starrett discovers that Doctor Richard Bailey's medical certificate was forged. Bailey is accused of hiring Haade to murder Starrett, Chandler and Gould. Bailey then planned to marry Hyer and gain control of the mine. Haade is arrested. Bailey attempts to escape in a stagecoach. The stagecoach crashes, killing Bailey.

Notes and Commentary: In addition to Charles Starrett, Martha Hyer would work with Tim Holt, Allan "Rocky" Lane and Kirby Grant in "B" westerns. In the mid- to late-'50s, Hyer graduated to big-budget features, receiving an Academy Award nomination for *Some Came Running* (Metro-Goldwyn-Mayer, 1958), co-starring Frank Sinatra, Dean Martin and Shirley MacLaine.

Reviews: "Another good action entry in 'The Durango Kid' series." *Western Movies*, Pitts

"Footage is about par for the Durango Kid series turned out at Columbia," *Variety*, 05/17/50

Summation: This film was unavailable for viewing by the author.

TEXAS DYNAMO
Columbia (June 1950)

Crackling with action and song!

Alternate Title: Suspected

Cast: Steve Drake/The Durango Kid, Charles Starrett; Julia Beck, Lois Hall; Bill Beck, Jock O'Mahoney; Slim, Slim Duncan; Smiley, Smiley Burnette// "Raider"; Stanton, John Dehner; Luke, Gregg Barton; Kroger, George Chesebro; Walt, Marshall Bradford; Turkey, Emil Sitka; Hawkins, Fred Sears; Texas Dynamo, Ethan Laidlow

Credits: Director, Ray Nazarro; Producer, Colbert Clark; Screenwriter, Barry Shipman; Editor, Paul Borofsky; Art Director, Charles Clague; Set Decorator, George Montgomery; Cinematography, Fayte Browne

Songs: "Fickle Finger of Fate" (Burnette) sung by Smiley Burnette; "Kitty Loved the Calliope" (Burnette) sung by Smiley Burnette; "Let's Rally One and All" (Clark) sung by Slim Duncan

Location Filming: Iverson, California

Production Dates: February 14, 1950–February 21, 1950

Running Time: 54 min

Story: Lois Hall's father sends for Charles Starrett to help rid the town of Beckton of its lawless element. Hall's father is murdered by vigilante leader John Dehner. The vigilantes are outlaws who pretend to be on the side of law and order. Under Dehner's direction, Hall is elected mayor and has her issue a decree that only Dehner and his close associates can legally carry firearms. Starrett, as the Durango Kid, is accused of Hall's father's murder. To capture Starrett, Dehner sends for gunman Ethan Laidlaw. Starrett finds Laidlaw dying of a snakebite and decides to take on his identity. Dehner places him in charge of the vigilantes. The vigilantes rob a bank and frame Hall's brother, Jock O'Mahoney. As Durango, Starrett reveals that the vigilantes are outlaws, with Dehner as their leader and the murderer of Hall's father.

Notes and Commentary: Lois Hall's career spanned 58 years. Fans of "B" movies remember her appearances in westerns with Charles Starrett, Jimmy Wakely, Whip Wilson and Johnny Mack Brown. Hall played Ann Howe Palooka in *Joe Palooka in the Squared Circle* (Monogram, 1950). Hall appeared in two serials, *The Adventures of Sir Galahad* (Columbia, 1949) and *Pirates of the High Seas* (Columbia, 1950).

Reviews: "This is a thoroughly confusing oater." *Motion Picture Guide*, Nash and Ross

"Pretty fair Charles Starrett series entry with strong work by John Dehner as the town boss." *Western Movies*, Pitts

"A dull affair, of interest only because Shipman managed to give Starrett three roles to play." *The Western*, Hardy

"There's little in 'Texas Dynamo' to distinguish it from other Charles Starrett westerns. It's standard for the series." *Variety*, 06-14-50

Summation: This film was unavailable for viewing by the author.

STREETS OF GHOST TOWN
Columbia (August 1950)

Bullet-haunted thrills and rhythms!

Cast: Steve Woods/The Durango Kid, Charles Starrett; Bill Donner, George Chesebro; Doris Donner, Mary Ellen Kay; Bart Selby, Frank Fenton; Tommy Donner, "Brown Jug" Don Reynolds; Ozie Waters and His Colorado Rangers; Smiley, Smiley Burnette// "Raider"; "Ring-Eye"; "Bullet"; Wicks, John Cason; Kirby, Jack Ingram; Henchman, Bob Kortman; Jenkins, Nolan Leary; Banker, Dick Rush; Newspaper woman, Doris Houck; The stranger, Paul Campbell

Credits: Director, Ray Nazarro; Producer, Colbert Clark; Screenwriter, Barry Shipman; Editor, Paul Borofsky; Art Director, Charles Clague; Set Decorator, George Montgomery; Cinematographer, Fayte Browne

Songs: "Streets of Laredo (The Cowboy's Lament)" (traditional, with additional lyrics by Burnette) sung by Smiley Burnette; "Oh! Susanna" (Foster) sung by Ozie Waters with His Colorado Rangers

Location Filming: Iverson, California

Production Dates: March 7–March 13, 1950

Running Time: 54 min.

Story: Charles Starrett, Smiley Burnette and Sheriff Stanley Andrews ride into Shadeville, a ghost town, looking for over a million dollars in stolen money. Outlaw leader Frank Fenton is trying to beat the law to the money. Years before, gang member George Chesebro hijacked the money from Fenton and hid it in a locked room in a Spanish mine called the Devil's Cave. Fenton later captured Chesebro. Chesebro refused to reveal the location of the money even under torture, which left him blind. Chesebro escaped, only to be captured by the law. Chesebro, it was reported, died in a prison fire. When their supplies are stolen, Starrett, Burnette and Andrews are forced to leave for more supplies. On the return trip, Chesebro's niece, Mary Ellen Kay, accompanies Starrett and his party. Kay believes Chesebro is still alive and her brother Don Reynolds is now acting as Chesebro's eyes. In the ghost town, Reynolds has found where the money is hidden and goes to Chesebro. Fenton follows Reynolds. Fenton captures Reynolds and shoots Chesebro, wounding him. After Fenton captures Kay, Reynolds leads him to the stolen money. When Fenton opens the door to the room, a crazed Chesebro is waiting. Fenton finally fires the shot that kills him. Kay and Reynolds run away with Fenton chasing them. Starrett, as the Durango Kid, appears and in an exchange of shots, ends Fenton's outlaw career.

Notes and Commentary: Stock footage from *Landrush* (Columbia, 1946) and *Gunning for Vengeance* was used. Ozie Waters' rendition of "Oh! Susanna" was lifted from *Landrush*. The Durango Kid's alter-ego character name in *Landrush* was Steve Harmon.

Production goof: Look at the scene in which Don Reynolds enters the room occupied by George Chesebro. Take a close look at the background scenery to see the roll of material on the sound stage floor.

Reviews: "A muddled plot that needed lots of action to make it passable. Confusing western." *Motion Picture Guide*, Nash and Ross

"The mystery element adds some life to this 'Charles Starrett' outing." *Western Movies*, Pitts

"A mighty confusing sagebrusher. Only recommendation is plenty of action." *Variety*, 08-16-50

Summation: Speedy Durango Kid western feature interspersed with stock footage from previous Durango Kid films. Performances are up to par, with George Chesebro a standout as a man slowly going mad.

ACROSS THE BADLANDS
Columbia (September 1950)

Blasting to new action and rhythm highs!

Alternate Title: The Challenge

Cast: Steve Ransom/The Durango Kid, Charles Starrett; Eileen Carson, Helen Mowery; Rufus Downey, Dick Elliott; Harmonica Bill, Harmonica Bill; Smiley, Smiley Burnette// "Raider"; Sheriff Crocker, Stanley Andrews; Duke Jackson/Keno Jackson, Bob Wilke; Jeff Carson, Hugh Prosser; Bart, Robert S. Cavendish; Gregory Banion, Charles Evans; Pete, Paul Campbell; Tough, Dick Alexander

Credits: Director, Fred F. Sears; Producer, Colbert Clark; Story and Screenwriter, Barry Shipman; Editor, Paul Borofsky; Art Director, Charles Clague; Set Decorator, Fay Babcock; Cinematographer, Fayte Browne; Sound, Jack Haynes

Songs: "I'm Telling Myself I Ain't Afraid" (Burnette) sung by Smiley Burnette; "Harmonica Bill" (Burnette) performed by Smiley Burnette and Harmonica Bill

Location Filming: Iverson, California

Production Dates: March 31, 1950–April 7, 1950

Running Time: 55 min.

Story: The Ranahan Trail, supposedly a shortcut across the badlands to San Feliz, is the subject of a search by masked raiders. Railroad surveyors are being attacked. Railroad man Charles Evans sends for Charles Starrett, an ex-Texas Ranger, to prove stagecoach operator Hugh Prosser is behind the attacks. Outlaws jump Starrett and, in the melee, one of the outlaw's guns ends up in Starrett's possession. The gun belonged to Prosser, who claims he lost it. Robert S. Cavendish, one of the outlaw gang, heads up a mob to lynch Prosser. Starrett, in his guise of the Durango Kid, rescues Prosser. He tells Starrett that he believes there is no Ranahan Trail. Starrett discovers that Sheriff Stanley Andrews is behind the attacks on the surveyors, and that there is, indeed, no Ranahan Trail. He is able to bring Andrews to justice. Then Starrett, as the Durango Kid, rounds up the rest of the gang.

Reviews: "A disjointed, erratically constructed film that also has Burnette performing his cornball comedy with chubby cheer. Not one of Starrett's better efforts." *Motion Picture Guide*, Nash and Ross

"Well done entry in the 'Durango Kid' series." *Western Movies*, Pitts

"A superior series entry from Starrett." *The Western*, Hardy

"Film doesn't take time for proper introduction, and the finale is likely to leave the viewer slightly bewildered. However, the action sequences and excellent photography give this an overall par rating." *Variety*, 09-20-50

Summation: The film was not available for viewing by the author.

RAIDERS OF TOMAHAWK CREEK
Columbia (October 1950)

Cowboy-and-Indian action and song!

Alternate Title: Circle of Fear

Cast: Steve Blake/The Durango Kid, Charles Starrett; Randolph Dike, Edgar Dearing; Janet Clayton, Kay Buckley; Smiley, Smiley Burnette// "Raider"; Billy Calhoun, Billy Kimbley: Chief Flying Arrow, Paul Marion; Sheriff, Paul McGuire; Jeff, Bill Hale; Saunders, Lee Morgan

Credits: Director, Fred F. Sears; Producer, Colbert Clark; Story, Eric Freiwald and Robert Schaefer; Screenwriter, Barry Shipman; Editor, Paul Borofsky; Art Director, Charles Clague; Set Decorator, Louis Diage; Cinematographer, Fayte Browne; Sound, Russ Malmgren

Songs: "I'm Too Smart for That" (Burnette) sung by Smiley Burnette; "The Grasshopper Polka" (Burnette) sung by Smiley Burnette

Location Filming: Iverson, California

Production Dates: June 6, 1950–June 13, 1950

Running Time: 55 min.

Story: Charles Starrett is the new Indian agent, replacing Edgar Dearing who was fired for excessive drinking. Rancher Bill Hale's ranch is partly on Indian territory. To placate Chief Paul Marion, Starrett tells Hale he can give him comparable property on the other side of Tomahawk Creek. During the discussion, Marion notices that Hale is wearing a ring made by the tribal medicine man. This is one of five rings that were made. Hale is murdered with a medicine man's tomahawk. Starrett discovers Hale's ring is missing. Three other men who had similar rings are murdered. Since Starrett has the fifth ring, he is arrested for the murders. Dearing and his accomplice, Lee Morgan, are behind the murders. Starrett, as the Durango Kid, is able to bring Dearing and Morgan to justice and retrieve the four stolen rings. Still as Durango, Starrett shows Marion that the five rings, when put together, show the location of a silver mine on Indian land.

Notes And Comentary: A poster for *Raiders of Tomahawk Creek* can be seen in *The Sniper* (Columbia, 1952) as Arthur Franz walks by a movie theater.

Reviews: "Action-packed Starrett oater." *Motion Picture Guide*, Nash and Ross

"Okay 'Durango Kid' series actioner." *Western Movies*, Pitts

"This is an entertaining Starrett series Western directed with real zest by Sears." *The Western*, Hardy

"This latest Charles Starrett western wears a better entertainment brand than some of his recent entries from Columbia." *Variety*, 11-08-50

Summation: This film was unavailable for viewing by the author.

LIGHTNING GUNS
Columbia (December 1950)

Routing valley gangsters!

Alternate Title: Taking Sides

Cast: Steve Brandon/The Durango Kid, Charles Starrett; Susan Atkins, Gloria Henry; Luke Atkins, William Norton Bailey; Musician, Ken Houchins; Smiley, Smiley Burnette// "Raider"; Captain Dan Saunders, Edgar Dearing; Jud Norton, Raymond Bond; Sheriff Ron Saunders, Jock O'Mahoney; Hank Burch, Chuck Robertson; Jim Otis, Frank Griffin; Crawley, Joel Friedkin; Blake, George Chesebro; Lookout, Billy Williams

Credits: Director, Fred F. Sears; Producer, Colbert Clark; Story, Bill Milligan; Screenwriter, Victor Arthur; Editor, Paul Borofsky; Art Director, Charles Clague; Set Decorator, George Montgomery; Cinematography, Fayte Browne; Sound, George Cooper

Songs: "Bathtub King" (Burnette) sung by Smiley Burnette; "Our Whole Family's Smart" (Burnette) sung by Smiley Burnette; "Ramblin' Blood in My Veins" (Burnette) sung by Smiley Burnette (Note: Ken Houchins assisted on some or all of the musical numbers)

Location Filming: Iverson, California

Production Dates: May 16, 1950–May 24, 1950

Running Time: 55 min.

Story: Edgar Dearing opposes the construction of a dam by rancher William Norton Bailey to conserve water. Masked raiders attack the dam site, only to be thwarted by Charles Starrett as the Durango Kid. Starrett has come to visit his friend Dearing, who is arrested for the raid and the murder of the town banker. In exchange for the mortgage on Bailey's ranch, general store owner Raymond Bond makes money available to complete the dam. Bond, the outlaw leader, orders his men to break Dearing out of jail. The dam is raided again, with the blame placed on Dearing. As Durango, Starrett follows the raiders to their hideout only to find that Bond is behind the raids. Starrett, still as Durango, rounds up the gang members and proves that Bond is the culprit. The dam can now be completed.

Notes and Commentary: Gloria Henry was a leading lady in "B" features at Columbia (1947–50), co-starring in westerns with Gene Autry and Charles Starrett, and appearing in various entries of the Bulldog Drummond, Rusty and Counterspy series. Henry is best known for her role as Alice Mitchell on the television series, *Dennis the Menace* (CBS, 1959–63).

Reviews: "A good entry in Columbia's 'Durango Kid' series. Plenty of action and good comic relief by Burnette." *Motion Picture Guide*, Nash and Ross

"Well done 'Durango Kid' series segment." *Western Movies*, Pitts

"A fast-paced addition to the Charles Starrett series, 'Lightning Guns' should have little difficulty roping in western addicts and action fans. Film starts off on an exciting note and is maintained throughout." *Variety*, 12-06-50

Summation: This film was not available for viewing by the author.

PRAIRIE ROUNDUP
Columbia (January 1951)

Outshooting big-time robber barons!

Cast: Steve Carson/The Durango Kid, Charles Starrett; Toni Eaton, Mary Castle; Buck Prescott, Frank Fenton; Singing cowhands, The Sunshine Boys (Ace Richmond, Eddie Wallace, J.D. Sumner, Freddie Daniel); Smiley, Smiley Burnette// "Raider," "Ring-Eye"; "Bullet"; Sheriff, Frank Sully; Fake Durango Kid, Al Wyatt; Hawk Edwards, Don Harvey; Poker Joe, Paul Campbell; Red Dawson, Lane Chandler; Barton, John Cason; Jim Eaton, George Baxter; Dan Kelly, Forrest Taylor; Pete, Glenn Thompson

Prairie Roundup (1951) title card—(left, top to bottom) Mary Castle, Smiley Burnette, Charles Starrett.

Credits: Director, Fred F. Sears; Producer, Colbert Clark; Screenwriter, Joseph O'Donnell; Editor, Paul Borofsky; Art Director, Charles Clague; Set Decorator, Dave Montrose; Cinematographer, Fayte Browne, Musical Director, Mischa Bakaleinikoff

Songs: "Deep Froggie Blues" (Burnette) sung by Smiley Burnette; "Press Along to the Big Corral" (traditional) sung by the Sunshine Boys; "Ride on the Golden Range in the Sky" sung by the Sunshine Boys; "Snack Happy" (Burnette) sung by Smiley Burnette with the Sunshine Boys

Location Filming: Iverson, California

Production Dates: July 11, 1950–July 18, 1950

Running Time: 53 min.

Story: Don Harvey and Paul Campbell frame ex–Texas Ranger Charles Starrett for the murder of Al Wyatt, who was dressed as the Durango Kid. Sentenced to hang, Starrett has Smiley Burnette break him out of jail. Burnette has information that Harvey and Campbell work for Starrett's old nemesis, Frank Fenton, in Santa Fe. Fenton's men stampede cattle herds coming into Santa Fe, pay low prices for the cattle that the trail herders recover and take the stampeded cattle. On the way to Santa Fe, Starrett and Burnette take jobs with George Baxter, who is taking a mixed branded herd to Santa Fe. Despite Starrett's best efforts, Fenton's men stampede Baxter's herd. Baxter's daughter, Mary Castle, has seen a reward poster for Starrett and believes he's in league with the rustlers. Starrett has Burnette form a cattle patrol to stop attacks on future herds coming to Santa Fe. Fenton's men try to capture Starrett but he is able to capture Campbell. Harvey follows the trail to a shack where Campbell is being held prisoner. Fenton has Harvey get a gun to Campbell. Starrett, as the Durango Kid, arrives at the shack to question him. Harvey fires shots to distract Starrett. Campbell pulls the gun from concealment and fires point blank at Starrett. Starrett returns fire, wounding Campbell. Burnette checks Campbell's pistol and finds it was loaded with blanks. Campbell confesses everything, he even tells where Baxter's herd is hidden. Starrett, still as Durango, goes to town to settle the score with Fenton. Meanwhile, Castle has decided to sell the remainder of her herd to Fenton. Starrett arrives in time to stop the sale. He then enters into a fierce hand-to-hand struggle with Fenton. Starrett is victorious and leaves Castle, with gun drawn to keep Fenton under guard until Starrett can return as Durango's alter ego. Desperate, Fenton snatches the gun from Castle's hand and races after Starrett. The two men fire at each other. Starrett's bullet finds it mark, killing Fenton. Starrett plans to return to Texas to clear his name.

Notes and Commentary: There was new opening credit music for the Durango Kid entry.

The cattle stampede sequence was lifted from *Arizona* (Columbia, 1940).

Reviews: "One of the best efforts of the 'Durango Kid' series. Some interesting plot twists and a variety of camera angles uncommon to westerns of this nature make this production an intriguing actioner." *Motion Picture Guide*, Nash and Ross

"Fast moving entry in the 'Durango Kid' series." *Western Movies*, Pitts

"Possibly Sears' best film with Starrett, *Prairie Roundup* sees its director confident enough to choose unusual angles for the action sequences." *The Western*, Hardy

"Columbia's Durango Kid series with Charles Starrett gets into high gear with 'Prairie Roundup,' an oater well above any recent entries in the group. Plenty of action, an okay plot and good use of the sagebrush formula. Should rate this one a neat reception in the program western market. Unusual for the scries oater field are the interesting camera angles and other marks of intelligent use of the lens displayed by Fayte Brown." *Variety*, 01-24-51

Summation: A superior "B" western. Everything falls into place in this one. Charles Starrett gives one of his best performances. Smiley Burnette is a believable sidekick, a real help to Starrett and he can handle himself in the fisticuffs department. Director Fred F. Sears is at the top of his game, conveying the tension found in screenwriter Joseph O'Donnell's fine screenplay while keeping the action flowing. Sears works with cinematographer Fayte Browne to use some interesting camera angles in the action sequences. Note Sears' adroit handling of close-ups to intensify the action. The music is top-flight, with Burnette's playing and singing of "Deep Froggie Blues" a true delight. A neat touch: look for the bartender to pour a sleeping drunk's whiskey back in the bottle! Don't miss this one.

RIDIN' THE OUTLAW TRAIL
Columbia (February 1951)

Starrett's a six-gun terror! Smiley's a riot of fun!

Cast: Steve Forsythe/The Durango Kid, Charles Starrett; Betsy Willard, Sunny Vickers; Pop Willard, Edgar Dearing; Pee Wee King and His Golden West Cowboys; Smiley, Smiley Burnette// "Raider"; Sheriff Tom Chapman, Peter Thompson; Ace Donley, Jim Bannon; Sam Barton, Lee Morgan; Reno, Chuck Roberson; Henchmen, Ethan Laidlaw and Frank McCarroll

Credits: Director, Fred F. Sears; Producer, Colbert Clark; Screenwriter, Victor Arthur; Editor, Paul Borofsky; Art Director, Charles Clague; Set Decorator, George Montgomery; Cinematographer, Fayte Brown; Sound, Howard Fogetti

Songs: "I'm a Sucker For a Bargain" (Burnette) sung by Smiley Burnette with Pee Wee King and His Golden West Cowboys; "Rack-a-Bye-Baby" (Burnette) sung by Smiley Burnette

Location Filming: Iverson, California

Production Dates: August 10, 1950–August 18, 1950

Running Time: 55 min.

Story: Texas Ranger Charles Starrett is after outlaw Lee Morgan. Morgan has stolen $20,000 in gold pieces. Outlaw leader Jim Bannon and his chief henchman Chuck Robertson murder Morgan and take the gold. Bannon forces blacksmith Smiley Burnette to melt gold into bullion. The gold is hidden in an old mine. Prospector Edgar Dearing has hidden his past prison record from his daughter, Sunny Vickers. Bannon threatens to tell Vickers unless Dearing pretends to make a gold strike. Burnette informs Starrett about Bannon and the gold. As Durango, Starrett breaks up the melting operations at the mine. With Sheriff Peter Thompson's help, Bannon and Morgan are brought to justice. Dearing's past is kept from Vickers. Starrett returns to Texas with the gold.

Notes and Commentary: This film is a loose remake of an earlier Durango Kid western, *Both Barrels Blazing* (Columbia, 1946).

Reviews: "This is a well-paced, exciting entry in the popular 'Durango Kid' series." *Motion Picture Guide*, Nash and Ross

"Fairly complicated, but okay, 'Durango Kid' actioner." *Western Movies*, Pitts

"Another superior Starrett series Western." *The Western*, Hardy

"A stock entry in the film cowpoke's Columbia oater series." *Variety*, 02-14-51

Summation: This film was not available for viewing by the author.

FORT SAVAGE RAIDERS
Columbia (March 1951)

Gunplay! Horseplay!

Cast: Steve Drake/The Durango Kid, Charles Starrett; Capt. Michael Craydon, John Dehner; Old Cuss, Trevor Bardette; Dusty Walker; Smiley, Smiley Burnette// "Raider"; Lt. James Sutter, Peter Thompson; Col. Sutter, Fred F. Sears; Jug, John Cason; Rog Beck, Frank Griffin; Col. Markham, Sam Flint

Credits: Director, Ray Nazarro; Producer, Colbert Clark; Screenwriter, Barry Shipman; Editor, Paul Borofsky; Art Director, Charles Clague; Set Decorator, George Montgomery; Cinematographer, Henry Freulich; Sound, George Cooper

Song: "Full Steam Ahead" (Burnette) sung by Smiley Burnette

Location Filming: Corriganville, California

Production Dates: September 13, 1950–September 21, 1950

Running Time: 54 min.

Story: Captain John Dehner goes AWOL to see his ailing child. Dehner is captured and placed in the garrison at Fort Savage. Dehner's mind snaps and he engineers a jailbreak with the other prisoners. Dehner's gang, the Fort Savage Raiders, begins violent raids. Charles Starrett is asked to break up the gang. Starrett gets his friends Smiley Burnette and Trevor Bardette to help him. As this is a military matter, young and inexperienced Lt. Peter Thompson is selected as leader. Thompson's mistake puts the men in peril, but Starrett, as the Durango Kid, rescues them. Thompson wants to arrest Durango. Starrett can take Thompson's attitude no longer and challenges him to a fistfight. Starrett is the victor. Using Starrett's plan, Dehner is trapped in a cave. In a gunfight, Starrett kills him.

Notes and Commentary: John Dehner was a consummate character actor. He originated the role of Paladin on the radio version of *Have Gun—Will Travel* (CBS, 1958–60). Dehner appeared in many television productions, but is best known for playing Duke Williams on *The Roaring 20s* (ABC, Warner Bros., 1960–62) and Cyril Bennett on *The Doris Day Show* (CBS, 1971–73).

Reviews: "A surprisingly intense Starrett western which sports a fine performance by Dehner as a crazed Army officer." *Motion Picture Guide*, Nash and Ross

"Well made 'Durango Kid' series episode with a sympathetic villain excellently played by John Dehner." *Western Movies*, Pitts

"Dehner, who brings a real depth to his role, and Shipman's intriguing script give the movie some of the edge of the superior *The Man from Colorado* (Columbia, 1948)." *The Western*, Hardy

"Typical western, okay for action spots." *Variety*, 03-14-51

Summation: This film was unavailable for viewing by the author.

SNAKE RIVER DESPERADOES
Columbia (May 1951)

Guns blazing! Fun amazing!

Cast: Steve Reynolds/The Durango Kid, Charles Starrett; Little Hawk, Don Reynolds "Brown Jug"; Billy Haverly, Tommy Ivo; Jim Haverly, Monte Blue; Smiley Burnette, Smiley

Burnette// "Raider"; "Ring Eye"; Josh Haverly, George Chesebro; Jason Fox, Sam Flint; Chief Black Eagle, Charles Hovarth; Dodds, John Pickard; Brandt, Boyd "Red" Morgan

Credits: Director, Fred Sears; Producer, Colbert Clark; Screenwriter, Barry Shipman; Editor, Paul Borofsky; Art Director, Charles Clague; Set Decorator, George Montgomery; Cinematographer, Fatye Browne; Musical Director, Ross DiMaggio; Music Supervisor, Paul Mertz

Location Filming: Iverson, California

Songs: "Listen to the Mockingbird" (Hawthorne) played by Smiley Burnette and band; "Brass Band Polka" (Burnette) sung by Smiley Burnette with band; "For He's a Jolly Good Fellow" (traditional) played by Smiley Burnette and band; "Blue Tail Fly" (traditional) played by Smiley Burnette and band

Running Time: 54 minutes

Production Dates: October 18, 1950–October 26, 1950

Story: Young Indian boy Don Reynolds tells Charles Starrett, in his Durango Kid guise, that white men are selling guns to his tribe, and that he wants him to prevent an Indian uprising. Starrett enlists the help of trader Monte Blue in calming the Indian tribe, not realizing that Blue is behind the trouble. Starrett persuades Chief Charles Hovarth to sign a peace treaty. Blue has his men dress as Indians and sack the town. Starrett rallies the townspeople and the outlaws are driven off. Starrett stops Blue's last effort to start an Indian war, and with a well-placed bullet, ends Blue's lawless career.

Notes and Commentary: In the segment when the fake Indians raid the town, footage from *Badlands of Dakota* (Universal, 1941), *Raiders of Ghost City* (Universal, 1943) and *Gun Town* (Universal, 1945) is used.

Reviews: "Well done actioner in the 'Durango Kid' series." *Western Movies*, Pitts

Charles Starrett's saddle heroics come off nicely in this sagebrusher, shaping it as okay for the program western field." *Variety*, 05-16-51

Summation: Fast, action-packed and well above-average Durango Kid film. Charles Starrett throws more punches than usual as director Fred F. Sears keeps proceedings moving at a breakneck pace. The performances are standard, with a nod to Don Reynolds for his athleticism.

BONANZA TOWN

Columbia (July 1951)

Charles Starrett cracks down on a frame-up and
Smiley Burnette bobs up as a barbarous barber!

Alternate Title: Two-Fisted Agent

Cast: Steve Ramsay/The Durango Kid, Charles Starrett; Henry Hardison, Fred F. Sears; Judge Anthony Dillon, Luther Crockett; Krag Boseman, Myron Healey, Smoker, Charles Horvath; Slim, Slim Duncan; Smiley, Smiley Burnette// "Raider"; "Bullet"; "Ring-Eye"; Marshal John Read, Paul McGuire; Bill Trotter, Al Wyatt; Bob Dillon, Ted Jordan; Krag's henchmen, George Magrill and Guy Teague; Whiskers, Vernon Dent; John Avery, Nolan Leary; Dirk, Zon Murray; Flint, Marshall Reed; Stage driver, Bud Osborne; Anne Avery, Nancy Saunders; Hod, George Chesebro; Danny Avery, Glen Stuart; Borger, I. Stanford Jolley; Borger's henchman, Bob Wilke; Sheriff, Steve Clark

Credits: Director, Fred F. Sears; Producer, Colbert Clark; Screenwriter, Barry Shipman and Bert Horswell; Editor, Paul Borofsky; Art Director, Charles Clague; Set Decorator, George Montgomery; Cinematography, Henry Freulich; Musical Director, Mischa Bakaleinikoff

Songs: "It All Goes to Show You" (Burnette) sung by Smiley Burnette and Slim Duncan; "Rooty-Toot" (Burnette) sung by Smiley Burnette and Slim Duncan

Location Filming: Iverson, California

Production Dates: November 14, 1950–November 18, 1950

Running Time: 56 min.

Story: Treasury Agent Charles Starrett is on the trail of Fred F. Sears, who stole $30,000. Sears had supposedly died in a flood some years earlier, but Starrett believes him to be in Bonanza Town. Bonanza Town is under the control of Myron Healey and his henchmen. Because of a crime he committed, Judge Luther Crockett is under the control of both Sears and Healey. Crockett's son, Ted Jordan, sends for Starrett, as the Durango Kid, to end the lawlessness. Starrett reports to Crockett and tells him of his mission. Overhearing the conversation, Sears realizes that Starrett is dangerous and plans to get rid of him. A trap is set to get rid of both Starrett and the Durango Kid. Crockett tips off Starrett that Sears is in hiding, waiting to kill him. Starrett attempts to capture Sears, but Sears is able to escape. Changing into his Durango Kid outfit, Starrett captures Healey and his henchmen. Sears returns to Crockett's house and shoots him for tipping off Starrett. Sears grabs his stolen money and tries to get out of town. Starrett, as Durango, fires a shot that ends Sears' criminal career.

Notes and Commentary: *Bonanza Town* is a sequel to *West of Dodge City* (Columbia, 1947) using about 19 minutes of footage from the original. In the cast listing above, actors from Nolan Leary to Steve Clark are only seen in the stock footage. In the sequel, Starrett relates that Fred Sears drowned in the floodwaters. In *Dodge City*, Sears survived to clear Glen Stuart of robbery charges.

The opening scene of Smiley Burnette's runaway wagon with Charles Starrett as Durango in pursuit was originally seen in *Whirlwind Raiders* (Columbia, 1948).

Co-screenwriter Bert Horswell wrote the screenplay for *West of Dodge City*.

Reviews: "Cheapie vehicle for Starrett." *Motion Picture Guide*, Nash and Ross

"Average 'Durango Kid' actioner." *Western Movies*, Pitts

"Average Charles Starrett western with Smiley Burnette." *Variety*, 07-18-51

Summation: Threadbare Durango Kid entry with only minimal entertainment value. Smiley Burnette's "funnies" are not so funny in this one. With the use of stock footage from two previous Durango Kid films and the time devoted to Burnette's comedy, there's not much time left for a new story.

CYCLONE FURY

Columbia (August 1951)

Charles Starrett rounds up hijacked horses ... Smiley Burnette ... horses around!

Cast: Steve Reynolds/The Durango Kid, Charles Starrett; Captain Barham, Fred F. Sears; Grat Hanlon, Clayton Moore; Bunco, Bob Wilke; Merle Travis and his Bronco Busters; Smiley, Smiley Burnette// "Raider"; "Ring-Eye"; "Bullet"; Brock Masters, Mark

Roberts; Henchmen, Lane Bradford; Wyatt, Ray Bennett; Bret Fuller, George Chesebro; Johnny Masters, Louis Lettieri; Henchman who attacks Johnny, Richard Alexander; Doctor, Frank O'Connor; Krag, Kermit Maynard; Regan, John Merton; Barstow, Edmund Cobb; Running Wolf, Jay Silverheels; Indian Chief, Paul Marion

Credits: Director, Ray Nazarro; Producer, Colbert Clark; Screenwriter, Barry Shipman and Ed. Earl Repp; Editor, Paul Borofsky; Art Director, Charles Clague; Set Decorator, George Montgomery; Cinematographer, Henry Freulich; Musical Supervisor, Paul Mertz; Musical Director, Mischa Bakaleinikoff

Songs: "Getting Some Sleep" (Burnette) sung by Smiley Burnette with Merle Travis and his Bronco Busters; "Hear the Wind (Singing a Cowboy Song)" (Burnette) sung by Smiley Burnette with Merle Travis and his Bronco Busters

Location Filming: Iverson and Corriganville, California

Production Dates: January 8, 1951–January 11, 1951

Running Time: 53 min.

Story: Charles Starrett is responsible for finding sources of horses for the Army. Mark Roberts, who has a large herd of wild mustangs on his ranch, receives a government contract. Before Roberts can deliver horses, news of his death is brought by his rival, Clayton Moore. Moore wants the Army contract. Starrett introduces Roberts's adopted son, Louis Lettieri, as the heir to the ranch. Lettieri has a deadline to provide at least 300 mustangs to the Army. Moore sends his henchman, Bob Wilke, to stampede the horses. The cowboys, led by Starrett as the Durango Kid, repulse the attack and rout the raiders. Seeing that all is lost, Moore attempts to escape. Starrett, as Durango, follows Moore to his office. A rugged fistfight ensues with Starrett emerging victorious. The mustangs are herded into the Army corral just in time to save Lettieri's contract.

Notes and Commentary: The working title was "Cyclone Canyon."

Footage from previous Durango Kid films, *Prairie Raiders* (Columbia, 1947), *Galloping Thunder* (Columbia, 1946), *Laramie* (Columbia, 1949), and the Randolph Scott-Glenn Ford western *The Desperadoes* (Columbia, 1943) was used. Interestingly, the villain's character name in *Galloping Thunder* was also Grat Hanlon.

The song "Hear the Wind (Singing a Cowboy Song)" was lifted from *Galloping Thunder*.

Reviews: "An interesting oater from the Durango Kid series." *Motion Picture Guide*, Nash and Ross

"Fairly good 'Durango Kid' series film." *Western Movies*, Pitts

"Charles Starrett has only a fair oater in his latest Columbia entry." *Variety*, 08-15-51

Summation: Another paste-up entry in the Durango Kid series with way too much stock footage. I can't believe it took even five days to complete filming in this one. Some entertainment values, but in the end, not truly satisfying.

THE KID FROM AMARILLO

Columbia (October 1951)

Starrett scores a bull's-eye — Smiley shoots the bull!

Alternate Title: Silver Chains

Cast: Steve Ransom/The Durango Kid, Charles Starrett; The Cass County Boys (Jerry Scoggins [guitar], Fred Martin [accordion] and Bert Dodson [bass]); Smiley, Smiley Burnette//

"Raider"; Tom Mallory, Harry Lauter; Jonathan Cole, Fred F. Sears; Rakin, Don Megowan; Snead, Scott Lee; Dirk, Guy Teague; Jason Summerville, Charles Evans; Don Jose Figaroa, George J. Lewis; Zeno, Henry Kulky; El Lobo, George Chesebro

Credits: Director, Ray Nazarro; Producer, Colbert Clark; Screenwriter, Barry Shipman; Editor, Paul Borofsky; Art Director, Charles Clague; Set Decorator, James Crowe; Cinematographer, Fayte Browne; Sound, Lambert Day

Songs: "The Great Burnette from Chihuahua" (Burnette) sung by Smiley Burnette; "Ziekel Saw the Wheel" (traditional) sung by Smiley Burnette and The Cass County Boys; "Old Colville Jail" (traditional) sung by The Cass County Boys

Location Filming: Iverson, California

Production Dates: May 17, 1951–May 25, 1951

Running Time: 56 min.

Story: Treasury Agent Charles Starrett is assigned to break up Fred F. Sears' silver smuggling ring. Agent Harry Lauter (posing as a fighter, "The Kid from Amarillo") is able to join Sears' gang. Sears runs a penal colony. Prisoners are taken into Mexico to build roads. Starrett notices the prisoners wear chains as they go to work, but not when they come back. Another agent, Smiley Burnette, begins investigating Sears but is captured. Sears learns Lauter's true identity. As captives, Lauter and Burnette see silver being made into the prisoner' chains. As the Durango Kid, Starrett stops a wagon loaded with chains and forces the men to take him to Sears' hideout. Starrett frees Lauter and Burnette. With the assistance of Mexican authorities, Sears' gang is captured. Starrett rides to Sears' ranch and brings him to justice.

Notes and Commentary: The Cass County Boys were known for their close association with Gene Autry. They traveled with Autry on his personal-appearance tours and appeared with him in nine feature films and on nine television shows.

Reviews: "Probably one of the worst of Starrett's Durango Kid films." *Motion Picture Guide*, Nash and Ross

"Fair actioner in the 'Durango Kid' series." *Western Movies*, Pitts

"Carelessly made, routine western. This is one of the poorest in the long string of oats operas in which Charles Starrett has been starred." *Variety*, 10-10-51

Summation: This film was unavailable for viewing by the author.

PECOS RIVER

Columbia (December 1951)

Be there when the shootin' starts!

Alternate Title: Without Risk

Cast: Steve Baldwin/The Durango Kid, Charles Starrett; Jack Mahoney, Jack Mahoney; Betty Coulter, Delores Sidener; Pop Rockland, Steve Darrell; Henry Mahoney, Edgar Dearing; Sheriff Denning, Frank Jenks; Bill, Harmonica Bill; "Raider"; "Bullet"; Smiley, Smiley Burnette// "Ring-Eye"; Mrs. Peck, Maudie Prickett; Mose Rockland, Zon Murray; Sniffy Rockland, Paul Campbell; Mr. Gray, Eddie Fetherston; Townsman, Blackie Whiteford

Credits: Director, Fred F. Sears; Producer, Colbert Clark; Screenwriter, Barry Shipman; Editor, Paul Borofsky; Art Director, Charles Clague; Set Decorator, James M. Crowe; Cinematographer, Fayte Browne; Musical Director, Mischa Bakaleinikoff

Songs: "The Eye Song" (music adapted from "Three Blind Mice" [traditional], lyrics by Burnette) sung by Smiley Burnette and Harmonica Bill; "New Outlook on Life" (music adapted from "Oh Where, Oh Where Has My Little Dog Gone" adapted from "Symphony No. 6 [Pastoria]" [Beethoven], lyrics by Burnette) sung by Smiley Burnette and Harmonica Bill; "Get Together, Stay Together" (Burnette) with passages from "Old Folks at Home" (Foster) and "Swanee River" (Foster) sung by Smiley Burnette and Harmonica Bill

Location Filming: Iverson, Corriganville, California

Production Dates: January 21, 1951–January 29, 1951

Running Time: 54 min.

Story: In a holdup attempt gone wrong, gang leader Steve Darrell's son is mortally wounded by stagecoach driver Edgar Dearing. Postal inspector Charles Starrett, looking for mail robbers, comes to town as a former outlaw. Dearing, the only person who knows Starrett is a lawman, gets Starrett a job with Delores Sidener's stagecoach line. Dearing's son Jack Mahoney returns home after completing his education in the East. When Starrett takes Mahoney to see Dearing, they find that Dearing has been murdered. Darrell killed him to avenge his son's death. Starrett, as the Durango Kid, promises to help Mahoney track down Dearing's murderer. Darrell learns the stagecoach line will be carrying mine payrolls. Believing that Starrett has a crooked past, Darrell wants him to give him information about the payroll shipments. At first, Mahoney thinks Starrett is crooked, but Starrett proves to him and Sidener that he is setting a trap for Darrell. Darrell and his sons, Paul Campbell and Zon Murray, with the rest of the gang attack the stagecoach which Mahoney is driving. Sheriff Frank Jenks is a passenger. An outlaw's bullet wounds Jenks. Starrett, as Durango, comes to Mahoney's aid. The stagecoach races to disaster by traveling over a bridge which is about to be dynamited. Mahoney jumps from the coach to bulldog Darrell from his saddle. The two men fight, and Mahoney emerges victorious. Campbell and Murray show up with the intent of gunning Mahoney down. Sidener, who has been following the coach, arrives to fire a well placed shot that wounds Campbell and then gets the drop on the outlaws. Starrett is able to get Jenks out of the coach before it goes onto the bridge. With Darrell's gang captured, Starrett rides to new adventures.

Notes and Commentary: As he became a regular for the final seven entries of the Durango Kid series, Jock O'Mahoney became Jack Mahoney.

The "Dead-Eye Dick" dime novel used for target practice in *Pecos River* was first seen in the earlier Durango Kid feature *Challenge of the Range* (Columbia, 1949)

The destruction of the bridge with the stagecoach falling into the water was first seen in the serial *The Great Adventures of Wild Bill Hickok* (Columbia, 1938). This scene was also used in *Blazing the Western Trail* (Columbia, 1945).

Reviews: "Okay action entry in the 'Durango Kid' series." *Western Movies*, Pitts

"A tight script by Barry Shipman is somewhat diluted by a screwball comedy ending. Despite this, 'Pecos River' shapes up as one of Starrett's stronger cowboy pix." *Variety*, 11-29-51

Summation: Rousing Durango Kid entry, full of action. Smiley Burnette's comedic interludes are amusing, with a neat touch at the end by having Smiley Burnette talk directly to the camera. Director Fred F. Sears keeps the story moving and the action humming. Even though Charles Starrett receives top billing, Jack Mahoney is the real show. Kudos to cinematographer Fayte Browne's handling of the chase scenes. His fine camera work adds to the excitement.

SMOKY CANYON

Columbia (January 1952)

Range war splits the great Montana divide!

Cast: Steve Brent/The Durango Kid, Charles Starrett; Jack Mahoney, Jack Mahoney; Roberta Woodstock, Dani Sue Nolan; Carl Buckley, Tristram Coffin; Sheriff Bogart, Larry Hudson; "Raider"; "Bullet"; Smiley, Smiley Burnette// "Ring-Eye", Chris Alcaide; Ace, Leroy Johnson; Joe, Boyd "Red" Morgan; Johnny Big Foot, Charles Stevens; Wyler, Forrest Taylor; Spade, Sandy Saunders; Jim Woodstock, Frank O'Connor

Credits: Director, Fred F. Sears; Producer, Colbert Clark; Screenwriter, Barry Shipman; Editor, Paul Borofsky; Art Director, Charles Clague; Set Decorator, Louis Diage; Cinematographer, Fayte Browne; Musical Director, Mischa Bakaleinikoff

Songs: "It's Got to Get Better Before It Gets Worse" (Burnette) sung by Smiley Burnette; "Daydream Lariat" (Burnette) sung by Smiley Burnette

Location Filming: Iverson, California

Production Dates: July 12,1951–July 19, 1951

Running Time: 55 min.

Story: Tristram Coffin and Sheriff Larry Hudson are instigating a range war between the cattlemen and sheepmen. They are being paid by an eastern syndicate to prevent Montana cattle from coming to market in order to keep cattle prices high. Charles Starrett, as the Durango Kid, is trying to end the range war. Starrett is aided by sheepman Jack Mahoney, who has been falsely accused of the murder of Dani Sue Nolan's father. Coffin has henchman Chris Alcaide burn both sheep and cattle to escalate the range war. Starrett, pretending to be a gun for hire, is hired by Coffin to stop the Durango Kid. Starrett finds that, though on opposite sides of the trouble, Mahoney and Nolan still love each other. Starrett, as Durango, confronts Coffin in Nolan's presence and take a ledger proving that he's behind the range war. Nolan overhears Coffin's plan to destroy more cattle and, with Mahoney, rides to stop him. Mahoney and Nolan are captured. Coffin plans to set off dynamite charges at the rim of the canyon to stampede the cattle. Alcaide forces Mahoney and Nolan to the canyon floor to be trampled by the cattle. Mahoney and Alcaide fight, with Mahoney victorious. The dynamite is set off. The cattle stampede. Starrett, as Durango, is able to take Mahoney and Nolan to safety but Alcaide meets his death under the cattle's hoofs. The blast of the dynamite causes a landslide that engulfs Coffin and Hudson. The range war is ended, but Mahoney is determined to capture gunman Starrett. Knowing Nolan and Mahoney are to marry, Starrett lowers his mask and asks Nolan to prevent Mahoney from looking for him. Nolan agrees and Starrett, as Durango, rides to new adventures.

Notes and Commentary: Co-hero Jack Mahoney gets to kiss Dani Sue Nolan twice. These are Mahoney's first screen kisses.

Reviews: "Fast moving and compact 'Durango Kid' series episode." *Western Movies*, Pitts "Routine oater." *Variety*, 01-23-52

Summation: An excellent Durango Kid film with Charles Starrett and Jack Mahoney making a good action duo. Smiley Burnette chips in with a good performance, and director Fred F. Sears and Screenwriter Barry Shipman allow Burnette to be handy in the fisticuffs department. Sears, who had grown more confident behind the camera, puts his stamp on this film with interesting camera angles to intensify the action. Don't miss this one.

THE HAWK OF WILD RIVER

Columbia (February 1952)

It's a slugfest to the finish!

Cast: Steve Martin/The Durango Kid, Charles Starrett; Jack Mahoney, Jack Mahoney; The Hawk, Clayton Moore; Skeeter, Eddie Parker; Al Travis, Jim Diehl; "Raider," "Bullet"; Smiley, Smiley Burnette// "Ring-Eye"; Duke, John Cason; Smoky, Leroy Johnson; Pete, Jack Carry; Donna, Donna Hall; Clark Mahoney, Sam Flint; George, Lane Chandler; Yank-Em-Out Kennedy, Syd Saylor

Credits: Director, Fred F. Sears; Producer, Colbert Clark; Screenwriter, Howard J. Green; Editor, Paul Borofsky; Art Director, Charles Clague; Set Decorator, David Montrose; Cinematographer, Fayte Browne; Musical Director, Mischa Bakaleinikoff

Song: "Pedro Enchilada" (Burnette) sung by Smiley Burnette

Location Filming: Iverson, California

Production Dates: July 30, 1951–August 7, 1951

Running Time: 54 min.

Story: Texas Ranger Charles Starrett is assigned to capture Clayton Moore and stop the robberies by Moore's gang in the Wild River area. With a bow and arrow, Moore murders the sheriffs. As the Durango Kid, Starrett prevents the death of Sheriff Jack Mahoney and later captures Moore. Starrett wants to bring all of the gang to justice and recover the stolen money, so he allows himself to be arrested. Starrett then engineers a jailbreak taking Moore with him. Starrett becomes a member of the gang. He then tips off Mahoney about Moore's next raid. As Durango, Starrett kills Moore and gangmember Leroy Johnson while Mahoney rounds up the rest of the gang.

Notes and Commentary: Some sources indicate that Smiley Burnette sang "Chief Pocatello from the Cherokees," but the song doesn't appear in the print viewed by the author.

Reviews: "Fast moving 'Durango Kid' series film." *Western Movies*, Pitts

"Results are in the routine groove for program oaters." *Variety*, 02-13-52

Summation: Strong, fast-paced Durango Kid entry buoyed by a neat performance by Clayton Moore.

LARAMIE MOUNTAINS

Columbia (April 1952)

Your favorite gun-and-fun team!

Alternate Title: Mountain Desperadoes

Cast: Steve Holden/The Durango Kid, Charles Starrett; Swift Eagle, Jack Mahoney; Major Markham, Fred Sears; Lieutenant Pierce, Marshall Reed; Paul Drake, Rory Mallinson; Carson, Zon Murray; "Raider"; "Bullet"; Smiley, Smiley Burnette// "Ring-Eye" (dog); Corporal, Boyd Stockman; Henry Mandel, Bob Wilke; Chief Lone Tree, John War Eagle; Cruller, Boyd "Red" Morgan

Credits: Director, Ray Nazarro; Producer, Colbert Clark; Screenwriter, Barry Shipman; Editor, Paul Borofsky; Art Director, Charles Clague; Set Decorator, James Crowe; Cinematographer, Fayte Browne; Musical Director, Mischa Bakaleinikoff

Songs: "Come to the Mess" (Burnette) sung by Smiley Burnette; "With a Sloop, Sloop, Sloop" (Burnette) sung by Smiley Burnette

Location Filming: Corriganville, California

Production Dates: late October 1951–early November 1951

Running Time: 54 min.

Story: Bob Wilke, with key henchmen Rory Mallison and Zon Murray, are stirring up trouble with the Indians to start a full-scale Indian War. Wilke has discovered gold on the Indian lands. Mallinson and Murray are able to sign on as army scouts with the Indian-hating Major Fred Sears. Charles Starrett is assigned to bring peace to the area. Using his persona as the Durango Kid, Starrett and Jack Mahoney — a white man living with the Indian tribe — decide to work together to bring peace. To escalate hostilities, Wilke has army soldiers murdered with Indian arrows and make an attempt on Chief John War Eagle's life. Starrett finds the outlaw hideout. Having been blamed for the murder of the soldiers, he can't go directly to Sears. Starrett gives a map to the hideout to the company cook, Smiley Burnette. Starrett and Mahoney go back to the hideout and are captured. They break free and a battle rages in the hideout. Starrett and Mahoney are using Indian weapons against outlaw guns. Finally, Burnette convinces the soldiers to ride to the cave to help round up Wilke and his gang. Peace is restored and Mahoney is commissioned to help the Indians with their newfound riches. Starrett rides to new adventures.

Notes and Commentary: Even though Smiley Burnette's horse, Ring-Eye, is mentioned in the film, we only have Ring-Eye, the dog, this time out.

Watch when Charles Starrett rides into his cave to change into his Durango outfit as he's chasing Jack Mahoney. Courtesy of a reverse negative, Starrett's gun is on his left hip, the rock is on the left and the brush is on the right. As Starrett rides out as Durango, the rock and brush are reversed.

Reviews: "Stale directing and routine performances make this a below par addition to the series." *Motion Picture Guide*, Nash and Ross

"Fair 'Durango Kid' series segment." *Western Movies*, Pitts

"*Laramie Mountains* is well below the average outing." *The Western*, Hardy

"Below-par entry in the Durango Kid series. Slim plot and routine thesping make it only so-so for the western field." *Variety*, 04-09-52

Summation: Although not in the preferred western class, *Laramie Mountains* nonetheless is an engaging western, with enough action to get by. The main problem is Ray Nazarro's direction. Unlike director Fred F. Sears' style, Nazarro is unable to generate visuals to pump up the action and generate tension.

THE ROUGH, TOUGH WEST

Columbia (June 1952)

Gold grabbers on the run!

Cast: Steve Holden/The Durango Kid, Charles Starrett; Big Jack Mahoney, Jack Mahoney; Carolina, Carolina Cotton; Pee Wee King and his Golden West Cowboys (Pee Wee King [accordion], Redd Stewart [fiddle], Hank Garland [guitar] other members unknown); "Raider"; "Bullet"; Smiley, Smiley Burnette// Jordan McCrea, Burt Arnold; Bill, Boyd "Red" Morgan; Fulton, Marshall Reed; Pete Walker/Doctor, Fred Sears; Saloon patron, Frank Ellis; Buzzy Bartlett, Tommy Ivo; Matty Bartlett, Valerie Fisher; Miner, Ben Corbett; Henchmen, Boyd Stockman and Bob Woodward

Credits: Director, Ray Nazarro; Producer, Colbert Clark; Screenwriter, Barry Shipman;

Editor, Paul Borofsky; Art Director, Charles Clague; Set Decorator, Frank Tuttle; Cinematographer, Fayte Browne; Musical Director, Mischa Bakaleinikoff

Songs: "You Gotta Get a Guy With a Gun" (Cotton) sung by Carolina Cotton with Pee Wee King and his Golden West Cowboys; "The Fire of '41" (Burnette) sung by Smiley Burnette with Pee Wee King and his Golden West Cowboys; "Cause I'm in Love" (Jones) sung by Carolina Cotton with Smiley Burnette and Pee Wee West and his Golden West Cowboys; "You Don't Need My Love Anymore" (King and Stewart) sung by Redd Stewart, Pee Wee King and Hank Garland with the Golden West Cowboys; "The More We Get Together" (Roberts and Fisher) sung by Smiley Burnette and Pee Wee King and his Golden West Cowboys

Location Filming: Iverson, California

Production Dates: November 27, 1951–December 4, 1951

Running Time: 54 min.

Story: Jack Mahoney has been using ruthless tactics to gain control of Hard Rock and the surrounding mining area. To ensure his success, Mahoney sends for former Texas Ranger Charles Starrett. Starrett take the job of town marshal. Miners, tired of Mahoney's oppression, send Burt Arnold to kill him. Although pretty well hated by most of the citizens, the newspaperwoman's crippled grandson, Tommy Ivo, thinks Mahoney is a great man. Mahoney gets control of the road leading out of the area and charges a toll to freight ore. The miners are ready to fight, but Starrett, as the Durango Kid, tells the miners to wait. Starrett has a plan to allow the miners to ship their ore without paying a toll. Starrett's plan is to use a pack train and an alternate route. Mahoney's chief henchman, Marshall Reed, learns of the plan. Reed finally persuades Mahoney to let him lead his men on an attack on the miners and to steal the valuable ore. Ivo overhears the plan and rides to warn the miners. As Ivo arrives, he sees Starrett, as Durango, in a running gun fight with the outlaws. A stray bullet wounds Ivo. Ivo's wound affects Mahoney deeply. When Reed shows up with the ore, and the miners in pursuit, Mahoney tells Reed he's going to return the ore to the miners. Mahoney and Reed fight first with fists and then with guns. Reed is able to wound Mahoney. As Reed and his henchman attempt to leave, Starrett shows up. A gunfight begins, in which the miners join with Starrett against the outlaws. To get away, Reed sets the town on fire. Starrett catches up to Reed before he can return to his men. Starrett and Reed have a vicious fight which Starrett wins. He then gets the drop on the henchmen. With the town on fire, the wounded and crippled Ivo is trapped in a building. The wounded Mahoney goes into the flaming building to rescue him, but is overcome by the smoke and heat. Starrett then enters the building and brings Ivo and Mahoney out to safety. Mahoney now realize how ruthless he'd become and now wants to work with the Hard Rock citizens to rebuild.

Notes and Commentary: When Jack Mahoney and Tommy Ivo begin the horse ride, Mahoney says, "Let's go, Tommy" instead of calling him by his screen name, "Buzzy."

Fred Sears does double duty in this film as miner Pete Walker and the town's doctor.

The song, "The More We Get Together" was sung by Smiley Burnette and the Sunshine Boys in *Challenge of the Range* (Columbia, 1949).

Reviews: "Fast moving and actionful 'Durango Kid' film." *Western Movies*, Pitts

"As programmer westerns go, this is a minor entry for the oater market featuring tame action and obscure plotting." *Variety*, 06-25-52

Summation: This is a surprisingly effective Durango Kid entry. Ray Nazarro does a good job of directing with better use of inventive camera angles. Jack Mahoney gives a fine performance as a ruthless town boss who ultimately reforms. On the lighter side, the musical interludes with Carolina Cotton, Pee Wee King and Smiley Burnette are quite good.

JUNCTION CITY

Columbia (July 1952)

Dropping Killers and Copping Laughs!

Cast: Steve Rollins/The Durango Kid, Charles Starrett; Jack Mahoney, Jack Mahoney; Penny, Kathleen Case; Emmet Sanderson, John Dehner; Black Murphy, Steve Darrell; "Raider"; "Bullet"; Smiley, Smiley Burnette// Sheriff Jeff Clinton, George Chesebro; Penelope Clinton, Anita Castle; Ella Sanderson, Mary Newton; Bleaker, Robert Bice; Sheriff, Hal Price; Sandy Clinton, Hal Taliaferro; Jarvis, Chris Alcaide; Keely, Bob Woodward; Boggs, Joel Friedkin; Giles, Harry Tyler; The Sunshine Boys (Ace Richmond, Freddie Daniel, Eddie Wallace and J.D. Sumner)

Credits: Director, Ray Nazarro; Producer, Colbert Clark; Screenwriter, Barry Shipman; Editor, Paul Borofsky; Art Director, Charles Clague; Set Decorator, Frank Tuttle; Cinematographer, Henry Freulich; Musical Director, Mischa Balaleinikoff

Songs: "Li'l Injun" (Burnette) sung by Smiley Burnette; "Glory Train" (traditional) sung by The Sunshine Boys

Production Dates: January 7, 1952–January 11, 1952

Running Time: 54 min.

Story: Kathleen Case has disappeared and stage driver Jack Mahoney is arrested, first for her kidnapping then, when her body cannot be found, for her murder. Charles Starrett, a friend of Case, has come to visit. Starrett believes Mahoney to be innocent. Starrett tells Mahoney that, years earlier, he helped Case gain ownership of a gold mine. Starrett discovers Case's guardians, John Dehner and Mary Newton, have made Case's life miserable. Before Mahoney can be hanged for the crimes, Starrett, as the Durango Kid, finds Case. Starrett proves that Dehner and Newton were trying to get possession of the mine.

Notes and Commentary: *Junction City* is a sequel to *West of Sonora* (Columbia, 1948). Footage from *West of Sonora* is used in the flashback sequences. Both songs had been featured in *West of Sonora.*

Reviews: "A poor oater in which the hand of the screenwriter comes through clearly and is told unconvincingly in flashbacks." *Motion Picture Guide*, Nash and Ross

"Passable 'Durango Kid' film from late in the series." *Western Movies*, Pitts

"Routine oater action of the also-ran category barely gets 'Junction City' by in its classification as a western programmer. The pace is slow and plot very involved, making for a long 54 minutes." *Variety*, 07-09-52

Summation: This film was not available for viewing by the author.

THE KID FROM BROKEN GUN

Columbia (August 1952)

They're beating a murder rap for a fighting pal!

Cast: Steve Reynolds, Charles Starrett; Jack Mahoney, Jack Mahoney; Gail Kingston, Angela Stevens; Martin Donohugh, Tristram Coffin; Kiefer, Myron Healey; Dixie King, Helen Mowery; "Raider"; "Bullet"; Smiley Burnette, Smiley Burnette// Judge Halloway, Edgar Dearing; Sheriff, Mauritz Hugo; Matt Fallon, Chris Alcaide; Chuck, John Cason;

Doc Handy, Pat O'Malley; Al, Eddie Parker; Joe, Charles Horvath; Jury Foreman, Edward Hearn; Cimarron Dobbs, Emmett Lynn; Rankin, George Chesebro; Monroe, Robert Filmer; Slade, Zon Murray; The Printer, Ernie Adams

Credits: Director, Fred F. Sears; Producer, Colbert Clark; Screenwriters, Barry Shipman and Ed. Earl Repp; Editor, Paul Borofsky; Art Director, Charles Clague; Set Decorator, Frank Tuttle; Cinematographer, Fayte Browne; Musical Director, Mischa Bakaleinikoff

Song: "It's the Law" (Burnette) sung by Smiley Burnette

Production Dates: March 31, 1952–April 4, 1952

Running Time: 55 min.

Story: Jack Mahoney is arrested for the murder of Chris Alcaide. Mahoney had threatened to kill Alcaide if he continued to bother attorney Angela Stevens. Alcaide is found murdered in Tristram Coffin's express office, and a strong box has gone missing. Mahoney's friends Charles Starrett and Smiley Burnette arrive for the trial. As the Durango Kid, Starrett finds a Spanish coin in Coffin's office. On the witness stand, Starrett tells the story of the discovery of Santa Ana's treasure and the duplicity of saloon girl Helen Mowery. Mahoney testifies that he heard Stevens' cry for help from the express office and raced to her rescue. Upon entering the office, Mahoney said he was struck on the head and dumped in the woods. The jury doesn't believe his story and sentences him to hang. The Santa Ana treasure is in the strong box, which is in the hands of Stevens and Coffin. Starrett, as Durango, breaks Mahoney out of jail. Starrett decides to hold a new trial and brings Sheriff Mauritz Hugo, the jury, Stevens and Coffin to the courthouse in the middle of the night. First, Starrett proves that Stevens is Mowery's sister. Then Starrett accuses Coffin of murder. Coffin reveals that Stevens is the real murderer. Mahoney is released from jail.

Notes and Commentary: With this entry, the Durango Kid ceased to ride. Instead of Charles Starrett riding to new adventures at the film's conclusion, Starrett and Smiley Burnette stand at a hitching rail and watch Jack Mahoney follow an attractive young lady in hopes of a new romance.

Helen Mowery receives billing even though all her scenes are from *The Fighting Frontiersman* (Columbia, 1946). Also seen from this film, though unbilled, are Emmett Lynn, George Chesebro, Robert Filmer, Zon Murray and Ernie Adams.

Reviews: "Last of the seven-year-long Durango Kid series and a very weak ending at that." *Motion Picture Guide*, Nash and Ross

"Sturdy series finale to 'The Durango Kid.'" *Western Movies*, Pitts

"Although it isn't a particularly good outing, it is scripted by Shipman and directed by Sears. Padded with too much stock footage. It is a typically fantastical Shipman and Repp screenplay, though sadly Sears' direction lacks the energy he'd given to earlier outings with Starrett." *The Western*, Hardy

"This is a complicated program western in the Charles Starrett series that will only get a mild reception from juve oater fans. The plot is too involved, and too much of the action is talked out, making for a slow 55 minutes." *Variety*, 08-13-52

Summation: This is an okay end to the Durango Kid series. *The Kid from Broken Gun* is a sequel to *The Fighting Frontiersman*, with copious stock footage from that film. In fact, this could be considered a double feature in the 55-minute running time. Thanks to Jack Mahoney, the film holds the viewer's interest, with more fistfights and stunts than usual in a later Durango Kid film. Just watch Mahoney's leap from one roof to another across the length of the livery stable. WOW!

Ellery Queen

I dedicate this program to the fight against crime, not merely crimes
of violence and crimes of dishonesty but crimes of intolerance,
discrimination and bad citizenship ... crimes against America!

—Introduction to Ellery Queen's radio program.

In 1928, *McClure's Magazine* and Frederick A. Stokes Publishers jointly sponsored a
contest for an original mystery novel, the winner of which would collect $7,500. Avid detective fiction buffs Frederic Dannay and his cousin Manfred B. Lee decided to enter. As one
of the contest rules was that the entry had to be submitted under a pseudonym, Dannay
and Lee chose the name "Ellery Queen" for both the author and the fictional detective.
Their entry, "The Roman Hat Mystery," won. Unfortunately, before the outcome could be
announced, *McClure's Magazine* was taken over by another, *Smart Set*. The new owners
decided to award the prize to another author whose novel would have greater acceptance
by female readers. All was not lost: Frederick A. Stokes decided to publish their novel. Dannay and Lee each received $200.

More Ellery Queen novels followed with increasing popularity. The strong point of
their works was a completely fair rendering of the story. All the clues were there for the
reader to reveal the murderer before Queen's denouncement. Characterization was minimal.
Queen, of course was the focal point, but other main characters included his father, Inspector
Richard Queen, Sergeant Velie, the coroner Doc Prouty and Djuna, the Queens' house boy.

In 1935, Queen joined the ranks of the screen sleuths, first in *The Spanish Cape Mystery*
(Republic, 1935) with Donald Cook, and then in *The Mandarin Mystery* (Republic, 1936)
with Eddie Quillan. Queen then temporarily left the screen. Next it was radio's turn for
the great detective. Producer/director George Zachary brought Ellery Queen to the airwaves
on CBS. Hugh Marlowe was Ellery; Santos Ortega played Inspector Queen; Howard Smith
was Sergeant Velie; and Robert Strauss took the part of Doc Prouty. One major change
brought a love interest to Ellery in the personage of Nikki Porter, played by Marian Shockley.
In the radio version, Nikki was a professional typist, whose service was used by Ellery.
Nikki convinced Ellery it would be better if she became his secretary so he could dictate
his stories. *The Adventures of Ellery Queen* began as a 60-minute show. The gimmick had
a break in the story so various guests could discuss and make their guess as to the identity
of the murderer. The show would then resume, with Ellery making his denouncement. On
February 25, 1940, the show moved into a 30-minute format. The program moved to NBC
for its second season.

In 1940 and 1942, Ellery Queen would be the subject of two Better Little Books from
Whitman Publishing. Also, in 1940, Ellery Queen would again come to the silver screen.

Columbia Pictures would release the feature films to be produced by Larry Darmour. Darmour acquired the rights to over 30 Queen novels and the weekly transcontinental radio broadcasts in February 1940, with plans for Columbia distribution. (Darmour had taken over serial production at Columbia in 1938, with *The Great Adventures of Wild Bill Hickok*. Darmour's production company also provided Columbia with some of their western films with such cowboy stars as Bob Allen, Ken Maynard, Jack Luden and Bill Elliott. Beginning with *North of Nome* [Columbia, 1936] Darmour produced Jack Holt's action films.) Ralph Bellamy was assigned the role of Ellery. This was Bellamy's second shot at a mystery series, having previously played Inspector Trent. In between series, Bellamy would have leading man status in "B" films and support status in some "A" features. (Bellamy was, in fact, nominated for an Academy Award for best supporting actor for his role in *The Awful Truth* [Columbia, 1937].) Bellamy played Ellery in four entries, after which he was replaced by William Gargan. Bellamy moved his services over to Universal to no great advantage and would be seen as part of an ensemble cast in the horror films, *The Wolf Man* (Universal, 1942) and *The Ghost of Frankenstein* (Universal, 1942) and a western, *Men of Texas* (Universal, 1942). Bellamy returned to the Broadway stage before entering television in 1950. Bellamy would have his finest hours in his portrayal of Franklin Delano Roosevelt in *Sunrise at Campobello* (Warner Bros., 1960) and, prior to that, in a stage production for which he received a Tony award.

Margaret Lindsay played Nikki Porter, Ellery's secretary. In the initial film, Nikki was an unsuccessful mystery writer who became the primary murder suspect. Ellery uncovers the real murderer and, in the process, hires Nikki to be his secretary. Lindsay had been a contract player at Warner Bros. and, like Bellamy, received leading roles in the lower budget pictures. Lindsay brought a freshness to the series that helped salvage a few entries. Other regulars were Charlie Grapewin as Inspector Queen, James Burke as Sergeant Velie and Charles Lane as Doc Prouty. With Bellamy's departure, Gargan took over and played Ellery in three films. Dannay and Lee were pressuring the studio to produce four films per year. Columbia disagreed and the series was discontinued. Gargan and Lindsay were quickly teamed in *No Place for a Lady* (Columbia, 1943). Nikki Porter finally appeared in print in the 1943 novel, *There Was an Old Woman*. Nikki's real name was Sheila Potts. Because of the notoriety from the murder case, Sheila became Nikki Porter. Even though a millionaire, Nikki decided to take the job as Ellery's secretary. She would only be featured in the short story anthology, *Calendar of Crime* and the novel, *Scarlet Letters*. Ellery Queen's radio program remained popular and had a nine year run. The last program was broadcast on May 27, 1948. Ellery Queen appeared sporadically on television during the '50s, portrayed by Richard Hart, Lee Bowman, Hugh Marlowe, George Nader and Lee Phillips.

The novels kept coming through the '60s and into the early '70s, most with the help of ghostwriters. Ellery Queen returned to radio in the '70s in the syndicated, *Ellery Queen's Minute Mysteries*, wherein a mystery would be presented in one minute. Listeners would then call in with their solutions. The first listener with the correct answer would win a prize. The radio station would then play Ellery's solution as confirmation. In 1971, Peter Lawford played the celebrated detective in the TV movie, *Ellery Queen: Don't Look Behind You* (Universal, 1971). It took the casting of Jim Hutton to become what is arguably the definitive Ellery Queen. First, Hutton starred in a made-for-TV movie *Ellery Queen: Too Many Suspects* (Universal, 1975), which led to a short-lived series on NBC. The series had an interesting twist. After all the significant clues had been presented, Hutton reviewed them, giving the audience a chance to guess the murderer before his denouncement. Hutton had excellent support, with David Wayne as Inspector Queen and Tom Reese as Sergeant Velie.

Ellery Queen still shows up in print from time to time. The most recent, in 2005, a collection of 14 radio programs in *The Adventure of the Murdered Moths: And Other Radio Mysteries*.

ELLERY QUEEN, MASTER DETECTIVE
Columbia (November 1940)

You've heard him on the air! You've read his stories! Now see Ellery Queen on the screen!

Cast: Ellery Queen, Ralph Bellamy; Nikki Porter, Margaret Lindsay; Inspector Queen, Charley Grapewin; Sergeant Velie, James Burke; Dr. James Rogers, Michael Whalen; Barbara Braun, Marsha Hunt; John Braun, Fred Niblo; Dr. Prouty, Charles Lane; Lydia Braun, Ann Shoemaker; Cornelia, Marion Mason; Rocky Taylor, Douglas Fowley; Zachary, Morgan Wallace; Amos, Byron Foulger; Valerie Norris, Katherine DeMille// Consultant physician, Jack Rice; Flynn, Lee Phelps

Credits: Director, Kurt Neumann; Story, Ellery Queen; Screenplay, Eric Taylor; Editor, Dwight Caldwell; Cinematographer, James S. Brown, Jr.; Music, Lee Zahler

Production Dates: September 16, 1940–October 2, 1940

Ellery Queen, Master Detective (1940) scene card — (left) Ralph Bellamy, Margaret Lindsay, (center) Margaret Lindsay, Ralph Bellamy.

Running Time: 67 min.

Story: Health guru Fred Niblo receives word that his health has deteriorated to a point that he only has a month to live. His wife, Ann Shoemaker, wants Inspector Charley Grapewin to search for their missing daughter, Marsha Hunt. Hunt left the house when Niblo broke up a romance between Hunt and his physician, Michael Whalen. Grapewin's son, mystery writer Ralph Bellamy, decides to beat the police in locating Hunt. Hunt, recovering from an illness, has been staying with a friend, aspiring mystery writer Margaret Lindsay. Bellamy follows Whalen to Lindsay's apartment and mistakes her for Shoemaker's daughter. Bellamy forces Lindsay to go to Niblo's estate where Lindsay, saying she is there to meet Whalen, is escorted to Whalen's office. In hiding, Lindsay hears Niblo cut all his staff out of his will, leaving everything to Shoemaker. The staff leaves. Before Lindsay can leave, Niblo locks the door to the hall and retires to his study. While trying to figure how to leave, an unanswered phone in Niblo's study piques Lindsay's curiosity. Lindsay finds Niblo's dead body with his jugular vein slashed. There's no trace of a murder weapon and there are bars on the only window—a classic locked-room mystery. When Bellamy learns of his mistake, he hurries to Niblo's estate where he encounters Lindsay. Bellamy believes Lindsay to be innocent and hides her in his and Grapewin's apartment. Lindsay poses as the cook. Strange things happen with Niblo's body. First, a statue (taking the place of the body) ends up in the morgue. Then, when the body is rediscovered and placed in a police vehicle, the vehicle is stolen. Bellamy decides to solve the murder. He determines that caretaker Byron Foulger's raven, attracted to the bright metal of a letter opener (the murder weapon) flew through the bars of the open window and took it and Niblo's will. Lindsay, trying to avoid the long arm of the law, spots the stolen police vehicle on the Niblo premises. Lindsay is kidnapped by the murderer and tries to escape in the vehicle. Both Bellamy, in his car, and Grapewin, in a police car, give chase. Bellamy catches up to the now-stopped vehicle and goes to Lindsay's rescue. The murderer takes Bellamy's car and is pursued by Grapewin. In the high-speed chase, Bellamy's car crashes, killing the murderer. The murderer is Whalen, who faked the fatal diagnosis of Niblo knowing Niblo's pride would make him take his own life. With the case solved, Bellamy asks Lindsay to become his secretary.

Notes and Commentary: The working title was "John Braun's Body."

Ellery Queen's *The Door Between* (*Cosmopolitan* magazine, 1936; J.B. Lippincott, 1937) was the basis for this screenplay. The basic plot devices are present in both the story and the film. The gender of the "murder" victim is female in the novel. There is a comely young lady, not Nikki Porter, who discovers the dead body and is accused of murder. Championing her cause is a young private detective, not Ellery Queen. Queen proves the death is a suicide and that a bird removed the suicide weapon from the enclosed room through a barred window. Finally, he deduces that the victim's physician had her believing she had a short time to live and would choose to end her life.

The movie was novelized in 1941(Grosset and Dunlap), and a Pyramid paperback, retitled *The Vanishing Corpse*, was published in May 1968.

This is Kurt Neumann's only directorial effort in the Ellery Queen series. With the next entry, James Hogan would take over for the rest of the series.

Author Ellery Queen was the pseudonym of Frederic Dannay and Manfred Lee.

Reviews: "A bad start to a bad series except for the inspired touch of having Bellamy meet Lindsay, who promises to become his secretary." *Motion Picture Guide*, Nash and Ross

"Weak film debut for the w.k. [well known] radio and fiction mystery-solver." *Variety*, 12/25/40

Summation: This not a well-written mystery. There are too many plot holes: how, for example, can the mystery villain always seem to be at the right place at the right time, and the coincidental manner in which the murder weapon disappears. Ralph Bellamy is just okay as Ellery Queen, no more. Margaret Lindsay's energetic performance gives the film the only spark it has, but it is not enough to save it. Too much silly "comedy" mars this feature.

ELLERY QUEEN'S PENTHOUSE MYSTERY
Columbia (March 1941)

Oriental terror prowls New York's guilded towers!

Cast: Ellery Queen, Ralph Bellamy; Nikki Porter, Margaret Lindsay; Inspector Queen, Charley Grapewin; Lois Ling, Anna May Wong; Sergeant Velie, James Burke; Count Brett, Edward Ciannelli; Sanders, Frank Albertson; Sheila Cobb, Ann Doran; Gordon Cobb, Noel Madison; Doc Prouty, Charles Lane; Walsh, Russell Hicks; McGrath, Tom Dugan; Roy, Mantan Moreland; Jim Ritter, Theodore von Eltz// Excellency, Richard Loo; Chinese businessman, Chester Gan

Credits: Director, James Hogan; Story, Ellery Queen; Screenwriter, Eric Taylor; Editor, Dwight Caldwell; Cinematographer, James S. Brown, Jr.; Music, Lee Zahler

Production Dates: January 4, 1941–January 18, 1941

Running Time: 69 min.

Story: Prominent Chinese citizens ask ventriloquist Noel Madison to undertake a perilous assignment: take valuable jewelry to America to purchase much-needed food and supplies. Upon his arrival in New York, Madison calls Anna May Wong to come to his hotel. Madison disappears. His daughter, Ann Doran, comes to Ralph Bellamy's secretary, Margaret Lindsay, for help. After someone attempts to steal Doran's purse, Bellamy reluctantly takes Doran to Madison's hotel room. Bellamy finds Madison's dead body in a steamer trunk. An empty jewel box is found. Bellamy alerts his father, Inspector Charley Grapewin, and tells him to find the ventriloquist dummy. Madison's agent, Russell Hicks, is notified and can offer no help. Later, Hicks and Count Edward Ciannelli, who had followed Madison from China, accuse each other of Madison's murder and of taking the jewels. Hicks's confederate in a crooked card game scheme, Theodore von Eltz, overhears the conversation. At the hotel, bellhop Frank Albertson turns out to be an investigative reporter. Eltz takes some of Madison's belongings from Ciannelli's room. In Eltz's apartment, a mysterious intruder is searching Madison's belongings when Eltz returns. There is a struggle and Eltz is killed. Bellamy gathers all the suspects. First, he finds (through Wong) that another courier brought the jewels to America. Then he proves Eltz murdered Madison and that Albertson was Eltz's assailant. Love begins to blossom between Bellmay and Lindsay.

Notes and Commentary: The film was adapted from the *Adventures of Ellery Queen* radio program, "The Three Scratches" that aired on the CBS radio network on December 17, 1939.

A novelization of *Ellery Queen's Penthouse Mystery* was published in 1941.

Ann Doran mentions the murder of John Braun that took place in *Ellery Queen, Master Detective* (Columbia, 1940).

Reviews: "Above average for the series, but that's not saying much." *Motion Picture Guide*, Nash and Ross

"Excellent programmer." *Variety*, 03/12/41

Summation: Bland murder mystery. The performers try hard but are ultimately defeated by the script and the indifferent direction by James Hogan. The "comedy" monologue delivered by Tom Dugan helps sink this one. Someone missed a golden opportunity by not spotlighting Mantan Moreland like Monogram would have done. That might have given the story some added energy.

ELLERY QUEEN AND THE PERFECT CRIME
Columbia (August 1941)

The strange mystery of the playful monkey ... the falling dagger ... the fateful arrow!

Alternate Title: The Perfect Crime

Cast: Ellery Queen, Ralph Bellamy; Nikki Porter, Margaret Lindsay; Inspector Queen, Charley Grapewin; Carlotta Emerson, Spring Byington; Ray Jardin, H.B. Warner; Sergeant Velie, James Burke; John Matthews, Douglass Dumbrille; Walter Matthews, John Beal; Marian Jardin, Linda Hayes; Anthony Rhodes, Sidney Blackmer; Henry, Walter Kingsford; Lee, Honorable Wu; Prouty, Charles Lane// Book salesman, Arthur Q. Bryan; Rufus Smith, Charles Halton; Moving men, Al Hill and Frank O'Connor

Credits: Director, James Hogan; Story, Ellery Queen; Screenwriter, Eric Taylor; Editor, Dwight Caldwell; Cinematographer, James S. Brown, Jr.; Music, Lee Zahler

Song: "My Old Kentucky Home" (Foster) sung by Honorable Wu (Sung in Chinese)

Production Dates: May 9, 1941–May 22, 1941

Running Time: 68 min.

Story: Receiving news that a storm will destroy the South Valley Power project, Douglass Dumbrille quickly disposes of all his holdings while insisting to H.B. Warner and other stockholders that there is nothing to worry about. Dumbrille's son, John Beal, is disgusted with his father's action and leaves home. Warner is broke and has to sell his home and all of his possessions and must discharge all servants. Warner's butler, Walter Kingsford, asks to stay on with Warner. Beal, who is in love with Warner's daughter, Linda Hayes, tells him that Dumbrille knew the truth about the storm and was able to turn adversity to his financial advantage. Beal is a friend of author Ralph Bellamy. Dumbrille asks Bellamy to find Beal so they can patch matters up. Bellamy advises Beal to meet with Dumbrille, but Beal refuses. Later, Beal decides to go, at which time finds his father's dead body. Beal changes the crime scene to make the death look like suicide by a self-inflicted dagger wound. An autopsy shows the dagger wound was not deep enough to have caused serious injury. Dumbrille's death was caused by poison. Bellamy reveals that an arrow, owned by Warner, had been dipped in a deadly poison and shot into Dumbrille's body, killing him instantly. In pursuing an investigation into the arrow, an attempt is made on Bellamy's life by Kingsford. Kingsford wanted revenge because he, too, lost his life's savings when the power project was destroyed. With the mystery solved, Beal and Hayes plan to marry.

Notes and Commentary: The working titles for "The Devil Pays" and "The Devil to Pay."

This film was based on Ellery Queen's *The Devil to Pay* (*Cosmopolitan* magazine, 1936; Frederick Stokes, 1938)

The film follows the plot of the novel fairly closely. The novel takes place in Hollywood instead of New York. Also, Inspector Queen and Sergeant Velie are not present. Most character names are changed, except that of Ray Jardin. Again, Jardin's close employee and associate almost commits the perfect crime.

The Perfect Crime, written in 1942, and published in paperback by Pyramid in June 1968, used elements from the film.

Reviews: "Clumsy series entry. The film is a waste of time except for an able supporting cast." *Motion Picture Guide*, Nash and Ross

"Acceptable program item for the rurals. It's an unpretentious effort, shrewdly scripted, and, with certain exceptions, skillfully made." *Variety*, 08/13/41

Summation: The third time is a charm. This time out, Ellery Queen has a winner. This is a well-crafted story with good direction by James Hogan and good performances by all concerned. The comedy touches will bring at least a smile, and perhaps a chuckle or two.

ELLERY QUEEN AND THE MURDER RING
Columbia (November 1941)

See the ace amateur sleuth of radio and fiction solve the
strange slaying of Wall Street's richest widow!

Alternate Title: The Murder Ring

Cast: Ellery Queen, Ralph Bellamy; Nikki Porter, Margaret Lindsay; Inspector Queen, Charley Grapewin; Miss Tracy, Mona Barrie; Page, Paul Hurst; Sergeant Velie, James Burke; Dr. Jannery, George Zucco; Mrs. Stack, Blanche Yurka; Thomas, Tom Dugan; John Stack, Leon Ames; Alice Stack, Joan Fenwick; Dr. Williams, Olin Howland; Dr. Dunn, Dennis Moore; Miss Fox, Charlotte Wynters; Crothers, Pierre Watkin// Motorcycle cop, Edgar Dearing; Elevator repairman, Harrison Greene; Martin, Barlowe Borland; Hospital desk supervisor, Don Brodie; Nurse in corridor, Claire Du Brey; Ambulance attendants, Pat West and George Lloyd; Male nurse, Byron Foulger; Henchmen, Edward Gargan and Harry Tyler

Credits: Director, James Hogan; Story, Ellery Queen; Screenplay, Eric Taylor and Gertrude Purcell; Editor, Dwight Caldwell; Cinematographer, James S. Brown, Jr.; Music, Lee Zahler

Production Dates: July 22, 1941–August 2, 1941

Running Time: 65 min.

Story: Blanche Yurka wants the police to investigate her hospital and, in particular, head surgeon George Zucco. Yurka's son, Leon Ames, owes money to gangster Paul Hurst. To settle up with Hurst, Ames asks him to cause an automobile accident that would be fatal to Yurka. Yurka survives the accident, but needs an operation. At the conclusion of the surgery, Yurka is found dead by suffocation. Operating room nurse Charlotte Wynters is questioned and finally states she went to sleep for a few moments. An autopsy shows Yurka was strangled. Inspector Charley Grapewin has his son, author and police consultant Ralph Bellamy, go to Wynters's apartment. Bellamy discovers her dead body. Wynters left a note which states that she had left the operating room for ten minutes. When Yurka's will shows Zucco is the primary heir, suspicion shifts to him. Bellamy's secretary, Margaret Lindsay, believes Zucco to be innocent. Nurse Mona Barrie learns that Zucco, not Ames, will inherit

Yurka's estate. Barrie, who secretly has been carrying on a romance with Ames, tells him the contents of the will. Barrie accuses Ames of plotting to kill his mother. Ames commits suicide. Lindsay goes to Barrie's apartment to see if she can help clear Zucco. Lindsay begins to suspect Barrie of murdering Yurka and Wynters. Barrie pulls a gun and locks Lindsay in a steamer trunk. Meanwhile, Bellamy finds a clue that leads him to Barrie. With Sergeant James Burke in tow, Bellamy hurries to Barrie's apartment. Bellamy rescues Lindsay and Burke arrests Barrie.

Notes and Commentary: A poster for *Ellery Queen and the Murder Ring* can be seen in the Lone Wolf feature, *Counter-Espionage* (Columbia, 1942) with Warren William.

The working title was "The Dutch Shoe Mystery." The movie was very loosely based on Ellery Queen's novel, *The Dutch Shoe Mystery* (Frederick Stokes, 1931). The plot lines taken from the novel included a wealthy female owner of a prestigious hospital who is strangled in the operating area of her hospital after an accident; one of her heirs, her son, is in debt to gangsters; a major character is Dr. Jannery; and the murderess, a nurse, killed so the man she loves would come into money. In the movie script, character names are changed; the head gangster and his subordinates play no important part in the story; Dr. Jannery is also strangled; and a major character in the novel is eliminated. When this novel was written there was no Nikki Porter. With this exception, the screenwriter should have paid more attention to the novel.

This would be Ralph Bellamy's last appearance as Ellery Queen. In the next film, William Gargan would take over in the title role.

Reviews: "More comedy than mystery here." *Motion Picture Guide*, Nash and Ross

"The adventure, with its sideline comedy byplay, is generally acceptable diverting fare." *Variety*, 09/24/41

Summation: This is a mishmash of a story. To pad the story to feature length there's too much unfunny and predictable Three Stooges-like comedy and especially too much Tom Dugan. About halfway through the proceedings, one of the actors exclaims, "I don't think I can take anymore." The author truly agreed, but plodded on to the dismal end. To top it off, Margaret Lindsay solves the mystery before Ralph Bellamy. Of all the Bellamy Ellery Queen entries, this one is the worst.

A CLOSE CALL FOR ELLERY QUEEN
Columbia (January 1942)

Fiction and Radio's Foremost Mystery Buster Tackles His Most Baffling Case

Alternate Title: A Close Call

Cast: Ellery Queen, William Gargan; Nikki Porter, Margaret Lindsay; Inspector Queen, Charley Grapewin; Alan Rogers, Ralph Morgan; Margo Rogers, Kay Linaker; Stewart Cole, Edward Norris; Sergeant Velie, James Burke; Lester Young, Addison Richards; Corday, Charles Judels; Bates, Andrew Tombes; Housekeeper, Claire Du Brey; Marie Dubois, Micheline Cheirel; Fisherman, Ben Welden; Butler, Milton Parsons// Mr. Crandall, Hobart Cavanaugh; Boggs, Edward Hearn; Tattoo artist, Harry Tyler

Credits: Director, James Hogan; Story, Ellery Queen; Screenwriter, Eric Taylor; Additional dialogue, Gertrude Purcell; Editor, Dwight Caldwell; Cinematographer, James S. Brown, Jr.; Music, Lee Zahler

Production Dates: October 28, 1941–November 11, 1941

Running Time: 65 min.

Story: Edward Norris comes to William Gargan for help. Norris tells Gargan that two men, Charles Judels and Andrew Tombes, are intimidating his employer, Ralph Morgan. Judels and Tombes are now "guests" of Morgan. Morgan's chief concern is to locate his long-lost daughter, Micheline Cheirel. Morgan was just recently reunited with his other daughter, Kay Linaker. Cheirel arrives in New York and meets Gargan's secretary, Margaret Lindsay. When Lindsay learns that Cheirel received a threatening letter, she offers to meet Morgan and see if the danger is real. Because of old grudges, Judels and Tombes demand blackmail money from Morgan, who can only give them $50,000. Morgan welcomes Lindsay as his daughter and wants to make her his heir, along with Linaker. Lindsay becomes nervous and asks Gargan to bring Cheirel to Morgan's estate. Gargan is unable to locate Cheriel, so Lindsay has to continue her impersonation. Morgan obtains the blackmail money from his lawyer Addison Richards. Going to a seedy bar, Morgan pays off Judels and Tombes. Inspector Charley Grapewin is summoned to the bar to investigate the murders of Judels and Tombes. Gargan tells Grapewin that he believed the murderer held up the men through a window, took the money and, because the men could identify him, shot them. Gargan goes to Morgan's estate and tells him of the murders. Grapewin arrives to find that Morgan had been murdered by a quick-acting poison. After Morgan's murder, Cheirel appears. Cheriel was hidden by the housekeeper, Claire Du Brey. Du Brey believed Lindsay and Gargen were trying to get Morgan's money. Du Brey shows Gargan proof that Linaker is not Morgan's daughter. Gargan and Grapewin accuse Linaker of murdering Judels and Tombes, but had an accomplice to forge documents showing Morgan was her father. The lights go out, and Gargan foils an attempt on Linaker's life. Gargan reveals the murderer to be Linaker's accomplice, Norris. Cheriel will inherit Morgan's estate.

Notes and Commentary: This was William Gargan's first outing as Ellery Queen, replacing Ralph Bellamy.

This film was very loosely based on the Ellery Queen novel, *The Dragon's Teeth: A Problem in Deduction* (Frederick Stokes, 1939). In the novel, Queen's partner, a character who doesn't appear in the movie, takes on most of the action. The millionaire, who dies of natural causes early in the story, has two heirs, children of siblings. One turns out to be an impostor who was working with the deceased's lawyer. The impostor tries unsuccessfully to murder the legitimate heir, and in turn is murdered by the lawyer. Queen's deductions bring the guilty party to justice.

Reviews: "Gargan does a nice job in bringing the amateur sleuth's intelligence and wit to a mediocre script." *Motion Picture Guide*, Nash and Ross

"Latest in the series shapes up as strong whodunit as support in duals." *Variety*, 03/11/42

Summation: This is just a so-so murder-mystery, enlivened by Margaret Lindsay's performance. To pad this feature, again unfunny and obvious "comedy" is used. When the film finally gets down to the mystery segment, the story is rushed to its conclusion.

A DESPERATE CHANCE FOR ELLERY QUEEN

Columbia (May 1942)

Ellery Queen untangles a web of mystery!

Alternate Title: A Desperate Chance

Cast: Ellery Queen, William Gargan; Nikki Porter, Margaret Lindsay; Inspector

A Desperate Chance for Ellery Queen (1942) scene card — (left to right) unknown actor, Frank Thomas, William Gargan, Charley Grapewin, unknown actor.

Queen, Charley Grapewin; Norman Hadley, John Litel; Adele Belden, Lilian Bond; Sergeant Velie, James Burke; Tommy Gould, Jack La Rue; Ray Stafford, Morgan Conway; George Belden, Noel Madison; Captain H.T. Daley, Frank Thomas; Mrs. Irene Evington Hadley, Charlotte Wynters// Burlesque house barker, Donald Kerr; Fingers Muldoon, Syd Saylor; Ticket clerk, Jack Rice; Doorman, Harry Tenbrook; Riley, Johnny Arthur; Reporter, William Newell; Detective, Guy Usher; Mrs. Plumpkin, Virginia Sale; Chinese waiter, Willie Fung; Motel landlady, Marie Blake; Quarantine sign poster, Billy Bletcher; Waymond Wadcwiff, Arthur Q. Bryan; Freddy Froelich, Byron Foulger; Hotel manager, Matt McHugh; Charlie, Harrison Greene; Nightclub patron with tires, Bernard Gorcey

    Credits: Director, James Hogan; Story, Ellery Queen; Screenwriter, Eric Taylor; Editor, Dwight Caldwell; Art Director, Richard Irvine; Cinematographer, James S. Brown, Jr.; Music, Lee Zahler

    Song: "Two Against One" (Pollack, Gilbert and Meroff) sung by Lilian Bond

    Production Dates: January 26, 1942–February 7, 1942

    Running Time: 70 min.

    Story: Burlesque star Lilian Bond threatens to leave her husband, Noel Madison, unless he starts spending the money he embezzled. Bond and Madison decide to go across country to San Francisco to begin using the money. Novelist and criminologist William Gargan is planning to go to San Francisco to get background information for a new mystery story.

Socialite Charlotte Wynters has received word that her supposedly deceased husband, John Litel, is alive and living in San Francisco, and so she asks Gargan to investigate. Gargan has his secretary, Margaret Lindsay, accompany him and impersonate Wynters in order to draw out Litel. Litel takes the bait and Gargan tries to persuade him to return home. Before Litel can agree, Gargan's father, Inspector Charley Grapewin, arrives from New York looking for Litel on suspicion of embezzlement. Litel returns to his apartment and finds Madison's dead body. Litel calls Gargan and tells him that he believes Madison was the embezzler. Gargan believes Litel to be innocent and hides him from the clutches of the law. Bond falls into the clutches of nightclub owner and gangster Morgan Conway and his henchman, Jack La Rue. Conway wants the money Madison embezzled and will pay her 50 cents on the dollar. Gargan's investigation leads him to Conway's nightclub. In the club, Gargan makes the acquaintance of Bond, who introduces him to Conway. Gargan enters Conway's office and, at gunpoint, looks through Conway's safe where he finds the "hot" money. Bond enters Conway's office followed by La Rue. Lights go out. Guns flash. Gargan leaves the office with Bond in tow, followed by La Rue. Gargan takes Bond to Litel's apartment where he proves Bond murdered Madison. Bond confesses because she sees La Rue through the kitchen window. La Rue fires a shot at Gargen, but misses. In trying to escape, La Rue is cut down by police bullets.

Notes and Commentary: The working title was "Ellery Queen and the Living Corpse."

This film was based on the *Adventures of Ellery Queen* radio program, "A Good Samaritan" (CBS, June 9, 1940). Extensive changes were made to the story before it reached the screen. The radio show had Ellery tracking down the individual who was sending stolen $100 bills to tenants in a particular tenement building.

Review: "Poor mystery that was the penultimate in an almost lifeless series." *Motion Picture Guide*, Nash and Ross

Summation: So far, the best entry in the series. The story moves nicely, and the few comedy moments are unobtrusive. William Gargan settles into the role of Ellery Queen comfortably and the chemistry with Margaret Lindsay really clicks in this one. Villainy is in the capable hands of Jack La Rue and Morgan Conway, both of whom are properly tough. Director James Hogan guides this episode in fine style, pacing it adroitly.

ENEMY AGENTS MEET ELLERY QUEEN
Columbia *(July 1942)*

Ellery pits Yankee brains against Nazi cunning ... to bring you thrills!

Alternate Title: The Lido Mystery

Cast: Ellery Queen, William Gargan; Nikki Porter, Margaret Lindsay; Inspector Queen, Charley Grapewin; Mrs. Van Dorn, Gale Sondergaard; Paul Gillette, Gilbert Roland; Heinrich, Sig Ruman; Sergeant Velie, James Burke; Morse, Ernest Dorian; Helm, Felix Basch; Commander Lang, Minor Watson; Commissioner Bracken, John Hamilton; Sergeant Stevens, James Seay; Reece, Louis Donath; Sailor, Dick Wessel// Khalkis, Maurice Cass; Ticket agent, Jack Rice; Porter, Fred Toones; Cleaning lady, Ellen Corby; Tenant, William Newell; Lido desk clerk, Arthur Space; Marine corporal, Harry Strang; Small sailor, Billy Bletcher

Credits: Director, James Hogan; Story, Ellery Queen; Screenwriter, Eric Taylor; Additional dialogue, Arthur Strawn; Editor, Dwight Caldwell; Art Director, Richard Irvine; Interior Decorator, Emile Kuri; Cinematographer, James S. Brown, Jr.; Music, Lee Zahler

Production Dates: May 11, 1942–May 23, 1942

Running Time: 64 min.

Story: During the beginning of World War II, Germans allow a ship carrying crates from Cairo to the Khalkis museum in New York to pass safely. The ship docks in New London, Connecticut, with the crates to be transported by train the rest of the journey. On the same train Sergeant James Burke is bringing a prisoner, Louis Donath, back to New York for the murder of Gale Sondergaard's husband. Entering their compartment on the train, Burke is rendered unconscious by Nazi leader Sig Ruman. Ruman, promising safety to Donath, confirms that the package in which the Germans are interested is hidden in the mummy case. Ruman then has Donath thrown from the train to his death. Inspector Charley Grapewin believes Burke was negligent and has him suspended from the force. William Gargan and Margaret Lindsay believe Burke was blameless and begin an investigation to have him reinstated. Gargan, Lindsay and Burke go to Sondergaard's office. Lindsay sees Gilbert Roland, whom she thinks may have some bearing on the case, and begins her own investigation. Roland believes Lindsay is a Nazi spy and imprisons her. Gargan is able to rescue Lindsay. A mummy case is stolen from the museum. Gargan and Lindsay search for the case in a nearby cemetery. The case is found with Roland's dead body inside. Gargan finally is able to see Sondergaard, running a bluff, finds there was a packet containing valuable diamonds. Sondergaard was going to sell the diamonds to raise money for the Netherland's fight for freedom. Sondergaard tells Gargan that the Lido Club would be worth investigating. The club turns out to be a hot bed of Nazi spies. Gargan is captured by Ruman, but breaks away long enough to get the attention of Marine Sergeant James Seay. Seay rounds up three other servicemen who race to Gargan's rescue. After a wild fistic brawl, all the spies are captured and the diamonds are recovered. Burke is reinstated.

Notes and Commentary: The working title was "Ellery Queen Across the Atlantic."

The film was very loosely based on the novel *The Greek Coffin Mystery* (Frederick Stokes, 1932). The basic premise of the mystery was promptly discarded. The only elements that remained were Khalkis as the owner of an art gallery, a murdered man unexpectedly found in a coffin and two characters who were Dutch.

The *Variety* reviewer had knowledge that this was the final film of the series.

Before World War II, Ernest Dorian was billed as Ernst Deutsch and Louis Donath was Ludwig Donath.

Reviews: "A fitting and inauspicious end to a mercifully brief series." *Motion Picture Guide*, Nash and Ross

"A slam-bang brawl provides virtually the only life to a feeble washup of what had become a tired series. A weak dualer." *Variety*, 08/26/42

Summation: This was a speedy but not well-written episode. Through most of the movie, the story is played for suspense with a few comic breaks. The ending is pure slapstick designed to break out the patriotic fervor of the audience, ruining the tone of the story. Sig Ruman, who was known for playing villainous Nazis, ended up as a poor comic character better found in a 3 Stooges comedy. Also, no groundwork was laid for Minor Watson's character to be revealed as a traitor to the United States.

The Five Little Peppers

In 1878, Harriett Mulford Stone, using the pseudonym Margaret Sidney, sent stories revolving around the lives of a fictitious family called the Peppers, to *Wide Awake* magazine. After the success of "Polly Pepper's Chicken Pie" and "Phronsie Pepper's New Shoes," publisher Daniel Lothrop asked Sidney to send more stories of the Pepper family. She finally began writing the Five Little Peppers series. The first book was her most famous, *Five Little Peppers and How They Grew*, published in 1881. This story told how the impoverished Pepper family became entwined with the well-to-do King family. Sidney's books were published by the D. Lothrop Company of Boston. (Lothrup, by this time, was Sidney's husband.) There were 11 books in the Peppers series. There were individual books devoted to Ben, Joel, Phronsie and, of course, Polly. After the eleventh, *Five Little Peppers in the Brown House* (Lothrup, Lee & Shepard Co., 1907) was published, Sidney thought that was last of the Pepper family. The public clamored for a book about the fifth Pepper, Davie. Finally *Our Davie Pepper* (Lothrup, Lee & Shapard Co., 1916) was published. This proved to be the last of the chronicles of the Pepper and King families. Many of the books continued to be reprinted.

The popularity convinced Columbia Pictures that a movie series would be successful. While Sidney's books took place around the turn of the century, Columbia decided to update them to the present day, which now was 1939. In the initial entry, *Five Little Peppers and How They Grew*, some plot elements from the original source were used, but most of the story and the remaining three films came from the screenwriters' imagination. Edith Fellows was an excellent choice to play Polly. Fellows was signed to a seven-year contract with Columbia in 1935. Her best-known film was *Pennies from Heaven* (Columbia, 1936) with Bing Crosby. (After leaving Columbia, Fellows made two appearances with Gene Autry at Republic. She worked sporadically until 1981 when she resumed her career and could be seen on many television programs.) Getting almost as much attention in the series was four-year-old Dorothy Ann Seese as Phronsie Pepper. After the first film, Seese received second billing, and would do so for the rest of the series. (Seese's film career was quite short, after the Pepper series she would be seen in two unbilled appearances in the Blondie series. Seese was fourth billed in her last Columbia picture, *Let's Have Fun* [1943]. Her last screen appearance would be an unbilled role in Randolph Scott's *The Bounty Hunter* [Warner Bros., 1954]. Seese then left films to become a business system analyst. Later she turned to the legal field, working as a legal secretary, legal assistant and paralegal.)

Character actress Dorothy Peterson played the part of Mrs. Pepper, which was probably the high point of her long screen career. Mr. King was first played by Clarence Kolb, best known for his role of George Honeywell on the television series, *My Little Margie* (NBC, CBS, 1952–55). After two episodes, Pierre Watkin took over the role of Mr. King.

(Although Watkin could play rich, influential business men, he was probably best known as Mr. Skinner, the bank president with the "hearty handclasp" in *The Bank Dick* (Universal, 1940). He also played Uncle Jim Fairchild in the serial *Jack Armstrong* [Columbia, 1947], and was the screen's first Perry White in the serials *Superman* [Columbia, 1948] and *Atom Man vs. Superman* [Columbia, 1950].) Ronald Sinclair, who played Jasper King, had only a six-year career as an actor before turning to the other side of the camera as a film editor. Clarence Peck, as Ben, was mostly uncredited in his film career with the exception of the Pepper series. Tommy Bond, who played Joey, had two different roles in the Our Gang and Little Rascals comedies. (Bond initially played Tommy and then, after being away from the series a few years, came back to play the role of Butch the bully. Later in his career, Bond was the first Jimmy Olsen on the screen in the serials *Superman* [Columbia, 1948] and *Atom Man vs. Superman* [Columbia, 1950].) Jimmy Leake's only screen role was as Davie. After *Five Little Peppers and How They Grew*, he was replaced by Bobby Larson. Larson's career began with the Charles Starrett western, *Down the Wyoming Trail* (Columbia, 1939) and lasted until an unbilled role in *Pride of Maryland* (Republic, 1951). Mr. King's valet, Martin, was first played by Leonard Carey. Rex Evans replaced Carey for the last three entries. Both actors had long film careers, primarily playing butlers or valets.

FIVE LITTLE PEPPERS AND HOW THEY GREW
Columbia (November 1939)

You asked to meet all of them again ... so here they are!

Cast: Polly Pepper, Edith Fellows; Mr. King, Clarence Kolb; Mrs. Pepper, Dorothy Peterson; Jasper, Ronald Sinclair; Ben Pepper, Charles Peck; Joey Pepper, Tommy Bond; Davie Pepper, Jimmy Leake; Phronsie Pepper, Dorothy Ann Seese; Martin, Leonard Carey// Barker, Jack Rice; Mrs. Peters's maid, Flo Campbell; Tom, Bruce Bennett; Miss Mary, Betty Roadman; Assistant Cook, Bess Wade; Caretaker, Harry Bernard; Delivery Man, George Lloyd; Dr. Spence, Harry Hayden; Dr. Emery, Edward LeSaint; Nurse, Dorothy Comingore; Hart, Maurice Costello; Townsend, Paul Everton

Credits: Director, Charles Barton; Story, J. Robert Bren and Gladys Atwater; Screenwriters, Nathalie Bucknall and Jefferson Parker; Editor, James Sweeney; Art Director, Lionel Banks; Cinematographer, Henry Freulich; Musical Director, M.W. Stoloff

    Song: "Wiegenlied (Brahms' Lullaby), Op. 49, No. 4" (Brahms) sung by Edith Fellows
    Source: Based on the novel, *Five Little Peppers and How They Grew* by Margaret Sidney
    Production Dates: June 28, 1939–July 24, 1939
    Running Time: 58 min.
    Story: Mining financier Clarence Kolb only owns 50 percent of a mining claim and needs the balance. Edith Fellows, daughter of Dorothy Peterson, is the eldest of five children. By chance, Fellows meets the grandson of Kolb, Ronald Sinclair, and tells him about the mining claim she owns. Fellows tells Kolb and he becomes friendly with Fellows and her siblings in order to obtain the stock as cheaply as he can. While visiting the family, the youngest child, Dorothy Ann Seese, comes down with the measles. Doctor Harry Hayden quarantines the premises. Kolb has to stay until the quarantine is lifted and, little by little, comes to care for the family. Fellows's brothers also come down with measles. In tending to her siblings, Fellows works herself into a state of exhaustion; she finally collapses and

loses her sight. Advised to remove Fellows from her poverty environment, Kolb invites Peterson to bring her family to his mansion. Kolb grows to love the family, and especially his role as father figure to Seese. Finally, Fellows regains her sight. A business rival of Kolb, Paul Everton, comes to the mansion and accuses Kolb of underhanded tactics in attempting to obtain the mining stock from Fellows. Fellows overhears this exchange and runs away when Kolb fails to deny the accusation. Fellows does not hear Kolb tell Everton that he changed his mind. Kolb will give Fellows $25,000 over Everton's best offer. Refusing to listen to him, Fellows and her family move back to their home after giving Kolb the mining stock certificate. Sinclair goes to Fellows and convinces her to listen to Kolb, and she relents. Kolb offers Fellows a check for $75,000 but Fellows says she would rather be Kolb's partner in the mine. Kolb then asks the family to permanently move in with him.

Notes and Commentary: Dorothy Comingore was best known for her role as Susan Alexander, Orson Welles's mistress in the classic, *Citizen Kane* (RKO, 1941). Earlier in her career she was known as Linda Winters in the Wild Bill Saunders series entry, *Pioneers of the Frontier* (Columbia, 1940).

Screenwriters cherry-picked some elements from Margaret Sidney's novel. First, the story was updated from the 1890s to the 1930s. The measles incident and Polly's blindness were retained. A new stove was provided (in the novel) by Dr. Fisher (a character not in the film), not Mr. King. The eldest boy, Ben, meets Jasper King and his dog, Prince, after they rescue Phronsie from an itinerant organ grinder. Through Jasper's friendship with Polly, Mrs. Pepper and her other children come to live with Mr. King. The relationship is further cemented when it's revealed that Mrs. Pepper is a cousin of Mr. King's son-in-law.

Tom, the chauffeur played by a youthful Bruce Bennett, is an elderly gentleman in the novel.

Reviews: "Routine family film about Mrs. Pepper and her five kids." *Motion Picture Guide*, Nash and Ross

"Excellent comedy-drama for the family and juvenile trade. New family series gets fine launching." *Variety*, 09/06/39

Summation: Overly sentimental, the film is a real tearjerker. Edith Fellows overcomes the maudlin script with an expert performance to make the story acceptable entertainment. Precious little Dorothy Ann Seese is a real scene-stealer.

FIVE LITTLE PEPPERS AT HOME
Columbia (February 1940)

That family is here again ... straight out of the famous stories beloved by millions!

Cast: Polly Pepper, Edith Fellows; Phronsie Pepper, Dorothy Ann Seese; Mr. King, Clarence Kolb; Mrs. Pepper, Dorothy Peterson; Jasper King, Ronald Sinclair; Ben Pepper, Charles Peck; Joey Pepper, Tommy Bond; Davie Pepper, Bobby Larson; Martin, Rex Evans; Mr. Decker, Herbert Rawlinson; Aunt Martha, Laura Treadwell// Bainbridge, Jack Rice; Dr. Emery, Edward LeSaint; Nurse, Ann Doran; Townsend, Paul Everton; Aunt Martha's chauffeur, Richard Fiske; Miner, Tom London

Credits: Director, Charles Barton; Screenwriter, Harry Sauber; Editor, Viola Lawrence, Art Director; Lionel Banks, Cinematographer; Allen G. Siegler; Musical Director, M.W. Stoloff

Source: Based on a book by Margaret Sidney
Production Dates: November 27, 1939–December 26, 1939
Running Time: 67 min.

Story: In an attempt to find copper in a mine owned in partnership with Edith Fellows, Clarence Kolb is near bankruptcy. In order to save his mansion and other holdings, Kolb convinces Fellows that they must take Paul Everton's offer for the mine. The stress of the situation leaves Kolb bedridden. Fellows goes to Everton's office to sell the mine, but Everton withdraws his offer. Everton believes that if he waits until the bank forecloses he can buy it at his own price. As time for the foreclosure draws near, Fellows learns that Rex Evans, Kolb's gentleman's gentleman, has knowledge of geology. Fellows asks Evans to go into the mine to see if he can find any evidence of a copper vein. Fellows, her siblings and Evans go down into the mine. The eldest boy, Charles Peck, drifts away from the others and, in his enthusiasm to find copper, causes the tunnel to cave in, trapping the others. In trying to dig his way out, Evans discovers a rich copper vein. Peck goes to town and brings the towns-people, who are able to rescue Fellows and her companions. Kolb decides to sell his mansion and build a new home in Gusty Corners and live with Fellows and her family.

Notes and Commentary: This film was supposedly based on Margaret Sidney's novel, *Five Little Peppers Midway* (Boston, 1890). "Five Little Peppers Midway" was the film's working title. Nothing from the original source material was used, therefore the title change.

Jack Rice's character name was Barker in *Five Little Peppers and How They Grew*.

Reviews: "Continues where *Five Little Peppers* left off, but far less entertaining." *Motion Picture Guide*, Nash and Ross

" A sweet-as-saccharine, less-effective episode." *The Columbia Story*, Hirshhorn

"Continues where Five Little Peppers left off, but far less entertaining." *Motion Picture Guide*, Nash and Ross

"More fatal about the second 'Pepper' story is its tediousness and with one or two exceptions, the dullness of the characters. Weak." *Variety*, 03/06/40

Summation: Overly sentimental and saccharine, the film plods along until the final reel, which generates a little suspense as Edith Fellows and her companions are trapped in a mine tunnel cave-in. The scriptwriter, Henry Sauber, conveniently allows a rich copper vein to be found to ensure a happy ending. Most of the film's running time is padded with scenes involving little Dorothy Ann Seese. These scenes probably were the part of the film that interested most moviegoers of the period.

OUT WEST WITH THE PEPPERS
Columbia (June 1940)

A raft of fun! ... the Peppers spice it with a generous dash of adventure!

Cast: Polly Pepper, Edith Fellows; Phronsie Pepper, Dorothy Ann Seese; Mrs. Pepper, Dorothy Peterson; Ben Pepper, Charles Peck; Joey Pepper, Tommy Bond; David Pepper, Bobby Larson; Jim Anderson, Victor Kilian; Ole, Emory Parnell; Alice Anderson, Helen Brown; Mr. King, Pierre Watkin; Jasper King, Ronald Sinclair; Caleb, Walter Soderling; Tom, Roger Gray; Bill, Hal Price// Martin, Rex Evans; Frenchman, Andre Cheron; Ship steward, John Rogers; Abbie, Kathryn Sheldon; Oscar, Ernie Adams

Credits: Director, Charles Barton; Screenwriter, Harry Rebaus; Editor, James Sweeney;

Art Director, Lionel Banks; Cinematographer, Benjamin Kline; Musical Director, M.W. Stoloff

Source: Based on a book by Margaret Sidney

Production Dates: mid–April 1940–mid–May 1940

Running Time: 62 min.

Story: Dorothy Peterson becomes ill and is advised to move to a higher climate and rest for a year. Peterson's sister, Helen Brown, lives in Oregon. Daughter Edith Fellows writes Brown and asks if they can stay with her. Brown tells Fellows to come, to the displeasure of her husband, Victor Kilian. Peterson, Fellows, Charles Peck, Tommy Bond, Bobby Larson and Dorothy Ann Seese arrive only to find that Brown runs a boarding house for lumberjacks in the area. One of the lumberjacks, Emory Parnell, tells Bond and Larson that he used to be a pirate and he can help them build a raft. Fellows makes a picnic lunch. Parnell takes Fellows, Bond, Larson and Seese down to the river. Kilian tags along. Parnell and Bond build a raft. Bond, Larson and Seese climb on the raft while Parnell goes to bring lunch back for them. The raft gets loose and drifts out into the middle of the river. Meanwhile, loggers have started logs moving and the raft is headed right in the middle of them. Parnell tries to swim to the raft but can't make it. Exhausted, Parnell holds on to a floating log to keep from drowning. Fellows sees the dilemma and asks Kilian to help. Kilian swims to the raft and fashions a rudder so the raft will head for shore. Kilian sees the helpless Parnell and swims to his aid. Kilian has undergone a change of heart and is happy that Fellows and her family are staying with them.

Notes and Commentary: This film was based on Margaret Sidney's novel, *Five Little Peppers Abroad* (Boston, 1902). "Five Little Peppers Abroad" was the film's working title. The only thing taken from Sidney's book is the fact that Mr. King took some of the Pepper family to Europe. In the book, Mrs. Pepper doesn't fall ill and return to America on the next steamer. In fact, the book ends with Polly going to Dresden, Germany, to study piano.

Reviews: "Based on the characters from Margaret Sidney's book, the film is soaked in sweetness and lacks the life of the [Andy] Hardy clan." *Motion Picture Guide*, Nash and Ross

"The weakest of the series." *The Columbia Story*, Hirshhorn

"Third of the series. The most inferior of the lot. Tasteless fare from beginning to end." *Variety*, 07/10/40

Summation: This is a pedestrian effort until the final reel when some mild excitement erupts. This offering, again, offers a lot of tedious "funny" business with Dorothy Ann Seese. Thanks to scriptwriter Harry Rebaus, Victor Kilian undergoes an unbelievable transition from a mean-spirited to a loving individual. Pure nonsense.

FIVE LITTLE PEPPERS IN TROUBLE

Columbia (September 1940)

They may be small ... but what a big wallop they pack!
Smashing straight to your heart ... while your sides ache with laughter!

Cast: Polly Pepper, Edith Fellows; Phronsie Pepper, Dorothy Ann Seese; Mrs. Pepper, Dorothy Peterson; Mr. King, Pierre Watkin; Jasper King, Ronald Sinclair; Ben Pepper, Charles Peck; Joey Pepper, Tommy Bond; Davie Pepper, Bobby Larson; Martin, Rex Evans;

Five Little Peppers in Trouble (1940) scene card —(left) Edith Fellows, (center, left to right) Ronald Sinclair, Edith Fellows, Charles Peck, (bottom, left to right) Bobby Larson, Tommy Bond, Charles Peck, Ronald Sinclair.

Mrs. Martha Wilcox, Kathleen Howard; Mrs. Lansdowne, Mary Currier; Miss Roland, Helen Brown; May, Betty Jane Graham; June, Shirley Mills; Kiki, Shirley Jean Rickert; Pam, Antonia Oland; Peggy, Rita Quigley// Cynthia, Ann Barlow; Miss Simpson, Ruth Robinson; Mrs. Wilcox's chauffeur, Eddie Laughton; Process server, Don Beddoe; Jim, Robert Carson; Mr. Barnes, Carlton Griffin; Mr. Corman, Reginald Simpson; Miss Roberts, Bess Flowers

    Credits: Director, Charles Barton; Screenwriter, Harry Rebuas; Editor, Robert Fantl; Art Director, Lionel Banks; Cinematographer, Benjamin Kline

    Song: "The Blue Danube Waltz, Opus 314" (Strauss) sung by Edith Fellows and accompanied by Shirley Jean Rickert on piano

    Source: Based on a book by Margaret Sidney

    Production Dates: May 22, 1940–June 17, 1940

    Running Time: 64 min.

    Story: Kathleen Howard, Ronald Sinclair's aunt, returns to take Sinclair to live with her. She believes Sinclair's grandfather, Pierre Watkin, cannot properly take care of him. Howard gets a court order to get control of Sinclair. To prevent this, Watkin has enrolled Sinclair, Edith Fellows, Charles Peck, Tommy Bond, Bobby Larson and Dorothy Ann Seese in Mary Currier's exclusive private school. The group has to interact with a bunch of snobs who give them a rough time. One of the snobs, Shirley Mills, plans to empty the swimming pool on the night the girls plan a forbidden midnight swim. Two of the girls suffer injuries and Fellows is blamed for the incident. Only one teacher, Helen Brown, believes in Fellows. Currier phones Watkin to pick up his charges. Mills gloats as the group leaves, prompting Brown to slap her. Howard makes a try in assuming custody of Sinclair. Watkin convinces the judge that he is best suited to bring up Sinclair. To celebrate, Watkin plans to take all of them to Paris.

Notes and Commentary: This film was supposedly based on Margaret Sidney's novel, *Five Little Peppers at School* (Boston, 1903). No part of the book was used in the final production. In the book, only three Peppers attend school. Joey and Davey go away from home to attend Dr. Marks's school. Polly Pepper stays at home as a student at Miss Salisbury's school. "Five Little Peppers at School" was the film's working title but, understandably, it was changed.

Dorothy Ann Seese recites Robert Louis Stevenson's *My Shadow*. The poem was published in Stevenson's *A Child's Garden of Verses* in 1885.

It looks like Columbia released the third and fourth films out of sequence. At the end of *Five Little Peppers in Trouble*, Watkins is taking the whole family to Paris. At the beginning of *Out West with the Peppers*, the family is returning from Paris.

Screenwriter Harry Sauber also received billing as Harry Rebaus and Harry Rebuas in this series.

Reviews: "The main trouble with this film is that there exists no reason for it." *Motion Picture Guide*, Nash and Ross

"A less than scintillating script. Little Dorothy Ann Seese pilfered the show with all the best lines." *The Columbia Story*, Hirshhorn

"Weakest in the Pepper series. The film continues the screen's most drab family in a very weak story." *Variety*, 09/18/40

Summation: Not too bad this time out; more melodramatic than overly sentimental and saccharine like the previous entries. Edith Fellows carries the lead very well and even is allowed to sing. Dorothy Ann Seese's role is more under control and therefore very effective. A neat twist in the screenplay is that Fellows is not cleared of emptying the swimming pool even though family and friends know she's innocent.

Gasoline Alley

Frank King's *Gasoline Alley* began on November 24, 1918, as a one panel strip, one-fourth of a page in the *Chicago Tribune* called "The Rectangle." King's strip consisted of four friends — Doc, Avery, Bill and Walt Wallet — discussing their cars. The popularity increased to the point that *Gasoline Alley* appeared daily beginning, as has been stated by many sources, on August 25, 1919. It didn't take long after that until *Gasoline Alley* received its own full-page, color strip in the Sunday edition. To add women readers, it was suggested that Walt be a father. Since Walt was a bachelor, a baby boy was mysteriously left on his doorstep. Walt decided to adopt the little baby and named him Skeezix, which is cowboy slang for a motherless calf. From this time, *Gasoline Alley* became a soap opera in the comic strips. The characters would age in real time. In later years, Walt married Phyllis Blossom. They had a son, Corky, and later adopted a little girl, Judy, who was found on the running board of Walt's car. By the 1940s, the strip concentrated on Skeezix. He was also the focus of four *Gasoline Alley* Better Little Books published by Whitman from 1934 to 1943.

Gasoline Alley was heard on radio from 1941 to 1949, and was sponsored by Autolite. The focus again was on Skeezix, played by both Bill Idelson and Jimmy McCallion during the course of the show's life. Skeezix would marry Nina Clock, and the couple would have two children, Chip and Clovia. By the early '50s, the strip's emphasis would be on Corky. There was a short-lived comic book that lasted two issues, in late 1950; these books reprinted old newspaper strips.

The popularity of the strip was a deciding factor to begin a movie series in 1951, and would replace the Blondie series. Audience reception to the series was disappointing and only two films were produced. Even though the series centered on Corky, regulars Skeezix, Walt, Phyllis, Nina, Chip, Clovia and Corky's wife, Hope, were present. Former popular child star Scotty Beckett was picked to play Corky. (Beginning his film career at the age of three, Beckett was a member of Hal Roach's Our Gang from 1934–1936. He went on to play in such memorable films as *Anthony Adverse* [Warner Bros., 1936], *The Charge of the Light Brigade* [Warner Bros., 1936] and *King's Row* [Warner Bros., 1942]. By the late '40s, Beckett was at Metro-Goldwyn-Mayer, co-starring with the likes of Elizabeth Taylor, Van Johnson and Clark Gable. After his "Gasoline Alley" films, Beckett was most noted for his role of Winky on the syndicated "Rocky Jones, Space Ranger" television show. Beckett's rocky personal life with drugs and alcohol led to his tragic death.)

Jimmy Lydon took the part of Skeezix. (Lydon began his show business career as a teenage star on Broadway and on radio. In the early '40s, Lydon was Henry Aldrich in nine films for Paramount. Lydon's talents were recognized on the screen in the late '40s playing Clarence in *Life with Father* [Warner Bros., 1947], Ricky in *Cynthia* [Metro-Goldwyn-Mayer, 1947], in which he gave Elizabeth Taylor her first screen kiss, and as Dudley Raoul

Bostwick in *The Time of Your Life* [United Artists, 1948]. After the Gasoline Alley series, Lydon was kept busy on television with occasional appearances in feature films. Lydon is remembered by television space buffs as Biff Cardoza on *Rocky Jones, Space Ranger.* By the late–'50s, Lydon had moved to the other side of the camera as a writer and producer.) Character actor Don Beddoe was Walt Wallet. (Beddoe began his career as a Broadway actor in 1929 and turned to films in 1938, working primarily at Columbia Pictures. After the Gasoline Alley series, Beddoe worked steadily in films and television. He got top billing in *The Boy Who Caught a Crook* [United Artists, 1961] and *Saintly Sinners* [United Artists, 1962]. Beddoe's last film was *Nickel Mountain* [ZIV International, 1984] when he was 84.) In 1951, Frank King turned over the Sunday strip to his assistant, Bill Perry. Dick Moores took over the daily strip in 1959, when King retired. When Perry retired in 1975, Moores drew the Sunday strip. Critics have noted that Moores sustained and possibly exceeded the quality for which King had been praised. With Moores's death in 1986, his assistant Jim Scancarelli became the strip's cartoonist. Thanks to Scancarelli, the Gasoline Alley comic strip is still a regular feature in many newspapers. In 2003, the first of four volumes of *Frank King's Gasoline Alley Nostalgia Journal* was published by Spec Productions. The volumes began with the first strip from November 24, 1918 and continued through December 31, 1920. Four books have been published in the "Walt and Skeezix" series, covering Skeezix' first appearance in 1921 through 1928. It has been announced that volume five, covering 1929–30 will be released on April 12, 2011. The early Sunday strips haven't been ignored with "Sundays with Walt and Skeezix" (Sunday Press Book, 2007).

GASOLINE ALLEY
Columbia (January 1951)

At last — America's most beloved "Funnies" family on the screen!

Cast: Corky, Scotty Beckett; Skeezix, Jimmy Lydon; Hope, Susan Morrow; Walt Wallet, Don Beddoe; Judy, Patti Brady; Phyllis, Madelon Mitchel; Pudge, Dick Wessel; Joe Allen, Gus Schilling// Nina, Kay Christopher; Charles D. Haven, Byron Foulger; Carol, Virginia Toland; Harry Dorsey, Jimmy Lloyd; Hacker, William Forrest; Reddick, Ralph Peters; Pettit, Charles Halton; Mortie, Charles Williams; Myrtle, Christine McIntyre; Con Man, Murray Alper; Mrs. Finch, Helen Dickson; Harold Simms, William E. Green; Chuck, Lee Morgan; Smite, Fred F. Sears; Mr. Upton, Ted Stanhope; Mr. Flask, Harry Tyler

Credits: Director, Edward Bernds; Producer, Milton Feldman; Story and Screenwriter, Edward Bernds; Editor, Aaron Stell; Art Director, Victor Greene; Set Decorator, James Crowe; Cinematographer, Lester White; Musical Director, Mischa Bakaleinikoff

Production Dates: September 20, 1950–October 3, 1950

Source: Based on the Comic Strip *Gasoline Alley* by Frank O. King. Distributed by *Chicago Tribune-New York News* Syndicate, Inc.

Running Time: 77 min.

Story: Scotty Beckett drops out of college and returns home, newly married to Susan Morrow. This worries his father, Don Beddoe, and brother, Jimmy Lydon, who are concerned about how he can support a wife. Both want to offer him jobs, but Beckett wants to open his own restaurant and needs Lydon's financial assistance to do so. William Forrest, who owns a chain of drive-in restaurants, wants to acquire the property. Beckett refuses to give up his option to the premises. Lydon, who owns the option, believes Beckett's restaurant

Gasoline Alley (1951) title card—(top, left to right) Don Beddoe, Patti Brady, Scotty Beckett, Susan Morrow, Jimmy Lydon (bottom right, top row, left to right) Don Beddoe, unknown actor, Gus Shilling, (middle row, left to right), Kay Christopher, Jimmy Lydon, unknown actor, (bottom row, left to right) Patti Brady, Scotty Beckett, Don Beddoe, Susan Morrow.

will ultimately fail. Lydon is set to sign over the option to Forrest. Charles Halton wants to purchase an adjacent lot that Beckett owns. Before Lydon can sign over the option, Halton arrives in time to give Beckett a check that will be sufficient to make Beckett's restaurant solvent.

Notes and Commentary: The *Variety* reviewer noted that Columbia would make two Gasoline Alley episodes and carried an option for more if the initial entries were successful.

Review: "Good family comedy based on the comic strip." *Variety*, 01/17/51

Summation: This is an entertaining little comedy with engaging performances by Scott Beckett and Dick Wessel. The plot may be predictable, but who cares. Just relax and enjoy the film. An aside: the makeup worn by Don Beddoe as Walt Wallet makes him look very much like the beloved comic strip character.

CORKY OF GASOLINE ALLEY

Columbia (September 1951)

Corky uncorks a new laugh riot!

Cast: Corky, Scotty Beckett; Skeezix, Jimmy Lydon; Walt Wallet, Don Beddoe; Elwood Martin, Gordon Jones; Judy, Patti Brady; Hope, Susan Morrow; Nina, Kay Christopher; Phyllis, Madelon Mitchel; Pudge, Dick Wessel// Cab driver, Phil Arnold; Chipper, Rudy

Lee; Clovia, Mimi Gibson; Avery, Harry Tyler; Larry, Ralph Voltrian; Mortie, Charles Williams; Rocky, John Doucette; Ellis, Lester Matthews; Donald, Tony Taylor; Ames, Jack Rice; House painter, Emil Sitka; Dr. Bloom, Harry Harvey; Stuffy, Ronnie Ralph; Dr. Hammerschlag, Ludwig Stossel; Mrs. Noble, Ruth Warren; Jefferson Jay, John Dehner; Hull, Lewis L. Russell

Credits: Director, Edward Bernds; Producer, Wallace MacDonald; Screenwriter, Edward Bernds; Editor, Jerome Thoms; Art Director, George Brooks; Set Decorator, James Crowe; Cinematographer, Henry Freulich; Musical Director, Mischa Bakaleinikoff

Production Dates: early June 1951

Source: Based on the Comic Strip *Gasoline Alley* by Frank O. King Distributed by *Chicago Tribune-New York News* Syndicate, Inc.

Running Time: 80 min.

Story: Gordon Jones shows up at the doorstep of Don Beddoe's house. Since he's a relative of Susan Morrow, Beddoe invites Jones to stay, not realizing that he is a freeloader who plans to stay for quite a while. Morrow tells her husband, Scotty Beckett, that Jones is the black sheep of the family. The decision is made to put Jones to work. Beckett first uses Jones at his diner where Jones causes an explosion in the kitchen. Since Jones is familiar with electronics, Lydon puts Jones to work in his fix-it shop repairing televisions. Jones is more interested in perfecting a "power pill" to increase the octane rating of gasoline. The "power pill" is placed in the gasoline tank of a car, with disastrous results. The car is totaled and smoke is emanated, covering the other cars in the garage. The result is that paint wipes off easily. To stay at Beddoe's house, Jones fakes a back injury. Jones had concealed a microphone in the living room so he can eavesdrop on conversations and hears exactly how to simulate the injury. Knowing that Jones is faking, Beckett's sister, Patti Brady, (with Beckett's help) finds the microphone. Beckett talks about selling Jones's formula without notifying him. Jones comes charging downstairs. Now everyone knows that he has been faking, and the offer turns out to be false. One of Lydon's customers, Lewis L. Russell, arrives and offers to buy Jones's formula for the "power pill." Jones doesn't realize the offer is valid and gathers his belongings and leaves. Russell realizes the formula's worth as a paint remover. Lydon, Beddoe and Beckett will make sure Jones gets the money for the formula less payment for all the damages he's incurred.

Notes and Commentary: As a review of the first episode, *Gasoline Alley*, footage from that film is used.

Gordon Jones was the screen's first Green Hornet in the Universal serial, *The Green Hornet* (Universal, 1940). Western fans remember Jones as Roy Rogers's sidekick, "Splinters" McGonigle in six feature films at Republic (1950–51). Jones is probably best known as Mike the Cop in 22 episodes of *The Abbott and Costello Show* (CBS, 1952–53).

Reviews: "Full of clichés and platitudes." *The Columbia Story*, Hirshhorn

"A few bright moments but basically over long and heavy-handed." *Motion Picture Guide*, Nash and Ross

"A relatively weak comedy." *Variety*, 09/12/51

Summation: This is another entertaining comedy thanks to Jimmy Lydon, Scotty Beckett, Gordon Jones and the rest of a fine cast. Jones garners most of the laughs as the boastful freeloader.

I Love a Mystery

Carlton E. Morse created the unusual radio program concerning three former soldiers of fortune who formed the A-1 Detective Agency. The stories varied from straight mystery and adventure to those that bordered on the supernatural. The trio was headed by tough Jack Packard and included the red-headed, woman-chasing Texan Doc Long and the cool British Reggie York. The series debuted on NBC on January 16, 1939 with 15-minute broadcasts, five times weekly. On September 30, 1940, the series changed to 30-minute stories, twice a week. When the series moved to CBS on March 2, 1943, it reverted to the 15-minute, five-times-a-week format. Michael Raffretto played Jack, Barton Yarborough was Doc and Walter Patterson took the role of Reggie. Patterson committed suicide in 1942. As he had been a close friend of Morse, he decided to write Reggie out of the series. The agency's secretary, Gerry Booker, played by Gloria Blondell, joined Jack and Doc on some of their adventures. (The sister of Joan Blondell, she was the voice of Daisy Duck from 1945–1950.)

I Love a Mystery lasted on CBS until December 29, 1944. Even when the show went off the air, Columbia decided to begin a movie series and cast Jim Bannon as Jack. Bannon, a former stuntman, had played leads in a few "B" features at Columbia before snagging the lead in *I Love a Mystery* (Columbia, 1945). Barton Yarborough, as he had been doing on radio, played Doc. The series was short lived, with only three episodes produced. A few years later, Bannon played Red Ryder for Eagle-Lion. Jack, Doc and Reggie surfaced again on *I Love Adventure*. Raffetto and Yarborough were back as Jack and Doc. Tom Collins played Reggie. The show appeared on ABC from April 25, 1948 to July 18, 1948. *I Love a Mystery* resumed on the Mutual network from September 3, 1949 to December 26, 1952. Almost all of the trio's adventures had been used in the initial run. Russell Thorson was Jack, with Jim Boles as Doc and Tony Randall as Reggie. After Reggie had been written out of the story, Gerry Booker returned. This time Gerry was played by Athena Lord. In 1967, the series was revived in a television movie, *I Love a Mystery* (Universal). Les Crane played Jack, with David Hartman as Doc and Hagan Beggs as Reggie. The story was a reworking of the radio script, "The Thing That Cries in the Night," using the characters Randolph, Job, Faith, Hope and Charity. Also, Alexander Archer and the mountain lions from "The Fear That Crept Like a Cat" were present. The producers must have had second thoughts about the film, as it took six years to reach television audiences. From time to time, *I Love a Mystery* showed up in various media, first as a comic book from Editors Press Service in 1984, then as a novel, "Stuff the Lady's Hatbox" (Seven Stones, 1988). Moonstone Comics issued "I Love a Mystery: The Fear That Crept Like a Cat" was issued in 2004.

I LOVE A MYSTERY
Columbia (January 1945)

When the temple bells toll four times ... you will die!

Cast: Jack Packard, Jim Bannon; Ellen Monk, Nina Foch; Jefferson Monk, George Macready; Doc Long, Barton Yarborough; Jean Anderson, Carole Mathews; Justin Reeves, Lester Matthews// Gimpy, Ernie Adams; Vovaritch, Leo Mostovoy; Miss Osgood, Isabel Withers; Street musician, Pietro Sosso; Mr. G's doorkeeper, Harry Semels; Dr. Han, Gregory Gay; Captain Quinn, Joseph Crehan; "Pegleg" James Anderson, Frank O'Connor

Credits: Director, Henry Levin; Producer, Wallace MacDonald; Screenwriter, Charles O'Neal; Editor, Aaron Stell; Art Director, George Brooks; Set Decorator, Joseph Kish; Cinematography, Burnett Guffey; Sound, Edward Bernds

Production Dates: October 23, 1944–November 9, 1944

Source: Based upon the original radio program *I Love a Mystery*, written and directed by Carlton E. Morse

Running Time: 70 min.

COLUMBIA PICTURES presents
"I LOVE A MYSTERY"

Hypnotized by the witch doctor of the Orient!

This advertising is the property of Columbia Pictures Corporation and is leased pursuant to an agreement for use only in connection with the exhibition of the above motion picture and prohibiting its sub-lease or resale.

PRINTED IN U.S.A.

Copyright Columbia Pictures Corp. 1945

I Love a Mystery (1945) scene card —(left to right) George Macready, Jim Bannon, Barton Yarbrough.

Story: A car crashes and the sole occupant is killed. The dead body of George Macready is taken to the morgue. At the Silver Samovar nightclub, detectives Jim Bannon and Barton Yarborough rehash the events of the past three days. The detectives meet Macready and his companion, Carole Mathews. Macready tells them that he's scheduled to die in three days and a peglegged man with a large satchel is following him. Bannon and Yarborough agree to help Macready. Leaving the nightclub with C. Mathews, Macready is followed. The detectives confront the peglegged man, Frank O'Connor, but he manages to get away. Macready tells the detectives that problems began when he and his wife, Nina Foch, were on a trip to the orient. They were followed by a mysterious street musician, Pietro Sosso, all the way back to the streets of San Francisco. Sosso confronts Macready and leads him to a meeting with Lester Matthews, who states he is the leader of the Barokan, a secret society. Matthews offers to pay Macready $10,000 for his head, which is needed as a replacement for the deceased Sacred One. Later, Nina Foch received a letter prophesying that she would be an invalid in three days. Dr. Gregory Gay, who is working with Foch, verifies that she is indeed paralyzed. Bannon figures out that Foch is faking: in the event of a divorce, the estate of the couple will go to charity. Only by death can the survivor inherit the money. In his investigation, he encounters an Oriental seller who knows Foch. Bannon suspects that Matthews is the leader of the Barokan. Bannon has a plan to draw out O'Connor, but C. Mathews interferes. O'Connor retreats to his rooming house not realizing that he's being followed and is brutally murdered. C. Mathews then meets the same fate. With the cooperation of the police, Bannon has telegrams sent to Foch, L. Matthews and Gay, telling them he knows who the murderer is and asking the culprit to meet him at one of Macready's warehouses. The three secretly meet in Foch's bedroom, knowing that not one of them is the murderer, and refuse to rise to the bait. L. Matthews is ready to back out of the scheme, but Foch wants to carry it through. As he leaves Macready's house, he's murdered. Macready confronts Foch and tells her that he is the murderer and will one day kill her. Afraid that Bannon will figure out his scheme, Macready goes to the warehouse to kill Bannon. Bannon and Macready scuffle, but Macready is able to get away. In his haste to escape, his car crashes and he is killed. Yarborough notes that everything is neatly wrapped up. Bannon states there's still one loose end. No one knows what happened to Macready's head.

Notes and Commentary: This initial entry of the series was based on the episode, "The Head of Jonathan Monk." The character's name in the film was changed to Jefferson Monk.

Variety indicated that Columbia intended to produce two films annually for five years. The series was terminated after only three episodes.

Jim Bannon would have his own series again in 1949 when he would play Red Ryder in four films for Eagle-Lion.

The notes played by the street musician were lifted from Tchaikovsky's *Fifth Symphony*.

Reviews: "A preposterous, thoroughly tasteless and rather nasty little thriller." *The Columbia Story*, Hirshhorn

"Shaky direction and script, but good performances from Bannon and Foch." *Motion Picture Guide*, Nash and Ross

"Fairly suspenseful low-budget chiller." *Variety*, 02/28/45

Summation: This is a good story. It is a film-noirish murder-mystery with supernatural overtones in the tradition of the popular radio show. Jim Bannon and Barton Yarborough stand out as the detectives, but it's George Macready's show as the beleaguered man marked for death. Director Henry Levin paces the story nicely to its wow finish.

THE DEVIL'S MASK

Columbia (May 1946)

A weird jungle curse haunted this beauty! Maddened this scientist!
Shocked the detective! ... the eeriest mystery you'll ever see!

Cast: Janet Mitchell, Anita Louise; Jack Packard, Jim Bannon; Rex Kennedy, Michael Duane; Louise Mitchell, Mona Barrie; Doc Long, Barton Yarborough; Dr. Karger, Ludwig Donath; Leon Hartman, Paul E. Burns; Professor Arthur Logan, Frank Wilcox// Narrator, Frank Martin; Willard, Edward Earle; Mendoza, Fred Godoy; Halliday, Richard Hale; Museum guard, Bud Averill; Frank, Coulter Irwin; Captain Quinn, Thomas E. Jackson; Quentin Mitchell, Frank Mayo; John, John Elliott; Karger's nurse, Mary Newton; Brophy, Harry Strang

Credits: Director, Henry Levin; Producer, Wallace MacDonald; Screenwriter, Charles O'Neal; Additional dialogue, Dwight Babcock; Editor, Jerome Thoms; Art Director, Robert Peterson; Set Decorator, George Montgomery; Cinematographer, Henry Freulich; Musical Director, Mischa Bakaleinikoff

Production Dates: February 6, 1946–February 23, 1946

Source: Based upon the original radio program *I Love a Mystery*, written and directed by Carlton E. Morse

Running Time: 66 min.

Story: A plane, in flight to South America, crashes on takeoff. No lives are lost, but all baggage is destroyed except for a box containing a shrunken head. The head is take to the local museum. At the museum, private detectives Jim Bannon and Barton Yarbrough meet Mona Barrie, whose husband owned the museum. Among the exhibits is a case with five Jivaro shrunken heads and a Jivaro blowgun. Barrie is being followed by Michael Duane, and thinks she is in danger of being killed. Duane is the boyfriend of Anita Louise, Barrie's stepdaughter. Duane and Barrie visit her uncle, Paul E. Burns, a taxidermist. His shop is decorated like a jungle, with many stuffed animals and one live black leopard, a present from Louise's father, Frank Mayo. Louise tells Burns that she hates Barrie and Professor Frank Wilcox, whom she suspects are lovers based on some love letters from Wilcox to Barrie she found. Louise told Mayo about the letters. Louise also believes Barrie murdered Mayo when they were on an expedition to South America. Barrie has Wilcox show slide photos of Mayo on the expedition that show to Bannon and Yarborough he was a happy man and had no reason to disappear. While the lights are out, a mysterious figure, using a blowgun, shoots a poison dart into the room, narrowly missing Barrie and Wilcox. As the figure make his getaway he is confronted by the butler, John Elliott, who recognizes the intruder. A dart from the blowgun kills Elliott instantly. Louise now believes Mayo is alive and that he is the murderer. A headless body is found and it is thought to be that of Mayo. Bannon and Yarborough go to Burns's shop to verify that the head found in the plane wreckage was that of a Jivaro native. The detectives go to the museum to examine the heads on exhibit. One of the heads has red hair, just like Mayo. Bannon examines the cords on the lips of the head and finds a clue that takes him to Burns. Duane is already confronting Burns, telling him that he murdered Mayo. Louise arrives at the taxidermist shop and tells Duane that he must be mistaken. Duane picks up the phone to call the police, but Burns has cut the phone cord. Burns then admits that he killed Mayo. Mayo disappeared in South America only to come back to San Francisco to see if Barrie and Wilcox were carrying on an affair. Mayo came to Burns. Burns took this opportunity to kill him because he killed animals for sport. Bannon arrives at the shop. Burns has already wounded Duane and turns his attention on Bannon. Bannon hides in the jungle, so Burns unleashes his leopard to finish him off. Bannon is able to get to the shop and close the door, leaving Burns to face the wild animal. Bannon decides to save Burns's life by killing the leopard. But he is too late: the animal has ended Burns's life. Louise discovers that the letters in question were written prior to Barrie meeting Mayo, and stepmother and stepdaughter are reconciled. In addition, Louise and Duane have fallen in love.

Notes and Commentary: The working title was "The Head."

Reviews: "An unassuming whodunit." *The Columbia Story*, Hirshhorn

"Enjoyable programmer from the short-lived 'I Love a Mystery' series." *Motion Picture Guide*, Nash and Ross

Summation: Screenwriters Charles O'Neal and Dwight Babcock have fashioned a neat, suspenseful murder-mystery, and Henry Levin has directed the tale nicely. The overall acting of the competent cast is up to standard, with Jim Bannon and Barton Yarborough in fine form as the detectives. Also, a special nod to Anita Louise, who brings off her role convincingly, ranging from anger and revenge to hysteria to, finally, peace within herself. Cinematographer Henry Freulich's camera work adds to the dark mood of this story, especially in the hypnosis scene with Louise.

THE UNKNOWN

Columbia (July 1946)

Murder stalks every shadow!

Cast: Rachel Martin, Karen Morley; Jack Packard, Jim Bannon; Nina Arnold, Jeff Donnell; Reed Cawthorne, Robert Scott; Richard Arnold, Robert Wilcox; Doc Long, Barton Yarborough; Edward Martin, James Bell; Ralph Martin, Wilton Graff; Phoebe Martin, Helen Freeman// Joshua, J. Louis Jackson; Captain Selby Martin, Boyd Davis; Colonel Wetherford, Russell Hicks; James Wetherford, Robert Stevens

Credits: Director, Henry Levin; Producer, Wallace MacDonald; Screenwriters, Malcolm Stuart Boylan and Julian Harmon; Adaptation, Charles O'Neal and Dwight Babcock; Editor, Arthur Seid; Art Director, George Brooks; Set Decorator, George Montgomery; Cinematography, Henry Freulich; Musical Director, Mischa Bakaleinikoff

Production Dates: March 25, 1946–April 15, 1946

Source: Based upon the original radio program *I Love a Mystery*, written and directed by Carlton E. Morse

Running Time: 70 min.

Story: Private detectives Jim Bannon and Barton Yarborough escort Jeff Donnell to a Southern mansion in Kentucky. Donnell is present for the reading of her grandmother Helen Freeman's will. Living in the house is Karen Morley, Donnell's mother, who is in a confused and disturbed mental state and still thinks her child is a baby; two uncles, Wilton Graff and James Bell; and a longtime servant, J. Louis Johnson. Lawyer Robert Scott is a guest. Morley's mental state is a result of an incident that occurred 20 years earlier. It seems that Morley and Wilcox, who are secretly wed, are about to leave the mansion when her father, Boyd Davis, comes into the room. Davis orders Wilcox out of the house, at gunpoint.

A struggle ensues; a shot is fired as Freeman enters. Freeman orders Morley to her room. After Morley leaves, Davis collapses, mortally wounded. Freeman says she'll accuse Wilcox of murder if he doesn't leave without Morley. Davis is laid to rest behind the brick fireplace. Now back to present time, that night, Morley hears a baby's cry and thinks it belongs to her child. Morley comes to Donnell's room. Because of her mental state, Morley still does not recognize Donnell as her child. Graff forces Scott to read the will at midnight, but the will is missing from his briefcase. In their investigation, Bannon and Yarborough see a prowler enter the mausoleum on the premises. They follow and find a secret passageway. Meanwhile, an attempt is made on Donnell's life. Believing Wilcox will come to take her away, Morley receives a note to meet Wilcox in the mausoleum. The detectives follow Morley and find Bell stabbed to death and Graff hiding in a crypt. Bannon asks Jackson to go to town and summon the police. Wilcox has received a letter in which he is promised money, and he returns to the mansion. Wilcox and Morley meet but she doesn't recognize him. Bannon goes to the room where Davis was killed and finds Freeman, who had faked her death (with Jackson's help). Before she dies, Freeman wants to make amends for the wrongs she's committed. A mysterious intruder silently enters the room through a secret panel, knocks Bannon unconscious and carries Freeman away. Bannon and Yarborough race to the mausoleum where they find her body. Freeman had died of shock. They enter the secret passageway and find a room with a doll used to torment Morley. Suddenly, the door is closed and barred. Again, Morley is lured to the mausoleum, followed by Donnell. They are confronted by Graff, who tells them that he killed Bell and now plans to kill them. Jackson frees Bannon and Yarborough. Bannon and Yarborough prevent the murders and, with Jackson's help, capture Graff. In Graff's pocket is the missing will. Freeman's wish is for Morley to find happiness and love with Wilcox and Donnell and live in the mansion.

Notes and Commentary: The working title was "The Coffin." The screenplay was based on Malcolm Stuart Boylan's radio play, *Faith, Hope and Charity Sisters*.

During his fourteen-year career, Robert Stevens was also billed as Robert Kellard. He was known to avid serial enthusiasts as the young hero in *Drums of Fu Manchu* (Republic, 1940) and the star of *Perils of the Royal Mounted* (Columbia, 1942) and *Tex Granger* (Columbia, 1948).

Reviews: "A familiar brew of chills and thrills." *The Columbia Story*, Hirshhorn

"The story is filled with all the things that are guaranteed to make audiences jump out of their seats." *Motion Picture Guide*, Nash and Ross

"The film shapes up as effective spine-tingling fare for the horror hounds." *Variety*, 07/24/46

Summation: This time out, the series turns to a gothic mystery story, with an old Southern mansion complete with secret passageways, secret rooms, sliding walls and a secret kept from the outside world. This results in another entertaining story. The cast performs well with Jim Bannon and Barton Yarborough in top form. Karen Morley is a standout as the mentally disturbed mother with problems only true love can cure. Henry Levin guides the story firmly aided by the fine camerawork of cinematographer Henry Freulich.

Inspector Trent

Inspector Steve Trent was Columbia's third try at a mystery series. This time, instead of using established characters familiar to movie going audiences, an original character was scripted. Screenwriter Robert Quigley was responsible for the first film, with Harold Shumate taking over for the final three. Columbia picked Ralph Bellamy to play the brilliant detective. Bellamy was a workaholic, having appeared in 23 feature films for various studios since his first screen appearance in 1931. Usually appearing as the second lead, Bellamy did manage to snag the lead in a few films, one of which was *Parole Girl* (Columbia, 1933). In the first of the Trent series, *Before Midnight* (Columbia, 1933), the detective was in New York State but, by the third, *The Crime of Helen Stanley*, he had moved to Hollywood. There were no other regulars in the series, although lovely Shirley Grey was Bellamy's leading lady in the final three.

BEFORE MIDNIGHT
Columbia (November 1933)

Murder by the clock!

Cast: Trent, Ralph Bellamy; Janet, June Collyer; Fry, Claude Gillingwater; Smith, Bradley Page; Mavis, Betty Blythe; Doctor, Arthur Pierson; Stubby, George Cooper; Arnold, William Jeffrey; Captain Flynn, Joseph Crehan; Kono, Otto Yamaoka// Taxi Driver, Fred Toones; Harry Graham, Edward LeSaint; Housekeeper, Mary Foy, Plainclothes detective, Bob Kortman; Jack, Kit Guard

Credits: Director, Lambert Hillyer; Screenwriter, Robert Quigley; Editor, Otto Meyer; Cinematographer, John Stumar

Production Dates: October 5, 1933–October 17, 1933

Running Time: 63 min.

Story: Inspector Ralph Bellamy is called to William Jeffrey's estate. Jeffery writes a check for Betty Blythe, who is waiting anxiously to leave. Jeffrey tells Bellamy he's marked for murder and, within minutes, he falls to the floor. Doctor Arthur Pierson had come to the estate to see Jeffrey's ward, June Collyer. Pierson and Collier are in love but Jeffrey blocked their marriage. Pierson tells Bellamy that Jeffrey died of heart failure. Bellamy disagrees and proves Jeffrey was killed by an injection of a poison in the bloodstream. Bellamy finds that Jeffrey and Claude Gillingwater, Blythe's husband, have been close friends for 15 years. Blythe didn't love Gillingwater and she hated Jeffrey. She received money to leave the estate. Jeffrey's lawyer, Bradley Page, sneaks into the house and takes a diary. Collyer learns that she's the primary heir to Jeffrey's estate. Bellamy deduces that, prior to returning to the States from China, Gillingwater and Jeffrey switched identities. Gillingwater had a fear of a curse that followed the family. Houseboy Otto Yamoaka starts to tell Bellamy the murderer's identity when a knife in his back silences him. Blythe knows that Page has the diary and retrieves it at gunpoint. As she leaves his office, plainclothes detective Bob Kortman takes the diary and sees that it reaches Bellamy. After reading the diary, Bellamy knows the motive. Investigating Jeffrey's desk, Bellamy finds an ink pen with a poisoned needle. He calls Gillingwater and has him use the pen; he tells him that the poison has been removed from the pen. Gillingwater confesses that he murdered Jeffrey because Jeffrey and Page were blackmailing him. Also, Jeffrey planned to murder Gillingwater and then blackmail Collyer. Gillingwater doesn't want his case to come to trial because contents of the diary that belonged to Collyer's mother will be read in court. Bellamy leaves the room, knowing there's a loaded gun in a desk drawer. A shot is heard. Gillingwater has committed suicide. Bellamy burns the diary to conceal the fact that Gillingwater was Collyer's father without benefit of clergy. Later, Collyer and Pierson wed.

Notes and Commentary: In the Canadian television series, *Wind at My Back* (Canadian Broadcasting Corporation, 1996–01), which is set in the Depression era, *Before Midnight* is playing at a local movie theater. This happens in the episode, "New Directions," which first aired March 21, 1999.

Reviews: "No names to attract and double murder plot is unconvincing. Bellamy tries hard as the detective but doesn't succeed." *Variety*, 1/16/34

"A tale of double murder and mayhem, told confusingly in flashback." *The Columbia Story*, Hirshhorn

"Run-of-the-mill mystery with some confusing flashbacks." *Motion Picture Guide*, Nash and Ross

Summation: A convoluted but entertaining murder mystery. Of course, we have a mysterious murder weapon, plenty of suspects and a couple of novel twists. The acting is par for the course, Ralph Bellamy is likable, but postures a little too much. Director Lambert Hillyer keeps the story moving steadily to a satisfactory conclusion.

ONE IS GUILTY
Columbia (March 1934)

Hair-trigger suspense! Startling thrills! Intriguing romance!

Cast: Inspector Trent, Ralph Bellamy; Sally Grey, Shirley Grey; Walters, Warren Hymer; Lola Deveroux, Rita La Roy; Jack Allen, J. Carrol Naish; Toledo Eddie, Wheeler Oakman; Miss Mabel Kane, Ruth Abbott; Wells Deveroux, Willard Robertson; Pop Dailey, Ralph Remley; William Malcolm, Vincent Sherman; Danny, Harry Todd// Coroner, Sam Flint, Waiter, Frank Yaconelli

Credits: Director, Lambert Hillyer; Supervisor, Irving Briskin; Story and Screenplay, Harold Shumate; Cinematography, John Stumar

Production Dates: December 5, 1933–December 17, 1933

Running Time: 63 min.

Story: A boxing champion is found murdered in an empty apartment. In his possession is a letter to his manager, J. Carrol Naish, and some ladies jewelry. Inspector Ralph Bellamy is called in to investigate and finds a ladies scarf and a lipstick-stained cigarette butt. Bellamy's initial suspect is Shirley Grey, who has an apartment in the building. He catches Rita La Roy, wife of apartment owner Willard Robertson, sneaking into the apartment. La Roy admits that the scarf and cigarette butt belong to her. Bellamy goes to the apartment of the murdered man's girlfriend, Ruth Abbott, and finds Naish visiting Abbott. Naish and Abbott provide alibis that do not match. Bellamy goes back to the murdered man's apartment and finds a theater ticket stub. A mysterious intruder attacks Bellamy and knocks him out. Bellamy remembers the seat number and police begin looking for those who attended the performance. Naish is murdered, and a lipstick-stained cigarette butt is found near the body. Further questioning of La Roy reveals that she was having an affair with the murdered man but denies killing him. Police question a theater patron who remembers the man who had the seat in question had a wrist watch that was missing the minute hand. That watch belongs to Robertson. Bellamy accuses Robertson of murdering the fighter out of jealousy and killing Naish because he discovered Robertson was the killer. Robertson attempts to escape, bur Bellamy apprehends him.

Notes and Commentary: The working title was "Murder at Rexford Arms."

Reviews: "Simple detective mystery. One of the Inspector Trent series with Ralph Bellamy. Neatly done." *Variety*, 5/29/34

"A run-of-the-mill detective yarn." *The Columbia Story*, Hirshhorn

"Evenly paced schemer, which manages a few thrills to keep the suspense flowing." *Motion Picture Guide*, Nash and Ross

Summation: This film was not available for viewing by the author.

THE CRIME OF HELEN STANLEY
Columbia (April 1934)

Lights! Camera! Murder!

Cast: Trent, Ralph Bellamy; Betty, Shirley Grey; Helen Stanley, Gail Patrick; Lee Davis, Kane Richmond; George Noel, Bradley Page; Karl Williams, Vincent Sherman; Larry King, Clifford Jones; Jimmy, Arthur Rankin; Gibson, Lucien Prival; Jack Baker, Ward Bond; Jessie, Helen Eby-Rock// Wallach, Alden Chase; Doctor, William Humphrey; Richardson, Edward Keane; Reilly, Hal Price; Ballistic expert, Frank O'Connor; Police radio operator, Lee Shumway; Electrician, Edmund Cobb; O'Hara, Robert Paige

Credits: Director, D. Ross Lederman; Story, Charles R. Condon; Screenwriter, Harold Shumate; Editor, Otto Meyer; Cinematographer, Al Siegler

Production Dates: March 2, 1934–March 13, 1934

Running Time: 58 min.

Story: Movie star Gail Patrick threatens to have her ex-lover, Kane Richmond, removed as cameraman for her new picture because he plans to marry her sister, Shirley Grey. Patrick's manager, Bradley Page, needs to explain what he's done with $60,000 or he will be fired. Feeling threatened, Patrick asks Inspector Ralph Bellamy to come to the studio. Patrick has a scene in which she's to be shot with a blank but a real bullet is fired, ending Patrick's life. Grey goes to Patrick's house to search for her diary. Bellamy arrests Richmond for the crime, but when he finds that Richmond and Grey are already married, he releases him. Grey finds the diary, but a mysterious intruder attacks her, and the diary is stolen. Cameraman Ward

Bond discovers how the murder was committed but is killed before he can speak to Bellamy. The diary is found in the possession of Patrick's bodyguard, Vincent Sherman. Bellamy decides to reconstruct the scene of the crime. Bellamy asks a studio employee, Clifford Jones, to take Patrick's role. Jones falls to the floor as a bullet sails over his head. A camera had been rigged so that, after a certain number of resolutions, a bullet would be fired. From the diary Bellamy learns that Patrick caused a former director to commit suicide. Jones had sworn vengeance because the director was his brother. Bellamy arrests Jones for the murders.

Notes and Commentary: The working title was "Murder in the Studio."

The Crime of Helen Stanley was remade as *Who Killed Gail Preston* (Columbia, 1938) with Don Terry and Rita Hayworth. *Preston* was set in a nightclub instead of a movie studio. Columbia tried to disguise the remake as an original screen story, "Murder in Swingtime" by Henry Taylor. Taylor borrowed from the original almost scene for scene.

Reviews: "Standard pattern murder mystery. Ralph Bellamy gets little chance as the detective, but a better break than the others. That's not very much." *Variety,* 8/21/34

"Preposterous thriller." *The Columbia Story,* Hirshhorn

"Poor murder mystery." *Motion Picture Guide,* Nash and Ross

Summation: This is a subpar murder-mystery. Most of the acting is poor. Even Ralph Bellamy is not up to his usual high standard.

GIRL IN DANGER

Columbia (August 1934)

Excitement! Adventure! She staked all — just for a thrill!

Cast: Inspector Trent, Ralph Bellamy; Gloria Gale, Shirley Grey; Mike Russo, J. Carrol Naish; Dan Torrence, Charles Sabin; Beckett, Arthur Hohl// Wynkoski, Ward Bond; Chief O'Brien, Edward LeSaint; Willie Tolini, Vincent Sherman; Tony, Francis McDonald; Thornton, Edward Keane; Rollins, Pat O'Malley; Secretary, Geneva Mitchell; Waiter, Frank Yaconelli; Headwaiter, Steve Clark

Credits: Director, D. Ross Lederman; Screenwriter, Harold Shumate; Editor, Otto Meyer; Cinematographer, Benjamin Kline

Production Dates: June 4, 1934–June 13, 1934

Running Time: 57 min.

Story: Thrill-seeking socialite Shirley Grey helps gangster Charles Sabin steal the Cortez Emerald. The jewel is left with Grey, and one of Sabin's men is set to retrieve it the next day. Inspector Ralph Bellamy calls on Grey. She thinks Bellamy works for Sabin and goes with him to a nightclub. During this time, police search Grey's apartment for the emerald. Sabin sees Grey with Bellamy and is able to tell her who Bellamy really is. Grey promises to give the jewel to Bellamy but slips away. Sabin is killed by underworld boss J. Carrol Naish who believes Sabin is double-crossing him. Naish's henchman, Vincent Sherman, kidnaps Grey. Then Grey is sent back to her apartment to retrieve the emerald. Bellamy is in the apartment, waiting. Grey gives Bellamy the jewel. Naish shows up, shoots Bellamy and takes Grey and the emerald to his hideout. Newspapers report Bellamy's murder. Russo has his lawyer, Arthur Hohl, make a deal with the insurance company to return the emerald for $250,000. A meeting is set at a roadhouse. Bellamy, who was not killed, is waiting and

Girl in Danger (1934) scene card —(left) Ralph Bellamy, Shirley Grey, (center), (left to right) Rita La Roy, Frank Yaconelli, Ralph Bellamy.

arrests Naish, Sherman and Hohl. Bellamy learns that Grey is a captive and will be killed if Naish is arrested. As the gangsters are getting ready to kill her, Bellamy and the police arrive. For her help in apprehending Naish and his gang, Grey will not be prosecuted. Grey tells Bellamy her thrill-seeking days are over.

Notes and Commentary: The working title was "By Persons Unknown."

Reviews: "Double feature candidate on racketeering. Mild under average screen diversion. Ralph Bellamy smoothly carries out Inspector Trent." *Variety*, 11/6/34

"Ralph Bellamy starred in *Girl in Danger* though really, in truth, it was the audiences who are really in danger; of dying of boredom." *The Columbia Story*, Hirshhorn

"A second-rate entry in the popular Inspector Trent series." *Motion Picture Guide*, Nash and Ross

Summation: This film was not available for viewing by the author.

Jess Arno

With the Ellery Queen series discontinued, Columbia still had William Gargan and Margaret Lindsay under contract. A decision was made to create a new series for them. Eric Taylor, who was the screenwriter for the Queen series, got the assignment. The new series would feature Jess Arno (a.k.a. the Front Page Detective) and his fiancée, June Terry. In the course of solving the crime, the couple would have misunderstandings, verbally sparring with each other before having their relationship on course by the picture's end. The first picture, *No Place for a Lady*, would be the last in the series for Gargan and Lindsay. Gargan would move on to a new series, Night Editor, and Lindsay would be assigned to Crime Doctor. In 1949, Jess Arno would be resurrected, not as a private detective, but as an insurance investigator. Again, Eric Taylor was the screenwriter. Warner Baxter, late of the Crime Doctor series, played Arno. The film, *The Devil's Henchman*, was a decided improvement over the Gargan effort. But this was the last Arno feature. (Saddled with arthritis, Baxter would make two more "B" features before undergoing a lobotomy procedure to relieve the pain. Due to complications, Baxter died of pneumonia.)

No Place for a Lady
Columbia (February 1943)

Maybe Woman's Place Is In The Home.... But not In The Cellar ... murder!

Cast: Jess Arno, William Gargan; June Terry, Margaret Lindsay; Dolly Adair, Phyllis Brooks; Randy Brooke, Dick Purcell; Eddie Moore, Jerome Cowan; Mario, Edward Norris; Moriarity, James Burke; Wembley, Frank Thomas; Captain Baker, Thomas Jackson; Evelyn Harris, Doris Lloyd; Thomas, William Hunter; Yvonne, Chester Clute// Hartley, Emmett Vogan; Hal, Ralph Sanford; Jules, Eddie Kane; Reporter, Dennis Moore; Air raid warden, Tom London

Credits: Director, James Hogan; Story and Screenwriter, Eric Taylor; Editor, Dwight Caldwell; Art Director, Richard Irvine; Cinematographer, James S. Brown; Music Director, Lee Zahler

Song: "A Cottage by the Sea" (Grossman and Hegyl) sung by Jerome Cowan

Production Dates: September 2, 1942–September 16, 1942

Running Time: 66 min.

Story: Tire factory owner Doris Lloyd, along with her boyfriend, nightclub singer Jerome Cowan, and henchman Edward Norris, are involved in a scheme by nightclub owner Frank Thomas to take over a shipment of tires. The tires are replaced with worn-out used

No Place for a Lady (1943) movie still — (left to right) William Gargan, Margaret Lindsay, Dick Purcell.

ones, which are subsequently destroyed in an arson fire. Lloyd received $50,000 and plans to go with Cowan to New York. En route, Cowan stops at deserted beach cottage belonging to private investigator William Gargan. Gargan decides to bring along his current client, Phyllis Brooks, to the displeasure of Gargan's fiancée, Margaret Lindsay. In the cellar, Gargan discovers Lloyd's body. When the police arrive, the body is missing. Gargan focuses on Cowan and follows him to his apartment where he finds the money. Gargan is told that Thomas was behind the scheme, and where Lloyd's body was moved. Cowan overpowers Gargan. He tries to escape but is murdered by Thomas and Norris. Gargan goes to Thomas's nightclub and demands $15,000. Lindsay interrupts Gargan's confrontation with Thomas and Norris. Gargan sends Lindsay away. Lindsay realizes Gargan is in trouble and goes to the police. In the meantime, he is able to capture Thomas and Norris. Gargan and Lindsay plan to finally marry.

Notes and Commentary: The *Hollywood Reporter* stated that this was to be the first of a new series. The picture was not successful and the series was discontinued. The character Jess Arno would show up six years later in *The Devil's Henchman.*

The working title was "Thirteen Steps to Heaven."

Jerome Cowan mouths the words of *A Cottage by the Sea,* it is evident that his voice was dubbed.

Throughout the film, Gargan is referred to as the "Front Page Detective" four different times. One statement notes that Gargan "is known to local officers as the Front Page Detective."

The author's guess is this is how the series would be known had the initial episode been successful.

Reviews: "*No Place for a Lady* was no film for the connoisseur. A threadbare mystery which kept audiences wondering why they'd bothered to waste their time and money on it." *The Columbia Story*, Hirschhorn

"A murder mystery of mediocre quality." *Variety*, 05/26/43

Summation: This is an okay but undistinguished murder-mystery. William Gargan and the lovely Margaret Lindsay make acceptable leads but, in the end, screenwriter Eric Taylor lets the principals down, with too much unfunny comedy. Having Gargan hide in a stack of tires and be able to freely move around seems more appropriate in a Three Stooges comedy than in a serious murder mystery.

THE DEVIL'S HENCHMEN
Columbia (September 1949)

Terror prowls the port of thieves where law and murder clash!

Cast: Jess Arno, Warner Baxter; Silky, Mary Beth Hughes; Rhino, Mike Mazurki; Connie, Peggy Converse; Tip Banning, Regis Toomey; Captain, Harry Shannon; Sergeant Briggs, James Flavin// Murray, Julian Rivero; Bill Falls, Paul Marion; May, Ann Lawrence; Baggy, George Lloyd; Dock police guard, Lee Phelps; Detective Whalen, Ken Christy; Anderson, William Forrest; Elmer Hood, Al Bridge; Sailor, Ethan Laidlaw

Credits: Director, Seymour Friedman; Producer, Rudolph C. Flothow; Screenwriter, Eric Taylor; Editor, Richard Fantl; Art Director, Harold MacArthur; Set Decorator, James Crowe; Cinematography, Henry Freulich; Musical Director, Mischa Bakaleinikoff

Production Dates: October 21, 1948–November 3, 1948

Running Time: 68 min.

Story: Warner Baxter is selling salvage, supposedly plucked out of the harbor, to Regis Toomey. Toomey and Mary Beth Hughes are mixed up in a scheme, selling stolen furs being transported by freighters. The owner of a waterfront café, Peggy Converse, wants to be cut in on the racket. One ship's third mate, Paul Marion, wants a larger cut for his participation. Toomey has Hughes escort Marion to a deserted warehouse where she is murdered. Baxter was following Marion and is accosted by strong man Mike Mazurki. Baxter thinks fast and becomes friends with Mazurki. When Toomey learns Baxter has a third mate's paper, he wants Baxter to work for him. Baxter is an insurance investigator trying to find out who is stealing cargo from the ships. He theorizes that the switch is happening at sea. Baxter's contact person is Julian Rivero, an organ grinder, who is leaving notes in his pet monkey's hat. Captain Harry Shannon, a customer at the café, believes he knows Baxter from the past. With police investigating Marion's murder, Toomey decides they'll make one last haul and leave the area. Investigating, Baxter believes the stolen cargo is being brought into Al Bridge's shop. Baxter is picked to participate in the heist but Mazurki is ordered to stay with Baxter. Needing to get information to the authorities, Baxter purchases Rivero's monkey. Baxter puts a note in the monkey's cap, but Converse intercepts the note. The brains behind the operation is Harry Shannon. Shannon accompanies Baxter and Mazurki, and the heist goes off without a problem. Arriving at Bridge's shop, Baxter is surprised that the authorities aren't present. Suddenly the police arrive: there is an exchange of bullets; Mazurki is killed

The Devil's Henchmen (1949) title card — (left) Warner Baxter, (lower left center) Mary Beth Hughes, (right, center) Mike Mazurki, (lower right, left to right) James Flavin, Ken Christy, Warner Baxter (kneeling), unidentified actor, Mary Beth Hughes, Regis Toomey, Al Bridge (hat only), Harry Shannon, unidentified actor, Mike Mazurki (bottom of scene with hands raised).

and the rest of the gang is arrested. Converse had taken the note to the police. Her husband had been killed by the gang a few years back, and she was trying to bring the gang to justice. Baxter and Converse plan to see each other socially.

Notes and Commentary: A *Variety* reviewer incorrectly identifies the film as the "latest in the Crime Doctor series."

Reviews: "A decent programmer." *Motion Picture Guide*, Nash and Ross

"The action, and there's plenty of it, is centered on seashore and shipping and gives out with enough suspense and capable acting to rate a good secondary spot on the double bill in first run houses." *Variety*, 07/23/52

Summation: This is a good "B" mystery. Warner Baxter, in his first role after the completion of the Crime Doctor series, seems comfortable in the role of Jess Arno. Some familiar faces of lower budget features have prominent parts, and all perform capably. Seymour Friedman's direction provides both the necessary pace and resulting suspense. This is a decided improvement of the previous Arno caper, *No Place for a Lady* (Columbia, 1943).

Jungle Jim

The Jungle Jim comic strip was created by pulp writer Don Moore and illustrator Alex Raymond, creator of the comic strip *Flash Gordon*. Jungle Jim Bradley was a gentleman adventurer who became a true friend of all good men and a relentless enemy of all bad men, no matter their race or creed. He was aided by his huge native friend, Kolu. The strip made its debut on January 7, 1934, as a topper to Flash Gordon, also making its debut in the comic strips. (A topper was a comic strip that appeared at the top of the page of a major strip. This was a common practice at the time.) Even though popular, *Jungle Jim* would be a Sunday-only strip and never appeared in the daily papers.

The *Jungle Jim* comic strip was so popular that it spawned a radio program. The program came into being in a most unusual fashion. On October 12, 1935, the radio program, *The Amazing Interplanetary Adventures of Flash Gordon*, became *The Adventures of Flash Gordon and Jungle Jim*. Flash Gordon, Dale Arden and Zarkov crash land in the Malaysian jungles and meet Jim, Kolu and Reverend Chalmers. On the October 26th program, Chalmers performs the marriage ceremony that makes Flash and Dale man and wife. The following week, on November 2, 1935, *The Adventures of Jungle Jim* aired. Jim was played by Matt Crowley (except for a short stint by Gerald Mohr) through the duration of the show. Kolu was played by Juano Hernandez and the sinister but lovely femme fatale Shanghai Lil (Lille DeVrille) was played first by Vicki Vola and then Franc Hale. This 15-minute radio program was very popular and had its final broadcast on August 1, 1954. Jungle Jim was also featured in two Whitman Big Little Books, *Jungle Jim* (1936) and *Jungle Jim and the Vampire Woman* (1937). Jim appeared in comic books, Ace Comics reprinted stories from the comic strip. From 1949 to 1951, Standard Comics published 11 original comic books. From Dell, 20 issues appeared from 1953 to 1959. One was issued by King Features in 1967, a reprint of a Dell comic. The final comic book run for Jim consisted of seven issues published by Charlton between 1969–70.

Jim came to the silver screen in *Jungle Jim* (Universal, 1937), a 12-chapter serial with Grant Withers in the lead. In the cast were Evelyn Brent as Shanghai Lil, Al Duvall as Kolu and Paul Sutton as LaBat, a despicable, vicious character who loved Lil.

Jim would again come to the movie screen in the feature film, *Jungle Jim* (Columbia, 1948) with Johnny Weissmuller in the title role. The faithful Kolu, played by Rick Vallin, was only in the initial entry. For the first four entries, Weissmuller had as his companions, Skipper, the dog, and Caw Caw, a crow. In the fifth feature, *Pygmy Island* (Columbia, 1950), Weissmuller's only companion was his chimpanzee, Tamba. Unlike the Jungle Jim of the comic strips who brandished a .45 automatic, Weissmuller's choice of weapons was his knife. It was now complete; Weissmuller really *was* Tarzan with clothes on. (Weissmuller had been an Olympic swimming champion, winning five gold medals and one bronze during the 1920s. In 1932, Metro-Goldwyn-Mayer had signed him to a seven-year contract to play the Lord of the Jungle, Tarzan. He made six films. In 1942, the series moved to RKO, and through 1946, Weissmuller made six addition Tarzan features before the decision was made to replace him. A younger, slimmer Tarzan was wanted.) Weissmuller had completed 13 Jungle Jim films before Columbia sold the rights to the character to their television subsidiary, Screen Gems. Screen Gems refused to allow their parent company to use the name Jungle Jim, so in the last three films remaining on his contract, Weissmuller would simply play Johnny Weissmuller. The name of Weissmuller's pet chimp had been changed to Kimba. With the screen ventures ended, Weissmuller was cast as Jim in the television series. He now had a son, Skipper, played by Martin Huston; Kaseem, who was played by Norman Fredric, later known as Dean Fredericks; and a pet chimp, Tamba. Only 26 episodes were filmed, but they were rerun constantly through the '50s.

JUNGLE JIM
Columbia (December 1948)

Adventure idol of millions ... on the screen at last!

Cast: Jungle Jim, Johnny Weissmuller; Dr. Hilary Parker, Virginia Grey; Bruce Edwards, George Reeves; Zia, Lita Baron; Kolu, Rick Vallin; Commissioner Geoffrey Marsden, Holmes Herbert// "Skipper"; Caw-Caw, Jimmy the Crow; Frightened native, Neyle Morrow; Chief Devil Doctor, Tex Mooney

Credits: Director, William Berke; Producer, Sam Katzman; Story and Screenplay, Carroll Young; Editor, Aaron Stell; Art Director, Paul Palmentola; Set Decorator, Sidney Clifford; Cinematographer, Lester White; Musical Director, Mischa Bakaleinikoff

Location Filming: Corriganville and Los Angeles County Arboretum & Botanic Garden, California

Production Dates: August 5, 1948–August 19, 1948

Running Time: 73 min.

Source: Based upon the newspaper feature *Jungle Jim*, owned and copyrighted by King Features Syndicate, and which appears regularly in "Puck" the comic weekly.

Story: Seeing a frightened native, Neyle Morrow, Johnny Weissmuller goes to his aid. Before Weissmuller can reach Morrow, a tiger mauls him. In the dead man's hand is a gold vial, with strange markings, containing a sticky black substance. This find sparks an archaeological expedition headed by Dr. Virginia Grey and guided by Weissmuller. The strange markings on the vial indicate that it came from the temple of Zimbalu, which is rumored to hold great treasures. Most importantly, the mysterious substance, though deadly in large doses, may be a cure for infantile paralysis. The safari encounters an elephant stampede and falling rocks. Weissmuller booby-traps their camp and jungle photographer George Reeves is caught in one of the snares. Grey, needing a photographer, asks Reeves to accompany the expedition. Through Reeves's "carelessness," Weissmuller nearly meets death twice. As the party nears the temple, Reeves quietly slips away. The entire party is captured by the devil doctors of the temple except for Weissmuller and his pet crow, Jimmy. The devil doctors consider Reeves a god because he can take their pictures. Weissmuller comes to the temple to rescue his friends. Reeves has put his camera down to steal the treasure, and mischievous Jimmy the Crow steals the lens from the camera. Chief Devil Doctor Tex Mooney wants his picture taken. When Reeves can't comply, the devil doctors become angry and Reeves is forced to flee. During the commotion, Weissmuller frees his friends. Reeves makes a last attempt to retrieve the treasure, but is killed by two devil doctors. Weissmuller and his party overpower the remaining devil doctors. With the valuable drug and the treasure safely in hand, Weissmuller is off to new adventures.

Notes and Commentary: Virginia Grey was Johnny Weissmuller's leading lady in *Swamp Fire* (Paramount, 1946).

Skipper the dog and Jimmy the crow appeared in *Enchanted Valley* (Eagle-Lion, 1947).

To simplify matters it seems, producer Sam Katzman dropped Jungle Jim's sir name of Bradley.

Kolu, Jim's companion in the comic strips, radio and in the serial, *Jungle Jim* (Universal, 1937), is dropped after this initial entry.

Reviews: "First in the string of successful Saturday matinee films." *Motion Picture Guide*, Nash and Ross

"'Jungle Jim' is completely juvenile and for that reason should get by in the Saturday matinee market." *Variety*, 12/22/48

Summation: This is a good beginning to the Jungle Jim series. Johnny Weissmuller is fine as Jungle Jim and he receives good support from Virginia Grey and George Reeves. Director William Berke paces the film nicely, even generating suspense in some of the scenes. Kudos to cinematographer Lester White, who is able to give the perception of depth in many of jungle scenes. Only negatives are the obvious padding in a scene with Skipper the dog with a chimpanzee and a dance sequence with the lovely Lita Baron. On second thought, maybe the latter wasn't a bad idea for the adult males in the audience after all.

THE LOST TRIBE
Columbia (May 1949)

Jungle Jim's mightiest adventure!

Cast: Jungle Jim, Johnny Weissmuller; Norina, Myrna Dell; Li Wanna, Elena Verdugo; Calhoun, Joseph Vitale; Captain Rawlins, Ralph Dunn; Chot, Paul Marion; Zoron, Nelson Leigh; Wilson, George J. Lewis// "Skipper," Caw Caw, Jimmy the Crow; Narrator, Holmes Herbert; Avery, Lee Roberts; Welker, Wally West; Zulta, Jody Gilbert; Dojek, Gil Perkins; Lerch, Charles Schaeffer; Kesler, John Merton

Credits: Director, William Berke; Producer, Sam Katzman; Story, Arthur Hoerl; Screenwriters, Arthur Hoerl and Don Martin; Editor, Aaron Stell; Art Director, Paul Palmentola; Set Decorator, Sidney Clifford; Cinematographer, Ira H. Morgan; Musical Director, Mischa Bakaleinikoff

Location Filming: Corriganville, California

Production Dates: September 8, 1948–September 20, 1948

Running Time: 72 min.

Source: Based upon the newspaper feature *Jungle Jim* owned and copyrighted by King Features Syndicate, and which appears regularly in "Puck" the comic weekly.

Story: Paul Marion, son of Nelson Leigh, leader of the people of Dzamm, has fallen in love with an outsider, Myrna Dell, from a nearby coastal settlement. Marion has told Dell about the riches of Dzamm. Dell is working with Joseph Vitale and Captain Ralph

Dunn to find the way to Dzamm so they can plunder their treasures. Learning that outsiders know of their riches, Leigh's daughter, Elena Verdugo, is sent to find Johnny Weissmuller. Leigh wants Weissmuller to take diamonds to Vitale and Dunn in hopes that they will leave Dzamm alone. Vitale and Dunn capture Verdugo when she comes to the settlement. Weissmuller attempts to rescue her, but both are captured. To prevent Verdugo from being tortured, Weissmuller agrees to lead Vitale, Dunn and their men to Dzamm. The men arrive in Dzamm and begin looting the temple. Through Weissmuller's pet crow, Jimmy, a tribe of gorillas is summoned to Dzamm to help Weissmuller. The gorillas decimate the invaders. Weissmuller leaves Dzamm for other adventures.

Notes and Commentary: The working title was "Jungle Jim's Adventure."

Paul Stader was Johnny Weissmuller's double.

An interesting tidbit: in a few websites, George J. Lewis's character is listed as Whip Wilson. At no time in the film is Lewis addressed as Whip, nor does Lewis ever use a whip.

Reviews: "Par for the jungle course." *The Columbia Story*, Hirschhorn

"Kids will enjoy this pre-Raiders of the Lost Ark adventure." *Motion Picture Guide*, Nash and Ross

"Action-packed, surefire entertainment for youthful filmgoers." *Variety*, 04/20/49

Summation: This is an exciting, fast-moving Jungle Jim adventure. Johnny Weissmuller is in fine form as the hero. The rest of the cast performs adequately. Director William Berke keeps the story continuously on the move.

MARK OF THE GORILLA
Columbia (February 1950)

Johnny snatches jungle beauty from gold-looting gorilla-men!

Cast: Jungle Jim, Johnny Weissmuller; Barbara Bentley, Trudy Marshall; Nyobi, Suzanne Dalbert; Brandt, Onslow Stevens; Kramer, Robert Purcell; Gibbs, Pierce Lyden; Head ranger, Neyle Morrow; Warden Bentley, Selmer Jackson// "Skipper"; Caw Caw, Jimmy the Crow; Narrator, Holmes Herbert

Credits: Director, William Berke; Producer, Sam Katzman; Screenwriter, Carroll Young; Editor, Henry Batista; Art Director, Paul Palmentola; Set Decorator, George Montgomery; Cinematographer, Ira H. Morgan; Unit Manager, Herbert Leonard; Musical Director, Mischa Bakaleinikoff

Location Filming: Corriganville and Bronson Canyon, California

Production Dates: September 14, 1949–September 23, 1949

Running Time: 69 min.

Source: Based upon the newspaper feature *Jungle Jim*, owned and copyrighted by King Features Syndicate, and which appears regularly in "Puck" the comic weekly.

Story: Alerted by Jimmy the Crow, Johnny Weissmuller finds a dead ranger from the wild game preserve and a letter addressed to him from Warden Selmer Jackson. En route to the wild game preserve headquarters, Weissmuller rescues Suzanne Dalbert from a gorilla attack. At park headquarters, he finds Jackson is seriously ill and is being treated by Onslow Stevens. Jackson tells Weissmuller that Nazi soldiers stole $1 million in gold bullion from the country of Shalikari and that the gold was hidden somewhere on the game preserve. Stevens, the leader of a gang digging for the stolen gold, has three of his men dress as gorillas to scare natives away. Stevens has henchman Robert Purcell murder Jackson. Weissmuller,

Mark of the Gorilla (1950) scene card — Johnny Weissmuller, Trudy Marshall.

Jackson's niece, Trudy Marshall, Suzanne Dalbert and park rangers try to locate the murderer. At the last minute, Stevens joins the party, which pleases Weissmuller, since he suspects Stevens of duplicity. Stevens is able to capture Weissmuller, Marshall and Dalbert and readies for his getaway when rangers show up. A ferocious gunfight ensues, with many casualties on both sides. Weissmuller, thanks to help form Jimmy the Crow, is able to get free of his bonds and overcome his captors. Seeing the rangers will win, Stevens tries to escape with some of the gold bullion. Weissmuller gives chase and causes him to fall to his death. Dalbert turns out to be the princess of Shalikari, and the gold bullion will be returned to her country.

Notes and Commentary: An interesting bit of dialogue is uttered by Johnny Weissmuller to villain Onslow Stevens, "Brant, I'm going to kill you." This is not typical in a "B" film based on a comic strip character.

Reviews: "Far-fetched screenplay." *The Columbia Story*, Hirshhorn

"Performances are convincing, with good production, considering the modest budget." *Motion Picture Guide*, Nash and Ross

"Followers of the cartoon series from which it has been fashioned, will find it exciting." *Variety*, 02/22/50

Summation: Overall, this is a good, entertaining Jungle Jim adventure, once you get through some unnecessary padding at the film's start. First, there is a sequence documenting wildlife in Africa and secondly, a comedy sequence with a chimpanzee stealing fish from Johnny Weissmuller, adding a interfering lion and ending with Weissmuller's dog, Skipper, biting the lion's tail. Weissmuller is good in the hero's role, delivering some lines with a welcome harshness not seen in previous outings. Director William Berke is able to pace the film nicely with exciting and suspenseful action sequences, especially the gunfight at the film's climax.

CAPTIVE GIRL
Columbia (July 1950)

Johnny unleashes the jungle's wildest fury to save blonde leopard girl!

Alternate Title: Jungle Jim in Captive Girl

Cast: Jungle Jim, Johnny Weissmuller; Barton, Buster Crabbe; Joan Martindale, Anita Lhoest; Mahala, Rick Vallin; Hakim, John Dehner; Silva, Rusty Westcoatt// "Skipper"; Caw Caw, Jimmy the Crow; "Tamba"; Reverend, Nelson Leigh; Village drummer, Stanley Price; Village elder, Frank Lackteen

Credits: Director, William Berke; Producer, Sam Katzman; Screenwriter, Carroll Young; Editor, Henry Batista; Art Director, Paul Palmentola; Set Decorator, James Crowe; Cinematographer, Ira H. Morgan; Unit Manager, Herbert Leonard; Musical Director, Mischa Bakaleinikoff

Location Filming: Corriganville and Los Angeles County Arboretum & Botanic Garden, California

Production Dates: October 4, 1949–October 13, 1949

Running Time: 73 min.

Source: Based upon the newspaper feature *Jungle Jim*, owned and copyrighted by King Features Syndicate, and which appears regularly in "Puck" the comic weekly.

Story: Johnny Weissmuller learns of a mysterious wild girl, Anita Lhoest, who has been plaguing a tribal witch doctor, John Dehner. It is feared that Dehner will attempt to kill Lhoest. Dehner murdered Lhoest's archaeologist parents. Weissmuller is aided in his quest by tribal chief, Rick Vallin, and his pets, Jimmy (a crow), Skipper (a dog) and Tamba (a chimpanzee). On the trail, Weissmuller meets Buster Crabbe: he and his men are searching for the Lagoon of Death and the treasures it holds. Trailing Lhoest, Weissmuller and Crabbe find the lagoon. Weissmuller continues his search for Lhoest, while Crabbe begins retrieving the treasure. Dehner and his followers confront Crabbe and his men. Both want Lhoest dead: Crabbe, so he can keep the treasure, Dehner, so he won't be arrested and tried for murder. Dehner also wants to kill Vallin to become the chief of the tribe. Dehner captures Lhoest and Vallin, as Weissmuller falls over a cliff and lies unconscious on a rock outcropping. Dehner sends a man to make certain that he is dead, but Skipper and Tamba intervene, saving Weissmuller's life. Dehner throws Lhoest and Vallin to their deaths into the lagoon, but Weissmuller rescues them. In the lagoon, Crabbe is retrieving the treasure and he stops to kill Weissmuller. In the ensuing battle, Crabbe is trapped underwater and drowns. Weissmuller, Vallin and some tribesmen battle Dehner and his followers. In the battle, Dehner also drowns in the lagoon, and his followers are defeated. Lhoest gives Vallin the treasure before returning to relatives in America.

Notes and Commentary: This film boasted three swimming champions: Weissmuller,

Crabbe and Lhoest. Johnny Weissmuller, who won five Olympic gold medals 1924–28. He also won every free style race in which he participated, from 1921–29. He was inducted as a charter member into the Olympic Hall of Fame in 1983.

Buster Crabbe was a gold medal winner in the summer Olympics of 1932. He also won a bronze medal in 1500-meter freestyle at Amsterdam. Anita Lhoest won the national championship in the 100-meter freestyle and set the national record in the 440-meter freestyle event in 1947. She was considered a prospect for the 1948 Olympics.

Buster Crabbe was Johnny Weissmuller's nemesis in *Swamp Fire* (Paramount, 1946).

In the scene in which simians attack John Dehner's followers, footage from *The Jungle Princess* (Paramount, 1936) was utilized.

Though billed as Tamba, the chimpanzee's name was Peggy.

After this film, Skipper and Jimmy the Crow were dropped from the series.

Reviews: "A routine adventure film at best." *Motion Picture Herald*

"For the juve trade, it is satisfactory." *Variety*, 04/19/50

"Usual jungle nonsense made somewhat interesting by the presence of Weissmuller and Crabbe, both former Tarzans, in the same movie." *Motion Picture Guide*, Nash and Ross

Summation: This is a satisfactory Jungle Jim adventure, buoyed by the presence of Buster Crabbe, as the villain. Johnny Weissmuller registers strongly as the hero, while Crabbe relishes his role of Weissmuller's antagonist. Again, the direction is in the capable hands of William Berke, who does well with a routine script. The fine cinematography of Ira H. Morgan is a decided asset.

PYGMY ISLAND
Columbia (November 1950)

Ambush! Pygmy Attack!

Cast: Jungle Jim, Johnny Weissmuller; Captain Ann Kingsley, Ann Savage; Major Bolton, David Bruce; Leon Marko, Steven Geray; Kruger, William Tannen; Novak, Tris Coffin; Makuba, Billy Curtis// "Tamba"; Army officers, Selmer Jackson and Larry Steers; Anders, Rusty Wescoatt; Lucas, Pierce Lyden; Army captain, Tommy Farrell; Kimba, Billy Barty; Henchman with machine gun, Harry Wilson

Credits: Director, William Berke; Producer, Sam Katzman; Screenwriter, Carroll Young; Editor, Jerome Thoms; Art Director, Paul Palmentola; Set Decorator, Sidney Clifford; Cinematographer, Ira H. Morgan; Unit Manager, Herbert Leonard; Musical Director, Mischa Bakaleinikoff

Location Filming: Corriganville and the Los Angeles County Arboretum & Botanic Garden, California

Production Dates: June 5, 1950–June 15, 1950

Running Time: 70 min.

Source: Based upon the newspaper feature *Jungle Jim*, owned and copyrighted by King Features Syndicate, and which appears regularly in "Puck" the comic weekly.

Story: Captain Ann Savage, sent on a confidential mission to find the ngoma plant, mysteriously disappears. The ngoma plant has many military uses and is desired by a foreign power. Major David Bruce is sent with a detail to find Savage, with Johnny Weissmuller as their guide. Savage is living with Billy Curtis's tribe, who saved her from death from Bush

Devils. The Bush Devils are actually henchmen of trader Steven Geray, who is a foreign agent. Savage tries to reach the settlement with Curtis's help. Both almost fall into the hands of Geray, but this is prevented by Weissmuller. It now becomes a race between Geray and Weissmuller to gain control of the ngoma plants. Geray reaches the plants first. Bruce, ignoring Weissmuller's warning, walks into a trap and has to retreat. Weissmuller is captured by Geray and is used as a hostage to allow Geray to escape with the plants. Curtis and his tribe help Weissmuller bring Geray and his gang to justice. Curtis pledges that all the ngoma plants will be a gift to the United States.

Notes and Commentary: Both Billy Curtis and Ann Savage starred in cult classic films. Billy Curtis was the hero in *The Terror of Tiny Town* (Columbia, 1938); Ann Savage was the femme fatale in the film noir classic, *Detour* (PRC, 1945).

With *Pygmy Island*, Tamba became Johnny Weissmuller's only animal companion.

The whistle used by Anita Lhoest in *Captive Girl* is heard in *Pygmy Island*.

Reviews: "Its all routine stuff with the standard amounts of wild beasties, cutthroat bad guys, and uncivilized natives." *Motion Picture Guide*, Nash and Ross

"Mild entry in Johnny Weissmuller's 'Jungle Jim' series." *Variety*, 11/22/50

Summation: This a good Jungle Jim adventure, with plenty of excitement, action and suspense. Johnny Weissmuller is again in fine form as the hero, but how many times do we have to see the same crocodile fight? Weissmuller has a good supporting cast; Steven Geray makes a worthwhile villain; the beautiful Ann Savage is a strong leading lady; and Billy Curtis gives good support as Weissmuller's side-kick. William Berke's direction is up to his usual standard, which makes for good entertainment.

FURY OF THE CONGO
Columbia (February 1951)

Johnny's strangest adventure!

Cast: Jungle Jim, Johnny Weissmuller; Leta, Sherry Moreland; Cameron, William Henry; Grant, Lyle Talbot; Professor Dunham, Joel Friedkin; Barnes, George Eldredge; Magruder, Rusty Westcoatt; Raadi, Paul Marion// "Tamba"; Narrator, James Seay; Mahara, Blance Vischer; Allen, Pierce Lyden; Henchman, John Hart

Credits: Director, William Berke; Producer, Sam Katzman; Screenwriter, Carroll Young; Editor, Richard Fantl; Art Director, Paul Palmentola; Set Decorator, Sidney Clifford; Cinematographer, Ira H. Morgan; Unit Manager, Herbert Leonard; Musical Director, Mischa Bakaleinikoff

Location Filming: Corriganville and Vasquez Rocks, California

Production Dates: late June 1950

Running Time: 69 min.

Source: Based upon the newspaper feature *Jungle Jim*, owned and copyrighted by King Features Syndicate, and which appears regularly in "Puck" the comic weekly.

Story: A plane crashes in the middle of an African lake. Johnny Weissmuller rescues pilot William Henry. Henry tells Weissmuller that he is with the territorial police and is searching for Professor Joel Friedkin. Friedkin is looking for a rare animal, the Okongo, which is the source of a powerful narcotic. Weissmuller and Henry reach the Okongo native village, where a maiden, Sherry Moreland, tells them that evil white men have kidnapped all the Okongo men. Moreland joins Weissmuller and Henry as they now try to find Friedkin, Chief Paul Marion and the Okongo men. Friedkin, a slave to henchmen Lyle Talbot and George Eldredge, is made to extract the valuable narcotic from a certain gland of an Okongo. William Henry is the real leader of the gang. When the gang members and their slaves, the Okongo tribesmen, leave camp to capture the Okongo herd, Friedkin makes his escape. Friedkin falls unconscious at the feet of Weissmuller, Henry and Moreland. Weissmuller leaves the unconscious Friedkin in Henry's care while he scouts ahead. On regaining consciousness, Friedkin recognizes Henry as the leader of the gang. On hearing this, Moreland runs away. Weissmuller tries to free Marion and his men. Weissmuller is captured and made to track the Okongo herd. On the trail, Weissmuller and the Okongo tribesmen make their escape. Moreland and the Okongo women, now armed, return to help free the captives. A pitched battle ensues, with Okongo tribe routing Henry's gang. Weissmuller engages in a bitter hand-to-hand struggle with Henry. In the fight, Henry falls into the path of the stampeding Okongos and is trampled to death. Friedkin and Weissmuller bid goodbye to the Okongo tribes people, with Weissmuller promising to return.

Notes and Commentary: The working title was "Jungle Menace."

Reviews: "A few minor thrills and chills." *The Columbia Story*, Hirschhorn

"Standard jungle genre." *Motion Picture Guide*, Nash and Ross

"Results just get by as programmer fare for the smaller situation." *Variety*, 02/21/51

Summation: This is another okay entry in the Jungle Jim series. Johnny Weissmuller is fine in the lead and receives adequate support from his co-stars. The story is entertaining, but nothing special this time out.

JUNGLE MANHUNT
Columbia (October 1951)

Tom-toms wail the war chant as Johnny wrecks a renegade empire of slaves

Cast: Jungle Jim, Johnny Weissmuller; Bob Miller, Bob Waterfield; Anne Lawrence, Sheila Ryan; Bono, Rick Vallin; Dr. Mitchell Heller, Lyle Talbot; "Tamba"// Maklee chief, Billy Wilkerson; Maklee tribesman, Rusty Westcoatt

Credits: Director, Lew Landers; Producer, Sam Katzman; Screenwriter, Samuel Newman; Editor, Henry Batista; Art Director, Paul Palmentola; Set Decorator, Sidney Clifford; Cinematographer, William Whitley; Musical Director, Mischa Bakaleinikoff

Location Filming: Corriganville and Los Angeles County Arboretum & Botanic Garden, California

Production Dates: early May 1951–mid–May 1951

Running Time: 66 min.

Source: Based upon the newspaper feature *Jungle Jim*, owned and copyrighted by King Features Syndicate, and which appears regularly in "Puck" the comic weekly.

Story: The unfriendly Maklee tribe led by skeleton men and a mysterious white man attacks the Matusa tribe. Chief Rick Vallin is shot, but manages to crawl to safety. The men of the tribe are captured and spirited away. Sheila Ryan, a free-lance photographer, is searching for pilot Bob Waterfield, who has been missing for nine years. Thinking Waterfield might be the mysterious white man, Johnny Weissmuller agrees to help find both the white man and the men of the Matusa tribe. Vallin and Ryan join him in the search. The mysterious white man, Lyle Talbot, forces the captured men to dig for a mysterious ore that possesses radioactive waves. Constant exposure to the radioactivity causes weakness and death. Needing additional men, the skeleton men attack another village where Weissmuller, Vallin and Ryan have stopped to rest. The trio makes their escape, which is successful due to the timely intervention of Waterfield. Waterfield, considered a god in his village, is not interested in aiding Weissmuller until the skeleton men and the Maklee tribe attack his village. In pursuing the skeleton men, Weissmulller, Waterfield, Vallin and Ryan are captured. They learn that Talbot has found a way to convert the radioactive ore into synthetic diamonds. Weissmuller is able to escape and form a battle plan that defeats Talbot's men. Talbot attempts to escape with some of his synthetic diamonds. Weissmuller gives chase. In trying to elude Weissmuller, Talbot falls from a high cliff to his death. Ryan and Waterfield have fallen in love and she will remain in the jungle with him.

Notes and Commentary: This is the first film in which Tamba receives onscreen billing.

The credits state "Introducing Bob Waterfield" when, in fact, he had been one of 11 pro football players in *Triple Threat* (Columbia, 1948).

At the time Waterfield made *Jungle Manhunt*, he was the starting quarterback for the Los Angeles Rams; he was also married to screen star Jane Russell.

Reviews: "Feeble entry." *The Columbia Story*, Hirschhorn

"A plot involving synthetic diamonds adds a bit more intrigue." *Motion Picture Guide*, Nash and Ross

"This is a routine series entry of the cliffhanger type." *Variety*, 10/03/51

Summation: This is an exciting Jungle Jim adventure. Producer Sam Katzman hired director Lew Landers and screenwriter Samuel Newman for the series, with telling results. The film is infused with an energy not seen in the previous couple of outings. Granted Bob Waterfield's acting is a little suspect, but the rest of the cast, especially Johnny Weissmuller, performs admirably. Director Landers keeps the story continuously on the move.

JUNGLE JIM IN THE FORBIDDEN LAND
Columbia (March 1952)

Se Jungle Jim, the giant killer, drive million-year-old man monsters back to their caves

Cast: Jungle Jim, Johnny Weissmuller; Dr. Linda Roberts, Angela Greene; Denise, Jean Willes; Commissioner Kingston, Lester Matthews; "Doc" Edwards, William Tannen; Fred Lewis, George Eldredge; Zulu, Frederic Berest; "Tamba"// Old One, William Fawcett; Quigley, Frank Jaquet; Giant man, Clem Erickson; Giant woman, Irmgard Helen H. Raschke

Credits: Director, Lew Landers; Producer, Sam Katzman; Screenwriter, Samuel Newman; Editor, Henry Batista; Art Director, Paul Palmentola; Set Decorator, Sidney Clifford; Cinematographer, Fayte Browne; Unit Manager, Herbert Leonard; Musical Director, Mischa Bakaleinikoff

Location Filming: Corriganville, California
Production Dates: began mid–April 1951
Running Time: 65 min.
Source: Based upon the newspaper feature *Jungle Jim*, owned and copyrighted by King Features Syndicate, and which appears regularly in "Puck" the comic weekly.

Jungle Jim in the Forbidden Land (1951) scene card —(center) Johnny Weissmuller and two unidentified actors, (right) Johnny Weissmuller, Angela Greene, "Tamba."

Story: Both anthropologist Angela Greene and Commissioner Lester Matthews want Johnny Weissmuller to lead them to the Land of Giants. Greene wants to study the inhabitants; Matthews wants to find a passageway elephants can travel to avoid being killed by unscrupulous hunters. Weissmuller refuses. He sees natives, led by Frederic Berest, stealing some of George Eldredge's ivory tusks that he is selling to Frank Jaquet. Jaquet wants more ivory but Eldredge has reached his quota and refuses. Eldredge's niece, Jean Willes, and his associate, William Tannen, see this as an opportunity to make some easy money and make a deal with Berest to slaughter more elephants to obtain the ivory. Matthews had captured two giants. Tannen suggests he could use the truth serum to sedate the giants, then let them go so they could follow them home. The male, Clem Erickson, escapes and returns to free the female, Irmgard Helen H. Raschke. Eldredge finds out about Willes and Tannen's scheme and plans to tell Matthews but is killed by Berest. Tannen captures Weissmuller and, with the truth serum, finds the way to the Land of Giants. Tannen also arranges to frame Weissmuller for Eldredge's murder. Greene rescues Weissmuller and they travel to the Land of Giants to prevent the slaughter. Willes and Tannen encounter Erickson and Raschke. Willes kills Raschke and wounds Erickson. Weissmuller arrives in time to prevent the elephant slaughter and defeat Tannen in a fistfight. Willes tries to escape but is confronted by Raschke, who wraps his arms around Willes and plunges over a cliff to their deaths.

Notes and Commentary: Working titles were "The Forbidden Land" and "Jungle Safari." This was the only film listed for the real-life giant people, Clem Erickson and Irmgard Helen H. Raschke. After viewing this film, I can understand why they terminated their screen careers.

Review: "Okay Jungle Jim programmer with Johnny Weissmuller." *Variety*, 03/05/52

Summation: This entry is not up to standard this time out. The plot is more disjointed, and the makeup of the giants is unrealistic. Johnny Weissmuller does all he can do with this tired script. Only Angela Greene stands out from the rest of a cast. Tamba is okay for some needed comic relief. Lew Landers's direction is not as sharp as in his previous outing.

VOODOO TIGER

Columbia (November 1952)

Voodoo vengeance runs riot!

Cast: Jungle Jim, Johnny Weissmuller; Phyllis Bruce, Jean Byron; Abel Peterson, James Seay; Shalimar, Jeanne Dean; Wombulu, Charles Horvath; Major Bill Green, Robert Bray; Heinrich Schultz, Michael Fox; Sgt. Bono, Rick Vallin; "Tamba"// Jerry Masters, John L. Cason; Michael Kovacs, Paul Hoffman; Co-pilot, William Klein; Commissioner Kingston, Richard Kipling; Native leader, Alex Montoya

Credits: Director, Spencer G. Bennet; Assistant Director, Charles S. Gould; Producer, Sam Katzman; Screenwriter, Samuel Newman; Editor, Gene Havlick; Art Director, Paul Palmentola; Set Decorator, Sidney Clifford; Cinematographer, William Whitley; Unit Manager, Herbert Leonard; Musical Director, Mischa Bakaleinikoff

Location Filming: Corriganville, California

Production Dates: June 9, 1952–June 17, 1952

Running Time: 68 min.

Source: Based upon the newspaper feature *Jungle Jim*, owned and copyrighted by King Features Syndicate, and which appears regularly in "Puck" the comic weekly.

Story: Johnny Weissmuller and police sergeant Rick Vallin are guiding research writer Jean Byron (of the British Museum) through the jungle when they come upon a sacrificial ritual to the voodoo tiger. Weissmuller stops the rites and orders Charles Horvath and his followers to renounce their voodoo practices. Weissmuller receives a message that Commissioner Kipling needs him to guide him to Michael Fox's trading post. U.S. Major Robert Bray is traveling with Kipling. At the trading post, Bray accuses Fox of being a Nazi war criminal with knowledge of the location of the Schulman art collection. International criminals James Seay, John L. Cason and Paul Hoffman arrive to kidnap Fox. A fight breaks out. Fox takes the opportunity to escape. Seay and his men gain the upper hand and leave as well. Fox hijacks a plane at a nearby airfield. Jeanne Dean, her trained tiger and the showgirls in her act are passengers. The plane has engine problems and is forced to land in headhunter country. The group is about to be killed when the tiger stalks out of the train. The natives are worshipers of the voodoo tiger and think this tiger is the reincarnation of their god. Seay has formed an alliance with Horvath, who plans to take them to Fox. Weissmuller leads a party to overtake them. Seay plans a dynamite trap to wipe out Weissmuller and his party. Weissmuller's pet chimpanzee, Tamba, reveals the trap to him, and he defuses it. In the village, the enraged tiger begins mauling the natives, including Horvath. In the confusion, Seay, Cason and Hoffman spirit Fox away. Weissmuller and his party also make their way out of the village. Weissmuller and Bray catch up with Seay, Cason and Hoffman. Weissmuller and Bray efficiently overcome the criminals and take Fox with them. No longer under Horvath's protection, the headhunters kill Seay and his confederates and then chase after Weissmuller and his party. Weissmuller reattaches the dynamite trap. The dynamite explodes, causing a massive landslide which kills all the headhunters. The group returns to civilization where Bray and Byron have fallen in love.

Notes and Commentary: Veteran director Spencer G. Bennet took over the helm for this Jungle Jim adventure and would go on to direct three additional episodes. Bennet started his directorial career with *Behold the Man* (Pathé, 1921) and retired after helming *The Bounty Killer* (Embassy, 1965). Bennet began his association with Sam Katzman when he directed the serial *Brick Bradford* (Columbia, 1947). During his association with Katzman, Bennet would direct a total of 21 serials and one western, *Brave Warrior* (Columbia, 1952) in addition to the Jungle Jim films.

Voodoo Tiger marked Jean Byron's film debut. Byron will always be known as Natalie Lane, the mother of Patty Duke, in all 87 episodes of *The Patty Duke Show* (ABC, 1963–66).

Reviews: "Moribund jungle caper." *The Columbia Story*, Hirschhorn

"This routine fare come complete with the usual leaf-and-lion footage." *Motion Picture Guide*, Nash and Ross

"Based on the 'Jungle Jim' comic strip, 'Voodoo Tiger' stacks up as okay program filler." *Variety*, 10/08/52

Summation: This is an above-average Jungle Jim story. Again, Johnny Weissmuller fits the title role perfectly. The cast, including Tamba, is effective in their roles. Veteran director Spencer G. Bennet moves the story well with no dull spots.

SAVAGE MUTINY
Columbia (February 1953)

A-bombs over Africa!

Cast: Jungle Jim, Johnny Weissmuller; Joan Harris, Angela Stevens; Major Walsh, Lester Matthews; Dr. Parker, Nelson Leigh; Chief Wamai, Charles Stevens; Lutembi, Paul Marion; Carl Kroman, Gregory Gay; Emil Bruno, Leonard Penn; Paul Benek, Ted Thorpe; "Tamba"// Johnson, George Robotham

Credits: Director, Spencer G. Bennet; Assistant Director, Carter DeHaven; Producer, Sam Katzman; Screenwriter, Sol Shor; Editor, Henry Batista; Art Director, Paul Palmentola; Set Decorator, Sidney Clifford; Cinematographer, William Whitley; Unit Manager, Herbert Leonard; Musical Director, Mischa Bakaleinikoff

Location Filming: Corriganville, California

Production Dates: June 24, 1952–July 2, 1952

Running Time: 73 min.

Source: Based upon the newspaper feature *Jungle Jim*, owned and copyrighted by King Features Syndicate, and which appears regularly in "Puck" the comic weekly.

Story: Believing all foreign agents have been eliminated in Mogamba territory, Dr. Nelson Leigh plans to conduct the first Anglo-American atom bomb test in Africa. The bomb will be exploded on Tulonga Island and Johnny Weissmuller is given the assignment to evacuate the natives. Angela Stevens, with the World Health Organization, is sent to inoculate the natives. Traders Gregory Gay and Leonard Penn attempt to stop the evacuation, but Weissmuller thwarts their plans. After the natives relocate in Dangor, Gay has a plane fly over their encampment and spread the area with radioactive particles, making the natives sick. Gay learns the exact time the atom bomb is to be dropped. He convinces the natives to return to Tulonga. The natives take Leigh and Stevens hostage so their return will not be stopped. Weissmuller has a plan to prevent their return. Gay and Penn see Weissmuller canoeing down a river and they attempt to stop him. There is a fight in the middle of the river and Weissmuller kills both foreign agents. Weissmuller reaches the beach ahead of the natives and turns their boats loose. He then tells the natives that the great fire bird will come in the morning. The natives hold Weissmuller, Stevens and Leigh hostage and threatens to kill them if the great fire bird does not come. As the natives raise their spears, the plane flies over the island and drops the atom bomb. Thanks to Weissmuller, the project is successful.

Notes and Commentary: The atom bomb explosion was previously used in the opening credits of the serial *Atom Man vs. Superman* (Columbia, 1950).

Review: "Exotically campy outing which takes a childish approach to the bleak Cold War situation." *Motion Picture Guide*, Nash and Ross

"Below level entry in 'Jungle Jim' series for program market." *Variety*, 01/21/53

Summation: This is a pretty good Jungle Jim adventure thanks primarily to Sol Shor's economical screenplay which allows Johnny Weissmuller to focus on one primary problem. As usual, Weissmuller is okay in the title role and is surrounded with a more than capable cast. There are some good action sequences as well, with Weissmuller punching out all comers. Spencer G. Bennet's straightforward direction guides the story through its satisfactory paces.

VALLEY OF HEAD HUNTERS
Columbia (August 1953)

Jolting jungle thrills!

Alternate Title: Valley of the Head Hunters

Cast: Jungle Jim, Johnny Weissmuller; Ellen Shaw, Christine Larson; Arco, Robert C. Foulk; Lt. Barry, Steven Ritch; Mr. Bradley, Nelson Leigh; Pico Church, Joseph Allen, Jr.; Commissioner Kingston, George Eldredge; Native, Neyle Morrow; M'Gono, Vince M. Townsend, Jr.; "Tamba"// Chief Bagava, Don Blackman; Chief Gitzhak, Paul Thompson

Credits: Director, William Berke; Assistant Director, Carter DeHaven, Jr.; Producer, Sam Katzman; Screenwriter, Samuel Newman; Editor, Gene Havlick; Art Director, Paul Palmentola; Set Decorator, Sidney Clifford; Cinematographer, William Whitley; Unit Manager, Herbert Leonard; Sound, Lambert Day; Musical Director, Mischa Bakaleinikoff

Location Filming: Corriganville, California

Production Dates: February 24, 1953– March 4, 1953

Running Time: 67 min.

Source: Based upon the newspaper feature *Jungle Jim*, owned and copyrighted by King Features Syndicate, and which appears regularly in "Puck" the comic weekly.

Story: Nelson Leigh has the assignment to get mineral rights treaties signed by native tribes living in the Valley of Head Hunters. The region has deposits of copper that is badly needed. Johnny Weissmuller and Lt. Steven Ritch are assigned to guide Leigh, with Christine Larson going along as interpreter. Unscrupulous lawyer Robert C. Foulk learns there is oil in that region and he wants the mineral rights. Working with his henchman, Joseph Allen, Jr., and native chief Vince Townsend, Jr., Foulk plots to have some of Townsend's tribesman terrorize the other tribes as headhunters. Foulk is able to convince all the chiefs except two, Don Blackman and Paul Thompson, that Weissmuller and Ritch brought the headhunters back to the valley. Townsend is voted to be head chief. Weissmuller is able to capture Allen and force him to confess that Foulk is behind the trouble. Blackman and Thompson hear the confession and realize that Weissmuller is innocent. Foulk captures the group and plans to launch an attack on Blackman's village, placing blame on Weissmuller and his friends. With help from his pet chimpanzee, Tamba, Weissmuller gets the upper hand and outlines a plan of defense for Foulk's attack. Weissmuller's plan is successful. In the battle, he kills Townsend in hand-to-hand combat; meanwhile, Blackman's tribesmen kill Allen. Weissmuller, with timely help from Tamba, brings Foulk to justice. Leigh is able to get the mineral rights leases signed.

Notes and Commentary: Paul Stader was Johnny Weissmuller's double in this film.

Review: "It's passable for booking in the programmer market." *Variety*, 07/29/53

Summation: This is another entertaining Jungle Jim episode. Johnny Weissmuller plays the lead with ease. The competent supporting cast is highlighted by Robert C. Foulk as the chief heavy and Steven Ritch as a novice officer. Director William Berke's direction is competent. The main drawback is some unnecessary "comic" interludes with Tamba.

KILLER APE

Columbia (December 1953)

Drug-mad beasts ravage human prey!

Cast: Jungle Jim, Johnny Weissmuller; Shari, Carol Thurston; Man Ape, Max Palmer; Ramada, Burt Wenland; Dr. Andrews, Nestor Paiva; Mahara, Paul Marion; Achmed, Eddie Foster; Perry, Rory Mallinson; Norley, Ray Corrigan; Maron, Nick Stuart, "Tamba"// Medical officer, Michael Fox; Magi, Pedro Regas; Henchman, Harry Wilson

Credits: Director, Spencer G. Bennet; Assistant Director, Carter DeHaven, Jr.; Producer, Sam Katzman; Story, Carroll Young: Screenwriters, Carroll Young and Arthur Hoerl; Editor, Gene Havlick; Art Director, Paul Palmentola; Set Decorator, Sidney Clifford; Cinematographer, William Whitley; Unit Manager, Herbert Leonard; Sound, Josh Westmoreland; Musical Director, Mischa Bakaleinikoff

Location Filming: Corriganville, California

Production Dates: February 5, 1953– February 12, 1953

Running Time: 68 min.

Source: Based upon the newspaper feature *Jungle Jim*, owned and copyrighted by King Features Syndicate, and which appears regularly in "Puck" the comic weekly.

Story: While investigating strange activity of some of the jungle animals, Weissmuller warns a wandering native tribe, led by Paul Marion, to stay out of the Canyon of the Man Ape. Later, Weissmuller warns scientist Nestor Paiva to leave the canyon. Paiva is conducting experiments with the jungle animals to develop germ-warfare drugs to sell to the highest bidder. The Man Ape, Max Palmer, disrupts Paiva's camp and wrecks his laboratory. Marion wants to see if Weissmuller's claim is valid. He runs into Palmer. Weissmuller comes to

Marion's aid but is knocked unconscious. Palmer kills Marion. Marion's sister, Carol Thurston, and her finance, Burt Wenland, accuse Weissmuller of the crime and take him captive. Weissmuller's chimpanzee, Tamba, causes a diversion and Weissmuller escapes. Thurston, intent on killing Weissmuller, follows him but he overcomes her and takes her to his camp. At the camp, Palmer tries to abduct Thurston, but Weissmuller uses fire to drive him away. Weissmuller takes Thurston back to her camp and leaves to obtain Wenland's help in fighting Palmer. Palmer comes to Thurston's camp and kidnaps her. Wenland decides not to provide animals to Paiva. Paiva, enraged, has his men gun down Wenland's men, then captures Wenland and a tribal elder, Eddie Foster. Weissmuller tries to free Wenland and is captured. Palmer brings Thurston to the canyon and Paiva's men capture both. Tamba has his simian friends attack Paiva's camp. In the confusion, Tamba frees Weissmuller and the others are able to escape. Palmer frees himself and begins killing Paiva's men. Palmer grabs Paiva and throws him in a cage with a black panther. Weissmuller, Wenland and Thurston return to fight Paiva's men. Palmer again captures Thurston; Weissmuller rescues Thurston and uses fire to destroy Palmer.

Notes and Commentary: Footage of the simians attacking Paiva's camp was previously used in *Captive Girl*.

Reviews: "More talk than action characterized this adventure." *The Columbia Story*, Hirschhorn

"It's a cliché tour-de-force replete with bad acting and apathetic direction." *Motion Picture Guide*, Nash and Ross

"Stereotyped entry in Johnny Weissmuller's 'Jungle Jim' series of programmers." *Variety*, 11/25/53

Summation: This Jungle Jim adventure has a preposterous plot but it's a lot of fun. Carroll Young and Arthur Hoerl's screenplay makes use of the old "Beauty and the Beast" theme, and fire is used to destroy the monster, a device seen in countless horror films. The cast takes the story in stride and the results are more than satisfactory. The Columbia makeup department does a much better job on the Man Ape's makeup than they did with the two giants in *Jungle Jim in the Forbidden Land*.

JUNGLE MAN-EATERS
Columbia (June 1954)

Jungle Jim against the cannibals ... to free their human prey!

Cast: Jungle Jim, Johnny Weissmuller; Dr. Bonnie Crandall, Karin Booth; Inspector Jeffrey Bernard, Richard Stapley; Zuwaba, Bernard Hamilton; Leroux, Gregory Gay; Commissioner Kingston, Lester Matthews; Zulu, Paul Thompson; Chief Boganda, Vince M. Townsend, Jr.; N'Gala, Louise Franklin, "Tamba"// Crewman, John Merton; Native escort, Woody Strode

Credits: Director, Lee Sholem; Assistant Director, Charles S. Gould; Producer, Sam Katzman; Story and Screenplay, Samuel Newman; Editor, Gene Havlich; Art Director, Paul Palmentola; Set Decorator, Sidney Clifford; Cinematographer, Henry Freulich; Special Effects, Jack Erickson; Unit Manager, Herbert Leonard; Sound, Josh Westmoreland; Musical Director, Mischa Bakaleinikoff

Location Filming: Corriganville, California
Production Dates: early–December 1953

Running Time: 68 min.

Source: Based upon the newspaper feature Jungle Jim owned and copyrighted by King Features Syndicate and which appears regularly in "Puck" the comic weekly.

Story: Bernard Hamilton is happy that Johnny Weissmuller and Commissioner Lester Matthews will attend the coronation of his father, Vincent M. Townsend. Doctor Karin Booth and Scotland Yard detective Richard Stapley wander from Matthews's camp and are attacked by the evil native Paul Thompson and some of his tribesmen. Weissmuller sees the attack, routs the natives and captures Thompson. At the camp is Gregory Gay from the Diamond Syndicate, who tells the party that unscrupulous people have found a rich diamond mine and plans to flood the market, making all diamonds worthless. Actually, Gay wants the diamonds for himself. Gay frees Thompson and forms an alliance with him. Gay locates the diamond mine. Gay has Thompson set fire to Townsend's village to force the tribe to leave the area and take the royal family hostage. Weissmuller, Booth, Stapley and Weissmuller's pet chimpanzee, Tamba, return to help Townsend. Instead they find him murdered and learn that Hamilton and his pregnant wife, Louise Franklin, are being held captive. Hamilton and Franklin are taken aboard a freighter. Weissmuller rescues them. Franklin is taken to a hospital, where she dies while delivering a baby boy. At the native village, Thompson kidnaps Booth and the baby. Weissmuller goes into action. He and Stapley locate the diamond mine. Weissmuller takes dynamite from Gay's camp to set a trap to prevent Thompson's men from raiding Hamilton's village. Weissmuller and Stapley rescue Booth and the baby. Weissmuller stays behind to deal with Gay and Thompson. Weissmuller kills Thompson in a short hand-to-hand struggle. Weissmuller chases Gay up into the mountains, where Gay falls to his death in a fight with Weissmuller. Hamilton sets off the dynamite charge, causing a landslide to destroy Thompson's camp and his tribesmen. Hamilton becomes the new chief of the tribe. Booth and Stapley fall in love. Tamba even finds a girlfriend.

Notes and Commentary: This would be the last official Jungle Jim feature film. Johnny Weissmuller would play himself in the final three episodes. With these finished, Weissmuller would then star in the Jungle Jim television series.

Most of the footage of Weissmuller rescue of Bernard Hamilton and Louise Franklin was lifted from an earlier episode, *The Lost Tribe*.

Sam Katzman hired Lee Sholem to direct *Jungle Man-Eaters* and the subsequence entry, *Cannibal Attack*. Sholem was known as "Roll 'Em" Sholem who, in his long directing career (1949–72) of directing feature films and television episodes, was always fast and efficient, never going over schedule.

Review: "Standard Jungle Jim programmer with Johnny Weissmuller for lower case bookings." *Variety*, 06-09-54

Summation: This is a fast-moving Jungle Jim adventure, loaded with stock footage. In director Lee Sholem's capable hands, the results are satisfactory. The acting is par for the series.

CANNIBAL ATTACK

Columbia (November 1954)

Out of the blackest jungle ... a white-out thrill adventure

Cast: Johnny Weissmuller, Johnny Weissmuller; Luora, Judy Walsh; Arnold King, David Bruce; Rovak, Bruce Cowling; Commissioner, Charles Evans; John King, Stevan Darrell; Jason, Joseph A. Allen, Jr.; "Kimba"// Narrator, Michael Granger

Credits: Director, Lee Sholem; Assistant Director, Abner Singer; Producer, Sam Katzman; Story and Screenwriter, Carroll Young; Editor, Edwin Bryant; Art Director, Paul Palmentola; Set Decorator, Sidney Clifford; Cinematographer, Henry Freulich; Special Effects, Jack Erickson; Unit Manager, Leon Chooluck; Sound, John Livadary and Harry Mills; Musical Director, Mischa Bakaleinikoff

Location Filming: Los Angeles County Arboretum & Botanic Garden, California
Production Dates: shooting began April 27, 1954
Running Time: 70 min.

Story: Stevan Darrell established a colony at the Magi River and opened a mine that will provide needed cobalt to the English government. Commissioner Charles Evans is on hand for the arrival of the first shipment. Johnny Weissmuller finds a dead man, one of the guards of the cobalt shipment, apparently killed by crocodiles. Judy Walsh, ward of Darrell, confronts Weissmuller with a rifle in his back. Weissmuller grabs the rifle and Walsh takes to the water. Weissmuller follows but is almost run down by a boat piloted by Bruce Cowling, The cobalt shipment is missing. Darrell's right-hand man, Cowling, takes some men to search for the cobalt. Weissmuller, with his per chimpanzee, Kimba, starts a search on his own. Weissmuller meets David Bruce, Darrell's brother. In a show of power, Darrell has banished Bruce to the mine. Weissmuller believes there is a connection between the Shenzi tribes — former cannibals who have power over crocodiles — and the cobalt theft. Cowling is an agent of a foreign government sent to steal the cobalt. A second shipment is sent. This time Cowling has the Shenzi send real crocodiles. Darrell's boat has motor trouble and sends the boat, led by Bruce, ahead. The crocodiles attack and only Bruce is able to escape. The raft with the cobalt falls into Cowling's hands. A third shipment is planned. Cowling tells Walsh, who is a Shenzi princess working with him, to request Darrell to send only high-grade ore. Darrell is in love with Walsh and is working with Cowling to help him set up his own empire with Walsh at his side. Weissmuller and Bruce, along with Kimba, find Cowling's hideout, but they are captured. Weissmuller and Bruce are set to be mauled by an angry crocodile. Kimba comes to cut Weissmuller's bonds. Weissmuller kills the crocodile. Knowing Weissmuller has escaped the death trap, Cowling and Walsh decide to attack the convoy and steal the cobalt. Weissmuller has set up a counter-attack and begins to rout the attackers. Darrell, who has confessed his part in the scheme, fights with Weissmuller. Enraged, Walsh kills Darrell and is promptly shot by Evans. Seeing that all is lost, Cowling tries to escape, but Weissmuller jumps on board. The ensuing fight ends in the river, with both men going under water. Only Weissmuller coming to the surface. Bruce succeeds Darrell as leader of the colony.

Notes and Commentary: This is the fist pseudo Jungle Jim film, with Johnny Weissmuller using his own name. The chimpanzee's name is now Kimba and Commissioner Kingston is now, simply, Commissioner.

Stevan Darrell was usually billed as Steve in his motion picture career.

Stock footage was used liberally: Weissmuller's fight with the leopard was lifted from *Jungle Jim*; *Mark of the Gorilla* was the source for Weissmuller's fight with the eagle; Weissmuller's fight with a crocodile in *The Lost Tribe* became David Bruce's fight in this film.

Reviews: "The latest in Sam Katzman's jungle series for Columbia, 'Cannibal Attack' is a standard mixture of studio action and jungle stock shots. However, dyed-in-the-wool action fans should be compensated by the innumerable clashes between man and beast, and man and man." *Motion Picture Herald*

"A Johnny Weissmuller starrer, 'Cannibal Attack' is standard action-adventure material for juvenile audiences. As such there is nothing pretentious about this Sam Katzman production but it will comfortably fill demands of the secondary situations." *Variety*

"Pretty decent." *Motion Picture Guide*, Nash and Ross

Summation: The first of the pseudo Jungle Jim films is a winner. Lee Sholem directs briskly and economically, keeping the pace at breakneck speed. Johnny Weissmuller delivers his usually fine job in the title role and the supporting cast is more than adequate. The comedy of Kimba is portioned out sparingly, which made it all the more welcome.

JUNGLE MOON MEN
Columbia (April 1955)
Strange jungle adventure!

Cast: Johnny Weissmuller, Johnny Weissmuller; Ellen Marsten, Jean Byron; Oma, Helen Stanton; Bob Prentice, Bill Henry; Santo, Myron Healey; Damu, Billy Curtis; Nolimo, Michael Granger; Max, Frank Sully; Marro, Benjamin F. Chapman, Jr.; Link, Kenneth L. Smith; Regan, Ed Hinton; "Kimba"// Commissioner Jones, Rory Mallinson

Credits: Director, Charles S. Gould; Assistant Director, Eddie Saeta; Producer, Sam Katzman; Story, Jo Pagano; Screenwriters, Jo Pagano and Dwight V. Babcock; Editor, Henry Batista; Art Director, Paul Palmentola; Set Decorator, Sidney Clifford; Cinematographer, Henry Freulich; Special Effects, Jack Erickson; Unit manager, Leon Chooluck; Sound, Josh Westmoreland; Musical Director, Mischa Bakaleinikoff

Location Filming: Corriganville and Iverson, California

Production Dates: May 19, 1954–May 25, 1954

Running Time: 70 min.

Story: Pygmies, known as "moon men" to other jungle inhabitants, capture Benjamin F. Chapman, Jr., to be the high priest to Helen Stanton, the high priestess of Baku. Egyptologist Jean Byron wants Johnny Weissmuller to guide her to Baku. Weissmuller relents when native chief Michael Granger wants Weissmuller to find his son. The safari starts out and is joined by Bill Henry, a friend of Byron's. The devious Myron Healey, whom Weissmuller dislikes, drove Henry to Weissmuller's party. Chapman escapes from Baku but dies in the attempt. The "moon men" chased Chapman. One of the "moon men," Billy Curtis, is captured by Weissmuller. Curtis states that Chapman was given a potion which becomes deadly only when a person leaves Baku. In Chapman's possession is a diamond pendant, which greatly interests Healey. "Moon men" rescue Curtis and, in the process, take Henry to be the next high priest. Weissmuller, Byron and Weissmuller's pet chimpanzee, Kimba, arrive at the Temple of the Moon Goddess. Kimba discovers how to open the door. As Weissmuller and Byron start to enter, Healey and his confederate, Frank Sully, arrive and force Weissmuller to lead the way. The party is captured by the "moon men" and taken to Stanton. Stanton reveals that she has discovered the secret of eternal youth but cannot venture into the sunlight. A drugged Henry states that he wants to remain in Baku with Stanton. Later, Weissmuller learns the truth that Henry wants to leave with Byron. Weissmuller tells Stanton that he'll remain to be the high priest if the rest are allowed to leave Baku. Weissmuller directs Henry to go to the police and bring them back to free him. Greed overcomes Healey. He attempts to steal valuable diamonds and is caught by Weissmuller. The men fight. Weissmuller is trying to return the jewels when he is intercepted by the "moon men." Both men are accused of stealing diamonds and the entire party is sentenced to die by mauling by wild lions. Before the lions can be released, Kimba frees Weissmuller, who releases the others. The lions are unleashed. Weissmuller directs every one to remain motionless and the lions pass by them. Knowing there is a secret passageway out of Baku, Weissmuller forces Stanton to reveal the way out. Healey and Sully have gone after the diamonds but meet a deadly fate as the lions maul them. Weissmuller, Byron and Henry leave Baku and Weissmuller forces Stanton to go with them. In the sunlight, Stanton turns to dust. Byron needs some proof to write the story of Baku, and Kimba brings it: the valuable diamond pendant is hanging around his neck.

Notes and Commentary: Look closely: When the pygmies try to capture Benjamin F. Chapman, Jr., by immobilizing him with a poison dart, the dart strikes an area on his chest covered by his shield.

Reviews: "This Sam Katzman production was made on a small budget for the small fry Saturday matinee trade; but even evaluated on this basis it fails to meet a minimum standard, having been negligently written and executed." *Hollywood Reporter*

"The story, which runs a terse 70 minutes, has been padded, but not too extensively, by some effective shots of wild animals on the prowl." *Motion Picture Herald*

"Writers of this Johnny Weissmuller jungle starrier borrow generously from H. Rider Haggard for plot material, but film fits into the groove of past offerings in the Sam Katzman series and should do the same type of biz in program situations." *Variety*

Summation: Okay, the story may be farfetched — as much science-fiction as jungle adventure — but, in the final analysis, it isn't dull. Charles S. Gould does a good job directing this story which is a knockoff of H. Rider Haggard's *She* (Graphic Magazine, 1886–87). The acting of the principals is up to par, with Johnny Weissmuller in fine form, as always. The cinematography of Henry Freulich enhances the story, especially in the land of Baku. Lighting in these scenes is superb.

DEVIL GODDESS
Columbia (October 1955)

Thundering With Jungle Adventure.... Throbbing With Jungle Thrills

Cast: Johnny Weissmuller, Johnny Weissmuller; Nora Blakely, Angela Stevens; Professor Carl Blakely, Selmer Jackson; Nels Comstock, William Tannen; Leopold, Ed Hinton; Professor Dixon, William M. Griffith; Teinusi, Abel M. Fernandez; Nkruma, Frank Lackteen; Sarabna, Vera M. Francis; "Kimba"// Native, Paul Marion; Henchman, John Cason; Kirundis chief, Max Reid

Credits: Director, Spencer G. Bennet; Assistant Director, Leonard Katzman; Producer, Sam Katzman; Story, Dwight Babcock; Screenwriter, George Plympton; Editor, Aaron Stell; Art Director, Paul Palmentola; Set Decorator, Sidney Clifford; Cinematographer, Ira Morgan; Special Effects, Jack Erickson; Unit Manager, Leon Chooluck; Sound, Harry R. Smith; Musical conductor, Mischa Bakaleinikoff

Location Filming: Bronson Canyon, California

Production Dates: December 14, 1954–December 21, 1954

Running Time: 68 min.

Story: Professor Selmer Jackson wants Johnny Weissmuller to take him to the Mountain of Explosive Fire in the land of the Kirundi to find a colleague, William M. Griffith. The

Devil Goddess (1955) title card. Left (top to bottom) — Kimba, William M. Griffin, Vera M. Francis, Angela Greene (tied to stake), others unidentified. Right center (top to bottom) — Kimba, unidentified actors, Johnny Weissmuller.

natives in that area worship a fire demon, a man who can control fire. A native, Frank Lackteen, trades a jeweled scimitar with William Tannen. Tannen and his boss, Ed Hinton realize the value of the weapon and believes other riches may be present. Both parties reach the land of the Kirundi. Tannen, Hinton and their henchmen discover the treasure. Weissmuller finds a native friend, Abel M. Fernandez, who tells him that his sweetheart, Vera M. Francis, is to be sacrificed to the fire demon, Griffith. Weissmuller initially stops the ritual, but eventually Francis ends up in the hands of Griffith. He does not harm Francis, but uses his control to prevent sacrificial deaths. Weissmuller and Jackson end up in the lair of the fire demon and plan to take Griffith and Francis to safety when an active volcano begins to erupt. Previously angered at all white men, the natives overcome and kill Tannen, Hinton and his henchmen. Griffith appears to the Kirundi and persuades them leave the valley to safety. The natives are grateful to Griffin and offer him their treasure. Griffith plans to give it to a museum.

Notes and Commentary: The initial footage of Angela Stevens and Johnny Weissmuller journeying into the jungle was lifted from *Savage Mutiny* (1953). Left in was Stevens's reference to a pouch with vaccine, which was integral to the plot of that film but of no reference to the plot of *Devil Goddess*.

Borrowed from other Jungle Jim films is footage from *Mark of the Gorilla* (1950), *Captive Girl* (1950), *Pygmy Island* (1950), *Jungle Manhunt* (1951), *Voodoo Tiger* (1952) and *Killer Ape* (1953).

Reviews: "This is a tongue-in-cheek adventure, in the best old-fashioned traditional classification." *Motion Picture Herald*

"There was a time, long ago, when the Tarzan pix and similar adventure yarns used to be fun. But this latest Sam Katzman entry, 'Devil Goddess,' is a plodding, almost amateurish attempt at making a formula theme pay off." *Variety*

"Silly jungle film." *Motion Picture Herald*, Nash and Ross

Summation: It looks like all life is gone from the series with this entry. From some unfunny monkeyshines with Kimba and two simian pals drinking alcohol, to the weaving in copious stock footage from previous Jungle Jim adventures, the film limps to its obvious conclusion. Johnny Weissmuller's derring-do is mostly recycled footage resulting in a lackluster performance from the star. Director Spencer G. Bennet could have phoned in his effort. A sorry end to a largely enjoyable series.

The Lone Wolf

Author Louis Joseph Vance's 14th novel, *The Lone Wolf* registered well with the adventure-loving readers. The story told of a young man, Michael Lanyard, trained in the ways of theft who became the world's most notorious jewel thief. The love of a good woman caused him to leave his life of crime. The second installment, *False Faces* was published in 1918. Six additional novels followed from 1921 to 1934.

Hollywood became interested in the Lone Wolf character and in 1917, *The Lone Wolf* (Herbert Brenon Film Corp./Selznick Distributing Corporation) with Bert Lytell was released. *The False Faces* (Thomas H. Ince/Paramount, 1919) with Henry B. Walthall followed. Bertram Grassby played Lanyard in *The Lone Wolf's Daughter* (Pathé, 1919) and action star Jack Holt had the honors in a retelling of the original story, *The Lone Wolf* (John McKeown/Associated Exhibitors, 1924). Columbia took over the character and began the first true series with *The Lone Wolf Returns* (1926). Bert Lytell, the first screen Lone Wolf, again reprised the role. (Lytell was also the first screen's Boston Blackie, with *Boston Blackie's Little Pal* [Metro, 1918].) Three additional films followed with Lytell in the lead. His final appearance as the Lone Wolf was *The Last of the Lone Wolf* (Columbia, 1930), the first all-talking feature in the series. At that time, Columbia lost interest in the character. (Lytell would star in a few more films before retiring from the screen. In the late '40s, Lytell would become a regular on the television program, *One Man's Family* (NBC) and could be seen on *The Philco Television Playhouse* [NBC].)

Thomas Meighan took the role in *Cheaters at Play* (Fox, 1932). Columbia became interested in the character again with the suave Melvyn Douglas in the lead for *The Lone Wolf Returns* (1935), a remake of Bert Lytell's entry. (Douglas began his film career in 1931, making films for Paramount, Universal, RKO, Majestic and Columbia and co-starring with Barbara Stanwyck, Sylvia Sidney, John Barrymore, Claudette Colbert, Virginia Bruce and Boris Karloff. His best known films to this time were *Tonight or Never* [United Artists, 1931] with Gloria Swanson and *As You Desire Me* [Metro-Goldwyn-Mayer, 1932] with Greta Garbo.) In *The Lone Wolf Returns*, Lanyard gained a gentleman's gentleman and co-conspirator in Jenkins, played by Raymond Walburn. Inspector Crane was on hand as the police inspector who doesn't quite buy Lanyard's reformation. Character actor Thurston Hall took the role and would play the part in seven films. Francis Lederer assumed the role in *The Lone Wolf in Paris* (1938). (Lederer began his career in German silent films, gaining recognition for his role as Alwa Schoen in *Pandora's Box* (Nero-Film AG, 1928) with Louise Brooks. In 1934, Lederer appeared in American films, working for RKO, Paramount, Fox, United Artists and Columbia. Lederer would have a long career in films and television. He taught acting until his death at 100 years of age.) In *The Lone Wolf in Paris*, Jenkins was still present, this time in the personage of Olaf Hytten.

The definitive Lone Wolf came to the screen in the next in the series, *The Lone Wolf Spy Hunt* (Columbia, 1939). Warren William played Lanyard in this and eight more entries. (William was a top leading man in the early '30s usually paying a cad who despoiled beautiful young ladies. With the enaction of the Production Code, William's stock diminished though he remained a leading man in lower-budget features. William was the screen's first Perry Mason. He, also, played sleuth Philo Vance. With *Passport to Suez* [Columbia, 1943], William left the series. William appeared in three films before retiring from the screen. William passed away on September 12, 1948, due to multiple myeloma.) William's valet in *Spy Hunt* was Leonard Carey. Lanyard's valet had a name change to Jameson. In the next entry, *The Lone Wolf Strikes* (Columbia, 1940), William was paired with Eric Blore as Jamison (note the change in spelling). This turned out to be inspired casting as the chemistry between them clicked. Blore would appear in eleven films in the series. (Blore gained prominence with his comedic presence in five of the nine Fred Astaire-Ginger Rogers films of the '30s. After Blore left the Lone Wolf series, his roles in films lessened. Blore was the voice of Mr. Toad in Walt Disney's *The Adventures of Ichabod and Mr. Toad* [RKO, 1949]. Blore's last screen appearance was in the role of a genie in the Bowery Boys' film, *Bowery to Bagdad* [Allied Artists, 1955].) William and Blore played the roles of Lanyard and Jamison on the first radio broadcast of the Lone Wolf. The radio program *Suspense* had the duo involved in murder at a society party in the story "Murder Goes for a Swim," on July 20, 1943.

Columbia decided to resume the series with *The Notorious Lone Wolf* (1946) with Gerald Mohr in the lead. (Mohr was primarily a radio actor in the '40s. Early film roles had him playing villains as in the serial *Jungle Girl* [Republic, 1941] and *King of the Cowboys* [Republic, 1943] with Roy Rogers. Mohr served in the Air Force during World War II. Upon discharge, Mohr landed the role of the Lone Wolf and played the part in three films. He also played Lanyard in the radio series which began on the Mutual network in 1948. After leaving the series Mohr had a long career in films and television.) In 1947, a new Lone Wolf book was published. Carl W. Smith wrote *The Lone Wolf and the Hidden Empire* (Whitman). During the course of the radio series, Walter Coy replaced Mohr. Lanyard's new choice of beverage was now milkshakes. The last program was broadcasted on January 1, 1949.

Columbia decided to give the series one more try. Ron Randell took over as Lanyard and noted character actor Alan Mowbray played Jamison. Randell had previously played Bulldog Drummond for Columbia. Randell then had major roles in *It Had to Be You* (Columbia, 1947) with Ginger Rogers and Cornel Wilde, and *The Mating of Millie* (Columbia, 1948) with Glenn Ford and Evelyn Keyes. Unfortunately Randell's entry, *The Lone Wolf and His Lady* (Columbia, 1949) would end the series. The Lone Wolf would have one last hurrah when former Simon Templar (the Saint) Louis Hayward starred in the television series *The Lone Wolf* (Gross-Krasne Productions). Some 39 episodes were filmed, airing from 1954–55. The series was also known as *Streets of Danger*.

Almost like the Lone Ranger with his silver bullet, Lanyard had a wolf's head medallion as his calling card.

THE LONE WOLF RETURNS

Columbia (August 1926)

Pleasurably exciting! Grippingly romantic! Amazingly different!

Alternate Title: The Return of the Lone Wolf

Cast: Michael Lanyard, Bert Lytell; Marcia Mayfair, Billie Dove; Mallison, Freeman Wood; Morphew, Gustav von Seyffertitz; Liane De Lorme, Gwen Lee; Crane, Alphonse Ethier

Credits: Director, Ralph Ince; Supervisor, Harry Cohn; Screenwriter, J. Grubb Alexander; Cinematographer, J.O. Taylor

Source: based on a work by Louis Joseph Vance

Running Time: 70 min.

Story: Bert Lytell steals a valuable necklace. With the police nearby, Lytell enters a house in which a masked ball is in progress. Lytell joins the party and dances with the owner, Billie Dove. Detective Alphonse Ethier and his men arrive and force the guests to unmask. Ethier is unable to find the necklace on Lytell, which is hidden in his cigarette case. Because of Dove's influence, Lytell replaces the necklace. Lytell and Dove go to a bohemian resort where gang leader Gustav von Seyffertitz confronts them and threatens Lytell. The place is raided. Lytell and Dove elude the police. Love's jewels are stolen and she suspects Lytell. Lytell retrieves the jewels from Seyffertitz and brings him to justice.

Notes and Commentary: This is a silent film.

This film was remade as *The Lone Wolf Returns* (Columbia, 1935) with Melvyn Douglas as the Lone Wolf.

Louis Joseph Vance's book, *The Lone Wolf Returns*, was the basis for this film, but only the title and some of the character's names (Mallison, Morphew, Liane De Lorme and Crane) are used.

Summation: This film was not available for review by the author.

ALIAS THE LONE WOLF
Columbia (August 1927)

As a gentleman adventurer, "The Lone Wolf" again becomes
involved in a series of gripping events. Packed with mystery and romance.

Cast: Michael Lanyard, Bert Lytell; Eve de Montalais, Lois Wilson; Whitaker Monk, William V. Mong; Phinuit, Ned Sparks; Popinot, James Mason; Liane De Lorme, Paulette Duval; Fifi, Ann Brody; Inspector Crane, Alphonse Ethier

Credits: Director, Edward H. Griffith; Assistant Director, Joe Cooke; Producer, Harry Cohn; Screenwriters, Edward H. Griffith and Dorothy Howell; Art Director, Robert E. Lee; Cinematography, J.O. Taylor

Source: based on a work by Louis Joseph Vance

Running Time: 65 min.

Story: Lois Wilson is determined to smuggle her jewels into the United States in order to help her brother. Paulette Duval and James Mason plan to steal the jewels. Bert Lytell's timely intervention upsets their plans and helps Wilson bring the jewels ashore. At a nightclub, Duval tells Wilson that Lytell is a notorious jewel thief. William V. Mong poses as a customs inspector and requests that Wilson hand over the jewels. Wilson discovers Mong's duplicity and escapes. Lytell declares the jewels to customs officials and the police round up the thieves. Lytell reveals to Wilson that he is a Secret Service agent. Lytell and Wilson now have time for romance.

Notes and Commentary: This is a silent film.

The film is based on Louis Joseph Vance's novel, *Alias the Lone Wolf,* but not too closely. The main character names are retained. The novel has Whitaker Monk, Phinuit and Liane De Lorme steal Eve de Montalais' jewels, hoping to place the blame on Michael Lanyard. Lanyard goes after the jewels, ultimately outwitting the villainous trio and returning them to de Montalais. Inspector Crane does not appear in the novel.

Reviews: "As long as one is not too inquisitive as to how Michael Lanyard escapes from the toils of the eager diamond thieves, *Alias the Lone Wolf* may be quite diverting. It has its flaws, but it is well photographed and not at all badly acted." *New York Times,* 9/19/27

"It's simple and insipid, loosely directed and more loosely played with the "detective situations" at times quite irritating." *Variety,* 10/05/27

Summation: This film was not available for review by the author.

THE LONE WOLF'S DAUGHTER
Columbia (February 1929)

The "Lone Wolf" is Back in Louis Joseph Vance's Latest Romantic Thriller.

Cast: Michael Lanyard, Bert Lytell; Helen Fairchild, Gertrude Olmstead; Count Polinac, Charles Gerard; Velma, Lilyan Tashman; Bobby Crenshaw, Donald Keith; Adrienne, Florence Allen; Ethier, Robert Elliott; Mrs. Crenshaw, Ruth Cherrington

The Lone Wolf's Daughter (1929) movie still — Bert Lytell, Gertrude Olmstead.

Credits: Director, Albert S. Rogell; Assistant Director, Tenny Wright; Presenter, Harry Cohn; Screenwriter, Sig Herzig; Dialogue, Harry Revier; Editor, William Hamilton; Art Director, Harrison Wiley; Cinematographer, James Van Trees

Source: based on a work by Louis Joseph Vance

Running Time: 72 min.

Story: Bert Lytell adopts Florence Allen as a favor to an old friend. Allen is engaged to marry Donald Keith, scion of a wealthy family. International jewel thieves Charles Gerard and Lilyan Tashman threaten to expose Lytell's past if he doesn't open the safe containing the guests' jewelry. Lytell is able to protect the jewels. Gerard and Tashman are arrested. Lytell's past is not revealed to Keith's family.

Notes and Commentary: Except for an opening dialogue sequence, this was a silent film.

The title is all that is left of Louis Joseph Vance's short novel. In the story, Michael Lanyard is the father of his daughter, Sophia — not Adrienne, as in the film. The story dealt with Lanyard's archenemy, Victor Vassilyevski, using Sophia unsuccessfully as a pawn to further his plot to bring Russian rule to England.

The Lone Wolf's Daughter was remade as *The Lone Wolf Spy Hunt* with Warren William as the Lone Wolf.

Review: "Old fashioned film fare. Not a week run picture." *Variety*, 03/06/29

Summation: This film was not available for review by the author.

THE LAST OF THE LONE WOLF

Columbia (August 1930)

Romantic crook drama

Cast: Michael Lanyard, Bert Lytell; Stephanie, Patsy Ruth Miller; Varril, Lucien Prival; Prime Minister, Otto Matieson; King, Alfred Hickman; Queen, Maryland Morne; Camilla, Halie Sullivan; Master of Ceremonies, Pietro Sosso; Count von Rimpau, Henry Daniell; Hoffman, James Liddy

Credits: Director, Richard Bolesalvsky; Assistant Director, C.C. Coleman; Producer, Harry Cohn; Adaptation, John Thomas Neville; Screenplay, Dorothy Howell; Editor, David Berg; Art Director, Edward Jewell; Cinematographer, Ben Kline; Sound, Russell Malmgren; Technical Director, Edward Shulter; Dialogue Director, Stuart Walker

Source: Based on a work by Louis Joseph Vance

Running Time: 70 min.

Story: Prime Minister Otto Matieson tells King Alfred Hickman that Queen Maryland Morne has given a ring to Henry Daniell. Hickman wants the ring recovered. Bert Lytell has been arrested. Lytell is offered his freedom by Matieson if he can retrieve the ring. Morne has commissioned her lady-in-waiting, Patsy Ruth Miller, to get the ring. Lucien Prival is sent to watch Lytell, but Lytell throws him off the train. Lytell gains admittance to the embassy and steals the ring. Under suspicion, Lytell returns the ring. Miller tells Lytell that failure to retrieve the ring would be detrimental to Morne. Lytell again steals the ring. Prival captures Lytell. Lytell is able to escape and gets the ring to Morne at the last possible moment. Lytell receives immunity and begins a romance with Miller.

Notes and Commentary: This was the first all-talking film in the Lone Wolf series.

This film would be remade as *The Lone Wolf in Paris* (Columbia, 1938) with Francis Lederer.

This was the last of the Lone Wolf series for five years. In 1935 Melvyn Douglas starred in *The Lone Wolf Returns*.

Review: "Bert Lytell gives his customary good performance, but the Lone Wolf here is limited. It's a cut-and-dried role, without much of the suavity and adventure the predecessors possessed." *Variety*, 10/22/30

Summation: This film was not available for review by the author.

THE LONE WOLF RETURNS

Columbia (December 1935)

Debonair — dangerous — always one step ahead of the police

Cast: Michael, Melvyn Douglas; Marcia, Gail Patrick; Liane, Tala Birell; Mallison, Henry Mollison; Crane, Thurston Hall; Jenkins, Raymond Walburn; Morpheux, Douglass Dumbrille; Aunt Julie, Nana Bryant; McGowan, Robert Middlemass; Benson, Robert Emmett O'Connor// Policemen, Jack Clifford, Hal Price, Lee Shumway and Kernan Cripps; Bancroft's butler, Olaf Hytten; Marjorie, Dorothy Bay; Mr. Cole, Wyrley Birch; Detectives, Eddy Chandler and William Gould; Flute player, Gennaro Curci; Reporter, Eddie Fetherston; Photographer, Harry Harvey; Crooner, Mort Greene; Party guest, Bess Flowers; "Nero," Harry Holman; "Robin Hood," David Horsley; "Jackass," Arthur Stuart Hull; "Gladiator," Pat Somerset; "Tarzan," George Webb; Drunk on stairs, Lloyd Whitlock; Customs officials, Lew Kelly and Monte Vandergrift; Baby, Lois Lindsay; Oscar, Arthur Loft; French official, Fred Malatesta; Maestro, George McKay; Koster, Gene Morgan; Suburbanites,

The Lone Wolf Returns (1935) movie still — Gail Patrick, Melvyn Douglas.

Ned Norton and Henry Roquemore; Stewart's butler, Vesey O'Davoren; Official's aide, John Picorri; Old man, Thomas Pogue; Fat woman, Maude Truex; Coleman, Frank Reicher; Terry, Archie Robbins; Mugg, Pat West

Credits: Director, Roy William Neill; Screenwriters, Joseph Krumgold, Bruce Manning and Lionel Houser; Editor, Viola Lawrence; Cinematographer, Henry Freulich; Costumes, Samuel Lange; Musical Director, Howard Jackson

Production Dates: September 3, 1935–October 22, 1935

Running Time: 69 min.

Source: Based on a story by Louis Joseph Vance

Story: After stealing the Bancroft pearls, Melvyn Douglas crashes the masquerade party at the neighboring estate. There, he steals a valuable necklace belonging to Gail Patrick. Party guests Henry Mollison and Tala Birell want the pearls for themselves. After meeting Patrick, Douglas returns the necklace to Patrick's safe. Thurston Hall is brought back out of retirement to catch Melvyn Douglas. Douglas declares to Hall that he is finished with crime and that the Bancroft pearls have been returned. Douglass Dumbrille is upset when Mollison and Birell return without the necklace. Douglas and Patrick begin to fall in love. Dumbrille tells Patrick that Douglas is a notorious international jewel thief. Dumbrille steals the jewels. Hall thinks Douglas is the culprit. Framed by Dumbrille, Douglas tells Hall that he'll bring the guilty party to justice by midnight. Dumbrille plans to sail to Europe with Patrick at his side. Hall gets the proof that Dumbrille stole the jewels. Douglas returns the jewels to Patrick. Douglas and Patrick plan to marry.

Notes and Commentary: This is a remake of *The Lone Wolf Returns* (Columbia, 1926) with Bert Lytell as the Lone Wolf. Again, only the title and some of the character names are taken from Vance's novel.

Reviews: "Louis Joseph Vance society crook story, well conceived and executed by capable cast topped by Melvyn Douglas and Gail Patrick." *Variety*, 2/5/36

"A moderately involving mystery." *The Columbia Story*, Hirshhorn

"One of the better films in the 'Lone Wolf' series, with Douglas doing a fine job as the title character. Above-average B production." *Motion Picture Guide*, Nash and Ross

"We thought the Lone Wolf had picked the wrong night to howl — wrong by fifteen years." *New York Times*, 2/4/36

Summation: This is an engaging, well-done mystery adventure. Melvyn Douglas is a delight as the sophisticated Lone Wolf. Gail Patrick matches him as the woman who reforms him. In the excellent supporting cast, Raymond Walburn as Douglas' trusty valet and Thurston Hall as Detective Crane are impressive. Deftly directed by Roy William Neill, this is one of the best Lone Wolf episodes.

THE LONE WOLF IN PARIS

Columbia (May 1938)

Love makes the Lone Wolf a thief once more!

Cast: Michael Lanyard, Francis Lederer; Princess Thania, Frances Drake; Jenkins, Olaf Hytten; Grand Duke Gregor, Walter Kingsford; Baroness Gambrell, Leona Maricle; Marquis de Meyerson, Albert Van Dekker; M. Fromont, Maurice Cass; Davna, Bess Flowers; Queen Regent, Ruth Robinson; King, Pio Peretti; Mace, Eddie Fetherston// Peter, Otto Fries;

The Lone Wolf in Paris (1938) movie still — Francis Lederer, Frances Drake.

Carl, Roger Gray; Hotel desk manager, George Andre Beranger; Rene Ledaux, Vernon Dent; Vault guard, Dick Curtis; Hilda, Lucille Ward; Bertha, Aileen Carlyle; Headwaiter, Eugene Borden; Otto, Al Herman; Dmitri, Frank Leigh

Credits: Director, Albert S. Rogell; Associate Producer, Wallace MacDonald; Screenwriter, Arthur T. Horman; Editor, Otto Meyer; Art Director, Stephen Goosson; Cinematographer, Lucien Ballard; Costumes, Kalloch; Musical Director, Morris Stoloff

Production Dates: December 9, 1937–January 6, 1938

Running Time: 67 min.

Source: Based on a story by Louis Joseph Vance

Story: Princess Frances Drake steals paste imitations of the crown jewels of Arvonne from Albert Van Dekker. Walter Kingsford, Dekker and Leona Maricle want Drake to advise Ruth Robinson to have her son, Pio Peretti, abdicate the throne. If Robinson refuses, a rumor will be spread that Robinson stole the jewels. Francis Lederer becomes interested in Drake's problem. Lederer steals jewels from Dekker, Kingsford and Maricle and replaces them with pastes. Lederer, Drake and Lederer's valet, Olaf Hytten, leave by plane to Arvonne, not realizing Kingsford's henchman, Eddie Fetherston, is aboard. Fetherston hijacks the plane and flies to Kingsford's hunting lodge. Lederer, Drake and Hytten are held captive. Kingsford regains possession of the jewels and travels to Arvonne. Lederer is able to escape and follows Kingsford. Through a ruse, Lederer has the jewels restored to Robinson and Kingsford is arrested. Peretti is crowned king. Lederer is allowed to secretly leave the country.

Notes and Commentary: The working title was "The Lone Wolf."

Plot elements were borrowed from *The Last of the Lone Wolf* (Columbia, 1930) with Bert Lytell

Reviews: "Fast paced thriller." *The Columbia Story*, Hirshhorn

"Francis Lederer makes a charming and of course unoutwittable addition to the top hat and flowing cape school of thievery." *New York Times*, 5/23/38

"Fair 'B' costumer with a good cast. One virtue is the fact there's a good deal of action crowded into the 67 minutes." *Variety*, 05/25/38

Summation: This is a bright adventure, reminiscent of Anthony Hope's *The Prisoner of Zenda*. Francis Lederer makes an impressive Lone Wolf and Olaf Hytten turns in a nice job as his valet. The supporting cast is impressive, with a special nod to Walter Kingsford as the arch villain. Director Albert S. Rogell keeps the interesting story moving throughout.

THE LONE WOLF SPY HUNT

Columbia (January 1939)

The Lone Wolf's turned spy-smasher!

Alternate Titles: The Lone Wolf's Daughter, The Lone Wolf

Cast: Michael Lanyard, Warren William; Val Carson, Ida Lupino; Karen, Rita Hayworth; Patricia, Virginia Weidler; Spiro, Ralph Morgan; Sergeant Devan, Tom Dugan; Inspector Thomas; Don Beddoe; Jameson, Leonard Carey; Jenks, Ben Welden; Senator Carson, Brandon Tynan; Marie Templeton, Helen Lynd// Girl in nightclub, Lorna Gray; Agnus Palmer, Forbes Murray; Henchman, Marc Lawrence; Doorman, I. Stanford Jolley; Charlie Fenton, Jack Norton; Party guest, James Craig; Fat party guest, Vernon Dent; Patrol sergeant at restaurant, Irving Bacon; Patrol officer at restaurant, Dick Elliott; Fagin, Herbert Evans; Marriage License Bureau clerk, Alec Craig; Detective with note, Edmund Cobb

Credits: Director, Peter Godfrey; Associate Producer, Joseph Sistrom; Screenwriter, Jonathan Latimer; Editor, Otto Meyer; Art Director, Lionel Banks; Cinematography, Allen G. Siegler; Gowns, Kalloch; Musical Director, Morris Stoloff

Production Dates: November 21, 1938–December 12, 1938

Running Time: 67 min.

Source: Based on a work by Louis Joseph Vance

Story: Ralph Morgan plans to steal secret plans from the War Department and frame Warren William for the crime. Morgan is able to obtain only part of the plans. The rest of the plans are in Inventor Forbes Murray's safe. William is kidnapped and is forced to open the safe. By a ruse, William takes the real plans and substitutes others to be taken to Morgan. Morgan, posing as an influential personage, gives a masquerade party. William crashes the party and takes the plans. At the same time, Morgan's henchmen grab the plans William had. Morgan sends Rita Hayworth to enlist William to sell the plans to a foreign power. William turns down the offer. Hayworth leaves, not realizing Williams's daughter, Virginia Weidler, has secreted herself in the trunk of her car. Weidler is found and taken captive. William follows and he, too, is captured. William starts a fight with Morgan's henchmen, giving Weidler a chance to escape with all of the plans. Police arrive and arrest Morgan and his gang. William is cleared of all charges against him.

Notes and Commentary: *The Lone Wolf Spy Hunt* is a remake of *The Lone Wolf's Daughter* (Columbia, 1929).

Reviews: "A neat blend of comedy and thrills." *The Columbia Story*, Hirshhorn

"The best of the 'Lone Wolf' series. One of the best things about the picture is its natural blending of action and comedy." *Motion Picture Guide*, Nash and Ross

"All the kiddies may be sure that a great treat is in store for them when the Lone Wolf howls." *New York Times*, 3/6/39

"Lone Wolf gets comedy treatment, mildly entertaining for the duals." *Variety*, 01/25/39

Summation: Warren William makes his debut as the Lone Wolf in this bright, fast-moving blend of adventure and comedy. William is a standout as the debonair adventurer and easily makes the role his own. Other performances are up to par except that of Ida Lupino. Lupino's role is written as an empty-headed socialite whose main purpose in the film is to make additional trouble for William. Otherwise, director Peter Godfrey guides the story nicely to its satisfactory conclusion.

THE LONE WOLF STRIKES
Columbia (January 1940)

The Lone Wolf can take it — if it isn't nailed down!

Cast: Michael Lanyard, Warren William; Delia Jordan, Joan Perry; Jamison, Eric Blore; Jim Ryder, Alan Baxter; Binnie Weldon, Astrid Allwyn; Emil Gorlick, Montagu Love; Ralph Bolton, Robert Wilcox; Conroy, Don Beddoe; Dickens, Fred Kelsey; Stanley Young, Addison Richards; Phillip Jordan, Roy Gordon; Alberts, Harland Tucker; Dorgan, Peter Lynn// Jewelry store clerk, Robert Noble; Martier's jeweler, Maurice Cass; Frederick, Cyril Thornton; House detective, Robert Emmett O'Connor; Hotel manager, Julius Tannen; Hotel doorman, Vernon Dent; Pete, Murray Alper; Bill, William Lally; Poker game dealer, Harry A. Bailey; Tony's doorman, Ralph Peters; Policeman in cellar of apartment building, Edmund Cobb

Credits: Director, Sidney Salkow; Producer, Fred Kohlmar; Story, Dalton Trumbo; Screenwriters, Albert Duffy and Harry Segall; Editor, Al Clark; Art Director, Lionel Banks; Cinematographer, Henry Freulich; Gowns, Kalloch; Musical Director, Morris Stoloff

Production Dates: November 15, 1939–December 9, 1939

Running Time: 67 min.

Source: Based on a work by Louis Joseph Vance

Story: Addison Richards asks his good friend, Warren William, to investigate the death of his partner, Roy Gordon, and retrieve valuable pearls that were stolen from him. Gordon's acquaintance, Astrid Allwyn, switched the real pearls for fake ones and gave them to her lover, Alan Baxter. The pearls now belong to Gordon's daughter, Joan Perry. Her boyfriend is working with Harland Tucker's gang to get possession of the pearls. By a ruse, William takes the real pearls from Baxter and gives them to Richards. Tucker murders Richards to get the pearls. William convinces Tucker that the pearls he stole were fake. William delivers Baxter and Allwyn to the police. William then arranges to have Tucker arrested with the real pearls in his possession. William and Perry begin a romantic relationship.

Notes and Commentary: This was Eric Blore's initial entry as the Lone Wolf's "gentleman's gentleman." Blore would play in seven more with William and then three additional entries with Gerald Mohr. There was a change in spelling of Blore's character name from *The Lone Wolf Spy Hunt* from Jameson to Jamison.

Don Beddoe was Inspector Thomas in *The Lone Wolf Spy Hunt* and Inspector Conroy in *The Lone Wolf Strikes*.

Reviews: "A neat and nifty quickie that never over-reached its modest expectations." *The Columbia Story*, Hirshhorn

"Above par for the Lone Wolf series. Its content of suspense and suave detecting will provide adequate program entertainment." *Variety*, 01/24/40

Summation: This is a good entry in the Lone Wolf series. The addition of Eric Blore to the proceedings was a masterstroke. The chemistry between Warren William and Blore is perfect, adding a spark to the story. Joan Perry is very appealing and effective as the woman who finally trusts William. The story is just okay, but the lead performers elevate it to loftier levels.

THE LONE WOLF MEETS A LADY
Columbia (May 1940)

Wanted by the police ... and every woman he meets!

Cast: Michael Lanyard, Warren William; Joan Bradley, Jean Muir; Jamison, Eric Blore; Clay Beaudine, Victor Jory; Peter Rennick, Roger Pryor; Bob Penyon, Warren Hull; Inspector Crane, Thurston Hall; Dickens, Fred A. Kelsey; Peter Van Wyck, Robert Emmett Keane; Mrs. Penyon, Georgia Caine; Arthur Trent, William Forrest; Rose Waverly, Marla Shelton; McManus (Motorcycle policeman), Bruce Bennett// Police doctor, Don Beddoe; Nick, George McKay; Joe, Shemp Howard; N. Pappakontous, Luis Alberni; Mrs. Pappakontous, Nellie V. Nichols; Diver, Houghton Ralph; Air pump operator, Roger Gray

Credits: Director, Sidney Salkow; Story, John Larkin; Screenwriters, Wolfe Kaufman and John Larkin; Editor, Al Clark; Art Director, Lionel Banks; Cinematography, Henry Freulich; Gowns, Kalloch; Musical Director, Morris Stoloff

Songs: "Believe Me if All Those Endearing Young Charms" (Moore, Irish melody) sung by Eric Blore; "Bury Me Not on the Lone Prairie" (traditional) sung by Eric Blore

Production Dates: March 15, 1940–April 6, 1940

Running Time: 71 min.

Source: Based on a story by Louis Joseph Vance

Story: Jean Muir, fiancée of Warren Hull, has possession of a valuable necklace belonging to his mother, Georgia Caine. Her supposedly deceased husband, Roger Pryor, overpowers Muir and takes the necklace. An unknown assailant kills Pryor before he can leave Muir's apartment. Muir tells Warren William and Eric Blore that she may be arrested for murder. William decides to help Muir and sets up an alibi for her. The alibi collapses when the key to her apartment is found on Pryor's body. Muir eludes the police and goes to Warren's apartment. Warren determines that to solve the mystery, the necklace must be found. Through underworld sources Warren finds the necklace had been broken up and sold a year ago. Warren deduces that the necklace Muir had must have been an imitation, and the murderer must have thrown it out of Muir's apartment into the river below. Muir tells Warren that, besides Hull, only Georgia Caine, Robert Emmett Keane, Marla Shelton and William Forrest knew she had the necklace. Gathering the suspects together, Caine remembers that Keane placed the necklace in the safe and that it hadn't been removed until it had been given to Muir. Keane attempts to escape but runs into the hands of the police.

Notes and Commentary: Three former serial heroes appeared in this Lone Wolf entry: Warren Hull, Victor Jory and Bruce Bennett.

Warren Hull played serial heroes in *The Spider's Web* (Columbia, 1938), *The Spider Returns* (Columbia, 1941), *Mandrake the Magician* (Columbia, 1939) and *The Green Hornet Strikes Again* (Universal, 1941).

Victor Jory had the lead in *The Shadow* (Columbia, 1940) and *The Green Archer* (Columbia, 1940). Bruce Bennett, as Herman Brix, starred in *The New Adventures of Tarzan* (Burroughs-Tarzan Enterprises, Inc., 1935) and *Hawk of the Wilderness* (Republic, 1938).

Reviews: "Capably scripted thriller." *The Columbia Story*, Hirshhorn

"The Lone Wolf's latest escapade emerges as a better than average example of the pre-fabricated mystery thriller." *New York Times*, 6/17/40

"Good entertainment. The film maintains suspense strength all the way." *Variety*, 06/12/40

Summation: This is a first-rate Lone Wolf adventure full of comedy and mystery. The outing provides a genuine murder-mystery story with Warren William and Eric Blore providing some welcome and funny comedy in the process. Jean Muir makes an excellent heroine. Muir is an actress of some talent that for some strange reason never made it to the higher echelon. Inspector Crane is back in the series in the welcome personage of Thurston Hall. Director Sidney Salkow keeps the film moving briskly with no dull moments. This is the best of the William Lone Wolf episodes to date.

THE LONE WOLF KEEPS A DATE
Columbia (January 1941)

He's giving the cops the slip ... ladies the works ... and killers the business!

Alternate Titles: Alias the Lone Wolf, Revenge of the Lone Wolf

Cast: Michael Lanyard, Warren William; Patricia Lawrence, Frances Robinson; Scotty, Bruce Bennett; Jamison, Eric Blore; Inspector Crane, Thurston Hall; Capt. Moon, Jed Prouty; Dickens, Fred Kelsey; Big Joe Brady, Don Beddoe; Mr. Lee, Lester Matthews; Chimp, Edward Gargan; Measles, Eddie Laughton; Mrs. Colby, Mary Sevoss//Manuel, Alberto Morin; Sam, Charles R. Moore; Clerk helping William, Jack Rice; Second clerk, Jay Eaton; Department store cashier, Evelyn Young; Paper boy, James "Hambone" Robinson; Motor policemen, Steve Benson, Leon Davidson, Gayle DeCamp and Jay Gudelia; Cyrus Colby, Henry Hebert; Dock attendant, Harry Strang; Croupier, Richard Fiske; Morgue attendant, Herbert Ashley; Headwaiter, Dudley Dickerson; Santos, Francis McDonald; Hotel desk clerk, George Dobbs; Night watchman, Walter Baldwin

Credits: Director, Sidney Salkow; Screenwriters, Earl Felton and Sidney Salkow; Editor, Richard Fantl; Art Director, Lionel Banks; Cinematography, Barney McGill; Gowns, Kalloch; Musical Director, Morris Stoloff

Production Dates: August 21, 1940–mid–September 1940

Running Time: 65 min.

Source: Based on a work by Louis Joseph Vance

Story: After purchasing a stamp in Havana to complete his collection, Warren William meets the lovely Frances Robinson. On arrival in Miami, Robinson is almost kidnapped. In the struggle, Williams's stamp collection is taken by the kidnappers. Robinson brought

$100,000 from Cuba, the exact amount of the money paid in the kidnapping of Henry Hebert. William decides to help Robinson and her fiancé, Bruce Bennett, find Hebert and, in the process, retrieve his stamp collection. The trail leads to casino boss, Don Beddoe. Beddoe gets the money and plans to murder Hebert and William. William is able to get a code message to Eric Blore, his valet, and Robinson. Police arrive in time to prevent the murder of William and Hebert and round up Beddoe and his gang. Robinson and Bennett plan to marry.

Notes and Commentary: Jed Prouty, usually a character actor, received the starring role as pharmacist John Jones in the Jones Family series. The Jones Family series, produced by 20th Century–Fox, ran for 16 entries, from 1936 to 1940.

Review: "Weakest of the series, not in cast, but in story." *Variety*, 12/18/40

Summation: This is a lesser entry in the Lone Wolf series. Warren William and Eric Blore try their best, but neither a good script nor crisp direction is present. Too many unfunny comedy moments mar this entry. The lovely Frances Robinson is just fine as the lady in distress.

THE LONE WOLF TAKES A CHANCE
Columbia (March 1941)

The Lone Wolf can't leave crime alone!.... It may be a cops' conspiracy,
but once more he's knee-deep in homicide and exciting villainy!

Cast: Michael Lanyard, Warren William; Gloria Foster, June Storey; Frank Jordan, Henry Wilcoxon; Jamison, Eric Blore; Inspector Crane, Thurston Hall; Sheriff Haggerty, Don Beddoe; Evelyn Jordan, Evalyn Knapp; Dickens, Fred Kelsey; Vic Hilton, William Forrest; Dr. Hooper Tupman, Walter Kingsford; Johnny Baker, Lloyd Bridges; Conductor, Ben Taggart; Brakeman, Richard Fiske// Policeman outside jewelry store, Tom London; First jewelry clerk, Corbet Morris; Police sergeant, John Tyrell; Wallace, Regis Toomey; Hotel manager, Cyril Ring; McKay, George McKay; Newsstand clerk, Ernie Adams; Desk sergeant, Ralph Sanford; Projectionist, Irving Bacon; Usher, George Hickman; Newsreel announcer, Art Gilmore; Pilot, Harry Strang; Detective in charge of opening vault, Edmund Cobb; Man with blow torch, I. Stanford Jolley

Credits: Director, Sidney Salkow; Screenwriters, Earl Felton and Sidney Salkow; Editor, Viola Lawrence; Art Direction, Lionel Banks; Cinematographer, John Stumar; Musical Director, Morris Stoloff

Production Dates: December 19, 1941–January 14, 1941

Running Time: 76 min.

Source: Based on a work by Louis Joseph Vance

Story: Inspector Thurston Hall bets Warren William that William can't stay out of trouble for 24 hours. Henry Wilcoxon and his men kidnap inventor Lloyd Bridges. In the process, private investigator Regis Toomey is murdered. William is accused of the crime. Bridges has invented a burglary-proof railway car that will carry engraving plates from New York to San Francisco. When anyone tries to open the car without the combination, poison gas will fill the car. Bridges is taken on the train with the car. William, his valet Eric Blore and Bridges's girlfriend, June Story, follow. As they are about to rescue Bridges, William and Blore are arrested; Wilcoxon's gang takes Story captive. Before the actual gang leader,

Walter Kingsford, can force Bridges to open the mail car, Hall and the police board the train. This action gives William and Blore an opportunity to escape. William and Blore trail the gang to an abandoned farmhouse where they learn the gang has the plates and Bridges is locked in the mail car. William and Blore rescue Story. Blore tricks the gang and retrieves the plates. William and Blore take the gang's vehicle and leave them stranded. The gang is arrested, but protest their innocence. William knows that when the mail car is forced open, Bridges will be overcome by the gas. Reviewing a newsreel, William gets the combination to the mail car. William races to it and opens it just in time to save Bridges.

Notes and Commentary: June Storey is known to western fans as Gene Autry's leading lady in ten films at Republic from 1939–40. June even got to vocalize with Autry in seven entries.

Reviews: "The pace is breakneck, but the story can't keep up." *Motion Picture Guide*, Nash and Ross

"The pace of *The Lone Wolf Takes a Chance* varies from fast to slow." *New York Times*, 4/7/41

"Overplayed cops-and-robbers tale." *Variety*, 03/12/41

Summation: No mystery this time out, just a straightforward adventure tale sparkling with comedy. Warren William and Eric Blore are in fine form, with the rest of the cast delivering only adequate performances. Sidney Salkow's direction is fine. The film moves swiftly with moments of genuine suspense.

SECRETS OF THE LONE WOLF
Columbia (November 1941)

The Lone Wolf's giving lessons in larceny ... and his pupil's are the cops!

Cast: Michael Lanyard, Warren William; Helene de Leon, Ruth Ford; Paul Benoit, Roger Clark; "Dapper" Dan Streever, Victor Jory; Jamison, Eric Blore; Inspector Crane, Thurston Hall; Dickens, Fred Kelsey// Colonel Costals, Victor Kilian; "Bubbles" Deegan, Mario Dwyer; Deputy Duval, Lester Scharff; Mr. Evans, Irving Mitchell; Uptown Bernie, John Harmon; Bob McGarth, Joe McGuinn; Squad car officer, Walter Sande

Credits: Director, Edward Dmytryk; Producer, Jack Fier; Story and Screenplay, Stuart Palmer; Editor, Richard Fantl; Art Direction, Lionel Banks; Cinematographer, Philip Tannura; Musical Director, M.W. Stoloff

Production Notes: July 29, 1941–August 14, 1941

Running Time: 67 min.

Source: Based on a novel by Louis Joseph Vance

Story: A gang, led by Victor Jory, mistakes Eric Blore for the famous international jewel thief. Jory wants Blore to steal valuable jewels from a refugee ship. Warren William is working with Inspector Thurston Hall to set up a defense against thieves. Blore gets away from the crooks. Jory decides to steal the jewels using a method associated with William. William is arrested but is able to prove Jory is the thief.

Notes and Commentary: The working title was "The Lone Wolf's Double Cross."

This movie was filmed at Fine Arts Studio; there was no available space on the Columbia lot.

Reviews: "One of the best of the 'Lone Wolf' series of detective films, and the first

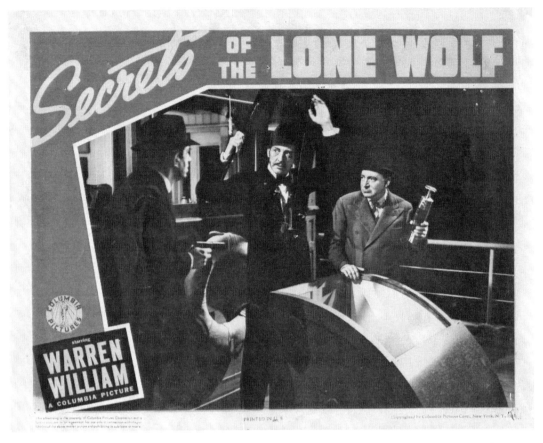

Secrets of the Lone Wolf (1941) scene card — (left to right) Victor Killian, Warren William, Eric Blore.

directed by Edward Dmytryk, who injected some clever humor into the series." *Motion Picture Guide*, Nash and Ross

"Top flight whodunit with Warren William." *Variety*, 11/26/41

Summation: This is a good, fast-moving Lone Wolf episode, but with too much "humor" from Fred Kelsey. Both Eric Blore and Warren William are in good form. It's nice to see their roles reversed for a few reels when Blore is mistaken for the Lone Wolf.

COUNTER-ESPIONAGE

Columbia (September 1942)

The Lone Wolf turns spy to make Nazis turn pale ... and cops turn green with envy!

Alternate Title: The Lone Wolf in Scotland Yard

Cast: Michael Lanyard, Warren William; Jameson, Eric Blore; Pamela, Hillary Brooke; Inspector Crane, Thurston Hall; Dickens, Fred Kelsey; Anton Schugg, Forrest Tucker; Inspector Stephens, Matthew Boulton; Gustav Soessel, Kurt Katch; Kent Wells, Morton Lowry; Harvey Leeds, Leslie Denison; George Barrow, Billy Bevan; Sir Stafford Hart, Stanley Logan; Police Constable Hopkins, Tom Stevenson// Barrow's daughter, Heather Wilde;

Newspaper vendor, Robert Hale; Maître d', Wyndham Standing; Waiter, Lloyd Bridges; Heinrich, Eddie Laughton; Air Warden Williams, Keith Hitchcock; Von Ruhoff, Wilhelm von Brincken; German telegrapher, William Yetter, Sr.

Credits: Director, Edward Dmytryk; Producer, Wallace MacDonald; Screenwriter, Aubrey Wisberg; Editor, Gene Havlick; Art Directors, Lionel Banks and Robert Peterson; Cinematography, Philip Tannura; Musical Director, M.W. Stoloff

Production Dates: April 10, 1942–April 28, 1942

Source: Based on a work by Louis Joseph Vance

Running Time: 73 min.

Story: In war-torn London, Warren Williams steals the Beam Detector plan from Stanley Logan's safe. Scotland Yard Inspector Matthew Boulton arrests Williams but not before he passes the plans to his valet, Eric Blore. William escapes from Scotland Yard only to find German Agent Forrest Tucker is waiting for him. Tucker takes William to the head of the spy ring, Kurt Katch. William agrees to sell the plans to Katch. Boulton is killed and his secretary, Milton Lowry, a German spy, finds proof that William is working for the British government. William discovers the lair of the German spies and is captured. With timely intervention from Blore and Air Raid Warden Billy Bevan, Katch and his spy ring are rounded up.

Notes and Commentary: Eric Blore's character name is listed as Jameson instead of Jamison, as it has been if the earlier series entries. Leonard Carey was Jameson in *The Lone Wolf Spy Hunt* (Columbia, 1939).

There has been a discussion as to whether Lloyd Bridges appeared in the film or not. It is obviously Bridges, with a mustache, as a German agent in the English pub.

Reviews: "Above average series entry." *Motion Picture Guide*, Nash and Ross

"But even that added complication (dealing with Nazi agents and a police dragnet) fails to raise the entertainment quotient of this labored melodrama." *New York Times*, 9/28/42

"One of the best in the Lone Wolf series." *Variety*, 09/30/42

Summation: This is a first-rate Lone Wolf entry with the accent on adventure and suspense, with comedy almost non-existent this time out. Warren William and Eric Blore are perfect in their roles. The rest of the cast acquit themselves well, especially Hillary Brooke and Billy Bevan. Edward Dmytryk's direction is on target, as he paces in fine fashion.

ONE DANGEROUS NIGHT

Columbia (January 1943)

The Lone Wolf goes on a woman-hunt ... but is trapped in the toils of feminine arms!

Cast: Michael Lanyard, Warren William; Eve Andrews, Marguerite Chapman; Jamison, Eric Blore; Jane Merrick, Mona Barrie; Sonia Budenny, Tala Birell; Patricia Blake, Margaret Hayes; Vivian, Ann Savage; Inspector Crane, Thurston Hall; Sidney Shannon, Warren Ashe; Dickens, Fred Kelsey; Hartzog, Frank Sully; Mac, Eddie Marr; Harry Cooper, Gerald Mohr; Arthur, Louis Jean Heydt; John Sheldon II, Roger Clark; Dr. Eric Budenny, Gregory Gaye; Drunk, Eddie Laughton// Woman at hotel, Symona Boniface; Airline gate attendant, Lloyd Bridges; Headwaiter, George Calliga; Elsie, Ann Hunter; Motorcycle cop, Joe

McGuinn; House detective, Ralph Peters; Doorman at theater, Hal Price; Doorman, Dick Rush; Attendant, John Tyrell

Credits: Director, Michael Gordon; Producer, David Chatkin; Story, Arnold Phillips and Max Nosseck; Screenwriter, Donald Davis; Editor, Viola Lawrence; Art Directors, Lionel Banks and Robert Peterson; Interior Decorator, George Montgomery; Cinematographer, L.W. O'Connell: Musical Director, M.W. Stoloff

Production Dates: September 10, 1942–September 29, 1942

Running Time: 77 min.

Source: Based on a work by Louis Joseph Vance

Story: Warren William and Eric Blore give Marguerite Chapman a ride to Gerald Mohr's house. Mohr is not only blackmailing Chapman, but also Tala Birell and Mona Barrie. The lights go out, a shot is fired and Mohr is killed. William and Blore return to Mohr's house and discover the body. The police arrive at the scene and believe William is the culprit. William eludes capture, but newspaper columnist Warren Ashe attaches himself to William, looking for a bigger story. William's sleuthing causes the killer to take a shot at him. He deduces that Ashe is the murderer because his wife was going to run off with Mohr.

Notes and Commentary: The working title was "The Lone Wolf Goes to a Party."

One Dangerous Night was Ann Savage's screen debut. Savage will remain a cult favorite as the femme fatale in *Detour* (PRC, 1945).

Reviews: "Competent second feature. William's seventh appearance as the Lone Wolf is an entertaining diversion." *Motion Picture Guide*, Nash and Ross

"Modest mystery from the Lone Wolf series." *Blockbuster Video Guide to Movies and Videos, 1995*, Castell

Summation: This is a decent and very enjoyable murder-mystery. Again, the comedy is pretty much put on hold except some droll comments by the principals, Warren William and Eric Blore, who turn in their usual fine work. Director Michael Gordon keeps the story moving at a rapid pace.

PASSPORT TO SUEZ

Columbia (August 1943)

The most furious battle of the Lone Wolf's thrill-lashed career!

Cast: Michael Lanyard, Warren William; Valerie King, Ann Savage; Llewellyn Jamison, Eric Blore; Donald Jamison, Robert Stanford; Johnny Booth, Sheldon Leonard; Fritz, Lloyd Bridges; Karl, Gavin Muir// Rembrandt, Louis Merrill; Whistler, Sig Arno; Sir Roger Wembley, Frederick Worlock; Cezanne, Jay Norvello; Chinese girl, Frances Chan; Egyptian bellboys, Darby Jones and Floyd Shackelford; Laundry proprietor, Frank Lackteen; Hotel night clerk, Jack Rice; Wembley agents, Frank O'Connor and John Tyrell; Bartender, Gene Stone; Chauffeur, Mal Merrihugh

Credits: Director, Andre De Toth; Producer, Wallace MacDonald; Story, Alden Nash; Screenwriter, John Stone; Editor, Mel Thorsen; Art Direction, Lionel Banks and Paul Murphy; Set Decorator, Joseph Kish; Cinematographer, L.W. O'Connell; Musical Director, M.W. Stoloff

Production Dates: April 29, 1943–May 18, 1943

Running Time: 71 min.

Source: Based on a work by Louis Joseph Vance

Story: Warren William is in Egypt to work for the British government. German spies kidnap William's valet, Eric Blore. To save his life, William agrees to steal secret British secret documents. Blore is released to work with William. Blore's son, Navy Lieutenant Robert Stanford, is stationed in Egypt. Stanford's fiancée, Ann Savage, has accompanied him. Savage plans to be a war correspondent, but she is actually working with the German spies reporting to Gavin Muir. William pulls off the job only to find that he was duped. The plans for the Suez minefield were stolen. William and Blore are arrested as traitors. They escape to clear their names and bring the spies to justice. Stanford realizes Savage played him for a fool and joins forces with William. Savage has the plans in her watch. Louis Merrill, a double agent, murders Savage and takes the plans. Merrill and Muir plan to take the plans out of Egypt by car. William is able to borrow a training plane with machine guns. William catches up, using the machine guns, and forces the car over an embankment. The spies are killed. The British government needs William for another mission.

Notes and Commentary: Working titles were "A Night of Adventure" and "The Clock Strikes Twelve."

It has been documented that the Los Angeles Board of Review did not favor the export of *Passport to Suez* as it portrays British Intelligence as ineffectual and naïve.

Reviews: "A good amount of gunplay and chase scenes — including one outstanding chase in airplanes — can't breathe life into this film." *Motion Picture Guide*, Nash and Ross

"Standard Lone Wolf sleuth thriller." *Variety*, 08/18/43

Summation: This film has strong atmosphere and an exciting story aided by good direction from Andre De Toth and fine cinematography by L.W. O'Connell. *Passport to Suez* delivers good entertainment, again almost devoid of comedy. There is none of Fred Kelsey's inane humor to mar this outing.

THE NOTORIOUS LONE WOLF
Columbia (February 1946)

It's triple-trouble for the Lone Wolf ... Blonde-Trouble ... Jewel-Trouble ... Killer-Trouble!

Cast: Michael Lanyard, Gerald Mohr; Carla Winter, Janis Carter; Jamison, Eric Blore; Lal Bara, John Abbott; Inspector Crane, William Davidson; Stonely, Don Beddoe; Rita Hale, Adele Roberts; Dick Hale, Robert Scott; Harvey Beaumont, Peter Whitney// Prince of Rapur, Olaf Hytten; Adam Wainwright, Ian Wolfe; Olga, Edith Evanson; Assistant hotel manager, Maurice Cass; Jones, Eddie Acuff; Lili, Virginia Hunter; Pierre, John Tyrell; Brooklynese bystander, Lew Harvey; Grand Dame at airport, Symona Boniface; Fireman, Cy Malis; Waiter, Joe Palma; Wainwright's assistant, Jeffrey Sayre; Room clerk, Fred Amsel; Night clerk, Billy Snyder; Plainclothesman, Bob Ryan; House detective, Eddy Chandler

Credits: Director, D. Ross Lederman; Producer, Ted Richmond; Story, William J. Bowers; Adaptation, Garnett Graham; Screenwriters, Martin Berkeley and Edward Dein; Editor, Richard Fantl; Art Director, Perry Smith; Set Decorator, Frank Kramer; Cinematographer, Burnett Guffey; Sound, Jack Goodrich; Musical Director, Mischa Bakaleinikoff

Production Dates: October 22, 1945–November 5, 1945
Running Time: 64 min.
Source: Based on a work by Louis Joseph Vance
Story: Gerald Mohr returns to New York after four years service in the Armed Services. All Mohr has on his mind is to resume his romance with Janis Carter. Inspector William Davidson informs Mohr that the Shalimar Diamond was stolen from John Abbott and Olaf Hytten. Carter's sister, Adele Roberts, asks Mohr to persuade her husband, Robert Scott, to end his affair with dancer Virginia Hunter. Hunter's boss, nightclub owner Don Beddoe, stole the diamond. Mohr and Scott go to the nightclub. Before they can talk with Hunter, she's murdered. The diamond was stolen again, this time from Hunter's costume. Mohr is accused of the murder but escapes to prove his innocence. Impersonating Abbott, Mohr receives a visit from jeweler Ian Wolfe. Wolfe is acting as an intermediary from the thief and can produce the diamond for a proposed reward. Before the transaction can take place in Wolfe's jewelry store, Beddoe comes in and takes the diamond. Mohr arranges for Beddoe and Wolfe's capture. Wolfe confesses to the murder. Mohr and Carter try to renew their romance. Carter's apartment building catches fire. Fireman Cy Malis carries Carter to safety, to Mohr's obvious displeasure.

Notes and Commentary: The working title was "The Lone Wolf on Broadway."

The theme song from the Blondie series is played when Gerald Mohr enters Don Beddoe's nightclub.

In a daring scene in a B movie in the '40s, Mohr and Janis Carter kiss. There is a fade out, fade in; perhaps Mohr and Carter made love.

Reviews: "After a short hiatus, the 'Lone Wolf' film series returned with the character more debonair than ever." *Motion Picture Guide*, Nash and Ross

"Comedy whodunit with able cast and high-polished routine material." *Variety*, 03/13/46

Summation: This is a so-so effort in the renewal of the Lone Wolf series. Gerald Mohr lacks the sophistication needed for the part. The chemistry that was present between Warren William and Eric Blore is sadly missing between Mohr and Blore. The comedy is clumsy and forced. The story has too many holes, e.g., Robert Scott was with Mohr when the shot was fired that killed Virginia Hunter and could have immediately cleared Mohr. Veteran director D. Ross Lederman couldn't completely salvage this one. Eric Blore is the only bright spot in this episode.

THE LONE WOLF IN MEXICO
Columbia (January 1947)

No wonder women won't let The Lone Wolf alone ... with another woman ... the wolf!!!

Cast: Michael Lanyard, Gerald Mohr; Sharon Montgomery, Sheila Ryan; Liliane Dumont, Jacqueline deWit; Jamison, Eric Blore; Captain Carlos Rodriguez, Nestor Paiva; Henderson, John Gallaudet; Leon Dumont, Bernard Nedell; Agatha Van Weir, Winifred Harris// Emil, Peter Brocco; Charles Montgomery, Alan Edwards; Captain Mendez, Fred Godoy; Cab driver, Chris-Pin Martin; Watchman, Theodore Gottlieb; Hotel maid, Nita Bieber; Hotel Manager, Lee Lenoir; Police chauffeur, Nacho Galindo; Headwaiter, Cosmo Sardo; Policemen at hotel, Jose Portugal and John Dutriz

Credits: Director, D. Ross Lederman; Producer, Sanford Cummings; Story, Phil Magee; Screenwriters, Maurice Tombragel and Martin Goldsmith; Editor, William Lyon; Art Director, Charles Clague; Set Decorator, Louis Diage; Cinematographer, Allen Siegler; Musical Director, Mischa Bakaleinikoff

Production Dates: September 4, 1946–September 18, 1946

Running Time: 69 min.

Source: Based on a work by Louis Joseph Vance

Story: Gerald Mohr and Eric Blore go to Mexico City on vacation. Jacqueline deWit, one of Mohr's old flames, and Winifred Harris invite Mohr and Blore to dinner at John Gallaudet's nightclub. Blore takes Sheila Ryan, a party guest, home. Ryan slips a valuable compact in Blore's coat pocket. Bernard Nedell, deWit's husband, tries to enlist Mohr in a caper. An unknown assailant shoots Nedell. Ryan accuses Blore of stealing her compact and tells him to recover jewels she lost at gambling at Gallaudet's nightclub. Mohr steals the jewels, discovers they're paste and replaces them in Gallaudet's safe. Winifred Harris admits to Mohr that she's heavily in debt to Gallaudet. Galluadet wants Harris's necklace in exchange for her gambling debts. Ryan shakes down Gallaudet for $10,000. Ryan tries to give Mohr some information but is shot before she can talk. Mohr rigs the crooked roulette wheel so Harris can recoup her losses. Gallaudet and deWit, in partnership, decide to steal Harris's necklace, not realizing it is paste. Mohr discovers that deWit murdered both Nedell and Ryan. Mohr helps the police bring Gallaudet and deWit to justice.

Notes and Commentary: The working title was "The Lone Wolf's Invitation to Murder."

Review: "The series was becoming increasingly prosaic." *1996 Movie & Video Guide*, Maltin

Summation: The series is back on track. Gerald Mohr gains sophistication in this one, though not up to Warren William's level, but extremely adequate. Eric Blore is shown to good advantage. The supporting cast, especially Winifred Harris, is quite satisfactory. The storyline is good and D. Ross Lederman's direction is on target, keeping the story moving briskly along.

THE LONE WOLF IN LONDON

Columbia (November 1947)

The Lone Wolf's Got a Way with Women Who Try to Get Away with murder!

Cast: Michael Lanyard, Gerald Mohr; Ann Klemscott, Nancy Saunders; Claudius Jamison, Eric Blore; Iris Chatham, Evelyn Ankers; David Woolerton, Richard Fraser; Lily, Queenie Leonard; Monty Beresford, Alan Napier; Inspector Garvey, Denis Green// Inspector Broome, Frederick Worlock; Henry Robards, Tom Stevenson; Sir John Klemscott, Vernon Steele; Bruce Tang, Paul Fung; Detective Mitchum, Guy Kingsford; Cab driver, Charles Coleman; Airport security guard, Frank O'Connor; Maid, Heather Wilde

Credits: Director, Leslie Goodwins; Producers, Ted Richmond and Robert Cohn; Story, Brenda Weisberg and Arthur E. Orloff; Screenwriter, Arthur E. Orloff; Editor, Henry Batista; Art Director, Robert Peterson; Set Decorator, James Crowe; Cinematographer, Henry Freulich; Musical Director, Mischa Bakaleinikoff

Production Dates: May 19, 1947–May 29, 1947

The Lone Wolf in London (1947) title card — Evelyn Ankers, Gerald Mohr.

Running Time: 68 min.

Source: Based on a work by Louis Joseph Vance

Story: Gerald Mohr is writing a book on famous jewels and needs to view the Eyes of the Nile. The jewel is stolen. Mohr and his valet, Eric Blore, in need of money, are invited by Nancy Saunders to come to her father Vernon Steel's home. Steele wants Mohr to find a dealer for some jewels he has to sell. Inspector Denis Green believes Mohr wants to steal Steel's jewels. Steel's butler, Tom Stevenson, is married to stage star Evelyn Ankers, a gold-digger. Ankers meets with Mohr and asks him to stay away from Steel's house. Stevenson wants to reconcile with Ankers, but she wants Stevenson to commit a crime. Mohr decides to honor Steel's request. Steel entrusts the jewels to Stevenson to take to Mohr. Before Stevenson leaves, he finds the supposedly stolen Eyes of the Nile on Steel's safe and takes them. Saunders' fiancé, Richard Fraser, decides to accompany Stevenson. When the car arrives at the meeting place with Mohr, Stevenson is found at the wheel, dead. Fraser reports that Stevenson pushed him out of the car on the way to meet Mohr. Mohr goes to Ankers's apartment where he overhears Ankers tell her boyfriend, Alan Napier, to steal the jewels from Mohr. Mohr finds the jewels sewn into the sleeve in Ankers's coat. Later, Mohr has Napier reveal that Ankers murdered Stevenson. Mohr also retrieves the jewels.

Notes and Commentary: Eric Blore was Llewellyn Jamison in *Passport to Suez* (Columbia, 1943) and renamed Claudius Jamison in this film.

Jean Gillie was initially announced to play the part of Iris Chatham.

Alan Napier will be primarily remembered as the butler Alfred Pennyworth in the *Batman* television series (20th Century–Fox/ABC, 1966–68).

Reviews: "The film's plot keeps tripping over itself with story twists and subplots. Mohr is one of the weaker actors to play the Lone Wolf character." *Motion Picture Guide*, Nash and Ross

"A standard mystery, hackneyed plot." *New York Times*, 11/22/47

"Okay as solid support in duals." *Variety*, 11/26/47

Summation: This is a decent Lone Wolf episode. Gerald Mohr still doesn't fully fill the bill as the sophisticated adventurer, but is generally okay. Eric Blore is still marvelous as Mohr's man Jamison. The rest of the cast is adequate. The story line is sometimes hard to follow but director Leslie Goodwins guides the players through the story adequately.

THE LONE WOLF AND HIS LADY
Columbia (August 1949)

Bullets and mystery pursue ... the Lone Wolf and His Lady

Cast: Michael Lanyard, Ron Randell; Grace Duffy, June Vincent; Jamison, Alan Mowbray; Inspector J.D. Crane, William Frawley, Marta Frisbie, Collette Lyons; John J. Murdock, Douglass Dumbrille; Tanner, James Todd; Myriber Van Groot, Steven Geray; Steve Taylor, Robert H. Barrat// Fisher, Arthur Space; Joe Brewster, Philip Van Zandt; Bill Slovak, Jack Overman; Sergeant Henderson, Lee Phelps; Lt. Martin, Robert Williams; Tex Talbot, Fred F. Sears; Managing editor, George M. Carleton; Ava Rockling, William Newell; Paul Braud, George Tyne; Shamus O'Brien, Harry Hayden; Guards, I. Stanford Jolley and Allen Mathews; Policemen, Lane Chandler and Kernan Cripps; Messenger, David Fresco; Police broadcaster, Charles Jordan; Street cleaner, Heine Conklin

Credits: Director, John Hoffman; Producer, Rudolph C. Flothow; Story, Edward Dein; Screenwriter, Malcolm Stuart Boylan; Editor, James Sweeney; Art Director, Sturges Carne; Set Decorator, James Crowe; Cinematographer, Philip Tannura; Musical Director, Mischa Bakaleinikoff

Production Dates: August 9, 1948–August 20, 1948

Running Time: 60 min.

Source: Based on a work by Louis Joseph Vance

Story: Newspaper reporter June Vincent gets Ron Randell to cover the unveiling of the Tahara diamond. At the show, Robert H. Barret and Philip Van Zandt steal the diamond. Inspector William Frawley arrests Randell. On the rooftop, Randell's valet, Alan Mowbray, sees two suspicious men in a building across the street. Also, Mowbray believes Steven Gerey, the jeweler who cut the stone, is the key to the robbery. Barret wants Geray to recut the diamond. Randell, who has escaped from the police, finds the room with Barrat, Geray and the diamond. Mowbray joins Randell. In the encounter, Mowbray throws the diamond out of the window. The diamond is retrieved by Vincent, who hides the stone. Vincent gets the diamond back into Randell's hands. The diamond is a fake. Randell finds the real diamond in Geray's tool kit. Frawley arrests Geray.

The Lone Wolf and His Lady (1949) scene card —(left to right) Jack Overman, Philip Van Zandt, Robert H. Barrat, Ron Randell, Alan Mowbray.

Notes and Commentary: Ron Randell was Bulldog Drummond in a short series for Columbia in 1947.

William Frawley played Inspector J.D. Crane. In the silent film, *The False Faces* (Paramount/Artcraft, 1919), the character was Robert T. Crane.

Review: "A fast 60 minutes of cops-and-robbers adventure." *Variety*, 03/23/49

Summation: In viewing the film, fans of the Lone Wolf will want to like the film more than they should. Ron Randell displays the necessary athleticism, but he, like Gerald Mohr who preceded him, lacks the necessary sophistication for the role. Alan Mowbray is fine as Jamison, but he's no Eric Blore. The story is on the weak side, displaying its "B" roots, relying too much on chance to solve the crime. Bottom line: just okay, no more.

The Medico

In James L. Rubel's first novel, *The Medico of Painted Springs*, his protagonist, Cliff Monroe, is a county health officer, assigned to practice in Painted Springs. Rubel's stories are like action-packed soap operas. Throughout Rubel's stories, Monroe not only has to deal with medical emergencies, but all sorts of lawlessness, e.g. cattlemen against sheepmen, cattlemen against nesters and a ghostly apparition assisting a reign of terror. Monroe and Nancy Starweather fall in and out of love, primarily because of Nancy's jealousy and her selfishness. The rights to Rubel's first three Medico novels were purchased by Columbia, but only the first had any plot resemblance to the source. All the novels take place in the vicinity of Painted Springs. At the end of the third novel *The Medico on the Trail*, Nancy has only animosity for Monroe. This further accentuates the soap-opera aspect of the series. Three years after the conclusion of the Columbia series, Rubel, under the pseudonym Mason MacRae, wrote *The Doctor of Painted Springs*. Thanks to an extremely helpful Mrs. Elaine Brown, Assistant, Reference Services, National Library of Scotland, I was able to obtain a synopsis of this novel.

> Nancy has married a crooked banker, Forseman. In the course of events, Monroe has to perform an emergency appendectomy to save Nancy's life. Nancy's husband attempts to repay Monroe by framing him for arson. In a rapid series of events, Nancy again needs medical assistance from Monroe and her private nurse, Shan Jungward, Forseman makes two unsuccessful attempts to kill Monroe, dying in the second try. At the novel's end, Nancy is underwriting Shan's medical training. When Shan returns to Painted Springs, it is to be with and practice medicine with Monroe. Throughout the novel, the underlying story is the push for a railroad to come through Painted Springs and Forseman's attempt to gain control of nester's land to sell at an exorbitant price to the railroad.

When Columbia purchased the rights, they envisioned a new type of western starring Charles Starrett. In the early '30s, Starrett had mainly secondary roles in big-budget films and starring roles in programmers. When Columbia signed Starrett to become their new saddle ace, he had only appeared in one pseudo-western, a modern Mountie film, *Undercover Man* (Dominion, 1934). Starrett's first western for Columbia was *The Gallant Defender* (1935). He quickly became a top western star, but exhibitors were complaining of the sameness of the plots. The Medico series was bought to change this. The main character's name was changed from Cliff Monroe to Steve Monroe. Screenwriters found the Rubel novels hard to adapt to the screen, especially with a 60-minute running time. The second and third films of the series had working titles of the second and third books, but nothing from those sources was used. It has been noted that Columbia had legal issues with Rubel, and the series was discontinued. In the author's opinion, Rubel was probably appalled at how his character was presented and refused to allow any future use. The series had settled down to a typical "B" western entry. Some critics thought it moved slower than previous Starrett outings. There was only one other series character, Bones, played by comedian-singer Cliff Edwards, who never appeared in any of the novels. Starrett would play various range defenders over the next four years before settling in as The Durango Kid.

Rubel was a prolific author of westerns and mysteries. He used two pseudonyms, Mason Macrae and Timothy Hayes, at various times in his career, depending on who the agent was. Most of his novels were written as Macrae. His career spanned from 1934 to 1960.

THE MEDICO OF PAINTED SPRINGS
Columbia (June 1941)

Blasting his way through gun-roaring, song-soaring adventures ... in a new kind of role!

Alternate Title: Doctor's Alibi

Cast: Dr. Steven Monroe, Charles Starrett; Nancy Richards, Terry Walker; John Richards, Ben Taggart; Ed Gordon, Ray Bennett; Fred Burns, Wheeler Oakman; Kentucky Lane, Richard Fiske; Sheriff, Edmund Cobb; Maw Blane, Edythe Elliott; Karns, Bud Osborne; Ellis, Steve Clark; Pete, Charles Hamilton; Joe, George Chesebro; The Simp-Phonies

Credits: Director, Lambert Hillyer; Producer, Jack Fier; Story, Wyndham Gittens;

The Medico of Painted Springs (1941) scene card—(left to right) Richard Fiske, Charles Starrett, Terry Walker.

Screenwriters, Wyndham Gittens and Winston Miller; Editor, Mel Thorsen; Cinematographer, Benjamin Kline

Songs: "We'd Just as Soon Fiddle as Fight" (Wilder) sung by the Simp-Phonies; "Lonely Rangeland" (Cunningham) sung by the Simp-Phonies; "Rocking and Rolling in the Saddle" (Busse) sung by the Simp-Phonies; "Corny Troubles" (the Simp-Phonies) sung by the Simp-Phonies

Production Dates: May 5, 1941–May 14, 1941

Source: Based on the novel *The Medico of Painted Springs* by James L. Rubel

Running Time: 58 min.

Story: Dr. Charles Starrett has the assignment of examining recruits for Teddy Roosevelt's Rough Riders. As Starrett arrives by stagecoach in Painted Springs, a gunfight between cattlemen and sheepmen breaks out. Cattleman Ben Taggart's daughter, Terry Walker (a passenger on the coach), and sheepman Ray Bennett are wounded. Starrett treats both patients. Wheeler Oakman is responsible for the trouble between the two factions. Oakman plans to steal Taggart's cattle and place the blame on Bennett. Walker is fond of both Starrett and foreman Richard Fiske. Henchman Charles Hamilton shoots Fiske and places the blame on Starrett. Near death, Fiske is revived by Starrett long enough for him to name Hamilton as the man who shot him. Tensions have reached a fever pitch between the cattlemen and the sheepmen and Taggart's men are poised to wipe out Bennett's men. Starrett arrives in time to prevent hostilities. Meanwhile, Walker accuses Oakman of rustling. Oakman puts Walker in Hamilton's hands and Hamilton rides off with her. Taggart's men arrive to take Oakman into custody. Starrett races after Hamilton. Starrett rescues Walker and forces Hamilton to reveal Oakman's crooked schemes. The cattlemen and sheepmen decide they can live together. Starrett rides off to continue his assignment of examining recruits.

Notes and Commentary: The Medico received a name change from Cliff Monroe to Steven Monroe as he moved from the written page to the silver screen. In addition, Nancy Starweather became Nancy Richards; Puff Gordon became Ed Gordon; and Kentucky Landers became Kentucky Lane. Maw Blane's name remained the same. Other character names did not appear in the novel.

In the novel, Cliff Monroe is the county health officer, assigned to practice in Painted Springs. Monroe has to straddle the fence in the midst of a range war between the cattlemen and the sheepmen. In the course of bringing an end to hostilities, Monroe has to deal with hoof and mouth disease, small pox, and being framed for murder before ending the criminal career of Puff Gordon. In addition, Monroe and sheepman's daughter, Nancy Starweather, fall in love and it looks like wedding bells will ring at the novel's end.

James Rubel was living in Newport Beach, California, when the film was completed. A local movie house, the Lido Theater, was the site of the film's premiere. *The Medico of Painted Springs* was the only one of Rubel's novels to be made into a movie.

Some sources indicate Enright Busse wrote the song, "Lonely Rangeland."

Reviews: "Pretty good actioner in Charles Starrett's Columbia series." *Western Movies,* Pitts

"The picture's main failing is Miller and Gittens' dialogue which has Starrett oscillate between being a brash cowboy and a mild-mannered medico." *The Western,* Hardy

"Saddled with sophomoric episodes and dialog *The Medico of Painted Springs* will find a groove for the Saturday matinees, where the kids stand for anything as long as it's a western." *Variety,* 6/25/41

Summation: The picture was not available for viewing by the author.

THUNDER OVER THE PRAIRIE

Columbia (July 1941)

Bullets barking! Knuckles cracking! Rhythms ringing!

Cast: Dr. Steven Monroe, Charles Starrett; Bones Malloy, Cliff Edwards; Nona Mandan, Eileen O'Hearn; Roy Mandan, Stanley Brown; Timmy Wheeler, Danny Mummert; Clay Mandan, David Sharpe; Hartley, Joe McGuinn; Taylor, Donald Curtis; Dave Wheeler, Ted Adams; Henry Clayton, Jack Rockwell; Judge Merryweather, Budd Buster; Cal Shrun and His Rhythm Rangers

Credits: Director, Lambert Hillyer; Producer, William Berke; Screenwriter, Betty Burbridge; Editor, Burton Kramer; Cinematographer, Benjamin Kline

Songs: "Saddle Tramps" (Hughes and Shrum); "Diggin' in the Cold, Cold Ground" (Hughes and Shrum); "Headin' for Home" (Hughes and Shrum)

Location Filming: Iverson, California

Source: Based on the novel *The Medico Rides* by James L. Rubel

Running Time: 60 min.

Story: Indian Stanley Brown returns to Rock City from medical school — without completing his studies — when he receives word that his father is near death. Drought has devastated the community. Brown finds his brother, David Sharpe, digging ditches on an irrigation project run by Jack Rockwell, the unscrupulous project boss. Brown's college roommate, Charles Starrett, comes to Rock City. His medical assistance is needed and he works tirelessly with most of the patients unable to pay him. Brown and Sharpe get into an altercation with Rockwell's henchmen, Joe McGuinn and Donald Curtis, and are fired. Brown and Sharpe decide to make a living by breaking and selling wild horses to the construction company. The first herd they bring in has two horses with the construction company's brand and they're branded as rustlers. In escaping from the law, Brown is seriously wounded. Starrett is brought to the brother's hideout. Starrett successfully operates on Brown. Starrett tries to make the brothers give themselves up and show that they are innocent. A violent storm begins to erode the dam, due to the use of substandard materials. The dam is dynamited and Rockwell accuses Brown and Sharpe. One of the workmen, Ted Adams, testifies for Rockwell. Starrett, called in to treat Adams's son, Danny Mummert, realizes Adams's testimony was false, and makes him confess the truth. Brown has been captured and forced to stand trial. In an attempt to free his brother, Sharpe and some Indian comrades round up another herd of horses and stampede them into town. In the turmoil, Brown mortally wounds McGuinn. Mummert is badly hurt and dies in Starrett's arms. Before he dies, McGuinn confesses and names Rockwell as his crooked leader. Brown and Sharpe are declared innocent of all crimes. Starrett rides off to new adventures.

Notes and Commentary: From the working title, "The Medico Rides," it appears the book of the same name would be used. Since the screenwriters scrapped the book entirely, James L. Rubel's title went also.

Reviews: "Okay Charles Starrett vehicle." *Western Movies*, Pitts

"The script is superior to the first in the series, *The Medico of Painted Springs*, concentrating as it does more on action and less on the bedside-manner aspect of doctoring." *The Western*, Hardy

"Picture is strictly a filler for the action houses and the juve matinees." *Variety*, 7/30/41

Summation: Having seen this film only once about 50 years ago, nothing about it stands out in my memory as being any more than average fare.

PRAIRIE STRANGER
Columbia (September 1941)

Bullets blazing to the tempo of torrid tunes!

Cast: Dr. Steven Monroe, Charles Starrett; "Bones," Cliff Edwards; Sue Evans, Patti McCarty; Jud Evans, Forbes Murray; Jim Dawson, Frank LaRue; Barton, Archie Twitchell; Craig, Francis Walker; Dr. Westridge, Edmund Cobb; Undertaker, Jim Corey; Whittling Jones, Russ Powell; Lew Preston and His Ranch Hands

Credits: Director, Lambert Hillyer; Producer, William Berke; Screenwriter, Winston Miller; Editor, James Sweeney; Cinematography, Benjamin Kline

Songs: "I'll Be a Cowboy 'Till I Die" (Preston and Willingham) sung by Cliff Edwards with Lew Preston and His Ranch Hands; "Doin' It Right" (Preston and Willingham) played by Lew Preston and His Ranch Hands; "It's Just a Small Town" (Preston and Willingham) played by Lew Preston and His Ranch Hands; "Ride, Cowboy, Ride" played by Lew Preston and His Ranch Hands; "Scallywag" sung by Cliff Edwards with Lew Preston and His Ranch Hands

Source: Based on the novel *The Medico On the Trail* by James L. Rubel

Running Time: 58 min.

Story: Seeing that the town of Red Fork needs a doctor, Charles Starrett and his pal, Cliff Edwards, decide to set up practice there. The townspeople believe Starrett is too young. When an older physician, Edmund Cobb, arrives, the townspeople switch their loyalties to him. This forces Starrett and Edwards to take jobs as cowboys on Forbes Murray's ranch. A rival rancher, Frank LaRue, plots to destroy Forbes's cattle. LaRue blackmails Cobb, who is an ex-convict, to manufacture a poison to kill Forbes's cattle. Forbes's foreman, Archie Twitchell, is working for LaRue. Twitchell takes the poison and hides it in his bunk. Edwards finds the bottle and takes it to Starrett to analyze the contents. LaRue finds that Starrett is in possession of the poison and accuses him of poisoning cattle. Starrett escapes to prove his innocence. Fearing Cobb will talk, LaRue has Twitchell kill him. Starrett and Edwards gain possession of the fatal bullet. At a dance, Edwards takes all the guns and Starrett is able to prove Twitchell's gun killed Cobb. Twitchell tries to escape, but Starrett brings him to justice.

Notes and Commentary: The working title was "The Medico Rides the Trail." The storyline of James L. Rubel's book again was completely eliminated, as was the book's title.

Reviews: "Average Charles Starrett western." *Western Movies*, Pitts

"Unexciting outing in the short-lived Doctor Monroe series. The plot drags on, offering a few moments of adventure near the ending." *Motion Picture Guide*, Nash and Ross

"Rebounding from a decline following the striking opener of the series, Columbia's 'Medico' sequence of westerns starring Charles Starrett levels off in this number to a pitch of entertainment promising sustained popularity." *Motion Picture Herald Product Digest*, 9/6/41

"Actionless western starring Charles Starrett.... Weak entry." *Variety*, 09/03/41

Summation: The picture was not available for viewing by the author.

Mr. District Attorney

Champion of the people! Defender of truth! Guardian of our fundamental rights to life, liberty, and the pursuit of happiness! ... and it shall be my duty as district attorney not only to prosecute to the limit of the law all persons accused of crimes perpetrated within this county, but to defend with equal vigor the rights and privileges of all its citizens.

This series was inspired by the exploits of Thomas E. Dewey. During the 1930s Dewey had been both a special and federal prosecutor before becoming the district attorney of Manhattan, New York. Dewey had become nationally recognized for his convictions of gangsters Waxey Gordon and Lucky Luciano. He also cracked down on both white- and blue-collar criminals.

Ed Byron created the concept for a radio series and brought it to the attention of Phillips H. Lord, who helped with its development. It was Lord who came up with the show's title. It began on April 3, 1939 as a 15-minute serial with Dwight Weist in the title role. Three months later, it became a 30-minute, self-contained series, now starring Raymond Edward Johnson. In 1940, Jay Jostyn took over the role as Mr. District Attorney, a part he would keep through the life of the radio show. When *Mr. District Attorney* transferred to television on October 1, 1951, Jostyn was still in the title role. Also in the cast were radio regulars Vicki Vola as Miss Miller and Len Doyle as Harrington. A Whitman Big Little Book, *Mr. District Attorney* was published in 1941. Republic Pictures decided a movie series was in order but made some drastic changes. Mr. District Attorney now had a name, Tom F. Winton, and his chief assistant was P. Cadwallader Jones. Not present were Miss Miller and Harrington. In the radio series, Mr. District Attorney was called either, Chief, Mr. D.A., or Boss. In the initial entry, *Mr. District Attorney* (Republic, 1941), Stanley Ridges played Winton and Dennis O'Keefe was Jones. In the second of the series, *Mr. District Attorney in the Carter Case* (Republic, 1941), Paul Harvey was Winton and James Ellison (Johnny Nelson of the early Hopalong Cassidy sagas) took on the role of Jones. There was a third in the series, *Secrets of the Underground* (Republic, 1942) that probably left the Mr. District Attorney fans shaking their heads. Winton was now played by the unbilled Pierre Watkin. When the character was called to Washington, D.C. for wartime duty, the district attorney mantle was transferred to Jones, now played by John Hubbard. The series was then cancelled.

In 1947, *Mr. District Attorney* (Columbia) returned to the screen with Adolphe Menjou. This was Menjou's first crack at a series since Thatcher Colt in 1932–33. Menjou's district attorney was named Craig Warren. Present in this story were Harrington, played by veteran actor Michael O'Shea, and pert Jeff Donnell took the part of Miss Miller. As in the first version, Dennis O'Keefe played the part of a novice assistant, almost succumbing to the murderous charms of Marguerite Chapman. Though intended as a series of seven features, only the one film was made. In 1948 with the January–February issue, National Periodic Publications began a long-running comic book series based on the radio program. The series ran for 67 issues, ending with the January–February 1959 issue. This was not the district attorney's first comic book appearance; he was in issue 35 of *The Funnies* (Dell, September 1939) and *Mr. District Attorney No. 13* (Dell, 1942). Jostyn's television series for ABC was cancelled after the June 23, 1952 program. Ziv Television Programs produced a syndicated show in 1954 with David Brian in the lead role of District Attorney Paul Garrett, with Jackie Loughery as Miss Miller. This would be the last appearance of Mr. District Attorney on any screen.

MR. DISTRICT ATTORNEY
Columbia (February 1947)

Hunted men and their women — one step ahead of the relentless pursuit of the law

Alternate Title: District Attorney

Cast: Steve Bennett, Dennis O'Keefe; Craig Warren, Adolphe Menjou; Marcia Manning, Marguerite Chapman; Harrington, Michael O'Shea; James Randolph, George Coulouris; Miss Miller, Jeff Donnell; Berotti, Steven Geray; Ed Jamison, Ralph Morgan; Franzen, John Kellogg// Marsden, Ralf Harolde; Mrs. Marsden, Joan Blair; Longfield, Charles Trowbridge; Gang Leader, Robert Barron; Defense Attorney, Frank Wilcox; Gallentyne, Holmes Herbert; Captain Lambert, Cliff Clark; Party guest, Arthur Space; Peter Lantz, Frank Reicher; Judge, Forbes Murray; Newsboy, Johnny Duncan; Doorman, Gene Roth

Credits: Director, Robert B. Sinclair; Assistant Director, James Nicholson; Producer, Samuel Bischoff; Story, Sidney Marshall; Adaptation, Ben Markson; Screenwriter, Ian McLellan Hunter; Editor, William Lyon; Art Directors, Stephen Goosson and George Brooks; Set Decorator, Earl Teass; Cinematographer, Bert Glennon; Gowns, Jean Louis; Sound, Jack Goodrich; Musical Director, M.W. Stoloff

Source: Based on the radio program *Mr. District Attorney* created by Phillips H. Lord

Production Dates: July 29, 1946–September 5, 1946

Running Time: 81 min.

Story: Marguerite Chapman, a suspected murderess, has a key position with racketeer George Coulouris. In addition, Coulouris wants to begin an affair with Chapman, but she wants marriage and wealth before love. District Attorney Adolphe Menjou's assistant, Dennis O'Keefe, is prosecuting one of Coulouris's associates. Chapman begins an affair with O'Keefe and obtains information that destroys his case. O'Keefe proposes to Chapman, but she rejects him. Menjou interferes and forces Chapman to give up O'Keefe. Chapman marries Coulouris. O'Keefe learns what Menjou did and resigns. Chapman murders another of Coulouris's associates when he decides to give information to Menjou. Chapman arranges for O'Keefe to work for Coulouris. She also verifies that O'Keefe still loves her. Coulouris is murdered and O'Keefe is thought to be the murderer. Nightclub owner Steven Geray observed the murder and goes to Chapman's apartment. Geray accuses Chapman of the crime. Menjou arrives and Geray gets the drop on him. Chapman shoots Geray, telling Menjou that she did it to save his life. Menjou believes O'Keefe to be innocent. Wearing a wire, O'Keefe goes to see Chapman, who confesses. She wants to marry O'Keefe and take over Coulouris's rackets. O'Keefe plans to turn Chapman in. She tries to push O'Keefe off

The underworld crumples under Mr. District Attorney's hammer blows!

Copyright 1946 Columbia Pictures Corp.   PRINTED IN U S A   7   46/992

Mr. District Attorney (1947) scene card — Adolphe Menjou (center) with gun on Robert Barron (left center), Dennis O'Keefe (over Menjou's left shoulder), other actors unidentified.

the eighth-story balcony, but he moves aside and Chapman plunges to her death. Menjou welcomes O'Keefe back as his assistant.

Notes and Commentary: The film begins with the same opening lines as the radio program.

Mr. District Attorney is given a name in this film unlike the radio program that called him either "Mr. D.A." or "Boss."

The producers wanted Tallulah Bankhead and Edward G. Robinson for roles in this film.

This was director Robert B. Sinclair's first postwar film assignment.

Reviews: "Phillips H. Lord's popular radio show *Mr. District Attorney* provided the inspiration for a lukewarm thriller." *The Columbia Story*, Hirschhorn

"Decent performances and good production, unfortunately, are lost in a haphazard script." *Motion Picture Guide*, Nash and Ross

"It is a rather haphazard version of the ether whodunit with cloudy storyline that will not always be clear to ticket buyers." *Variety*, 12/25/46

Summation: This is a good crime melodrama that is faithful to the radio program. The taut screenplay emphasizes the film noir genre highlighted by Robert B. Sinclair's direction and Bert Glennon's cinematography. The acting is first-rate. Marguerite Chapman scores strongly as a femme fatale who will stop at nothing to get what she wants. Dennis O'Keefe matches Chapman as an aspiring assistant district attorney who is out of his depth in his dealings with Chapman. Adolphe Menjou sparkles as Mr. District Attorney.

Nero Wolfe

Fer-de-Lance (Farrar & Rinehart, 1934), by author Rex Stout, introduced mystery readers to the corpulent, eccentric detective Nero Wolfe. Wolfe has a particular distaste for leaving his brownstone on W. 35th Street in New York City. Wolfe balances his daily routine with tending to his orchids and actually working on a case. He loves gourmet food and beer. Since Wolfe rarely leaves the sanctity of his home, most of legwork is left to his assistant, Archie Goodwin. Archie spins the yarn in his breezy, often humorous style. Archie is blessed with the ability to remember long conversations with many participants verbatim. He also has a unique fighting style, planting a hard right to the kidney of his opponent, rendering him temporarily immobile. The Wolfe and Goodwin tandem immediately became popular. Stout followed with another well-received novel in 1935, *The League of Frightened Men*.

For $7,500 Columbia attained the screen rights to *Fer-de-Lance* and the option to purchase additional stories. Rex Stout stated that Charles Laughton would make the perfect Wolfe on the screen. Laughton was asked to portray Wolfe and said that he would consent to do one but not a series. Columbia decided to cast Edward Arnold, thinking that he could play Wolfe between bigger budgeted features. (Arnold's career began in silents in 1916. He became a star with *Diamond Jim* [Universal, 1935].) Arnold decided he didn't want to be a series star and bowed out. By 1938, Arnold realized his career rested with character roles and his talents were in demand. Interestingly he did take the lead in two Duncan Maclain mysteries in the '40s. Arnold was replaced by Walter Connolly, who was thought would have played the role in the first place. A noted character actor, Connolly, like Arnold, began his career in silents. Connolly physically fit the part but his high-pitched voice could not effectively properly convey the character. (Connolly did play a famous detective. He took the role of Charlie Chan on radio from 1932–1938.) Lionel Stander played Archie in both Columbia entries, although he did not meet Stout's conception of Archie. After the two films, Stout would not agree to let the series continue. One would surmise that Stout did not like how the Columbia screenwriters were bringing Wolfe and Archie to the screen. Stout was a prolific writer, with 33 novels and 41 short stories. His final work, *A Family Affair* (The Viking Press) was published in 1975.

The Adventures of Nero Wolfe came to radio in 1943–44 with J.B. Williams, Santos Ortega and Luis Van Rooten, portraying at various times, Wolfe. Wolfe was back on radio in 1946 as *The Amazing Nero Wolfe* with Francis X. Bushman in the lead. *The New Adventures of Nero Wolfe* aired on October 20, 1950 starring Sydney Greenstreet. The series never really caught on; Greenstreet blamed the low ratings on the actors who played Archie. It must have sounded like Archie de jour. In the six-month run, there were five actors in the role: Gerald Mohr, Herb Ellis, Larry Dobkin, Wally Maher and Harry Bartell.

In late November 1957 into 1958, a Nero Wolfe comic strip was syndicated by Columbia Features. The comic strip was the basis for a Miller Series comic book published in 1959. There was a name change for the corpulent detective to Theo Drake, but Archie's name remained unchanged.

Nero Wolfe came to the television screen in 1979, four years after Stout's death. Wolfe was played by Thayer David, with Tom Mason as Archie. A series may have resulted, but halted due to David's untimely death. In 1981, William Conrad would be the next Wolfe. Conrad was a good choice physically, but Conrad's facial hair and cuteness in interpreting the role put off Wolfe aficionados. Lee Horsely was Archie. Wolfe returned to novel form in 1985, with new stories by Robert Goldsborough. Goldsborough wrote seven novels, the last being *The Missing Chapter* (Bantam) in 1994. Wolfe left the printed page but returned to television on the A & E network in March 2000 with the movie, *The Golden Spiders: A Nero Wolfe Mystery*. The film was successful, and a Nero Wolfe series was launched in 2001. There was impeccable casting with Timothy Hutton as Archie and Maury Chaykin as Wolfe. Stout's stories formed the basis for the television programs, even to the point of utilizing Stout's dialogue. Wolfe may be off the screen, but his exploits are still being read and reread.

MEET NERO WOLFE
Columbia (July 1936)

Slyest of sleuths!

A B.P. Schulberg Production

Cast: Nero Wolfe, Edward Arnold; Archie Goodwin, Lionel Stander; Ellen Barstow, Joan Perry; Claude Roberts, Victor Jory; Sarah Barstow, Nana Bryant; Mazie Gray, Dennie Moore; Manuel Kimball, Russell Hardie; E.J. Kimball, Walter Kingsford; Prof. Barstow, Boyd Irwin; Olaf, John Qualen; O'Grady, Gene Morgan; Maria, Rita Cansino; Dr. Bradford, Frank Conroy// Golf starter, Eddy Waller; Johnny, William Benedict; Carlo, Juan Torena; Apartment house maid, Martha Tibbetts; Mike, George Offerman, Jr.; Tommy, Raymond Borzage; Bill, William Anderson; Kimball's chauffer, David Worth; Kimball's butler, Eric Wilton

Credits: Director, Herbert Biberman; Story, Rex Stout; Screenwriters, Howard J. Green, Bruce Manning and Joseph Anthony; Editor, Otto Meyer; Art Director, Stephen Goosson; Cinematographer, Henry Freulich; Costume, Lon Anthony; Musical Director, Howard Jackson

Production Dates: April 1, 1936–April 27, 1936

Running Time: 70 min.

Story: Boyd Irwin dies on a golf course. Then Juan Torena is murdered. In his hand was the newspaper article of Irwin's murder, that the murderer removes from his hands. Torena's sister, Rita Cansino, hires renowned private detective Edward Arnold, who deduces that the deaths of Irwin and Torena were connected. Irwin's wife, Nana Bryant, offers Arnold $50,000 to uncover the murderer's identity. Arnold's investigation leads to the conclusion that Walter Kingsford was the intended victim, not Irwin. Kingsford is skeptical until a deadly snake, a Fer-de-lance, kills his chauffeur, David Worth. After another attempt to murder Kingsford, Arnold gathers all the suspects together in his house. An attempt to murder Arnold fails. Arnold reveals Kingsford's son, Russell Hardie, is the murderer. Hardie believed his father murdered his mother and wanted revenge.

Meet Nero Wolfe (1936) movie still—(left to right) Lionel Stander, Dennie Moore, Edward Arnold, Victor Jory, Joan Perry, Frank Conroy, John Qualen, Nana Bryant, Walter Kingsford, Russell Hardie.

Notes and Commentary: The working title for the film was "Fer-de-Lance," the title of the novel by Rex Stout. The story was published in abridged form in the March 1934 issue of *American Magazine* before being released in hardcover by Farrar & Rinehart on September 17, 1934. Although the basic premise of the story is maintained, there are some major differences: the daughter and the widow's first names were switched; there was no second murder; and Nero Wolfe allows the murderer to commit suicide, thereby avenging the death of his mother and also ending the life of his father. The Swiss chef and housekeeper, Fritz Brenner, became Olaf, a Scandinavian. The character of Archie Goodwin is far more polished in the novel than what is shown on the screen. How did the screenwriters come up with "comic" interludes of Archie wanting to get married to Mazie Gray? Archie had no steady romantic interest until he met Lily Rowan in *Some Buried Caesar* (Farrar & Rinehart, 1939).

Rita Cansino would become a legend as screen goddess Rita Hayworth.

It has been said Harry Cohn had both Joan Perry and Rita Cansino in his office. He told Cansino that he would make her a star. To Perry he said she would become his wife. Both predictions came true.

Reviews: "Strong whodunit fare, thickly studded with comedy and with Edward Arnold registering solidly in the name role." *Variety*, 7/22/36

"Arnold is outstanding as the beer-gulping, orchid-growing sleuth. The tension and mystery are well conceived and sustained by director Biberman, and the script is taut and true to Stout's novel." *Motion Picture Guide*, Nash and Ross

Summation: *Meet Nero Wolfe* is a good murder-mystery, with Edward Arnold most effective in the title role. Unfortunately the script has Arnold too jovial and laughing too much, a trait definitely not found in Rex Stout's stories. Certainly Arnold fit the part physically and shows the necessary toughness when the part calls for it. Lionel Stander is adequate as Archie. At this stage in the novels, Archie was still rough around the edges but not as rough as Stander portrays him. The script has Stander getting married at the fade-out, something Stout would never have his Archie do. The supporting cast gives ample support with Victor Jory and Walter Kingsford singled out for acting honors.

THE LEAGUE OF FRIGHTENED MEN
Columbia (May 1937)

Detective Nero Wolfe reveals....

Cast: Nero Wolfe, Walter Connolly; Archie Goodwin, Lionel Stander; Paul Chapin, Eduardo Ciannelli; Evelyn Hibbard, Irene Hervey; Pitney Scott, Victor Kilian; Agnes Burton, Nana Bryant; Mark Chapin, Allen Brook; Ferdinand Bowen, Walter Kingsford; Professor Hibbard, Leonard Mudie; Dr. Burton, Kenneth Hunter; Augustus Farrell, Charles Irwin; Dora Chapin, Rafaela Ottiano; Inspector Cramer, Edward McNamara; Michael Ayers, Jamison Thomas; Nicholas Cabot, Ian Wolfe; Alexander Drummond, Jonathan Hale; Fritz, Herbert Ashley; Joe, James Flavin// Book shop owner, Clara Blandick; Policeman, Ed Cobb

Credits: Director, Alfred E. Green; Associate Producer, Edward Chodorov; Screenwriters, Eugene Solow and Guy Endore; Editor, Gene Milford; Art Director, Stephen Goosson; Cinematographer, Henry Freulich; Gowns, Kalloch

Production Dates: February 17, 1937–mid–March 1937

Source: Novel, *The League of Frightened Men* by Rex Stout

Running Time: 71 min.

Story: A college-hazing incident by ten students went awry, and Eduardo Ciannelli is permanently injured. Years later, two of the students are dead and the remaining eight have received threatening notes. Worried, Professor Leonard Mudie hires Walter Connolly to find the sender. Mudie then disappears. Connelly requests the remaining seven come to his office. All comply except Victor Kilian. At the meeting, banker Walter Kingsford notes that the two men died penniless. Ciannelli goes to Dr. Kenneth Hunter's house. While Ciannelli is in the house, Hunter is killed with his own gun. Connolly defends Ciannelli and postulates the murderer was hiding in a closet and waited until Ciannelli arrives before murdering Hunter. In his investigation, Connolly reveals Ciannelli did write the threatening letters. Kingsford took advantage of this situation to begin his murder spree and had hoped to place the guilt of Ciannelli. Kingsford had misappropriated the funds his fellow classmates had left in his custody. Mudie reappears, having dropped out of sight to find proof against Ciannelli.

Notes and Commentary: Walter Connolly took over the role of Nero Wolfe in this entry. Connolly is physically suited to the part, although he had a high-pitched voice that is foreign to Stout's character.

Columbia's screenwriters made a few significant changes: the league was decreased from

The League of Frightened Men (1937) scene card —(lower left) Allen Brook, Irene Hervey, (center, left to right) Rafaela Ottiano, Lionel Stander, Walter Connolly, Eduardo Cianelli, (far right, top to bottom) Lionel Stander, Walter Connolly.

29 to just ten members; and all of the deaths in the film were murders while in the novel, the first two were accidents and only the final death was a murder.

Columbia bowed to the Production Code and had Nero Wolfe drink hot chocolate instead of his usual beer. Egad!

The screenwriters made additional changes in the Wolfe character as created by Rex Stout. They had Wolfe getup from his desk to receive a visitor, actually perform some of his own investigations and at the fade, had Wolfe and Archie going out for a drink. The screenwriters, also, had Archie, in conversations with suspects, refer to Wolfe as Nero — something Archie would never do in the novels.

For the second in the series, chef and housekeeper Olaf is gone and Fritz, from Rex Stout's novels, is listed in the credits (as played by Herbert Ashley). Throughout the film, Ashley is called Butch, who is an ex-pug.

In the series previous entry, Archie wanted to get married to Mazie Gray. Thankfully that subplot was dropped.

Reviews: "Hardly any audience likes to watch a character who just sits and thinks. Thus, 'League of Frightened Men' suffers from inactivity. He [Nero Wolfe] drinks beer in the novel but hot chocolate in the picture. That's the best explanation of what's wrong with the film." *Variety,* 6/16/37

"A boring mystery with Connolly playing Nero Wolfe and solving the case from his study. Action is limited and the villain is obvious from the beginning of the film." *Motion Picture Guide*, Nash and Ross

Summation: The picture proved to be a pleasant surprise. Walter Connolly is adequate as Wolfe, despite his high-pitched voice. Lionel Stander makes a better Archie this time out. Eduardo Ciannelli captures the character of Paul Chapin and is the standout actor in the film. Director Alfred E. Green keeps the film moving briskly to keep the audience's interest.

Night Editor

Hal Burdick created the *Night Editor* radio program that featured short stories with an ironic twist. The program first aired in 1934 and was popular enough to run until 1948 on the NBC network. All programs were fifteen minutes long. Burdick, using his own name, played the Night Editor who told his stories to Bobby, a fellow newspaperman, over a cup of Edwards coffee (of course, the show's sponsor). As Burdick told the story, he was the voice of all the characters. Stories ran the gamut of all genres, from high adventure to human interest. The popularity of the show encouraged Columbia to develop a movie series. The initial entry falls into the film noir genre. The Night Editor's name was changed to Crane Stewart and was played by Charles D. Brown. When audience's failed to respond, the proposed series was discontinued. *Night Editor* made a stab at television with Burdick back in the lead role. The show aired on the Dumont network. The final broadcast date was September 8, 1954.

NIGHT EDITOR

Columbia (March 1946)

In the middle of a kiss ... murder! The thrill of the year in emotional tenseness!
Radio's Night Editor ... in the middle of his first blazing screen adventure!

Alternate Title: The Trespasser
Cast: Tony Cochrane, William Gargan; Jill Merrill, Janis Carter; Martha Cochrane, Jeff Donnell; Johnny, Coulter Irwin; Crane Stewart, Charles D. Brown; Ole Strom, Paul E. Burns; Capt. Lawrence, Harry Shannon; Douglas Loring, Frank Wilcox; Doc Cochrane, Robert Kellard// Street sweeper driver, John Tyrell; Max, Robert Emmett Keane; Swanson, Charles Marsh; Necktie, Lou Lubin; Doc Cochran as a boy, Michael Chapin; Tusco, Anthony Caruso; Coroner, Emmett Vogan; Dickstein, Ed Chandler; Butler, Frank Dae; Benjamin Merrill, Roy Gordon; Bank manager, Douglas Woods; Phillips, Charles Waggenheim; Heavyset man in library, Vernon Dent; Clerk, Jimmy Lloyd; Luke, Murray Leonard; Bartender, Harry Tyler; District Attorney Halloran, Jack Davis
Credits: Director, Henry Levin; Producer, Ted Richmond; Story, Scott Littleton, Screenwriter, Hal Smith; Editor, Richard Fantl; Art Director, Robert Peterson; Set Decorator, James Crowe; Cinematographers, Burnett Guffey and Philip Tannura; Sound, Lambert Day; Musical Director; Mischa Bakaleinikoff
Source: Based on the radio program *Night Editor* by Hal Burdick
Production Dates: December 26, 1945–January 12, 1946

Running Time: 68 min.

Story: Night editor Charles D. Brown tells reporter Coulter Irwin the story of policeman William Gargan's affair with socialite Janis Carter. Irwin has not been home for a week and is now afraid to go. Gargan and Carter are both married. Gargan takes Carter to a secluded spot to break off the affair. Carter is able to seduce Gargan. In the throes of their lovemaking, another car pulls up. A woman is murdered. Gargan lets the murderer escape to avoid a personal scandal. Gargan is assigned to the case and learns that Carter knew the murdered woman — as well as the murderer. The murderer is bank president Frank Wilcox, whom Gargan also recognizes. Gargan wants Carter to go with him to police headquarters, but she refuses. When an innocent man is accused of the crime, Gargan looks for other evidence to convict Wilcox. Carter is now having an affair with Wilcox and provides an alibi for him. Gargan has no other choice but to come forward. Gargan goes to arrest Wilcox and finds him in a passionate embrace with Carter. Enraged, Carter stabs Gargan in the back with an ice pick. Gargan hands over his prisoners and surrenders his badge before collapsing. As the story ends, Irwin leaves the newsroom. In the lobby, Irwin realizes the cigar stand owner is Gargan and that his family stood by him. Irwin now knows the importance of family and decides to go home.

Notes and Commentary: The working title was "Inside Story," which had been heard on the *Night Editor* radio program.

Night Editor was released on DVD as a part of the *Columbia Bad Girls of Film Noir Collection* in 2010.

Night Editor (1946) title card — (left to right) William Gargan, Janis Carter, Harry Shannon.

Reviews: "An inept cop drama." *The Columbia Story*, Hirschhorn

"This is a classic example of film noir with its analogies between sex and violence, women who use sex to get what they want, and basic negativity toward people in general. Gargan is dull and ineffectual in his role as detective-narrator, but this may have been the intention." *Motion Picture Guide*, Nash and Ross [Author's note: the narrator was newspaper editor Crane Stewart, played by Charles D. Brown.]

"Cockeyed police-sleuth meller. It's an instance of a good idea gone haywire via slipshod production and faulty direction." *Variety*, 04/03/46

Summation: This is a good film noir that was supposed to be the first of an anthology series similar to that of The Whistler. Henry Levin nicely directs the story with flawless performances by William Gargan and Janis Carter. The cinematography by Burnett Guffey and Philip Tannura is first-rate. The delicate shadings of black and white add immensely to the film noir tale. On a minor note: it would have been stronger film noir if Gargan had succumbed to Carter's murder attempt, and if the wraparound story had been eliminated.

Robin Hood

The debate still rages as to whether Robin Hood was real or just a fictional character. The earliest references date back to the late 13th century. From the late 14th- to the early-15th century ballads about Robin Hood began to be heard. It was noted that Robin was a skilled archer and swordsman. In the earliest stories, he was a commoner. Later he became a yeoman, and finally an aristocrat disposed of his land and branded an outlaw. At first Robin's named companions were Will Scarlet, Little John and Much the Miller's Son. Later stories added Maid Marion and Alan-a-Dale. To add more adventure and excitement, Robin's stories departed from just local adventure to taking arms against King John while the true king, Richard, is participating in the Crusades. In the 19th century, books were

The Bandit of Sherwood Forest (1946) title card — (center left) Cornel Wilde, (lower right) Anita Louise, Cornell Wilde.

271

written about Robin but geared to children's tastes. Two such books were *The Merry Adventures of Robin Hood* by Howard Pyle and *The Prince of Thieves* by Alexandre Dumas.

Robin Hood has been a screen favorite for almost 100 years. Robert Frazer, an actor familiar to serial and western film lovers, was the first screen Robin in *Robin Hood* (Universal Film Manufacturing Co., 1912). The silent screen's definitive Robin was Douglas Fairbanks in *Robin Hood* (United Artists, 1922). It took Errol Flynn to set the screen's standards in *The Adventures of Robin Hood* (Warner Bros., 1938). Robin next appeared as a father figure but still went into action in the personage of Russell Hicks in *The Bandit of Sherwood Forest* (Columbia, 1946). The film focused on Robin's son, Robert, played by Cornel Wilde. Jon Hall was the next Robin in *The Prince of Thieves* (Columbia, 1948). (Hall had gained fame as Maria Montez's co-star in six sex-and-sand epics for Universal from 1942–45. Later Hall gain additional recognition as Ramar in the television *Ramar of the Jungle* (Arrow Productions, 1952–54). The next Columbia entry that took place in Sherwood Forest dealt on with Robin's son, also named Robin, in *The Rogues of Sherwood Forest* (1950). John Derek took the lead. Other notable appearances of Robin include *The Story of Robin Hood and His Merrie Men* (Disney, RKO, 1952); the television series *Adventures of Robin Hood* (CBS, 1955–58) with Richard Green; the 1960 British feature *Sword of Sherwood Forest*, also with Richard Greene; Walt Disney's animated feature *Robin Hood* (Buena Vista, 1973) with the voice of Brian Bedford as Robin; *Robin and Marion* (Columbia, 1976) with Sean Connery; *Robin Hood: Prince of Thieves* (Warner Bros., 1991) with Kevin Costner, and *Robin Hood* (Universal, 2010) with Russell Crowe.

THE BANDIT OF SHERWOOD FOREST
Columbia (February 1946)

And now the Son of Robin Hood ... dashing lover ... adventurer ... outlaw!

Alternate Title: The Son of Robin Hood

Cast: Lady Catherine, Anita Louise; Queen Mother, Jill Esmond; Friar Tuck, Edgar Buchanan; Robert of Nottingham, Cornel Wilde; William of Pembroke, Henry Daniell; Fitz-Herbert, George Macready; Robin Hood, Russell Hicks; Will Scarlett, John Abbott; Sheriff of Nottingham, Lloyd Corrigan; Mother Meg, Eva Moore// Lord Warrick, Miles Mander; Little John, Ray Teal; Allan-A-Dale, Leslie Denison; Lord Mortimer, Ian Wolfe; The king, Maurice Tauzin; Men-at-Arms, Mauritz Hugo and Ben Corbett; Prioress Guards, Philip Van Zandt, Robert Williams and Harry Cording; Robin Hood's men, Robert Scott, George Eldredge, Ross Hunter and Nelson Leigh; Innkeeper, Ferdinand Munier; Jailer, Gene Stutenroth; Outlaws, Lane Chandler, Dan Stowell and Blackie Whiteford; Crossbowman, Jimmy Lloyd; Castle gate guard, Dick Curtis

Credits: Directors, George Sherman and Henry Levin; Assistant Director, Wilbur McGaugh; Producers, Leonard S. Picker and Clifford Sanforth; Story, Paul A. Castleton; Screenwriters, Paul A. Castleton, Melvin Levy and Wilfred A. Petitt; Editor, Richard Fantl; Art Directors, Stephen Goosson and Rudolph Sternad; Set Decorator, Frank Kramer; Cinematographers, Tony Gaudio, William Snyder and George B. Meehan, Jr.; Costumes, Jean Louis; Makeup, Clay Campbell; Hair Stylist, Helen Hunt; Sound, Lambert Day; Musical Director, M.W. Stoloff; Technical Advisor, Howard H. Hill; Technicolor Color Director, Natalie Kalmus; Associate Color Director, Francis Cugat

Location Filming: Corriganville, California

Production Dates: March 20, 1945–May 21, 1945

Source: Novel, *The Son of Robinhood* by Paul A. Castleton

Running Time: 86 min.

Color by Technicolor

Story: Russell Hicks fears that tyranny has returned to England under the rule of Henry Daniell. Daniell refuses to be bound by the Magna Carta. Hicks defies Daniell and pledges his support to the boy king, Maurice Tauzin. Tauzin's mother and Anita Louise escape to Hicks's camp with the help of his son, Cornel Wilde. Daniell plans to have Tauzin murdered. Wilde engineers a plan to rescue Tauzin. Tauzin is rescued but Wilde and Louise are captured. Wilde demands trial by combat. Daniell plans to fight Wilde after he's been deprived of food or drink for three days. Louise is able to smuggle both food and water to Wilde. Prior to the duel, Hicks and his men gain access to the castle. Wilde defeats Daniell and marries Louise.

Notes and Commentary: Columbia planned to call the film "The Son of Robin Hood," but Metro-Goldwyn-Mayer insisted they owned the rights to the name Robin Hood. Columbia then renamed the film, *The Bandit of Sherwood Forest*. In any event, Castleton's story, written for the juvenile reader, told of Robin Hood's son's journey into manhood with his teenager friend, Dick o' the Lea, with no involvement with tyranny in England. Obviously, all Columbia wanted was the rights to the book's title. Castleton gave Robin Hood's son the name of Merion, not Robert.

Columbia was one of the first studios to use a helicopter in the filming of a scene in a movie. A specially designed helicopter was used in the filming of Cornel Wilde's men seizing the castle.

A poster for *The Bandit of Sherwood Forest* can be seen on a movie theater in *Crime Doctor's Man Hunt* (Columbia, 1946).

Reviews: "Beautifully photographed in Technicolor, George Sherman and Henry Levin directed with immense panache." *The Columbia Story*, Hirshhorn

"Nice color photography, decent sets and a good cast of character actors help this average story line." *Motion Picture Guide*, Nash and Ross

"Technicolor swashbuckler with name strength to see it through. It stands up as okay escapist fare for the non-too-critical." *Variety*, 02/20/46

Summation: Though not up to the Errol Flynn classic, *Bandit of Sherwood Forest* is a neat bit of derring-do. Cornel Wilde plays young Robin to a T, with able support from the beautiful Anita Louise as his love interest, Henry Daniell and George Macready supplying the necessary villainy and Russell Hicks scores nicely as the elder Robin. Directors George Sherman and Henry Levin keep the story moving and the action flowing.

THE PRINCE OF THIEVES

Columbia (January 1948)

Revealing new daring adventures of Robin Hood!

Alternate Title: Alexandre Dumas' The Prince of Thieves

Cast: Robin Hood, Jon Hall; Lady Marian, Patricia Morison; Lady Christabel, Adele Jergens; The Friar, Alan Mowbray; Sir Allan Claire, Michael Duane; Gilbert Head, H.B.

The Prince of Thieves (1948) movie still — (left to right) H.B. Warner, Jon Hall, Patricia Morrison, Belle Mitchell.

Warner; Sir Phillip, Lowell Gilmore// Bowman, I. Stanford Jolley; Will Scarlett, Syd Saylor; Little John, Walter Sande; Margaret Head, Belle Mitchell, Sir Fitz-Alwin, Lewis L. Russell; Baron Tristram, Gavin Muir; Maude, Robin Raymond; Lindsay, Fred Santley

   Credits: Director, Howard Bretherton; Associate Director, Derwin Abrahams; Producer, Sam Katzman; Adaptation, Charles H. Schneer; Screenwriter, Maurice Tombragel; Editor, James Sweeney; Art Director, Paul Palmentola; Set Decorator, Sidney Moore; Cinematographer, Fred H. Jackman, Jr.; Production Manager, Herbert Leonard; Musical Director, Mischa Bakaleinikoff; Cinecolor Supervisor, Gar Gilbert

   Location Filming: Corriganville, California
   Production Dates: April 30, 1947–June 5, 1947
   Running Time: 72 min.
   Color by Cinecolor
   Story: Michael Duane is traveling with his sister, Patricia Morison, to Lewis L. Russell's castle to marry his daughter, Adele Jergens. En route, bowman I. Stanford Jolley draws aim to send an arrow into Duane's back. Jon Hall intervenes, saving Duane's life. Hall and Duane become friends. Hall breaks the news to Duane that, in a political move, Jergens is to marry Baron Gavin Muir. Hall and Duane plan to sneak into Russell's castle and bring Jergens to Hall's Sherwood Forest hideout. The plans fails: while Duane escapes, Hall is captured. Jergens' handmaiden, Robin Raymond, helps Hall to escape with Jergens and Raymond. Muir gives chase and recaptures Jergens. Later, Morison is captured by Muir's

men. Muir offers to trade Morison's freedom for Hall's capture. Hall agrees, but finds that the bargain is a hoax. Morison is to marry Muir's henchman, Lowell Gilmore. Hall is to be hanged, but his men capture the castle. Muir and Gillmore have taken Jergens and Morison to the nearby village for the marriage ceremony. Hall and Duane get to the village in time to stop the wedding. Hall and Duane engage Muir and Gilmore in sword fights. Hall and Duane emerge victorious. A marriage ceremony is held, with Hall marrying Morison and Duane wedding Jergens. Before they can go on their honeymoons, Hall and Duane are called to take up the fight against tyranny.

Notes and Commentary: Some sources state that Alexandre Dumas never wrote a book about Robin Hood, but his novel, *Robin Hood le proscrit*, was published in Paris in 1863. "Le proscit" translates to "the outlaw" in English. English translation have titled the book either *Robin Hood: Prince of Outlaws* or *Robin Hood: Prince of Thieves*. Screenwriter Maurice Tombragel followed the first half of the book fairly closely, the exception being that Robin was older and already the leader of the men hiding in Sherwood Forest. The latter half of Dumas's novel was scrapped as it told of King Henry proclaiming Robin an outlaw to prevent him from claiming his rightful title of the Earl of Huntingdon. At the novel's end, Robin and his followers take refuge in Sherwood Forest, after Robin has told Marian that now they cannot wed. In the other subplot, Sir Philip's daughter, Christabel, has taken refuge in a French convent. After seven years she can leave to marry Allen.

Stuntman Jock Mahoney doubled Jon Hall in this picture.

Reviews: "Cinecolor came to the aid of *The Prince of Thieves* under Howard Bretherton's flaccid direction." *The Columbia Story*, Hirshhorn

"Of the Merry Men, it is Mowbray as Friar Tuck who steals the show with a performance that borders on slapstick. Mainly a kiddie picture." *Motion Picture Guide*, Nash and Ross

"This version boils down to nothing more than a typical western transplanted to King Arthur's era. Despite the fact there's action aplenty, principal failing is the fantasy is never punched across." *Variety*, 01/14/48

Summation: Columbia's second entry in the Robin Hood legend is strictly "B" fodder for the Saturday matinee and action audiences. This is a fast-moving entry. There is not much in plot development, but there is plenty of action. A minor carp: the dispatching of Muir by Hall is offscreen. The screenplay is not written for character development, so don't expect any great shakes in the acting department, but the performances are adequate.

ROGUES OF SHERWOOD FOREST
Columbia (July 1950)

Thrills with the son of Robin Hood! Dashing deeds of daring!

Cast: Robin, John Derek; Lady Marianne, Diana Lynn; King John, George Macready; Little John, Alan Hale; Sir Giles, Paul Cavanagh; Count of Flanders, Lowell Gilmore; Friar Tuck, Billy House; Alan-A-Dale, Lester Matthews; Will Scarlett, William Bevan; Baron Fitzwalter, Wilton Graff; Archbishop Stephen Langton, Donald Randolph// Sir Baldric, John Dehner; Office posting decree, Harry Cording; Abbot, Matthew Bolton; Pretty girl, Lois Hall; Little boy, Christopher Cook; Baron Alfred, Gavin Muir; Baron Chandos, Tim Huntley; Baron Benedict, Nelson Leigh; Charcoal burner, Olaf Hytten; Charcoal burner's wife, Symona Boniface

Rogues of Sherwood Forest (1950) scene card — Diana Lynn and John Derek.

Credits: Director, Gordon Douglas; Assistant Director, Wilbur McGaugh; Producer, Fred M. Packard; Story, Ralph Bettinson; Screenwriter, George Bruce; Editor, Gene Havlick; Art Director, Harold MacArthur; Set Decorator, James Crowe; Cinematographer, Charles Lawton, Jr.; Sound, Jack Goodrich; Gowns, Jean Louis; Makeup, Clay Campbell; Hair Stylist, Helen Hunt; Musical Director, Morris Stoloff; Musical Score, Heinz Roemheld and Arthur Morton; Technicolor Color Consultant, Francis Cugat

Location Filming: Corriganville, California

Production Dates: August 22, 1949–September 29, 1949

Running Time: 80 min.

Color by Technicolor

Story: George Macready plans a reign of terror to gain more power as king. Macready strikes a bargain with the Count of Flanders, Lowell Gilmore, to pay 100,000 gold coins for 5,000 soldiers. To obtain this sum, Macready decides to tax his subjects heavily. John Derek and Alan Hale happen upon soldiers collecting taxes in Nottingham and engage them in combat. Finally the odds are too great: Derek and Hale are captured and sentenced to hang. Lady Diana Lynn, Macready's ward, helps Derek and Hale escape. Macready brands Derek an outlaw. Derek decides to bring together his father's Merry Men to oppose Macready's tyranny. Derek needs knowledge of Macready's actions and is able to get homing pigeons in Lynn's possession. Macready's co-conspirator, Paul Cavanaugh, believes Lynn is sending messages to Derek by way of the pigeons. Lynn outsmarts Cavanaugh and sends a pigeon without a message before releasing one with important information. Macready invites the barons to a gala dinner. Derek stops them and warns them of a trap. The barons refuse to listen. After dinner, Macready's archers shoot the barons. The barons' bodies are placed on the road and Derek will be blamed for the crime. One baron, Wilton Graff, survives and tells his story to Derek and Abbot Mathew Bolton. Bolton is charged with drawing up a covenant of the peoples' rights. Macready desperately needs Gilmore's soldiers but doesn't have the necessary funds. Gilmore decides to help Macready in return for Lynn's hand in marriage. Lynn balks, but a note from Derek tells her to play along and insists she be married at the Cathedral. Derek and his men attack the wedding party. Lynn is rescued. Gilmore chases Derek. The two men fight, with Derek finally victorious. Macready is allowed to remain as king only if he signs the covenant, now known as the Magna Carta. Derek and Lynn plan to wed.

Notes and Commentary: Columbia assigned Gig Young to play a heavy in this picture. Young refused and was suspended.

Rogues of Sherwood Forest was Alan Hale's last film. He played the part of Little John three times: in *Robin Hood* (United Artists, 1922) with Douglas Fairbanks and *The Adventures of Robin Hood* (Warner Bros., 1938) with Errol Flynn. Alan Hale utters some wonderful last lines, "Everything has been said. Everything has been done."

David Sharpe doubled John Derek in this film.

Reviews: "The son of Robin Hood as played by the good looking John Derek with all the Technicolor swash and buckle the role demanded. Under Gordon Douglas' full-blooded and picturesque direction the cast gave their all." *The Columbia Story*, Hirshhorn

"John Derek adds little to this familiar tale in which he is cast as Robin Hood's son." *Motion Picture Guide*, Nash and Ross

"Okay swashbuckler for the general trade." *Variety*, 06-21-50

Summation: What a delight! Director Gordon Douglas brings freshness and excitement to this action tale. John Derek seems conformable as Robin. Even though he can't match Errol Flynn's classic performance, he does fine and looks like he could be Flynn's son. Diana Lynn gives a sensitive, thoughtful performance as Lady Marianne. Villainy is in the fine hands of George Macready, Lowell Gilmore and Paul Cavanaugh. Alan Hale and Billy House add strong support and some welcome humorous moments.

Rusty

Screenwriter Al Martin wrote the story for *Adventures of Rusty*. In the future adventures of Rusty and his master Danny Mitchell, Martin would receive credit for creating the characters. The stories were written as morality plays, emphasizing the right way to live your life, e.g., the adverse effects of slander, lying and prejudgment of others. Martin had a long career in motion pictures. He started in 1920 writing title cards for silent films. With the advent of talkies, Martin began writing stories, dialogue and screenplays. When working for Columbia, Martin created the "Rusty" characters. The stories centered around a boy, Danny Mitchell, and his dog Rusty. In the initial entry, Rusty was played by Ace, the Wonder Dog. Ace was well known as "Devil" in the serial, *The Phantom* (Columbia, 1943).

Adventures of Rusty (1945) title card (lower left) Arno Frey and "Ace," (center) Ted Donaldson, "Ace," (lower right) Margaret Lindsay, Conrad Nagel.

278

Flame played Rusty in five entries. Flame was quite busy; in addition to playing Rusty, he was Pal in some short subjects for RKO, and Shep at Screen Guild Productions. Ted Donaldson was cast as Danny. Prior to the Rusty series, he had been seen to good advantage in *Once Upon a Time* (Columbia, 1944), with Cary Grant, and *A Tree Grows in Brooklyn* (20th Century–Fox, 1945). Danny's father, Hugh Mitchell, was first played by Conrad Nagel. Other actors cast in the role were Tom Powers (twice) and John Litel (five times). John Litel had a long career in movies and later television. (He entered films in 1929, becoming a member of the Warner Bros. stock company in the mid- to late-'30s. Freelancing in the '40s, he took on the role of Sam Aldrich in Paramount's Henry Aldrich series [1943–44]. After the Rusty series, Litel would appear in three television series: as Mr. Thackery on *My Hero* [NBC, 1952–53], the governor on *Zorro* [Disney, 1959] and Dan Murchison on *Stagecoach West* [ABC, 1960-61].) The first actress to play Danny's mother was Margaret Lindsay. This was Lindsay's third role in a series opener since the Ellery Queen series and as in the previous two, it was one appearance and out. Danny mother was called Ann in the opening saga. No first name was given in the second, *The Return of Rusty* (Columbia, 1946), with the role being played by Barbara Woodall. For the last six films, Danny's mother (now known as Ethel) was played by Ann Doran. (Doran was a prolific actress. Some state Doran appeared in over 500 films and as many television shows. She played Martha Brown on *National Velvet* [NBC, 1960–62], Mrs. Kingston on *Longstreet* [ABC, 1971–72] and Charlotte McHenry on *Shirley* [NBC, 1979–80]. Doran's career spanned over fifty years in sound films alone.) Many child actors had various parts in the series. Most notable were Dwayne Hickman (Nip, Bobby), David Ackles (Tuck, Peanuts), Mickey McGuire (Porky, Gerald), Ronnie Ralph (Gerald) and Teddy Infuhr (Herbie, Timmy, Squeaky).

ADVENTURES OF RUSTY
Columbia (September 1945)

The high-spirited story of two thoroughbreds!

Cast: Danny Mitchell, Ted Donaldson; Ann Mitchell, Margaret Lindsay; Hugh Mitchell, Conrad Nagel; Louise Hover, Gloria Holden; Will Nelson, Robert Williams; Dr. Banning, Addison Richards; Tausig, Arno Frey; Ehrlich, Eddie Parker; Rusty, Ace, the Wonder Dog// Harry, Billy Gray; Herbie, Gary Gray; Mrs. Florence Nelson, Ruth Warren; Minister, Lloyd Ingraham; Henry, Bobby Larson; Billy, Douglas Madore

Credits: Director, Paul Burnford; Producer, Rudolph C. Flothow; Story, Al Martin; Screenplay, Aubrey Weisberg; Editor, Reg Browne; Cinematographer, L.W. O'Connell; Sound, Howard Gogetti; Musical Director, M.R. Bakaleinikoff

Production Dates: April 9, 1945–April 26, 1945

Running Time: 67 min.

Story: Widower Conrad Nagel marries Margaret Lindsay, much to the disappointment of his son, Ted Donaldson. Donaldson's dog is killed by a hit-and-run driver. Donaldson becomes despondent due to the loss of his dog and having to share Nagel with Lindsay. Donaldson takes a liking to neighbor Robert Williams's dog, Ace. Ace was trained by Nazis and is branded as a vicious dog. Ace is injured as he escapes confinement. Donaldson finds Ace and brings him home. Nagel and Lindsay think Ace is too dangerous and tell Donaldson to return him. Donaldson convinces Williams to let him take care of Ace. With advice from

Dr. Addison Richards, Donaldson begins to work with Ace. Lindsay also receives advice from Richards on how to work with Donaldson. Meanwhile, two German spies, Arno Frey and Eddie Parker, land on the beach and grab Ace when he runs away from Donaldson. Donaldson enlists the help of neighborhood boys to search for the dog. Donaldson finds Ace but meets up with Parker. Ace prevents Parker from shooting Donaldson. Donaldson and Ace capture Parker. Then Ace helps the neighborhood boys capture Frey. When Donaldson returns home, he finds Lindsay has left Nagel. Donaldson goes to Lindsay and asks her to come back home, which she does.

Notes and Commentary: The working titles were "For the Love of Rusty" and "Rusty." *For the Love of Rusty* was finally used as the title for the third entry in the series.

Veteran director George Sherman was initially signed to the film. Sherman had to bow out because of a prior commitment, giving Paul Burnford a chance to direct his first feature film.

Reviews: "Pleasant programmer. There are some funny bits but most of the film drops along until the dog springs into action." *Motion Picture Guide*, Nash and Ross

"Weak 'B' boy-and-his-dog melodrama born of a bad script." *Variety*, 08/15/45

Summation: A good boy-and-his-dog story. Ted Donaldson and Margaret Lindsay give good performances, but the primary acting honors go to Ace as the troubled dog that is rehabilitated. This is a good story well directed by Paul Burnford.

THE RETURN OF RUSTY
Columbia (June 1946)

No boy is an outcast ... while a faithful dog trots by his side!

Cast: Denny Mitchell, Ted Donaldson; Hugh Mitchell, John Litel; Loddy Bicek, Mark Dennis; Mrs. Mitchell, Barbara Woodell; Sgt. Jack Beals, Robert Stevens; Marty Connors, Mickey Kuhn; Herbie, Teddy Infuhr; Bobby, Dwayne Hickman; Porky, Mickey McGuire; Skinny, Gene Collins; Peanuts, David Ackles; Trailer boy, Donald Davis; "Rusty"// Motor Policeman, Eddie Parker; Detective, Fred F. Sears; MPs, Leo Kaye, George Turner and Joseph Palma; Driver, Ernie Adams; Gas station attendant, Victor Potel; Policeman, Bob Ryan; Veteran, Tom Daly; Nurse, Adele Roberts; Wife, Mary Emery; Steve, Georgie Nokes; Judge, Frank Dae; Mrs. Connors, Isabel Withers; Immigration officer, Pat O'Malley, Major, Kernan Cripps; Music teacher, Rose Plummer; Col. Malcolm, Emmett Vogan; Newsboy, Walter Marx

Credits: Director, William Castle; Producer, Leonard S. Picker; Story, Lewis Helmer Herman; Screenwriter, William B. Sackheim: Editor, James Sweeney; Art Director, Hans Radon; Set Decorator, Robert Bradfield: Cinematographer, Philip Tannura; Music Director, Mischa Bakaleinikoff

Production Dates: March 15, 1946–April 4, 1946

Running Time: 64 min.

Source: Based on characters created by Al Martin.

Story: Czechoslovakian war orphan Mark Dennis is a stowaway on an Army transport ship. In New York, Dennis is apprehended by military police. Army Sergeant Robert Stevens wants to adopt Dennis and arranges his escape. Dennis is told to go to Stevens's hometown of Lawtonville. Once there, Ted Donaldson and his dog, Rusty, befriend Dennis. When detectives come looking for Dennis, Donaldson hides him in their cave clubhouse. Stevens is arrested on suspicion of helping Dennis escape. Dennis leaves the clubhouse with Rusty to help Stevens. Dennis and Rusty are separated. Donaldson's pal, Mickey Kuhn, finds Rusty. Kuhn, who doesn't like Dennis, gives Rusty away and tells Donaldson that Dennis stole the dog. Dennis retrieves Rusty, but Donaldson still believes Kuhn's story. Dennis confronts Kuhn. Frightened, Kuhn runs from Dennis and falls down a steep ravine. Dennis and Rusty climb down to help him, but Dennis is unable to climb out. Rusty is able to make his way up and go for help. Meanwhile, Dennis administers first-aid to Kuhn. Rusty finds Donaldson, who sees a note on Rusty's collar. The boys are rescued. Stevens has been absolved of guilt and is able to adopt Dennis.

Notes and Commentary: John Litel took over the role of Hugh Mitchell from Conrad Nagel. Barbara Woodell became the new Mrs. Mitchell, replacing Margaret Lindsay. Ace was Rusty in the first episode, *The Adventures of Rusty* (Columbia, 1945), and Flame took over in *For the Love of Rusty* (Columbia, 1947). Print resources only state the dog's name in *The Return of Rusty* as "Rusty."

Summation: This film was unavailable for viewing by the author.

FOR THE LOVE OF RUSTY
Columbia (May 1947)

A thrilling blend of action and comedy!

Cast: Danny Mitchell, Ted Donaldson; Hugh Mitchell, Tom Powers; Ethel Mitchell, Ann Doran; Dr. Francis Xavier Fay, Aubrey Mather; Moe Hatch, Sid Tomack; J. Cecil Rinehardt, George Meader; Gerald Hebble, Mickey McGuire; Rusty, Flame// Mr. Hebble, Harry Hayden; Doc Levy, Fred Sears; Bill Worden, Dick Elliott; Frank Foley, Olin Howland; Tommy Worden, Teddy Infuhr; Doc Levy, Jr., Dwayne Hickman; Squeaky, Georgie Nokes; Sarah Johnson, Almira Sessions; Policeman, Ralph Dunn; Barker, Eddie Fetherston

Credits: Director, John Sturges; Producer, John Haggott; Screenwriter, Malcolm Stuart Boylan; Editor, James Sweeney; Art Director, Hans Radon; Set Decorator, Frank Kramer; Cinematographer, Vincent Farrar; Musical Director, Mischa Bakaleinikoff

Production Dates: December 5, 1946–December 21, 1946

Running Time: 69 min.

Source: Based on characters created by Al Martin.

Story: Ted Donaldson and his father, Tom Powers, have grown distant in their relationship. Donaldson and his dog, Flame, meet Aubrey Mather. Mather introduces Donaldson to stargazing. Donaldson and Mather become friends, to the consternation of Powers. Donaldson's mother, Ann Doran, invites Mather to dinner. Mather is most engaging and intelligent and becomes the hit of the evening. To get closer to Donaldson, Powers takes Donaldson and Flame to a local carnival. Pitchman Sid Tomack takes exception to Flame being at the carnival and kicks at him. Flame lunges at Tomack. Because of the altercation, Powers decides Flame must wear a muzzle. Angry with Powers, Donaldson decides to live with Mather. Powers talks with Mather, and tells Powers that all Donaldson needs is a father. Mather retires to his trailer where he is overcome by gas from his stove. Flame goes to the rescue and, in the process, Flame's leg is injured. Mather contrives to have Donaldson and Powers talk to each other while he attends to Flame's injury. It turns out that Flame's injury was non-existent, but it brought father and son together. On this pleasant note, Mather leaves town.

Notes and Commentary: Again we have cast changes. Tom Powers takes over as Hugh Mitchell and Ann Doran is now Mrs. Mitchell. Mrs. Mitchell's first name is Ethel, and will remain so for the rest of the series.

Reviews: "Not a lot of plot, just a lot of boy and a lot of dog." *Motion Picture Guide*, Nash and Ross

"The latest in Columbia's series around a boy and his dog furnishes tiptop entertainment." *Variety*, 07/02/47

Summation: Another fine entry in the Rusty series. The story drags a little in the first half but all is made up with a good second half. Aubrey Mather as a wandering scholar and veterinarian, and Ann Doran as Ted Donaldson's mother steal the acting honors. Tom Powers is saddled with a part that makes him seem too unintelligent for such an intelligent man. Ted Donaldson and Flame contribute adequate performances. The end result is an overly sentimental, but fairly effective, drama.

THE SON OF RUSTY
Columbia (August 1947)

A heart-warming adventure in living....

Cast: Danny Mitchell, Ted Donaldson; Jed Barlow, Stephen Dunne; Hugh Mitchell, Tom Powers; Ethel Mitchell, Ann Doran; Franklyn P. Gibson, Thurston Hall; Luther Hebble, Matt Willis; Gono, Rudy Robles; "Rusty"// Squeaky Foley, Teddy Infuhr; Gerald Hebble, Ronnie Ralph; Nip Worden, Dwayne Hickman; Tuck Worden, David Ackles; Dr. McNamara, Harlan Briggs; Judge, Griff Barnett; Mr. Carpenter, Walter Soderling; Mrs. Hebble, Edythe Elliott; Postmaster, Ernie Adams; Police chief, Kenneth MacDonald; E.A. Thompson, Fred Sears; Sammy, Norman Ollestad; Bakery clerk, Chester Conklin; Mayor, Dick Elliott; Townswoman, Minta Durfee; Townsmen, Frank O'Connor and Edward Piel, Sr.; Gossiper, Blackie Whiteford

Credits: Director, Lew Landers; Producer, Wallace MacDonald; Screenwriter, Malcolm Stuart Boylan; Editor, Aaron Stell; Art Director, Sturges Carne; Set Decorator, Frank Tuttle; Cinematography, Henry Freulich; Musical Director, Mischa Bakaleinikoff

Production Dates: April 10, 1947–April 21, 1947

Running Time: 69 min.

Source: Based on characters created by Al Martin.

Story: Thurston Hall catches Ted Donaldson, Rusty and the gang trespassing on his property and then leases the property to them for 99 years. Stephen Dunne comes to town with his dog. Dunne is unfriendly and doesn't want to make friends. Donaldson and his pals decide to keep an eye on him. Since Dunne received a letter from a military prison, Matt Willis starts a campaign against Dunne, thinking that he is a jailbird. Donaldson helps Dunne when he has a bout of malaria, and they become friends. After a fight between Dunne and Willis, Powers asks Donaldson to stay away from Dunne's farm. Rusty goes to the farm and is injured by an explosion. Donaldson believes Dunne tried to kill Rusty. Dunne is arrested for careless handling of explosives. Donaldson and Dunne renew their friendship and Dunne asks Donaldson to take care of his dog. Donaldson retains Hall to defend Dunne. Dunne testifies that an emotional breakup with his girlfriend caused him to become bitter toward the world. Through Hall's successful litigation, Dunne is only fined $100 and becomes a member of the community. Willis is charged with slander. Rusty and Dunne's dog are proud parents of puppies. For his fee, Hall takes the puppy that looks most like Rusty.

Notes and Commentary: Thurston Hall had a long and distinguished career, appearing in over 250 feature films and television programs from 1915–1958. Hall was best known as Mr. Schuyler on *Topper* (CBS, 1953–54), and Diet Smith on *Dick Tracy* (ABC, 1950).

Summation: Top-notch Rusty episode, with fine performances by Thurston Hall as a retired lawyer and Stephen Dunne as an embittered man wanted to live a solitary existence. Ted Donaldson and Rusty also chip in with good performances. This entry presents a successful diatribe on the harmful effects of gossip. Lew Landers directs confidently with an excellent story by Malcolm Stuart Boylan.

MY DOG RUSTY
Columbia (April 1948)

The Way to a Boy's Heart is Through His Dog!

Cast: Danny Mitchell, Ted Donaldson; Hugh Mitchell, John Litel; Ethel Mitchell, Ann Doran; Dr. Toni Cordell, Mona Barrie; Joshua Michael Tucker, Whitford Kane; Rodney Pyle, Jimmy Lloyd; Mayor Fulderwilder, Lewis L. Russell; Rusty, Flame// Frank Foley, Olin Howland; Mr. Hebble, Harry Harvey; Bill Worden, Ferris Taylor; Squeaky Foley, Teddy Infuhr; Nip Worden, Dwayne Hickman; Gerald Hebble, Michael McGuire; Tuck Worden, David Ackles; Jack, Jack Rice; Mrs. Laura Foley, Minta Durfee; Mrs. Stokes, Jessie Arnold; Telephone gossip, Cecil Weston; Truck driver, Fred Aldrich; Voice of radio announcer, Frank Martin

Credits: Director, Lew Landers; Producer, Wallace MacDonald; Story, William Sackheim and Brenda Weisberg; Screenwriter, Brenda Weisberg; Editor, Jerome Thoms; Art Director, George Brooks; Set Decorator, James Crowe; Cinematography, Vincent Farrar; Musical Director, Mischa Bakaleinikoff

Production Dates: November 3, 1947–November 14, 1947

Running Time: 67 min.

Source: Based on characters created by Al Martin.

Story: Ted Donaldson's constant lying infuriates his father, John Litel. Litel's harsh response puts a strain on the father-son relationship. Because Lawtonville needs a physician, Litel enlists the services of an old flame, Mona Barrie, who is a good friend of his wife, Ann Doran. Because of Donaldson's skill in treating animals, Barrie allows Donaldson to assist her in her office. Some of Donaldson's friends come down with a mysterious illness, and Barrie suspects the drinking water is the cause. Mayor Lewis L. Russell's company is responsible for water purification. Barrie has samples ready to test, but Flame knocks them over, spilling them. Because Flame was not supposed to be in the lab, Donaldson fills them with contaminated water from an off-limits swimming hole. Barrie's experiments state the town's drinking water is contaminated. Russell and his nephew, Jimmy Lloyd, gain possession of the original container. Litel is Russell's opponent in the mayoral election. The day before the election, Lloyd accuses Litel, Barrie and Citizen of the Year Whitford Kane of slandering his campaign. Litel asks Donaldson if he has any knowledge of the disputed water samples and Donaldson denies any involvement. Feeling remorseful, Donaldson runs away. Litel is livid until both Kane and Doran ask him not to be harsh with Donaldson. Doran sends Flame to find Donaldson. Before Donaldson and Flame can return home, a rattlesnake bites the dog. Donaldson performs first-aid and goes to Barrie for medical help. Litel greets Donaldson with a smile and Donaldson realizes that Litel still loves him. Barrie and Doran go to help Flame. Donaldson tells Litel that he was afraid, and that's why he didn't tell the truth. Litel arranges to have Donaldson admit his involvement in the water contamination scandal, thereby exonerating Litel, Barrie and Kane. Even though the election results are close, Russell is the victor. Litel believes he's the victor because now Donaldson knows he should always tell the truth.

Notes and Commentary: In 1933, Mona Barrie came to the United States from England by way of Australia, and signed a contract with the Fox Film Corporation. Barrie would enjoy a 20-year career in motion pictures, often taking time out to appear on Broadway. By the '40s, Barrie was featured in productions by Republic, Monogram and PRC. In addition, she made the rounds in various Columbia series productions appearing on Ellery Queen, the Lone Wolf, the Crime Doctor, I Love a Mystery, the Whistler and Rusty. *My Dog Rusty* would be Barrie's last film for about four years. She appeared as a tourist in *Plunder of the Sun* (Warner Bros, 1953) which was her last film.

Reviews: "Overly cute, with mediocre production values, this is a minor and forgettable 'boy and his dog' film. Donaldson is completely inept." *Motion Picture Guide*, Nash and Ross

"Sentimental entry in Columbia's series of kid-dog supporting features. Modest tear-jerker." *Variety*, 06/09/48

Summation: It may be overly sentimental, but it sure is a good, well-written and acted story. Fine performances by Ted Donaldson, John Litel, Ann Doran and Whitford Kane spark the story. Of course, Flame is there to steal scenes from the human performers.

RUSTY LEADS THE WAY
Columbia (October 1948)

A boy's best friend ... and a kid's only hope!

Cast: Danny Mitchell, Ted Donaldson; Penny Waters, Sharyn Moffett; Hugh Mitchell, John Litel; Ethel Mitchell, Ann Doran; Louise Adams, Paula Raymond; Mrs. Waters, Peggy Converse; Rusty, Flame// Tuck Worden, David Ackles; Nip Worden, Dwayne Hickman; Squeaky, Teddy Infuhr; Gerald, Michael McGuire; Mrs. Mungy, Ida Moore; Miss Davis, Mary Currier; Harry Ainesworth, Harry Hayden; Board members, Dick Elliott and John Hamilton; Mitchell's secretary, Wanda Perry; Jack Coleman, Fred Sears; Postman, Paul E. Burns; Gas station attendant, Al Thompson

Credits: Director, Will Jason; Producer, Robert Cohn; Story, Nedrick Young; Screenwriter, Arthur Ross; Editor, James Sweeney; Art Director, George Brooks; Set Decorator, Frank Tuttle; Cinematography, Vincent Farrar; Technical Director, George Coulouris; Musical Director, Mischa Bakaleinikoff

Production Dates: February 23, 1948–March 4, 1948
Running Time: 59 min.

Source: Based on characters created by Al Martin.

Story: Ted Donaldson and Flame meet a new citizen, Sharyn Moffett, in Lawtonville. Moffett is vision-impaired and the school board wants to send her to a state school for similar students. Donaldson believes that if Moffett had a guide dog, she could attend the local school with sighted students. Donaldson's father, John Litel, convinces the school board to give this a try. Moffett goes to the Reed Institute for Guide Dogs, headed by Fred Sears. Trainer Paula Raymond gives Moffett her favorite dog, Tubby. Moffett is afraid of failure and thinks Tubby still loves Raymond. On Moffett's first solo trip in town, noises confuse her and she starts running. To protect her, Tubby knocks her down and protects her until Raymond comes to help. Moffett just wants to go home. Raymond and Sears take Tubby along on the trip to Lawtonville. Once home, Moffett runs from Tubby. Donaldson learns that Moffett is home and is slated to attend the state school. Donaldson and Flame take Moffett for a walk. On the trip back to the Reed Institute, Sears and Raymond stop at a gas station. Tubby takes the opportunity to return to Moffett. As Tubby gets close, his harness gets caught on a log. Flame hears Tubby's cry for help and races to the rescue. Flame frees Tubby. The dogs race to Donaldson and Moffett. Moffett knows Tubby now loves her, and she is now ready to face life.

Notes and Commentary: The working title was "Rusty Takes a Walk."

In the previous entry, *My Pal Rusty*, Harry Hayden played Michael McGuire's father, Mr. Hebble. This time out Hayden is the school board superintendent, Harry Ainesworth.

Review: "Only the very little might buy this trite material." *Motion Picture Guide*, Nash and Ross

"Good entry in "Rusty" series." *Variety*, 07/28/48

SUMMMATION: Although slow getting started, director Will Jason guides the story to a most satisfying conclusion. Sharyn Moffett shines as a young vision impaired girl who finally learns to live and overcome her handicap. Ted Donaldson and Flame lend good support.

RUSTY SAVES A LIFE
Columbia (1949)

Grand new thrills from your favorite boy and dog!

Cast: Danny Mitchell, Ted Donaldson; Lyddy Hazard, Gloria Henry; Fred Gibson, Stephen Dunne; Hugh Mitchell, John Litel; Ethel Mitchell, Ann Doran; Frank A. Gibson, Thurston Hall; Gono Sandoval, Rudy Robles; Rusty, Flame// Nip Worden, Dwayne Hickman; Tuck Worden, David Ackles, Gerald Hebble, Ronnie Ralph; Squeaky Foley, Robert Scott; Dr. McNamara, Harlan Briggs; Miss Simmons, Ellen Corby; Roy Hebble, Harry Harvey; Mr. Foley, Emmett Vogan

Credits: Director, Seymour Friedman; Producer, Wallace MacDonald; Screenwriter, Brenda Weisberg; Editor, Gene Havlick; Art Director, Sturges Carne; Set Decorator, James Crowe; Cinematographer, Henry Freulich; Musical Director, Mischa Bakaleinikoff

Production Dates: May 10, 1948–May 20, 1948

Running Time: 68 min.

Source: Based on characters created by Al Martin.

Story: Believing his nephew Stephen Dunne doesn't like him, Thurston Hall decides to make a new will reducing his inheritance. Hull plans to leave his land, house and Pottery Works to Ted Donaldson and his four friends. Hall writes his new will that night and places it in the book he's reading. Hall dies before he can sign the will. The boys meet Dunne when his car hits Flame. The will is read, Dunne inherits everything only if he lives in Lawtonville for one full year and continues Hall's Sunday night dinners with Donaldson and his pals. Dunne acknowledges that the boys have a right to use the clubhouse on his property but denies them access. Ronnie Ralph convinces Donaldson and the other boys to initiate a campaign of vandalism to drive Dunne away. While touring his property, Dunne meets artist Gloria Henry and is immediately infatuated. Believing animals are infesting his property, Dunne buys traps. When it's Donaldson's turn to vandalize Dunne's property, Flame is caught in one of the traps. Donaldson accidentally starts a fire while trying to release Flame from the trap. Dunne declines to press charges against Donaldson for $500 restitution. Dunne starts for Chicago to see if the conditions of the will can be broken. Driving recklessly, Dunne's car plunges into a river. Ted Donaldson, Robert Scott and Flame are close by. Flame is first on the scene. Overcoming his dislike for Dunne, Flame swims to the rescue. Meanwhile, Henry tells the leading citizens that they have been unfair to Dunne. Dunne recovers and receives gifts and well wishes from the Lawtonville citizens. Hall's unsigned will is found and given to Donaldson, who burns the will. Learning about this, Dunne gives the land to Donaldson and the boys. Dunne and Henry plan to cultivate a romance. The citizens of Lawtonville and Dunne become friends.

Notes and Commentary: After playing the school board superintendent in the last film, *Rusty Leads the Way*, Harry Harvey is back as Roy Hebble.

Review: "Another maudlin tale of impossible moppets. Strictly for padding out a double bill, and thin padding at that." *Variety*, 02/09/49

Summation: Neat Rusty story, only mildly sentimental this time out. Acting is par except for Flame, who steals practically every scene he's in.

RUSTY'S BIRTHDAY
Columbia (November 1949)

When two fellers need the same dog ... only Rusty knows how to make them both happy!

Cast: Danny Mitchell, Ted Donaldson; Hugh Mitchell, John Litel; Ethel Mitchell, Ann Doran; Jeff Neeley, Jimmy Hunt; Bill Neeley, Mark Dennis; Virgil Neeley, Ray Teal; Carrie Simmons, Lillian Bronson; Rusty, Flame// Vagrant, Robert Williams; Jack Wiggins, Myron Healey; Amos Wembley, Raymond Largay; Ella Mae Wembley, Lelah Tyler; Nip Worden, Dwayne Hickman; Tuck Worden, David Ackles; Squeaky Foley, Teddy Infuhr; Gerald Hebble, Ronnie Ralph; Motor Patrolman, Jim Nolan; Policeman, Fred Sears

Credits: Director, Seymour Friedman; Producer, Wallace MacDonald; Screenwriter, Brenda Weisberg; Editor, James Sweeney; Art Director, Harold MacArthur; Set Decorator, Frank Tuttle; Cinematographer, Henry Freulich; Musical Director, Mischa Bakaleinikoff

Song: "Beautiful Dreamer" (Foster) sung by Lillian Bronson

Production Dates: February 8, 1949–February 18, 1949

Running Time: 60 min.

Source: based on characters created by Al Martin.

Story: Vagrant Robert Williams is able to sell Ted Donaldson's dog, Flame, to an unsuspecting elderly couple, Raymond Largay and Lelah Tyler. When the couple makes a stop, Flame makes a break for home. On the way, Flame meets an itinerant migrant farm worker, Ray Teal, and his two sons, Mark Dennis and Jimmy Hunt. Since Flame doesn't have a collar, Hunt claims him as his dog. Teal arrives in Donaldson's hometown where Donaldson has been searching feverishly for Flame. Donaldson accuses Teal and his sons of stealing Flame. The altercation costs Teal a job that employment agency manager Lillian Bronson had found for him. Donaldson's father, John Litel, offers Teal a job working a section of land that he owns. Teal is hit with an attack of appendicitis. Meanwhile, Williams is arrested for attempted robbery and, when threatened by Flame, admits he's the one who stole Flame. Donaldson apologizes to Dennis for thinking him a thief and the two become friends. When Teal's condition gets worse, he calls for his youngest son, Hunt, who had been staying with Litel temporarily. When Donaldson and Dennis look for him, they find he's gone, having taken Flame. Hunt and Flame go to the shack where Teal and Dennis have been staying. Bronson finds Hunt and, when seeing he is exhausted, puts him to bed. Hunt wishes Bronson could be his mother. Before Dennis can take Hunt to Teal, they get word that the crisis has passed and that Teal is on the road to recovery. Hunt finally gets his own dog as Flame becomes a father again and Hunt is given one of the puppies. It looks like Hunt will get a mother after all as Teal and Bronson have become engaged.

Notes and Commentary: *Hollywood Reporter* named Richard Fantl as the editor on this film. James Sweeney gets screen credit.

Review: "Okay programmer for the 'Rusty' series." *Variety*, 10/12/49

Summation: Nice ending to the Rusty series. *Rusty's Birthday* is well written, though sentimental. Director Seymour Friedman competently moves the film to its happy conclusion. The acting is up to par with nods to Jimmy Hunt as a little boy looking for both a dog and a mother and Flame, who registers the proper emotions throughout.

Sally and Bill Reardon

Wilson Collison's "There's Always a Woman" appeared in the January 1937 issue of *American Magazine*. The short story featured the happily married private investigators Donna and Bill Blake, with the emphasis on Donna. Screenwriter Gladys Lehman was given the task of instigating a new series to rival Metro-Goldwyn-Mayer's Thin Man stories. Once Collison's property was optioned, Lehman made some changes to the protagonists' name, and the married couple became Sally and Bill Reardon. Columbia borrowed Joan Blondell from Warner Bros. to play Sally. The lovely, sexy Blondell was a mainstay in the Warners films and provides a wonderful spark in the series' opener, *There's Always a Woman* (Columbia, 1939). Talented Melvyn Douglas, who had recently played jewel thieves Lone Wolf and Arsène Lupin, took on the role of Bill. The movie was popular and on December 17, 1939, Orson Welles presented the story on his *Campbell Playhouse*. Welles played Bill and the future *My Friend Irma* star Marie Wilson was Sally. Columbia wanted a long-running series, but since Blondell was not available Virginia Bruce was picked to take over the role as Sally. Unfortunately, the chemistry that Blondell and Douglas had in the initial entry failed to carry over with Bruce and Douglas. Also, the weak script that Lehman presented spelled doom for the series. Douglas went on to become a very respected actor, winning Best Supporting Actor Academy Awards for *Hud* (Paramount, 1963) and *Being There* (United Artists, 1979); and an Academy Award nomination for Best Actor for *I Never Sang for My Father* (Columbia, 1970). Blondell went on a to have very distinguished career as well, garnering an Academy Award nomination for Best Supporting Actress for *The Blue Veil* (RKO, 1951). Collison was a prolific playwright and author. Some of his plays that were made into films were *Red Dust*, *Getting Gertie's Garter* and *Up in Mabel's Room*. A novel, *Dark Dame* (Claude Kendall and Willoughby Sharp, 1935) was the basis for Metro-Goldwyn-Mayer's successful Maisie series with Ann Southern.

THERE'S ALWAYS A WOMAN
Columbia (March 1938)

Concentrated amusement ... a clever blend of mystery-melodrama — comedy at its height for those who enjoy combined suspense and swift action — deftly played by a cast of skilled performers at their very best.

Cast: Sally Reardon, Joan Blondell; William Reardon, Melvyn Douglas; Lola Fraser, Mary Astor; Anne Calhoun, Frances Drake; Nick Shane, Jerome Cowan; Jerry Marlowe, Robert Paige; District Attorney, Thurston Hall; Mr. Ketterling, Pierre Watkin; Grigson,

There's Always a Woman (1938) scene card — (left) Joan Blondell, (center) Joan Blondell, Melvyn Douglas, (lower right) Melvyn Douglas.

Walter Kingsford; Walter Fraser, Lester Matthews// Radio patrolman, Arthur Loft; Radio car driver, Wade Boteler; Miss Jacobs, Wyn Cahoon; Rent collector, William H. Strauss; Headwaiter, Marek Windham; City editor, Robert Emmett Keane; Newspaper reporter, John Gallaudet; News photographer, Eddie Fetherston; Mary, Rita Hayworth; Flannigan, Tom Dugan; Fogarty, Gene Morgan; Police broadcaster, Lee Phelps; Bellhop, Billy Benedict

Credits: Director, Alexander Hall; Producer, William Perlberg; Story, Wilson Collison; Screenwriter, Gladys Lehman; Editor, Viola Lawrence; Art Directors, Stephen Goosson and Lionel Banks; Cinematography, Henry Freulich; Gowns, Kalloch; Musical Director, Morris Stoloff

Running Time: 81 min.

Production Dates: January 5, 1938–February 17, 1938

Running Time: 81 min.

Story: Not being able to make a living as a private detective, Melvyn Douglas decides to return to his old job in the District Attorney's office. Douglas's wife, Joan Blondell, decides to take over the agency. She is hired by Mary Astor to follow Frances Drake, whom Astor thinks is having an affair with her husband, Lester Matthews. At the Skyline club, Matthews slips an envelope to Drake. Drake passes something to club owner Jerome Cowan.

Drake's fiancé, Robert Paige, threatens to kill Matthews if he keeps showing an interest in Drake. Matthews is shot in Paige's apartment and Blondell decides to solve the crime. Both Blondell and Douglas search Matthews's apartment. Drake arrives and removes a letter from Matthews's desk. Blondell gains possession of the letter and leaves the apartment. Drake owed Cowan money and Matthews gave it to her to pay off the debt. Astor owes Cowan $50,000. Blondell learns that Cowan was in Matthews's apartment at the time of the murder. Blondell goes to the apartment where she finds the dead body of Cowan, and detects the smell of perfume in the air. Blondell accuses Astor of the murder and gains a confession. Douglas finds proof that Astor hired Cowan to murder Matthews. Cowan, in turn, was murdered by Astor. Astor realized that she would be blackmailed by him.

Notes and Commentary: It has been reported that Rita Hayworth's role was cut to a brief bit when the decision was made to make a series of Sally and Bill Reardon features.

The film was based on a story in the *American Magazine* (January 1937) entitled "There's Always a Woman." In the story the detectives are Bill Rendon and his blonde wife Donna Blake Rendon. There is only one murder. Nick Shane shoots Fraser because he shows a romantic interest in his ex-wife. The emphasis in the story is centered on the Donna Blake character.

Orson Welles's *Campbell Playhouse* presented *There's Always a Woman* on December 17, 1939 with the following cast: Sally Reardon, Marie Wilson; Bill Reardon, Orson Welles; Shane, Ray Collins; Grigson, Everett Sloane; Jerry Marlowe, Edgar Barrier; Lola Fraser, Mary Taylor; Anne Calhoun, Georgia Backus; District Attorney, Frank Riddick; Walter Fraser, Richard Wilson.

Reviews: "The script was surprisingly good, largely due to the uncredited efforts of Ryskind, Sayre and Rapp. The teaming of Blondell and Douglas worked quite well." Motion Picture Guide, Nash and Ross

"It is one of the lightest and most engaging affairs of recent months. Deft direction, a neat dovetailing of comically epigrammatic scenes and incidents and the really superb work of Joan Blondell have resulted in an excellent job of all-around spoofing — a *Thin Man* of the lower income brackets." New York Times, 4/28/38

"A breezy comedy thriller. The script's tongue-in-cheek approach to the mayhem at hand kept the audiences chuckling while, at the same time, managed to spoof the crime-melodrama genre." *The Columbia Story*, Hirshhorn

"It's a briskly paced, battle-of-the-sexes-comedy against the background of a murder mystery." *Variety*, 05/04/38

Summation: This is a delightful comedy-mystery. The pairing of Joan Blondell and Melvyn Douglas has the right chemistry, but it is the performance of Blondell that electrifies the picture. A good script, direction and fine performances make this outing a winner.

There's That Woman Again
Columbia (*January 1939*)

Comedy that cleverly combines mystery and frivolity ... suspense ... laughter ... the misadventures of a gay, engaging detective couple ... played with zest and delightful humor.

Alternate Title: What a Woman
Cast: Bill Reardon, Melvyn Douglas; Sally Reardon, Virginia Bruce; Mrs. Nacelle,

Margaret Lindsay; Tony Croy, Stanley Ridges; Charles Crenshaw, Gordon Oliver; Flannigan, Tom Dugan; Johnson, Don Beddoe; Rolfe Davis, Jonathan Hale; Mr. Nacelle, Pierre Watkin; Stone, Paul Harvey// Receptionist, Lucille Lund; Porter, Mantan Moreland; Waiter, William Newell; Fat woman, June Gittelson; Police captain, Charles C. Wilson; Hat check girl, Lola Jensen; Tony Lombardi, Harry Burns; Stevens, Marc Lawrence

Credits: Director, Alexander Hall; Associate Producer, B.B. Kahane; Story, Gladys Lehman; Editor, Viola Lawrence; Art Director, Lionel Banks; Interior Director, Babs Johnstone; Cinematographer, Joseph Walker; Gowns, Kalloch; Jewels, Laykin et Cie; Musical Director, M.W. Stoloff

Song: "Rock-a-Bye Baby" sung by Melvyn Douglas

Production Dates: September 29, 1938–November 4, 1938

Source: play by Ken Englund, Philip G. Epstein and James Edward Grant and from a work by Wilson Collison

Running Time: 72 min.

Story: Melvyn Douglas is trying to find who is stealing jewelry from Jonathan Hale's store. The prime suspect is employee Gordon Oliver. Hale's partner, Margaret Lindsay, suspects Hale of being the thief. Oliver comes to Douglas's partner and wife, Virginia Bruce, and asks her to find the thief. Jewelry is found in Oliver's apartment and he is arrested. Hale intercepts a note meant for gangster Stanley Ridges which takes him back to the jewelry store, where he is shot by Ridges. He accuses Lindsay of murdering Hale and stealing the jewels. Lindsay had been stealing the jewels to stop Ridges from telling her husband, Pierre Watkin, that she never got a divorce from Ridges. He is shot and Lindsay implicates Watkin. Douglas gets Oliver to confess that he was Lindsay's confederate in the thefts. In her investigation, Bruce learns of Lindsay's relationship with Ridges and suspects Lindsay of the murders. Lindsay plans to murder Bruce before she can relay this information to Douglas. Douglas arrives in time to save Bruce's life.

Notes and Commentary: With Joan Blondell unavailable, Virginia Bruce, who had co-starred with Douglas in other films, was signed for the role of Sally Reardon.

Reviews: "The picture is no THE THIN MAN and ultimately rings hollow in its attempt to be a light, charming murder mystery. Things are a just a little too cute for their own good and the story is filled with too many implausibilities. The sequel is a poor follow up to a clever effort." *Motion Picture Guide*, Nash and Ross

"The screenplay was sardine-packed with clichés and inconsistencies." *The Columbia Story*, Hirshhorn

"Sequel to the zany 'There's Always a Woman' is effective comedy and b.o. [box office]." *Variety*, 01/11/39

Summation: *There's That Woman* again — Why? After a delightful initial entry, this film is a big disappointment. The chemistry between Joan Blondell and Melvyn Douglas does not carry over to the Douglas and Virginia Bruce tandem. The comedy is forced and unfunny. The story lets the viewer down when the murderer is revealed long before Douglas comes up with the solution. No wonder the series was cancelled after this one.

Thatcher Colt

About the Murder of Geraldine Foster introduced Police Commissioner Thatcher Colt to the mystery-reading public. The author was Fulton Oursler, who used the pseudonym Anthony Abbot. Oursler made the decision to use an author's name beginning with "A" and a book title also beginning with "A" to ensure both would be at the top of an alphabetized list. Colt was an unusual commissioner who liked to solve the crime rather than leave things to his subordinates. Colt was a complex individual, multilingual, adept in wrestling and able to read lips. Abbot's books were popular; four Colt mysteries had been published by 1932 alone.

In 1932 Hollywood beckoned and Columbia decided to make a short series with Adolphe Menjou in the lead. Three films were scheduled but only two were made. Since Colt was urbane and sophisticated, Menjou was an excellent choice. (Menjou began his 47 year career in 1914. By 1921, he began getting excellent parts and soon became a leading man. When sound came in, Menjou still starred in lower-budget films and had substantial supporting roles in the more important pictures.) In the first film of the Colt series, *The Night Club Lady*, Skeets Gallagher plays Tony Abbott, a friend of Colt's. The only character who appeared in both films was Kelly, Colt's secretary, played by Ruthelma Stevens. It was interesting to have Colt and Kelly go on a vacation together in *The Circus Queen Murder*. The true relationship between the two is not quite spelled out, but it is obvious the two have more than a fondness for each other. The Thatcher Colt films were probably the highlight of Stevens's film career. She appeared in films until 1937 and then resumed her career for three years in 1949.

After the Columbia series, Abbot wrote four more mystery novels, the last in 1943. Critics are undecided as to whether Abbot wrote the final two entries or if they were ghost-written. Thatcher Colt had his farewell on the Hollywood scene with *The Panther's Claw* with Sidney Blackmer as Colt and Rick Vallin as Tony Abbot. Oursler was probably best known for his religious books, *The Greatest Story Ever Told* (Doubleday & Company, 1949), *The Greatest Book Ever Written* (Doubleday & Company, 1949) and co-authored (with April Oursler Armstrong) *The Greatest Faith Ever Known* (Doubleday & Company, 1949).

THE NIGHT CLUB LADY
Columbia (August 1932)

Who killed beautiful Lola Carewe as the clock struck midnight

Cast: Thatcher Colt, Adolphe Menjou; Lola Carewe, Mayo Methot; Tony, Skeets Gallagher; Kelly, Ruthelma Stevens; Mrs. Carewe, Blanche Friderici; Mike, Nat Pendleton;

Rowland, Albert Conti; Eunice, Greta Gransted// Mura, Teru Shimada; Bill, Ed Brady; Joe, Lee Phelps; Dr. Lengle, Wilhelm von Bricken; Dr. Baldwin, Niles Welch; Andre, George Humbert; Everett, Gerald Fielding; Dr. Magnus, Frank Darien

Credits: Director, Irving Cummings; Story, Anthony Abbot; Screenplay, Robert Riskin; Editor, Maurice Wright; Cinematographer, Ted Tetzlaff

Source: Novel, *About the Murder of the Night Club Lady* by Anthony·Abbot

Production Dates: June 8, 1932–June 24, 1932

Running Time: 66 min.

Story: Mayo Methot is receiving threatening letters, but goes to her night club anyway. One of the patrons is Police Commissioner Adolphe Menjou. By reading lips, Menjou realizes Methot's life is in danger. Menjou escorts Methot to her penthouse apartment and places her under police guard. Despite all precautions, Methot is murdered. Methot was a ruthless blackmailer and had many enemies. After two additional murders, Menjou discovers the instrument of death was a scorpion. In a reenactment of Methot's murder, an attempt is made on Menjou's life. The murderess is Blanche Friderici, thought to be Methot's mother, but is really her stage mother. Friderici was the mother of a man Methot drove to suicide. Friderici breaks away from Menjou and plunges to her death from Methot's penthouse apartment.

Notes and Commentary: Anthony Abbot was a pseudonym for Fulton Oursler.

The screenwriters were pretty faithful to the novel. There were some exceptions. Tony, in the novels, was Tony Abbot, Thatcher Colt's confidential secretary instead of just being Colt's best friend and a wastrel with a propensity for alcohol. Ruthelma Stevens, as Kelly, became Thatcher Colt's secretary, a character not found in the novel. Dr. Baldwin, instead of being Lola Carewe's physician, is the medical examiner. To add additional suspense, there is an attempt on Thatcher Colt's life, a scene not in the novel. Probably to avoid any racial overtones, Lola's hold on actor Guy Everett is his past as a jailbird in the movie. In the novel Lola discovered Everett had Negro blood in him, which would have ruined his show business career.

Reviews: "Pace is somewhat slack, with a lot of attention given to extraneous details that add nothing to the story." *Motion Picture Guide*, Nash and Ross

"Save for slowness through detail, a murder mystery that holds the interest." *Variety*, 08/30/32

Summation: This is a solid murder-mystery with Adolphe Menjou in top form as the authoritative police commissioner, Thatcher Colt. Ruthelma Stevens chips in with a good performance as Menjou's secretary. Skeets Gallagher, playing the part of a man who dearly loves his alcohol, is somewhat irritating as Menjou's best friend. Gallagher played Tony or Anthony Abbot, the author of the Thatcher Colt mystery series.

THE CIRCUS QUEEN MURDER
Columbia (April 1933)

Murder before your very eyes!
But how? Why? By whom?

Cast: Thatcher Colt, Adolphe Menjou; Sebastian, Donald Cook; La Tour, Greta Nissen; Kelly, Ruthelma Stevens; Flandrin, Dwight Frye; Dugan, Harry Holman; Rainey,

The Circus Queen Murder (1933) title card–Adolphe Menjou, Ruthelma Stevens.

George Rosener// Crying woman, Helene Chadwick; Roustabouts, Eddy Chandler, Bud Geary and Clarence Muse; Lubbell, Clay Clement; Krumpz, Adolph Miller; Circus man at washtub, Frank Mills; Reporter, Lee Phelps

   Credits: Director, Roy William Neill; Screenplay, Jo Swerling; Editor, Richard Cahoon; Cinematography, Joseph August

   Source: from the *Liberty* magazine story by Anthony Abbot

   Production Dates: February 6, 1933–February 24, 1933

   Running Time: 65 min.

   Story: New York Police Commissioner Adolphe Menjou and his secretary Ruthelma Stevens go on vacation to a small New York town. Arriving in town is George Rosener's circus, which is filled with intrigue. Rosener wants star aerialist Greta Nissen to play up to financial backer Clay Clement so he will keep investing in his circus. Nissen is married to Dwight Frye, but is in love with fellow circus performer Donald Cook. In the circus parade, Stevens lip-reads Frye telling Nissen that he will kill Cook and her. Press agent Harold Holman recognizes Menjou and asks him to help with the trouble the circus is having. Menjou meets with Rosener and finds that all the star performers have received threatening notes warning them not to perform. Stevens tells about Frye's threats. Menjou and the circus personnel hurry to Frye's wagon when they find a bullet hole in the window and blood on the bed sheets, but no body. Frye disguises himself as one of the African cannibals traveling with the circus. At the first performance, Frye has climbed on top of the Big Top where he can look down on the performers. Aerialist Cook has a near-fatal accident when a rope snaps. Nissen performs next. As she finishes her act, Frye shoots a poisoned dart into her back. Nissen falls to the circus floor, dead. Stevens sees movement on top of the tent and goes to investigate. After Nissen's body has been taken to another tent, Menjou notices Stevens is missing and starts to look for her. Fyre stops Menjou at gunpoint; he wants Menjou to request that everyone leave Nissen's tent except Cook. Frye plans to enter the tent and kill Cook and then himself. To ensure that Menjou will carry out his request, Frye shows Menjou that Stevens is his captive. Menjou does as Frye requested. Frye enters the tent and sees a prostrate form holding Nissen's dead body. Frye puts three bullets into the form. Stevens enters the tent to find the form is Menjou with protective armor. Frye goes to the Big Top to perform his aerial act. Menjou introduces Frye as a part of the act. At the end of the act, Frye shoots himself and falls to the circus floor. Menjou plans to return to New York for his vacation.

Notes and Commentary: Screenwriter Jo Swerling only used the characters La Tour, Sebastian and Flandrin from the novel. In both the book and the movie, La Tour is murdered during her high wire routine; only in the book she is killed by a tear gas bomb. Circus owner Tod Robinson, a character not in the film, was the murderer. La Tour discovered Robinson was responsible for the many "accidents" that befell the circus. Robinson was trying to gain total control of the circus.

This movie had a tie-in with Borden's Richer Malted Milk. The ad showed a picture of Adolphe Menjou and Greta Nissen having lunch with the caption, "If we lose our figures ... we lose our jobs."

Footage from *Rain or Shine* (Columbia, 1930) was used to good advantage. In both films the name of the Circus is the Rainey Circus.

The version currently available is the 1938 re-release print. It now meets the new Production Code standards.

Reviews: "Adolphe Menjou ran away with the acting honors in *Circus Queen Murder*, under Roy William Neill's nifty direction." *The Columbia Story*, Hirshhorn

"Fast moving yarn. Menjou in his waxed black mustache and impeccable wardrobe won raves for his role as the police commissioner on vacation." *Motion Picture Guide*, Nash and Ross

"Well knitted and above average circus mystery." *Variety*, 05/09/33

Summation: *The Circus Queen Murder* is not so much a murder mystery as a study of a man's descent into insanity with the purpose of bring down those who have done him an injustice. Adolphe Menjou is the perfect choice as Anthony Abbot's Thatcher Colt. Ruthelma Stevens plays his right-hand "man" to perfection. The knowledge of the identity of the murderer doesn't hamper the suspense of who will be killed and how. Dwight Frye turns in an excellent performance as the tormented circus performer. The other cast members are more than adequate in there roles. Director Roy William Neill is able to convey some suspense in this well-scripted narrative, with one caveat: the audience never understands what message Stevens conveys to Menjou when being held captive by Frye. Like Menjou's character, I guess the audience must also be able to lip read.

Tillie the Toiler

Russ Westover's popular comic strip came to newspaper readers on January 3, 1921. Its instant popularity led to Tillie appearing in the Sunday comics on October 12, 1922. Tillie Jones worked for a women's clothing company run by J. Simpkins. Tillie would have a myriad of boyfriends but the one who really loved was her quiet unassuming co-worker, Clarence "Mac" MacDougall. Throughout the comic strip, Tillie would have a rocky relationship with Simpkins, alternately quitting her job or getting fired. In all instances, Tillie would get her job back. In 1925, Tillie made her first appearance in comic book form from Cupples & Leon, with eight issues from 1925 to 1933.

Tillie the Toiler (1941) scene card —(left, top to bottom) William Tracy, George Watts, Daphne Pollard, Jack Arnold, Kay Harris, (center) William Tracy, Kay Harris, unidentified actresses.

Tillie's popularity caught Hollywood's eye and Marion Davies had the title role in *Tillie the Toiler* (Metro-Goldwyn-Mayer, 1927) with Matt Moore as Mac and George Fawcett as Mr. Simpkins. In 1941, Tillie returned to the comic books for 14 issues, published by Dell from 1941–49, a Whitman hard-cover book, *Tillie the Toiler and the Wild Man of Desert Island*, and a radio program that lasted less than a year. On the air, Caryl Smith was Tillie, with Billy Lynn as Mac and John Brown as Simpkins. Most importantly, her second feature film was released. Newcomer Kay Harris played Tillie. Tillie, for some strange reason was now Tompkins instead of Jones. (Harris, a secretary in Cincinnati, was discovered by Penny Singleton. Singleton was the wife of producer Robert Sparks and recommended Harris for the role of Tillie. Harris's time in Hollywood was short-lived; she appeared in seven more features for Columbia before ending her career.) William Tracy appeared as Mac. (Tracy is known to serial fans as the lead in *Terry and the Pirates* [Columbia, 1940] and as Sergeant "Dodo" Doubleday in a series of Hal Roach wartime comedies. His last role of note was that of Hot Shot Charlie in the television series, *Terry and the Pirates* [Dumont, 1952].) George Watts played Simpkins. (Vaudevillian George Watts had a short undistinguished career, appearing in 39 feature films from 1941–41, many in which he was uncredited.) *Tillie the Toiler* was the first and last entry in the proposed series; the poor reception to the film ended all hopes of continuing.

In the film, Mac is the object of Tillie's affections at the end, something that took almost twenty years to happen in the strip. The comic strip lasted until March 15, 1959. Westover's assistant, Bob Gustafson, took over the strip in 1951. On the last day of the strip, Tillie finally accepted Mac's marriage proposal, a happy ending to the long running strip.

TILLIE THE TOILER

Columbia (August 1941)

The honey of the "funnies"—now the scream of the screen!

Cast: Tillie Tompkins, Kay Harris; Mac, William Tracy; Simpkins, George Watts; Mumsy, Daphne Pollard; Wally Whipple, Jack Arnold; Bubbles, Marjorie Reynolds; Glennie, Bennie Bartlett; Ted Williams, Stanley Brown; George Winkler, Ernest Truex; Perry Tweedale, Franklin Pangborn; Teacher, Sylvia Field; Policeman, Edward Gargan; Pop Tompkins, Harry Tyler

Credits: Director, Sidney Salkow; Producer, Robert Sparks; Story, Karen DeWolf; Screenwriters, Karen DeWolf and Francis Martin; Editor, Gene Milford; Art Director, Lionel Banks; Cinematographers, Henry Freulich and Philip Tannura; Gowns, Monica; Musical Director, M.W. Stoloff

Production Dates: April 28, 1941–May 29, 1941

Source: Based on the comic strip *Tillie the Toiler* created by Russ Westover, copyrighted by King Features Syndicate, Inc.

Running Time: 67 min.

Story: George Watts of the Simpkins Dress Company is looking for a secretary. William Tracy, who is smitten with Kay Harris, recommends her for the position. Office manager Jack Arnold soon becomes Tracy's rival for Harris's affections. Harris sends a letter to Ernest Truex, a potential partner of Watts that contains some of Watts' negative comments on Truex. Truex cancels negotiations and steals the upcoming season's fashion designs. Harris is about to be fired when Watts learns that Truex is a crook. Watts goes on a business trip, leaving Tracy in charge. A budding dress designer, Stanley Brown, comes into the office with his portfolio of designs. Harris, mistakenly thinks these are the dress designs Watts wants promoted. Harris convinces Tracy to put on a fashion show. Watts returns to a barrage of bill collectors, wanting to be paid for their services for the show. Watts is about to cancel the show when he finds Truex is putting on a fashion show with the stolen designs. Watts allows Harris to go on as scheduled. Brown's designs are a huge hit. Tracy is promoted to general manager and Harris is now responsible for style promotion. Tracy no longer has a rival for Harris's affection when Arnold is drafted into the army.

Notes and Commentary: Tillie's last name was originally Jones, but was changed to Tompkins for the film.

Review: "Broadly sketching the comedy factors in elemental fashion, picture will slip by satisfactorily in the secondary and family houses as supporting attraction." *Variety*, 08/13/41

Summation: This film was unavailable for viewing by the author.

The Whistler

I am the Whistler, and I know many things, for I walk by night. I know many strange tales, hidden in the hearts of men and women who have stepped into the shadows. Yes ... I know the nameless terrors of which they dare not speak.

Thus begins the many tales of the Whistler on radio, in the movies and on television. To add to the eerie quality of the program was Wilbur Hatch's 13-note theme whistled by Dorothy Roberts. (Roberts would perform this function for 13 years. *The Whistler* was primarily a West Coast program, with the exception of the summer of 1946, and in 1947 and 1948. The first show aired on May 16, 1942. For the first two years, J. Donald Wilson was the writer-producer. Producer-director George Allen took over in 1944. Later, Sterling Tracy and Sherman Marks directed show, with Joel Malone and Harold Swanton providing scripts. Bill Foreman was the initial voice of the Whistler; others were Gale Gordon, Joseph Kearns, Marvin Miller, Bill Johnstone and Everett Clarke. Columbia decided to produce a series based on the radio program in 1944. Otto Forrest was the voice of the Whistler on the screen. Richard Dix was signed to star in the series, playing different parts in seven entries. (Dix began his film career in 1917. In the silent era, he was noted for his performances as John McTavish in *The Ten Commandments* [Famous Players-Lasky/Paramount, 1923] and as Nophaie in *The Vanishing American* [Famous Players-Lasky/Paramount, 1925]. Dix made the transfer to sound, receiving an Academy Award nomination for best actor as Yancey Cravet in *Cimarron* (Radio Pictures, 1931). Later in the 30's, Dix remained a leading man at RKO, although his films were primarily in the "B" category. In 1940, he began a collaboration with producer Harry Sherman, starring in six westerns. In 1944, Dix made his first Whistler film and concentrated on that series until his retirement from motion pictures in 1947.) An eighth film, *The Return of the Whistler* (Columbia, 1948), starring Michael Duane, ended the series. The last radio program was broadcast on September 22, 1955. *The Whistler* came to television on July 13, 1954, and 39 episodes were produced. The last one aired on June 24, 1955. The program was scheduled to have a second season. It was popular but conflict over costs between CBS Television Film Sales and Lindsley Parsons, who produced the first 13 episodes, hastened the demise of the show. Writer and producer Joel Malone took over the production reins with the 14th episode. Even though Malone was the producer through the remainder of the series, beginning with episode 27, the series was copyrighted by Columbia Television Film Sales, Inc.

THE WHISTLER

Columbia (March 1944)

Radio's Master of Mystery ... now on the Screen!

Cast: Earl C. Conrad, Richard Dix; Alice Walker, Gloria Stuart; "Smith," J. Carrol Naish; Gorman, Alan Dinehart/Voice of the Whistler, Otto Forrest; Lefty Vigran, Don Costello; Gus, Cy Kendall; Deaf-mute, Billy Benedict; Police Detective in alley, Pat O'Malley; Jennings, Charles Coleman; Charlie McNair, Robert Emmett Keane; Telephone Repairman, Clancy Cooper; Bill Tomley, George Lloyd; Antoinette Vigran, Joan Woodbury; Plainclothes Detective, Jack Ingram; Flop-house Desk Clerk, Byron Foulger; Bum in next bed, Trevor Bardette; Dock Watchman, Robert Homans; Ship's Purser, Charles Waggenheim; Detective at dock, Kermit Maynard

Credits: Director, William Castle; Producer, Rudolph C. Flothow; Story, J. Donald Wilson; Screenwriter, Eric Taylor; Editor, Jerome Thoms; Art Direction, George Van Marter; Set Decorator, Sidney Clifford; Cinematographer, James S. Brown; Original Theme and Score, Wilbur Hatch

Production Dates: January 21, 1944–February 7, 1944

Running Time: 59 min.

Source: Suggested by the Columbia Broadcasting System program *The Whistler.*

Story: Despondent over his wife's death, Richard Dix hires an unknown killer to murder him. Dix then receives a telegram, informing him that his wife is still alive. He tries to reach the killer to rescind the agreement. The killer, J. Carroll Naish plans to murder Dix by frightening him to death. Dix finally meets Naish and asks to call off the arrangement. Since Naish knows Dix has seen him kill another man, he is afraid Dix will go to the police. Dix's secretary, Gloria Stuart, brings him another telegram, stating that his wife died on the journey home. Dix now wants to live, having found a new love in Stuart. Naish fires a shot at Dix, one that misses. Naish is killed by Kermit Maynard, a detective stationed at the dock.

Notes and Commentary: Richard Dix's health wouldn't allow him to continue to star in action films. He signed a contract with Columbia to headline the Whistler series.

To get the desired effect of a mood of desperation from Dix, director William Castle first made him go on a diet and give up smoking. Next, Castle gave Dix early calls and then made him wait to late in the day for his scenes. This made Dix nervous and jumpy, which allowed Castle to get the reactions he wanted.

Director William Castle's place in cinema history rests primarily with his gimmicky horror films, including *House on Haunted Hill* (Allied Artists, 1959), *13 Ghosts* (Columbia, 1960) and *Mr. Sardonicus* (Columbia, 1961).

Gloria Stuart received an Academy Award nomination for Best Supporting Actress in *Titanic* (20th Century–Fox/Paramount, 1997). Stuart played Rose, the 100-year-old survivor.

The first telegram received by Richard Dix has the date March 8, 1944 — the month and year the film was released.

Reviews: "Tense little programmer. Castle never did anything else as effective as this. Dix is excellent as the man terrorized and unable to do anything to stop it. The production values, considering that the film was shot on a budget of less than $75,000, are excellent.

A perfect example of the art that could be created in the strictures of studio B-unit production." *Motion Picture Guide*, Nash and Ross

"Richard Dix in stout supporting gangster meller for duals." *Variety*, 05/03/44

Summation: *The Whistler* is a winner. Richard Dix gives a fine performance as a man with mental problems who first wants to be murdered and then changes his mind. J. Carrol Naish gives a strong performance as a cold-blooded killer. The story does not disappoint. The viewer knows that Naish's efforts to murder Dix would be futile. The fun is in seeing how Naish would be tripped up at the last moment.

THE MARK OF THE WHISTLER

Columbia (October 1944)

Radio's mystery master in a thrilling tale of murder!

Cast: Lee Selfridge Nugent, Richard Dix; Pat Henley, Janis Carter; Joe Sorsby, Porter Hall; "Limpy" Smith, Paul Guilfoyle; Eddie Donnelly, John Calvert/Voice of the Whistler, Otto Forrest; Landlady, Minerva Urecal; Fireman, Walter Baldwin; Children's Aid Society

The Mark of the Whistler (1944) scene card —(left to right) John Calvert, Richard Dix.

Woman, Edna Holland; Mailman, Jack Rice; Bank Guard, Edgar Dearing; M.K. Simmons, Howard Freeman; Newspaper Photographer, Donald Kerr; Haberdasher, Eddie Kane; Perry Donnelly, Matt Willis; Sellers, Arthur Space; Tom, Matt McHugh; Men's Room Attendant, Willie Best; Truck Driver, Bill Raisch

Credits: Director, William Castle; Producer, Rudolph C. Flothow; Story, Cornell Woolrich; Screenwriter, George Bricker; Editor, Reg Browne; Art Director, John Datu; Set Decoration, Sidney Clifford; Cinematographer, George Meehan; "Whistler" theme music, Wilbur Hatch

Production Dates: July 31, 1944–August 14, 1944

Running Time: 61 min.

Source: Suggested by the Columbia Broadcasting System program *The Whistler*.

Story: Richard Dix, down on his luck, decides to claim a dormant account since he has the same name. After careful preparation and giving the right answers, Dix receives over $29,000. Leaving the bank in a hurry and not wanting to be photographed for the newspapers, Dix accidently knocks over a crippled street beggar, Paul Guilfoyle. After seeing Dix's picture in the paper, John Calvert and his brother Matt Willis plan to murder Dix. Calvert finds Dix in a nightclub with newspaper reporter Janis Carter. Sensing trouble, Dix is able to leave the club by a hidden back window. Before he can reach his hotel, Dix is joined in his cab by Guilfoyle, who tells him that men are waiting for him. Dix asks Guilfoyle to enter his hotel room and retrieve a small box for him. When Guilfoyle takes the box, the top opens and Guilfoyle sees the money. Leaving the hotel, Guilfoyle is trailed by Calvert. Guilfoyle gives the box to Dix and tells him if he's in trouble to come to his apartment. When Guilfoyle leaves, Calvert introduces himself to Dix as a policeman and tells him he's under arrest. Dix is taken to Calvert's home. Calvert believes Dix is the true owner of the dormant account and tells him that because of his father's duplicity, Calvert's father was falsely imprisoned and consequently lost his mind. Calvert plans to exact his revenge on Dix. Dix tries to tell Calvert he's not the person he's looking for to no avail. Transporting Dix to a secluded area to kill him, Calvert's vehicle is involved in a traffic accident, giving Dix a chance to escape. As fate would have it, Dix is on the street where Guilfoyle resides. Dix goes to Guilfoyle's apartment where he finds that Guilfoyle is the real owner of the account. As Calvert tries to break into the apartment, the police arrive. In a gunfight, Calvert is killed. Dix will have to serve prison time for fraud even though Guilfoyle tried to have the charges dropped. Guilfoyle had removed the money from the box before giving it to him. Guilfoyle tells Dix they will go into business together when he is released from prison. Also, Carter wants to renew a budding romance with Dix.

Notes and Commentary: The film is based on the short story, "Dormant Account" by Cornell Woolrich. The story appeared in the May 1942 issue of *Black Mask* magazine. Screenwriter George Bricker followed Woolrich's story closely, with only a few changes. Bricker named his protagonist Lee Selfridge Nugent instead of George Palmer. A female newspaper reporter is added as a possible romantic interest for Nugent. At the end of the screenplay the bank insists Nugent must serve prison time for fraud even though Limpy wanted charges dropped, whereas in Woolrich's story Limpy's pleas are successful and no jail time is imposed.

"Dormant Account" was also the working title for this film.

Reviews: "Direction is evenly paced and performances are up to par." *Motion Picture Guide*, Nash and Ross

"Moderately entertaining." *Variety*, 11/15/44

Summation: Another good Whistler film, in which director William Castle builds the suspense nicely. Richard Dix is fine in the lead, and John Calvert is properly sinister. Cinematographer George Meehan chips in with some great camera work, especially in scene in the dark with Dix and Paul Guilfoyle.

THE POWER OF THE WHISTLER
Columbia (April 1945)

Radio's Mystery Man Will Hold You Spellbound!

Cast: William Everest, Richard Dix; Jean Lang, Janis Carter; "Francie" Lang, Jeff Donnell; Charlie Kent, Loren Tindall; Constantina Ivaneska, Tala Birell; Kaspar Andropolous, John Abbott/Voice of the Whistler, Otto Forrest; Motorist, I. Stanford Jolley; Stage Door Guard, Forrest Taylor; Flotilda, Nina Mae McKinney; Locksmith, Jack George; Richards, Stanley Price; Pharmacist, Cy Kendall; Joe Blainey, Murray Alper; Cake Delivery Man, Frank Hagney; Police Captain; Crane Whitley; Western Union Agent, Walter Baldwin; John Crawford, Kenneth MacDonald; Highway Patrolman, Robert Williams; Motorcycle Patrolmen, Eddie Parker and Frank J. Scannell

Credits: Director, Lew Landers; Producer, Leonard S. Picker; Screenwriter, Aubrey Wisberg; Editor, Reg Browne; Art Director, John Tatu; Set Decorator, Sidney Clifford; Cinematographer, L.W. O'Connell; "Whistler" theme music, Wilbur Hatch

Production Dates: December 6, 1944–December 20, 1944

Running Time: 66 min.

Source: Suggested by the Columbia Broadcasting System program *The Whistler*.

Story: While crossing a street, Richard Dix is hit by a car. Falling backward, Dix hits his head on a lamppost, causing amnesia. In a Greenwich Village café, Janis Carter sees Dix and reads his fortune, using a deck of cards. Carter warns Dix that he will die within 24 hours. Learning that Dix has amnesia, Carter decides to help him and enlists her sister, Jeff Donnell, to help. During the search for Dix's identity, small animals are found, dead. Donnell discovers that Dix had a prescription filled for a deadly poison and then had a birthday cake sent to Doctor Kenneth MacDonald at the Hudson Mental Institute in Woodville. Unbeknownst to Carter, Dix regains his memory, including the fact that he wants to murder the judge who had him committed to the mental institution. Dix convinces Carter to travel with him. Donnell goes to the police with information that proves him to be a homicidal maniac. On the way to the judge's house, Carter becomes suspicious and breaks away. Dix stalks Carter as the police close in. Dix traps Carter in a barn. As Dix comes closer to Carter, Carter seizes a pitchfork and drives it into Dix's body, killing him.

Notes and Commentary: As a pharmacist, I couldn't help but notice that Cy Kendall filled a prescription for a deadly poison without knowing the patient's name and that the physician was deceased. In this case, the physician had been dead for about 50 years.

Reviews: "Chilling suspense story. Dix is cast in a tough part which he is unable to pull off." *Motion Picture Guide*, Nash and Ross

"Fair mystery chiller for the duals." *Variety*, 03/28/45

Summation: The story builds well to a harrowing suspenseful conclusion. Richard Dix delivers a competent performance as a homicidal maniac; Janis Carter is also excellent. Lew Landers does a fine job of directing, with excellent cinematography by L.W. O'Connell.

THE VOICE OF THE WHISTLER
Columbia (October 1945)

The Strange Case of the haunted Lighthouse!

Cast: John Sinclair, Richard Dix; Joan Martin, Lynn Merrick; Ernie Sparrow, Rhys Williams; Fred Graham, James Cardwell; Ferdinand, Tom Kennedy/Voice of the Whistler, Otto Forrest; Sinclair Executives, Stuart Holmes, Wilbur Mack, Charles Marsh, Harold Miller and Forbes Murray; Paul Kitridge, Douglas Wood; Doctor, John Hamilton; Train Porter, Clinton Rosemond; Tony, Martin Garralaga; Bobbie, Gigi Perreau; Dr. Rose, Frank Reicher; Georgie, Byron Foulger; Georgie's wife, Minerva Urecal; Waitress, Doris Houck; Pharmacist, Robert Williams

Credits: Director, William Castle; Producer, Rudolph C. Flothow; Story, Allan Radar; Screenwriters, Wilfred H. Pettitt and William Castle; Editor, Dwight Caldwell; Cinematographer, George Meehan; Sound, Jack Goodrich; Musical Director, M.R. Bakaleinikoff; "Whistler" theme music, Wilbur Hatch

Production Dates: July 23, 1945–August 7, 1945

Running Time: 60 min.

Source: Suggested by the Columbia Broadcasting System program *The Whistler*.

Story: At the pinnacle of his financial career, Richard Dix decides wants nothing to interfere with his personal life. Due to stress, Dix collapses and is told by his physician, John Hamilton, to take a vacation trip. In Chicago, Dix lapses into unconsciousness and is aided by cab driver Rhys Williams. Williams takes Dix to a clinic, where Dix meets nurse Lynn Merrick. Dix is told that he needs good sea air and friends. Dix convinces Williams to accompany him. Believing that he only has months to live, Dix asks Merrick to marry him. Thinking the marriage will be short and that she will soon inherit Dix's fortune, Merrick accepts his proposal. Then, when Dix dies, Merrick will then be free to marry her true love, James Cardwell. Dix converts an abandoned lighthouse into a beach resort. Dix's health miraculously improves and Merrick finds herself in a loveless marriage. Cardwell comes to visit. Marrick and Cardwell rediscover their love for each other. Merrick wants to stay with Dix and see Cardwell on the sly. Dix becomes aware of the situation and tells Cardwell how he could murder Cardwell without being caught. Cardwell plans to use the scheme to murder Dix, but he turns the tables and murders him. Merrick sees what happened and calls the police. Dix is sentenced and executed. Even though Merrick inherits Dix's money, fate dooms her to a life of solitude in the lighthouse.

Notes and Commentary: The working title was "Checkmate for Murder."

A pharmacist plays a part in the unfolding of this tale. He supplies a prescription without any label as to ingredients, strength, directions, patient's name and authorization from a physician.

Reviews: "Despite a good idea and the proper atmosphere, the story is not brought to the screen effectively, making for tough going as the plot drags itself out." *Motion Picture Guide*, Nash and Ross

"So-so whodunit of its type." *Variety*, 12/26/45

Summation: While not as suspenseful as the previous Whistler entries, the film is very well done.

MYSTERIOUS INTRUDER
Columbia (April 1946)

Radio's master of mystery ... in his most thrilling case!

Cast: Don Gale, Richard Dix; Detective Taggart, Barton MacLane; Joan Hill, Nina Vale; James Summers, Regis Toomey; Freda Hanson, Helen Mowery; Harry Pontos, Mike Mazurki; Elora Lund, Pamela Blake; Detective Burns, Charles Lane/Voice of the Whistler, Otto Forrest; Edward Stillwell, Paul E. Burns; Reporters, Donald Kerr and Dan Stowell; Desk Clerk, Charles Jordan; Woman in Window, Jessie Arnold; Dr. Connell, Selmer Jackson; Rose Denning, Kathleen Howard; Mr. Brown, Harlan Briggs; Kelly, Kernan Cripps; Henry, Stanley Blystone; Police Desk Sergeant, Harry Strang; Miss Gordon, Isabel Withers; Jimmy, Jack Carrington; Policeman outside Stillwell's store, Joe Palma; Davis, Arthur Space

Credits: Director, William Castle; Producer, Rudolph C. Flothow; Story and Screenwriter, Eric Taylor; Editor, Dwight Caldwell; Art Director, Hans Radon; Set Decorator, Robert Priestly; Cinematography, Philip Tannura; Sound, Jack Haynes; Musical Director, Mischa Bakaleinikoff; "Whistler" theme music, Wilbur Hatch

Production Dates: December 6, 1945–December 20, 1945

Running Time: 61 min.

Source: Suggested by the Columbia Broadcasting System program *The Whistler*.

Story: Seedy private investigator Richard Dix is hired by Paul E. Burns to find Pamela Blake who he has not seen for many years. Burns has some of Blake's mother's heirlooms that might be worth a fortune. Dix decides to pass Helen Mowery off as the heir. When Mowery meets Burns, tough guy Mike Mazurki shows up and murders Burns and takes Mowery. Mowery returns to Dix when he tells reporters Mowery was only pretending to be the heir. Mowery leads Dix to Mazurki. Dix breaks into the house and finds Mazurki passed out. Police detectives Barton MacLane and Charles Lane arrive. Shots are fired. Mazurki is killed. Dix is seen leaving the house and is arrested. Blake sees the newspaper article about Burns's death and calls the police. Dix is released. Blake is instructed to meet with Dix to find the valuable heirloom; Dix tells Blake that he will find it. Dix confronts Mowery and makes her confess that she was working with Mazurki and that she had her boyfriend call the police. Mowery hoped the police would shoot Dix. Mowery also shows Dix a newspaper clipping about some rare Jenny Lind recordings, worth $200,000. Someone comes to Mowery's door and Dix leaves through the back entrance. From Harlan Briggs, who owns the shop next door, Dix is shown a secret passage into Burns's store. Dix learns that Mowery was murdered. Apartment manager Regis Toomey found her body. Dix decides to enter the store, where he finds Briggs's body. In Burns's store, Toomey and a confederate, Arthur Space, are looking for the Jenny Lind recordings. Toomey and Space locate the recordings and start to leave, only to be confronted by Dix. It turns out that Toomey was working with Mowery and wants to make a deal with Dix. Dix takes the box with the recordings. Shots are exchanged and it appears that Toomey and Space are hit. From a tip, MacLane and Lane enter the store through the front door. Dix leaves by the secret passage and calls the police. Dix hears someone coming through the passage, and thinking it's the killers, fires a shot. Shots are returned. One bullet goes through the box, smashing the recordings and into Dix's body, killing him. MacLane and Lane fired the shots.

Notes and Commentary: The working title was "Murder Is Unpredictable."

Reviews: "Though routine in plot, this is a well-paced film with some good moments of suspense. Though classically hard-boiled, Dix's characterization has a soft spot, as well as providing some humor within the mystery. Some interesting camera work and a tightly plotted script make this a nifty programmer." *Motion Picture Guide*, Nash and Ross

"Nicely paced whodunit with Richard Dix, *Mysterious Intruder* provides a consistently entertaining hour's entertainment." *Variety*, 03/27/46

Summation: This is a fine mystery and film noir. Richard Dix's portrayal of a private investigator working on the edge of the law is excellent. Dix is given a fine supporting cast, including such worthies as Barton MacLane, Regis Toomey, Mike Mazurki, Pamela Blake and Charles Lane. William Castle's direction and Philip Tannura's cinematography complement Eric Taylor's first-rate story.

THE SECRET OF THE WHISTLER
Columbia (November 1946)

The whistler's greatest love murder!

Cast: Ralph Harrison, Richard Dix; Kay Morrell, Leslie Brooks; Jim Calhoun, Michael Duane; Edith Harrison, Mary Currier; Linda Vail, Mona Barrie; Joe Conroy, Ray Walker; Laura, Claire Du Brey/Voice of the Whistler, Otto Forrest; Jorgensen, Byron Foulger; Girls at party, Doris Houck and Nancy Saunders; Dr, Winthrop, Charles Trowbridge; Fred, Fred "Snowflake" Toones; McLaren, John Hamilton; Messenger boy, Fred Amsel; Dr. Gunther, Arthur Space; Miss Bailey, Barbara Woodell; George, Ernie Adams; Henry Loring, Jack Davis; Butler, Ernest Hilliard; Detective Lieutenant, Pat Lane; Detective, Tony Shaw

Credits: Director, George Sherman; Producer, Rudolph C. Flothow; Story, Richard H. Landau; Screenwriter, Raymond L. Schrock; Editor, Dwight Caldwell; Art Director, Hans Radon; Set Decorator, Robert Bradfield; Cinematographer, Allen Siegler; Musical Director, Mischa Bakaleinikoff; "Whistler" theme music, Wilbur Hatch

Production Dates: July 15, 1946–August 1, 1946

Running Time: 65 min.

Source: Suggested by the Columbia Broadcasting System program *The Whistler*.

Story: Mary Currier, who has a heart problem, purchases a tombstone for herself. Her husband, Richard Dix, is an untalented artist who lives on her money. Dix learns Currier has a short time to live. He begins an affair with gold digger Leslie Brooks and wants to marry her. Under the care of a new physician, Currier returns to good health. She also discovers Dix's affair with Brooks and plans to divorce him. Dix decides to murder Currier before she can begin divorce proceedings; he adds poison to one of her medications. Housekeeper Claire Du Brey finds Currier's dead body. The death is attributed to Currier's heart condition. In her diary, Currier stated that she is going to divorce Dix and that he put something in her medication. Brooks finds the prescription bottle and has it analyzed. Brooks receives a phone call that verifies poison was put in the medication. Dix overhears the conversation and goes into a rage and strangles Brooks. Brooks had called the police. The police arrive and shoot Dix as he tries to escape. The irony is that the page in the diary would have exonerated him.

Reviews: "One of the best of the series." *The Columbia Story*, Hirshhorn

"Engrossing as usual and well acted." *Motion Picture Guide*, Nash and Ross

Summation: This was another fine entry in the Whistler series. Buoyed by George Sherman's direction, telling performances by Richard Dix, Leslie Brooks, Mary Currier and Claire Du Brey, the film generates genuine suspense. Raymond L. Schrock's screenplay adaptation of Richard H. Landau's story keeps you guessing to the end as to how fate will trip up Dix.

THE THIRTEENTH HOUR
Columbia (February 1947)

Murder on a one-way highway ... to the gallows!

Alternate Title: The 13th Hour

Cast: Steve Reynolds, Richard Dix; Eileen Blair, Karen Morley; Charlie Cook, John Kellogg; Jerry Mason, Jim Bannon; Don Parker, Regis Toomey; Mabel Sands, Bernadene Hayes; Tommy Blair, Mark Dennis/Voice of the Whistler, Otto Forrest; Truck Driver/Waiter, George Lloyd; Truck Driver, Eddie Parker; Jimmy, Paul Campbell; Donna, Nancy Saunders; Ranford, Anthony Warde; McCabe, Ernie Adams; Judge Collins, Selmer Jackson; Bernie, Charles Jordan; Motorist who gets license number, Robert Kellard; Stack, Jack Carrington; Berger, Robert Williams; Secretary, Lillian Wells; Captain Linfield, Cliff Clark; Detectives, Pat O'Malley and Stanley Blystone; Policeman, Kernan Cripps

Credits: Director, William Clements; Producer, Rudolph C. Flothow; Story, Leslie Edgley; Screenwriters, Edward Bock and Raymond L. Schrock; Editor, Dwight Caldwell; Art Director, Hans Radon; Set Decorator, Albert Rickerd; Cinematographer, Vincent Farrar; Musical Director, Mischa Bakaleinikoff; "Whistler" theme music, Wilbur Hatch

Production Dates: October 3, 1946–October 22, 1946

Running Time: 65 min.

Source: Suggested by the Columbia Broadcasting System program *The Whistler*.

Story: Freight line owner Richard Dix is framed for the murder of police officer Regis Toomey. Toomey was Dix's rival for the affections of café owner Karen Morley. Before the murderer knocked him out, Dix tore a glove off one of the murderer's hands, indicating the murderer was missing a thumb. Dix has Morley hide the glove. Afraid the police won't believe him innocent, Dix goes on the run. About to give himself up, Dix spots an unscrupulous freight line run by Jim Bannon and learns that he is the head of a car-stealing racket. Dix gets his mechanic, John Kellogg, to get a job with Bannon. Kellogg tells Dix that stolen cars have been brought into Bannon's garage and that one of the drivers was missing a thumb. Kellogg tells Dix to get the glove and come to the garage to catch the murderer red-handed. Dix comes to the garage without the glove and finds Bannon's body; he also finds that his safe ransacked. As Dix is investigating, a mysterious figure sneaks up behind him and knocks him out. The intruder goes through Dix's pockets. Kellogg tells the now-conscious Dix that he has been attacked. Kellogg encourages him to stay on the run. Dix goes to Morley to retrieve the glove, and Morley and her son, Mark Dennis, show him a cylinder in the glove containing diamonds. Dennis believes that one of the employees, Bernadene Hayes, is working with the murderer. Dix follows Hayes to her apartment and overhears her calling the murderer. Dix enlists Kellogg to help him capture him, not realizing that Kellogg is the guilty party. Kellogg forces Dix to write a note that will enable him to retrieve the glove. Dix had removed the diamonds from the glove and had placed them in his tobacco pouch. Morley insists on accompanying Kellogg when he again talks to Dix. Finding that the diamonds aren't in the glove, Kellogg begins to rough up Morley. Dix gives Kellogg the diamonds. Kellogg and Hayes walk out of the apartment and are arrested. Dennis had alerted the police that Morley and Dix were in danger. Kellogg murdered Toomey because he knew Kellogg was a wanted man and was blackmailing him. Dix will receive a substantial reward for the recovery of the diamonds. Dix plans to get back in the trucking business and marry Morley.

Notes and Commentary: The working titles were "The Hunter Is a Fugitive" and "Whistler's Destiny."

This was the last film for series star Richard Dix; he died on September 20, 1949.

George Lloyd had two roles in the film: a truck driver in the opening scene, and then later as a waiter.

Review: "Efficient entry in the Whistler series." *1996 Movie & Video Guide*, Maltin

Summation: Neat Whistler story with fate entering Richard Dix's life at the beginning of the story instead the end. Dix is fine as the fugitive on the run. Again Dix is given good support, especially by John Kellogg, Karen Morley and Mark Dennis.

THE RETURN OF THE WHISTLER
Columbia (March 1948)

Her wedding night ... a nightmare of terror!

Cast: Ted Nichols, Michael Duane; Alice Dupres Barkley, Lenore Aubert; Gaylord Traynor, Richard Lane; Charlie Barkley, James Cardwell; Mrs. Barkley, Ann Shoemaker; Mrs. Hulskamp, Sarah Padden/Voice of the Whistler, Otto Forrest; Jeff Anderson, Olin Howland; Hotel Painter, William Newell; Crandall, Fred Sears; Hart, Robert Emmett Keane; Captain Griggs, Edgar Dearing; George Sawyer, Jack Rice; Sam, Eddy Waller; Sybil, Ann Doran; Arnold, Trevor Bardette; Traynor's Secretary, Abigail Adams; Older Nurse, Isabel Winters; Dr. Grantland, Wilton Graff; Male Nurses, Steve Benton and Kenner G. Kemp; Nurse, Dolores Castle; Police Sergeant, Harry Strang

Credits: Director, D. Ross Lederman; Producer, Rudolph C. Flothow; Story, Cornell Woolrich; Screenwriter, Edward Bock and Maurice Tombragel; Editor, Dwight Caldwell; Art Director, George Brooks; Set Decorator, James Crowe; Cinematographer, Philip Tannura; Musical Director, Mischa Bakaleinikoff; "Whistler" theme music, Wilbur Hatch

Production Dates: October 13, 1947–October 23, 1947

Running Time: 63 min.

Source: Suggested by the Columbia Broadcasting System program *The Whistler*.

Story: Michael Duane and Lenore Aubert decide to get married, but the justice of the peace has been called away. Meanwhile, two mysterious men disable their car. Duane and Aubert barely make it to The Inn, where only Aubert is able to get a room. The next morning, she is missing. Private Investigator Richard Lane offers to help Duane find her. Duane tells Lane that Aubert had been married to an American soldier who had been killed on their wedding day. Aubert came to the United States recently to be with her late husband's relatives. At his apartment, Duane finds Aubert's marriage certificate. Lane hits Duane and takes the certificate. Duane manages to track down Aubert's former in-laws. Duane meets James Cardwell, who tells him that *he* is Aubert's husband. Duane is allowed to see Aubert,

The Return of the Whistler (1948) title card — (center) Lenore Aubert, (right) Michael Duane.

who verifies this fact. After he leaves, it becomes evident that Aubert was forced to lie at gunpoint. Cardwell and his mother, Ann Shoemaker, are behind a scheme to take away a fortune that belongs to Aubert. Cardwell then meets Lane, who hands him the marriage certificate. Duane discovers Cardwell had lied to him and plans to talk to Aubert. Meanwhile, Lane finds that Cardwell is *not* Aubert's husband and begins his investigation. Aubert has been taken to a sanitarium. Duane is able to rescue her before Cardwell confronts him. Duane defeats Cardwell in a fistfight. As orderlies begin to subdue Duane, Lane shows up with the police. Cardwell, Shoemaker and other family members are arrested. Duane and Aubert finally marry.

Notes and Commentary: The screenplay was adapted from Cornell Woolrich's story, "All at Once, No Alice," first published in the March 2, 1940, issue of *Argosy*. Significant changes are made in bringing Woolrich's story to the screen, but the basic premise is maintained. The names of the couple in the short story are James Cannon and Alice Brown. In the story, the couple is married by the justice of the peace. They are unable to find a suitable room for the night's lodging. Alice is able to spend the night in a small closet in a local hotel; James finds a room at the YMCA. The next morning the hotel employees and the justice of the peace insist they have never heard of her. The police become involved. Finally Detective Ainslie sees proof that Alice exists. James remembers that Alice told him that she worked as a maid for a Beresford family. In following up, James and Ainslie discover that

Alice's real name is Alma Beresford. Alma was rich but told James she was a maid so as not to frighten him away because of their difference in social standing. Alma had loved James and wanted to marry him. Alma's guardian, Hastings, planned to murder Alma to inherit her fortune. Hastings had bribed the hotel employees and the justice of the peace to deny any knowledge of Alma. Hastings's plans are thwarted by Ainslie and James. James plans to legally marry Alma, with Ainslie as best man.

Review: "Shoddy script has a hard time holding any level of suspense." *Motion Picture Guide*, Nash and Ross

"Fairish whodunit. With some judicious editing the film could have been a superior suspense thriller." *Variety*, 03/03/48

Summation: Engrossing Whistler episode. Not as much suspense as some previous entries but the story unfolds at a nice pace and holds the viewer's interest. Acting is up to par for the series, but Richard Dix is sorely missed.

Wild Bill Hickok

James Butler "Wild Bill" Hickok was a Civil war scout and spy, U.S. deputy marshal, county sheriff and town marshal as various times in his life. Hickok was said to have an unerring skill with both a pistol and a rifle. He preferred to fight man-to-man with his fists, using pistols as a last resort. Hickok carried Colt Model 1851 Navy revolvers, butt forward in a sash or belt with open-top holsters. Famed in fact and fiction as a notorious lawman, Hickok became legendary when he was murdered by Jack McCall while playing poker in a Deadwood saloon.

In 1923, William S. Hart had the title role in *Wild Bill Hickok* (Famous Players-Lasky/Paramount, 1923). The first major sound feature in which Hickok was a character was *The Plainsman* (Paramount, 1936) with Gary Cooper. Cooper was an obvious influence on Gordon (later Bill) Elliott in the serial *The Great Adventures of Wild Bill Hickok* (Columbia, 1938). The serial launched Elliott's career as a western star. By 1940, Columbia decided to change Elliott's series character from Wild Bill Saunders to Wild Bill Hickok. In *The Return of Wild Bill* (Columbia, 1940), Elliott as Saunders rides to new adventures in Kansas. When Elliott arrives in Kansas in *Prairie Schooner* (Columbia, 1940), he is now Hickok. In his eight features in the 1940–41 season, only six would feature Elliott as Hickok. The two remaining features had Hickok as descendents of Davy Crockett and Daniel Boone. The series had only one other continuing character, Cannonball, played by Dub Taylor. Taylor had scored well in Frank Capra's *You Can't Take it With You* (Columbia, 1938) and was assigned to play Elliott's sidekick in his Wild Bill Saunders series, which carried over to the Hickok series. For his 1941–42 series, Elliott had a co-star, Tex Ritter. Ritter came to Columbia from his successful run of pictures for Monogram. In the eight features, Elliott would play Hickok only six times. After the first entry, *King of Dodge City* (Columbia, 1941), Taylor was replaced by Frank Mitchell. The acrobatic Mitchell would provide pratfalls designed to elicit laughter from the younger audience members. Although Elliott and Ritter were friends, neither one wanted a co-star in their series. Elliott managed to get out of his Columbia contract and signed with Republic Pictures, where he became best known as Red Ryder. The Wild Bill Hickok series was then discontinued. In 1946, Elliott was promoted to big-budget westerns. In 1950, he left Republic and made his last western series in a group of intelligent lower-budget features for Monogram and the parent company, Allied Artists. In 1954, the era of series "B" pictures was all but over and Elliott finished out his contract and motion picture career with five nicely turned detective stories.

There were some interesting films featuring Wild Bill Hickok in the '40s, including Richard Dix in *Badlands of Dakota* (Universal, 1941) and Bruce Cabot in *Wild Bill Hickok Rides* (Warner Bros., 1941). In the art work for *Rides*, the artist's interpretation of Hickok had Hickok looking just like Elliott instead of Cabot.

311

The next major appearance of Hickok was the television series, *The Adventures of Wild Bill Hickok* (Screen Gems, 1951–58) with Guy Madison in the lead role and Andy Devine as his sidekick, Jingles P. Jones. Madison and Devine also starred in a radio show on the Mutual Network. The show lasted 271 episodes, airing from April 1, 1951 to December 31, 1954. From 1952–56, executive producers got extra duty from the series by pairing two television episodes to be released to theaters as a western feature presentation. A total of 16 feature films were released by Monogram (and then Allied Artists) from 1952–55. Wild Bill and Jingles would be seen in *Cowboy Western Comics* beginning with issue number 67. With issue 68 (August 1958), the title was changed to "Wild Bill Hickok and Jingles" which lasted for seven issues (December 1959).

Later Wild Bill Hickok interpretations include Robert Culp in *The Raiders* (Universal, 1963), Don Murray in *The Plainsman* (Universal, 1966), Jeff Bridges in *Wild Bill* (United Artists, 1995) and Keith Carradine in the television series, *Deadwood* (HBO, 2004).

PRAIRIE SCHOONERS

Columbia (September 1940)

Hot Lead Flies ... on the Bullet-Ridden Plains!

Cast: Wild Bill Hickok, Bill Elliott; Virginia Benton, Evelyn Young; Cannonball, Dub Taylor; Dalton Stull, Kenneth Harlan; Wolf Tanner, Ray Teal; Jim Gibbs, Bob Burns; Cora Gibbs, Neta Parker; Adams, Richard Fiske; Rusty, Edmund Cobb; Chief Sanche, Jim Thorpe// "Sonny"; Farmer, Jim Corey; Dude Geeter, Sammy Stein; Skinny Hutch, Ned Glass; Mack, Merrill McCormick; Pawnee boy, Lucien Maxell

Credits: Director, Sam Nelson; Story, George Cory Franklin: Screenwriters, Robert Lee Johnson and Fred Myton; Editor, Al Clark; Cinematography, George Meehan
LOCATION FILMING: Iverson and Lone Pine, California
Production Dates: July 26, 1940–August 2, 1940
Running Time: 56 min.

Story: The Kansas farmers have their backs to the wall, given a severe drought and their debt to Kenneth Harlan. Harlan wants the land, knowing it will be valuable in the future. Bill Elliott, spokesman for the farmers, is unable to work out a settlement with him. Elliott persuades the farmers to pull up stakes and relocate to Colorado. Rancher Evelyn Young gives the farmers money to pay their debts on all supplies. Harlan is happy to see the farmers leave — until he learns they're heading for Colorado. Harlan's partner, Ray Teal, has been supplying guns to the Sioux, enemy of the Pawnees, and buying valuable furs from them for less than their true value. Settlers in Colorado will ruin this lucrative business. Elliott leads farmers through various perils until they arrive in Pawnee country. Harlan entices Pawnee Chief Jim Thorpe to attack the settlers. The attack is called off when Young is kidnapped. Elliott follows and is captured also. Harlan tells Elliott that Young will be released only if the farmers return to Kansas. Elliott agrees but changes his mind when he learns Teal is a blood brother of the Sioux. Harlan and Teal try to escape but are stopped by the Pawnees. The settlers continue on their trek. Elliott decides to settle down, but Young tells him he never will, not as long as he can throw a leg over a saddle.

Notes and Commentary: The working title was "Into the Crimson West."

Stock footage from *End of the Trail* (Columbia, 1933) is used when the Indians leave their village.

Jim Thorpe, a Native-American who played the part of Chief Sanche, was a 1912 Olympic Champion. He was also a major league outfielder for seven years, playing for the New York Giants, Cincinnati Reds and the Boston Braves. He also played half back for 14 years with the Canton Bulldogs, Cleveland Indians, Oorang Indians, Rock Island Independents, New York Giants and Chicago Cardinals. In 1963, Thorpe became a charter member of the Pro Football Hall of Fame. In 1931, he began a 20-year career in films, usually playing an Indian in "B" westerns. Because Thorpe played in a professional sport prior to his appearance in the Olympics, he was stripped of his medals, which were later returned to his family in the early 1990s. Thorpe was named America's greatest athlete of the first half of the 20th Century.

Reviews: "Latest Wild Bill Hickok thriller gives Bill Elliott a break showing him a comer in the horse opera rank. As much can't be said for the rambling, implausible yarn. Bill Elliott again as Wild Bill Hickok besides looking like a cowboy, he is a first-rate thespian." *Variety*, 11/13/40

"Actionful Bill Elliott vehicle." *Western Movies*, Pitts

Summation: This is a better-than-average western, but with a weak ending. Bill Elliott is perfect as the hero in his first Wild Bill Hickok adventure. The chemistry between Elliott and leading lady Evelyn Young is right on target. (Just look at the way Young touches Elliott's arm as he rides to talk with Kenneth Harlan, and the way she looks at him when the wagon train rolls through Lone Pine.) Stock footage makes the film more impressive, even though at times it doesn't match well. Dub Taylor does well after some unfunny slapstick in his first few scenes. The film would have received a higher rating if there had been a final confrontation between Elliott and villains Harlan and Ray Teal.

BEYOND THE SACRAMENTO

Columbia (November 1940)

A Frontier Threatened by Trigger Treachery!

Cast: Wild Bill Hickok, Bill Elliott; Lynn Perry, Evelyn Keyes; Cannonball, Dub Taylor; Jason Perry, John Dilson; Cord Crowley, Bradley Page; Jeff Adams, Frank LaRue; Nelson, Norman Willis; Curly, Steve Clark; Sheriff, Jack Clifford; Warden McKay, Don Beddoe; Storekeeper, Harry Bailey// "Sonny"; "Lightning"; Joe, Bud Osborne; Henchman, Art Mix; Tom Jimson, Olin Francis; George (Bartender), George McKay; Tex/Townsman, Tex Cooper; George (Bank Teller), Ned Glass

Credits: Director, Lambert Hillyer; Screenwriter, Luci Ward; Editor, James Sweeney; Cinematographer, George Meehan

Songs: "Riding for the Law" sung by Dub Taylor; "The West Gets Under My Skin" sung by Dub Taylor

Location Filming: Iverson and Corriganville, California

Production Dates: August 15, 1940–August 28, 1940

Running Time: 58 min.

Story: In Lodestone, Dub Taylor learns that two confidence man, saloon owner Bradley Page and newspaper editor Frank LaRue, are masquerading as leading citizens, and sends for Bill Elliott. Page, LaRue and banker John Dilson are promoting a phony bond issue. Elliott has been looking for Page and LaRue since he spoiled their scheme to defraud citizens of Albuquerque. Unaware of Dilson's involvement with Page, Elliott tries to convince Dilson that Page and LaRue are crooks. Dilson's daughter, Evelyn Keyes, thinks Elliott may be right. Elliott and Taylor break into LaRue's newspaper office and reprint the front page, indicting LaRue as a crook. With the townspeople wanting an explanation from LaRue, Elliott offers him a way out by turning state's evidence. LaRue refuses and Elliott leaves him locked in his office. Not seeing any other way out, LaRue commits suicide. Dilson goes to Page, and Page gets Dilson to stall Elliott. Page has his men hold up Dilson's bank. Thanks to Keyes' quick action, the holdup is thwarted, but she is shot. Dilson goes to the saloon for vengeance, and is promptly shot down by Page. In a blazing gunfight, Elliott dispatches Page and two henchmen. Keyes recovers from her wound and wants Elliott to work in the bank with her. Although tempted, Elliott has to leave when he learns that his brother needs his help.

Notes and Commentary: The working title was "Ghost Guns."

The post card Bill Elliott receives at the story's end is the outline of the plot for *The Wildcat of Tucson* (Columbia, 1940). This would be the next Wild Bill Hickok adventure to be released.

Evelyn Keyes, known for role as Scarlett O'Hara's sister, Suellen, in *Gone With the Wind* (Selznick/Metro-Goldwyn-Mayer, 1939) is Bill Elliott's leading lady in this episode. It has been reported that the kiss Keyes gives Elliott at the end of the film was not in the script. Look at Elliott's stunned reaction. This would be Keyes's only appearance in a "B" western, but she would be in two big-budget color westerns, *The Desperadoes* (Columbia, 1943), with Randolph Scott and Glenn Ford, and *Renegades* (Columbia, 1946) with Willard Parker and Larry Parks.

Stage driver Tex Cooper is handed a bundle of newspapers to deliver as he drives out of town. A few scenes later, Cooper is seen as one of the townsmen.

Reviews: "A standard giddyapper boasting one unique twist. This will get by for satisfactory results with cowhand and junior trade. Elliott makes the proper and omniscient and omnipotent hero." *Variety,* 5/7/41

"Fast paced Bill Elliott vehicle." *Western Movies,* Pitts

Summation: Bill Elliott is handed a basically town-bound western, and his forceful personality makes this picture work. Elliott is given only three action sequences, and he carries them off in fine style. The rest of the time, Elliott's acting and personality keeps the audience interested. Sidekick Dub Taylor is given a neat running gag with a flea-infested cowhide vest. Evelyn Keyes does a nice job as Elliott's leading lady.

The Wildcat of Tucson
Columbia (December 1940)

It's Show-Down Time ... Out Where the West Begins!

Alternate Title: Promise Fulfilled

Cast: Wild Bill Hickok, Bill Elliott; Vivian Barlow, Evelyn Young; Dave Hickok, Stanley Brown; Cannonball, Dub Taylor; Rance McKee, Kenneth MacDonald; Judge Barlow, Ben Taggart; Seth Harper, Edmund Cobb; U.S. Marshal, George Lloyd; Gus Logan, Sammy Stein// "Sonny"; Bobby, Robert Winkler; Tough in newspaper office, Francis Walker; Charlie (Newspaper Editor), Forrest Taylor; Henchman, George Chesebro; Doctor, Murdock MacQuarrie; Vigilantes, Steve Clark and Jim Corey

Credits: Director, Lambert Hillyer; Screenwriter, Fred Myton; Editor, Charles Nelson; Cinematography, George Meehan

Songs: "Wild Bill and Me" sung by Dub Taylor; "Looking Out and Looking In" sung by Dub Taylor

Location Filming: Iverson, California

Production Dates: September 11, 1940–September 19, 1940

Running Time: 59 min.

Story: Kenneth MacDonald is systematically taking ranches from their lawful owners, with help from Judge Ben Taggart and U.S. Marshal George Lloyd. In preventing Lloyd and MacDonald's henchman, Sammy Stein, from taking possession of Edmund Cobb's ranch, Stanley Brown is arrested and convicted of attempted murder. Dub Taylor gets Brown's brother, Bill Elliott, to lend a hand. Elliott surmises that MacDonald is behind Brown's problems. Brown escapes from jail, making him an outlaw. Finding where Brown is hiding, Elliott and Brown's sweetheart, Evelyn Young, ride to convince him to turn himself in. Brown refuses, accusing Elliott of wanting him in jail so Elliott can romance Young. In truth, Young has romantic designs on Elliott, but he isn't interested. Elliott discovers Taggert is in league with MacDonald and makes him sign a document to that effect. MacDonald decides to have Taggart killed by Stein. Brown comes to town and Stein shoots Brown, only wounding him. Taylor returns fire, killing Stein. Taggart tells Elliott that all charges will be dropped against Brown. Elliott meets MacDonald in his office. In a gun duel, Elliott is the victor. Brown recovers, soon to be married to Young. Elliott rides off to new adventures.

Notes and Commentary: Newt Kirby doubled Bill Elliott; Dorothy Andre doubled Evelyn Young; John Daheim doubled Stanley Brown; and Bert Young doubled Dub Taylor.

Reviews: "Fairly actionful Bill Elliott vehicle." *Western Movies*, Pitts

"An indifferent series entry for Elliott, distinguished only by his final exciting showdown with MacDonald." *The Western*, Hardy

Summation: Bill Elliott's presence, with a matching performance by Kenneth Mac-Donald, brings this western saga satisfactorily to the screen. Elliott, tight-lipped and grim, but with a touch of humor towards youngsters and friends, is in fine form as Wild Bill Hickok. MacDonald, almost as equally tight-lipped, makes a worthy villain. The final confrontation between the two adversaries is beautifully constructed. An interesting subplot has heroine Evelyn Young momentarily switching her affection from Stanley Brown to his brother, Elliott. Lambert Hillyer's direction is first-rate.

ACROSS THE SIERRAS

Columbia (February 1941)

"Outlaws, My Six-Guns Are Beggin' for a red Hot Chat with You ... !"
The Hardest Ridin', Toughest Fightin' Hombre in the West Hits the Thrill Trail!

Alternate Title: Welcome Stranger

Cast: Wild Bill Hickok, Bill Elliott; Larry Armstrong, Richard Fiske; Anne, Luana Walters; Cannonball, Dub Taylor; Mitch Carew, Dick Curtis; Stringer, LeRoy Mason; Lu Woodworth, Ruth Robinson; Dan Woodworth, John Dilson; Sheriff, Milton Kibbee; Hobie, Ralph Peters// "Sonny"; Townsman with baton, Tex Cooper; Man on wagon, James Pierce;

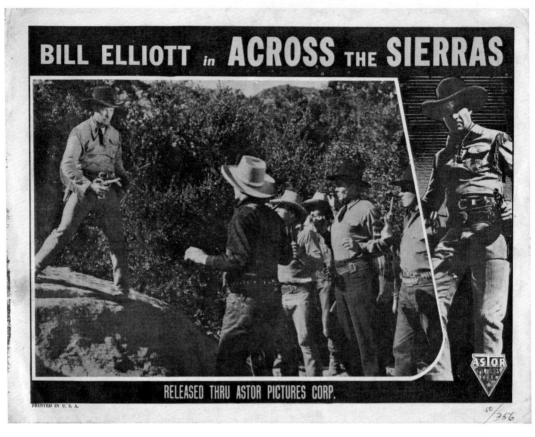

Across the Sierras (1941) scene card — (left) Bill Elliott, (second right) Dick Curtis, (right) Bill Elliott.

Fawcett, Edmund Cobb; Ed, Cobb's cowhand, Eddie Laughton; Bartender, Lew Meehan; Ed, the stage driver, Art Mix; Doctor, Edward Coxen; Blackjack, Blackjack Ward

    Credits: Director, D. Ross Lederman; Screenwriter, Paul Franklin; Editor, James Sweeney; Cinematographer, George Meehan

    Songs: "Star-Spangled Prairie" (Drake) sung by Dub Taylor; "I Gotta Make Music" (Drake) sung by Dub Taylor; "Honeymoon Ranch" (Drake) sung by Dub Taylor

    Location Filming: Iverson, California

    Production Dates: October 10, 1940–October 19, 1940

    Running Time: 59 min.

    Story: After saving Richard Fiske from being lynched, Bill Elliott brings him to Arroyo, where Elliott plans to settle down and begin life as a rancher. Waiting in Arroyo is an old enemy of Elliott's, Dick Curtis, who plans to kill him. (Elliott had arrested Curtis on a robbery charge six years earlier.) Curtis's terrifying presence forced John Dilson (whose testimony convicted Curtis) to draw first, only to be shot down in self-defense. In Arroyo, Elliott meets Dilson's niece, Luana Walters, from Boston, and the two quickly fall in love. Fiske, looking to get rich quick, joins up with Curtis and participates in a stage holdup. During the robbery, Fiske is called by his first name, and Elliott seeks to persuade him to leave the country. Elliott finds Fiske, and the two men talk, with Elliott unaware that Curtis and henchman LeRoy Mason are hiding behind some nearby rocks. Fiske refuses Elliott's advice and Elliott turns his back to leave. Mason, seizing the opportunity, takes a shot at Elliott, which misses. Elliott turns and, thinking his friend had turned on him, fires a shot that mortally wounds Fiske. Fiske's death shakes Elliott, and he decides to give up his guns, buy a ranch and marry Walters. Curtis sends word by Elliott's pal, Dub Taylor, that he's waiting to shoot it out. Elliott refuses to leave town in disgrace and be thought of as a coward. He straps on his guns for what he hopes will be the last time. Elliott and Curtis meet, with Elliott ending Curtis's criminal career with a well-placed bullet. Because of their different attitudes towards violence, Elliott knows he can never make Walters happy, and he rides away.

Notes and Commentary: Stage driver Art Mix is called "Obie" by Dub Taylor, but a few scenes later he is called "Ed" by Milton Kibbee and Bill Elliott.

Reviews: "A concoction with average chances in the action bracket." *Variety*, 4/16/41

"Surprisingly austere 'Wild Bill Hickok' entry, a very good programmer." *Western Movies*, Pitts

Summation: *Across the Sierras* is an adult "B" western in the William S. Hart or Buck Jones tradition. Bill Elliott and Dick Curtis make worthy adversaries, and both acquit themselves well. The film is well directed by D. Ross Lederman, who uses George Meehan's excellent cinematography to fine advantage. Note the unusual but effective camera angles when Elliott and Curtis exchange words in the saloon. Elliott's performance is one of his best, as he portrays a man who wants to give up his guns for the woman he loves, with circumstances not permitting him to fully renounce his old life. A must-see picture. With the adult slant, it makes one wonder if the juvenile trade bought into this one.

NORTH FROM THE LONE STAR
Columbia (March 1941)

Watch Bandits Run to Cover ... When "Wild Bill" Starts Taking Over!

Cast: Wild Bill Hickok, Bill Elliott; Clint Wilson, Richard Fiske; Madge Wilson, Dorothy Fay; Cannonball, Dub Taylor; "Flash" Kirby, Arthur Loft; "Rawhide" Fenton, Jack Roper; Spike, Chuck Morrison; Lucy Belle, Claire Rochelle; Slats, Al Rhein; Dusty Daggett, Edmund Cobb// "Sonny"; Saloon patron, Lane Bradford; Bartender, Hank Bell; Henchmen, Steve Clark and Art Mix; Saloon brawler, Francis Walker

Credits: Director, Lambert Hillyer; Producer, Leon Barsha; Screenwriter, Charles Francis Royal; Editor, Mel Thorsen; Cinematographer, Benjamin Kline

Songs: "Home on the Range" (Traditional) played by Dub Taylor; "Of Course, It's Your Horse" (Drake) sung and played by Dub Taylor; "Saturday Night in San Antone" (Drake) sung and played by Dub Taylor

Location Filming: Iverson, California

Production Dates: February 6, 1941–February 15, 1941

Running Time: 58 min.

Story: Bill Elliott arrives in Deadwood to settle down. He finds an old nemesis, Arthur Loft, taking over all the businesses. When Loft tries to gain control of Richard Fiske's livery stable, Elliott steps in and stops Loft's henchmen. Loft offers Elliott the marshal's job and Elliott finally accepts. When Elliott arrests Fiske for shooting one of Loft's henchmen, Loft believes Elliott is working with him. Actually, Elliott jailed Fiske to prevent him from being lynched. Fiske's sister, Dorothy Fay, tries to break him out of jail, but Elliott had him removed to a neighboring county. With Loft out of town, Elliott finds the gambling in Loft's saloon is crooked and closes down the establishment. Elliott and Loft give each other 30 minutes to leave town. Elliott and his deputy, Dub Taylor, go to Fiske's livery stable, where Fay is being held prisoner. A gunfight ensues and Loft is about to get Elliott under his gunsight. Fiske, who has escaped from the neighboring county's jail, returns in time to help Elliott. Loft and Fiske exchange shots, killing each other. Realizing he cannot settle down in Deadwood, Elliott rides off to new adventures.

Notes and Commentary: Dorothy Fay would become the wife of the western star great Tex Ritter.

Reviews: "Nicely made western, chock-full of swift action, nicely compact script job. Besides Bill Elliott's neat portrayal of the Wild Bill Hickok role, Dub Taylor provides essential comic relief as Cannonball, his sidekick." *Variety*, 6/25/41

"Actionful Bill Elliott vehicle with a well staged saloon fight sequence." *Western Movies*, Pitts

Summation: This is another good Wild Bill Hickok adventure. Bill Elliott carries off the action and acting capably, having to fend off two lovely ladies, Dorothy Fay and Claire Rochelle, in this one. A nicely crafted gunfight in the final reel greatly enhances this western. *North from the Lone Star* is a town-bound western, one which Lambert Hillyer paces adroitly.

HANDS ACROSS THE ROCKIES
Columbia (June 1941)

See Him Out-Shoot an Outlaw Band ... to Outdo All His Past Hits for Thrills!

Cast: Wild Bill Hickok, Bill Elliott; Marsha, Mary Daily; Cannonball, Dub Taylor; "Juneau" Jessup, Kenneth MacDonald; Rufe Crawley, Frank LaRue; Dade Crawley, Donald Curtis; Hi Crawley, Tom Moray; Johnny Peale, Stanley Brown; Marshal Bemis, Slim Whitaker; Abel Finney, Harrison Greene; Red, Art Mix; Judge Plunkett, Eddy Waller; Cash Jennings, Hugh Prosser// Stage passenger, John Tyrell; Ranger, Edmund Cobb; Bartender, Ethan Laidlaw; Court clerk, Eddie Laughton; Jury foreman, George Morrell; Jurors, Buck Moulton, George Chesebro and Tex Cooper; Callie, Kathryn Bates

Credits: Director, Lambert Hillyer; Producer, Leon Barsha; Screenwriter, Paul Franklin; Editor, Mel Thorsen; Cinematographer, Benjamin Kline

Songs: "While the Stage Went Bumping Along" sung by Dub Taylor; "Ro-Ro-Rollin'" sung by Dub Taylor

Location Filming: Iverson, California

Production Dates: March 26, 1941–April 3, 1941

Running Time: 56 min.

Source: story by Norbert Davis

Story: Frank LaRue warns Stanley Brown to stay away from his niece, Mary Daily. Brown and Daily are in love and want to get married. Town boss Kenneth MacDonald wants to marry Daily so she can't be forced to testify that she saw him murder Dub Taylor's father. Taylor arrives in Independence with his pal, Bill Elliott, to find his father's killer. Brown tries to run away with Daily but is stopped by LaRue and arrested for kidnapping. Elliott believes that Daily holds the key to uncovering the murderer and appoints himself

Brown's lawyer. Elliott uncovers evidence to prove Brown innocent and announces that Daily can prove MacDonald murdered Taylor's father. MacDonald attempts to escape but falls before Elliott's gunfire. As Brown and Daily plan to marry, Elliott receives word that his services are needed elsewhere, and he and Taylor ride off to new adventures.

Notes and Commentary: *Hands Across the Rockies* was based on a short story from the October 1940 issue of *Dime Western Magazine*, "A Gunsmoke Case for Major Cain" by Norbert Davis. The basic premise of Davis's story is followed. There are some major differences. In the story, the protagonists are Cain and Stringer, who just happen to come to town. Screenwriters had to change the tie of the niece to Jessup. She was to be sold to Jessup to work in his saloon. This was a plot element not suitable for the younger moviegoers. Screenwriters *did* incorporate some of Davis's dialogue, especially having Elliott declare himself a counselor of gun-law.

Eddy Waller is best known to western fans as Nugget Clark, sidekick to Allan "Rocky" Lane in 32 western features for Republic (1947–50, 1952–53).

Review: "Pretty actionful Bill Elliott film." *Western Movies*, Pitts

Summation: This is one of the best and most enjoyable entries in Bill Elliott's Wild Bill Hickok series. Elliott's and Eddy Waller's performances, with able assistance from Dub Taylor and Kenneth MacDonald, bring first-rate entertainment to the screen. Elliott gives a fine performance as the tight-lipped agent of justice, delivering his lines forcefully or with compassion to meet the demands of the script. Waller matches Elliott as a cantankerous judge who will not stand for any nonsense in his courtroom. Taylor adds some nice comedic touches while being quite efficient as Elliott's sidekick. Don't miss this one.

KING OF DODGE CITY
Columbia (August 1941)

Your Two Favorite Western Stars in One Terrific Blast of Thrills and Range Melodies!

Cast: Wild Bill Hickok, Bill Elliott; Tex Rawlings, Tex Ritter; Janice Blair, Judith Linden; Cannonball, Dub Taylor; Morgan King, Guy Usher; Judge Lynch, Rick Anderson; Jeff Carruthers, Kenneth Harlan; Reynolds, Pierce Lyden; Carney, Francis Walker; Stephen Kimball, Harrison Greene; Martin, Jack Rockwell// "Sonny"; "White Flash"; Sheriff Daniels, Edward Coxen; Crooked gambler, Tristram Coffin; Gamblers, Edmund Cobb and George Chesebro; Bill Lang, Jack Ingram; Samuels, Steve Clark

Credits: Director, Lambert Hillyer; Producer, Leon Barsha; Screenwriter, Gerald Geraghty; Editor, Jerome Thomas; Cinematographer, Benjamin Kline

Songs: "There's an Empty Cot in the Bunkhouse Tonight" sung by Tex Ritter; "To Shoot a Low Down Skunk" sung by Tex Ritter; "Riding the Trail to Home" sung by Tex Ritter; "Riding the Trail to Home" (reprise) sung by Tex Ritter

Location Filming: Iverson and Monogram Ranch, California

Production Dates: May 20, 1941–May 29, 1941

Running Time: 63 min.

Story: Wanted for the murder of a crooked gambler in a lawless community, Bill Elliott is asked by government official Harrison Greene to break up the lawlessness in Kansas and bring Guy Usher to justice. In Abilene, Tex Ritter is the sheriff, and his actions lead Elliott to suspect he is in league with Usher. Elliott suspects Usher is misappropriating bank funds

King of Dodge City (1941) scene card — Tex Ritter (left), Bill Elliott (center), and an unidentified actor, discuss the murder of Steve Clark (on ground).

for his own purposes. Elliott is framed for murder. Ritter finds proof that Elliott is working for the state government. The two men join forces to bring Usher to justice. When Elliott and Ritter return to Abilene, they are met by a hail of bullets from Usher and his henchmen. Joined by the honest citizens, Elliott and Ritter begin to get the upper hand. Usher tries to escape but is shot down in a gunfight with Elliott. With Usher's reign of terror ended, Elliott and Ritter ride off to new adventures.

Notes and Commentary: Bill Elliott utters an interesting bit of dialogue when, as henchmen Francis Walker and Pierce Lyden level their guns at Tex Ritter, Elliott steps into the picture and says, "I'm superstitious. I hate to see anyone shot in the back."

Tex Ritter sports a bruise on his cheek after being hit by Bill Elliott.

Reviews: "Picture is an average shoots-and-saddles actioner. Lambert Hillyer's direction maintains a good tempo for an action western. Ritter suffers by comparison in the acting against the better performance by Elliott." *Variety*, 8/13/41

"Steady Bill Elliott-Tex Ritter outing but not one of their best vehicles." *Western Movies*, Pitts

Summation: This initial teaming of Bill Elliott and Tex Ritter makes for a sturdy western. Elliott is convincing as a man willing to take the law into his own hands, even if it means being branded as an outlaw. Ritter capably handles the action sequences. The movie moves well, but, like most in this series, has the two leads at odds until the final wrap-up, which, in this case, is too quickly accomplished.

ROARING FRONTIERS
Columbia (October 1941)

Bad News for Bandits ... but Good News for All Lovers of Rhythm and Thrills!

Alternate Title: Frontier

Cast: Wild Bill Hickok, Bill Elliott; Tex Martin, Tex Ritter; Reba Bailey, Ruth Ford; Cannonball, Frank Mitchell; Hawk Hammond, Bradley Page; Flint Adams, Tristram Coffin; Link Twaddle, Hal Taliaferro; Boot Hill, Francis Walker; Knuckles, Joe McGuinn; Red Thompson, George Chesebro; Moccasin, Charles Stevens// "Sonny"; "White Flash"; Sheriff, George Eldredge; Henchman, Jim Corey; Old Timer, Rick Anderson; Jailer, Ernie Adams; Hank, the stage driver, Hank Bell; Stage guard, Steve Clark

Credits: Director, Lambert Hillyer; Producer, Leon Barsha; Screenwriter, Robert Lee Johnson; Editor, Mel Thorsen; Cinematographer, Benjamin Kline

Songs: "You've Got to Come and Get Me, Boys" sung by Tex Ritter; "Judge Morrow Will Find the Truth and Set Me Free" sung by Tex Ritter; "Then You're a Part of the West" sung by Tex Ritter

Location Filming: Iverson, California

Production Dates: June 23, 1941–July 2, 1941

Running Time: 60 min.

Story: Trying to find his father's killer, Tex Ritter goes to see saloon owner Bradley Page. Page is talking with a stranger when Ritter enters his office. Sheriff George Eldredge, fearing trouble, comes into the room. The stranger breaks the solitary lamp, plunging the room into darkness, and fires a shot meant for Ritter; it kills Eldredge instead. Page then blames Ritter for the crime, forcing him to flee. Ritter's horse goes lame and he has to hole up in a blind canyon. Page's men bottle up Ritter. Marshal Bill Elliott arrives in Goldfield, and Page asks him to bring in Ritter. Through a ruse, Elliott is successful in arresting Ritter. In Goldfield, Elliott realizes Ritter will not receive a fair trial and grants Ritter's request to have his case heard at the county seat. Page sends a posse to kill Ritter, but Elliott intervenes. In the struggle, Ritter is shot in the leg, but Elliott and Ritter are able to get to the stagecoach traveling to the county seat. On the stage are three men and a woman. The woman, Ruth Ford, is a transplanted Easterner who can't understand the violence of the West. The other passengers are prospector Frank Mitchell, barber Hal Taliaferro and gambler Tristram Coffin. Forced to stop at a way station to rest the horses, Ritter's wound is attended to by Ford. Elliott learns there was another man in the room besides Page when Eldredge was killed and surmises that Coffin was that man. Knowing he's suspected by Elliott, Coffin steals a horse and rides to warn Page. Elliott and Ritter return to Goldfield and shoot it out with Page and his men. Ritter corners Page and Coffin in Page's office. The two men try to outgun Ritter, but are unsuccessful. Ritter becomes mayor of Goldfield, and Elliott rides off to new adventures.

Notes and Commentary: The working title was "A Star on Its Saddle."

In the cast listing, Tex Ritter's character name is given as Tex Rawlings, but in the film he plays Tex Martin.

Frank Mitchell replaced Dub Taylor in this film. Mitchell played his character straight until the final scene in which he and Tex Ritter staged a fake fight in an attempt to convince Bill Elliott to settle down. In the next six entries, Mitchell would demonstrate his acrobatic talents via many pratfalls.

Ritter's song, "Judge Morrow Will Fine the Truth and Set Me Free," was deleted from many TV prints.

Review: "Solid entertainment in the Bill Elliott – Tex Ritter Columbia series." *Western Movies*, Pitts.

Summation: This is a superior "B" western. Bill Elliott and Tex Ritter are handed a good script and make the most of it, both in the acting and action departments. Of particular note, the songs sung by Ritter reflect his thoughts at the time, and the dialogue is superior to that found in most "B" westerns. *Roaring Frontiers* is well directed by veteran director Lambert Hillyer.

THE LONE STAR VIGILANTES
Columbia (January 1942)

A Roaring Blast of Blazing Action!

Alternate Title: The Devil's Price

Cast: Wild Bill Hickok, Bill Elliott; Tex Martin, Tex Ritter; Cannonball, Frank Mitchell; Shary Monroe, Virginia Carpenter; Marcia Banning, Luana Walters; Colonel Monroe, Budd Buster; Dr. Banning, Forrest Taylor; Major Clark, Gavin Gordon; Peabody, Lowell Drew; Charlie Cobb, Edmund Cobb; Benson, Ethan Laidlaw; Lige Miller, Rick Anderson// "Sonny"; "White Flash"; Kellogg, Francis Walker; Pedro, Dick Botiller; Manton, Eddie Laughton; Jones, Steve Clark; Soldier, John Cason

Credits: Director, Wallace W. Fox; Producer, Leon Barsha; Screenwriter, Luci Ward; Editor, Mel Thorsen; Cinematography, Benjamin Kline

Songs: "Headin' Home to Texas" sung by Tex Ritter and Frank Mitchell; "When the Moon is Shining on the Old Corral" sung by Tex Ritter; "Going to Join the Rangers" sung by Tex Ritter

Location Filming: Corriganville, Burro Flats, Agoura and Iverson, California

Production Dates: July 21, 1941–July 30, 1941

Running Time: 58 min.

Story: Civil War veterans Bill Elliott, Tex Ritter and Frank Mitchell return to Texas. Even though they fought on the side of the Confederacy, the men realize it's now important to have but one nation. As wounds between neighbors are beginning to heal, Union Major Gavin Gordon announces that Winchester County is under martial law, and confiscates all weapons. Gordon plans to loot and gain control of all properties. Elliott and Ritter recognize one of Gordon's soldiers as a horse thief, and they have doubts about his intentions. Luana Walters, who was treated badly by Confederate sympathizers prior to the war, wants revenge and decides to work with Gordon. Elliott plans to expose Gordon as an impostor. Ritter decides to join vigilantes to fight Gordon with guns stolen from the Army. Walters informs Gordon about the vigilantes, and Ritter is arrested and sentenced to hang. Figuring Walters is an informant, Elliott gives her false information to draw Gordon and his men out of town. Elliott breaks Ritter out of jail and obtains proof that Gordon is an impostor and not an Army officer. Walters brings Gordon back in time to begin a gunfight with Ritter, Elliott, Mitchell and the Texans. A bullet takes Walters's life, and Ritter captures Gordon. With peace restored, Elliott, Ritter and Mitchell ride to join the Texas Rangers.

Notes and Commentary: The working title was "Law of the Winchester."

Even though Frank Mitchell was listed as playing "Cannonball" in the credits of the previous film, *Roaring Frontiers* (Columbia, 1941), he was never called by name in the film. In *The Lone Star Vigilantes*, Mitchell was introduced as Cannonball Q. Boggs.

Reviews: "*Lone Star Vigilantes* is the best of the first three Bill Elliott-Tex Ritter western series. Full of action, with plenty of gun pumping and heroics, picture is a good entry in the western field. Good western-type script accentuating action and excitement combined with fast-paced direction. Elliott is most prominent for heroics." *Variety*, 9/24/41

"Plenty of gun-fighting action." *Motion Picture Guide*, Nash and Ross

Summation: A strong story highlights this superior entry in the Bill Elliott-Tex Ritter series. The story spends little time with Elliott and Ritter on opposite sides of the fence. The stars complement each other well and the story benefits greatly. Elliott, again, is the stronger of the two in the acting category, but both overshadow a more than adequate supporting cast. Luana Walters gives a nifty performance as a Northern sympathizer who can't let old hurts heal. Wallace W. Fox's direction is up to the story's demands.

BULLETS FOR BANDITS

Columbia (February 1942)

Thrill as These Two Top Western Stars Rock the Screen
with Stirring Adventure and Song!

Cast: Wild Bill Hickok/Prince Katey, Bill Elliott; Tex Martin, Tex Ritter; Cannonball, Frank Mitchell; Dakota Brown, Dorothy Short; Clem Jeeter, Ralph Theodore; Queen Katey, Edythe Elliott; Bert Brown, Forrest Taylor// "Sonny"; "White Flash"; Cowhand who manhandles Cannonball, Bud Osborne; Croupier, Hal Taliaferro; Cheated gambler, Harry Harvey; Beetle, Joe McGuinn; Whit, Art Mix

Credits: Director, Wallace W. Fox; Producer, Leon Barsha; Screenwriter, Robert Lee Johnson; Editor, Mel Thorsen; Cinematographer, George Meehan

Songs: "Want My Boots on When I Die" sung by Tex Ritter; "Reelin' Rockin' Rollin' Down the Trail" sung by Tex Ritter; "Somewhere on the Lone Prairie" sung by Tex Ritter

Location Filming: Agoura, Corriganville and Iverson, California

Production Dates: August 11, 1941–August 21, 1941

Running Time: 55 min.

Story: Stopping off in a town in the Badlands, Bill Elliott sees a gunman who is his exact double. When gunman Elliott attempts to cheat another player at roulette, Elliott steps in and the two exchange shots. Gunman Elliott falls dead, but from a shot in the back from Joe McGuinn. McGuinn murdered gunman Elliott, at Ralph Theodore's direction, to prevent Edythe Elliott's foreman, Frank Mitchell, from bringing him back to stop Theodore from taking over E. Elliott's ranch. Mitchell mistakes Elliott for the man he was sent to get and persuades Elliott to come to E. Elliott's aid. Sheriff Tex Ritter goes after Elliott, as he suspects him in being involved in the killing. Elliott arrives in time to prevent Theodore's first attempt to grab E. Elliott's ranch. Theodore is also stirring up trouble between the homesteaders and E. Elliott. Ritter arrives and determines that Elliott is *not* the guilty party. The two men decide to work together. Theodore decides to lynch Elliott and brand him the guilty party. Theodore and his men lay siege to E. Elliott's ranch, with Elliott holding them at bay. Mitchell rides for Ritter's help. Ritter arrives and, with Elliott's help, arrests

Theodore and McGuinn. E. Elliott and the homesteaders can now live as peaceful neighbors.

Notes and Commentary: The working title was "Honor of the West."

Bill Elliott has his one and only turn at a double role, playing hero Wild Bill Hickok and notorious gunman Prince Katey. The shared screen time is brief, as they have an early shootout, with Katey being shot in the back by Joe McGuinn and Elliott thinking it was *his* bullet that ended Katey's life.

Famed badman of westerns and serials Lane Bradford doubles Bill Elliott in this production.

Review: "Somewhat uneven entry in the Bill Elliott-Tex Ritter starring series." *Western Movies*, Pitts

Summation: Okay entry in the Bill Elliott-Tex Ritter series due to Elliott's presence and some good running inserts. The slight storyline does give Elliott a chance to show his acting prowess, especially in his scenes with Edith Elliott. Ritter chips in with some good songs, but the script doesn't allow him to participate much in the action department this time out.

THE DEVIL'S TRAIL
Columbia (May 1942)

Hit the High Road to Thrills with Two Top Stars!

Alternate Titles: Rogue's Gallery and Devil's Canyon

Cast: Wild Bill Hickok, Bill Elliott; Tex Martin, Tex Ritter; Myra, Eileen O'Hearn; Cannonball, Frank Mitchell; Bull McQuade, Noah Beery; Ella, Ruth Ford; Dr. Willowby, Joel Friedkin; Jim Randall, Joe McGuinn; Sid Howland, Edmund Cobb; Ed Scott, Tristram Coffin; Blacksmith, Paul Newlan// "Sonny"; "White Flash"; Harris, Bud Osborne; Henchmen, Buck Moulton, Stanley Brown, Steve Clark and Art Mix

Credits: Director, Lambert Hillyer; Producer, Leon Barsha; Screenwriter, Philip Ketchum; Editor, Charles Nelson; Art Directors, Lionel Banks and Perry Smith; Cinematographer, George Meehan

Songs: "When the Sun Goes Down" sung by Tex Ritter; "Hi, Diddle Lum, Diddle Lum" sung by Tex Ritter

Location Filming: Iverson, California

Production Dates: October 27, 1941–November 5, 1941

Running Time: 61 min.

Source: Based on Philip Ketchum's story, "The Town in Hell's Backyard," as published in *Ten Story Western Magazine* by Popular Publications, Inc.

Story: Bill Elliott is hiding out in Tiburon until he can clear himself of a murder charge. Tiburon is under control of Noah Beery, who is plotting to have Kansas secede from the Union. Beery is holding Dr. Joel Friedkin and his daughter, Eileen O'Hearn, hostage. Marshal Tex Ritter arrives in Tiburon to arrest Elliott. Frank Mitchell, who is being held prisoner, helps Elliott escape. When Beery sends his men after Elliott, O'Hearn takes the opportunity to escape on foot. Beery's henchmen attempt to murder Ritter, but O'Hearn's intervention saves his life. O'Hearn convinces Ritter to join forces with Elliott and Mitchell. Elliott proves he's innocent of the murder charge. Elliot and Ritter return to Tiburon to rescue Friedkin and are trapped in the blacksmith shop. After a gunfight, Elliott and Ritter get the drop on Beery and his men.

Notes and Commentary: Here, Bill Elliott and Noah Beery are reunited (as antagonists) after 13 years. Elliott and Beery were rivals in the silent film *The Passion Song* (Excellent Pictures/Interstate Pictures, 1928). They both appeared in *Big Boy* (Warner Bros., 1930) as well, but had no scenes together.

Phillip Ketchum was the author of the short story, "The Town in Hell's Backyard," which appeared in the March 1939 issue of *Ten Story Western Magazine*. In Ketchum's story, Jeff Bannister (changed to Tex Martin in the film) comes to Tiburon, an outlaw stronghold, to tell his good friend Tex Lohman that he's no longer wanted for murder. Lohman is a minor player in the story as the emphasis is on Bannister. Most of the major character names are carried over from the story. The attempted murder of Martin was used, as was the animosity between Martin and Sid Howland, and a wounded Myra warning Ritter of danger. Ketchum rewrote the story to encompass the talents of Elliott and Ritter.

Paul Newlan's blacksmith character was named Ed Dawson.

Reviews: "Top notch effort in the Bill Elliott-Tex Ritter series." *Western Movies*, Pitts

"Even the considerable talents of Elliott and Ritter can't prevent this tepid oater from boring." *Motion Picture Guide*, Nash and Ross

Summation: *The Devil's Trail* is an actionful Bill Elliott-Tex Ritter western, but the story is marred by a mild windup in the capture of Noah Beery and his gang. Elliott and Ritter deliver fine performances in the action and dialogue sequences. Director Lambert Hillyer is able to generate good suspense, especially in the scene in which Edmund Cobb is attempting to force Ritter to fall from a cliff.

PRAIRIE GUNSMOKE
Columbia (July 1942)

Two Famous Stars Keep the Range Hummin' with Bullets and Songs!
Fists Crash ... . Hoofs Thunder ... Guns Blaze ... in a Hair-Raising Saga of the West!

Cast: Wild Bill Hickok, Bill Elliott; Tex Terrell, Tex Ritter; Cannonball, Frank Mitchell; Lucy Wade, Virginia Carroll; Henry Wade, Hal Price; Jim Kelton, Tristram Coffin; Spike Allen, Joe McGuinn; Sam, Frosty Royce; Dan Whipple, Rick Anderson// "Sonny"; "White Flash"; Buck Garrick, Steve Clark; Ranchers, Milburn Morante and Horace B. Carpenter; Henchmen, Art Mix and Francis Walker

Credits: Director, Lambert Hillyer; Producer, Leon Barsha; Story, Jack Ganzhorn; Screenwriter, Fred Myton; Editor, Arthur Seid; Cinematographer, Benjamin Kline

Songs: "Where the Buffalo Roam" sung by Tex Ritter; "Someone" sung by Tex Ritter

Location Filming: Iverson, California

Production Dates: December 12, 1941–December 20, 1941

Running Time: 56 min.

Story: Tristram Coffin wants to control the rangeland because of valuable ore deposits. The only rancher with this knowledge is Rick Anderson, who is murdered by Coffin's henchman Joe McGuinn. Rancher Tex Ritter plans to fight to keep his property. Bill Elliott rides in and is branded as one of Coffin's hired gunmen by Ritter, rancher Hal Price and Virginia Carroll, Price's daughter and Ritter's sweetheart. When he's not given a chance to explain,

Elliott decides to see Coffin. Coffin offers him the job of running Ritter off his ranch, which Elliott says he'll consider. In an abandoned tunnel on Ritter's ranch, Elliott finds some of the valuable ore. Elliott tells Coffin he wants to be a partner in his scheme. Coffin decides to move fast by ordering the destruction of Ritter's cattle and the kidnapping of both Price and Carroll. Elliott finds proof, implicating Coffin in Anderson's murder. Elliott tells Ritter that Anderson was his uncle, and the two men decide to work together. Elliott rescues Price while Ritter goes to Carroll's aid. Ritter and Carroll are pinned down in Anderson's cabin by Coffin and his men. Elliott arrives and the tide is turned. Elliott and Coffin fight. A blow by Elliott knocks Coffin down a mineshaft to his death. Elliott rides on, while Ritter and Carroll now have time for romance.

Notes and Commentary: Hal Price's character name in the cast list, is Bill Wade, but in the film Price is referred to as Henry.

Review: "Pretty good actioner in the Bill Elliott-Tex Ritter series." *Western Movies*, Pitts

Summation: This is an action-packed, fast-paced, superior western that effectively spotlights the talents of its stars, Bill Elliott and Tex Ritter. Elliott has the better of Ritter in the acting department, especially as he has to react to unfounded accusations about the type of person he really is. Branded a gunman by Ritter, Hal Price and Virginia Carroll, Elliott's disappointment in being unable to explain himself properly is evident in his reactions, both verbally and in his facial expressions. If you like fisticuffs, not to mention plenty of gunplay and hard riding, there is an abundance, making the film reminiscent of a Charles Starrett-Russell Hayden saga.

Wild Bill Saunders

After Bill Elliott had made a successful leading man debut in the serial *The Great Adventures of Wild Bill Hickok* (Columbia, 1938), Columbia decided that he was their new cowboy star. Larry Darmour produced four Elliot films that were released by Columbia. Elliott became a popular cowboy star and Columbia decided to make Elliot's vehicles in house, thus, the series, Wild Bill Saunders, was born. Amazingly, Elliot resembled the real Wild Bill Hickok, with guns reversed in his holsters. Screenwriters Charles Francis Royal, Robert Lee Johnson and Fred Myton were responsible for the fine scenarios. The only other series character was Dub Taylor as Cannonball. Taylor and his xylophone had registered well in Frank Capra's *You Can't Take It with You* (Columbia, 1938) which led him to be signed for the role. After the four films, Columbia decided that Elliott should have been Wild Bill Hickok all along. He went on to play Hickok in 14 of his remaining 16 features for the studio.

TAMING OF THE WEST
Columbia (October 1939)

The Law Reached Only as Far as His Guns Could Shoot!

Cast: Wild Bill Saunders, Bill Elliott; Pepper, Iris Meredith; Rawhide, Dick Curtis; Cannonball, Dub Taylor; Handy, James Craig; Slim, Stanley Brown; Judge Bailey, Ethan Allen; Blaisdale, Kenneth MacDonald; Cholly Wong, Victor Wong; Jackson, Charles King// "Sonny"; Blake, Richard Fiske; Blackie Gilbert, Art Mix; Townsman, Horace B. Carpenter; Turkey, Lane Chandler; Marshal, Hank Bell; Cheated gambler, John Tyrell; Mary Jenkins, Irene Herndon; Gun checker, Jack Kirk; Mrs. Gardner, Stella LeSaint; Shifty, Bob Woodward

Credits: Director, Norman Deming; Story, Robert Lee Johnson; Screenwriters, Charles Francis Royal and Robert Lee Johnson; Editor, Otto Meyer; Cinematographer, George Meehan

Location Filming: Iverson and Burro Flats, California

Production Dates: began early August 1939

Running Time: 55 min.

Story: Bill Elliott rides into the town of Prairie Port. When gambler Lane Chandler murders Marshal Hank Bell, Elliott gives chase. The two men fight, and in the struggle Chandler falls to his death. Elliott takes the job of marshal when outlaws Dick Curtis and James Craig kill restaurant owner Iris Meredith's sister, Irene Herndon. Elliott arrests gang members for various crimes. Banker Kenneth MacDonald, the outlaw leader, starts a wave of intimidation that gains freedom for his henchmen. Through a ruse, Elliott determines that MacDonald is the outlaw leader. Elliott quickly brings MacDonald and his men to justice before heading to new adventures.

Notes and Commentary: The working title was "Sundown in Helldorado."

After four features produced by Larry Darmour, Columbia now took over production of Bill Elliott's westerns. *Taming of the West* was the first in the series of four Wild Bill Saunders adventures.

At the picture's end, Bill Elliott receives a letter informing him that he has inherited a ranch, which is now an outlaw's headquarters. This sets the stage for the plot of Elliott's next Wild Bill Saunders adventure, *Pioneers of the Frontier* (Columbia, 1940).

Kenneth MacDonald would provide the villainy in four more Columbia entries, *Wildcat of Tucson* (1941), *Hands Across the Rockies* (1941), *Son of Davy Crockett* (1941) and *The Valley of Vanishing Men* (1942). MacDonald was most impressive in the latter two films. He had already appeared with Elliott in *Overland with Kit Carson* (Columbia, 1939), and would be featured in two Elliott big-budget films at Republic, *The Fabulous Texan* (1947) and *Hellfire* (1949).

Reviews: "'Taming of the West' is an above average horse opera. Bill Elliott, on top, is a type likely to become quite popular. He's more along the lines of William S. Hart and somewhat of a slugger with punches not always pulled." *Variety*, 10/11/39

"Bill Elliott fans will enjoy this actionful outing." *Western Movies*, Pitts

Summation: This was the first of the Columbia-produced Bill Elliott series westerns, and it is a winner. The film starts on a high note, which, unfortunately, is not sustained, with Elliott bringing Lane Chandler to justice. It then reverts to the standard plot of cleaning up the town, but it's put over with style thanks to Elliott's presence and the fine supporting cast, led by Iris Meredith. Elliott gets a chance to show his acting ability most convincingly in the scene in which he learns of the shooting of a courageous rancher. (Just look at how Elliott reveals and then quickly suppresses his anger over the incident.) A tip of the hat goes to George Meehan's cinematography, especially in the chase sequences, and to Norman Deming's efficient directorial effort.

PIONEERS OF THE FRONTIER

Columbia (February 1940)

Defying Death ... to Wipe Out a Swindling Gang of Cut-Throats!

Alternate Title: The Anchor

Cast: Wild Bill Saunders, Bill Elliott; Joan Darcey, Linda Winters; Matt Brawley, Dick Curtis; Cannonball, Dub Taylor; Dave, Stanley Brown; Bart, Richard Fiske; Jim Darcey, Carl Stockdale; Mort Saunders, Lafe McKee; Lem Wilkins, Ralph McCullough; Marshal Larsen, Al Bridge// "Sonny"; Settler, Hank Bell; Appleby, George Chesebro; Ed Carter, Edmund Cobb; Tommy, Buddy Cox; Stagecoach agent, Ralph Peters; Henchmen, Francis Walker and Blackjack Ward; Rancher, Jack Kirk; Townsmen, Jim Corey and Kenne Duncan

Credits: Director, Sam Nelson; Screenwriter, Fred Myton; Editor, James Sweeney; Cinematographer, George Meehan

Pioneers of the Frontier (1940) scene card—(left to right) Bill Elliott, Dick Curtis, Linda Winters.

Location Filming: Iverson, California
Production Dates: October 11, 1939–October 19, 1939
Running Time: 58 min.
Story: Dick Curtis murders Bill Elliott's uncle, Lafe McKee. Curtis then takes over McKee's spread. Linda Winters sends Elliott a letter, asking him to come home at once. Elliott finds that Curtis wants to be king of the vast area. With help from Winters and rancher Dub Taylor, Elliott sets a trap to catch Curtis and his men. Curtis is informed of the trap. He and his men trap Winters and the ranchers. Curtis and a few henchmen go after Elliott. Taylor warns Elliott. Elliott's quick thinking and his ability with his six-guns brings an end to Curtis's dreams of power. Elliott rides off to new adventures.
    Notes and Commentary: The working title was "Gun Lord of the Frontier."
    There is a continuity lapse: Stanley Brown is shown with his arm in a sling *before* Bill Elliott wounds him.
    Linda Winters was billed as Dorothy Comingore in the classic film *Citizen Kane* (RKO, 1941), Winters played Kane's mistress Susan Alexander, an untalented aspiring opera singer.
    Reviews: "Very good Bill Elliott actioner." *Western Movies*, Pitts
    "Action-packed Elliott entry." *The Western*, Hardy
    Summation: This is a good, fast-moving action western, bolstered by solid performances from Bill Elliott, Dick Curtis and Dub Taylor. Elliott is convincing as the stalwart hero, easily handling the action elements while delivering his lines in a convincing manner. Curtis is a strong adversary, and Taylor does a nice turn as Elliott's sidekick.

THE MAN FROM TUMBLEWEEDS
Columbia (May 1940)

He's Satan Himself ... Throwing Crimson Streaks of Death from His Blazing Six-Guns ... Blasting a Bandit's Reign of Terror from the Old West's Wildest Range!

Cast: Wild Bill Saunders, Bill Elliott; "Spunky" Cameron, Iris Meredith; Cannonball, Dub Taylor; Powder Kilgore, Raphael Bennett; Lightning Barloe, Francis Walker; Shifty Sheldon, Ernie Adams; Honest John, Al Hill; Slash, Stanley Brown; Dixon, Richard Fiske; Jeff Cameron, Edward LeSaint; Governor Dawson, Don Beddoe// "Sonny"; Jackson, Eddie Laughton; Bank Robbers, Olin Francis and George Chesebro; Marshal of Tumbleweeds, Steve Clark; Wilson, Edward Cecil; Prison warden, Bruce Bennett; Stage driver, Hank Bell; Henchman, Blackie Whiteford

Credits: Director, Joseph H. Lewis; Screenwriter, Charles Francis Royal; Editor, Charles Nelson; Cinematographer, George Meehan

Location Filming: Iverson, California

Production Dates: March 13, 1940–March 22, 1940

Running Time: 59 min.

Story: Raphael Bennett is behind the lawless activity in Gunsight. Bill Elliott is asked to help, but realizes one man can't stop Bennett and his gang. With backing from Governor Don Beddoe, Elliott is given a group of hardened convicts to become state rangers. One of the convicts, Al Hill, becomes Elliott's chief lieutenant. Elliott asks another convict, Ernie Adams, to infiltrate Bennett's gang, not knowing Adams is in league with Bennett. Bennett and Adams set a trap to murder Elliott. Hill and fellow convict Stanley Brown realize Elliott is riding into a trap, and ride to prevent Elliott from being ambushed. From a note sent to Adams, Elliott knows the location of Bennett's hideout. Elliott and Hill arrive at the hideout and a suspenseful gunfight ensues, resulting in Elliott bringing Bennett and his gang to justice. Elliott turns down the commission of commander-in-chief of the state rangers, and recommends Hill instead. Elliott rides off to new adventures.

Notes and Commentary: Joseph H. Lewis was noted for his edgy direction and unusual camera angles to enhance a story (e.g., shooting scenes through wagon wheels and windows). In his "B" western career, Lewis directed four Bob Bakers at Universal before moving to Columbia. At Columbia, he directed three Charles Starretts and two Bill Elliotts. He then moved back to Universal to direct three Johnny Mack Brown vehicles.

In an interesting scene from *The Man from Tumbleweeds*, chief villain Raphael Bennett tells one of his minions to climb up a ladder into a tree to draw a bead on Bill Elliott. Bennett asks, "Can you get him?" A shot rings out and the henchman's lifeless body falls to the ground.

Reviews: "This opus is a good one in its field. Elliott fits well into the leading role, a cool, slow-forming-opinion, fast on the draw individual. Bill Elliott finally hits his stride, coming up with a hard-shooting action pic." *Variety*, 5/29/40

"Speedy and entertaining Bill Elliott oater." *Western Movies*, Pitts

Summation: This is a forerunner of *The Dirty Dozen* (Metro-Goldwyn-Mayer, 1967), as Bill Elliott recruits convicts to fight lawlessness in this top-flight "B" western. Elliott brings some fine shading to his heroic characterization, which make his performance all the more enjoyable. Al Hill, the leader of the convicts picked to be state rangers, leads the competent supporting cast. The chemistry between Elliott and Hill is perfect and natural. Joseph H. Lewis's edgy direction is on target. Lewis has a number of scenes enhanced by innovative camera angles, including the fistfight between Elliott and Francis Walker, and the gunfight between Elliott and Walker.

THE RETURN OF WILD BILL
Columbia (June 1940)

The Most Feared Gunman in the West Adds Plenty to
His Reputation ... in the Most Exciting Gunfight in History!

Alternate Title: False Evidence

Cast: Wild Bill Saunders, Bill Elliott; Sammy Lou Griffin, Iris Meredith; Matt Kilgore, George Lloyd; Kate Kilgore, Luana Walters; Lige Saunders, Edward LeSaint; Ole Mitch, Frank LaRue; Jake Kilgore, Francis Walker; Bart, Chuck Morrison; Cannonball, Dub Taylor; Mike, Buel Bryant; Hep, William Kellogg// "Sonny"; Sam Griffin, John Ince; Sheriff, Jack Rockwell; Townsman, Tex Cooper; Dusty Donahue, John Merton; Blacksmith, Bill Nestell

Credits: Director, Joseph H. Lewis; Producer, Leo Barsha; Story, Walt Coburn; Screenwriters, Robert Lee Johnson and Fred Myton; Editor, Richard Fantl; Cinematographer, George Meehan

Location Filming: Iverson, California

Production Dates: April 8, 1940–April 18, 1940

Running Time: 60 min.

Story: George Lloyd and his gang, ruthless outlaws posing as vigilantes, hang an innocent John Ince for rustling Edward LeSaint's cattle, hoping to start a range war between Ince's daughter, Iris Meredith, and LeSaint. Warned of trouble by Lloyd's sister, Luana Walters, LeSaint sends for his son, Bill Elliott. Lloyd wants LeSaint's ranch and sends his brother, Francis Walker, to either buy the ranch or murder LeSaint. When LeSaint won't sell, Walker shoots him. Elliott arrives moments after the shooting and in time for LeSaint to tell who shot him and what Lloyd's up to. Elliott catches up to Walker. The two men fight and then struggle over Elliott's pistol. The gun discharges, killing Walker. Elliott teams up with Meredith and an old family friend, Frank LaRue, to organize the ranchers against Lloyd. Lloyd sends fake lawmen to arrest Elliott and bring him to Lloyd to be lynched. Walters reaches Meredith, LaRue and the ranchers, and takes them to Elliott in time to prevent the hanging. Lloyd attempts to shoot Elliott, but Walters intervenes. In a tussle with Lloyd, the trigger is pulled and Walters is killed. Elliott goes after Lloyd and two henchmen, bringing all three down in a gunfight. Elliott receives word that he's desperately needed in Kansas. He tells Meredith that he'll return one day to "hang lace curtains."

Notes and Commentary: The working title was "Block K Rides Tonight."

At the film's conclusion, as Bill Elliott is about to settle down with Iris Meredith, Dub Taylor arrives to tell Elliott that he's needed in Kansas because a lot of farmers and ranchers are in trouble. This sets the stage for Elliott's next release, *Prairie Schooners* (Columbia, 1940). There would be one significant change: Elliott begins his journey as Wild Bill Saunders, but when he arrives in Kansas he's now Wild Bill Hickok.

The fight scene between Bill Elliott and Francis Walker is utilized in *Meanwhile, Back at the Ranch* (Curtco & RCR Productions, 1977).

Reviews: "Lewis' edgy direction is absolutely the best thing about this film." *The Western*, Hardy

"Well made Bill Elliott vehicle." *Western Movies*, Pitts

Summation: This is one of the all-time best "B" westerns, featuring good acting, direction, writing and cinematography. Bill Elliott is even allowed to act. (Just look at him as he realizes that his father, Edward LeSaint, has died; Elliott captures the pain and sadness in his eyes and face.) Both leading ladies — Iris Meredith and Luana Walters — turn in fetching performances; they vividly portray jealous women who both love Elliott. Joseph H. Lewis's edgy direction works. His pacing is impeccable and his interesting use of the camera gives the story added punch.

Bibliography

Books

Abbot, Anthony. *About the Murder of the Night Club Lady*. New York: Covici-Friede, 1931.
_____. *About the Murder of the Circus Queen*. New York: Popular Library, 1971.
Barbour, Alan G. *The Wonderful World of B-Films*. Kew Gardens, NY: Screen Facts, 1968.
Blottner, Gene. *Wild Bill Elliott: The Complete Filmography*. Jefferson, NC: McFarland, 2007.
Boyle, Jack. *Boston Blackie*. Boston: Gregg, 1979.
Carman, Bob, and Dan Scapperotti. *The Adventures of the Durango Kid*. Rockledge, FL: Robert Carman, 1983.
Castell, Ron. *Blockbuster Video Guide to Movies and Videos, 1995*. New York: Dell, 1994.
Castleton, Paul. *The Son of Robin Hood*. New York, NY: Cupples & Leon, 1941.
Dick, Bernard F. *The Merchant Prince of Poverty Row: Harry Cohn of Columbia Pictures*. Lexington: University Press of Kentucky, 1993.
Dumas, Alexandre. *Robin Hood, Prince of Thieves*. New York: Dell, 1965.
Fernett, Gene. *American Film Studios: An Historical Encyclopedia*. Jefferson, NC: McFarland, 1988.
Hirschhorn, Clive. *The Columbia Story*. New York: Crown, 1989.
Kennedy, Matthew. *Joan Blondell: A Life Between Takes*. Jackson: University Press of Mississippi, 2007.
McAleer, John. *Rex Stout: A Biography*. Boston: Little, Brown, 1977.
McNeille, H.C. (Sapper). *Bulldog Drummond at Bay*. London: Hodder & Stroughton, 1935.
_____. *Bulldog Drummond Strikes Back*. Garden City, NY: Doubleday, Doran, 1933.
Messner-Loebs, William, and Brett Barkley. *Bulldog Drummond*. Calumet City, IL: Moonstone, 2002.
Miller, Don. *B Movies*. New York: Ballantine, 1988.
Overstreet, Robert M. *The Overstreet Comic Book Price Guide* (26th Ed.). New York: Avon, 1996.
Penzler, Otto, Chris Steinbrunner, Marvin Lachman, and Mill Roseman. *Detectionary*. New York: Ballantine, 1980.
Petrucha, Stefan, and Kirk Van Wormer. *Boston Blackie*. Calumet City, IL: Moonstone, 2004.
Pitts, Michael R. *Western Movies: A TV and Video Guide to 4200 Genre Films*. Jefferson, NC: McFarland, 1986.
Queen, Ellery. *The Devil to Pay*. New York: Frederick A. Stokes, 1938.
_____. *The Door Between*. New York: J.B. Lippincott, 1937.
_____. *The Dragon's Teeth: A Problem in Deduction*. New York: Frederick A. Stokes, 1939.
_____. *The Dutch Shoe Mystery*. New York: Frederick A. Stokes, 1931.
_____. *The Greek Coffin Mystery*. New York: Frederick A. Stokes, 1932.
_____. *There Was an Old Woman*. New York: Little, Brown, 1943.
Renzi, Thomas C. *Cornell Woolrich from Pulp Noir to Film Noir*. Jefferson, NC: McFarland, 2006.
Rubel, James. *The Medico of Painted Springs*. New York: Phoenix, 1934.
_____. *The Medico on the Trail*. New York: Phoenix, 1938.
_____. *The Medico Rides*. New York: Phoenix, 1935.
Sabatini, Rafael. *Captain Blood Returns*. New York: Grossett & Dunlap, 1930.

_____. *The Fortunes of Captain Blood*. New York: Grossett & Dunlap, 1936.
Sidney, Margaret. *Five Little Peppers Abroad*. Boston: D. Lothrop, 1902.
_____. *Five Little Peppers and How They Grew*. Boston: D. Lothrop, 1881.
_____. *Five Little Peppers at School*. Boston: D. Lothrop, 1903.
_____. *Five Little Peppers Midway*. Boston: D. Lothrop, 1890.
Stout, Rex. *Fer-de-lance*. New York: Bantam, 1983.
_____. *The League of Frightened Men*. New York: First Jove/HBJ, 1979.
Townsend, Charles R. *San Antonio Rose*. Urbana and Chicago: University of Illinois Press, 1986.
Tuska, Jon. *The Detective in Hollywood*. Garden City, NY: Doubleday, 1978.
Vance, Louis Joseph. *Alias the Lone Wolf*. New York: Grossett & Dunlap, 1927.
_____. *The Lone Wolf*. New York: Avon, 1914.
_____. *The Lone Wolf Returns*. New York: E.P. Dutton, 1923.
_____. *Red Masquerade*. Garden City, NY: Doubleday, Page, 1921.
Zinman, David. *Saturday Afternoon at the Bijou*. New Rochelle, NY: Arlington House, 1973.

Magazines

Collison, Wilson. "There's Always a Woman." *American Magazine*, January 1937.
Davis, Norbert. "A Gunsmoke Case for Major Cain." *Dime Western Magazine*, October 1940.
Dellinger, Paul. "Filmography: Charles Starrett, Part Three." *Under Western Skies*, September 1983.
Ketchum, Philip. "The Town in Hell's Backyard." *10 Story Western Magazine*, March 1939.

Index